MANAGERIAL ECONOMICS
SEVENTH EDITION

MANAGERIAL ECONOMICS
THEORY, APPLICATIONS, AND CASES

SEVENTH EDITION

W. Bruce Allen
The Wharton School
University of Pennsylvania

Neil A. Doherty
The Wharton School
University of Pennsylvania

Keith Weigelt
The Wharton School
University of Pennsylvania

Edwin Mansfield
late of the University of Pennsylvania

W. W. NORTON & COMPANY
NEW YORK · LONDON

W. W. Norton & Company has been independent since its founding in 1923, when William Warder Norton and Mary D. Herter Norton first published lectures delivered at the People's Institute, the adult education division of New York City's Cooper Union. The firm soon expanded its program beyond the Institute, publishing books by celebrated academics from America and abroad. By mid-century, the two major pillars of Norton's publishing program—trade books and college texts—were firmly established. In the 1950s, the Norton family transferred control of the company to its employees, and today—with a staff of four hundred and a comparable number of trade, college, and professional titles published each year—W. W. Norton & Company stands as the largest and oldest publishing house owned wholly by its employees.

Managerial Economics
Theory, Applications, and Cases, Seventh Edition

W. Bruce Allen, Neil A. Doherty, Keith Weigelt, Edwin Mansfield

Copyright © 2009, 2005, 2002, 1999, 1996, 1993, 1990 by W. W. Norton & Company, Inc.

The text of this book is composed in Minion and DIN.
Composition by Matrix

Manufacturing by Quebecor World—Taunton, MA
Book design by Binocular, New York
Design director: Rubina Yeh
Project editor: Melissa Atkin
Production managers: Jane Searle and Benjamin Reynolds

Library of Congress Cataloging-in-Publication Data
Mangerial economics : theory, applications, and cases / W. Bruce Allen . . .
[ed al.] — 7th ed.
        p. cm.
    Includes bibliographical references and index.
    ISBN 978-0-393-93224-9 (hardcover)
    1. Managerial economics.   I. Allen, W. Bruce.
    HD30.22.M354 2009
    338.5024′658--dc22

                                                2009004491

W. W. Norton & Company, Inc., 500 Fifth Avenue, New York, N.Y. 10110
www.wwnorton.com
W. W. Norton & Company Ltd., Castle House, 75/76 Wells Street, London W1T 3QT

2 3 4 5 6 7 8 9 0

To Edwin Mansfield, a pioneer of managerial economics

BRIEF CONTENTS

CONTENTS

CONTENTS

CONTENTS

PART 7: RISK, UNCERTAINTY, AND INCENTIVES   429

PREFACE

This edition of *Managerial Economics* represents our third revision since inheriting the text from the late Edwin Mansfield, a master economist and educator. When you inherit a book from another author, it is akin to purchasing his or her house. In a house, tastes and values differ, and the passing of time can cause once-current trends to look outdated. Books have similar features. And, as with a house, it takes the new owner time to make all the desired changes. In each of the two previous revisions, we significantly altered various chapters but not the overall tone of the book. This edition represents our finished house. It is our vision of how to integrate economics into the managerial world.

The three of us teach the Managerial Economics course at The Wharton School of Business. It is required for most MBA students and is taken during their first semesters. Our charge is to show students how to apply economic principles in their future management positions. We have designed this book to make it easier for them to do just that.

The text is structured on the following principles. First, in the managerial world, economic thinking is a component of decision making. Economics is best taught as a decision-making framework. Students must see past the equations and graphs and understand why they need to follow general precepts. For example, the tools of marginal analysis and backward induction need to be in every manager's intellectual toolbox.

Second, managerial economics is integrative in nature. Economic models permeate all business disciplines. We emphasize the integrative nature of economics in this book.

Third, the formal analysis of models adds value to managerial discussions; for without it, perceived knowledge is merely speculative. The managerial world is one of efficiency. Objectivity is generally desired in performance metrics. Our experience is that the objectivity of mathematics brings focus to a business discussion. Its mastery is essential to business decision making.

We recognize that managers are inherently rational. However, managers occasionally make mistakes in judgment. This book is intended to improve their judgment by providing the knowledge to avoid mistakes. We also acknowledge that managers are often faced with situations of conflicting interests. Managers, as agents, face conflicting desires in favoring their own interests over those of share-holders. In the last chapters, we address these difficult issues.

THE SEVENTH EDITION OF *MANAGERIAL ECONOMICS*

We have significantly improved the text in this seventh edition. Our changes follow three broad paths: a re-constructed table of contents; a tighter focus on managerial behavior; and an emphasis on the discrete over the continuous.

Table of Contents

Overall, we reduced the length of the book by more than twenty percent. Most of the reduction comes from eliminating four chapters that were periphery to our focus and were better served by more specialized books—the removed chapters were the ones on optimization techniques, estimating demand functions, forecasting, and industrial innovation. These chapters can still be found on the book's website for any instructor who wishes to use them. We also reduced the number of pages and increasing the clarity of ideas by being more concise. Finally, we dissolved a chapter and spread it throughout the entire book. The world has truly gone global since Professor Mansfield last edited *Managerial Economics*. We now take a global perspective throughout the entire book, rather than confining global issues to a single chapter.

All chapters were revised and had new content added. Much of the new content has a strategic focus, such as the discussions of gift giving and Bertrand pricing behavior. We also added more graphs to visually clarify principles and concepts.

Finally, we rethought how to best integrate principles with examples from the managerial world. We chose to emphasize the strategic nature of these principles. For this reason, our examples are highlighted in boxes titled Strategy Sessions. Each Strategy Session generally tells a story of how managers use economic principles to influence behavior. We hope these sessions help readers to visualize how certain principles are encountered in the managerial world.

Within the text we are also using boxes titled Problem Solved to illustrate how a recently discussed idea is actually used in making decisions. While we do not expect managers to always have such definitive knowledge in making a decision, they do need to understand the underlying dynamics.

Below are brief chapter summaries of what is new in each chapter relative to the last edition.

Chapter 1 – (**Introduction**) We changed the focus of the text from the behavior of organizations to the behavior of individuals within organizations, that is, managers. Our goal is to provide the knowledge that managers need for making decisions. New Strategy Sessions include looking at social consumerism ("Bono sees Red") to examining how the shifts in commodity prices influence consumer behavior ("Effects of High Commodity Prices").

Chapter 2 – (**Demand Theory**) This chapter looks at how changes in sales influence the behavior of managers. New Strategy Sessions include servicing low-profit customers ("The Customer is Always Right—Wrong") and the use of demand elasticity by managers ("Verizon").

Chapter 3 – (**Consumer Behavior and Rational Choice**) We continue by showing managers how aggregate demand is composed of consumer subgroups and how individuals make choices. We then introduce the goal of most market strategies— the capturing of consumer surplus. Here new Strategy Sessions look at manager behavior when choosing between organizational goals ("Managers Trade-off Between Profit and Output"), considering the trade-off between work and leisure ("Do I Stay or Do I Go"), and considering decisions within a global context ("Trade-off Between Risk and Return"). We also added sections to the text that show how managers influence consumer behavior with pricing schemes and in gift giving.

Chapter 4 – (**Production Theory**) Now we move to the supply side and discuss what managers should consider when making output decisions. We also show managers how to create competitive advantages using the economies of scale and scope.

Chapter 5 – (**The Analysis of Costs**) We show managers how to structure costs to move toward efficiency and higher profits. Understanding the nature of costs is essential for managers. Empirically, too many managers choose strategies without a good knowledge of costs. It is difficult to maximize profit in such a state. Because students often ask how managers should estimate cost functions, we move that discussion to a chapter appendix, which can be skipped without disturbing the flow of the text.

Chapter 6 – (**Perfect Competition**) We now apply the knowledge of the first five chapters to managerial behavior in perfectly competitive markets. We use the simple market structure to show managers how to integrate basic concepts like costs, revenues, and prices. Behavior in these markets is later used as a benchmark when we show how market power affects managers' decisions.

Chapter 7 – (**Monopoly and Monopolistic Competition**) Now we examine behavior in market structures where managers have market power. We show managers how to use this power to create competitive advantages for their companies. For example, how they should price to increase profit. One new Strategy Session shows managers how incentives influence managerial behavior ("Franchisees vs. Franchiser"). And, we expand our discussion by showing how managers want to behave when they are the only buyer (monopsony).

Chapters 8 – (**The Managerial Use of Price Discrimination**) We provide a greater focus on pricing strategies by splitting one chapter from the last edition into two chapters. Chapter 8 focuses on the strategies of price discrimination and bundling. We use multiple Strategy Sessions to illustrate how managers use these techniques to increase profit. We discuss the pricing power of a mouse ("That Darling Little Mouse"), the different prices for rental autos in the global market ("Hey Buddy, Want to Rent a Car"), and how managers use pricing to induce behavior from the consumer ("Why Do Your Laundry at 3 AM?").

Chapter 9 – (**Bundling and Intrafirm Pricing**) focuses on the strategy of two-part tariffs and shows managers how to choose efficient intra-firm pricing schemes. Again, we use multiple Strategy Sessions to illustrate concepts. From showing how Costco managers use pricing to capture consumer surplus ("Costco and the Two-Part Tariff"), to giving managers negotiation advice ("When Can You Haggle?"), to considering how human behavior influences the effects of pricing decisions ("Scientific Pricing – Even for Great Art?").

Chapter 10 – (**Oligopoly**) This chapter begins our focus on how managers must explicitly consider the interactive nature of the strategic world. Those managers who fail to develop an interactive mode of thinking will consistently make bad decisions. A new discussion shows managers how to reduce price competition through the use of differentiated products. We also show managers how to reduce the tensions of strictly competitive behavior through their actions (i.e., competing on quantity). Finally, we show how the timing of strategies affects firm payoffs by analyzing both simultaneous and sequential decision making.

Chapter 11 – (**Game Theory**) We focus this chapter on the behavioral aspects of interactive thinking. We use game theory less as a formal framework and more for illustrating why managers need to follow certain strategic principles like assessment and backward induction. We show how game theory can help managers categorize families of decisions, like repeated play, and leverage off their shared characteristics across contexts. Finally, we discuss the importance of reputations both at the personal and firm levels as assets that can generate future profits.

Chapter 12 – (**Auctions**) We show managers how to apply game theoretic principles in auction settings to improve their decision making. For example, in some auction designs, managers have a dominant strategy and do not care what others might bid. We also show managers how they can use auction designs to induce consumers to reveal their preferences prior to purchase. Managers can then use this information when setting prices to increase profit.

Chapter 13 – (**Risk Analysis**) Managers must learn how to integrate risk into their decision making. This chapter discusses basic strategies that managers need to consider. We also focus on the role of risk in determining structural characteristics of the financial crisis that began in 2007. It is impossible for managers to make good decisions if they do not know how risk influences their decision behavior.

Chapter 14 – (**Principal-Agent Issues and Managerial Compensation**) This chapter begins our study of how informational asymmetries affect managers' choices. The new title for this chapter indicates its focus on the effect of corporate incentives and information asymmetries on managerial behavior. The magnitude of how these issues affect corporate governance is easily shown in a series of Strategy Sessions. These sessions look at what shareholders get in return for their payment to managers ("Value of CEO Pay"), how to get board members to think about the long run ("Getting the Board to Focus"), how compensation compares across the globe ("Imitation is the Best Form"), and how incentives change managerial behavior ("The Good and Bad"). In the text, we have a new discussion on why some performance schemes have unintended consequences. Given the role of managers and moral-hazard issues in the current government bail-outs, we use examples to show how moral-hazard concerns changed managerial behavior.

Chapter 15 – (**Adverse Selection**) This chapter continues our look at how informational asymmetries affect managerial choice. It focuses on situations where one party knows more than another about the quality of an asset. While many models predict market failure, we show how managers choose strategies to create similar though different markets. For example, the use of certified warranty programs for pre-owned autos helps managers avoid the predicted market failure for used autos. We use Strategy Sessions to describe the diversity of decisions affected by adverse selection: from the use of store loyalty programs ("How Managers Gather Information") to internet shopping ("Using Search Engines"); from deciding the fate of abandoned property ("Information Asymmetries") to government prescription programs ("Adverse Selection and Government").

Chapter 16 – (**Government and Business**) This chapter shows the effect of government control on managerial behavior. Given the involvement of the U.S. government in the private sector in its bid to stave off financial disaster, it is more important than ever that managers understand the implications of government action. Recognizing the global nature of economies, we have added new sections on trade and trade policy. We also show the effect of government intervention on managerial pricing decisions. Strategy Sessions include a global discussion of anti-trust behavior ("Anti-trust on Both Sides of the Atlantic"), the use of incentives to encourage managers to become whistle blowers ("Making Whistle Blowing Pay"), and the perversity of anti-trust behavior ("From Factories to Breweries").

Focus on Managerial Behavior

A subtle but significant change throughout the book is the shift in focus from firm behavior to managerial behavior. This reflects our greater emphasis on the strategic nature of economics and its role in managerial decisions. We also believe that it more truly represents the causality of "firm" decisions.

Our intent is to show managers the many facets of economic reasoning and how to apply them to the managerial world. For example, managers can use economics to better understand the behavior of others. Another way is in the design of their pricing strategy. A third use is in the design of a compensation scheme. Game theory helps them find the optimal bidding strategy.

We also place great emphasis on explaining how information asymmetries affect managerial decisions. Informational asymmetries are common in the managerial world and managers need to understand how they affect behavior. Incentives, preferences, actions, and beliefs can all change in the presence of these asymmetries.

Discrete, Not Continuous

Most readers would probably think a change in mathematical operations from dP/dQ to $\Delta P/\Delta Q$ is rather subtle. On one level it simply changes the treatment of the material to discrete units, so managers can consider hiring either 5 or 6 new employees, but not 5.5. This subtlety in exposition masks a profound difference in problem-solving methodology, especially to economists. Algebra or calculus—does one trace its heritage to Diophantus or Newton? Clearly, the average college student prefers Diophantus.

However, we also know that some students march to the beat of a different drum. We did and find ourselves writing a book on economics. *Webster's Dictionary* defines a geek as "an expert especially in a technological field." We regard ourselves as geeky economists; after all, we have written a 500-page book on the subject. We understand that most students have no desire to become geeky economists, so the book's main focus is on these students. However, we do not want to ignore those students who aspire to become the next generation of geeky economists. As the older generation, we want to nurture those of the younger one.

To that end, we created what we call the Quant Option[1]. The discussions in these boxed inserts provide a richer mathematical treatment of the material just-presented. Often in them, we examine material using calculus, not algebra. The discussions do not interrupt the flow of the book, so they can be skipped without any penalty in understanding the material.

---

1. Our thanks to Barry Nalebuff for the name.

PART 1
THE NEED FOR A GUIDE

CHAPTER 1

INTRODUCTION

The main task of managers is to make good decisions. For better or worse, managers face a complex world, and they need a guide to help them choose well. This is that guide. Those who gain its understanding will increase the value of their decisions at personal and organizational levels.

This guide provides knowledge in the following sense. The ancient Chinese discuss knowledge as a temporal flow. Knowledge is not storage of memorized facts but an ability to understand the actions of others. With this knowledge, you better anticipate their behavior. Our guide will help you navigate through the managerial world of behavior.

We construct our guide within the framework of managerial economics. Managerial economics uses formal models to analyze managerial actions and their effect on firm performance. We use these models to shed light on business concepts such as cost, demand, profit, competition, pricing, compensation, market entry strategy, and auction strategy. All these concepts are under the control of managers, and they determine firm performance.

Contrary to the beliefs of many, managerial economics differs significantly from microeconomics: The focus of analysis is different. At best the focus in microeconomics is at the firm level; many times the analysis is at the market level.

In managerial economics, the focus is on managerial behavior. Managerial economics prescribes behavior, whereas the micro world describes the environment. This focus on managerial behavior provides powerful tools and frameworks to guide managers to better decisions. These tools allow managers to better identify the consequences of alternative courses of action.

Managerial economics plays two important roles in preparing students for managerial life. Concepts we will discuss in subsequent chapters are found in other functional business courses like accounting, finance, strategy, operations, and marketing. Our guide is what the great strategist Sun Tzu called the "general's seat," and it is characterized by what are known as economies of scope. That is, the better you understand the concepts we discuss, the easier will be your understanding of them when they arise in other business classes. And because managerial economics recognizes the complexity of the managerial world, it is arguably the most integrative of the functional business classes. This helps students learn the integrative mind-set that is essential for good management, and it also gets them to think past the short-term mentality and consider the long-term consequences.

THE THEORY OF THE FIRM

Managers work within a larger organization and ultimately determine its performance. To understand the behavioral world of managers, we must account for the behavior of firms. Of course firms really don't behave on their own; you might think of them as marionettes with managers controlling the strings. Some management teams are good at pulling these strings, while others can't seem to get it right. But although management styles differ greatly in the millions of firms across the globe, there is surprisingly little variance in the goals of managers. Overwhelmingly, managers choose actions they believe will increase the value of their organization. So in our theory of the firm, the goals of managers focus on increasing this value. We understand there are many ways to create value in an organization; for example, to a microcredit organization with a double bottom line, value from its lending practices might consist of a profit measure and the gains to a local community's economy. But our models must account for behavior across a great number of firms, so we take the view that managers in profit-oriented organizations try to increase the net present value of expected future cash flows. We can formally present this managerial effort in the following:

$$\text{Present value of expected future profits} = \frac{\pi_1}{1+i} + \frac{\pi_2}{(1+i)^2} + \cdots + \frac{\pi_n}{(1+i)^n}$$

$$\text{Present value of expected future profits} = \sum_{t=1}^{n} \frac{\pi_t}{(1+i)^t} \tag{1.1}$$

STRATEGY SESSION: Bono Sees Red and Corporate Participants See Black

In 2007, rock star Bono started Red, a campaign that combines consumerism with altruism. When a consumer buys a Dell RED computer, a Motorola Red Motorazr, red items from The Gap, uses an American Express Red card, or the like, a contribution is made into the global fund. Companies pay a licensing fee to label their products "Red" and then pay a portion of the sales from those products into the fund. Thus far over $59 million has gone into the fund, which fights AIDS, malaria, and tuberculosis in the African countries of Ghana, Rwanda, and Swaziland; $22 million has been generated to fight HIV and AIDS in Rwanda.

This concept has been branded "cause marketing" and was around long before Red—but without the publicity capable of being generated by a personality like Bono. For years McDonald's has sponsored Ronald McDonald houses, where parents of sick children can find respite (and support groups) near the hospitals where their children are patients. Why do firms participate in cause marketing? Clearly the compa-

nies can market themselves as being socially conscious. But equally clear is the cost of paying for the Red license and operating Ronald McDonald houses. Where's the tangible benefit? According to a 2006 poll by Cone Inc. (a Boston marketing agency), 89 percent of Americans aged 13 to 25 (a large consumer group and one swayed by Bono) would switch to a brand associated with a "good cause" if the products and prices were comparable. There's the benefit: Cause marketing also leads to a revenue stream (and presumably a profit stream).

So incurring Red leads to seeing black as profits increase because of such actions. Cause marketing is in harmony with profit maximization. Another phenomenon we are witnessing is the rise of "philantrepreneurs" such as Warren Buffet, Bill Gates, Richard Branson, and Ted Turner—individuals who make a lot of profit and then use that money for good causes.

Source: "Bottom Line for (Red)," *The New York Times*, February 6, 2008.

---

where π_t is the expected profit in year t, i is the interest rate, and t goes from 1 (next year) to n (the last year in the planning horizon). Because profit equals total revenue (TR) minus total cost (TC), this equation can also be expressed as

$$\text{Present value of expected future profits} = \sum_{t=1}^{n} \frac{TR_t - TC_t}{(1 + i)^t} \qquad (1.2)$$

where TR_t is the firm's total revenue in year t, and TC_t is its total cost in year t.

Equation (1.2) shows why managers influence firm performance. Managerial decisions clearly determine both the revenues and costs for an organization. Consider, for example, the Toyota Motor Company. Its marketing managers and sales representatives work hard to increase its total revenues, while its production managers and manufacturing engineers strive to reduce its total costs. At the same time, its financial managers play a major role in obtaining capital and hence influence equation (1.2); its research and development personnel invent new products and processes to increase total revenues and reduce total costs. Managers of all these diverse groups make decisions to affect Toyota Motor's value, defined here as the present value of expected future profits.

Although managers want to increase their firm's value, they do not have total control over the level of value. If managerial life were that simple, you would not have to go to school to learn business techniques. What complicates managerial life are the operating constraints managers face. One constraint is that most resources are scarce. Within the firm, managerial decision making often involves allocating scarce inputs to support the production, distribution, and sales of goods and services that are sold at a price that exceeds their costs.

Other constraints that limit managerial actions are legal or contractual. For example, managers may be bound to pay wages exceeding a certain level because minimum wage laws stipulate that they must do so. Also, they must pay taxes in accord with federal, state, and local laws. Further, managers must comply with contracts with customers and suppliers—or take the legal consequences. A wide variety of laws (ranging from environmental laws to antitrust laws to tax laws) limit what managers can do, and contracts and other legal agreements further constrain their actions.

WHAT IS PROFIT?

As we have seen, firm value is largely a function of **profit**. Unlike the accounting world, in the managerial economics framework, we measure profit after taking account of the capital and labor provided by the owners. For example, suppose a manager quits her position at a large firm to create a small start-up business. She receives no salary even though she puts in long hours trying to establish her business. If she worked these hours for her previous firm, she would have earned $65,000. And if she had invested the capital she used to begin her business in some alternative investment, she could have earned $24,000. Let's say in 2008 her start-up firm earned an accounting profit of $100,000. Her firm's profit in the managerial economics world is $100,000 − $65,000 − $24,000 = $11,000 rather than the $100,000 shown in accounting statements.

The differences between the profit concepts used by the accountant and the economist reflect the difference in their focus. The accountant is concerned with controlling the firm's day-to-day operations, detecting fraud or embezzlement, satisfying tax and other laws, and producing records for various interested groups. The economist is concerned with decision making and rational choice among strategies. Although most financial statements of firms conform to the accountant's and not the managerial economist's concept of profit, the latter is more relevant for managerial decisions. (And this, of course, is recognized by sophisticated accountants.) For example, suppose the woman we just discussed is trying to decide whether to continue operating her business. If she is interested in making as much money as possible, she should calculate her firm's profit based on our

Profit When economists speak of profit, they mean profit over and above what the owner's labor and capital employed in the business could earn elsewhere.

economist model. If the firm's economic profit is greater than zero, she should continue to operate the firm; otherwise she should close it down and pursue her other opportunities.

REASONS FOR THE EXISTENCE OF PROFIT

A firm's economic profit is generated by the actions of managers. Profit is one indicator of their decision-making skills. Three fertile profit-generating areas used by managers are innovation, risk, and market power. As we write this chapter, people are waiting in line for the chance to buy the iPhone, a new cellular phone from Apple. And airlines are committing billions of dollars to reserve the opportunity to purchase the 787 Dreamliner from Boeing. In both these markets, products already exist; but consumers apparently are more interested in new products. Both the iPhone and the 787 are considered product innovations. They push the frontier relative to existing products in terms of functionality, technology, and style. As we write today, these managerial efforts both generate high profit—reportedly up to 40 percent. Future value will depend on how each managerial team executes its market strategy.

A hallmark of managerial decision making is the need to make risky choices. For managers this risk takes many forms. They are asked to make decisions whose future outcomes are unknown (How successful will this product be in the market?) when they don't know the reactions of rivals (If I raise my price, will my rivals raise theirs?) and when they do not know the likelihood of a future event (How likely is it that a democrat will be elected our next president?). Profit is the reward to those who bear risk well.

As we will see later, managers also earn profit by exploiting market inefficiencies. Good managers understand how to create inefficiencies to give their firm a sustainable competitive advantage. Common tactics in this area include building market entry barriers, sophisticated pricing strategies, diversification efforts, and output decisions. Such tactics, if done well, can generate a long stream of profit for a firm.

MANAGERIAL INTERESTS AND THE PRINCIPAL-AGENT PROBLEM

Although managerial economists generally assume that managers want to maximize profit (and hence firm value, as defined in equation (1.1)), they recognize additional goals that managers may strive to achieve. Some of these goals may enhance the firm's long-term value, like building market share or establishing a brand name. Other managerial goals may have less to do with firm value and more to do with increasing managerial compensation.

As we will see, our model recognizes that preferences of firm owners and managers sometimes diverge. And when managers make choices between maximizing a firm's value and increasing the payoffs to a single manager or management team, some choose the selfish path. This too is a trait of managerial behavior. The tendency to focus on self-interest is growing in importance because the separation between the ownership and management of firms is continuing to increase on a global scale. The owners of the firm—the stockholders—usually have little detailed knowledge of the firm's operations. As we will see, even a firm's board of directors has limited information relative to the management team. Management is generally given a great deal of freedom as long as it seems to be performing adequately. Consequently, firm behavior may be driven by the interests of the nonowner management group. At the least, this behavior results in higher pay and more perquisites for managers; at worst, it creates an Enron spectacle.

Managerial economists call this **the principal–agent problem**. Managers are agents who work for the firm's owners, who are the shareholders or principals. The principal–agent problem centers on whether managers may pursue their own objectives at a cost to the owners. Consider the thoughts of Joseph Wagner, a manager of a local pharmaceutical firm. "Let me see. The cost of the company benefits (large staff, company-paid travel, and so on) I receive are borne entirely by the owners." We ask students in our class, "If we send you to Atlantic City with our money, would your behavior change?" Because the firm's owners find it difficult to distinguish between benefits that bolster profit and those that do not, managers have incentives to enrich themselves.

To deal with this problem, owners often use contracts to converge their preferences and those of their agents. For example, owners may give managers a financial stake in future firm success. Many corporations use stock option plans, whereby managers can purchase shares of common stock at less than market price. These plans give managers an incentive to increase firm profit and comply with owners' interest. There is some evidence these plans do change behavior. According to one study, if managers own between 5 and 20 percent of a firm, the firm is likely to perform better (that is, earn more profit) than if they own less than 5 percent. In some firms managers are forced to purchase stock, and boards of directors are compensated in stock. This and other moral hazard issues are discussed extensively in Chapter 14.

The principal–agent problem
When managers pursue their own objectives, even though this decreases the profit of the owners.

DEMAND AND SUPPLY: A FIRST LOOK

To understand behavior in any society, we must have a working knowledge of its institutions. The managerial world revolves around markets. Any manager, whether in Tokyo, New York, London, or Toronto, must understand basic market principles in order to anticipate behavior. A significant portion of this book is

STRATEGY SESSION: Baseball Discovers the Law of Supply and Demand

It started several years ago, with the Colorado Rockies looking for a way to obtain more revenue but at the same time not wishing to heap additional expense on their loyal season ticket holders (who buy tickets for every game or an aggregation of games as a bundle). As of the 2003 season, the Rockies were joined by 11 other teams—slightly less than half of the 30 major league baseball teams. Doing what? Practicing what they call variable pricing. In lay terms they are charging more for games with desirable teams as opponents, such as teams that are traditional rivals, teams with superstars, and the like.

Although this concept is nothing new for many other goods and services (Miami Beach hotel rooms cost more in February than in July, phone calls are more expensive in daytime hours than at night), it is new for baseball.

Historically the price for seat X in the stadium was price Y for each of the team's 81 home games. Now seat X is priced higher on opening day, on fireworks night, or when the New York Yankees or another traditional rival comes to town. The basic premise is the law of supply and demand. The number of seats in the ballpark remains fixed, but the attractiveness of a seat to a potential buyer is not constant.

Bill Iannicello, vice president of ticket sales for the New York Mets, stated, "The demand for games with particular opponents is certainly greater than for others. The same is true for summer versus spring or fall dates, and weekends versus weekdays. We tried to look at it on a game-by-game level."

Frank Maloney, the director of ticket sales for the Chicago Cubs, stated, "I think people understand the theory. If I'm a realistic fan, I know prices are going to go up one way or another. So when we raise prices on only 19 dates of 81, which is what we did, I think that they see that as a pretty good deal." Maloney adds that variable pricing is "an idea that makes too much sense."

All 12 teams have their own version of variable pricing. The Mets' scheme is the most sophisticated. There are four tiers: gold (17 dates), silver (21 dates), bronze (27

devoted to helping you understand the behavior of people in markets. We first give an overview of markets and then examine both the demand and supply sides of markets in greater detail.

One issue faced by managers long ago involved the facilitation of economic exchange. Whereas two individuals can negotiate face-to-face, coordination costs mount quickly as more people join the deal. So managers had to devise a plan to reduce coordination costs and encourage more trade. They chose to create a social institution called a **market**.

Market A group of firms and individuals that interact with each other to buy or sell a good.

A market exists when there is economic exchange; that is, multiple parties enter binding contracts. Today countless markets exist in the world. The business world operates within these markets, and we need to examine (and understand) behavior in them. Surprisingly, given the number and diversity of markets in the world, they all follow general principles. It is these principles we now focus on because understanding them is essential to understanding market behavior. We examine the behavior of individuals who enter contracts and on the aggregate effect that they create.

dates), and value (16 dates). In the 2002 season, before the Mets adopted variable pricing, all seats were priced at the bronze level. For the exact same seat, the gold price is $53, the silver price is $48, the bronze price is $43, and the value price is $38. Tampa Bay has 13 prime games, 55 regular games, and 13 value games. Weekday afternoon games in April are the cheapest way to see the Cubs play. The 18 summer weekend games and the season opener are the most expensive. The remainder of the games are at the regular price. St. Louis charges a $2 premium on seats between May 16 and August 28. Atlanta charges $3 extra for seats on Friday nights and Saturdays in the summer. San Francisco adds an extra $1 to $4 depending on the seat location for every weekend game and the season opener.

What is next? Teams play 162 games to determine who wins the division pennant (there are six divisions). Those winners plus two wild cards (teams with the best won–lost records who did not win their divisions) have the right to enter postseason play (which ultimately leads to two of the eight teams playing in the World Series, the winner being crowned World Champions). The divisions have "pennant races," which become evident in September. Some division winners are not determined until the last several games of the season. Right now variable pricing is based on preseason feelings about what games the fans will really want to see. True variable pricing will see price changing very close to game time. Teams that have a chance to win a division (those that are still in the pennant race in September) will be expected to raise prices on unsold tickets for those games. This will occur under other circumstances, too. If Ryan Howard is coming to town and already has 70 home runs, expect to see ticket prices rise. Coming to a ballpark near you: real-time variable pricing.

Source: "All Games Are Not Created Equal as Teams Turn to Variable Pricing," *Philadelphia Inquirer*, April 2, 2003, pp. E-1 and E-4.

THE DEMAND SIDE OF A MARKET

Every market consists of demanders and suppliers. A manager needs to know how potential customers value a product or service, and must be able to estimate the quantity of goods demanded at various prices. One goal of managers is to maximize firm value. The ability to focus on profit requires a thorough knowledge of demand, especially the behavior of revenue as price changes. Total revenue is equal to the number of units sold (Q) multiplied by the price (P) at which they were sold ($TR = P \times Q$).

The association of price and quantity demanded often depends on many variables, some controlled by the manager and some not. Possible influences include income and tastes, prices of substitutes and complementary products, advertising dollars, product quality (as well as the quality of substitutes and complements), and governmental fiat. The behavior of quantity demanded relative to price is called a firm's **demand function** (holding other possible influences constant).

A demand curve shows managers how many units they will sell at a given price. Consider Figure 1.1, which shows the demand curve for copper in the world

Demand function Quantity demanded relative to price, holding other possible influences constant.

FIGURE 1.1

The Market Demand Curve for Copper, World Market

The market demand curve for copper shows the amount of copper that buyers would like to purchase at various prices.

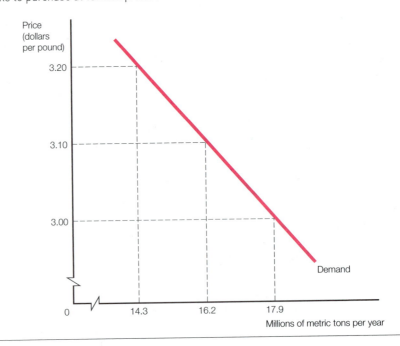

market in 2008. The figure shows that about 16.2 million metric tons of copper are demanded annually if the price is $3.10 per pound; about 14.3 million metric tons are demanded if the price is $3.20 per pound; and about 17.9 million metric tons are demanded if the price is $3.00 per pound. An important reason why copper has experienced recent growth in quantity demanded is its increasing use in emerging markets like China and India.

The demand curve in Figure 1.1 shows the global quantity demanded at all prices. Any demand curve pertains to a particular period of time, and the shape and position of the demand curve can depend on the period length. The demand curve for copper slopes downward to the right. In mathematical terms, we say it has a negative slope; that is, the quantity of copper demanded increases as the price falls. This is true of demand curves for most commodities: They almost always slope downward to the right. This makes sense; we would expect increases in a good's price to result in a smaller quantity demanded.

Any demand curve is based on the assumption that other influences like tastes and incomes are held constant. Changes in any of these factors are likely to shift the position of a commodity's demand curve. So if consumers' tastes shift toward

Although you can't get blood from a stone, you can get oil from shale. But it's expensive. When oil prices rise, entrepreneurs start looking at oil shale as a place to find more oil. When oil prices fall, they scrap those ideas. Oil shale has never paid off (except marginally) for most oil companies, which have lost considerably on their ventures into oil shale. From the 1950s to the 1980s, the major oil companies invested about $2 billion on experiments designed to extract oil from shale. The second Arab oil embargo in 1980 spurred the last major oil shale exploration (Colorado, Utah, and Wyoming are the target areas). But when prices fell after the embargo, the ventures there folded. It's not that there isn't oil there (the U.S. government estimates that 800 million barrels exist—more than triple the known reserves in Saudi Arabia); it's just that it's been so expensive to get out of the ground. The expense includes the energy needed to get the oil out of the ground, air pollution created in the extraction process, the devastation to surface lands, and pollution of adjacent scarce groundwater supplies.

Three companies (Shell, Chevron, and EGL Resources) feel that with new extraction technology (each company has a different one), the lower costs coupled with the high price of oil make the time for harvesting oil shale potentially ripe (by "ripe" they mean that work done now could bring the oil online by 2020). Each company's technique involves heating the organic material in the ground, melting it into oil, and pumping it to the surface; but the techniques for doing so are vastly different.

So what's going on here? When the price of oil exceeds a supplier's reservation price of producing oil, the supplier enters the market. Obviously this is a long-run view of the price of oil and the costs of extracting it, and the oil companies have been wrong before (oil prices fell, and the costs of extracting were higher than expected). What's different now? At least three things. The oil crises in 1972–1973 and in 1980 didn't raise prices for long. This latest price increase has lasted for a long time and shows no sign of abatement (at best fluctuation around a high number). Second, the political situations in major oil-producing countries (Iran, Iraq, Nigeria, Venezuela) are unstable, and the rest of the Middle East is also not a certainty. Finally, the companies believe they have cheaper, more efficient methods of extracting the shale oil.

Only time will tell. If oil prices fall and the cost estimates prove optimistic, we can again expect to see abandoned oil shale activities in the West.

Source: "The Cautious U.S. Boom in Oil Shale," *The New York Times*, December 21, 2006, www.nytimes.com/2006/12/21/business/21shale.html.

goods that use considerable copper or if consumers' incomes increase (and they thus buy more goods using copper), the demand curve for copper will shift to the right. In other words, holding the price of copper constant, more copper is demanded at any price. We will discuss this more fully in Chapter 2.

THE SUPPLY SIDE OF A MARKET

The supply side of a market is represented by a market supply curve that shows how many units of a commodity sellers will offer at any price. Figure 1.2 shows the supply curve for copper in the world market in 2008. According to the figure,

FIGURE 1.2

The Market Supply Curve for Copper, World Market

The market supply curve for copper shows the amount of copper that sellers would offer at various prices.

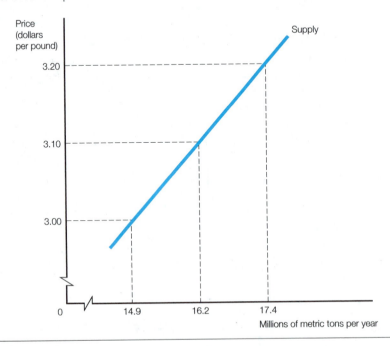

about 16.2 million metric tons of copper are supplied if the price of copper is $3.10 per pound, about 17.4 million tons if the price is $3.20 per pound, and about 14.9 million tons if the price is $3.00 per pound.

Note that the supply curve for copper slopes upward to the right. In mathematical terms, we say it has a positive slope; in other words, the quantity of copper supplied increases as the price rises. This seems plausible: Higher prices provide an incentive to suppliers to produce more copper to sell. Any supply curve is based on the assumption that production technology is held constant. If lower-cost production technology is developed, then managers will be willing to sell more units at any price. That is, technological change often causes a supply curve to shift to the right.

The supply curve for a product is affected by the cost of production inputs (labor, capital, and land). When costs of inputs decrease, managers realize lower production costs and are willing to supply a given amount at a lower price. So decreases in the cost of inputs cause supply curves to shift to the right. If input costs increase, managers are willing to supply a given amount only at a higher price (because their costs are higher). Hence the supply curve shifts to the left.

EQUILIBRIUM PRICE

Economists represent markets as the interaction of demand and supply curves. To illustrate, consider the world copper market shown in Figure 1.3. We construct the figure by overlaying the demand curve (Figure 1.1) with the supply curve (Figure 1.2). Now we can determine market behavior at various prices. For example, if the price of copper is $3.20 per pound, the demand curve indicates that 14.3 million metric tons of copper are demanded, while the supply curve indicates that 17.4 million metric tons are supplied. Therefore, if the market price is $3.20 per pound, there is a mismatch between the quantity supplied and the quantity demanded. Specifically, as shown in Figure 1.3, there is excess supply of 3.1 million metric tons. Some producers will not be able to sell all their inventories at this price; they may be tempted to cut their prices to reduce these inventories. Hence a market price of $3.20 per pound creates an unbalance in the market—there is too much supply. Because of this excess supply, producers will drop their prices, so $3.20 is not a sustainable market price.

FIGURE 1.3

Equilibrium Price of Copper, World Market

The equilibrium price is $3.10 per pound, since quantity demanded equals the quantity supplied at this price.

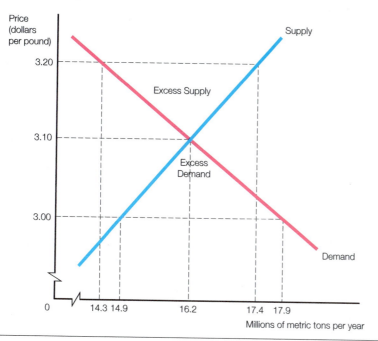

STRATEGY SESSION: Supply and Demand—We See It Working at the Pumps

Where some see a conspiracy of big oil companies to raise prices (they never seem to be guilty of anything when prices fall), economists see the power of the market at work. The person in the street feels that a pipeline shutdown or a refinery fire affects *tomorrow's* supply; but *today's* gas was produced with pre-event oil, so why should fuel prices go up today as a result of such events?

It's explained by a concept called storage arbitrage. Suppose you owned an acre of corn. Suppose corn prices today are $3 per bushel but everyone thinks that corn will sell for $3.50 per bushel tomorrow. You wouldn't sell your corn at $3 today. You'd just defer your harvest by a day and sell it tomorrow for $3.50 (as long as the costs of harvesting are not expected to go up by $0.50 per bushel overnight). But your fellow corn farmers also decide to wait until tomorrow. Thus corn becomes scarce today and today's price increases. To what price? To $3.50. That would induce the corn growers to sell today rather than wait until tomorrow.

The solution, conspiracy theorists propose, is a price ceiling—a price gas cannot exceed. But such a policy creates excess demand (shortages) and the attendant deadweight loss discussed in Chapter 16. A study of the impact of a price ceiling after Hurricanes Katrina and Rita concluded that such deadweight loss costs would be $1.9 billion.

The Federal Trade Commission investigated allegations of price gouging after Hurricanes Katrina and Rita in 2005 and found no widespread evidence of pricing abuse. The FTC and the Department of Energy have done numerous such studies and never found abuse, concluding that supply and demand determine the prices. A 2003 FTC study of gas price changes from 1991 through 2003 concluded that 85 percent of the variation in prices reflected price changes of crude oil. These changes are made not in the United States but in world markets and are influenced strongly by OPEC as a dominant firm price leader that controls about 40 percent of the market. Analogous to rent control, price control policies could discourage investment in refining capacity improvements.

The United States is highly dependent on foreign oil (most of which comes from Canada and Mexico). But the oil market is a world market. If prices in the rest of the world rise and in the United States are legislatively held low, where will the Canadians and Mexicans sell their oil? They like us, but not that much!

Sources: "The Rapidly Changing Signs at the Gas Station Show the Market at Work," *The New York Times*, August 24, 2006, at www.nytimes.com/2006/08/24/business/24scene.html; "Gasbags," *The Wall Street Journal*, April 19, 2007; "Oil Price 'Gouging': A Phantom Menace?", *The New York Times*, May 20, 2007, at www.nytimes.com/2007/05/20/business/yourmoney/20view.html.

If the price is $3.00 per pound, the demand curve indicates that 17.9 million metric tons are demanded, while the supply curve indicates that 14.9 million metric tons are supplied. So a market price of $3.00 also creates an unbalance in the market: There is not enough supply to satisfy demand. In fact, at this price consumers want to purchase an additional 3 million metric tons, but they can find no suppliers. When suppliers realize there is a shortage of copper they will increase their prices. Hence $3.00 is not a sustainable market price.

So what is a sustainable market price? A price is sustainable when the quantity demanded at a price is equal to the quantity supplied at that price. The market is in balance because everyone who wants to purchase the good can, and every seller who wants to sell the good can. We say the market is at **equilibrium**. In Figure 1.3, the price at which the quantity supplied equals the quantity demanded is $3.10 per pound. This is also the point where the two curves intersect.

Equilibrium When the market is in balance because everyone who wants to purchase the good can and every seller who wants to sell the good can.

ACTUAL PRICE

Of course price managers are interested in the actual price—the price that really prevails—not the equilibrium price. In general economists assume the actual price approximates the equilibrium price, which seems reasonable enough because the basic forces at work tend to push the actual price toward the equilibrium price. Therefore, if conditions remain fairly stable for a time, the actual price should move toward the equilibrium price.

To see this, consider the global market for copper, as described in Figure 1.3. What if the actual price of copper is $3.20 per pound? As we have seen, this price level will cause downward pressure on the price of copper. Suppose the price, responding to this pressure, falls to $3.15 per pound. Comparing the quantity demanded with the quantity supplied at $3.15 per pound, we see there is still downward pressure on price because the quantity supplied exceeds the quantity demanded. The price, responding to this pressure, may fall to $3.12 per pound; but comparing the quantity demanded with the quantity supplied at this price, we find there is still downward pressure on price.

As long as the actual price is greater than the equilibrium price, there is downward pressure on price. Similarly, as long as the actual price is less than the equilibrium price, there is upward pressure on price. Hence there is always a tendency for the actual price to move toward the equilibrium price. The speed of this adjustment can vary. Sometimes it takes a long time for the actual price to approach the equilibrium price, and sometimes it happens quickly.

This price adjustment process is what Adam Smith called the market's **invisible hand**. No governmental agency is needed to induce producers to drop or increase their prices. They act more or less in unison and cause the market price to change.

Invisible hand When no governmental agency is needed to induce producers to drop or increase their prices.

WHAT IF THE DEMAND CURVE SHIFTS?

Any supply and demand diagram like Figure 1.3 is essentially a snapshot of the situation during a particular time. The results in Figure 1.3 are limited to a particular period because demand and supply curves are not static; they shift in reaction to changes in the environment. What happens to the equilibrium price of a good when its demand curve changes? This is important to know because managers need to anticipate and forecast changes in prices.

STRATEGY SESSION: Life During a Market Movement

When the market moves, planets can tremble. In early spring 2008 shifting demand and supply curves were impacting every country. The global food supply was in disequilibrium, and it appeared that the world was in a panic. During one week in early spring 2008, major governments worldwide used their sovereign powers to restrict trade in basic foods. Saudi Arabia cut import taxes on basic foodstuffs, India removed tariffs on edible oils while banning rice exports, and Vietnam cut its rice exports by 22 percent. Political unrest was beginning to erupt in countries as diverse as Egypt and Mexico over the rising cost of food. What is perhaps a mere inconvenience of paying $4.25 for a gallon of milk in the United States is one of life or death to those who live on the fringes. For the 300 million Chinese who live in poverty, food accounts for 50 percent of household expenses.

Look at what caused this commotion. The figure shows the behavior of food prices prior to mid-2008.

You can clearly see the acceleration of prices across major food groups. This is a shift in the demand curve. The *Financial Times* reported that the Philippine government paid $700 per ton of rice—almost double the price the government paid in December 2007. The price of corn increased by 73 percent between April 2007 and April 2008 (from $3.46 a bushel to $6 a bushel). Wheat increased by 123 percent in this same period (from $5.63 to $12.57 a bushel). In China, the price of pork increased by 63 percent.

This rightward shift in the demand curve for food was attributed to several factors. One theory was that the mathematical doomsday machine of Thomas Malthus was finally reaching fruition. The world population continues to expand while agricultural acreage continues to shrink. Many governments in developing countries have focused efforts on economic development and not agriculture. A UN report shows the annual growth in agricultural productivity slowed to 1 percent by 2002. A growing middle class in large developing countries like China and India consumes more food. As people increase their income, they generally eat more food. In China consumption of meat has doubled as personal income has increased. Finally, the increased use of food stock, like corn, for the production of ethanol fuel has taken such products out of the food market. Also, more individuals are leaving rural areas (farms)

To illustrate the effects of a rightward shift of a demand curve, consider the copper industry in 2006. Housing starts were increasing on a global scale (copper tubing is often used for water lines), and the emerging markets of China and India were starting to expand. As indicated in the right panel of Figure 1.4, managers should have expected that such a rightward shift of the demand curve would cause an increase in the price of copper from P to P_2. In fact the global price of copper in 2006 was roughly $2.65 per pound. By 2008 this price had increased to $3.10.

In mid-2008, we see a leftward shift in the demand curve for copper as shown in the left panel of Figure 1.4. Because of slow economic growth in the United States and other countries, there was less demand for copper. This meant that the demand curve for copper shifted left, so there was less quantity demanded at any given price. Figure 1.4 shows a decrease in price from P to P_1.

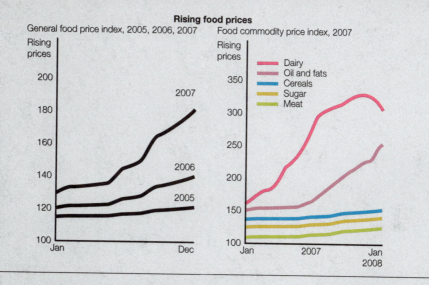

Rising food prices

General food price index, 2005, 2006, 2007

Food commodity price index, 2007

in developing countries and moving to urban areas. These trends are apt to move the supply curve to the left and the demand curve to the right and put further upward price pressure on food.

Sources: "Countries Rush to Restrict Trade in Basic Foods," *Financial Times*, April 2, 2008, p. 1; "Food Prices Give Asian Nations a Wake-Up Call," *Financial Times*, April 3, 2008, p. 4.

WHAT IF THE SUPPLY CURVE SHIFTS?

What happens to the equilibrium price of a product when its supply curve changes? For example, suppose that because of technological advances in copper production, large producers like Codelco of Chile can supply more copper at a given price than they used to. This will cause the supply curve to shift to the right, as shown in the right panel of Figure 1.5. How will this shift affect the equilibrium price? Clearly it will fall from P (where the original supply curve intersects the demand curve) to P_4 (where the new supply curve intersects the demand curve).

On the other hand, suppose there is a significant increase in the wage rates of copper workers. This increase will cause the supply curve to shift to the left, as shown in the left panel of Figure 1.5. This shift will cause the equilibrium price to

FIGURE 1.4

Effects of Leftward and Rightward Shifts of the Demand Curve on the Equilibrium Price of Copper

A leftward shift of the demand curve results in a decrease in the equilibrium price; a rightward shift results in an increase in the equilibrium price.

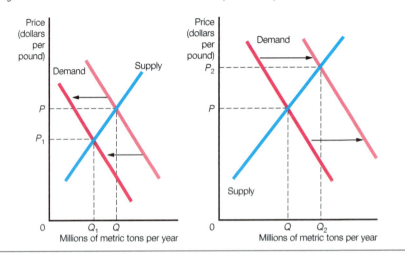

FIGURE 1.5

Effects of Leftward and Rightward Shifts of the Supply Curve on the Equilibrium Price of Copper

A leftward shift of the supply curve results in an increase in the equilibrium price; a rightward shift results in a decrease in the equilibrium price.

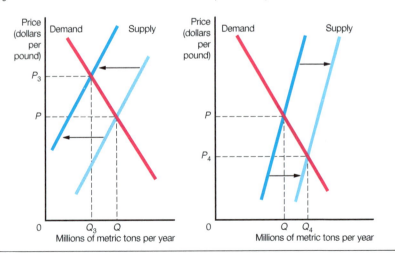

increase from P (where the original supply curve intersects the demand curve) to P_3 (where the new supply curve intersects the demand curve).

SUMMARY

1. The main task of managers is to make decisions. We offer a guide for that managerial world; it is based on the behavioral economics of the managerial model. In contrast to microeconomics, which is largely descriptive, managerial economics is prescriptive. Courses in managerial economics provide fundamental analytical tools as well as play a major integrating role. Our decision framework describes behavior found at a wide range of organizations, from nonbusiness organizations like government agencies to single-owner entrepreneurial efforts.

2. To apply economics to managerial behavior, we need a theory of the firm. The theory accepted by most managerial economists is that the owners want to maximize its value, defined as the present value of its expected future net cash flows (which for now are equated with profit). However, this maximization occurs subject to constraints because the firm has limited inputs, particularly in the very short run, and must comply with a variety of laws and contracts.

3. Managerial economists define profit somewhat differently from the way accountants do. When economists speak of profit, they mean profit over and above what the owners' labor and capital employed in the business could earn elsewhere. To a considerable extent, the differences between the concepts of profit used by the accountant and the economist reflect the difference in their functions.

4. Three important reasons for the existence of profit are innovation, risk, and monopoly power. Profit and loss are the mainspring of a free enterprise economy. They are signals showing where resources are needed and where they are too abundant. They are important incentives for innovation and risk taking. They are society's reward for efficiency.

5. Although managerial economists generally assume that owners want to maximize profit (and hence their value), a principal–agent problem arises if managers pursue their own interests, even though this decreases the profit of the owners. To address this problem, owners often give managers a financial stake in the future success of a firm.

6. Every market has a demand side and a supply side. The market demand curve shows the amount of a product buyers will purchase at various prices. The market supply curve shows the amount of a product producers are willing to sell at various prices. The equilibrium price is the price where the quantity demanded equals the quantity supplied. This price is also called the market-clearing price.

7. Both demand curves and supply curves can shift over time. This results in changes in a product's price. Rightward shifts in the demand curve (and leftward shifts in the supply curve) tend to increase price. Leftward shifts in the demand curve (and rightward shifts in the supply curve) tend to decrease price.

wwnorton.com/studyspace Ⓢ

PROBLEMS

1. A book is to be written by Britney Spears. Batman Books agrees to pay Britney $6 million for the rights to this not-yet-written memoir. According to one leading publisher, Batman Books could earn a profit of roughly $1.2 million if it sold 625,000 copies in hardcover. On the other hand, if it sold 375,000 copies, managers would lose about $1.3 million. Publishing executives stated that it was hard to sell more than 500,000 copies of a nonfiction hardcover book, and very exceptional to sell 1 million copies. Were Batman managers taking a substantial risk in publishing this book?

2. Some say that any self-respecting top manager joining a company does so with a front-end signing bonus. In many cases this bonus is in the seven figures. At the same time the entering manager may be given a bonus guarantee. No matter what happens to firm profit, he or she gets at least a percentage of that bonus. Do long-term bonus guarantees help to solve the principal–agent problem, or do they exacerbate it? Why?

3. If the interest rate is 10 percent, what is the present value of the Monroe Corporation's profit in the next 10 years?

Number of Years in the Future	Profit (Millions of Dollars)
1	8
2	10
3	12
4	14
5	15
6	16
7	17
8	15
9	13
10	10

4. Managers at Du Pont de Nemours and Company expect a profit of $2.9 billion in 2008. Does this mean that Du Pont's expected economic profit will equal $2.9 billion? Why or why not?

5. William Howe must decide whether to start a business renting beach umbrellas at an ocean resort during June, July, and August of next summer. He believes he can rent each umbrella to vacationers at $5 a day, and he intends to lease 50 umbrellas for the three-month period for $3,000. To operate this business, he does not have to hire anyone (but himself), and he has no expenses other than the leasing costs and a fee of $3,000 per month to rent the business location. Howe is a college student, and if he did not operate this business, he could earn $4,000 for the three-month period doing construction work.

a. If there are 80 days during the summer when beach umbrellas are demanded and Howe rents all 50 of his umbrellas on each of these days, what will be his accounting profit for the summer?

b. What will be his economic profit for the summer?

6. On March 3, 2008, a revival of *Gypsy*, the Stephen Sondheim musical, opened at the St. James Theater in New York. Ticket prices ranged from $117 to $42 per seat. The show's weekly gross revenues, operating costs, and profit were estimated as follows, depending on whether the average ticket price was $75 or $65:

	Average Price of $75	Average Price of $65
Gross revenues	$765,000	$680,000
Operating costs	600,000	600,000
Profit	165,000	80,000

a. With a cast of 71 people, a 30-piece orchestra, and more than 500 costumes, *Gypsy* cost more than $10 million to stage. This investment was in addition to the operating costs (such as salaries and theater rent). How many weeks would it take before the investors got their money back, according to these estimates, if the average price was $65? If it was $75?

b. George Wachtel, director of research for the League of American Theaters and Producers, has said that about one in three shows opening on Broadway in recent years has at least broken even. Were the investors in *Gypsy* taking a substantial risk?

c. According to one Broadway producer, "Broadway isn't where you make the money any more. It's where you establish the project so you can make the money. When you mount a show now, you really have to think about where it's going to play later." If so, should the profit figures here be interpreted with caution?

d. If the investors in this revival of *Gypsy* make a profit, will this profit be, at least in part, a reward for bearing risk?

7. If the demand curve for wheat in the United States is

$$P = 12.4 - Q_D$$

where P is the farm price of wheat (in dollars per bushel) and Q_D is the quantity of wheat demanded (in billions of bushels), and the supply curve for wheat in the United States is

$$P = -2.6 + 2Q_S$$

where Q_S is the quantity of wheat supplied (in billions of bushels), what is the equilibrium price of wheat? What is the equilibrium quantity of wheat sold? Must the actual price equal the equilibrium price? Why or why not?

8. The lumber industry was hit hard by the subprime mortgage turmoil in 2008. Prices plunged from $290 per thousand board feet to less than $200 per thousand board feet. Many observers believed this price decrease was caused by the slowing of new home construction because of the glut of unsold homes on the market. Was this price decrease caused by a shift in the supply or demand curve?

9. From November 2007 to March 2008 the price of gold increased from $865 per ounce to over $1,000 per ounce. Newspaper articles during this period said there was little increased demand from the jewelry industry but significantly more demand from investors who were purchasing gold because of the falling dollar.

   a. Was this price increase due to a shift in the demand curve for gold, a shift in the supply curve for gold, or both?

   b. Did this price increase affect the supply curve for gold jewelry? If so, how?

CHAPTER 2

DEMAND THEORY

An important determinant of profit is the nature of the demand for a firm's goods or services. It is imperative that managers understand this multidimensional concept if they are to positively influence firm performance. Good managers learn to understand the nature of demand for products and effectively manage it. Effective management requires more knowledge than understanding the directional impact on sales for a given price change. Many other factors besides price affect consumer demand. Some of these factors are controlled by managers, such as advertising, product quality, and distribution. Other factors, like the number of substitute goods, the prices of rival products, and the advertising of rivals, are part of the competitive dynamics of the product space. Finally, a few factors, like the state of the economy or the level of disposable consumer income, are macroeconomic and are not influenced by individual managers. Though these factors are outside their control, managers still need to predict how their changes affect demand.

This chapter explains how managers can more precisely predict changes in various environmental factors and quantify their impact on product demand. The nature of product demand is that it is a process—and as such is dynamic. Because many factors influence product demand, managers need to understand how changes in these factors affect product demand. Knowing the sensitivity of demand to changes in environmental factors lets a manager effectively respond to these changes. The sensitivity of one factor to another is called **elasticity**. Elasticity

Elasticity Elasticity measures the percentage change in one factor given a small (marginal) percentage change in another factor.

24

measures the percentage change in one factor given a small (marginal) percentage change in another factor. The concept of elasticity is widespread in the business world. For example, elasticity is the basis for both a firm's operating and financial leverage. It is also used by managers to determine a product's most efficient mix of inputs.

THE MARKET DEMAND CURVE

One way we can show how sales of a product are affected by its price is with a **market demand schedule**, which is a table showing the total quantity of the good purchased at each price. For example, suppose the market demand schedule for laptop computers in 2008 is as shown in Table 2.1. According to this table, 1.5 million laptop computers are demanded per year if the price is $2,000 per computer; 800,000 are demanded if the price is $3,000; and so on. Another way of presenting the data in Table 2.1 is with a **market demand curve**, which is a plot of the market demand schedule on a graph. The vertical axis of the graph measures the price per unit of the good, and the horizontal axis measures the quantity of the good demanded per unit of time. Figure 2.1 shows the market demand curve for laptop computers in 2008, based on the figures in Table 2.1.

In the previous chapter we introduced the concept of a market demand curve. Now we examine one in more detail. Note three things about Figure 2.1. First, the market demand curve shows the total quantity of laptop computers demanded at each price, not the quantity demanded from a particular firm. We discuss the demand for a particular firm's product later. Second, the market demand curve for laptops slopes downward to the right. That is, the quantity of laptops demanded increases as the price falls. As we pointed out in the last chapter, this is true for most products or services. Third, the market demand curve in Figure 2.1 pertains to a specified period: 2008. As you recall from the last chapter, any demand curve

Market demand schedule Table showing the total quantity of the good purchased at each price.

Market demand curve The plot of the market demand schedule on a graph.

TABLE 2.1

Market Demand Schedule for Laptops, 2008

Price per Laptop (Dollars)	Quantity Demanded (Thousands)
3,000	800
2,750	975
2,500	1,150
2,250	1,325
2,000	1,500

FIGURE 2.1

Demand Curve for Laptops

This demand curve is a graphical representation of the figures in Table 2.1.

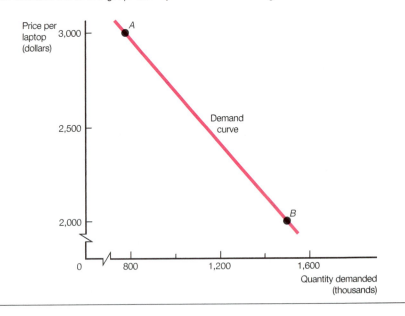

pertains to some particular time, and its shape and position depend on the length and other characteristics of this period. If we were to estimate the market demand curve for laptops for the first week in 2008, it would probably differ from the one in Figure 2.1. This difference arises partly because consumers adapt their purchases more fully to changes in the price of laptops in a year relative to a week.

In addition to the length of time, what factors determine the position and shape of a market demand curve? One important factor is the tastes of consumers. If consumers show an increasing preference for a product, the demand curve shifts to the right; that is, at each price consumers want to buy more than they did previously. Alternatively, for each quantity consumers are willing to pay a higher price. On the other hand, if consumers show a decreasing preference for a product, the demand curve shifts to the left because at each price consumers buy less than previously. Alternatively, for each quantity consumers are willing to pay only a lower price. For example, as shown in Figure 2.2, if people find that laptops are helpful and begin to use them more and give them in larger numbers to their children and others, the demand curve may shift to the right. The greater the shift in preferences, the farther the demand curve shifts.

Another factor that influences the position and shape of a product's market demand curve is the level of consumer incomes. For some products the demand

Some customers are viewed as angels. They purchase the big-ticket, big-markup items, want them right when they come out, and want each one of them. And some customers are viewed as devils. They wait for loss leader sales (items sold at a loss designed to entice consumers to the store, where the store hopes they will buy many other items—the devils only buy the loss leaders); buy items, return them, and then rebuy them as previously owned items at a discount; buy the most discounted items and then resell them (eliminating their customers from the store's pool); scour the Internet, circulars, and newspapers for the store's competitors' low prices and then make the store honor the competitors' prices because of the "we will not be undersold" pledge of the store; send in for rebates; and so on.

Big box electronics store Best Buy has had enough of the devils' tactics. Best Buy estimates that 20 percent of its store visits are by devils. And they'd like the devils to get out of their stores. They want to fire some of their customers! On the other hand, they have identified the true angels—the 20 percent of their customers that generate the bulk of their profits.

How do you get rid of the devils? You can't identify them and then not let them in your store. That would violate antidiscrimination laws. But you can eliminate the programs that draw them to your stores (and make sure they are not the same programs that draw the angels). For instance, stop direct mailing to the customers identified (by their past purchases) as devils; charge customers a restocking fee of 15 percent of the purchase price for returned items; prohibit reselling returned items on the Internet or at another store rather than at the original store; and break all ties with Internet sites (FatWallet.com, SlickDeals.net, TechBargains.com) that tipped the devils off to Best Buy bargains and buying strategies that Best Buy regarded as having a negative impact on profits. The financial services sector has solved this problem by catering to their angels (free checking for maintaining a certain balance) and penalizing the devils (transaction fees for ATM use, fees to deal with a teller, check fees, and so forth).

Source: "Analyzing Customers, Best Buy Decides Not All Are Welcome," *The Wall Street Journal*, November 8, 2004, A-1.

curve shifts to the right if per capita income increases, whereas for other products it shifts to the left if per capita income rises. In the case of laptops, we expect that an increase in per capita income will shift the demand curve to the right, as shown in Figure 2.3. Still another factor that influences the position and shape of a product's market demand curve is the level of other prices. For example, we expect the quantity of laptops demanded to increase if the price of computer software falls drastically.

Finally, the position and shape of a product's market demand curve are affected by the size of the population in the relevant market. If the number of consumers increases, we expect that, if all other factors are held equal, the quantity of laptops demanded will increase. Of course the population generally changes slowly, so this factor often has little effect in the short run.

FIGURE 2.2

Effect of an Increased Preference on the Market Demand Curve for Laptops

The demand curve for laptops shifts to the right.

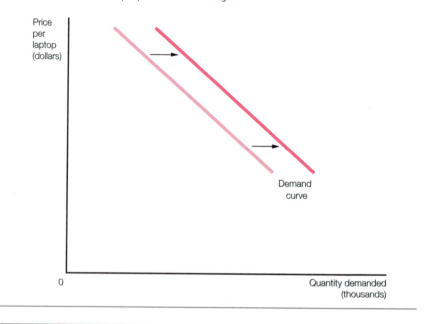

FIGURE 2.3

Effect of an Increase in Per Capita Income on the Market Demand Curve for Laptops

The demand curve shifts to the right.

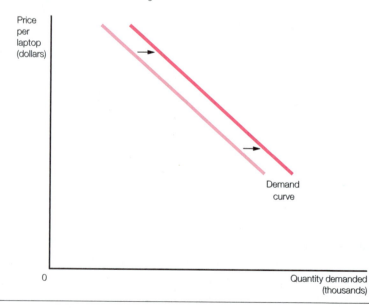

INDUSTRY AND FIRM DEMAND FUNCTIONS

Building on the results of the previous section, we define the **market demand function** for a product as the relationship between the quantity demanded and the various factors that influence this quantity. Put generally, this market demand function is written as

$$\text{Quantity demanded of good } X = Q = f \text{ (price of } X \text{, incomes of consumers, tastes of consumers, prices of other goods, population, advertising expenditures, and so forth)}$$

> **Market demand function** The relationship between the quantity demanded and the various factors that influence this quantity.

To be useful for analytical and forecasting purposes, this equation must be more specific. For example, if good X is laptop computers, the market demand function might be

$$Q = b_1 P + b_2 I + b_3 S + b_4 A \tag{2.1}$$

where in a particular year, Q equals the number of laptops demanded, P is the average price of laptops, I is per capita disposable income, S is the average price of software, and A is the amount spent on advertising by laptop producers. Equation (2.1) assumes that the relationship is linear. (Also, we assume the population in the relevant market is essentially constant.)

Going a step further, it generally is necessary for managers to obtain numerical estimates of the values of the b's in equation (2.1). Employing various statistical techniques, managers estimate these **parameters** of the demand function to increase their knowledge of the demand for their product. To illustrate the results we might obtain, we find that

> **Parameters** Constant or variable terms used in the function that helps managers determine the specific form of the function but not its general nature.

$$Q = -700P + 200I - 500S + 0.01A \tag{2.2}$$

According to equation (2.2), a \$1 increase in the price of a laptop computer decreases the quantity demanded by 700 units per year; a \$1 increase in per capita disposable income results in a 200-unit increase in the quantity demanded; a \$1 increase in the price of software reduces the quantity demanded by 500 units per year; and a \$1 increase in advertising raises the quantity demanded by 0.01 unit per year.

It is important to understand the relationship between the market demand function and the demand curve. The market demand curve shows the relationship between Q and P when all other relevant variables are held constant. For example, suppose we want to know the relationship between quantity demanded and price if per capita disposable income is \$13,000, the average price of software is \$400, and advertising expenditure is \$50 million. Because $I = 13,000$, $S = 400$, and $A = 50,000,000$, equation (2.2) becomes

$$Q = -700P + 200(13,000)$$
$$-500(400) + 0.01(50,000,000) \tag{2.3}$$

or

$$Q = 2,900,000 - 700P \qquad (2.4)$$

Solving this equation for P, we obtain

$$P = 4,143 - 0.001429Q$$

which is graphed in Figure 2.1. This is the demand curve for laptops, given that I, S, and A are held constant at the stipulated levels.

Given the market demand function, managers can better understand how changes in variables can shift the demand curve. For example, how much of a shift will occur in the demand curve if the price of software falls from $400 to $200? Inserting 200 (rather than 400) for S in equation (2.3), we find that

$$Q = 3,000,000 - 700P \qquad (2.5)$$

Solving this equation for P, we obtain

$$P = 4,286 - 0.001429Q \qquad (2.6)$$

which is graphed (together with the demand curve based on $S = 400$) in Figure 2.4. Clearly the demand curve has shifted to the right: The quantity demanded is 100,000 more than when $S = 400$ (if P is held constant).

FIGURE 2.4

Demand Curve for Laptops

If the price of software falls from $400 to $200, the demand curve shifts to the right by 100,000 units.

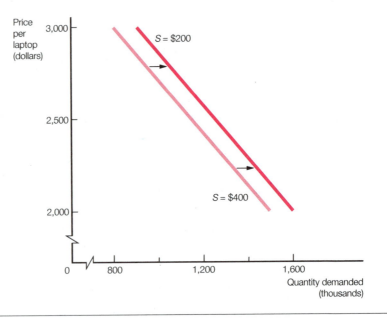

Managers are often more interested in the demand curves of their own brands rather than the market demand curve. We can derive these demand functions in a similar manner to predict the sales of an individual producer of laptop computers. In such an equation, the quantity demanded of the firm's product is still inversely related to its own price but is directly related to prices charged by its competitors. So if Dell increases its laptop prices, sales of Apple laptops will increase (all other factors being equal). It is important to distinguish between industry and firm demand functions because they are quite different. Although both are important for managers to understand, they are generally used for different purposes. Looking at the demand functions for individual firms is important in understanding the competitive dynamics of the market. Market demand curves tell managers more about substitute goods outside their product market and the general effects of macroeconomic factors like changes in disposable income on industry sales.

THE OWN-PRICE ELASTICITY OF DEMAND

The elasticity of a function is defined as the percentage change in the dependent variable in response to a 1 percent change in the independent variable. In $y = ax$, y is the dependent variable because by specifying x, we can determine y. A market demand curve is a function in which quantity demanded is dependent on a product's price. Market demand curves vary with regard to the sensitivity of quantity demanded to price. For some goods, a small price change results in a big change in quantity demanded; for other goods, a big price change results in a small change in quantity demanded. To indicate how sensitive quantity demanded is to price changes, economists use a measure called the **own-price elasticity of demand**. The word *own* is used to convey the idea that managers generally measure the price elasticity of demand for a product or service produced by their firm. More commonly, own-price elasticity of demand is simply referred to as the price elasticity of demand. The price elasticity of demand is defined as the percentage change in quantity demanded resulting from a 1 percent change in price. More precisely, it equals

Own-price elasticity of demand
More simply referred to as price elasticity of demand, this is the concept managers use to measure their own percentage change in quantity demanded resulting from a 1 percent change in their own price.

$$\eta = \left(\frac{P}{Q}\right)\frac{\Delta Q}{\Delta P} \tag{2.7}$$

$\Delta Q/\Delta P$ (horizontal change/vertical change) is the inverse of a line's slope. Because linear demand curves are downward-sloping, $\Delta Q/\Delta P$ is negative; hence the price elasticity of demand is expressed as a negative number. Suppose a 1 percent reduction in the price of Apple laptop computers results in a 1.3 percent increase in U.S. sales. If so, the price elasticity of demand for Apple laptops is -1.3. The price elasticity of demand generally changes as price varies along the demand curve. For instance, the price elasticity of demand may be higher in absolute value when the price of laptops is relatively high than when it is low. Similarly, the price elasticity

---

FIGURE 2.5

Demand Curves with Zero and Infinite Price Elasticities of Demand

The demand curve is a vertical line if the price elasticity is zero and a horizontal line if it is negative infinity.

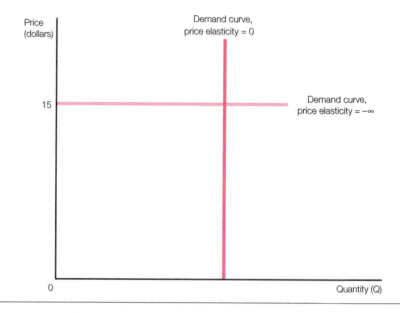

---

of demand varies from market to market. India probably has a different price elasticity of demand for laptops than that of the United States.

We can classify the price elasticity of demand as falling into one of three possible "buckets." When a 1 percent change in price leads to a more than 1 percent change in quantity demanded, we say demand is elastic. When a 1 percent change in price leads to a less than 1 percent change in quantity demanded, we say demand is **inelastic**. And when a 1 percent change in price leads to a 1 percent change in quantity demanded, we say demand is unitary elastic. Because the price elasticity of demand is always negative for linear demand, we express this information as follows: When demand is elastic, $\eta < -1$; when demand is inelastic, $\eta > -1$; and when demand is unitary elastic, $\eta = -1$.

The price elasticity of demand for a product must lie between zero and negative infinity. If the price elasticity is zero, the demand curve is a vertical line; that is, the quantity demanded is unaffected by price. If the price elasticity is negative infinity, the demand curve is a horizontal line; that is, an unlimited amount can be sold at a particular price ($15 in Figure 2.5), but nothing is sold if the price is raised even slightly. Figure 2.5 shows these two limiting cases.

We know that $\Delta Q/\Delta P$ is constant along a linear function. However, the price

Inelastic Inelastic is used to describe demand when a 1 percent change in price leads to a less than 1 percent change in quantity demanded.

FIGURE 2.6

Values of the Price Elasticity of Demand at Various Points along a Linear Demand Curve

The price elasticity increases in absolute value as price rises, approaching negative infinity as quantity approaches zero.

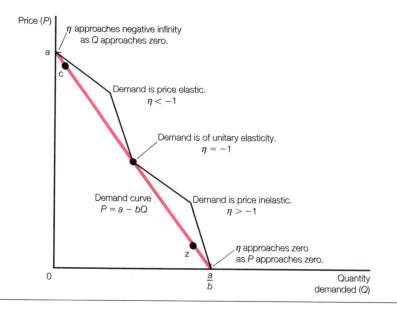

elasticity of demand even for linear demand is not constant because the ratio of price to quantity (P/Q) varies as we move along the demand curve. This is illustrated in Figure 2.6. Point c represents a point on the demand curve. Price is very high, and quantity demanded is very low. Hence P/Q is a large positive number, so elasticity must be low ($\eta < -1$, and demand is elastic). At point z the opposite is true. Price is very low, and quantity demanded is very high; hence P/Q is less than 1. So elasticity is high ($\eta > -1$, and demand is inelastic). Hence for linear demand curves, when P is high, the price elasticity of demand is large (in absolute value terms). As we move down the demand curve, P is decreasing and Q is increasing. This causes the price elasticity to monotonically increase. As we approach the horizontal axis, by definition, P is low and Q is high, so the demand is inelastic. Because the price elasticity is high (above -1) when P is low, and low (below -1) when P is high, at some point on any linear demand curve, the price elasticity must be equal to -1 (unitary elasticity).

An alternative way of seeing how the price elasticity changes as we move along the demand curve is the following. If

$$P = a - bQ$$

where a is the intercept of the demand curve on the price axis and b is the slope (in absolute terms) of the demand curve, it follows that

$$Q = \frac{a}{b} - \frac{1}{b} P$$

Therefore, the price elasticity of demand is

$$\left(\frac{\Delta Q}{\Delta P} \right) \left(\frac{P}{Q} \right) = \left(\frac{-1}{b} \right) \frac{a - bQ}{Q}$$

Clearly, if the demand curve is linear, the price elasticity approaches zero as $P\ (= a - bQ)$ gets very small and approaches negative infinity as Q gets very small.

So for most demand curves, the elasticity of demand varies with price. That is, the magnitude of the sales response to price changes does not remain constant. This makes it more difficult for managers to estimate the effects of price changes on sales levels.

POINT AND ARC ELASTICITIES

If we have a market demand schedule showing the quantity of a product demanded at various prices, how can we estimate the price elasticity of market demand? Let ΔP be a change in the price of the good and ΔQ the resulting change in its quantity demanded. If ΔP is very small, we can compute the point elasticity of demand:

$$\eta = \frac{\Delta Q}{Q} \div \frac{\Delta P}{P} \qquad (2.8)$$

For instance, consider Table 2.2, where data are given for very small increments in the price of a commodity. If we want to estimate the price elasticity of demand when the price is between $0.9995 and $1, we obtain

$$\eta = \frac{20,002 - 20,000}{20,000} \div \frac{99.95 - 100}{100} = -0.2$$

Note that we used $1 as P and 20,000 as Q. We could have used $0.9995 as P and 20,002 as Q, but it would have made no real difference to the answer.

But if we have data concerning only large changes in price (that is, ΔP and ΔQ are large), the answer may vary considerably depending on which values of P and Q are used in equation (2.8). Consider the example in Table 2.3. Suppose we want to estimate the price elasticity of demand in the price range between $4 and $5. Then, depending on which values of P and Q are used, the answer is

$$\eta = \frac{40 - 3}{3} \div \frac{4 - 5}{5} = -61.67$$

TABLE 2.2

Quantity Demanded at Various Prices (Small Increments in Price)

Price (Cents per Unit of Commodity)	Quantity Demanded per Unit of Time (Units of Commodity)
99.95	20,002
100.00	20,000
100.05	19,998

or

$$\eta = \frac{3 - 40}{40} \div \frac{5 - 4}{4} = -3.70$$

The difference between these two results is very large. To avoid this difficulty, it is advisable to compute the arc elasticity of demand, which uses the average values of P and Q:

$$\eta = \frac{\Delta Q}{(Q_1 + Q_2)/2} \div \frac{\Delta P}{(P_1 + P_2)/2}$$

$$\eta = \frac{\Delta Q(P_1 + P_2)}{\Delta P(Q_1 + Q_2)} \tag{2.9}$$

where P_1 and Q_1 are the first values of price and quantity demanded, and P_2 and Q_2 are the second set. Therefore, in Table 2.3,

$$\eta = \frac{40 - 3}{(40 + 3)/2} \div \frac{4 - 5}{(4 + 5)/2} = -7.74$$

TABLE 2.3

Quantity Demanded at Various Prices (Large Increments in Price)

Price (Dollars per Unit of Commodity)	Quantity Demanded per Unit of Time (Units of Commodity)
3	50
4	40
5	3

USING THE DEMAND FUNCTION TO CALCULATE THE PRICE ELASTICITY OF DEMAND

Managers often estimate a demand function for their products. In equation (2.2) we provided the following hypothetical demand function for laptop computers:

$$Q = -700P + 200I - 500S + 0.01A$$

Given such a demand function, how can we calculate the price elasticity of demand?

The first step is to specify the point on the demand curve at which price elasticity is to be measured. Assuming per capita disposable income (I) is $13,000, the average price of software (S) is $400, and advertising expenditure (A) is $50 million, we know from equation (2.4) that the relationship between quantity demanded and price is

$$Q = 2,900,000 - 700P \qquad (2.10)$$

Suppose we want to measure the price elasticity of demand when price equals $3,000. At this point on the demand curve (point A in Figure 2.1),

$$Q = 2,900,000 - 700(3,000)$$
$$= 800,000$$

We can express $\Delta Q/\Delta P$ as the inverse of the slope. Hence, in our example,

$$\frac{\Delta Q}{\Delta P} = -700$$

According to equation (2.7), to obtain the price elasticity of demand, we must multiply $\Delta Q/\Delta P$ by P/Q. Performing this multiplication, we get

$$-700\frac{3,000}{800,000} = -2.63$$

which means the price elasticity of demand equals -2.63.

As a further illustration, let us calculate the price elasticity of demand when price equals $2,000 rather than $3,000. At this point on the demand curve (point B in Figure 2.1),

$$Q = 2,900,000 - 700(2,000)$$
$$= 1,500,000$$

Because $\Delta Q/\Delta P = -700$,

$$\eta = \left(\frac{\Delta Q}{\Delta P}\right)\left(\frac{P}{Q}\right) = (-700)\frac{2,000}{1,500,000} = -0.93$$

Therefore, the price elasticity of demand equals -0.93.

THE EFFECT OF PRICE ELASTICITY ON THE FIRM'S REVENUE

As we have seen, estimating the price elasticity of demand helps managers predict how a given price change will affect sales. We can also use price elasticities to determine how a price change will affect a firm's total revenue. Total revenue is equal to the price per unit multiplied by the number of units sold ($TR = P \times Q$). So as managers change the price of a product, sales generally vary. Good managers need to consider whether a price change will increase the firm's total revenue if their decisions are to improve firm performance. And whether a price change increases total revenue depends on the price elasticity of demand.

Suppose at the current price, demand for a product is price elastic; that is, the price elasticity of demand is less than -1. In this situation, if the price is reduced, the percentage increase in quantity demanded is greater than the percentage reduction in price (this follows from the definition of elastic demand). That is, although all units are now being sold at a lower price, the increase in units sold because of the lower price more than makes up for the slightly lower unit price. Hence total revenue increases. Similarly, if demand is elastic at the current price and a manager increases the price, total revenue will decrease. Although we are selling each unit at a higher price, the decrease in sales (because of the higher price) more than offsets the slightly higher price per unit.

If the demand for the product at a given price is price inelastic, the price elasticity of demand is greater than -1. Following from our definition of inelastic demand, the percentage change in quantity is less than the percentage change in price. Hence if we increase price, total revenue will increase because the slightly higher price per unit sold will more than offset the decrease in units sold. If demand is inelastic and we decrease price, total revenue will decrease because the increase in units sold cannot offset the lower price per unit sold.

We can easily show this relationship formally. Let $TR = P \times Q$; then,

$$\frac{\Delta TR}{\Delta P} = Q\frac{\Delta P}{\Delta P} + P\frac{\Delta Q}{\Delta P}$$

$$Q\frac{\Delta P}{\Delta P} + Q\frac{P}{Q}\frac{\Delta Q}{\Delta P} = Q(1 + \eta)$$

$$\frac{\Delta TR/\Delta P}{Q} = 1 + \eta$$

Then if $\eta < -1$ (that is, elastic), $\frac{\Delta TR/\Delta P}{Q} < 0$ or $\frac{\Delta TR}{\Delta P} < 0$, so an increase in price will reduce TR. And if $\eta > -1$ (that is, inelastic), $\frac{\Delta TR/\Delta P}{Q} > 0$ or $\frac{\Delta TR}{\Delta P} > 0$, so an increase in price will increase TR.

QUANT OPTION

Although most students could hardly agree less, those who use calculus do find some measure of satisfaction in it. So here we derive the elasticity relationship using calculus:

$$\frac{dTR}{dP} = Q\frac{dP}{dP} + P\frac{dQ}{dP}$$

$$Q\frac{dP}{dP} + Q\frac{P}{Q}\frac{dQ}{dP} = Q(1 + \eta)$$

$$\frac{dTR/dP}{Q} = 1 + \eta$$

If $\eta < -1$ (that is, elastic), $\frac{dTR/dP}{Q} < 0$ or $\frac{dTR}{dP} < 0$, so an increase in price will reduce TR. And if $\eta > -1$ (that is, inelastic), $\frac{dTR/dP}{Q} > 0$ or $\frac{dTR}{dP} > 0$, so an increase in price will increase TR.

PROBLEM SOLVED: Price Elasticity of Demand: Philip Morris

In 1993 Philip Morris cut cigarette prices by 18 percent. Its major competitor (RJ Reynolds) matched the price cut. Not surprisingly, the quantity sold of Philip Morris cigarettes increased (by 12.5 percent). In a June 13, 1994, article referring to the perils of a price cut, *Fortune* reported that Philip Morris profits fell by 25 percent as the result of a bad pricing strategy. Is there any evidence to determine whether this decision by Philip Morris managers decreased firm performance?

Although all the information is not available, we are not surprised by this result. We estimate the price elasticity of demand for Philip Morris brands (including the iconic Marlboro Man) as revealed by the market:

$$\eta_p = \frac{\%\Delta Q}{\%\Delta P} = \frac{12.5\%}{-18\%} = -0.694$$

Demand is inelastic, so any drop in price should surely decrease firm revenue. Total revenue decreased and total costs increased (because more cigarettes were produced), so profit was destined to fall.

FUNDING PUBLIC TRANSIT

Consider an example in which we can predict market behavior based on estimates of elasticity measures. The fare (price) elasticity for public transportation in the United States is about -0.3 (that is, fairly inelastic). All transit systems in the United

States lose money. Keeping the deficit under control is a constant battle because the typical subsidizers (federal, state, and local governments) are often reluctant to fund public transit (because of their own deficit problems). Can we identify which transit systems have the most difficult time getting public funding?

We can use our knowledge of price elasticity of demand. Managers of transit systems depend on two sources of revenue: ticket sales and public funding. They know that increasing fares will result in higher revenues. Most likely costs will also drop because less capital and labor are used. However, increasing fares reduces ridership and makes public transit less affordable to many. So managers of transit systems that do not receive enough public funding must increase their fares to balance their budgets (and they know their revenues will increase because of their inelastic demand).

DETERMINANTS OF THE OWN-PRICE ELASTICITY OF DEMAND

Table 2.4 shows the price elasticity of demand for selected products in the United States. Managers need to understand the factors that determine a product's price elasticity of demand:

1. The price elasticity of demand for a product depends heavily on the number and similarity of available substitute products. A product with many close substitutes generally has elastic demand. If managers increase the product's price, consumers can easily switch to one of the several available substitutes. Conversely, if managers reduce the price of their product, they will see a significant increase in sales as consumers switch to their product. The extent to which a product has close substitutes largely depends on how well managers differentiate their product from similar ones.

2. The price elasticity of demand is also affected by a product's price relative to a consumer's total budget. Some claim that the demand for products like thimbles, rubber bands, and salt is quite inelastic, because the typical consumer spends only a very small fraction of her income on such goods. This is also why retail stores place items such as candy, soda, and magazines at the checkout counter. Because they are relatively inexpensive, consumers often buy them without thinking about the price. In contrast, products that command a larger percentage of the consumer's total budget tend to be more price elastic. Research has shown that when consumers consider purchasing items such as kitchen appliances or automobiles, they take the time to get several price quotes and gather information about brand attributes.

3. The price elasticity of demand for a product is also affected by the length of the period to which the demand curve pertains. For nondurable goods, demand is likely to be more elastic over a long period relative to a short period. This is because the longer the time period, the easier it is for consumers to substitute

TABLE 2.4

Own Price Elasticities of Demand, Selected Goods, and Services from Global Locations

Good/Service	Elasticity	Good/Service	Elasticity
Agricultural products		Cigarettes (U.S.)[7]	−0.107
Apples (U.S.)[1]	−1.159	Bread (U.K.)[3]	−0.26
Potatoes (U.K.)[3]	−0.13	Energy	
Oranges (U.S.)[2]	−0.62	Gasoline—short run (Canada)[8]	−0.01 to −0.2
Lettuce (U.S.)[2]	−2.58	Gasoline—long run (Canada)[8]	−0.4 to −0.8
Products from animals/fish		Transportation	
1 percent milk (U.S.)[5]	−0.54 to −0.74	Domestic cars (U.S.)[9]	−0.78
Cheese (U.K.)[3]	−1.36	European cars (U.S.)[9]	−1.09
Cheese (U.S.)[6]	−0.595	Other manufactured goods	
Meat (China)[4]	−0.06 to −0.18	Clothing and footwear (U.K./Ireland)[10]	−0.94
Beef/veal (U.K.)[3]	−1.45	Other goods (U.K./Ireland)[10]	−0.85
Manufactured agricultural products		Services	
Beer and malt beverages (U.S.)[6]	−2.83	Child care (North America)[11]	−0.570
Wine (U.K./Ireland)[7]	−1.12	Government health care (Kenya)[12]	−0.100
Wine and brandy (U.S.)[6]	−0.198		

[1]C. Elmore, Chapter 10, "Use of 2.4-D in Orchard, Vineyard, and Soft Fruit Production in the United States," *Phenoxy Herbicides*, December 20, 1998, found at *piked.agn.uiuc.edu/piap/assess2/ch10.htm*.

[2]D. Suits, "Agriculture," in Walter Adams and James Brock, eds., *The Structure of American Industry*, (10th ed.; Englewood Cliffs, NJ: Prentice-Hall, 2000).

[3]AEF116: 1.6: Major market response concepts and measures 1: The demand side and its elasticities found at *www.staff.ncl.ac.uk/davidharvey/AEF116/1.6/1.6/html*.

[4]Millennium Institute, China Agricultural Project found at *www.threshold21.com/chinaag/report/appendix.html*.

[5]A Regional Economic Analysis of Dairy Compacts: Implications for Missouri Dairy Producers, Section IV—Economic Analysis of Dairy Compact, circa 1999, found at *agebb.missouri.edu/commag/dairy/bailey/compact/sect4.htm*.

[6]Emilo Pagoulatos and Robert Sorensen, "What Determines the Elasticity of Industry Demand," *International Journal of Industrial Organization*, Vol. 4, 1986.

[7]C. O'Donoghue, "Carbon Dioxide, Energy Taxes, and Household Income," Department of Statistics and Social Policy, London School of Economics, October 13, 1998.

[8]"Potential for Fuel Taxes to Reduce Greenhouse Gas Emissions in Transportation," Hagler Bailly Canada for Department of Public Works and Government Services, Hull, Quebec, June 11, 1990 found at *www.tc.gc.ca/envaffairs/sub . . . udy1/Final report/Final Report.html*.

[9]P. McCarthy, "Market Price and Income Elasticities of New Vehicle Demands," *Review of Economics and Statistics*, Vol. 78(3), August 1996, 543–547.

[10]E. Brynjolfsson, "Some Estimates of the Contribution of Information Technology to Consumer Welfare," MIT Sloan School, Working Paper 3647-094, January 1994.

[11]D. Chaplin et al., "The Price Elasticity of Child Care Demand: A Sensitivity Analysis," found at *www.cpc.unc.edu/pubs/ppp_papers/1997/chaplin.html*.

[12]Section 4: The Basics of Markets and Health Care Markets: Box 4.4: Demand for Health Care in Kenya found at *www.worldbank.org/wbi/healthflagship/learning/module1/box4_4.htm*.

one good for another. If, for instance, the price of oil should decline relative to other fuels, the consumption of oil on the day after the price decline will probably increase very little. But over several years, people have an opportunity to react to the price decline in choosing types of home heating fuel; thus the price decline will have a greater effect on oil consumption than in the shorter period of one day. For durable goods, the opposite is true. Let's assume a consumer has just purchased a car. If the price of the car falls soon after the purchase, it is unlikely the consumer will run out and purchase another car; hence demand is inelastic.

THE STRATEGIC USE OF THE PRICE ELASTICITY OF DEMAND

Good managers not only display an avid interest in the price elasticity of demand for their products; they also take strategic actions to use the price elasticity to their benefit. Consider Table 2.5, which provides estimates of the price elasticity of demand for first-class, regular economy, and excursion air tickets between the United States and Europe. The price elasticity of demand for first-class air tickets is much lower in absolute value than for regular economy or excursion tickets, owing in part to the fact that the people who fly first class—often business travelers and relatively wealthy people—are unlikely to change their travel plans if moderate increases or decreases occur in the price of an air ticket. Airline executives study these data carefully and price these classes of tickets differently. For example, because the price elasticity of demand for first-class air tickets is relatively low in absolute value, they price these tickets relatively high. In early 2008 a consumer could purchase an economy airline ticket for a round-trip between Philadephia and Paris for under $500. A first-class ticket would cost the consumer more than $1,700.

Managers can also change the price elasticity of demand for their product. The most common way managers impact the price elasticity of their product is with

---

TABLE 2.5

Elasticities of Demand for Air Tickets between the United States and Europe

Type of Ticket	Price Elasticity	Income Elasticity
First class	−0.45	1.50
Regular economy	−1.30	1.38
Excursion	−1.83	2.37

Source: J. Cigliano, "Price and Income Elasticities for Airline Travel: The North Atlantic Market," *Business Economics,* September 1980.

STRATEGY SESSION: Elasticity in Use

Aside from the Wal-Mart Zorro price slasher cutting prices from levels like $12.79 to $10.56, most of us are accustomed to seeing prices that end in 0s, 5s, or 9s. But prices that end in any integer are becoming more common. In addition, prices for the exact same item may differ substantially in stores of the same chain, even if the stores are located close to one another. Why? Elasticity is being used to generate optimal (or closer to optimal) prices in a price optimization model. The model is designed to generate the ideal price for every item, in each store, at any given time. Longs Drug Stores, a U.S. drugstore chain with 390 stores in the lower 48 states, uses such a model. D'Agostino's, a 23-store grocery chain in New York, claims that such a model has increased unit revenues by 10 percent, unit volume by 6 percent, and net profits by 2 percent. ShopKo used a similar model in 141 stores and reports gross profit margins increased by 24 percent. Payback periods for the purchase and use of such pricing systems is estimated to be a year (despite their expensive price tags).

Rather than marking up costs, benchmarking competitors' prices, or guessing, price optimization models use data mining techniques. Scanned transactions from cash registers, responses to sales promotions, and the like are used to estimate an individual demand curve *for each product in each store*. Much of this modeling is based on airline yield management systems (see Chapter 8). The goal driving the modeling is to find the "crossover point between driving sales and giving away margin unnecessarily." That is consultant-speak. Let us put it in economist-speak.

Airline yield management models attempt to equate marginal expected revenues for each fare class. For instance, suppose two fare classes, 1 and 2, exist. As shown on page 47, marginal revenue (MR) is equal to $MR = P[1 + (1/\eta)]$, so equating marginal revenues for classes 1 and 2 yields

$$MR_1 = P_1[1 + (1/\eta_1)] = P_2[1 + (1/\eta_2)] = MR_2$$

Think about why a business with two different demand curves for the same product (such as business and leisure travelers for an airline seat, spring and summer demand for a bathing suit, location 1 and location 2 demand levels for Pampers) would want to equate the marginal revenues of those demand curves. If the marginal revenue on fare type 2 exceeds the marginal revenue on fare type 1, it would pay the airline to switch seats out of fare type 1 and into fare type 2. Because the cost of moving a person in fare type 1 is likely to be the same as the cost of moving a person in fare type 2, the

differentiation strategies. Managers who successfully increase the differentiation of their product decrease (in absolute value) its price elasticity of demand. Simply put, differentiation strategies convince consumers the product is unique; hence it has fewer substitutes. Because consumers perceive fewer substitutes, they act as if they are more price inelastic. This gives managers more freedom to increase price because sales will fall less.

It is important for managers to understand that differentiation is not effective if consumers do not perceive it. Conversely, differentiation does not require tangible differences in products. For example, bleach is a commodity product; its chemical formula is well known. However, Clorox Bleach is able to command a retail price that is 300 percent higher than other brands of bleach. Most

airline can increase revenues while leaving costs the same by such a switch. Such a move must increase the airline's bottom line. (If the equated marginal revenues equal the marginal cost of moving a passenger, profits are not only improved, they are maximized.)

How would an elasticity model do this in retailing? Consider the optimal discounting of a product over time. The subscript 1 stands for the first time period, and the subscript 2 stands for the second time period. If the marginal revenue is higher in period 2 than in period 1, you would want to shift some merchandise from period 1 to period 2 (or if 1 and 2 refer to stores, shift some product from store 1 to store 2).

Suppose that $\eta_1 = -2$ and $\eta_2 = -3$. Then

$$MR_1 = P_1[1 + (1/-2)] = P_1[1 - (1/2)] = P_1/2$$
$$= P_2[1 + (1/-3)] = P_2[1 - (1/3)] = 2P_2/3 = MR_2$$

Or $P_2 = 0.75P_1$; that is, the optimal discount on the product would be to sell the good in time period 2 for 25 percent off the price from time period 1. Lowering price increases the quantity demanded (because demand curves have an inverse relationship between price and quantity)—hence the term driving sales. But lowering price too much or too little will not give the seller the optimal profit margin—that is, the profit margin that

yields maximum profit. This can be done only where $MR_1 = MR_2 (= MC)$.

ShopKo, by analyzing several years' sales data, estimates a seasonal demand curve for each product (approximately 300 of them). The analysis predicts how many units will sell each week at various prices. The software uses sales history "to predict how sensitive customer demand would be to price changes, what economists call 'price elasticity.'" The software then uses the price elasticity information, the number of weeks until the product is outdated, and such factors in a system of mathematical models to determine the most profitable price cuts on each item.

An article in the *Economist* ("The Price Is Wrong") notes that supermarket chains "can quickly and easily track customers' 'elasticity'—how their buying habits change in response to a price rise or discount." Supermarkets such as D'Agostino's in New York and Dominicks in Chicago use elasticity-based models to help them make pricing decisions.

Source: "The Power of Optimal Pricing," *Business 2.0*, September, 2002, pp. 68–70; "Priced to Move: Retailers Try to Get Leg Up on Markdowns with New Software," *The Wall Street Journal*, August 7, 2001.

remarkably, this brand has been able to command such a high premium over several decades.

TOTAL REVENUE, MARGINAL REVENUE, AND PRICE ELASTICITY

We want to look more closely at the effect of the price elasticity of demand on a firm's total revenue. To a good's producers, the total amount of money paid by consumers equals the firm's revenue. Therefore, to the Toyota Motor Company, the total amount consumers spend on its cars is its total revenue. Suppose the demand curve for a firm's product is linear; that is,

$$P = a - bQ \tag{2.11}$$

In 2005 the U.S. federal government rescinded a fee (called the universal service fund fee) that it charged users of Internet services (to subsidize rural and low-income phone service). This charge amounted to $1.25 per month for users of Verizon's DSL service and $2.83 per month for their high-speed Internet service. Undoubtedly users thought they wouldn't have to pay this charge any more because it was no longer required by the government. But Verizon implemented its own supplier surcharges of $1.20 per month on DSL service and $2.70 per month on high-speed Internet.

If Verizon wanted to increase the price of its Internet services by $1.20 and $2.70, why didn't it do so when the surcharge existed? Assuming rationality, it would have done so if this would have increased net revenue. And why didn't Verizon reduce its fees by $1.25 and $2.83 when the surcharge was rescinded? Assuming rationality, it would have done so if this would have increased net revenue.

Consumers make decisions based on the prices they pay. This includes the base price of an item and any taxes. It was revealed to Verizon that consumers would buy DSL at $14.95 + $1.25 and DSL at $29.99 + $2.83. Verizon apparently decided that $14.95 + $1.20 and $29.99 + $2.70 would maximize net revenues. Verizon must have thought that it would add more revenue by increasing its own prices than by attracting more customers with lower prices. In terms of elasticity of demand, Verizon seems to have decided that the extra $1.20 and $2.70 from existing customers (which would go directly to the bottom line) could not be offset by any increase in revenue (and increase in cost) caused by attracting more users.

Source: "Verizon's Lesson about Elasticity of Demand," *Philadelphia Inquirer*, August 26, 2006, pp. C1, C7.

where a is the intercept on the price axis and b is the slope (in absolute terms), as shown in panel A of Figure 2.7. Thus the firm's total revenue equals

$$TR = PQ$$
$$= (a - bQ)Q$$
$$= aQ - bQ^2 \tag{2.12}$$

Marginal revenue The incremental revenue earned from selling the nth unit of output.

An important concept to managers is that of **marginal revenue**, which is the incremental revenue earned from selling the nth unit of output. As we will see, managers must understand marginal revenue to maximize the firm's profit. Because this concept is central to firm performance, we need to understand how the price elasticity of demand affects it. In the present case,

$$MR = \frac{\Delta TR}{\Delta Q}$$
$$= \frac{\Delta(aQ - bQ^2)}{\Delta Q}$$
$$= a - 2bQ \tag{2.13}$$

We can see this relationship more clearly using calculus:

$$MR = \frac{dTR}{dQ}$$

$$= \frac{d(aQ - bQ^2)}{dQ}$$

$$= a - 2bQ$$

---

which is also shown in panel A of Figure 2.7. Comparing the marginal revenue curve with the demand curve, we see that while both have the same intercept on the vertical axis (this intercept being a) the slope of the marginal revenue curve is twice that of the demand curve.

According to the definition in equation (2.7), the price elasticity of demand, η, equals $(\Delta Q/\Delta P)(P/Q)$. Because $\Delta Q/\Delta P = -1/b$ and $P = a - bQ$, it follows, in this case, that

$$\eta = \left(\frac{-1}{b} \right) \frac{a - bQ}{Q} \qquad (2.14)$$

Therefore, whether η is greater than, equal to, or less than -1 depends on whether Q is greater than, equal to, or less than $a/2b$. As shown in Figure 2.7, demand is price elastic if $Q < a/2b$; it is of unitary elasticity if $Q = a/2b$; and it is price inelastic if $Q > a/2b$.

Panel B in Figure 2.7 plots the firm's total revenue against the quantity demanded of its product. Remember that marginal revenue is the incremental revenue earned from selling the next unit of output. As long as marginal revenue is positive, an increase in sales raises total revenue. However, at outputs where the incremental revenue is negative, total revenue will decrease. Some may ask, how can incremental revenue be negative? If a firm sells one more unit, it must receive a positive revenue from the person it sells to (unless it pays the person to take the good). But think about the effect on total revenue of that last unit sold. If managers need to reduce the price to sell that last unit, they reduce the price of all the units sold. Hence selling one more unit can cause total revenue to be lower because the manager has reduced the price on all the units sold. Also, producing one more unit increases total costs. So if total revenue decreases and total cost increases, the manager is moving further from a profit-maximizing strategy. The important thing to remember is that managers do not want to produce at an output level where marginal revenue is negative.

Another thing to note about Figure 2.7 is that, at quantities where demand is price elastic, marginal revenue is positive; at quantities where it is of unitary

FIGURE 2.7

Relationship between Price Elasticity, Marginal Revenue, and Total Revenue

If demand is price elastic, marginal revenue is positive and increases in quantity result in higher total revenue. If demand is price inelastic, marginal revenue is negative and increases in quantity result in lower total revenue.

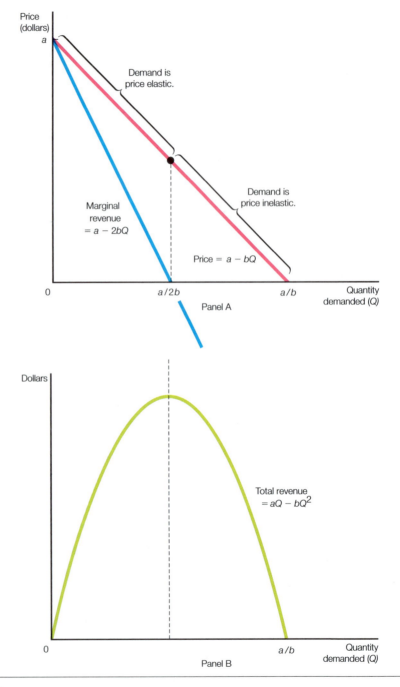

elasticity, marginal revenue is zero; and at quantities where it is price inelastic, marginal revenue is negative. This is no accident. In general, whether or not the demand curve is linear, this is the case. To see why, recall that by definition,

$$MR = \frac{\Delta TR}{\Delta Q}$$

Because total revenue equals price times quantity, it follows that

$$MR = \frac{\Delta(PQ)}{\Delta Q}$$

We can transform this into

$$MR = P\frac{\Delta Q}{\Delta Q} + Q\frac{\Delta P}{\Delta Q}$$

Because $\Delta Q/\Delta Q = 1$,

$$MR = P + Q\frac{\Delta P}{\Delta Q}$$

$$= P\left[1 + \left(\frac{Q}{P}\right)\left(\frac{\Delta P}{\Delta Q}\right)\right]$$

And because the definition of the price elasticity of demand implies that (Q/P) $(\Delta P/\Delta Q) = 1/\eta$,

$$MR = P\left(1 + \frac{1}{\eta}\right) \tag{2.15}$$

QUANT OPTION

Equation (2.15) is so famous that we think it deserves a formal derivation:

$$MR = \frac{dTR}{dQ}$$

$$MR = \frac{d(PQ)}{dQ}$$

$$MR = P\frac{dQ}{dQ} + Q\frac{dP}{dQ}$$

$$MR = P + Q\frac{dP}{dQ}$$

$$= P\left[1 + \left(\frac{Q}{P}\right)\left(\frac{dP}{dQ}\right)\right]$$

$$MR = P\left(1 + \frac{1}{\eta}\right)$$

Equation (2.15) shows that if $\eta < -1$, marginal revenue is positive; if $\eta > -1$, marginal revenue is negative; and if $\eta = -1$, marginal revenue is zero. In later chapters we use equation (2.15) repeatedly. Managers will find lots of uses for it. One way they use it is to estimate the value of marginal revenue. For example, what is the marginal revenue if the product price is $10 and the price elasticity of demand is -2? On the basis of equation (2.15), it equals $10(1 - 1/2) = \$5$.

THE INCOME ELASTICITY OF DEMAND

Price is not the only factor managers need to consider in predicting how many units they will sell. An important factor over which managers have little control is the level of consumer income. A consumer with relatively more money to spend is more likely to purchase various goods. For example, more cognac is sold on a per capita basis in cities populated by consumers with higher income levels, like New York City, then in cities like Fargo, ND, where consumers have lower income levels. Managers need to understand the sensitivity of demand to changes in consumer incomes.

Income elasticity of demand
The percentage change in quantity demanded resulting from a 1 percent change in consumers' income.

The **income elasticity of demand** for a particular good is defined as the percentage change in quantity demanded resulting from a 1 percent change in consumers' income. More precisely, it equals

$$\eta_I = \left(\frac{\Delta Q}{\Delta I} \right)\left(\frac{I}{Q} \right)$$

(2.16)

where Q is quantity demanded and I is consumers' income. For most products, the income elasticity of demand is positive. That is, when consumer incomes increase, they buy more of the product. Such goods are called normal goods. However, some products, called inferior goods, have negative income elasticities. For these goods, quantity demanded moves opposite to consumer incomes. When incomes increase, quantity demanded decreases; when incomes decrease, quantity demanded increases. Two examples of inferior goods in the United States are hamburgers and public transportation. When consumers' income increases, they generally consume fewer hamburgers. It is not that they eat less beef, but they eat steaks instead of burgers.

Managers must understand the impact of the income elasticity of demand on sales. Variance in sales is common in products with high income elasticities as sales react to the various stages of the business cycle. When the economy is expanding, products with high income elasticities will enjoy a significant increase in sales. However, when the economy enters a recession, these same products will see a significant decrease in sales. Though managers selling products with high income elasticities can do little to influence the business cycle, they can plan ahead to lessen the negative impact of economic fluctuations. For example, they can try

STRATEGY SESSION: Estimating the Demand for Amtrak Rail Passenger Business

Amtrak (the national passenger railroad in the United States) has used an aggregate demand model to forecast systemwide passenger revenues. The first part of its model was a multivariate linear regression that forecast its systemwide passenger miles—the dependent variable (a passenger mile is one passenger moved one mile). Explanatory variables were disposable personal income; Amtrak's average fare; the ratio of Amtrak's average fare to the airlines' average fare; retail gasoline prices; dummy variables to reflect such events as weather, holidays, strikes, and derailments; and dummy variables to reflect seasonal variation.

The most important determinant of rail passenger miles was disposable personal income (a proxy variable for the strength of the U.S. economy). From the regression, a 1 percent increase in disposable personal income was expected to yield a 1.8 percent increase in systemwide passenger miles.

1. Explain the rationale for each explanatory variable appearing in the model and what sign (positive or negative) you expect for its regression coefficient.

2. How did Amtrak use this forecast of systemwide passenger miles to obtain its estimate of systemwide passenger revenues?

3. What is Amtrak's estimate of income elasticity of demand for passenger service (based on the income level of the economy as a whole)? If U.S. disposable personal income per capita increases from $27,000 to $28,000, what's your prediction for the increase in train passenger miles in the new situation (all other independent variables remaining constant)? Will this prediction be 100 percent accurate? Why or why not?

4. Even though disposable personal income rose throughout the early 2000s, Amtrak's market share of intercity passenger miles decreased. Can you explain this?

to shift their cost structure toward fewer fixed costs and greater variable costs. One way of accomplishing this is by leasing capital goods instead of buying them. And in times of economic expansion, they must prepare for the probable significant increase in sales.

In forecasting the long-term growth of the quantity demanded for many major products, the income elasticity of demand is of key importance. According to studies done by the U.S. Department of Agriculture, the income elasticity of demand for milk is about 0.5, which means a 1 percent increase in disposable income is associated with about a 0.5 percent increase in the quantity demanded of milk. But in a study done in Britain, the income elasticity of bread was about −0.17, which means that a 1 percent increase in disposable income is associated with about a −0.17 percent decrease in the quantity demanded of bread. Table 2.5 shows that the income elasticity of demand for first-class air tickets between the United States and Europe is 1.5, which means that a 1 percent increase in disposable income is associated with a 1.5 percent increase in the quantity demanded of such tickets. Table 2.6 shows the income elasticity of demand for other commodities across the world. In measuring income elasticities, income can be defined as

---

TABLE 2.6

Income Elasticity of Demand, Selected Commodities, Global

Good	Elasticity
Agricultural products	
Grain (China)[1]	−0.12 to +0.15
Potatoes (U.K.)[2]	−0.32
Potatoes (U.S.)[3]	+0.15
Oranges (U.S.)[3]	+0.83
Apples (U.S.)[3]	+1.32
Lettuce (U.S.)[3]	+0.88
Animal products	
Meat (China)[1]	+0.1 to +1.2
Milk (U.K.)[2]	+0.05
Milk (U.S.)[3]	+0.50
Cream (U.S.)[3]	+1.72
Eggs (U.K.)[2]	−0.21
Eggs (U.S.)[3]	+0.57
Processed food products	
Bread (U.K.)[2]	−0.17
Other cereal products (U.K.)[2]	+0.18
Automobiles	
Domestic cars (U.S.)[4]	+1.62
European cars (U.S.)[4]	+1.93
Asian cars (U.S.)[4]	+1.65

---

[1]Millennium Institute, China Agricultural Project, found at *www.threshold21.com/chinaag/report/appendix.html.*
[2]AEF116: 1.6 "Major Market Response Concepts and Measures. 1: The Demand Side and Its Elasticities," found at *www.staff.ncl.ac.uk/david.harvey/AEF116/1.6/1.6.html.*
[3]D. Suits, "Agriculture," in *The Structure of American Industry*, ed. Adams and Brock.
[4]P. McCarthy, "Market Price and Income Elasticities of New Vehicle Demands."

the aggregate income of consumers (as in Table 2.6) or as per capita income (as in the next section), depending on the circumstances.

CROSS-PRICE ELASTICITIES OF DEMAND

In addition to price and income, another factor influencing the quantity demanded of a product is the prices of rivals. Holding constant the product's own price (as well as the level of income) and allowing the price of another product to vary may result in important effects on the quantity demanded of the product in ques-

PROBLEM SOLVED: Income Elasticity of Demand

In a previous section we learned how to calculate the price elasticity of demand based on a product's demand function. Here we see how to calculate the income elasticity of demand. Suppose the demand function for a product is

$$Q = 1,000 - 0.2P_X + 0.5P_Y + 0.04I$$

where Q is the quantity demanded of good X, P_X is the price of good X, P_Y is the price of good Y, and I is per capita disposable income. The income elasticity of demand is

$$\eta_I = \left(\frac{\Delta Q}{\Delta I}\right)\left(\frac{I}{Q}\right)$$

$$= 0.04\frac{I}{Q}$$

If $I = 10,000$ and $Q = 1,600$,

$$\eta_I = 0.04\left(\frac{10,000}{1,600}\right) = 0.25$$

The income elasticity of demand equals 0.25, which means that a 1 percent increase in per capita disposable income is associated with a 0.25 percent increase in the quantity demanded of product X.

---

tion. By observing these effects, we can classify pairs of products as substitutes or complements, and we can measure how close consumers perceive the relationship (either substitute or complementary). Consider products X and Y. If Y's price goes up, what is the effect on Q_X, the quantity of X demanded? The **cross-price elasticity of demand** is defined as the percentage change in the quantity demanded of good X resulting from a 1 percent change in the price of good Y:

$$\eta_{XY} = \left(\frac{\Delta Q_X}{\Delta P_Y}\right)\left(\frac{P_Y}{Q_X}\right) \tag{2.17}$$

Cross-price elasticity of demand
The percentage change in the quantity demanded of one good resulting from a 1 percent change in the price of another good.

Goods X and Y are classified as substitutes if the cross-price elasticity of demand is positive. For instance, an increase in the price of wheat, when the price of corn remains constant, tends to increase the quantity of corn demanded; therefore, η_{XY} is positive, and wheat and corn are classified as substitutes. On the other hand, if the cross-price elasticity of demand is negative, goods X and Y are classified as complements. For example, an increase in the price of software tends to decrease the purchase of laptop computers when the price of laptops remains constant; therefore, η_{XY} is negative, and software and laptops are classified as complements. If the cross-price elasticity of two products is around zero, then the products have independent demand levels. For example, if the price of butter increases, the demand for airline tickets remains constant.

To illustrate the calculation of cross-price elasticities, suppose once again the demand function for our product is

$$Q_X = 1{,}000 - 0.2P_X + 0.5P_Y + 0.04I$$

where Q_X is the quantity demanded of product X, P_X is the price of X, P_Y is the price of product Y, and I is per capita disposable income. The cross-price elasticity of demand between products X and Y is

$$\eta_{XY} = \left(\frac{\Delta Q_X}{\Delta P_Y}\right)\left(\frac{P_Y}{Q_X}\right)$$

$$= 0.5\frac{P_Y}{Q_X}$$

Although the value of the cross-price elasticity depends on the values of P_Y and Q_X, the goods are always substitutes because η_{XY} must be positive, regardless of the values of P_Y and Q_X. If $P_Y = 500$ and $Q_X = 2{,}000$,

$$\eta_{XY} = 0.5\left(\frac{500}{2{,}000}\right) = 0.125$$

The cross-price elasticity of demand is of fundamental importance to managers because they continually must do their best to anticipate what will happen to their own sales if rivals change their prices. To do so, they need information concerning the cross-price elasticities of demand. Table 2.7 shows the cross-price elasticities of demand for selected pairs of commodities.

The measure is also frequently used by antitrust authorities to evaluate merger applications. A high cross-price elasticity measure between products X and Y can cause concern that a merger between the producers of products X and Y might result in consumers experiencing higher prices and fewer brand choices. A low cross-price elasticity measure (a large negative η_{xy}) signifies that the products are strong complements. Here the authorities may be concerned that a merger between the products might lead to excessive control of the supply chain. That is, the merged firm may refuse to sell the intermediate product to other producers.

THE ADVERTISING ELASTICITY OF DEMAND

Advertising elasticity of demand
The percentage change in the quantity demanded of the product resulting from a 1 percent change in the advertising expenditure.

Although the price elasticity, income elasticity, and cross-price elasticities of demand are the most frequently used elasticity measures, they are not the only ones. For example, managers sometimes find it useful to calculate the **advertising elasticity of demand.** Suppose the demand function for a particular firm's product is

$$Q = 500 - 0.5P + 0.01I + 0.82A$$

where Q is the quantity demanded of the product, P is its price, I is per capita disposable income, and A is the firm's advertising expenditure. The advertising

TABLE 2.7

Cross-Price Elasticity of Demand, Selected Pairs of Commodities, Global

Change of Price of Good	Change of Quantity of Good	Cross-Price Elasticity
European/Asian cars	U.S. domestic cars	+0.28[1]
European/U.S. domestic cars	Asian cars	+0.61[1]
U.S. domestic/Asian cars	European cars	+0.76[1]
Australian public transit	Australian auto ownership	+0.1 to +0.3[2]
Irish coal	Irish natural gas	+0.4[3]
Irish coal	Irish oil	+0.7[3]
Kenyan government-provided health care	Mission- or private sector-provided health care in Kenya	+0.023[4]
U.S. durum wheat	U.S. hard red spring wheat	+0.04[5]
U.S. hard red winter wheat	U.S. white wheat	+1.80[5]
U.K. beef/veal	U.K. pork	0.00[6]
U.K. mutton/lamb	U.K. beef/veal	+0.25[6]

[1]P. McCarthy, "Market Price and Income Elasticities of New Vehicle Demand."
[2]J. Luk and S. Hepburn, "A Review of Australian Travel Demand Elasticities," Working Document No. TE 93/004, 1993, Australian Road Research Board.
[3]Competition Authority Decision of 30 January 1998, relating to a proceeding under Section 4 of the Competition Act 1991: Notification No. CA/15/97—Statoil Ireland Ltd./Clare Oil Company Ltd.— Share Purchase Agreement and Service Employment Agreement. Decision No. 490 found at *www. irlgov.ie/compauth/dec490.htm.*
[4]"Section 4: The Basics of Markets and Health Care Markets: Box 4.4: Demand for Health Care in Kenya," found at *www.worldbank.org/wbi/heathflagship/learning/module1/box4_4.htm.*
[5]Wheat Yearbook, March 30, 1998, Economic Research Services, U.S. Department of Agriculture, Washington, DC 20036-5831.
[6]AEF116: 1.6: "Major Market Response Concepts and Measures. 1: The Demand Side and Its Elasticities," found at *www.staff.ncl.ac.uk/david.harvey/AEF116/1.6/1.6.html.*

elasticity is defined as the percentage change in the quantity demanded of the product resulting from a 1 percent change in advertising expenditure. More precisely, it equals

$$\eta_A = \left(\frac{\Delta Q}{\Delta A} \right)\left(\frac{A}{Q} \right)$$

(2.18)

In this case, because $\Delta Q/\Delta A = 0.82$,

$$\eta_A = 0.82 \frac{A}{Q}$$

If A/Q, the amount of advertising per unit of the product demanded, is $2,

$$\eta_A = 0.82(2) = 1.64$$

This useful elasticity tells managers that a 1 percent increase in advertising expenditure results in a 1.64 percent increase in the quantity demanded. In later chapters we will see how information of this sort is used to help guide managerial decisions.

THE CONSTANT-ELASTICITY AND UNITARY ELASTIC DEMAND FUNCTION

Constant-elasticity demand function Mathematical form that always yields the same elasticity, regardless of the product's price and the consumers' income.

In this chapter, we generally assume the demand function is linear. That is, the quantity demanded of a product is assumed to be a linear function of its price, the prices of other goods, consumer income, and other variables. Another mathematical form frequently used is the **constant-elasticity demand function**. If the quantity demanded (Q) depends only on the product's price (P) and consumer income (I), this mathematical form is

$$Q = aP^{-b_1}I^{b_2} \tag{2.19}$$

Therefore, if $a = 200$, $b_1 = 0.3$, and $b_2 = 2$,

$$Q = 200P^{-0.3}I^2$$

An important property of this type of demand is that the price elasticity of demand equals $-b_1$, regardless of the value of P or I. (This accounts for it being called the constant-elasticity demand function.)

The constant-elasticity demand function is often used by managers and managerial economists for several reasons. First, in contrast to the linear demand function, this mathematical form explicitly recognizes that the effect of price on quantity demanded depends on income level and that the effect of income on quantity demanded depends on price. The multiplicative relationship in equation (2.19) is often more realistic than the additive relationship in equation (2.1). Second, like the linear demand function, the constant-elasticity demand function is relatively easy to estimate.

If the demand is of unitary elasticity (which means that the price elasticity of demand equals -1), an increase or decrease in price has no effect on the amount

---

QUANT OPTION

Here is the formal derivation of the constant elasticity.

$$\eta = (P/Q)(\partial Q/\partial P) = (P/aP^{-b_1}I^{b_2})(-ab_1P^{-b_1-1}I^{b_2}) = P(-b_1P^{-1}) = -b_1$$

FIGURE 2.8

Demand Curve with Unitary Elasticity at All Points

The demand curve is a rectangular hyperbola if the price elasticity of demand is always −1.

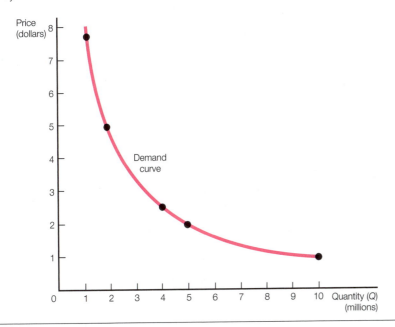

spent on the commodity. As an illustration, consider the case shown in Figure 2.8. The demand curve shown is a rectangular hyperbola, which means that

$$Q = \frac{m}{P} \qquad (2.20)$$

where Q is product demand, P is the price, and m is a constant. This type of demand is of unitary elasticity at all points. Hence changes in price have no effect on the total amount spent on the product. It is evident from equation (2.20) that, regardless of the price, the total expenditure for the product will be m ($10 million in Figure 2.8).

SUMMARY

1. The market demand curve for a product shows how much of the product is demanded at each price. The market demand curve shifts in response to changes in tastes, incomes, the prices of other products, advertising, and the size of the population.

2. The market demand function for a product is an equation showing how the quantity demanded depends on the product's price, the incomes of consum-

ers, the prices of other products, advertising expenditure, and additional factors. Holding all factors other than the product's price constant, we can draw the market demand curve for the product from the market demand function. Market demand functions are formulated for individual firms as well as for entire industries.

3. The own-price elasticity of demand is the percentage change in quantity demanded resulting from a 1 percent change in price; more precisely, it equals $(\Delta Q/\Delta P)(P/Q)$. Whether a price increase (or decrease) results in an increase in the total amount spent by consumers on a product depends on the own-price elasticity of demand.

4. Marginal revenue is the change in total revenue resulting from a one-unit increase in quantity. Marginal revenue equals $P(1 + 1/\eta)$, where P is price and η is the own-price elasticity of demand.

5. The own-price elasticity of demand for a product tends to be elastic if the product has many close substitutes. Also, it often tends to be more elastic in the long run than in the short run. It is sometimes asserted a product's demand is relatively price inelastic if the product accounts for a very small percentage of the typical consumer's budget, but this need not be the case.

6. The income elasticity of demand is the percentage change in quantity demanded resulting from a 1 percent change in consumer income; that is, it equals $(\Delta Q/\Delta I)(I/Q)$, where I is the income of consumers. The income elasticity of demand may be positive or negative. Like the price elasticity of demand, it is of major importance in forecasting the long-term growth in the quantity demanded for products.

7. The cross-price elasticity of demand is the percentage change in the quantity demanded of product X resulting from a 1 percent change in the price of product Y; in other words, it equals $(\Delta Q_X/\Delta P_Y)(P_Y/Q_X)$. If X and Y are substitutes, it is positive; if they are complements, it is negative. This elasticity is important for managers because they must understand and forecast the effects of changes in other firms' prices on their own firm's sales.

8. If a demand curve is linear, the own-price elasticity of demand varies from point to point on the demand curve. As price approaches zero, the own-price elasticity of demand also approaches zero. As quantity demanded approaches zero, the own-price elasticity approaches negative infinity. In contrast, for a constant-elasticity demand function, the own-price elasticity of demand is the same regardless of the product's price. Both linear demand functions and constant-elasticity demand functions are used frequently by managers and managerial economists.

wwnorton.com/studyspace ⑤

PROBLEMS

1. The Dolan Corporation, a maker of small engines, determines that in 2008 the demand curve for its product is

$$P = 2,000 - 50Q$$

where P is the price (in dollars) of an engine and Q is the number of engines sold per month.

   a. To sell 20 engines per month, what price would Dolan have to charge?

   b. If managers set a price of $500, how many engines will Dolan sell per month?

   c. What is the price elasticity of demand if price equals $500?

   d. At what price, if any, will the demand for Dolan's engines be of unitary elasticity?

2. The Johnson Robot Company's marketing managers estimate that the demand curve for the company's robots in 2008 is

$$P = 3,000 - 40Q$$

where P is the price of a robot and Q is the number sold per month.

   a. Derive the marginal revenue curve for the firm.

   b. At what prices is the demand for the firm's product price elastic?

   c. If the firm wants to maximize its dollar sales volume, what price should it charge?

3. After a careful statistical analysis, the Chidester Company concludes the demand function for its product is

$$Q = 500 - 3P + 2P_r + 0.1I$$

where Q is the quantity demanded of its product, P is the price of its product, P_r is the price of its rival's product, and I is per capita disposable income (in dollars). At present, $P = \$10$, $P_r = \$20$, and $I = \$6,000$.

   a. What is the price elasticity of demand for the firm's product?

   b. What is the income elasticity of demand for the firm's product?

   c. What is the cross-price elasticity of demand between its product and its rival's product?

   d. What is the implicit assumption regarding the population in the market?

4. The Haas Corporation's executive vice president circulates a memo to the firm's top management in which he argues for a reduction in the price of the firm's product. He says such a price cut will increase the firm's sales and profits.

   a. The firm's marketing manager responds with a memo pointing out that the price elasticity of demand for the firm's product is about -0.5. Why is this fact relevant?

   b. The firm's president concurs with the opinion of the executive vice president. Is she correct?

5. Managers of the Hanover Manufacturing Company believe the demand curve for its product is

$$P = 5 - Q$$

where P is the price of its product (in dollars) and Q is the number of millions of units of its product sold per day. It is currently charging $1 per unit for its product.

a. Evaluate the wisdom of the firm's pricing policy.

b. A marketing specialist says that the price elasticity of demand for the firm's product is -1.0. Is this correct?

6. On the basis of historical data, Richard Tennant has concluded, "The consumption of cigarettes is . . . [relatively] insensitive to changes in price. . . . In contrast, the demand for individual brands is highly elastic in its response to price. . . . In 1918, for example, Lucky Strike was sold for a short time at a higher retail price than Camel or Chesterfield and rapidly lost half its business."

a. Explain why the demand for a particular brand is more elastic than the demand for all cigarettes. If Lucky Strike raised its price by 1 percent in 1918, was the price elasticity of demand for its product greater than -2?

b. Do you think that the demand curve for cigarettes is the same now as it was in 1918? If not, describe in detail the factors that have shifted the demand curve and whether each has shifted it to the left or right.

7. According to S. Sackrin of the U.S. Department of Agriculture, the price elasticity of demand for cigarettes is between -0.3 and -0.4, and the income elasticity of demand is about 0.5.

a. Suppose the federal government, influenced by findings that link cigarettes and cancer, were to impose a tax on cigarettes that increased their price by 15 percent. What effect would this have on cigarette consumption?

b. Suppose a brokerage house advised you to buy cigarette stocks because if incomes were to rise by 50 percent in the next decade, cigarette sales would be bound to spurt enormously. What would be your reaction to this advice?

8. Using the PIMS (Profit Impact of Market Strategies) survey of major U.S. firms, Michael Hagerty, James Carman, and Gary Russell estimated that, on the average, the advertising elasticity of demand was only about 0.003. Doesn't this indicate that firms spend too much on advertising?

9. The McCauley Company hires a marketing consultant to estimate the demand function for its product. The consultant concludes that this demand function is

$$Q = 100P^{-3.1}I^{2.3}A^{0.1}$$

where Q is the quantity demanded per capita per month, P is the product's price (in dollars), I is per capita disposable income (in dollars), and A is the firm's advertising expenditures (in thousands of dollars).

a. What is the price elasticity of demand?

b. Will price increases result in increases or decreases in the amount spent on McCauley's product?

c. What is the income elasticity of demand?

d. What is the advertising elasticity of demand?

e. If the population in the market increases by 10 percent, what is the effect on the quantity demanded if P, I, and A are held constant?

10. The Schmidt Corporation estimates that its demand function is

$$Q = 400 - 3P + 4I + 0.6A$$

where Q is the quantity demanded per month, P is the product's price (in dollars), I is per capita disposable income (in thousands of dollars), and A is the firm's advertising expenditures (in thousands of dollars per month). Population is assumed to be constant.

a. During the next decade, per capita disposable income is expected to increase by $5,000. What effect will this have on the firm's sales?

b. If Schmidt wants to raise its price enough to offset the effect of the increase in per capita disposable income, by how much must it raise its price?

c. If Schmidt raises its price by this amount, will it increase or decrease the price elasticity of demand? Explain. Make sure your answers reflect the fact that elasticity is a negative number.

CHAPTER 3

CONSUMER BEHAVIOR AND RATIONAL CHOICE

We discussed market demand in Chapter 2. But as we will soon see, market demand for a product is the aggregate of individual demands. So managers need to understand how individuals choose products. As you read this chapter, think about how you make decisions; certainly we all purchase much in our lives. More important, you need to understand how the variables controlled and directed by managers (prices, advertising, etc.) influence consumer choice.

Our model for consumer behavior is part of a larger whole. All of us make decisions every day. Most are decided with little effort: Either the choice is obvious or the impact is limited, so deep thought is not warranted. Occasionally we encounter decisions that require more thought and have high impact; in these situations we are likely to think harder about possible choices and their consequences. But whether we make a snap judgment or a systematic analysis, we are governed by an internal classification scheme that tells us we prefer one choice over another. Without preference ordering, we are reduced to random choices without any future.

This chapter shows how economists model consumer purchase decisions. In later chapters we examine how individuals make decisions under risk (Chapter 13) and when they possess asymmetric information (Chapters 14 and 15).

Although some students may fret about the usefulness of economic principles in the business world, they cannot deny the usefulness of our decision models.

It should be obvious that managers constantly face limited budgets to allocate across different uses. You as a consumer face this decision daily. For a problem of this sort, the economist's model of consumer behavior provides some guidelines. And good managers understand that they can take actions to influence consumer choice. This is the idea underlying the use of marketing, pricing, and distributional strategies.

In subsequent chapters we explain how this decision framework is applied to help improve managerial decision making. For now, you may want to try Problem 11 at the end of this chapter. See if you can figure out how this model sheds light on a state's choice between mass transit and highways. (The answer is provided at the end of the book.)

In examining how consumers choose, we initially assume a consumer is rational and wishes to maximize his or her well-being. That is, to the best of their knowledge, consumers do not make choices that cause them harm. A consumer's well-being is a function of the goods she or he chooses to purchase. However, this well-being is not unconstrained. If it were, we would see many more people driving expensive cars like a Porsche or Bentley. Purchases are constrained by the income level of the consumer. A rational consumer maximizes his or her well-being given the prices of goods, personal tastes and preferences for goods, and income. We formally model this behavior by developing the concepts of utility functions, indifference curves, and budget lines. Using them, we derive the consumer's demand curve for products and show how demand shifts when income changes.

INDIFFERENCE CURVES

To clarify important ideas, we initially assume consumers can purchase only food products and clothing products. All the implications we discuss apply to the more complex setting of the world. Consumer choice is modeled as a series of indifference curves. An **indifference curve** contains points representing market bundles among which the consumer is indifferent. To illustrate, consider Jennifer Popovich, a consumer in South Pasadena, California. Certain market bundles—that is, combinations of food and clothing—are equally desirable to her. For example, she may have a hard time choosing between a market bundle containing 50 pounds of food and 5 pieces of clothing and one containing 100 pounds of food and 2 pieces of clothing. These two bundles are represented by two points, K and L, in Figure 3.1. In addition, other market bundles, each of which is represented by a point in Figure 3.1, are just as desirable to Ms. Popovich. If we connect all these points, we derive a curve that represents equally desirable bundles to Ms. P. Figure 3.1 maps these bundles as points on curve I_1 in Figure 3.1. Curve I_1 is an indifference curve.

Indifference curve Contains points representing market bundles among which the consumer is indifferent.

FIGURE 3.1

Two of Ms. Popovich's Indifference Curves

The curves I_1 and I_2 are two of Ms. Popovich's indifference curves. Each shows market bundles that are equally desirable to Ms. Popovich.

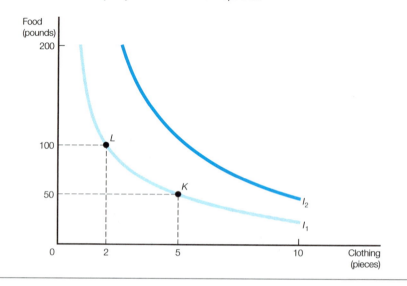

We need to understand three things when modeling consumer indifference curves:

1. *A consumer has many indifference curves.* If Ms. Popovich is indifferent among all the market bundles represented by points on I_2 in Figure 3.1, I_2 is another of her indifference curves. Moreover, one thing is certain. She prefers any I_2 bundle to any one on I_1, because I_2 has bundles with as much clothing as and more food than (or as much food as and more clothing than) bundles on I_1. Implicitly we assume that consumers are sometimes insatiable. (Of course consumers sometimes become so satiated with a product that they prefer less of it to more, but we assume for simplicity that this is not the case here.) Consequently, market bundles on higher indifference curves like I_2 are preferred to bundles on lower indifference curves like I_1.

2. *Every indifference curve must slope downward and to the right, so long as the consumer prefers more of each commodity to less.* If one market bundle on an indifference curve has more of one product than a second bundle, it must have less of the other product than the second bundle. This is true so long as more of each product is preferred.

3. *Indifference curves cannot intersect.* If they did, this would contradict the assumption that more of a product is preferred. For example, suppose that I_1 and

FIGURE 3.2

Intersecting Indifference Curves: A Contradiction

Indifference curves cannot intersect. If they did, the consumer would be indifferent between D and C because both are on indifference curve I_1, and between E and C because both are on indifference curve I_2. But this implies that he or she must be indifferent between D and E, which is impossible because E contains the same amount of food and two more pieces of clothing than D, and we are assuming that more of a commodity is preferred to less.

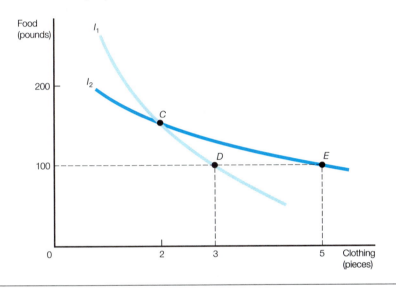

I_2 in Figure 3.2 are two intersecting indifference curves. If this is the case, the market bundle at point D is equivalent to the one represented by point C because both are on indifference curve I_1. Moreover, the market bundle represented by point E is equivalent in the eyes of the consumer to the one represented by point C because both are on indifference curve I_2. And this means the market bundle represented by point E is equivalent to the one represented by point D. But this is impossible because the bundle at E contains the same amount of food and two more pieces of clothing than bundle D. If we assume that more of a product is preferred, the bundle at E must be preferred to the bundle at D.

THE MARGINAL RATE OF SUBSTITUTION

Some consumers place a high value on obtaining an extra unit of a product; others place a low value on obtaining it. If managers are to understand consumer choice, it is useful to measure the relative importance a consumer places on acquiring an additional unit of a particular product. We measure this using what is called the marginal rate of substitution.

Marginal rate of substitution The number of units of product Y that must be given up if the consumer, after receiving an extra unit of product X, is to maintain a constant level of satisfaction.

The **marginal rate of substitution** of product X for product Y is defined as the number of units of product Y that must be given up if the consumer, after receiving an extra unit of product X, is to maintain a constant level of satisfaction. Obviously the more units of product Y the consumer is willing to give up to get an extra unit of X, the more important product X is (relative to Y) to the consumer. To estimate the marginal rate of substitution, we multiply the slope of the consumer's indifference curve by -1. This gives us the number of units of product Y the consumer is willing to give up for an extra unit of product X.

To illustrate, consider consumer preferences for attributes of automobiles. Two key attributes are stylishness and performance (for example, speed, gasoline mileage, and handling). Some consumers are willing to trade a lot of stylishness for a little extra performance. This behavior is shown in the left panel of Figure 3.3. The indifference curves here are steep. The marginal rate of substitution of performance for stylishness is relatively high because the slope of the indifference curves (times -1) is relatively large. Other consumers are willing to trade a lot of performance for a little extra stylishness. For these consumers the indifference curves in Figure 3.3 are relatively flat, as in the right panel of Figure 3.3. The marginal rate of substitution of performance for stylishness is relatively low because the slope of the indifference curves (times -1) is relatively small.

FIGURE 3.3

Indifference Curves of Consumers with High and Low Marginal Rates of Substitution of Performance for Stylishness

The left panel shows the indifference curves of consumers who are willing to trade a lot of stylishness for a little extra performance. The right panel shows the indifference curves of consumers who are willing to trade a lot of performance for a little extra stylishness.

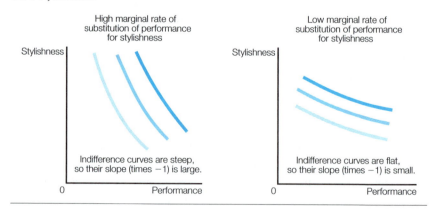

THE CONCEPT OF UTILITY

The consumer's indifference curves represent his or her tastes and preferences. Given all the indifference curves of a particular consumer, we attach a number, called a utility, to each of the available market bundles. **Utility** indicates the level of enjoyment or preference attached by a consumer to a particular market bundle. More specifically, it summarizes the preference ranking of market bundles; the higher the utility assigned to a bundle, the higher the level of satisfaction the consumer realizes from it. Because all market bundles on a given indifference curve yield the same amount of satisfaction, they all have the same utility. Market bundles on higher indifference curves have higher utilities than those on lower indifference curves.

When we assign utilities to market bundles, it tells us which bundles the consumer prefers. If the utility attached to one bundle is higher than that attached to another, the consumer prefers the first over the second. If the utility attached to the first bundle is lower than the second, he or she prefers the second over the first. If the utility attached to the first market bundle equals the second, he or she is indifferent between the two market bundles.

How do we rationally assign these utilities? Assume our consumer prefers market bundle R to bundle S, and bundle S to bundle T. The utility assigned to bundle R must be higher than that assigned to bundle S, while the utility assigned to bundle S must be higher than that assigned to bundle T. Any set of numbers conforming to these requirements is an adequate measure of utility. Therefore, the utility of market bundles R, S, and T may be 30, 20, and 10 or 6, 5, and 4, respectively. All that counts is that the utility of market bundle R is higher than that of bundle S, which in turn should be higher than that of bundle T. Put differently, both sets of utilities provide a correct ordering or ranking of market bundles in terms of levels of consumer satisfaction.

Indifference curves are also known as iso-utility curves. We can measure the slope described above as

$$-\Delta f/\Delta c = -(\Delta U/\Delta c)/(\Delta U/\Delta f) = -MU_c/MU_f$$

where MU_f is the marginal utility of food, i.e., the increase in Ms. Popovich's utility if she obtains one more unit of food (holding the amount of clothing she possesses constant), and where MU_c is the marginal utility of clothing, i.e., the increase in Ms. Popovich's utility if she obtains one more unit of clothing (holding the amount of food she possesses constant). Thus, Ms. Popovich's marginal rate of substitution is equal to the ratio of her marginal utility of clothing to her marginal utility of food. These marginal utilities are precisely what we were talking about earlier in this section when we referenced the value a consumer placed on obtaining an extra unit of a product.

Utility Indicates the level of enjoyment or preference attached by a consumer to a particular market bundle.

THE BUDGET LINE

Consumers wish to maximize their utility, which means they want to consume bundles from the highest possible indifference curve. But whether a particular indifference curve is attainable depends on a consumer's income and product prices. To make things concrete, we return to our consumer, Jennifer Popovich. Suppose her total income is $600 per week, and she spends it on only food and clothing.

How much of each product Ms. Popovich can buy depends on the prices of food and clothing. Suppose a pound of food costs $3 and a piece of clothing costs $60. Then, if she spent all her income on food, she could buy 200 pounds of food per week. On the other hand, if she spent all her income on clothing, she could buy 10 pieces of clothing per week. Or she could, if she wished, buy some food and some clothing. There are many combinations of food and clothing she could buy, and each such combination can be represented by a point on the line in Figure 3.4. This line is called her budget line. A consumer's **budget line** shows the market

Budget line Shows the market bundles that the consumer can purchase, given the consumer's income and prevailing market prices.

FIGURE 3.4

Ms. Popovich's Budget Line

The consumer's budget line shows the market bundles that can be purchased, given the consumer's income and prevailing commodity prices. This budget line assumes that Ms. Popovich's income is $600 per week, that the price of a pound of food is $3, and that the price of a piece of clothing is $60.

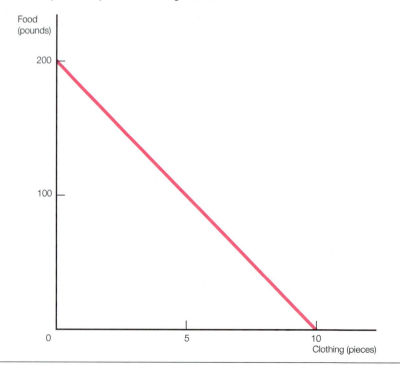

bundles that he or she can purchase, given the consumer's income and prevailing market prices.

To obtain the equation for Jennifer Popovich's budget line, note that

$$YP_f + XP_c = I \tag{3.1}$$

where Y is the amount of food she buys, X is the amount of clothing she buys, P_f is the price of food, P_c is the price of clothing, and I is her income. The left side of equation (3.1) equals the total amount she spends on food and clothing; what equation (3.1) says is that this amount must equal her income. For simplicity, we assume she saves nothing. (This assumption can be relaxed.) Solving equation (3.1) for Y, we obtain

$$Y = \frac{I}{P_f} - \frac{P_c}{P_f} X \tag{3.2}$$

which is the equation for her budget line.

A shift occurs in a consumer's budget line if changes occur in the consumer's income or product prices. In particular, an increase in income raises the budget line, whereas a decrease in income causes the budget line to fall (parallel to the original line because a change in I does not affect the slope). This is illustrated in Figure 3.5, which shows Ms. P's budget lines at incomes of $300, $600, and $900 per week. Her budget line moves upward as her income rises.

FIGURE 3.5

Ms. Popovich's Budget Lines at Incomes of $300, $600, and $900 per Week

The higher the consumer's income, the higher is the budget line. Holding commodity prices constant, the budget line's slope remains constant.

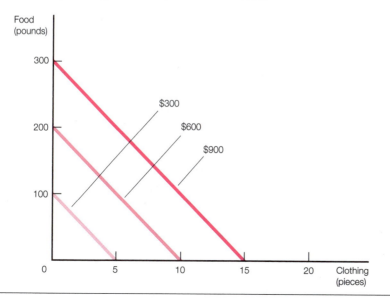

FIGURE 3.6

Ms. Popovich's Budget Line at Food Prices of $3 and $6 per Pound

Holding constant Ms. Popovich's income at $600 per week and the price of a piece of clothing at $60, the budget line intersects the vertical axis farther from the origin when the price of food is $3 than when it is $6.

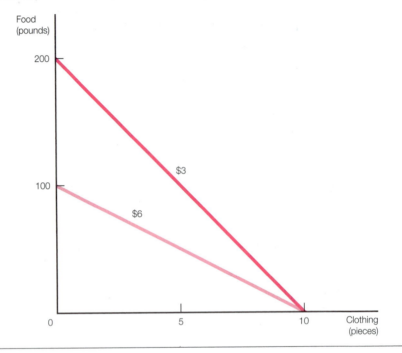

Also, the prices of products affect the budget line. A decrease in a product's price causes the budget line to intersect this product's axis at a point farther from the origin. Figure 3.6 shows Ms. Popovich's budget line when the price of a pound of food is $3 and when it is $6. You can see the budget line meets the vertical, or food, axis farther from the origin when the price of food is $3 per pound. This is because the change in the price of food alters the slope of the budget line, which equals $-P_c/P_f$ (as shown in equation (3.2)).

THE EQUILIBRIUM MARKET BUNDLE

Equilibrium market bundle The market bundle that, among all the items the consumer can purchase, yields the maximum utility.

Given a consumer's indifference curves and budget line, we can determine the consumer's **equilibrium market bundle**—the market bundle that, among all the items the consumer can purchase, yields the maximum utility. The first step is to combine the indifference curves with the budget line on the same graph. Figure 3.7 brings together Ms. Popovich's indifference curves (from Figure 3.1) and her budget line (from Figure 3.4). On the basis of the information assembled in Figure 3.7, it is a simple matter to determine her equilibrium market bundle. Her indifference curves show what she wants: Specifically, she wants to attain the highest possible indifference curve. Therefore, she would rather be on indifference curve I_2 than on indifference curve I_1 and on indifference curve I_3 than on indifference curve I_2. But she cannot choose any market bundle she likes. The budget line shows which market bundles her income and product prices permit her to buy. Consequently she must choose a bundle on her budget line.

Clearly the consumer's choice boils down to choosing the market bundle on the budget line that is on the highest indifference curve. This is the equilibrium market bundle. For example, Ms. P's equilibrium market bundle is at point H in Figure 3.7; it consists of 100 pounds of food and 5 pieces of clothing per week. This is her equilibrium market bundle because any other bundle on the budget line is on a lower indifference curve than point H. But will Ms. P choose this bun-

---

FIGURE 3.7

Equilibrium Market Bundle

Ms. Popovich's equilibrium market bundle is at point H, containing 100 pounds of food and 5 pieces of clothing. This is the point on her budget line that is on the highest indifference curve she can attain, I_2.

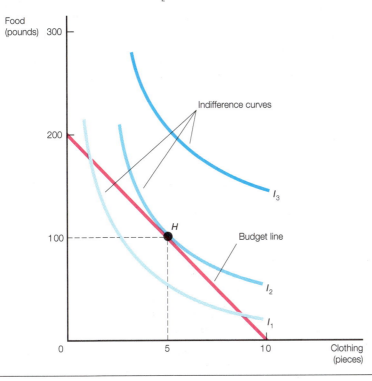

For consumers, time can be as important as money. For example, suppose Mildred Evans, an avid sports fan who goes regularly to baseball and football games, decides that she can devote no more than 24 hours per month to attending such games and that she can spend no more than $120 per month on baseball and football tickets. She lives much closer to the local baseball stadium than to the nearest football stadium, so it takes her 4 hours to see a baseball game but 6 hours to see a football game. The price of each baseball ticket is $10, and the price of each football ticket is $40.

Let B be the number of baseball games and F be the number of football games she attends per month. If she spends a total of $120 per month on tickets,

$$40F + 10B = 120 \qquad (3.3)$$

Why? Because $40F$ is the amount spent on football tickets, and $10B$ is the amount spent on baseball tickets, so $40F + 10B$ is the total amount spent per month on baseball and football tickets, which must equal $120. From equation (3.3), it follows that

$$F = 3 - B/4 \qquad (3.4)$$

This is the equation for the budget line, plotted in the following graph.

But this ignores the time constraint. If she spends a total of 24 hours per month at baseball and football games,

$$6F + 4B = 24 \qquad (3.5)$$

Why? Because $6F$ equals the number of hours spent at football games and $4B$ equals the number of hours spent at baseball games, so $6F + 4B$ equals the total number of hours spent at baseball and football games, which must equal 24. From equation (3.5), it follows that

$$F = 4 - 2B/3 \qquad (3.6)$$

This is the equation for the time constraint, plotted in the graph.

To keep within both the time and expenditure constraints, Mildred must pick a market bundle on line segment AE or line segment EC in the graph. Note that the time constraint cuts down on the number of feasible market bundles. Given that she wants to devote only 24 hours per month to attending baseball and football games, she must be content with market bundles along line segment EC rather than line segment ED, which would be available if there were no time constraint.

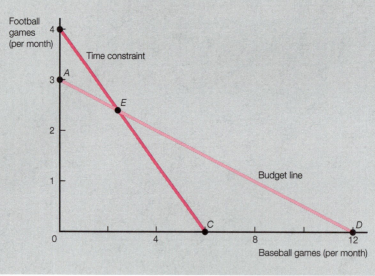

dle? It may take some time for her to realize this is the best market bundle under the circumstances, but eventually we should expect her to purchase this bundle.

MAXIMIZING UTILITY: A CLOSER LOOK

Let us look more closely at the equilibrium market bundle at point *H*, the one Ms. Popovich chooses. Clearly this bundle is at the point where the budget line is tangent to an indifference curve. Because the slope of the indifference curve equals -1 times the marginal rate of substitution of clothing for food (see page 64) and the slope of the budget line is $-P_c/P_f$ (see page 68), it follows that Ms. Popovich, if she maximizes utility, chooses in equilibrium to allocate her income between food and clothing so that

$$MRS = P_c/P_f \qquad (3.7)$$

where *MRS* is the marginal rate of substitution of clothing for food.

To understand what this means, recall that the marginal rate of substitution is the rate at which the consumer is willing to substitute clothing for food, holding her total level of satisfaction constant. Hence if the marginal rate of substitution is 4, the consumer is willing to give up 4 pounds of food to obtain 1 more piece of clothing. On the other hand, the price ratio, P_c/P_f, is the rate at which the consumer is able to substitute clothing for food. So if P_c/P_f is 4, the consumer *must* give up 4 pounds of food to obtain one more piece of clothing.

What equation (3.7) is saying is this: The rate at which the consumer is willing to substitute clothing for food (holding satisfaction constant) must equal the rate at which he or she is able to substitute clothing for food. Otherwise, it is always possible to find another market bundle that increases the consumer's satisfaction.

To illustrate, suppose Ms. Popovich chooses a market bundle for which the marginal rate of substitution of clothing for food is 4. Suppose the price ratio, P_c/P_f, is 3. If this is the case, Ms. Popovich can obtain an extra piece of clothing if she buys 3 fewer pounds of food because the price ratio is 3. But an extra piece of clothing is worth 4 pounds of food to Ms. P because the marginal rate of substitution is 4. Therefore, she can increase her satisfaction by substituting clothing for food—and this will continue to be the case so long as the marginal rate of substitution exceeds the price ratio. Conversely, if the marginal rate of substitution is less than the price ratio, Ms. Popovich can increase her satisfaction by substituting food for clothing. Only when the marginal rate of substitution equals the price ratio does her market bundle maximize her utility.

CORNER SOLUTIONS

Although in our example Ms. Popovich chooses the market bundle where the budget line is tangent to an indifference curve (the market basket at point *H* in Figure

In the corporate world managers are often asked to choose between multiple goals. We can use indifference curves to estimate this behavior. Let's say a manager is driven by two goals: (1) She wants to make a large profit, and (2) she also wants to be noticed. And small firms don't tend to get noticed while big firms do.

For simplicity, assume she is a monopolist, so the market demand curve is her firm demand curve. The demand curve is

$$P = a - bQ$$

Hence $P = a$ when $Q = 0$ and $Q = a/b$ when P is 0. Total revenues are 0 when $P = 0$ and 0 when $Q = 0$. She can maximize revenues at a price where $\eta = -1$. If it costs a constant k to make a unit of product, total costs are $TC = kQ$. The figure below visualizes total revenue, total cost, and profit (the difference between the two).

The manager's utility curves have the usual shape: Utility increases if output is held constant and profit increases, and utility increases if profit is held constant and output increases. Of course she is

happiest if both output and profit increase. The profit curve now is her constraint curve. She will maximize utility with profit of Π_2 and output of Q_2 generating utility of U_2. Note that she does not maximize profit (which gives utility of only U_1) or quantity (because that gives her utility of only U_0—we're constraining her output size objectives to profitable output).

Now let's say our manager works for a large, publicly held corporation. You are a shareholder of that company, and you'd prefer to maximize profit. There is ample evidence to support your preference because higher profit is strongly associated with higher stock prices. We have just shown that the manager does not want to maximize profit. What can the shareholder do to revise the behavior of our manager so she also wants to maximize profit?

Such issues are faced by shareholders of most publicly held corporations. We will discuss these behaviors in Chapter 14 when we discuss the principal–agent issue. But as we can see from the figure, if we tie the manager's compensation to firm profit, our manager would care more about maximizing profit.

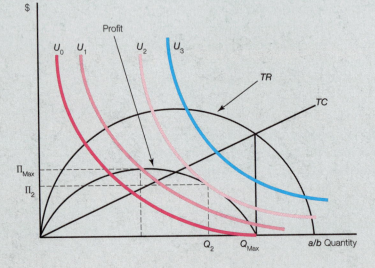

3.7), this is not always true. A consumer may consume none of some products because the cost does not justify the level of satisfaction they receive. For example, though many people have the income to afford a small amount of Beluga caviar, they do not purchase it because the cost is greater than the pleasure they receive from eating fish eggs.

Figure 3.8 shows this situation graphically. For simplicity, we assume the consumer can choose only between Beluga caviar and pizza. Given the position of these indifference curves, the consumer maximizes utility with bundle *W*, which contains all pizza and no Beluga caviar. This market bundle maximizes utility because it is on a higher indifference curve than any other bundle on the budget line. It is a **corner solution** in which the budget line touches the highest achievable indifference curve along an axis (in this case the vertical axis).

We previously showed that if the consumer purchases some of both goods to maximize utility, the marginal rate of substitution is equal to the price ratio. But if the consumer maximizes utility with a corner solution, this is not the case.

Corner solution When the budget line touches the highest achievable indifference curve along an axis.

FIGURE 3.8

Corner Solution

The market bundle that maximizes your utility is *W*, which lies on the vertical axis.

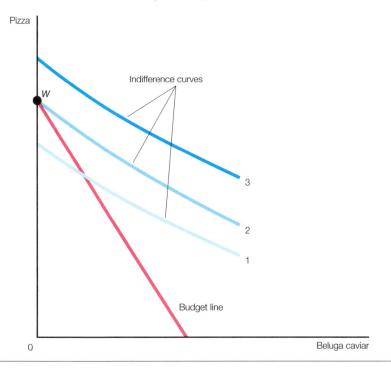

HOW MANAGERS CAN STRATEGICALLY INFLUENCE CONSUMER CHOICES

We just saw how Ms. P's purchase decisions are influenced by her preferences, her income, and product prices. Although managers can do little to change consumer incomes, they can influence preferences and the effect of a budget constraint. For example, advertising is a direct action to influence preferences; lowering prices may induce a consumer to purchase products. So managers can influence budget constraints with their pricing policies. We have just portrayed the budget constraint as linear to present the basic theory of consumer choice; but in the real world managers price in ways that are consciously designed to make the budget constraint nonlinear and to influence consumer choice.

A recent coupon offer by a leading grocery chain (Albertson's) offered its customers $18 off their grocery bill if they spent at least $180 in one store visit. Let's

---

FIGURE 3.9

Ms. Popovich's Utility-Maximizing Purchase of Clothing and Groceries before Receiving the Coupon

With a budget of $200 and the price of a unit of clothing and a unit of groceries each $1, Ms. Popovich rationally chooses to consume $C_{0'}$ units of clothing and $G_{0'}$ units of groceries, attaining a utility of $U_{0'}$.

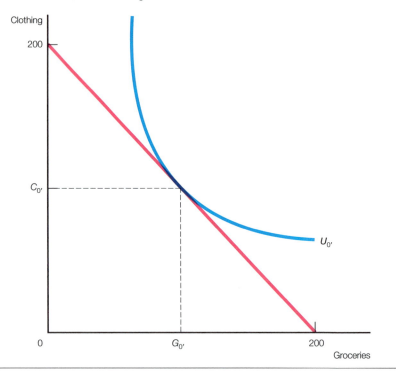

view the impact of such an offer on Ms. Popovich. Suppose her income is $200. She can consume groceries at $1 per unit or clothing at $1 per unit. Thus, before the coupon, her budget constraint and purchase decision (she purchases $C_{0'}$ units of clothing, $G_{0'}$ units of groceries, and attains utility level $U_{0'}$) appears in Figure 3.9.

By offering a coupon, Albertson's managers in effect shift Ms. P's budget constraint outward parallel to her old one. When her grocery bill reaches $180 (so she consumes $20 of clothing), she receives $18 back (or pays $162 to the grocery store) and now has the potential of spending $38 on clothing (if she spends all her savings on clothing). Alternatively, she could spend $218 on groceries (if she took her $18 in savings and spent it on more groceries). Her new budget constraint and purchase choices appear in Figure 3.10.

FIGURE 3.10

Ms. Popovich's Utility-Maximizing Purchase of Clothing and Groceries after Receiving the Coupon

Part of Ms. Popovich's budget line shifts outward, parallel to her budget line without the coupon. Depending on the shape of her indifference curves, the coupon may or may not influence her purchases of clothing and groceries. If her indifference curves are similar to the dashed line here, her behavior is uninfluenced; but if her indifference curves are like the solid line, the coupon increases her utility (and perhaps firm revenue).

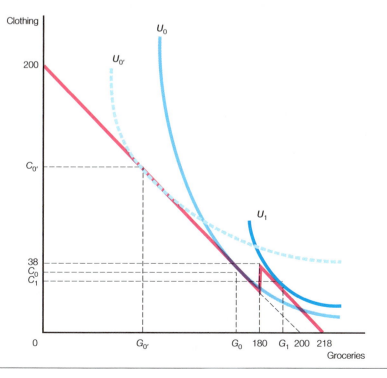

The coupon budget constraint looks like her no-coupon budget constraint until she spends at least $180 on groceries. Then her budget constraint shifts upward to the right by an additional $18. In effect, through their pricing decisions, Albertson's managers have shifted Ms. P's budget constraint. If Ms. P's indifference curves resemble the dashed line in Figure 3.10, the coupon does not affect her purchase behavior (her utility stays at $U_{0'}$ and her purchases are $C_{0'}$ and $G_{0'}$). Nothing was gained by Albertson's managers, but the cost was trivial (the printing of some coupons). However, had Ms. P's initial indifference curve been the solid U_0, the coupon would enable her to increase her utility to U_1. The coupon was a good deal for Ms. P. Was it a good strategy by Albertson's managers? Only if $G_1 - G_0 > 18$; that is, only if Ms. P spent over $18 more on groceries than she did without the coupon. Presumably the managers felt that most consumers would spend more than $18 extra on groceries as a result of the coupon. So we see that managers have a range of strategies they can use to change the purchasing decisions of consumers in addition to advertising and changing prices.

Another strategy for influencing the budget constraint of consumers is quantity discounts. Ms. P pays a visit to Dunking Donuts. A single donut costs $.50, a half dozen costs $2, and a dozen costs $3. Suppose Ms. P has $4 to spend on donuts and all other goods. The price of a unit of all other goods is $1. Thus if Ms. P buys one donut, she will have $3.50 to spend on all other goods. If she buys two donuts, she will have $3 to spend on all other goods. If Ms. P buys four donuts separately, she will spend $2 on donuts and $2 on all other goods—but she could buy a half dozen for $2. If more is indeed better (that is, if the marginal utility of donuts is positive), she should buy the half dozen rather than four or five donuts. If Ms. P wants seven donuts, she should buy the half dozen for $2 and one donut separately for $0.50; this will leave her with $1.50 for all other goods. Should she wish to buy eight donuts, she should buy the dozen for $3. She could spend $2 for a half dozen and $0.50 each for donuts seven and eight, or she could get a dozen for the same $3. Thus she should never buy 8, 9, 10, or 11 donuts. Her budget constraint will appear as the step function in Figure 3.11.

In effect, what is the influence of the pricing strategy? Selling a half dozen donuts for $2 reduces the price per donut to $0.33, and selling a dozen donuts for $3 reduces the price per donut to $0.25. Why should the managers offer this price decrease? Perhaps because of the diminishing marginal utility of donuts. Consumers are willing to pay a lot for the first donut. But donuts are filling (and fattening). As the marginal utility of donuts decreases, the Dunking managers must lower the price to entice buyers.

If the price of donuts was always $0.50/donut, Ms. P's budget constraint intercept on the donuts axis would occur at 8 donuts. With the quantity discount, her budget constraint intercept is at 14 donuts. If Ms. P's indifference curve is the dashed one, the quantity discount strategy will not change her behavior; but if it

FIGURE 3.11

Ms. Popovich's Utility-Maximizing Choices for Donuts and All Other Goods

The quantity discount for donuts creates a step function budget constraint and means that Ms. P will never purchase 4, 5, 8, 9, 10, or 11 donuts. The quantity discount doesn't change her behavior if her indifference curves resemble the dashed line but raises her utility if her indifference curves resemble the solid line.

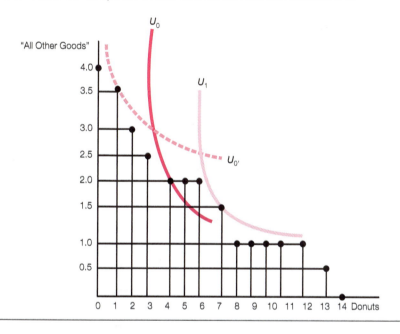

is the solid one, she is induced to move from buying 4 donuts to 7 while increasing her utility from U_0 to U_1. Both managers and consumers can benefit from this strategy.

You face this situation anytime you are offered a quantity discount. Remember this the next time you encounter one and see whether the pricing strategy changes your behavior.

We can also use shifts in the budget constraint to explain why most individuals prefer cash to a specific gift (unless they requested the gift). At every holiday season, consumers decide what gifts to buy for friends and family. Suppose Ms. Popovich is already maximizing her utility subject to her budget constraint (I_0) with A_0 units of all other goods and G_0 units of the gift good and receiving U_0 units of satisfaction. Let the unit price of all other goods, P_A, be 1. Suppose Ms. P's well-meaning mother-in-law gives her another unit of the gift item for the

FIGURE 3.12

Ms. P's Utility and Consumption of All Other Goods and Gift Goods under Various Scenarios of Gift Receiving

A gift will, at best, give Ms. P the exact consumption of the gift good and all other goods had Ms. P made the choice herself. But most likely a smaller cash gift from the gift giver will yield Ms. P the same utility as the gift; or a gift of cash to Ms. P equal to what the gift giver spent will yield a higher level of utility than did the gift.

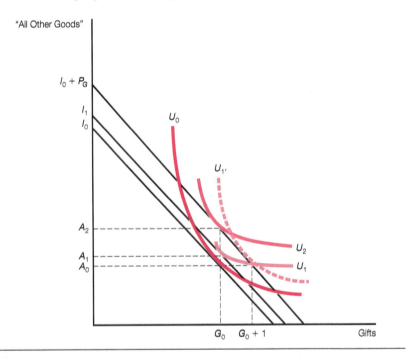

holidays. Assuming the marginal utility of the gift item is positive, Ms. P's utility has increased. Gift giving has been a success as far as her mother-in-law is concerned. But how about for Ms. Popovich? Consider the situation depicted in Figure 3.12.

After receiving the gift unit from her mother-in-law, if Ms. P's high-level utility resembles the dashed line, she will have A_0 units of all other goods and $G_0 + 1$ units of the gift good and will maximize her utility at level $U_{1'}$. By spending P_G on a gift unit, the mother-in law got it right on. The mother-in-law is happy that Ms. P appreciates the gift, and Ms. P is happy because her utility is increased. You will be lucky if all your gift giving turns out this way. Unfortunately, in many cases the most likely scenario is depicted by the solid higher-level indifference curves

(U_1 and U_2). We can state two things. If the mother-in-law's objective is to get Ms. Popovich to a level of satisfaction U_1, she could do so with a smaller expenditure ($I_1 < I_0 + P_G$), giving Ms. P no gift units and instead $A_1 - A_0$ units of all other goods. Ms. P will get the same level of utility as with the gift if she had A_1 units of all other goods and G_0 gift units. In general, from a utility standpoint, gift giving is more expensive than it has to be. A second point is that if the mother-in-law gives Ms. P the cash she spent on her gift (P_G), Ms. P's budget line will shift outward to $I_0 + P_G$ and Ms. P will maximize her utility by consuming A_2 units of all other goods and G_0 units of the gift good. That is, a cash gift equal to the unit cost of the gift good will increase Ms. P's utility to U_2, which is higher than the U_1 level attained with the gift. Thus the mother-in-law could spend less and give Ms. Popovich the same level of satisfaction by buying Ms. P more units of all other goods (that is, by giving cash) rather than the gift she bought her.

Our Wharton colleague Joel Waldfogel has received much "Grinch" publicity since his article about this deadweight loss of Christmas was published in 1993[1]. In fact, every year around Christmas he gets calls from newspapers looking for seasonal stories about Christmas. If you look at the proliferation of gift cards in recent years, you might conclude that his concept is getting through. However, gift cards tie the recipient to a particular store: A gift card to an apparel store may not be good if you really want electronics. General gift cards, like American Express, are less constraining but aren't universally accepted; cash is accepted in all brick-and-mortar stores. We should point out, though, that our analysis does not account for sentimental value. You may hate the gift that your grandmother gives you but be happy knowing that she loves you enough to select and purchase it.

DERIVING THE INDIVIDUAL DEMAND CURVE

A consumer's demand curve shows how much product a person will purchase at various prices (when other prices and income are held constant). It reveals the inner desires of purchase behavior. Let us return to Ms. Popovich.

Ms. P can choose between two products: food and clothing. Her weekly income is $600, and the price of clothing is $60 per piece. Ms. P's budget is budget line 1 in Figure 3.13 when the price of food is $3 per pound. As we saw in Figure 3.7, she will buy 100 pounds of food per week.

How will she purchase when the price of food increases to $6 per pound? If her income and the price of clothing remain constant, her budget is budget line 2 in Figure 3.14. She attains her greatest utility by reaching her highest indifference curve, I_1. She chooses the bundle at point K, which contains 50 pounds of food per week. If the price of food is $6 per pound, she will make a weekly purchase of 50 pounds of food per week.

1. J. Waldfogel, "The Deadweight Loss of Christmas," *American Economic Review* 83, no. 5 (December 1993), pp. 1328–1336.

PROBLEM SOLVED: Do I Stay or Do I Go? Use of Indifference Curves

Ms. Popovich is a self-employed business owner who is also raising a family. Her business is growing, and she finds it could literally demand 18–20 hours per day. Of course she feels the same about her children. What is she to do? We call the time spent engaged in business *work* and time spent not working *leisure*.[a] Unlike money budget constraints, which vary with an individual's income, the time constraint is a great equalizer: There are 24 hours each day whether you are rich or poor. Thus Ms. P is directed by a time budget constraint of $H_W + H_L = 24$, where H_W is the hours worked and H_L is the hours spent in leisure pursuits. We express hours worked as $H_W = 24 - H_L$.

In every hour working, Ms. P receives a wage of W. We use that knowledge to estimate a time budget constraint with income. Her utility (level of satisfaction) is a function of income (I) and leisure (L): $U = U(I, L)$. As in a purchase decision, she must choose between the two. For a given level of income, she'd be happier with more leisure, and for a given time in leisure, she'd be happier with more income. Her indifference curves are downward-sloping and convex to the origin (the "normal" shape).

We estimate Ms. P's income as the hourly wage (W) times the hours worked:

$$W \times (24 - H_L) = 24W - W \times H_L$$

We presuppose that time is money and show why with a budget constraint. If she chooses all work and no play, $H_W = 24$ and $H_L = 0$, her income is $24W$. If she chooses all play and no work, $H_W = 0$ and $H_L = 24$, her income is 0. Her utility-maximizing behavior is shown in the figure.

The slope of the time constraint is $-W = -24W/24$; that is, the market will pay her W to work an hour (or alternatively, she forgoes W for every hour of leisure). The slope of her indifference curve is

$$\frac{-\Delta I}{\Delta L} = \left(\frac{-\Delta I}{\Delta L}\right)\left(\frac{\Delta U}{\Delta U}\right)$$

$$= -\left(\frac{\Delta U}{\Delta L}\right)\Big/\left(\frac{\Delta U}{\Delta I}\right) = -\frac{MU_L}{MU_I}$$

Or more elegantly,

$$-\frac{MU_L}{MU_I} = -\left(\frac{dU}{dL}\right)\Big/\left(\frac{dU}{dL}\right)$$

We estimate that Ms. P will act as if setting $MU_L/MU_I = W$, the slope of the indifference curve, is equal to the slope of the constraint. That is, she works up to the point where her trade-off of leisure for income equals the wage rate. By changing the wage rate (for instance, from W to a greater rate W'), we can estimate how Ms. Popovich changes her demand for leisure (in this case choosing less of it, $H_{L'} < H_L$, and preferring more income). We can change the wage rate and virtually trace out Ms. P's supply curve for labor. But, if we pay Ms. P too much, she may actually choose to work less. She has attained enough income to make her comfortable and now wants to spend more time with her family. So if the wage rate rises to W'', Ms. Popovich will decrease her working time to $24 - H_L$ hours.

[a] Arguably, it might be the other way around.

Ms. P's Dilemma of Balancing Work and Leisure

Ms. P gets utility from work (income) and leisure (family and friends). If the wage rate is W, she will work $24 - H_L$ hours. If the wage rate increases to W', she will increase her work hours to $24 - H_{L'}$.

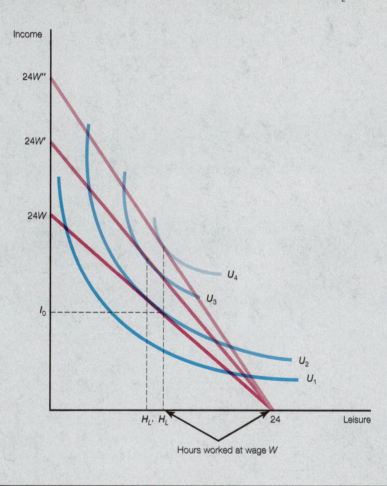

FIGURE 3.13

Effect of a Change in Price on Ms. Popovich's Equilibrium Market Bundle

If the price of a pound of food is $3, Ms. Popovich's budget line is such that her equilibrium market bundle is at point *H*, where she buys 100 pounds of food per week. If the price of a pound of food is $6, Ms. Popovich's budget line is such that her equilibrium market bundle is at point *K*, where she buys 50 pounds of food per week.

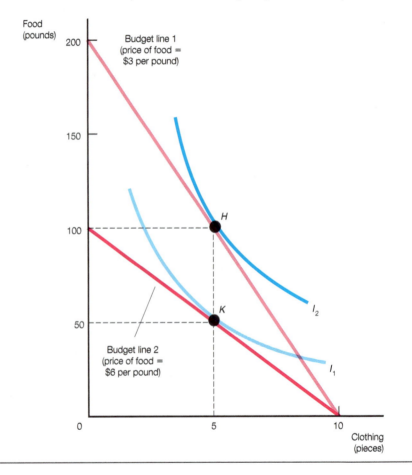

We have derived two points on Ms. P's demand curve for food, those corresponding to food prices of $3 and $6 per pound. Figure 3.14 shows these two points, *U* and *V*. To obtain more points on her demand curve, all we do is assume a particular price of food, construct the budget line corresponding to this price (holding her income and the price of clothing constant), and find the market bundle that is on her highest indifference curve. Plotting the level of food in this bun-

FIGURE 3.14

Ms. Popovich's Individual Demand Curve for Food

Ms. Popovich's individual demand curve for food shows the amount of food she would buy at various prices.

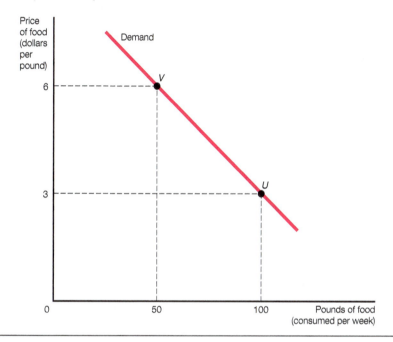

dle relative to the assumed price of food, we obtain a new point on her demand curve for food. Connecting all these points, we estimate her complete demand curve for food, in Figure 3.14. (In our scenario, the level of clothing consumed remains constant. This does not have to be the case.)

DERIVING THE MARKET DEMAND CURVE

We have just shown how to estimate a consumer's demand curve for a product, given the consumer's tastes and income as well as the prices of other products. What if we estimate the individual demand curve for each consumer in the market? How can they help us understand the market?

The answer is easy. Think of the market demand curve as representing the sum of tastes and preferences of individual consumers. It summarizes the demand curves of all individuals in the market. To derive the market demand curve, we estimate the horizontal sum of all the individual demand curves. At each pricing

TABLE 3.1

Individual Demand Curves and Market Demand Curve for Food

Price of Food (Dollars per Pound)	Individual Demand (Hundreds of Pounds per Month)				Market Demand
	Miller	Sarafian	Chase	Gruber	
3.00	51.0	45.0	5.0	2.0	103
3.20	43.0	44.0	4.2	1.8	93
3.40	36.0	43.0	3.4	1.6	84
3.60	30.0	42.0	2.6	1.4	76
3.80	26.0	41.4	2.4	1.2	71
4.00	21.0	41.0	2.0	1.0	65

point we estimate the market total by summing the purchases of all individuals at that price.

Table 3.1 shows the demand schedules for food of four families: the Millers, Sarafians, Chases, and Grubers. For simplicity, suppose these four families constitute the entire market for food; then the market demand curve for food is shown in the last column of Table 3.1. Figure 3.15 shows the families' demand curves for food as well as the resulting market demand curve. To illustrate how the market demand curve is derived, suppose the price of food is $3 per pound; the market quantity demanded is 103 hundreds of pounds per month. This is the sum of the quantities demanded by the four families. (As shown in Table 3.1, this sum equals 51.0 + 45.0 + 5.0 + 2.0, or 103 hundreds of pounds.)

Figure 3.15 clearly illustrates that within a single product market, demand is not composed of homogeneous buyers. A market is generally composed of buyers with different tastes and preferences. We will see later that managers can strategically exploit this heterogeneity by identifying submarkets and charging each submarket a different price.

We also see why managers like to expand their markets. As more consumers enter the market, the demand curve is pushed out to the right due to horizontal summation. As this occurs (and the supply curve remains constant), the market price increases.

Finally, while demand for a firm's product or service is necessarily a fraction of total market demand, the demand curve facing managers of a firm is generally not a parallel, scaled-down version of market demand. The choices of managers can significantly influence demand for their products. Managers who are better able to influence consumers realize higher performance relative to rivals.

FIGURE 3.15

Individual Demand Curves and Market Demand Curve for Food

The market demand curve is the horizontal sum of all the individual demand curves.

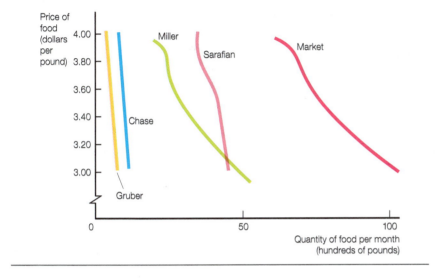

CONSUMER SURPLUS

One key insight managers need to understand is that many consumers value a product at a premium. They are willing to pay a higher price than that of the market, as illustrated in Figure 3.16. This is a simple but powerful (and potentially profitable) fact that managers need to exploit. An individual's demand curve estimates the unit price (P_X) she is willing to pay to purchase a given number of product units (say X). Because the demand curve (usually) is downward-sloping, the curve indicates that the consumer values products $X - 1$, $X - 2$, and so forth at a higher amount than the value of the Xth good purchased (say at values P_{X-1}, P_{X-2}). The price at which the consumer values each number of units demanded is called the **consumer's reservation price** for that particular unit of good. It is also known as the willingness to pay (WTP). The reservation price is the highest price the consumer is willing to pay for that unit of product or service. If we try to charge any price above the WTP, the consumer will not purchase from us.

The difference between what an individual is willing to pay and what that individual has to pay (the market price) for a product is called **consumer surplus.** It is the actual price paid subtracted from the reservation price.

When a market is at equilibrium, the marginal individuals to purchase are those whose reservation price just equals the market price. They receive no

Consumer's reservation price The price at which the consumer values each number of units demanded.

Consumer surplus The difference between what an individual is willing to pay (their reservation price) and what that individual has to pay (the market price) for a product.

STRATEGY SESSION: The Trade-Off between Risk and Return

As investors in developing countries like India and China begin to diversify their savings from simple saving accounts to bonds and stocks, they will show behavior regarding their risk–return profiles. A recent article in *The Times of India* discussed the need for investors to understand their "risk profile."[a] We can operationalize this risk profile using indifference curves.

Assume our investor Devi Bangerjee has $1 million, which she must allocate between stocks and government bonds. If she invests in government bonds, she will receive a return of 5 percent, and there is no risk. If she invests $1 million in common stock, she expects a return of 10 percent and endures considerable risk. If she invests half in bonds and half in common stocks, she expects a return of 7.5 percent and there is some risk. Line *RT* in the graph that follows shows her expected return with its corresponding risk for combinations of the two investments. People differ in their risk tolerance; this is part of human nature. We represent hers in the form of indifference curves.

But because we differ in risk tolerance does not mean we are totally idiosyncratic. For most of us, indifference curves slope upward to the right. Risk is fundamentally different from purchase decisions, for which indifference curves slope downward to the right.

The risk indifference curves slope upward to the right because Devi prefers less risk to more when the expected return is held constant. If there is an increase in risk, she needs a higher expected return to maintain the same level of satisfaction. She must choose some point on line *RT*. The point on *RT* that is tangent with the highest indifference curve is point *S*. Here her expected return is 7.5 percent. Hence she should purchase $500,000 of government bonds and $500,000 of common stock. We will look at such investment decisions in greater detail in Chapter 13.

There are Web sites around the globe (www.amp.conz; https://www.tools.asiapacific.hsbc.com) with risk profile calculators. Using a short series of questions, these calculators approximate the indifference curve of the investor.

[a]D. Ghosh, "Know Your Appetite for Risk-Taking," *The Times of India*, April 15, 2008.

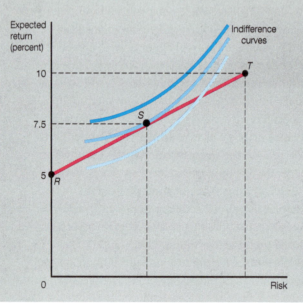

FIGURE 3.16

The Consumer Surplus for a Price of P_X

The consumer surplus for an individual is the area under the demand curve but above the price (P_x) paid (area A). The same definition holds for a market demand curve.

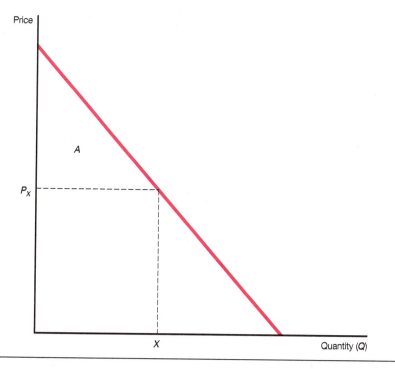

consumer surplus from the purchase; they value it for the amount of money they paid for it. But all other purchasers have reservation prices exceeding the market price. They all gained a surplus because they paid less for the product than they were willing to pay (they got what many term a "good deal"). If we aggregate all the individuals' consumer surpluses, we estimate the consumer surplus of the market at that given price. Visually, a product's consumer surplus is the area below the demand curve but above the market price (area A in Figure 3.16).

We will say more about consumer surplus later, when we introduce the analogous idea of producer surplus, and the summation of consumer and producer surplus, called the total surplus. Economists use these concepts to describe the efficiency of markets and the social benefits of market transactions. We draw a simpler observation. As long as the demand curve for a product is downward-sloping (and most are), a manager will generate more revenue if she charges each consumer his or her reservation price. Managers can also increase revenue by charging higher prices to consumers who value the product more highly. This is called price discrimination. Relative to a simple single-price strategy, this captures consumer surplus for the benefit of the firm. Even though various legal, practical, and economic constraints limit the extent to which managers can charge different prices for the same product, the practice is widespread. Examples include airline tickets, automobiles sold at dealerships where haggling is the norm, and goods and services offered at discounts through coupon systems and other special offers. We explore these strategies in greater detail later.

SUMMARY

1. An indifference curve contains points representing market bundles among which the consumer is indifferent. If the consumer prefers more to less of both commodities, an indifference curve must have a negative slope.

2. Market bundles on higher indifference curves provide more satisfaction than those on lower indifference curves. Utility is a number that indexes the level of satisfaction derived from a particular market bundle. Market bundles with higher utilities are preferred over those with lower utilities.

3. The marginal rate of substitution shows how many units of one good must be given up if the consumer, after getting an extra unit of another good, is to maintain a constant level of satisfaction. To obtain the marginal rate of substitution, multiply the slope of the indifference curve by -1.

4. The budget line contains all the market bundles the consumer can buy, given his or her money income and the level of each price. Increases in income push the budget line upward and parallel to the old budget line; changes in the price ratio alter the budget line's slope.

5. To attain the highest level of satisfaction compatible with the budget line, the consumer must choose the market bundle on the budget line that is on the highest indifference curve. This market bundle is at a point where the budget line is tangent to an indifference curve (unless there is a corner solution).

6. The consumer who maximizes utility will choose in equilibrium to allocate his or her income so that the marginal rate of substitution of one good for another good equals the ratio of the prices of the two goods (unless there is a corner solution).

7. The theory of consumer behavior is often used to represent the process of rational choice. Frequently a person or organization has a certain amount of money to spend and must decide how much to allocate to a number of different uses. This theory indicates how such decisions should be made.

8. A consumer's demand curve shows how much the consumer would purchase of a good at various prices of the good when other prices and the consumer's income are held constant. The theory of consumer behavior can be used to derive

the consumer's demand curve, and the market demand curve can be obtained by summing the individual demand curves horizontally.

9. Consumer surplus is the difference between what a consumer is willing to pay for a good and what the consumer pays for the good in the market. Clever managers want to figure out pricing policies to extract consumer surplus from consumers.

wwnorton.com/studyspace

PROBLEMS

1. The market for sports performance drinks experienced a big shift in 2008 as sales of low-calorie sports drinks grew by over 25 percent. Many attributed this shift to greater use by women who wanted a sports drink without many calories.
   a. If a woman desires two containers of low-calorie sports drink as much as one container of high-calorie sports drink, what do her indifference curves (between low- and high-calories sports drinks) look like?
   b. Do they have the typical shape of indifference curves? Why or why not?
2. In recent years fresh bagel sales have been growing at about 30 percent per year. Once considered an ethnic food to be eaten with cream cheese and lox, bagels now "have become the new donut to bring to the office," according to Michael Goldstein of Goldstein's Bagel Bakery in Pasadena, California. But one problem with bagels is that they get stale fast. In the words of Ray Lahvic, editor emeritus of *Bakery Production and Marketing*, "the worst thing in the world is a day-old bagel." If a market researcher asserts that the slope of the typical consumer's indifference curves between fresh bagels and day-old bagels is -1, would you agree with this assertion? Why or why not?
3. On a piece of graph paper, plot the quantity of lamb consumed by Ms. Turner along the vertical axis and the quantity of rice she consumes along the horizontal axis. Draw the indifference curve that includes the following market bundles. Each of these market bundles gives equal satisfaction:

Market Bundle	Lamb (Pounds)	Rice (Pounds)
1	2	8
2	3	7
3	4	6
4	5	5
5	6	4
6	7	3
7	8	2
8	9	1

4. In the previous question, what is the marginal rate of substitution of rice for lamb? How does the marginal rate of substitution vary as Ms. Turner consumes more lamb and less rice? Is this realistic?

5. Suppose Richard has an after-tax income of $500 per week and must spend it all on food or clothing. If food is $5 per pound and clothing is $10 per piece, draw his budget line on a piece of graph paper, where the amount of food is measured along the vertical axis and the amount of clothing is measured along the horizontal axis.

6. In the previous problem, what is the budget line if Richard's weekly income increases to $600? What is his budget line if his income is $500 but the price of food increases to $10 per pound? What is his budget line if his income is $500 but the price of clothing increases to $20 per piece? Draw each of these budget lines on the piece of graph paper used in the previous problem.

7. Maria has budgeted a total of $9 to spend on two goods: chips and salsa. She likes to consume a unit of chips in combination with a unit of salsa. Any unit of chips that she cannot consume in combination with a unit of salsa is useless. Similarly, any unit of salsa that she cannot consume in combination with a unit of chips is useless. If the price of a unit of chips is 50 cents and the price of a unit of salsa is 10 cents, how many units of each good does she purchase?

8. In the following diagram, we show one of Jane's indifference curves and her budget line.
   a. If the price of good X is $100, what is her income?
   b. What is the equation for her budget line?
   c. What is the slope of her budget line?
   d. What is the price of good Y?
   e. What is Jane's marginal rate of substitution in equilibrium?

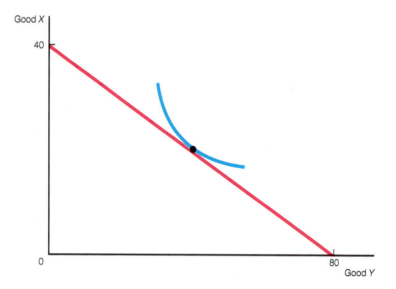

9. Sarah has $300 to allocate between opera tickets and movie tickets. The price of each opera ticket is $60, and the price of each movie ticket is $6. Her marginal rate of substitution of opera tickets for movie tickets equals 5, regardless of what market bundle she chooses. How many opera tickets does she purchase?

10. Suppose Milton has $50 to be divided between corn and beans and that the price of beans is $0.50 per pound. What will be the relationship between the price of corn and the amount of corn he will buy if $U = \log Q_c + 4 \log Q_b$, where U is his utility, Q_c is the quantity of corn he consumes (in pounds), and Q_b is the quantity of beans he consumes (in pounds)?

11. In 1993 the state of New York received $3 billion (from federal sources and a state petroleum tax) to be spent during the mid-1990s on highways and/or mass transit (subways, buses, and urban rail lines), both of which could be used to meet the transportation needs of the state's population.
    a. If each mile of mass transit costs $20 million, what is the maximum number of miles of mass transit that these funds would have enabled the state to construct?
    b. If each mile of highway costs $10 million, what is the maximum number of miles of highways that these funds would have enabled the state to construct?
    c. If the number of miles of mass transit constructed is put on the vertical axis of a graph and the number of miles of highways constucted is put on the horizontal axis, can a budget line (showing the maximum number of miles of mass transit that can be constructed, given each number of miles of highways constructed) be drawn for the state? If so, what is the slope of this budget line? (Assume that the $3 billion is the only source of funds for mass transit or highway construction.)
    d. If the public and the state government agree that every extra mile of mass transit adds three times as much to the state's transportation capability as an extra mile of highways, how much of the $3 billion should be spent on mass transit if the objective is to maximize transportation capability?

CHAPTER 4

PRODUCTION THEORY

Once managers determine the demand for the firm's product or service, their job is far from over. Now they must choose the optimal method to produce. Managers need to be as efficient as possible. Resources are costly, and using them wisely is the hallmark of good managers. Efficiency requires an understanding of the production process. Simply stated, a production process explains how scarce resources (inputs) are used to produce a good or service (output). The production function precisely specifies the relationship between inputs and outputs.

Production issues are not confined to the physical transformation of inputs into outputs. In business, production involves all activities associated with providing goods and services, such as employment practices, acquisition of capital resources, and product distribution. Today, at firms like investment banks and consulting practices, managers are concerned with efficiently producing intellectual resources.

Understanding the production process is fundamental to gaining insight into cost analysis. Control of costs, along with an understanding of demand, is required for managers to optimize profit. But costs evolve from the production process. Managers cannot understand their firm's cost structure unless they understand the production process.

STRATEGY SESSION: The Yankees' Deal for Alex Rodriguez

In February 2004 the New York Yankees assumed the richest contract in sports by trading players to the Texas Rangers for shortstop Alex Rodriguez. Rodriguez was working under a 10-year, $252 million contract that he signed with the Rangers in 2000. As soon as the deal was announced, commentators speculated about whether the contract was economically sensible. In fact, when we look at the underlying economics, the Yankees appear to have gotten the best player in baseball at a relatively bargain price.

First, the Yankees received $67 million in cash from the Rangers—the largest sum to trade hands in the history of baseball. This reduced the Yankees' liability to Rodriguez to roughly $112 million. The expected payouts to the players the Yankees got rid of in the trade were approximately $13.3 million. Rodriguez was to receive $15 million in 2004, but he agreed to defer $1 million. Hence the added cost of Rodriguez to the Yankees' payroll in 2004 was roughly $750,000.

For future years, the payouts to Rodriguez would be the following: $15 million for the next three seasons; $16 million in 2007–2008; $17 million in 2009; and $18 million in 2010. Rodriguez would defer $1 million for the first four years at no interest and receive the $4 million in 2011.

Because of their high payroll costs, the Yankees must pay a luxury tax (which is split among the other baseball teams). In 2004 the Yankees estimated their payroll would equal $190 million (this was higher than the 10 lowest-payroll teams). A payroll of $190 million would cost the Yankees $21 million in luxury taxes.

The total revenue for the Yankees was estimated to be $330 million in 2004. Approximately $110 million was generated from 3.5 million paying customers (ticket prices increased by an average of 10 percent for the 2004 season). The Yankees received $60 million from the YES Network, $10 million from WCBS radio, and over $30 million from national television, licensing, and sponsorship revenues. The team also received revenue from local sponsorships and game concessions.

The Yankees expected the addition of Alex Rodriguez to increase attendance even in the face of increasing ticket prices (after the trade was announced, the ticket office was swamped with ticket requests). These additional fans also presumably would spend more at the games on snacks, drinks, and merchandise.

After all the factors are considered, most experts believe the marginal benefit to the Yankees was greater than the additional costs for Rodriguez's contract.

Source: "Sports Business: Steinbrenner Has Got It, and He Loves to Flaunt It," *The New York Times*, February 17, 2004.

THE PRODUCTION FUNCTION WITH ONE VARIABLE INPUT

The production function is a table, a graph, or an equation showing the maximum product output achieved from any specified set of inputs. The function summarizes the characteristics of existing technology at a given time; it shows the technological constraints managers face. Any manager should want to use the most efficient process known. So we assume managers presuppose technical efficiency. Unfortunately many managers view processes as static. Production is dynamic:

Methods, designs, and factor costs change. Changes beget changes and may require different input mixes.

Say a process uses two inputs. If X_1 is the level of the first input and X_2 is the level of the second input, the production function is

$$Q = f(X_1, X_2) \tag{4.1}$$

where Q is the firm's output rate.

Cognitively, the simplest case has one input whose quantity is fixed and one input whose quantity is variable. Fixed inputs cannot be changed in the short run. To be sure, economists assume the time needed to change an asset is the beginning of what is called the long term. Fixed inputs often require capital (buildings, machinery, land). Variable inputs can be changed in the short run; labor is an example. In the long run, all inputs are variable.

John Thomas is an entrepreneur who currently owns five CNC machine tools. He works as a contractor in the airplane industry. He wants to know the effect

---

TABLE 4.1

Output of Metal Parts When Various Amounts of Labor Are Applied to Five Machine Tools, Thomas Machine Company

Amount of Labor (L)	Amount of Capital (Number of Machines)	Output of Parts (Q, hundreds per year)
0	5	0
1	5	49
2	5	132
3	5	243
4	5	376
5	5	525
6	5	684
6.67	5	792.59
7	5	847
8	5	1,008
9	5	1,161
10	5	1,300
11	5	1,419
12	5	1,512
13	5	1,573
14	5	1,596
15	5	1,575

---

on annual output if he were to hire various numbers of machinists. (Please note that the following output numbers are expressed in hundreds.) Thomas estimates that one machinist produces 49 parts per year. Thomas can produce more parts by hiring more workers, as we see in Table 4.1. This table represents a production function for Thomas Machine Company when five machine tools are used. More visually, the curve in Figure 4.1 presents exactly the same results. In fact, the

---

FIGURE 4.1

Relationship between Total Output and Amount of Labor Used on Five Machine Tools, Thomas Machine Company

Total output increases as labor increases at an increasing rate (up to 6.67 units of labor) and increases at a decreasing rate (until slightly more than 14 units of labor). Thereafter, output decreases as more units of labor are deployed. Managers will never willfully deploy labor in the latter circumstance. The production function shows the relationship between output (in this case number of parts produced) and input (in this case units of labor).

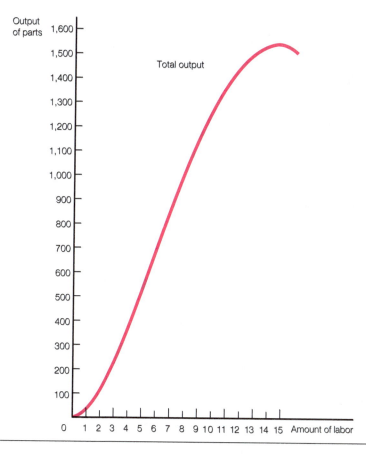

numbers in Table 4.1 (and Table 4.2) are derived from the production function equal to $Q = 30L + 20L^2 - L^3$. L is equal to the number of machinists.

We can think of the production function as giving insights into the manager's technology use. Thomas is clearly interested in knowing how output changes as the number of machinists varies. One common measure used by many managers is *output per worker*. This measure is what economists call **average product (AP)**. Because we are varying machinists, this is output per worker or

Average product (AP) Common measuring device for estimating the units of output, on average per input unit.

$$AP = \frac{Q}{X_1}, \text{ holding } X_2 \text{ constant}$$

Average product tells Thomas how many units of output, on average, each machinist is responsible for. If he wants a better metric to estimate the efficiency of each worker, he should use what economists call the **marginal product (MP)**. The input's MP is equal to the incremental change in output created by a small change in input:

Marginal product (MP) Metric for estimating the efficiency of each input in which the input's MP is equal to the incremental change in output created by a small change in the input.

$$MP = \frac{\Delta Q}{\Delta X_1}, \text{ holding } X_2 \text{ constant}$$

For machinists, the marginal product represents the impact on output of a unit change in machinists. If Thomas adds a machinist, the question is, "How many more units did we produce because I hired this last machinist?" If he must let one go, it is, "How many fewer units did we produce because I let this machinist go?" The marginal product is what Thomas wants to measure.

We calculate the average product and marginal product of labor, based on our estimated $Q = 30L + 20L^2 - L^3$. Both vary, of course, as we allocate the machinists to our five machines. If $Q(L)$ is total output with L units of labor per year, the average product is $Q(L)/L$. The marginal product of labor MP, when between L and $(L - 1)$ units of labor per year, is $Q(L) - Q(L - 1)$. From Table 4.2 we see that the average product of our first machinist is 49 parts and the marginal product is 83 parts per machinist between the first and second hires. Results for other machinist hires are shown in Table 4.2.

QUANT OPTION

More precisely, the marginal product of an input is the derivative of output with regard to the quantity of the input. That is, if Q is the output and x is the quantity of the input, the marginal product of the input equals dQ/dx if the quantities of all other inputs are fixed.

TABLE 4.2

Average and Marginal Products of Labor, Thomas Machine Company

Amount of Labor (Units)	Amount of Capital (Number of Machines)	Output of Parts (Q, Hundreds of Parts)	Average Product (Q/L)	Marginal Product ($\Delta Q/\Delta L$)[a]	Marginal Product (dQ/dL)[a]
0	5	0	—	—	—
1	5	49	49	49	67
2	5	132	66	83	98
3	5	243	81	111	123
4	5	376	94	133	142
5	5	525	105	149	155
6	5	684	114	159	162
6.67	5	792.59	118.89	162.89	163.33
7	5	847	121	<u>163</u>	163
8	5	1,008	126	161	158
9	5	1,161	129	153	147
10	5	1,300	<u>130</u>	139	<u>130</u>
11	5	1,419	129	119	107
12	5	1,512	126	93	78
13	5	1,573	121	61	43
14	5	1,596	114	23	2
15	5	1,575	105	−19	−45

[a] The figures in the $\Delta Q/\Delta L$ column pertain to the interval between the indicated amount of labor and one unit less than the indicated amount of labor. The figures in the dQ/dL column are the continuous marginal product—that is, $dQ/dL = MP_L = 30 + 40L - 3L^2$.

The average and marginal products of machinists are shown in Figure 4.2; the numbers are derived from Table 4.1. The curve is representative of most production processes. The average product of machinists (with five machines) reaches a maximum (at $L = 10$ and $Q/L = 130$), then falls. The marginal product of labor follows a similar pattern: It initially increases, reaches a maximum (at $L = 6.67$ and marginal product $= 163.33$), then falls. This, too, is typical of most production processes. Figure 4.2 shows that the marginal product equals the average product when the latter reaches a maximum; that is, $MP = AP = 130$ when $L = 10$.

We use two definitions of marginal product in Table 4.2. The first ($\Delta Q/\Delta L$) assumes that Thomas employs labor in discrete units, as in a machinist or a machinist-hour. This may be due to employment laws or negotiated contracts with labor.

FIGURE 4.2

Average and Marginal Product Curves for Labor

Marginal product exceeds average product when the latter is increasing and is less than average product when the latter is decreasing. (Output per unit of labor is measured in hundreds of parts.)

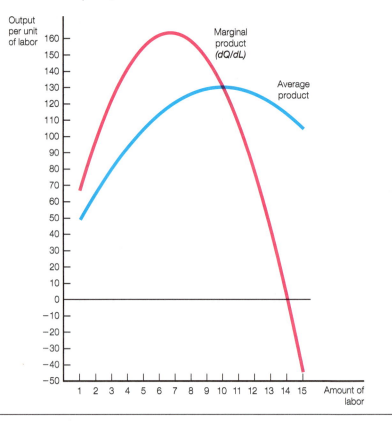

The second (dQ/dL) assumes that Thomas can employ labor continuously, as in 1.25 workers or 1.33 workers. This could be achieved by using part-time workers or workers who work more or less time than in a standard day's work.

We need to understand why MP equals AP when AP is maximized. A simple intuitive frame may help. Assume your professor is grading papers. She is keeping a running average of test scores by calculating a new average after each paper she corrects. After grading three papers her average is 86. If the next (marginal) test score is higher than 86, the average must increase. If it is lower than 86, the average must decrease. This is a natural law of mathematics. So as long as MP is greater than AP, AP must be increasing. When MP is less than AP, AP must be decreasing. MP intersects with AP when AP is at a maximum.

Enough chat; let's get serious. If x is the input with Q as the output, then AP is Q/x and MP is dQ/dx:

$$\frac{d(Q/x)}{dx} = \frac{x(dQ/dx) - Q(dx/dx)}{x^2}$$

$$= \frac{1}{x}\left(\frac{dQ}{dx} - \frac{Q}{x}\right)$$

When the average product is at a maximum, $d(Q/x)/dx$ equals zero. Therefore,

$$\frac{d(Q/x)}{dx} = \frac{1}{x}\left(\frac{dQ}{dx} - \frac{Q}{x}\right) = 0$$

And hence

$$MP = \frac{dQ}{dx} = \frac{Q}{x} = AP$$

THE LAW OF DIMINISHING MARGINAL RETURNS

The **law of diminishing returns** is a well-known constraint in managerial economics and a good one for managers to understand. It teaches managers to remain in balance. For most production processes, if managers add equal increments of an input while holding other input levels constant, the incremental gains (MP) to output get smaller, and if pushed to the extreme, are counterproductive. It is not hard to see why diminishing marginal returns are found in most production functions.

We see in Table 4.2 that if Thomas hires an eighth machinist, marginal product will decrease. Why? Because Thomas has only five machines. As more machinists are hired, they will have to ration machines, or new hires will be assigned to less important tasks.

Choosing the optimal input bundle is not an easy managerial task. Managers cannot hold all inputs but one constant; and they cannot expect that adding more units will always result in large increases in output. It is not as simple as that, as we will see later.

THE PRODUCTION FUNCTION WITH TWO VARIABLE INPUTS

Now we want to complicate John Thomas' world. With a longer time horizon, the formerly fixed input of five CNC machines becomes variable. Table 4.3 shows the

Law of diminishing returns
A well-known occurrence where when managers add equal increments of an input while holding other input levels constant, the incremental gains to output eventually get smaller.

TABLE 4.3

Production Function, Two Variable Inputs, Thomas Machine Company

Amount of Labor (Units)	Quantity of Machine Tools (Hundreds of Parts Produced per Year)			
	3	4	5	6
1	5	11	18	24
2	14	30	50	72
3	22	60	80	99
4	30	81	115	125
5	35	84	140	144

---

extra input combinations to consider. Though Thomas will have to consider more choices, the process is similar to that of the one-variable input case.

To illustrate, suppose Thomas is considering whether to purchase additional CNC machines. Engineers estimate the production function of additional machines and derive Table 4.3. The average product of either machine tools or machinists is computed by dividing the total output by the amount of either machine tools or machinists used. The marginal product of each input is obtained by holding the other input constant. For example, the marginal product of an additional machine tool when using four machinists and three machine tools is 5,100 parts per machine tool; the marginal product of an additional machinist when using three machinists and four CNC machines is 2,100 parts per unit. If X_1 is the amount of the first input and X_2 is the amount of the second input, the production function is

$$Q = f(X_1, X_2)$$

where Q is the firm's output rate. The marginal product of the first input is $\Delta Q/\Delta X_1$; the marginal product of the second input is $\Delta Q/\Delta X_2$.

QUANT OPTION

For the fastidious, we have

$$MP_1 = \frac{\partial Q}{\partial X_1} \qquad MP_2 = \frac{\partial Q}{\partial X_2}$$

FIGURE 4.3

Production Function, Two Variable Inputs

The production surface, *OAQB*, shows the amount of total output that can be obtained from various combinations of machine tools and labor.

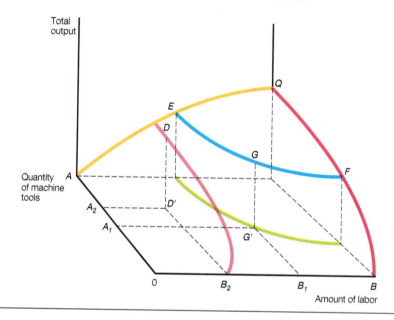

Visually, we can represent the production function by a surface, as shown in Figure 4.3. The production surface is *OAQB*.[1] We measure output for any input bundle as height on the surface. Dropping a perpendicular down from a point on the surface to the "floor" defines the corresponding input bundle. For example, producing $G'G$ units of output requires OB_1 ($= A_1G'$) machinists and OA_1 ($= B_1G'$) machine tools. Conversely, we can take any amounts of machine tools and machinists, say OA_2 machine tools and OB_2 machinists, and find their output levels by measuring the height of the production surface at D', the point where machinists is OB_2 and machine tool input is OA_2. According to Figure 4.3, the output equals $D'D$. Input bundles that produce identical output have the same height.

ISOQUANTS

An **isoquant** is a curve showing all possible (efficient) input bundles capable of producing a given output level. An isoquant is composed of all the points having the same height in the production surface of Figure 4.3. Suppose we want to find the isoquant corresponding to an output of $G'G$. All we need to do is cut the surface at the height of $G'G$ parallel to the base plane, the result being *EGF*, and drop

Isoquant Curve showing all possible (efficient) input bundles capable of producing a given output level.

1. This surface is not meant to represent the numerical values in Table 4.3 but is a general representation of how a production surface of this sort is likely to appear.

STRATEGY SESSION: How Nucor Stays on the Production Function

Nucor is one of the largest steel firms in the United States, although it did not focus on steel production until the 1960s. In 2008 its first quarter sales were approaching $5 billion; the firm achieved record first quarter net earnings for the fifth consecutive year. Managers have increased Nucor's dividend every year for the past thirty-five years. This performance has far outstripped that of more traditional (integrated) steel manufacturers like U.S.X. For example, when the average integrated steel company in the United States produced 400 tons of steel per employee, Nucor produced about 980 tons per employee. What actions have Nucor's managers implemented to achieve this superior performance?

One difference is that Nucor is a "minimill," not an integrated steel firm. Minimills have a different production function than do integrated mills. They use electric arc furnaces to make steel products from scrap metal. In 2007 Nucor was the nation's largest recycler, reprocessing one ton of steel every two seconds.

The primary reason for Nucor's outstanding performance is the company's focus on the efficient use of resources. Management has executed strategies that keep the company on an efficient production function. Being efficient is not caused by random luck. It is clearly governed by managerial decisions and requires an integrated set of policies. In Nucor's case, the firm employs over 7,000 people. How do Nucor managers keep employees focused on efficient production?

Nucor uses the following multipronged approach:

1. It maintains a simple, streamlined organizational structure that encourages decentralized decision making. Most divisions use only three layers of management. Each division is treated as a profit center and is expected to earn a 25 percent return on total assets.

2. The company acts as the general contractor in building new plants. It locates plants in rural areas where land is cheap (and unions are weak). Also, each plant is located near water and is served by at least two railroad lines to keep freight rates low. Nucor recruits employees to help build the plant; this allows it to observe the work habits of individuals. Those with good work habits are recruited to work in the plant when it opens. It also brings workers from other plants (who have already built plants) to join the constuction team. Using these methods, Nucor can build a plant at a lower cost and in about 33 percent less time than competitors.

3. All employees are subject to performance-related compensation plans. For example, production employees are paid weekly bonuses based on the productivity of their work group. Using this team approach, Nucor can lower its monitoring costs because employees monitor each other. Bonuses are based on the capabilities of the equipment and average 80 percent to 150 percent of an employee's base pay. The more output a team produces, the higher are its bonuses.

4. Nucor treats all employees equally. Benefits are the same regardless of organizational position. There are no company cars, executive dining rooms, or corporate jets.

5. The firm's focus on output does not mean that quality suffers. Employees are committed to providing the highest-quality steel at a competitive price. To reinforce this commitment to quality, most of Nucor's divisions are ISO 9000 certified.[a]

6. Finally, Nucor regards itself as a technological leader. It was the first firm to produce thin-slab casting at a minimill and searches worldwide for new developments in steel production. This emphasis on innovation is reinforced by the firm's flat organizational structure. Decisions can be made and implemented quickly.

[a]ISO 9000 is a set of quality standards. To receive ISO 9000 certification, managers must fulfill various quality assurance requirements and be audited by an external registrar. If a firm's quality assurance system is approved by this registrar, the firm is awarded an ISO 9000 certification and is allowed to advertise this fact to all customers.

perpendiculars from *EGF* to the base. Clearly this results in a curve that includes all efficient combinations of machine tools and machinists that can produce $G'G$ metal parts. Using the notation in equation (4.1), an isoquant shows all combinations of X_1 and X_2 such that $f(X_1, X_2)$ equals a certain output.

Several isoquants, each pertaining to a different output rate, are shown in Figure 4.4. The two axes measure the quantities of inputs. In contrast to the previous diagrams, we assume labor and capital—not machinists and machine tools (a particular form of labor and capital)—are the relevant inputs. The curves show the various input bundles that produce 100, 200, and 300 units of output. For example, consider the isoquant for 100 units of output. This isoquant shows it is possible to produce 100 units if L_0 units of labor and K_0 units of capital are used per time period. Alternatively, this output rate can be attained with L_1 units of labor and K_1 units of capital—or L_2 units of labor and K_2 units of capital.

Figure 4.4 illustrates several properties of isoquants. The farther the isoquant is from the origin, the greater the output it represents. Because we assume continuous production functions, we can draw an isoquant for any input bundle. Each isoquant represents an infinite number of possible input combinations. Isoquants are always downward-sloping and convex to the origin (we will see why in the next section).

FIGURE 4.4

Isoquants

These three isoquants show the various combinations of capital and labor that can produce 100, 200, and 300 units of output.

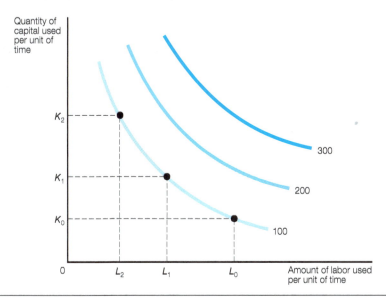

THE MARGINAL RATE OF TECHNICAL SUBSTITUTION

Marginal rate of technical substitution (MRTS) MRTS shows the rate at which one input is substituted for another (with output remaining constant).

Generally a particular output can be produced with a number of input bundles. As we move along a particular isoquant, the **marginal rate of technical substitution** (MRTS) shows the rate at which one input is substituted for another (with output remaining constant). If, as in equation (4.1), the output produced is a function of two inputs,

$$Q = f(X_1, X_2)$$

MRTS is

$$MRTS = -\frac{\Delta X_2}{\Delta X_1} \tag{4.2}$$

given that Q (output) is held constant.

Geometrically the marginal rate of technical substitution is -1 times the slope of the isoquant. This makes sense because $\Delta X_2/\Delta X_1$ measures the slope, which is downward or negative (so X_2 is on the y axis and X_1 is on the x axis).

It is useful for managers to think of MRTS as the ratio of marginal products, MP_1/MP_2, for inputs 1 and 2. Managers need to be efficient. The marginal product metric shows the incremental effect on output of the last unit of input. In spirit, managers want to increase the use of inputs with relatively high marginal products, though they must also consider the costs of inputs.

The rate of substitutability between inputs is varied. In some production processes, one type of labor is easily substituted for another; in others, specialized inputs are required. In extreme cases, no substitution among inputs is possible; to produce a unit of output, a fixed amount of each input is required, and inputs must be used in fixed proportions. Figure 4.5 shows the firm's isoquants in such a case; as you can see, they are right angles. Few production processes allow no substitution among inputs, but in some, substitutability is limited. If perfect

---

QUANT OPTION

It's time for some fun!

$$dQ = \left(\frac{\partial Q}{\partial X_1}\right) dX_1 + \left(\frac{\partial Q}{\partial X_2}\right) dX_2 = 0$$

Therefore,

$$\frac{dX_2}{dX_1} = \frac{-(\partial Q/\partial X_1)}{\partial Q/\partial X_2} = -\frac{MP_1}{MP_2} \tag{4.3}$$

FIGURE 4.5

Isoquants in the Case of Fixed Proportions

If inputs must be used in fixed proportions, the isoquants are right angles.

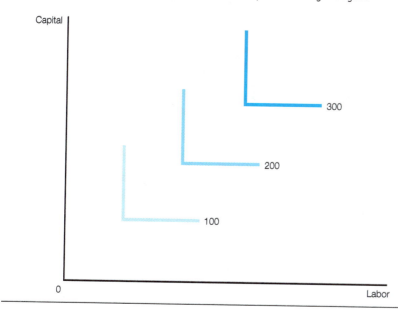

substitutability of inputs is possible, isoquants are straight lines connecting the two axes.

Mathematically, isoquants may have positively sloped segments or bend back on themselves, as shown in Figure 4.6. Above *OU* and below *OV*, the isoquant slopes are positive, implying that increases in both capital and labor are required to maintain a specified output rate. If this is the case, the marginal product of one or the other input is negative. Above *OU*, the marginal product of capital is negative; therefore, output increases if less capital is used while the level of labor is held constant. Below *OV*, the marginal product of labor is negative; output increases if less labor is used while the amount of capital is held constant. The lines *OU* and *OV* are called **ridge lines**.

No profit-maximizing manager will operate at a point outside the ridge lines because she can produce the same output with less of both inputs. This choice is strictly less costly. Consider point *H* in Figure 4.6. This point is located on a positively sloped segment of the isoquant (and so outside the ridge lines). It will always require greater levels of both labor and capital than a point inside the ridge lines (for example, point *E*) on the same isoquant. Because both capital and labor have positive prices, it is cheaper to operate at point *E* than at point *H*. The moral is this: Managers cannot use input bundles outside the ridge lines if they want to maximize profit.

Ridge lines The lines that profit-maximizing firms operate within, because outside of them, marginal products of inputs are negative.

FIGURE 4.6

Economic Region of Production

No profit-maximizing firm operates at a point outside the ridge lines, *OU* and *OV*.

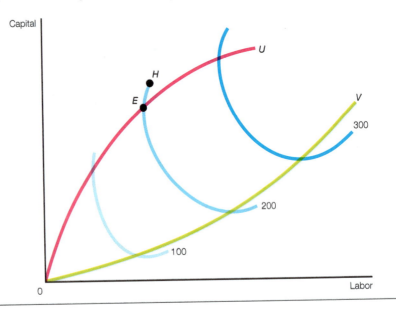

THE OPTIMAL COMBINATION OF INPUTS

The previous analysis did not include the costs of inputs. Managers must consider costs because the inputs are scarce. A manager who wants to maximize profit will try to minimize the cost of producing a given output or maximize the output derived from a given level of cost.[2] Suppose a manager takes input prices as given and uses two inputs, capital and labor, that vary in the relevant period. What combination of capital and labor should the manager choose to maximize the output derived from the given level of cost?

First we determine the various input combinations that can be obtained for a given cost. If capital and labor are the inputs and the price of labor is P_L per unit and the price of capital is P_K per unit, the input combinations that are obtained for a total outlay of M are such that

$$P_L L + P_K K = M \tag{4.4}$$

where L is the level of labor and K is the level of capital. Given M, P_L, and P_K, it follows that

$$K = \frac{M}{P_K} - \frac{P_L L}{P_K} \tag{4.5}$$

2. The conditions for minimizing the cost of producing a given output are the same as those for maximizing the output from a given cost. This is shown in the present section. Therefore, we can view the firm's problem in either way.

FIGURE 4.7

Isocost Curve

The isocost curve shows the combinations of inputs that can be obtained for a total outlay of M.

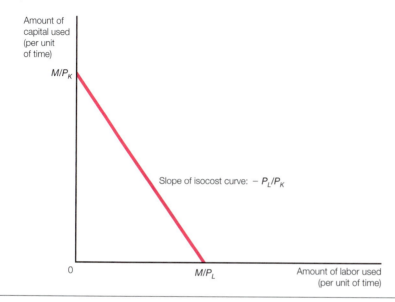

The various bundles of capital and labor that can be purchased, given P_L, P_K, and M, are represented by the straight line shown in Figure 4.7. (Capital is plotted on the vertical axis, and labor is plotted on the horizontal axis.) This line, which has an intercept on the vertical axis equal to M/P_K and a slope of $-P_L/P_K$, is called an **isocost curve**. It shows all the input bundles that can be purchased at a specified cost (M).

If we superimpose the relevant isocost curve on the isoquant map, we see the input bundle that maximizes output for a given cost. An efficient manager should choose the point on the isocost curve that is tangent to the highest-valued isoquant— for example, R in Figure 4.8. Because the slope of the isocost curve is the negative of P_L/P_K and the slope of the isoquant is the negative of MP_L/MP_K (as we pointed out in the previous section), it follows that the optimal combination of inputs is one where $MP_L/MP_K = P_L/P_K$. Put differently, the firm should choose an input combination where $MP_L/P_L = MP_K/P_K$.

So efficient managers need to choose an input bundle where the marginal products per dollar spent of labor and capital are identical. If they are not, the manager should increase the use of the input with the higher marginal per dollar value.

If there are more than two inputs, the manager maximizes output by distributing costs among the various inputs so the marginal product of a dollar's worth

Isocost curve Curve showing all the input bundles that can be purchased at a specified cost.

FIGURE 4.8

Maximization of Output for a Given Cost

To maximize the output for a given cost, the firm should choose the input combination at point R.

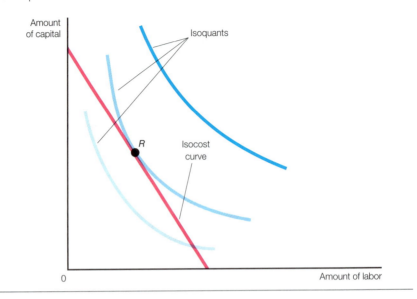

---

of one input is equal to the marginal product of a dollar's worth of any other input used. In spirit, the manager chooses an input bundle such that

$$\frac{MP_a}{P_a} = \frac{MP_b}{P_b} = \cdots = \frac{MP_n}{P_n} \qquad (4.6)$$

where $MP_a, MP_b, \ldots, MP_n$ are the marginal products of inputs $a, b, \ldots, n$; and $P_a, P_b, \ldots, P_n$ are the prices of inputs $a, b, \ldots, n$.

To determine the input bundle that minimizes production costs, we use a graph similar to Figure 4.8. Moving along the isoquant of the stipulated output level, we find the point that lies on the lowest isocost curve—for example, S in Figure 4.9. Input bundles on isocost curves like C_0 that lie below S are cheaper than S, but they cannot produce the desired output. Input bundles on isocost curves like C_2 that lie above S produce the desired output but at a higher cost than S. It is obvious that the optimal bundle S is a point where the isocost curve is tangent to the isoquant. Therefore, to minimize the cost of producing a given output or to maximize the output from a given cost outlay, the firm must equate MP_L/MP_K and P_L/P_K; this means that $MP_L/P_L = MP_K/P_K$. And if more than two inputs are needed, the manager must satisfy equation (4.6).

FIGURE 4.9

Minimization of Cost for a Given Output

To minimize the cost of producing the amount of output corresponding to this iso-quant, the firm should choose the input combination at point S.

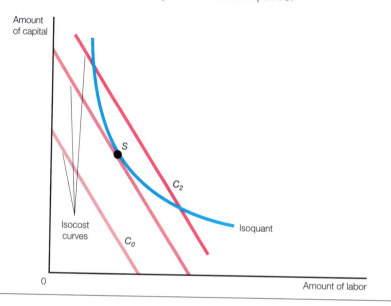

CORNER SOLUTIONS

Just as in consumption theory in Chapter 3, it is possible to have corner solutions—that is, optimal input bundles with just one input deployed. Given the production technology and the prices of the inputs, there may be no tangency of an isoquant with an isocost curve. In the two-input case, this means that just one input is used to produce the product in the least expensive way (or to produce the most output with a given cost). Equation 4.6 will now be an inequality reading $MP_K/P_K > MP_L/P_L$ for cases where just capital is used and $MP_K/P_K < MP_L/P_L$ for cases where just labor is used. The former case is shown in Figure 4.10.

RETURNS TO SCALE

We have seen how managers can represent technology as a production function and use concepts like marginal and average product to operate more efficiently. We want to continue this theme and examine some long-term considerations managers face. These focus on scale. Basically, what is the incremental change to output as managers increase their use of capital and labor?

FIGURE 4.10

A Corner Solution Where Only One Input Is Used

With outlay of M, the most that can be produced is Q_3 using only capital (M/P_K units). If only labor were used, the firm could produce only Q_1 units with outlay M. The cheapest way to produce Q_3 units is with just M/P_K units of capital and with no labor. Q_3 units could be produced with an outlay of $M' > M$ by using both capital and labor, but that would be inefficient.

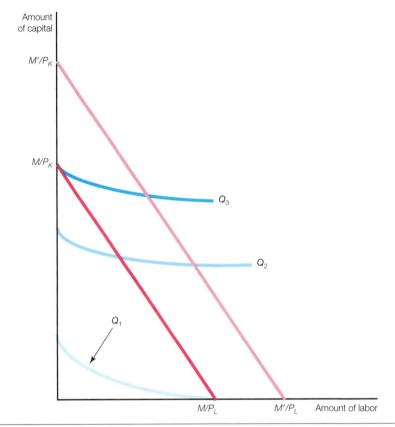

Suppose we consider a long-term situation where all inputs are variable, and managers increase the level of inputs by the same proportion. What will happen to output? Clearly there are three possibilities. First, output may increase by a larger proportion than inputs; for example, doubling all inputs may more than double output. This is the case of **increasing returns to scale**. Or output may increase by a smaller proportion than inputs; for example, doubling all inputs may lead to less than a doubling of output. This is the case of **decreasing returns to scale**. Finally, output may increase by exactly the same proportion as inputs;

Increasing return to scale When output increases by a larger proportion than inputs.

Decreasing returns to scale When output increases by a smaller proportion than inputs.

for example, doubling all inputs may double output. This is the case of **constant returns to scale.**

At first glance, some managers may believe that production functions necessarily exhibit constant returns to scale. After all, if a manager can build two factories with the same plant size and types of workers, can't she achieve the same output with a single plant twice the size? But things are not this simple. If managers double the size of a plant, they may employ techniques that are economically infeasible at the smaller scale. Some inputs are not available in small units; for example, we cannot install half a robot. Because of indivisibilities of this sort,

Constant returns to scale When output increases by exactly the same proportion as inputs.

PROBLEM SOLVED: What Skills Do We Need?

Consider the Beiswanger Company, a small firm engaged in engineering analysis. Beiswanger's president has estimated that the firm's output per month (Q) is related in the following way to the number of engineers (E) and technicians used (T):

$$Q = 20E - E^2 + 12T - 0.5T^2 \qquad (4.7)$$

The monthly wage of an engineer is \$4,000, and the monthly wage of a technician is \$2,000. If the president allots \$28,000 per month for the combined wages of engineers and technicians, what mix of engineers and technicians should he hire?

If the president is to maximize output (for his \$28,000 budget), he must choose a bundle of engineers and technicians such that

$$\frac{MP_E}{P_E} = \frac{MP_T}{P_T} \qquad (4.8)$$

where MP_E is the marginal product of an engineer, MP_T is the marginal product of a technician, P_E is the wage of an engineer, and P_T is the wage of a technician. Viewing the change in equation (4.7) with respect to E and T, we find that

$$MP_E = \frac{\Delta Q}{\Delta E} = 20 - 2E \qquad (4.9a)$$

$$MP_T = \frac{\Delta Q}{\Delta T} = 12 - T \qquad (4.9b)$$

Inserting these expressions for MP_E and MP_T into equation (4.8) and noting that $P_E = 4,000$ and $P_T = 2,000$, it follows that

$$\frac{20 - 2E}{4,000} = \frac{12 - T}{2,000}$$

$$\frac{2,000(20 - 2E)}{4,000} = 12 - T$$

$$10 - E = 12 - T$$

$$T = E + 2$$

Because Beiswanger allocates \$28,000 per month for the total wages of engineers and technicians, we have

$$4,000E + 2,000T = 28,000$$

Substituting ($E + 2$) for T gives us

$$4,000E + 2,000(E + 2) = 28,000$$

This means that $E = 4$ (and $T = 6$). So to maximize output from the \$28,000 outlay on wages, the president should hire 4 engineers and 6 technicians.

PROBLEM SOLVED: The Efficient Minds of Managers

Managers need to search for input bundles to minimize costs for a given output. Intuitively they need to balance the productivity of an input with its cost. As we will show in Chapter 5, there are easier metrics for managers to use, like costs. But the ability to control costs is enhanced by understanding production functions. Consider the issues facing managers at the Miller Company, for which the relationship between output per hour (Q) and the number of workers (L) and machines (K) used per hour is

$$Q = 10(LK)^{0.5}$$

The wage of a worker is \$80 per hour, and the price of a machine is \$20 per hour. If the Miller Company produces 800 units of output per hour, how many workers and machines should managers use?

According to equation (4.8), the Miller Company should choose an input combination such that

$$\frac{MP_L}{P_L} = \frac{MP_K}{P_K}$$

where MP_L is the marginal product of a worker, MP_K is the marginal product of a machine, P_L is the wage

of a worker, and P_K is the price of using a machine. Because $Q = 10(LK)^{0.5}$,

$$MP_L = \frac{\Delta Q}{\Delta L} = 5\left(\frac{K}{L}\right)^{0.5}$$

$$MP_K = \frac{\Delta Q}{\Delta K} = 5\left(\frac{L}{K}\right)^{0.5}$$

So if $MP_L/P_L = MP_K/P_K$

$$\frac{5(K/L)^{0.5}}{80} = \frac{5(L/K)^{0.5}}{20}$$

Multiplying both sides of this equation by $(K/L)^{0.5}$, we get

$$\frac{5K}{80L} = \frac{5}{20}$$

which means that $K = 4L$. Because $Q = 800$,

$$10(LK)^{0.5} = 800$$
$$10[L(4L)]^{0.5} = 800$$
$$L = 40$$
$$K = 160$$

Therefore, to minimize cost, managers at the Miller Company should hire 40 workers and use 160 machines.

---

larger plants may have increasing returns to scale. So when managers think about efficient choice, building one large factory relative to two smaller ones may be better.

Larger plants also let managers subdivide tasks and use inputs more narrowly. This specialization strategy increases production efficiency; so investment bankers specialize in designated areas, and airlines dedicate computers to handling reservations. Larger size may also generate probabilistic efficiencies; for example, because the aggregate behavior of a larger number of customers tends to be more stable, a firm's inventory may not have to increase in proportion to its sales.

Increasing returns to scale also arise because of certain geometrical relations. Because the volume of a box that is $2 \times 2 \times 2$ feet is eight times as great as the volume of a box that is $1 \times 1 \times 1$ foot, the former box can carry eight times as much as the latter box. But the area of the six sides of the $2 \times 2 \times 2$ box is 24 square feet and the area of the six sides of the $1 \times 1 \times 1$ box is six square feet, so the former box requires only four times as much wood as the latter.

It turns out that bigger is not always better; managers can experience decreasing returns to scale. The most common culprit is the challenge of coordinating a large organization. It can be difficult even in a small firm for managers to obtain the necessary information to make important decisions; in a large firm such problems tend to be greater. As we show in Chapter 14, managers often have difficulties in designing efficient incentive schemes in larger firms. Though the advantages of a large organization are obvious, scale can generate inefficiencies. For example, in certain kinds of research and development, large teams tend to be less effective than smaller ones.

Whether scale returns are constant, increasing, or decreasing is an empirical question that must be settled case by case. There is no simple, all-encompassing answer. In some industries the evidence suggests that returns increase over a certain range of output; but the answer is likely to depend on the output considered. There may be increasing returns to scale at small output levels and constant or decreasing returns to scale at higher levels. In addition, managers need to know how output changes when inputs are not all increased or decreased in the same proportion.

THE OUTPUT ELASTICITY

To measure whether there are increasing, decreasing, or constant returns to scale, the output elasticity is computed. The **output elasticity** is defined as the percentage of change in output resulting from a 1 percent increase in all inputs. If the output elasticity exceeds 1, there are increasing returns to scale; if it equals 1, there are constant returns to scale; and if it is less than 1, there are decreasing returns to scale.

As an illustration, consider the Lone Star Company, a maker of aircraft parts, which has the following production function:

$$Q = 0.8L^{0.3}K^{0.8}$$

Here Q is the number of parts produced per year (measured in millions of parts), L is the number of workers hired, and K is the amount of capital used. This is the commonly used Cobb-Douglas production function (named after Charles Cobb and Paul Douglas, who pioneered its application).

Output elasticity The percentage of change in output resulting from a 1 percent increase in all inputs.

STRATEGY SESSION: Economies in Oil Tankers

Over 65 percent of crude oil output is transported by oil tankers. Oil is the largest commodity in trans-ocean trade, accounting for 40 percent of all ocean shipments by weight. Oil tankers can be regarded as large cylinders. The surface area of a cylinder is not proportional to its volume; instead, as a cylinder's volume increases, its surface area goes up less than proportionately. Therefore, a tanker that can carry 300,000 deadweight tons (dwt) is only about twice as broad, long, and deep as one that can carry 30,000 tonnes.

Since the 1970s, the size of oil tankers has increased, as shown here:

Year	Average Oil Tanker Size (Thousands of dwt)
1973	64.0
1978	103.0
1985	146.0
2000	220.0
2008	273.0

There is a strong cost incentive for larger tankers to be built. The cost of constructing an oil tanker is largely based on the cost of steel. A manager can increase the capacity of a tanker eight times by only using four times the amount of steel. A 280,000 dwt tanker costs roughly $85 million to build, whereas a 28,000 dwt tanker costs roughly $20 million to build.

Larger tankers can also operate with relatively smaller crews. An oil tanker of over 200,000 dwt today operates with a crew of twenty-four—roughly half the crew size of a ship half that size in the 1980s. Onshore personnel costs are also relatively lower with larger tankers because these are based on the number of ships and not total tonnage. Finally, fuel costs of larger tankers are relatively lower. For example, a 60,000 dwt tanker generally requires 16,000 horsepower to travel at 15 knots. A 260,000 dwt tanker requires 42,500 horsepower to do the same. So 2.7 times the energy enables 4.3 times as much cargo to be shipped.

Sources: www.oceanatlas.org/unatlas/uses/transportation; www.eagibson.co.uk/posidonia.

To calculate the output elasticity at the Lone Star Company, let's see what will happen to Q if we multiply both inputs (L and K) by 1.01. Clearly the new value of Q (that is, Q') equals

$$Q' = 0.8(1.01L)^{0.3}(1.01K)^{0.8}$$
$$= 0.8(1.01)^{1.1}L^{0.3}K^{0.8}$$
$$= (1.01)^{1.1}(0.8L^{0.3}K^{0.8})$$
$$= (1.01)^{1.1}Q$$
$$= 1.011005484Q$$

Therefore, if a manager increases the use of both inputs by 1 percent, output increases by slightly more than 1.1 percent; this means the output elasticity is approximately 1.1. It is exactly 1.1 for an infinitesimal change in input use (of both inputs). Because a 1 percent change is larger than infinitesimal, the increase in output is slightly larger than 1.1.

ESTIMATIONS OF PRODUCTION FUNCTIONS

Managers need to estimate production functions. One of the first steps in estimating a production function is to choose its mathematical form. Managers commonly use the Cobb-Douglas form. With only two inputs, this form is

$$Q = aL^b K^c \qquad (4.10)$$

where Q is the number of parts produced per year (measured in millions of parts), L is the number of workers hired, and K is the amount of capital used. One advantage of this form is that the marginal productivity of each input depends on the level of all inputs employed, which is often realistic. Consider the marginal product of labor, which equals

---

QUANT OPTION

$$\partial Q/\partial L = baL^{b-1}K^c = baL^{b-1}K^c(L/L) = baL^b K^c/L = b(Q/L) = b(AP_L)$$

$$\frac{\Delta Q}{\Delta L} = baL^{b-1}K^c = b\left(\frac{Q}{L}\right) = b(AP_L)$$

Obviously the marginal product of labor depends on the values of both L and K. Another advantage is that if logarithms are taken of both sides of equation (4.10),

$$\log Q = \log a + b \log L + c \log K \qquad (4.11)$$

Note that if managers use the Cobb-Douglas form, they can easily estimate the returns to scale. If the sum of the exponents (that is, $b + c$) exceeds 1, increasing returns to scale are indicated; if the sum of the exponents equals 1, constant returns to scale prevail; and if the sum of the exponents is less than 1, decreasing returns to scale are indicated. This is true because if the Cobb-Douglas production function prevails, the output elasticity equals the sum of the exponents. For example, in the previous section the output elasticity of the Lone Star Company was 1.1, which equaled the sum of the exponents (0.3 and 0.8).

There is no cut-and-dried way to determine which mathematical form is best because the answer depends on the particular situation. Frequently a good procedure is to try more than one mathematical form and see which fits the data best. The important thing is that the chosen form provide a faithful representation of the actual situation. To determine whether this is the case, it often is useful to see how well a particular estimated production function can forecast the quantity of output resulting from the combination of inputs actually used.

PROBLEM SOLVED: Finding the Optimal Mix

Consider the production of broiler chickens, which is a big industry in the United States (2008 production value: $19.1 billion). At one company, managers ran an experiment in which broilers were fed various amounts of corn and soybean oilmeal and the gain in weight of each broiler was measured. The managers then used regression to estimate the production function for broilers:

$$G = 0.03 + 0.48C + 0.64S$$
$$- 0.02C^2 - 0.05S^2 - 0.02CS \quad (4.12)$$

Here G is the gain in weight (in pounds per broiler), C is pounds of corn per broiler, and S is pounds of soybean oilmeal per broiler. The multiple coefficient of determination (R^2) is very high—about 0.998.

Using equation (4.12), managers can estimate isoquants for poultry production. Suppose they want to estimate the isoquant pertaining to a weight gain of one pound. In other words, they want to find the various combinations of corn per broiler and soybean oilmeal per broiler that results in a weight gain per broiler of one pound. To find these combinations, set $G = 1$:

$$1 = 0.03 + 0.48C + 0.64S$$
$$- 0.02C^2 - 0.05S^2 - 0.02CS \quad (4.13)$$

Then we set C equal to various values and determine each resulting value of S. For example, suppose $C = 1$. Then

$$1 = 0.03 + 0.48(1) + 0.64S$$
$$- 0.02(1^2) - 0.05S^2 - 0.02(1)S$$

or

$$1 = 0.03 + 0.48 - 0.02 + (0.64 - 0.02)S - 0.05S^2$$

Solving $0.05S^2 - 0.62S + 0.51 = 0$ by the quadratic formula yields

$$S = [0.62 \pm (0.62^2 - 4(0.05)(0.51))^{0.5}]/2(0.05)$$
$$= [0.62 \pm (0.3844 - 0.0102)^{0.5}]/0.1$$
$$= [0.62 \pm (0.2824)^{0.5}]/0.1$$
$$= (0.62 \pm 0.5314)/0.1$$

Therefore, $S = 1.1514/0.1 = 11.514$, or $S = 0.08858/0.1 = 0.886$. Consequently, if a broiler is to gain one pound of weight, it must be fed 0.886 pounds of soybean oilmeal, as well as one pound of corn.[a]

If we let $C = 1.1$, we can find the corresponding value of S by substituting 1.1 for C in equation (4.13) and solving for S. If we let $C = 1.2$, we can find the corresponding value of S by substituting 1.2 for C in equation (4.13) and solving for S. Proceeding in this way, we can find more and more points on the isoquant corresponding to a weight gain of one pound. The resulting isoquant is shown in the figure. Isoquants of this sort are of great importance to managers. Coupled with data regarding input prices, they can be used to determine which input bundles will minimize costs (recall Figure 4.9).

Managers use the isoquant in the figure shown on page 119 to determine how much corn and soybean oilmeal to feed a broiler if they want a one-pound weight gain. To see how, suppose the price of a pound of corn is three-quarters the price of a pound of soybean oilmeal. Then the slope of each isocost curve in the figure equals −¾ because, as pointed out in Figure 4.7, the slope equals −1 times the price of the input on the horizontal axis (corn) divided by the price of the input on the vertical axis (soybean oilmeal). For the cost of the weight gain to be at a minimum, the isocost curve should be tangent to the isoquant; this means that the slope of the

Isoquant for a One-Pound Weight Gain for a Broiler and Isocost Curve If Corn Price Is ¾ of Soybean Oilmeal Price

The optimal input combination is 1.35 pounds of corn and 0.61 pounds of soybean oilmeal.
Source: Organization for Economic Cooperation and Development, Interdisciplinary Research

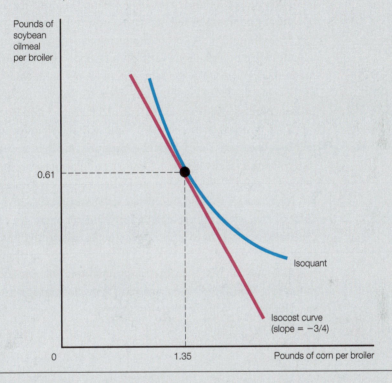

isoquant should also equal −¾. As shown in the figure, this occurs when 1.35 pounds of corn and 0.61 pounds of soybean oilmeal are used. Therefore, this is the optimal input combination if the price of a pound of corn is three-quarters the price of a pound of soybean oilmeal.

[a] There is another possible value of S, which corresponds to the use of the plus sign (rather than the minus sign) before $(b^2 - 4ac)^{0.5}$ in this formula; but this other value is not relevant here.

SUMMARY

1. The production function defines the relationship among various inputs and the maximum quantity of a good that can be produced. Managers study production functions to gain insights into the firm's cost structure.

2. An isoquant is a curve showing all possible (efficient) combinations of inputs capable of producing a particular quantity of output. The marginal rate of technical substitution shows the rate at which one input can be substituted for another input if output remains constant. No profit-maximizing manager will operate at a point where the isoquant is positively sloped.

3. To minimize the cost of producing a particular output, a manager should allocate expenditures among various inputs so that the ratio of the marginal product to the input price is the same for all inputs used. Graphically, this amounts to choosing the input combination where the relevant isoquant is tangent to an isocost curve.

4. If a manager increases all inputs by the same proportion and output increases by more (less) than this proportion, there are increasing (decreasing) returns to scale. Increasing returns to scale may occur because of indivisibility of inputs, various geometrical relations, or specialization. Decreasing returns to scale can also occur; the most frequently cited reason is the difficulty of managing a huge enterprise. Whether there are constant, increasing, or decreasing returns to scale is an empirical question that must be settled case by case.

5. Managers have estimated production functions in many firms and industries. Many studies show that a Cobb-Douglas function is the best fit for the data.

wwnorton.com/studyspace ⓢ

PROBLEMS

1. In the Elwyn Company, the relationship between output (Q) and the number of hours of skilled labor (S) and unskilled labor (U) is

$$Q = 300S + 200U - 0.2S^2 - 0.3U^2$$

The hourly wage of skilled labor is $10, and the hourly wage of unskilled labor is $5. The firm can hire as much labor as it wants at these wage rates.

a. Elwyn's chief engineer recommends that the firm hire 400 hours of skilled labor and 100 hours of unskilled labor. Evaluate this recommendation.

b. If the Elwyn Company decides to spend a total of $5,000 on skilled and unskilled labor, how many hours of each type of labor should it hire?

c. If the price of a unit of output is $10 (and does not vary with output level), how many hours of unskilled labor should the company hire?

2. A consulting firm specializing in agriculture determines that the following combinations of hay and grain consumption per lamb will result in a 25-pound gain for a lamb:

Pounds of Hay	Pounds of Grain
40	130.9
50	125.1
60	120.1
70	115.7
80	111.8
90	108.3
110	102.3
130	97.4
150	93.8

a. The firm's president wants to estimate the marginal product of a pound of grain in producing lamb. Can he do so on the basis of these data?

b. The firm's president is convinced that constant returns to scale prevail in lamb production. If this is true and hay and grain consumption per lamb are the only inputs, how much gain accrues if the hay consumption per lamb is 100 pounds and the grain consumption per lamb is 250.2 pounds?

c. What is the marginal rate of technical substitution of hay for grain when between 40 and 50 pounds of hay (and between 130.9 and 125.1 pounds of grain) are consumed per lamb?

d. A major advance in technology occurs that allows farmers to produce a 25-pound gain per lamb with less hay and grain than the preceding table indicates. If the marginal rate of technical substitution (at each rate of consumption of each input) is the same after the technological advance as before, can you draw the new isoquant corresponding to a 25-pound gain per lamb?

3. The Ascot Corporation, which produces stationery, hires a consultant to estimate its production function. The consultant concludes that

$$Q = 0.9P + 0.06L$$

where Q is the number of pounds of stationery produced by Ascot per year, L is the number of hours of labor per year, and P is the number of pounds of paper used per year.

a. Does this production function seem to include all the relevant inputs? Explain.

    b. Does this production function seem reasonable if it is applied to all possible values of L? Explain.

    c. Does this production function exhibit diminishing marginal returns?

4. A Cobb-Douglas production function was estimated for six types of farms. There were five inputs in the production function: (1) land, (2) labor, (3) equipment, (4) livestock and feed, and (5) other resource services. The exponent of each input was as follows:

| | | | Exponent | | |
Farm Type	Land	Labor	Equipment	Livestock and Feed	Other Resource Services
Crop farms	0.24	0.07	0.08	0.53	0.02
Hog farms	0.07	0.02	0.10	0.74	0.03
Dairy farms	0.10	0.01	0.06	0.63	0.02
General farms	0.17	0.12	0.16	0.46	0.03
Large farms	0.28	0.01	0.11	0.53	0.03
Small farms	0.21	0.05	0.08	0.43	0.03

    a. Do there appear to be increasing returns to scale in any of these six types of farms?

    b. In what type of farm does a 1 percent increase in labor have the largest percentage effect on output?

    c. Based on these results, would you expect output to increase if many of the farms included in this sample were merged?

5. According to the chief engineer at the Zodiac Company, $Q = AL^\alpha K^\beta$, where Q is the output rate, L is the rate of labor input, and K is the rate of capital input. Statistical analysis indicates that $\alpha = 0.8$ and $\beta = 0.3$. The firm's owner claims the plant has increasing returns to scale.

    a. Is the owner correct?

    b. If β were 0.2 rather than 0.3, would she be correct?

    c. Does output per unit of labor depend only on α and β? Why or why not?

6. According to data obtained by the U.S. Department of Agriculture, the relationship between a cow's total output of milk and the amount of grain it is fed is as follows:

Amount of Grain (Pounds)	Amount of Milk (Pounds)
1,200	5,917
1,800	7,250
2,400	8,379
3,000	9,371

(This relationship assumes that forage input is fixed at 6,500 pounds of hay.)

a. Calculate the average product of grain when each amount is used.

b. Estimate the marginal product of grain when between 1,200 and 1,800 pounds are fed, when between 1,800 and 2,400 pounds are fed, and when between 2,400 and 3,000 pounds are fed.

c. Does this production function exhibit diminishing marginal returns?

7. An electronics plant's production function is $Q = 5LK$, where Q is its output rate, L is the amount of labor it uses per period, and K is the amount of capital it uses per period. The price of labor is $1 per unit of labor, and the price of capital is $2 per unit of capital. The firm's vice president for manufacturing hires you to determine which combination of inputs the plant should use to produce 20 units of output per period.

a. What advice would you give him?

b. Suppose the price of labor increases to $2 per unit. What effect will this have on output per unit of labor?

c. Is this plant subject to decreasing returns to scale? Why or why not?

8. Volvo A.B., the Swedish auto firm, operated a car assembly plant at Uddevalla in 1988. The idea was to have a small team of highly skilled workers build an entire car. According to the proponents, this would reduce the tedium associated with the conventional assembly line and cut absenteeism and turnover among workers. In 1991 there were reports that it took 50 hours of labor to assemble a car at Uddevalla, in contrast to 25 hours at Volvo's conventional assembly plant at Ghent, Belgium. If you were Volvo's chief executive officer, what questions would you ask Uddevalla's managers, and what steps would you take?

APPENDIX: LAGRANGIAN MULTIPLIERS AND OPTIMAL INPUT COMBINATIONS

In this chapter we stated that equation (4.6) must be satisfied if a firm is to maximize output for a given expenditure level or if it is to minimize the cost of producing a specified amount of output. In this appendix we show how the decision rule in equation (4.6) is derived using the method of Lagrangian multipliers. To keep things relatively simple, we assume the manager is using only two inputs.

Maximizing Output from a Specified Expenditure Level

Suppose a firm's production function is

$$Q = f(X_1, X_2)$$

where Q is output, X_1 is the amount used of the first input, and X_2 is the amount used of the second input. The firm's total expenditure on both inputs is specified to equal E^*. Therefore,

$$X_1 P_1 + X_2 P_2 = E^*$$

where P_1 is the price of the first input and P_2 is the price of the second input. The manager seeks to maximize output for this specified level of expenditure. So she wants to maximize Q, where

$$Q = f(X_1, X_2)$$ (4.14)

subject to the constraint that

$$E^* - X_1 P_1 - X_2 P_2 = 0$$ (4.15)

We first construct the Lagrangian function, which is the right side of equation (4.14) plus λ times the left side of equation (4.15):

$$L_1 = f(X_1, X_2) + \lambda(E^* - X_1 P_1 - X_2 P_2)$$

where λ is the Lagrangian multiplier. Taking the partial derivatives of L_1 with respect to X_1, X_2, and λ and setting them all equal to zero, we obtain

$$\frac{\partial L_1}{\partial X_1} = \frac{\partial f(X_1, X_2)}{\partial X_1} - \lambda P_1 = 0$$ (4.16)

$$\frac{\partial L_1}{\partial X_2} = \frac{\partial f(X_1, X_2)}{\partial X_2} - \lambda P_2 = 0$$ (4.17)

$$\frac{\partial L_1}{\partial \lambda} = E^* - X_1 P_1 - X_2 P_2 = 0$$ (4.18)

These are the conditions for output maximization subject to the expenditure constraint.

MP_1 is the marginal product of input one and MP_2 is that for input two. By definition, we know the following is true:

$$\frac{\partial f(X_1, X_2)}{\partial X_1} = \frac{\partial Q}{\partial X_1} = MP_1$$

$$\frac{\partial f(X_1, X_2)}{\partial X_2} = \frac{\partial Q}{\partial X_2} = MP_2$$

Equations (4.16) and (4.17) can be restated as

$$MP_1 - \lambda P_1 = 0$$
$$MP_2 - \lambda P_2 = 0$$

which implies that

$$MP_1 = \lambda P_1$$ (4.19)
$$MP_2 = \lambda P_2$$ (4.20)

Dividing each side of equation (4.19) by the corresponding side of equation (4.20), we find that

$$\frac{MP_1}{MP_2} = \frac{P_1}{P_2}$$

or

$$\frac{MP_1}{P_1} = \frac{MP_2}{P_2} \qquad (4.21)$$

which is the decision rule in equation (4.6) when there are only two inputs. Thus we have shown why managers want to equate the marginal product per dollar spent across all inputs using the method of Lagrangian multipliers when the object is to maximize output subject to an expenditure constraint.

Minimizing the Cost of a Specified Amount of Output

Suppose a manager is committed to produce a specified quantity of output, Q^*, which means that

$$f(X_1, X_2) = Q^*$$

Her problem is to minimize costs, which equal

$$C = X_1 P_1 + X_2 P_2 \qquad (4.22)$$

subject to the constraint that

$$Q^* - f(X_1, X_2) = 0 \qquad (4.23)$$

We use Lagrangian multipliers to solve this problem. Again, we first construct the Lagrangian function, which is the right side of equation (4.22) plus λ times the left side of equation (4.23):

$$L_2 = X_1 P_1 + X_2 P_2 + \lambda[Q^* - f(X_1, X_2)]$$

where λ is the Lagrangian multiplier. Taking the partial derivatives of L_2 with respect to X_1, X_2, and λ and setting them all equal to zero, we obtain

$$\frac{\partial L_2}{\partial X_1} = P_1 - \lambda \frac{\partial f(X_1, X_2)}{\partial X_1} = 0 \qquad (4.24)$$

$$\frac{\partial L_2}{\partial X_2} = P_2 - \lambda \frac{\partial f(X_1, X_2)}{\partial X_2} = 0 \qquad (4.25)$$

$$\frac{\partial L_2}{\partial \lambda} = Q^* - f(X_1, X_2) = 0 \qquad (4.26)$$

These are the conditions for cost minimization subject to the output constraint.

Substituting MP_1 for $\partial f(X_1, X_2)/\partial X_1$ and MP_2 for $\partial f(X_1, X_2)/\partial X_2$ in equations (4.24) and (4.25), we get

$$P_1 - \lambda MP_1 = 0$$
$$P_2 - \lambda MP_2 = 0$$

which implies that

$$P_1 = \lambda MP_1 \tag{4.27}$$
$$P_2 = \lambda MP_2 \tag{4.28}$$

Dividing each side of equation (4.27) by the corresponding side of equation (4.28), we find that

$$\frac{P_1}{P_2} = \frac{MP_1}{MP_2}$$

or

$$\frac{MP_1}{P_1} = \frac{MP_2}{P_2}$$

which is our decision rule in equation (4.6).

THE ANALYSIS OF COSTS

Even a manager who fully understands the relationship between inputs and outputs still cannot make optimal (profit-maximizing) decisions without cost information. The key question managers must ponder is this: How are costs related to output? A full understanding of costs is necessary because virtually all business decisions require comparisons of costs and benefits. A manager wants to undertake an action if the additional (marginal) revenue attributable to that action exceeds its additional (marginal) cost. As we will see, to maximize profit, a manager wishes to produce at an output level where the marginal revenue equals the marginal cost. Obviously this calculation is not possible without a knowledge of the cost structure.

Cost (like many four-lettered words) invokes multiple interpretations. Managers find that what seems like a simple concept often provokes controversy over the nature of costs, how they are defined, and their scope and relevance in a decision (hence the basis for cost accounting in virtually every MBA program). A thorough understanding of cost is necessary for a variety of basic managerial decisions: pricing, output, transfer pricing, cost control, and planning for future production.

Managerial consideration of costs must include both short-run and long-run components. A focus on just one of these components, especially the short term, can have catastrophic consequences for an organization. As we detail in later chapters, most managerial decisions require long-term vision.

This chapter explains the basics of cost analysis and describes models to help managers create competitive advantages using cost analysis.

OPPORTUNITY COSTS

Managerial economists define the opportunity cost of producing a particular product as the revenue a manager could have received if she had used her resources to produce the next best alternative product or service. That is, opportunity costs are the revenues forgone if resources (inputs) are not optimally used. They are one reason why managers want to use resources as efficiently as possible; managers need to reduce opportunity costs.

We encounter opportunity costs throughout our lives. Those of you who were accepted at more than one college already have. Those of you who are married or in committed relationships also should understand the concept.

The opportunity cost of General Electric managers' decision to produce large gas turbines is the revenue they could have earned if the labor, equipment, and materials used in the production of turbines were used to produce another GE product—say debt financing. Or GE managers could even have invested outside their firm. Economists believe the true costs of inputs are their values when used in the most productive way. These costs, together with the firm's production costs (the accounting costs of producing a product), determine the economic cost of production. This is called the **opportunity cost doctrine**.

The opportunity cost of an input may not equal its **historical cost**, which is defined as the money managers actually paid for it. For example, if a manager invests $1 million in equipment that is quickly outmoded and inefficient relative to new equipment, its value is clearly not $1 million. Although conventional accounting rules place great emphasis on historical costs, managerial economists believe historical costs can be misleading.

Managers must be concerned with two types of costs, both of which are important. The first type is **explicit costs**, which are the ordinary items accountants include as the firm's expenses. These include the firm's payroll, payments for raw materials, and so on. The second type is **implicit costs**, which include the forgone value of resources that managers did not put to their best use. Unfortunately accountants and managers, in calculating the costs to a firm, often omit implicit costs.

Think of opportunity costs in the context of MBA students. The total cost (including room and board) of a year's schooling at The Wharton School is roughly $90,000. This is the cash outlay that most students pay. However, many MBA students held jobs before coming back to school. Assume the compensation of the average MBA student in the previous year was $70,000. If we asked an accountant the average yearly cost of attending Wharton, he would say about $90,000. If we pose that same question to economists, most would say $160,000.

Opportunity cost doctrine The inputs' values (when used in their most productive way) together with production costs (the accounting costs of producing a product) determine the economic cost of production.

Historical cost The money that managers actually paid for an input.

Explicit costs The ordinary items accountants include as the firm's expenses.

Implicit costs The forgone value of resources that managers did not put to their best use.

Consider John Harvey, the proprietor of a firm who invests his own labor and capital in the business. These inputs should be valued at the amount he would have received if he had used them in a different manner. If he could have received a salary of $65,000 working for someone else and he could have received dividends of $20,000 by investing his capital elsewhere, he should value his labor and capital at these rates. Excluding these implicit costs can be a serious mistake.

Economists also follow the doctrine of **sunk costs**. Sunk costs are resources that are spent and cannot be recovered. For example, if a company builds a plant for $12 million but then disposes of it for a price of $4 million, it incurs sunk costs of $8 million. Sunk costs equal the difference between what a resource costs and what it is sold for in the future.

Ignoring sunk costs is difficult for managers—and in fact perplexes most folks. Many people stay in unhealthy relationships because of the time they have invested. You may have given a partner the best five years of your life, but that is no reason to remain in a relationship you don't like. No matter what you do, you cannot recapture the five years, so ignore them in deciding your future.

Rational managers must ignore sunk costs and choose between possible strategies by evaluating only future costs and benefits. For example, if a manager has already spent $6 million on an advertising campaign, those costs are sunk (they cannot be recovered). So she cannot argue that she has already spent $6 million and needs only $1 million more to "turn the corner." The expected return of that $1 million in the campaign must be compared to the expected return of $1 million across alternative investments.

SHORT-RUN COST FUNCTIONS

Given a firm's cost of producing each level of output, we can define the firm's cost structure. A **cost function** shows various relationships between input costs and output rate. The firm's production function and the input prices determine the firm's cost structure.

Similar to what we saw with production functions, cost functions are either for the short or long run. The short run is a period so short that a manager cannot alter the quantity of some inputs. As the length of time increases, more inputs become variable. The time span between one where the quantity of no input is variable and one where the quantities of all inputs are variable is called the **short run**. However, a more restrictive definition is generally employed: We say the short run is the time interval so brief that a manager cannot alter the quantities of plant and equipment. These are the firm's **fixed inputs**, and they determine the firm's **scale of plant**. Inputs like labor, which a manager can vary in quantity in the short run, are the firm's **variable inputs**.

We consider three short-run cost concepts: fixed, variable, and total. **Total fixed cost** (*TFC*) is the total cost per period of time incurred for fixed inputs.

Sunk costs Sunk costs are resources that are spent and cannot be recovered.

Cost function Function showing various relationships between input costs and output rate.

Short run The time span between one where the quantity of no input is variable and one where the quantities of all inputs are variable.

Fixed inputs When the quantities of plant and equipment cannot be altered.

Scale of plant This scale is determined by fixed inputs.

Variable inputs Inputs that a manager can vary in quantity in the short run.

Total fixed cost (*TFC*) The total cost per period of time incurred for fixed inputs.

TABLE 5.1

Fixed, Variable, and Total Costs: Media Corporation

Units of Output Q	Total Fixed Cost (Dollars per Day) TFC	Total Variable Cost (Dollars per Day) TVC	Total Cost (Dollars per Day) TC
0	100	0	100
1	100	40	140
2	100	64	164
3	100	78	178
4	100	88	188
5	100	100	200
5.5	100	108.625	208.625
6	100	120	220
6.64	100	139.6	239.6
7	100	154	254
8	100	208	308
9	100	288	388
10	100	400	500

Because the level of fixed inputs is constant (by definition), the firm's total fixed cost does not vary with output. Examples of fixed costs are depreciation of plant and equipment and property taxes. Table 5.1 shows that the fixed cost of the Media Corporation, a producer of sofas, is $100 per day. This is visually shown in Figure 5.1. If Q is equal to total output, the values in Table 5.1 (and in Table 5.2) come from the total cost relationship

$$TC = 100 + 50Q - 11Q^2 + Q^3$$

Total variable cost *(TVC)* The total cost incurred by managers for variable inputs.

Total variable cost (TVC) is the total cost incurred by managers for variable inputs. They increase as output rises because greater output requires more inputs and higher variable costs. For example, the greater the output of a woolen mill, the larger the quantity of wool used and the higher the total cost of the wool. The Media Corporation's total variable cost schedule is shown in Table 5.1. Figure 5.1 shows the corresponding total variable cost function. Up to a particular output rate (four units of output), total variable costs rise at a decreasing rate; beyond that output level, they increase at an increasing rate. This characteristic of the total variable cost function follows from the law of diminishing marginal returns. At low levels of output, increasing the variable inputs may increase productivity, with

FIGURE 5.1

Fixed, Variable, and Total Costs: Media Corporation

Fixed costs do not vary with output, so the fixed cost curve is a horizontal line. Variable costs at first increase with output at a decreasing rate and then increase with output at an increasing rate. The total cost curve is the vertical summation of the fixed cost curve and the average variable cost curve. The total cost function and the total variable cost function have the same shape because they differ by only a constant amount, which is total fixed cost.

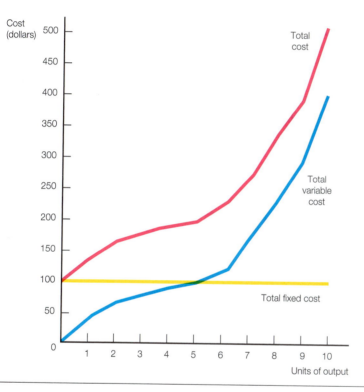

the result that total variable costs rise with output but at a decreasing rate. (More will be said about this later.)

Finally, **total cost** (*TC*) is the sum of total fixed and total variable costs. To derive the total cost column in Table 5.1, add the total fixed cost and total variable cost at each output level. The total cost function for the Media Corporation is also shown in Figure 5.1. The total cost function and the total variable cost function have the same shape because they differ by only a constant amount, which is total fixed cost.

Managers want to allocate resources efficiently (remember, they are scarce). They want to choose the input bundle that produces a given output at the lowest

Total cost (*TC*) The sum of total fixed and total variable costs.

possible cost. Costs are a function of the production process and input prices, so managers need to understand the behavior of costs as output changes. One indicator of this behavior is found in average and marginal costs.

AVERAGE AND MARGINAL COSTS

Average fixed cost (AFC) The total fixed cost divided by output.

Average variable cost (AVC) The total variable cost divided by output.

Although the total cost of producing a product is important, from an operational viewpoint, knowledge of the average and marginal cost functions is key. These functions predict the behavior of costs as output changes. There are three average cost functions, corresponding to the three total cost functions. **Average fixed cost** (AFC) is total fixed cost divided by output. AFC necessarily declines with increases in output; mathematically, the function is a rectangular hyperbola. Table 5.2 and Figure 5.2 show the AFC function for the Media Corporation.

Average variable cost (AVC) is total variable cost divided by output. This indicator tells managers the variable cost, on average, of each unit of output. For the Media Corporation, the AVC function is shown in Table 5.2 and Figure 5.2. Ini-

---

TABLE 5.2

Average and Marginal Costs: Media Corporation

Units of Output Q	Average Fixed Cost (Dollars) TFC/Q	Average Variable Cost (Dollars) TVC/Q	Average Total Cost (Dollars) TC/Q	Marginal Cost (Dollars) $\Delta TC/\Delta Q$ [a]	Marginal Cost (Dollars) dTC/dQ [a]
0	—	—	—	—	—
1	100	40	140	40	31
2	50	32	82	24	18
3	33.33	26	59.33	14	11
4	25	22	47	10	10
5	20	20	40	12	15
5.5	18.18	19.75	37.93		19.75
6	16.67	20	36.67	20	26
6.64	15.06	21.04	36.11		36.11
7	14.29	22	36.29	34	43
8	12.5	26	38.5	54	66
9	11.11	32	43.11	80	95
10	10	40	50	112	130

---

[a] The figures in the $\Delta TC/\Delta Q$ column pertain to the interval between the indicated amount of quantity and one unit less than the indicated amount of quantity. The figures in the dTC/dQ column are the continuous marginal cost—that is $dTC/dQ = MC = 50 - 22Q + 3Q^2$.

FIGURE 5.2

Average and Marginal Cost Curves: Media Corporation

Average fixed cost continually decreases as output increases. Average variable cost and average total cost at first decrease, reach a minimum, then increase as output increases. The minimum of the average total cost occurs at a higher output than the minimum of the average variable cost. The average total cost curve is the vertical summation of the average fixed cost and the average variable cost curves. Marginal cost passes through the minimum of both average cost curves, and when marginal cost is below the average cost, average cost falls and vice versa. Average total cost achieves its minimum at a higher output rate (6.64) than average variable cost (5.5) because the increases in average variable cost are, up to a point, more than offset by decreases in average fixed cost.

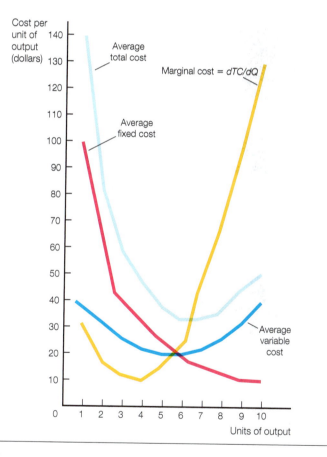

tially, increasing output results in decreases in *AVC*. However, as output increases, at some point of increased production, *AVC* rises, thus increasing the average variable cost per unit.

Last chapter we said the behavior of cost is largely determined by the production function. Now we can show you why. *AVC* is simply total variable cost divided by the number of units produced (TVC/Q). Let U be the number of input units used and W the cost per unit of input. It is then true that

$$AVC = \frac{TVC}{Q} = W \frac{U}{Q}$$

We defined average product in Chapter 4 as

$$AP = \frac{Q}{U}$$

Hence AP is the inverse of U/Q. Now we can express AVC as

$$AVC = W \frac{1}{AP} \tag{5.1}$$

So one way for managers to think of AVC is as the inverse of average product times the cost per unit of input. Recall the behavior of the average product. It initially increases with output, reaches a maximum, and then begins to decrease. Because of their inverse relationship, AVC mirrors the behavior of AP. When AP increases, AVC decreases; when AP decreases, AVC increases. So we expect AVC to initially decrease, hit a minimum, and then increase.

Average total cost (ATC) The total cost divided by output.

Average total cost (ATC) is total cost divided by output. For the Media Corporation, the ATC function is shown in Table 5.2 and Figure 5.2. ATC is simply the sum of $AFC + AVC$. Its shape is similar to AVC but higher at all output levels due to the effect of fixed costs. At output levels where both AFC and AVC decrease, ATC must decrease too. However, ATC reaches its minimum at output levels relatively higher than AVC because increases in average variable cost are for a time more than offset by decreases in average fixed cost (which must decrease as output increases).

Marginal cost (MC) The incremental cost of producing an additional unit of output.

Marginal cost (MC) is the incremental cost of producing an additional unit of output. If $C(Q)$ is the total cost of producing Q units of output, the marginal cost between Q and $(Q - 1)$ units of output is $C(Q) - C(Q - 1)$. For the Media Corporation, the marginal cost function is shown in Table 5.2 and Figure 5.2. At low output levels, MC may decrease (as it does in Figure 5.2) with increases in output; but after reaching a minimum, it increases (like AVC) with additional output. We saw why this is true last chapter when we discussed diminishing marginal returns. If ΔTVC is the change in total variable costs resulting from a change in output of ΔQ and if ΔTFC is the change in total fixed costs resulting from a change in output of ΔQ then

$$MC = \frac{\Delta TVC + \Delta TFC}{\Delta Q}$$

But ΔTFC is zero because fixed costs can't vary; therefore

$$MC = \frac{\Delta TVC}{\Delta Q}$$

Hence the cost of the input is given by $\Delta TVC = W(\Delta U)$, where W is the cost per unit of input and ΔU is the change in the units of input needed to produce the increase of ΔQ in output. Consequently,

$$MC = W \frac{\Delta U}{\Delta Q}$$

Last chapter we defined MP as

$$MP = \frac{\Delta Q}{\Delta L}$$

Hence we can define MC as

$$MC = W \frac{1}{MP}$$

So like the inverse nature of AP and AVC, the behavior of MP is inverse to that of MC. Marginal cost is simply the cost per unit of input times the inverse of its marginal product. Let's think about why this is true. Say a unit of labor costs $10. If the MP of a unit of labor is 10, the MC of producing the last unit of output is $1 ($10/10). But if the MP of that unit of labor is 1, the MC is $10. As MP increases, MC decreases; and when MP decreases, MC increases. We saw that the behavior of marginal product is to increase, attain a maximum, and then decline with increases in output; marginal cost normally decreases, attains a minimum, and then increases.

QUANT OPTION

If the total cost function is continuous, marginal cost is defined as dTC/dQ, where TC is total cost. Suppose, for example, using the Media Corporation's total cost function,

$$TC = 100 + 50Q - 11Q^2 + Q^3$$

where TC is expressed in thousands of dollars and Q is expressed in units of output. This firm's marginal cost function is

$$MC = \frac{dTC}{dQ} = 50 - 22Q + 3Q^2$$

TABLE 5.3

Relationship of Average Product and Marginal Product to Average Variable Cost and Marginal Cost: Thomas Machine Company

L	Q	AP_L	$MP_L =$ dQ/dL	W	$AVC =$ W/AP_L	$MC =$ W/MP_L
0	0	—	—	390	—	—
1	49	49	67	390	7.96	5.82
2	132	66	98	390	5.91	3.98
3	243	81	123	390	4.81	3.17
4	376	94	142	390	4.15	2.75
5	525	105	155	390	3.71	2.52
6	684	114	162	390	3.42	2.41
6.67	792.6	118.9	163.33	390	3.28	2.388←MP_L max
7	847	121	163	390	3.22	2.393 so MC min
8	1008	126	158	390	3.10	2.47
9	1161	129	147	390	3.02	2.65
10	1300	130	130	390	3.00	3.00←AP_L max
11	1419	129	107	390	3.02	3.64 so AVC min
12	1512	126	78	390	3.10	5.00
13	1573	121	43	390	3.22	9.07
14	1596	114	2	390	3.42	195.00
15	1575	105	−45	390	3.71	—

The relationship between production and cost is shown in Table 5.3. Consider the previous definitions of the production function of the Thomas Machine Company ($Q = 30L + 20L^2 - L^3$) from the last chapter. If the wage rate is 390, Table 5.3 shows the relationship between average product and average variable cost and between marginal product and marginal cost. As you can see, when AP is maximized, AVC is minimized. Likewise, we see that MC equals AVC when average variable cost is minimized. This is to be expected because $MP = AP$ when AP is maximized. Average product is maximized when 10 units of labor are employed (at 130); average variable cost is minimized when 10 units of labor are employed (at 3); and marginal cost is also equal to 3 when 10 units of labor are employed.

Marginal cost always equals average variable cost when the latter is at a minimum (because $MP = AP$, when AP is maximized). If the cost function of Thomas is $TC = 100 + 50Q - 11Q^2 + Q^3$, then the firm's AVC is

$$AVC = \frac{TVC}{Q} = 50 - 11Q + Q^2$$

If we take the ΔAVC with respect to ΔQ and set it equal to zero, we find the value of Q where AVC is at a minimum:

$$\frac{\Delta AVC}{\Delta Q} = -11 + 2Q = 0$$

$$Q = 5.5$$

When Q equals 5.5, both marginal cost and average variable cost equal \$19.75. (Substitute 5.5 for Q in the preceding equations for MC and AVC and see for yourself that this is true.) Therefore, as pointed out, $MC = AVC$ when AVC is at a minimum. Note also that marginal cost equals average total cost when the latter is at a minimum. The firm's average total cost is

$$ATC = (100/Q) + 50 - 11Q + Q^2$$

If we take ΔATC with respect to ΔQ and set it equal to zero, we find the value of Q where ATC is at a minimum:

$$\frac{\Delta ATC}{\Delta Q} = \left(\frac{-100}{Q^2}\right) - 11 + 2Q = 0$$

or

$$2Q^3 - 11Q^2 - 100 = 0$$

This is solved for $Q = 6.64$. Substituting 6.64 into the ATC and MC equations yields $MC = ATC = 36.11$.

QUANT OPTION

Here's some fun!

$$\frac{dAVC}{dQ} = \frac{d\left(\frac{VC}{Q}\right)}{dQ}$$

$$\frac{\left[Q\left(\frac{dVC}{dQ}\right) - VC\left(\frac{dQ}{dQ}\right)\right]}{Q^2}$$

$$\frac{\left[\left(\frac{dVC}{dQ}\right) - \left(\frac{VC}{Q}\right)\right]}{Q} = 0$$

which implies

$$\left(\frac{dVC}{dQ}\right) - \left(\frac{VC}{Q}\right) = MC - AVC = 0$$

or

$$MC = AVC$$

PROBLEM SOLVED: The Effects of Output on the Cost of Producing Aircraft

The National Research Council has made a study of the U.S. aircraft industry, which stresses the importance to airplane manufacturers of serving the entire world market. As evidence, the council presents the following graph.

Problems

1. As indicated in this graph, the cost per airplane of producing 525 aircraft of a particular type is about 10 percent higher than the cost per airplane of producing 700 aircraft of this type. Assuming this graph pertains to the short run, by what percentage does average fixed cost increase if 525 rather than 700 aircraft are produced?

2. If average fixed cost is 30 percent of average total cost if 700 aircraft are produced and 36 percent of average total cost if 525 aircraft are produced, is it true that average total cost is about 10 percent higher if 525 rather than 700 aircraft are produced?

Solutions

1. If the number of aircraft produced is 525 rather than 700, average fixed cost is $TFC/525$ rather than $TFC/700$, where TFC equals total fixed cost. Therefore, average fixed cost increases by 33 percent.

2. For 700 aircraft, average total cost equals $X/0.30 = 3.33X$, where X is average fixed cost when 700 aircraft are produced. For 525 aircraft, average total cost equals $1.33X/0.36 = 3.69X$ because average fixed cost equals $1.33X$ when 525 aircraft are produced. Therefore, average total cost increases by about 11 percent (from $3.33X$ to $3.69X$) if 525 rather than 700 aircraft are produced.

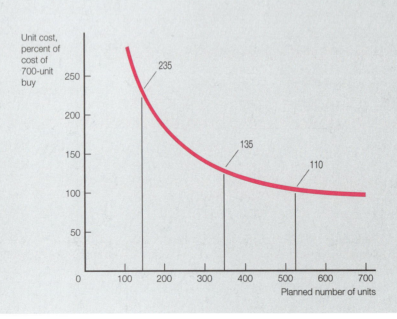

Note that we define marginal cost in two ways. The first ($\Delta TC/\Delta Q$) assumes we can produce only in discrete units, like a car or a cake. The second (dTC/dQ) assumes we can produce on a continuous basis, as in 3.14 tons of grain or 10.33 gallons of gasoline. Which definition managers use depends on the situation: Is the manager constrained to an integer output level or can she produce fractions of the product?

LONG-RUN COST FUNCTIONS

In the long run all inputs are variable, and managers can build any scale or type of plant. There are no fixed costs in the long run because no inputs are fixed; so there is nothing to stop a manager from being as efficient as possible. We can choose and implement the optimal input bundle. Thinking about the long run requires managers to focus more on the destination rather than the route. As we show in Chapter 11, managers need to actively anticipate the future and think toward it.

When Toyota managers consider building a new U.S. plant, they can build one of any size at any location; there are boundless choices. But once the investment is made, type and size of plant and equipment are to a considerable extent frozen.

Assume managers are looking to construct one of three alternative scales of plant; the short-run average cost functions for these scales of plant are represented by $G_1G_{1'}$, $G_2G_{2'}$, and $G_3G_{3'}$, in Figure 5.3. In the long run managers can choose any of the three plants. Which scale is most profitable? Obviously the answer depends on the manager's beliefs about long-run product demand because she needs to produce at the minimum average cost.

We can see this in Figure 5.3. If the manager anticipates product demand of around Q, she should build the smallest plant. At these sales, the average cost per unit sold is equal to C. If the manager builds the medium-sized or largest plant, the average cost per unit is higher. If the manager believes that demand will be equal to S, she should build the largest plant.

The **long-run average cost function** (*LAC*) shows the minimum cost per unit of all output levels when any desired size plant is built. In Figure 5.3 the long-run average cost function is the solid portion of the short-run average cost functions, G_1DEG_3'. Any point on the long-run average cost function is also a point on a short-run average cost function. In fact, it is a point on the lowest-cost short-run cost function for the given output level. So when given the freedom (that is, in the long run), managers want to choose the plant scale that minimizes average cost. The broken-line segments of the short-run functions are not included because they are not the lowest average costs, as is obvious from the figure.

Toyota managers can choose from more than three plant scales: They can choose from an infinite number of possibilities. However, managers must understand that once they commit funds to building a plant, they immediately shift to a short-run cost function. Figure 5.4 depicts this decision. The minimum average

Long-run average cost function (LAC) Function showing the minimum cost per unit of all output levels when any desired size plant is built.

FIGURE 5.3

Short-Run Average Cost Functions for Various Scales of Plant

The long-run average cost function is the solid portion of the short-run average cost functions, $G_1 DEG'_3$.

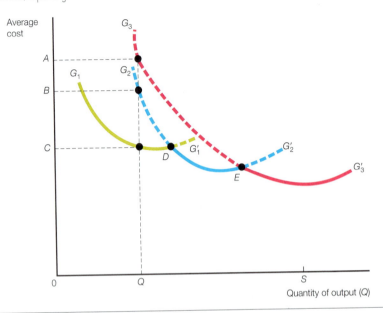

cost of producing all outputs is given by the long-run *AC* function, *LL'*. Each point on *LL'* is also a point on a short-run *AC* function. At that output level, it is a point on the lowest-cost short-run *AC* function; it is the best an efficient manager can do. The two functions are tangent at that point. (Mathematically, the long-run average cost function is the envelope of the short-run functions.)

Managers who estimate the long-run average cost of producing any given output can readily derive the long-run total cost of production: It is simply the product of long-run average cost and output. Figure 5.5 shows the relationship between long-run total cost and output; this relationship is called the **long-run total cost function.**

Managers can readily derive the **long-run marginal cost function.** This function represents how varying output affects the cost of producing the last unit if the manager has chosen the most efficient input bundle. This marginal cost function shows behavior similar to average costs. Long-run marginal cost is less than *LAC* when *LAC* is decreasing; it is equal to long-run *LAC* when *LAC* is at a minimum; and it is greater than *LAC* when *LAC* is increasing. When managers build the optimal scale of plant for producing a given level of output, long-run marginal cost is equal to short-run marginal cost at that output.

Long-run total cost function
The relationship between long-run total cost and output.

Long-run marginal cost function Function representing how varying output affects the cost of producing the last unit if the manager has chosen the most efficient input bundle.

FIGURE 5.4

Long-Run Average Cost Function

The long-run average cost function, which shows the minimum long-run cost per unit of producing each output level, is the envelope of the short-run functions.

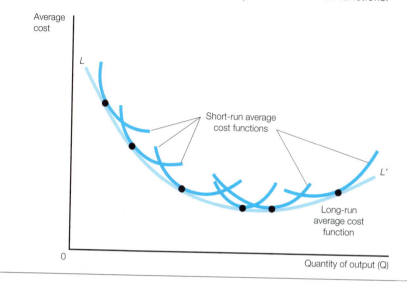

FIGURE 5.5

Long-Run Total Cost Function

The long-run total cost of a given output level equals the long-run average cost (given in Figure 5.4) times output.

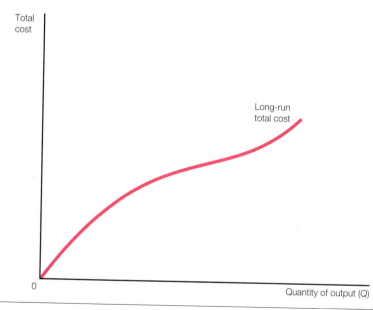

PROBLEM SOLVED: Managerial Use of Cost Functions

To illustrate the relationship between a firm's long-run and short-run cost functions, consider a Martin division that produces MP3 players. Managers have been told to cut costs, so they need to create an efficient input bundle. Engineers estimate the division's production function as

$$Q = 4(KL)^{0.5} \qquad (5.2)$$

where Q is output (in thousands of MP3 players per month), K is the capital used per month (in thousands of units), and L is the number of hours of labor employed per month (in thousands). Because laborers are paid $8 per hour and capital costs equal $2 per unit, Martin's total cost (in thousands of dollars per month) equals

$$TC = 8L + 2K = \frac{Q^2}{2K} + 2K \qquad (5.3)$$

Equation (5.2) implies that

$$L = \frac{Q^2}{16K}$$

In the short run, managers cannot vary their level of capital, so K is fixed. The division presently uses 10,000 units of capital ($K = 10$). Substituting 10 for K in equation (5.3), we find that the short-run cost function is

$$TC_S = \frac{Q^2}{20} + 20 \qquad (5.4)$$

where TC_S is short-run total cost. Therefore, the short-run average total cost function is

$$AC_S = \frac{TC_S}{Q} = \frac{Q}{20} + \frac{20}{Q}$$

and the short-run marginal cost function is

$$MC_S = \frac{\Delta TC_S}{\Delta Q} = \frac{Q}{10}$$

In the long run, managers can buy new machines or sell current ones, so no input is fixed. If Martin managers want to minimize total costs, they need to choose the optimal level of capital needed to produce Q MP3 players. Basing their estimates on equation (5.3), they find that

$$\frac{\Delta TC}{\Delta K} = -\frac{Q^2}{2K^2} + 2$$

Setting this equal to zero, we find that the cost-minimizing value of K is

$$K = \frac{Q}{2}$$

This decision rule tells the managers to estimate expected demand and then purchase capital equal to one-half of demand. Substituting $Q/2$ for K in equation (5.3), we see that the long-run cost function is

$$TC_L = 2Q \qquad (5.5)$$

where TC_L is long-run total cost. Because $TC_L/Q = 2$, the long-run average cost equals $2 per MP3 player. The long-run marginal cost is also $2 for MP3 players because $\Delta TC_L/\Delta Q = 2$.

Short-Run Average and Marginal Costs and Long-Run Average Cost, Martin Division

Because the long-run average cost function is horizontal, it is tangent to the short-run average cost function at the latter's minimum point.

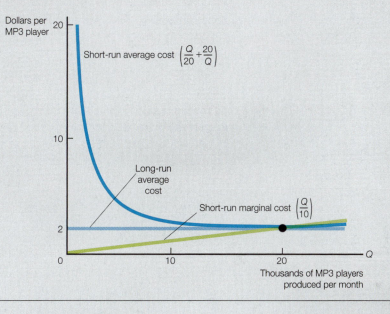

The figure shows the relationship between Martin's short-run average and marginal costs and its long-run average costs. As managers expect, the short-run marginal cost function intersects the short-run average cost function at its minimum point, where $Q = 20$ and $AC_S = 2$, in this case. Because it is horizontal (owing to constant returns to scale), the long-run average cost function is tangent to the short-run average cost function at the latter's minimum point. Many long-run average cost functions are not horizontal. Instead they have what we call *scale economies*: As the plant size varies, so does the average unit cost. As discussed in the following section, there are economies of scale (over at least some range of output) in a wide variety of markets and processes. Smart managers use these scale economies to create competitive advantage.

QUANT OPTION

Never believe everything you read; always ask for the proof.

Suppose the long-run average cost of producing an output rate of Q is $L(Q)$, and the short-run AC of producing it with the ith scale of plant is $A_i(Q)$. Let $M(Q)$ be the long-run MC and $R_i(Q)$ be the short-run MC with the ith scale of plant. If the manager maximizes profit, she is operating where short-run and long-run average costs are equal; in other words, $L(Q) = A_i(Q)$. This means that

$$\frac{dL(Q)}{dQ} = \frac{dA_i(Q)}{dQ} \text{ and } Q\frac{dL(Q)}{dQ} = Q\frac{dA_i(Q)}{dQ}$$

From these conditions, it is easy to prove that the long-run marginal cost, $M(Q)$, equals the short-run marginal cost, $R_i(Q)$:

$$M(Q) = \frac{d[QL(Q)]}{dQ} = L(Q) + \frac{QdL(Q)}{dQ}$$

$$R_i(Q) = \frac{d[QA_i(Q)]}{dQ} = A_iQ + \frac{QdA_i(Q)}{dQ}$$

We know from the previous paragraph that $L(Q) = A_i(Q)$ and $QdL(Q)/dQ = QdA_i(Q)/dQ$; so it follows that $R_i(Q)$ must equal $M(Q)$.

QUANT OPTION

$$dTC_S/dQ = Q/10$$

$$dTC/dK = -(Q^2/2K^2) + 2 = 0$$

$$dTC_L/dQ = 2$$

MANAGERIAL USE OF SCALE ECONOMIES

Economies of scale When the firm's average unit cost decreases as output increases.

Long-run average cost curves tell managers whether bigger is better: They show whether, and to what extent, larger plants have cost advantages over smaller ones. **Economies of scale** occur when the firm's average unit cost decreases as output increases. To illustrate, consider nursing homes, which make up an industry with

FIGURE 5.6

Long-Run Average Cost Curve for Texas Nursing Homes

For nursing homes with fewer than 60,000 patient–days, there seem to be substantial economies of scale.

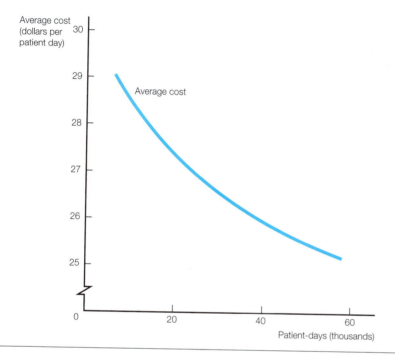

annual sales of over $75 billion. Figure 5.6 shows the long-run average cost curve for a nursing home.

As you can see, there are substantial economies of scale. If a nursing home provides 10,000 patient–days of service per year, the cost per patient–day is almost $29; if it provides about 50,000 patient–days of service per year, the cost per patient–day is under $26. Curves like Figure 5.6 are estimated by engineers and economists for a wide variety of plants and processes; they help managers choose optimal input bundles.

Scale economies are not confined to plants. In our global economy, managers often use more than one plant to produce their product. Nike is a good example. Managers at such companies have the opportunity to exploit possible scale economies at the firm level. For example, holding the size of each plant constant, average cost may decrease in response to increases in the number of plants operated by Nike. Managers could create such cost savings for several reasons, including centralized purchasing, better management techniques, or an improved ability to build or lease plants.

Managers use many sources of scale economies to create competitive advantages. Managers at UPS use them in their distribution network to decrease costs. Exxon Mobil managers use them to decrease costs in their refining and chemical process. Managers at BskyB, the British pay television server, can pay more for some content because of scale economies in its large network. Finally, the size of cruise ships keeps growing because larger ships have a lower cost per passenger thanks to scale economies. Royal Caribbean continues this trend with the launching of the *Genesis* ship in 2009; this 220,000-ton ship can carry 5,400 passengers. When asked why bigger is better, Harri Kulovaara of Royal Caribbean noted, "Having more real estate, we can provide more deck area. That means more entertainment options and better amenities."[1]

Managers must understand their cost relationships to recognize where to best exploit scale economies. As we have seen, scale economies are not confined to production; they are found in distribution, raising capital, advertising, and most business processes. All managers have the opportunity to exploit scale economies in some form, though some fail to recognize their opportunities.

However, bigger is not always better. As plants, distribution networks, or cruise ships get bigger, at some point managing them gets harder. Increasing size eventually causes **diseconomies of scale**: Average costs per unit of output increase, usually because of the complexity of managing and coordinating all the necessary activities.

Diseconomies of scale When the average costs per unit of output increase.

MANAGERIAL USE OF SCOPE ECONOMIES

Scale economies are not the only cost economies managers can exploit. A cost efficiency strategy available to managers of multiproduct firms is called **economies of scope**. These economies exist when the cost of producing two (or more) products jointly is less than the cost of producing each one alone. For example, suppose managers of the Martin Company can produce 1,000 milling machines and 500 lathes per year at a cost of $15 million, whereas if the firm produced only 1,000 milling machines, the cost would be $12 million, and if it produced only 500 lathes, the cost would be $6 million. In this case the cost of producing both the milling machines and the lathes is less than the total cost of producing each separately. Hence there are scope economies.

Economies of scope Exist when the cost of jointly producing two (or more) products is less than the cost of producing each one alone.

A simple way for managers to estimate the extent of their scope economies is to use the following measure:

$$S = \frac{C(Q_1) + C(Q_2) - C(Q_1 + Q_2)}{C(Q_1 + Q_2)} \tag{5.6}$$

Here S is the degree of economies of scope, $C(Q_1)$ is the cost of producing Q_1 units of the first product alone, $C(Q_2)$ is the cost of producing Q_2 units of the second product alone, and $C(Q_1 + Q_2)$ is the cost of producing Q_1 units of the first

1. J. Wise, "World's Largest Cruise Ship Pulls 360s with Joystick," *Popular Mechanics*, June 2007.

146

product in combination with Q_2 units of the second product. If there are economies of scope, S is greater than zero because the cost of producing both products together—$C(Q_1 + Q_2)$—is less than the cost of producing each alone—$C(Q_1)$ + $C(Q_2)$. Clearly S measures the percentage of saving that results from producing them jointly rather than individually. Managers of the Martin Company calculate the following:

$$S = \frac{\$12 \text{ million} + \$6 \text{ million} - \$15 \text{ million}}{\$15 \text{ million}} = 0.20$$

which means scope economies have lowered their costs by an estimated 20 percent. Strategically, managers of Martin have created a 20 percent cost advantage

STRATEGY SESSION: Economies of Scope in Advertising Agencies

In recent years there has been considerable controversy over the extent to which there are economies of scope in the advertising industry. An advertising agency can use many media, including network television, general magazines, newspapers, radio, outdoor ads, the Internet, and cell phones.

Researchers have looked at the percentage of cost reduction from joint production at several hundred advertising agencies and found the following cost savings.

As you can see, the cost savings from joint production of these products range from essentially zero to about 86 percent, depending on which advertising agency is considered. On the average, the cost saving is about 26 percent. Clearly advertising has very substantial economies of scope; and smaller firms seem to enjoy greater scope economies than larger firms.

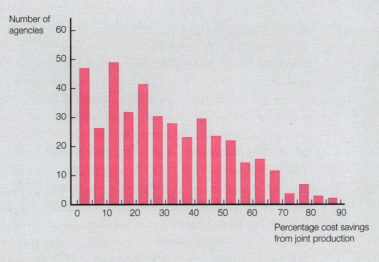

relative to managers of single-product firms. Obviously, the larger is the value of *S*, the greater are the scope economies.

Like scale economies, managers can exploit scope economies across a range of markets, processes, and behavior. Oil firms like Exxon Mobil and BP produce both petroleum and chemical products; drug firms like Merck and Glaxo SmithKline produce both vaccines and tranquilizers; and publisher W. W. Norton publishes both economics and literature textbooks. Both Coca-Cola and Pepsi use single trucks to deliver an assortment of flavors and sizes of drinks. Most airlines fly both passengers and cargo. Managers use scope economies to create cost advantages by producing multiple products rather than just one. Often these cost savings arise because the products share either processes (like distribution) or resources (such as components). However, just as with diseconomies of scale, there can be diseconomies of scope. Many conglomerates, e.g., G.E., continue to subtract (and add) from their lines of business when it is no longer profitable for them to produce a particular product.

MANAGERIAL USE OF BREAK-EVEN ANALYSIS

The concept of breaking even is a cost-based analysis that is both useful and simple. Break-even analysis looks at the relative positioning of costs and revenues; managers use it to estimate how possible pricing changes affect firm performance. Figure 5.7 shows the situation facing Martin divisional managers. They face fixed costs of $600,000 per month and average variable costs of $2 per unit. They sell their component for $3 per unit. Because average variable cost is constant, the cost of an extra unit (marginal cost) is also constant and equal to average variable cost. Given the $3 per-unit price, the revenue curve is a straight line through the origin. Martin managers create a break-even chart by plotting the firm's total revenue curve with its total cost function. The chart estimates monthly profit for all possible sales. For example, Figure 5.7 shows that if Martin managers have sales of 300,000 units per month, managers realize a loss of $300,000. The chart also estimates the **break-even point**, which is the output level that must be reached if managers are to avoid losses. This is the intersection of the cost and revenue functions; in Figure 5.7 the break-even point is 600,000 units. A useful way to represent the difference between a product's price and its average variable costs is as the money needed to "cover" the fixed costs. Once managers cover their fixed costs, the difference represents the profit per unit. For the Martin managers, each unit they sell can cover a dollar of fixed costs ($3 − $2). Because fixed costs are $600,000, they need to sell 600,000 units given this $1 difference. At the 600,000th unit, the firm's profit is $0; and after 600,000 units are sold, each unit increases profit by $1.

Break-even analysis offers useful estimates of the relationships among sales and costs, receipts, and profit. For example, managers use this analysis to predict how a projected decline in sales will impact profit. Or they use it to estimate how

Break-even point The output level that must be reached if managers are to avoid losses.

FIGURE 5.7

Break-Even Chart: Martin Company

The break-even point—the output level that must be reached if the firm is to avoid losses—is 600,000 units of output per month.

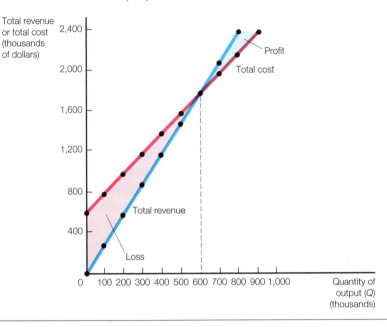

QUANT OPTION

Let P be the price of the component, Q the quantity sold, AVC the average variable cost, and TFC the fixed cost. The break-even unit is the output, Q_B, at which $TR = TC$. Because TR is PQ and total cost is $TFC + AVC(Q)$, it follows that

$$PQ_B = TFC + AVC \times (Q_B)$$

$$(P - AVC)Q_B = TFC$$

$$Q_B = \frac{TFC}{P - AVC} \qquad (5.7)$$

In the case of the Martin managers, $P = \$3$, $AVC = \$2$, and $TFC = \$600,000$. Consequently,

$$Q_B = \frac{\$600,000}{3 - 2} = 600,000$$

a price change might affect profit. Like most models, the analysis has limitations. High variance in prices or difficulties in estimating the cost structure can decrease the accuracy of results.

It is worth noting that although we worked with a linear cost function, this assumption is easily relaxed. Often a curvilinear cost function is used to estimate the cost structure. Many times, for fairly small changes in output, a linear approximation is good enough. This guideline is supported by many empirical studies suggesting that cost functions are often close to linear, as long as the firm is not operating at or close to capacity.

PROFIT CONTRIBUTION ANALYSIS

Profit contribution analysis A break-even analysis to understand the relationship between price and profit.

Managers also use break-even analysis to understand the relationship between price and profit; this analysis is known as **profit contribution analysis**. As we already discussed, profit contribution is the difference between total revenue and total variable cost; on a per-unit basis, it is equal to price minus average variable

---

STRATEGY SESSION: Mr. Martin Gets Chewed Out by the Boss

John Martin, an accountant at a small company that manufactures and sells three types of desks, constructed a break-even chart for the company as a whole. He used as a measure of output the total number of desks produced during each year. To estimate the average variable cost of a desk, he took the mean of the average variable costs of the three types of desks. To estimate the price of a desk, he took the mean of the prices of the three types of desks. Using these figures, he constructed a break-even chart (based on linear total cost and total revenue curves) indicating that the company was operating at an output level well above the break-even point and that profit would increase rapidly as output increased.

When Martin presented these findings, the company's president, Susan Rogers, said they were misleading because the analysis lumped together the three types of desks. For one type, the plant was operating at capacity, and marginal cost would increase substantially if output were increased. For another type of desk, it had become increasingly

obvious that the price was too high, and it was about to be reduced. For the third type of desk, only a few were produced, so it was incorrect to weight it as heavily as the other two types in the analysis. Rogers also pointed out that as the firm's output increased, the first and second types accounted for bigger and bigger shares of total output.

How should Martin respond to these comments? (Sometimes it is best just to admit you are wrong and thank the president for the information.) The fact that the product mix changes with increases in output is important, and Martin should have recognized this. It is also misleading to lump all three products together. And contrary to the assumption that the total cost curve is linear, the marginal cost of the first type of desk rises with increases in output. Finally, the price Martin used for the second type of desk is not the relevant one.

This section is based on an actual case, although the numbers and situation have been disguised somewhat.

cost. In the case of the Martin Company, price is $3 and average variable cost is $2, so the per-unit profit contribution is $3 − $2, or $1.

Suppose managers at Martin want to estimate the sales level that will earn them a profit of $1 million per month. The required sales equal

$$Q = \frac{\text{Total fixed cost + Profit target}}{\text{Profit contribution (per unit)}}$$

$$= \frac{\$600,000 + \$1,000,000}{\$1}$$

$$= 1,600,000 \text{ units}$$

Or if managers sell only 500,000 units per month, the firm loses $100,000. The marketing team hope to land an order for 50,000 units of product. How much will this order reduce the firm's loss? To find out, multiply the order size (50,000 units) by the per-unit profit contribution ($1) to get the increase in profit (or reduction in loss, which is the case here); the result is $50,000.

SUMMARY

1. Managerial economists define a product's opportunity cost as the value of other products that could have been produced with the money used to produce the product. Hence a product's opportunity cost may differ from its historical cost, which is generally the basis for accounting statements.

2. In the short run it is important to distinguish between a firm's fixed and variable costs. Managers should be able to chart total, average, and marginal costs against output. The resulting cost functions, or cost curves (as they are often called), show how changes in output affect a firm's costs.

3. The long-run average cost function shows the minimum cost per unit of producing a given output level when any desired scale of plant can be built. The long-run average cost function is tangent to each of the short-run average cost functions at the output where the plant corresponding to the short-run average cost function is optimal. The long-run average cost curve is important to managers because it shows the extent to which larger plants have cost advantages over smaller ones.

4. Economies of scope occur when the cost of producing two (or more) products jointly is less than the cost of producing them separately. Such economies may arise because the production facilities used to make one product can also be used to make another product, or by-products resulting from the making of one product can be useful in making other products.

5. Break-even analysis compares total revenue and total cost, graphically or algebraically. A break-even chart combines the total cost function and the total revenue curve, both of which are generally assumed to be linear, and shows the profit or loss resulting from each sales level. The break-even point is the sales level that must be achieved if the firm is to avoid losses. Managers often find it useful to

carry out various types of profit contribution analysis. The profit contribution is the difference between total revenue and total variable cost; on a per-unit basis, it is equal to price minus average variable cost.

wwnorton.com/studyspace Ⓢ

PROBLEMS

1. An MIT study has estimated costs for producing steel with three different technologies: (1) coke, blast furnace, basic oxygen furnace, ingots, and finishing mills; (2) coke, blast furnace, basic oxygen furnace, continuous casting, and finishing mills; and (3) steel scrap, electric arc furnace, continuous casting, and finishing mills. Under reasonable assumptions concerning input prices, the estimated average costs per ton are as follows:

Cost Category	Coke, Blast Furnace, Basic Oxygen Furnace, Ingots, Finishing Mills	Coke, Blast Furnace, Basic Oxygen Furnace, Continuous Casting, Finishing Mills	Steel Scrap, Electric Arc Furnace, Continuous Casting, Finishing Mills
Process materials	$148.34	$136.19	$122.78
Energy	21.15	15.98	41.58
Direct labor	83.43	75.09	67.43
Capital	102.06	99.93	54.08
Other	46.74	41.67	24.47
Total	$401.72	$368.86	$310.34

a. The MIT report concludes that "unless significant changes occur in other technologies, the electric-furnace continuous-casting route will dominate domestic production." Why?

b. At the same time, the report notes that the price of scrap (which is used in this route) "could increase as electric furnace production expands because of the increased demand." Why is this relevant?

c. The report also concludes that regardless of which of these technologies is used, cost per ton is about 25 to 30 percent higher if wages are $26 per hour rather than $2 per hour. What does this imply about the competitiveness of U.S. steel producers relative to producers in other countries that pay wages far below U.S. levels?

d. If these cost figures are long-run average costs, under what circumstances would they also equal long-run marginal costs?

2. The Haverford Company is considering three types of plants to make a particular electronic device. Plant A is much more highly automated than plant B, which in turn is more highly automated than plant C. For each type of plant,

average variable cost is constant so long as output is less than capacity, which is the maximum output of the plant. The cost structure for each type of plant is as follows:

Average Variable Costs	Plant A	Plant B	Plant C
Labor	$1.10	$2.40	$3.70
Materials	0.90	1.20	1.80
Other	0.50	2.40	2.00
Total	$2.50	$6.00	$7.50
Total fixed costs	$300,000	$ 75,000	$25,000
Annual capacity	200,000	100,000	50,000

  a. Derive the average costs of producing 100,000, 200,000, 300,000, and 400,000 devices per year with plant A. (For output exceeding the capacity of a single plant, assume that more than one plant of this type is built.)
  b. Derive the average costs of producing 100,000, 200,000, 300,000, and 400,000 devices per year with plant B.
  c. Derive the average costs of producing 100,000, 200,000, 300,000, and 400,000 devices per year with plant C.
  d. Using the results of parts (a) through (c), plot the points on the long-run average cost curve for the production of these electronic devices for outputs of 100,000, 200,000, 300,000 and 400,000 devices per year.

3. The Abner Corporation, a retail seller of television sets, wants to determine how many television sets it must sell to earn a profit of $10,000 per month. The price of each television set is $300, and the average variable cost is $100.
  a. What is the required sales volume if the Abner Corporation's monthly fixed costs are $5,000 per month?
  b. If the firm sells each television set at a price of $350 rather than $300, what is the required sales volume?
  c. If the price is $350, and if average variable cost is $85 rather than $100, what is the required sales volume?

4. According to a statistical study, the following relationship exists between an electric power plant's fuel costs (C) and its eight-hour output as a percentage of capacity (Q):

$$C = 16.68 + 0.125Q + 0.00439Q^2$$

  a. When Q increases from 50 to 51, what is the increase in the cost of fuel for this electric plant?
  b. Of what use might the result in part (a) be to the plant's managers?
  c. Derive the marginal (fuel) cost curve for this plant, and indicate how it might be used by the plant's managers.

5. The following table pertains to the Lincoln Company. Fill in the blanks:

Output	Total Cost	Total Fixed Cost	Total Variable Cost	Average Fixed Cost	Average Variable Cost
0	50	___	___	___	___
1	75	___	___	___	___
2	100	___	___	___	___
3	120	___	___	___	___
4	135	___	___	___	___
5	150	___	___	___	___
6	190	___	___	___	___
7	260	___	___	___	___

6. The Deering Manufacturing Company's short-run average cost function in 2008 was

$$AC = 3 + 4Q$$

where AC is the firm's average cost (in dollars per pound of the product), and Q is its output rate.
   a. Obtain an equation for the firm's short-run total cost function.
   b. Does the firm have any fixed costs? Explain.
   c. If the price of the Deering Manufacturing Company's product (per pound) is $3, is the firm making profit or loss? Explain.
   d. Derive an equation for the firm's marginal cost function.
7. The president of the Tacke Corporation believes that statistical research by his staff shows that the firm's long-run total cost curve can be represented as

$$TC = \alpha_0 Q^{\alpha 1} P_L^{\alpha 2} P_K^{\alpha 3}$$

where TC is the firm's total cost, Q is its output, P_L is the price of labor, and P_K is the price of capital.
   a. Tacke's president says that α_1 measures the elasticity of cost with respect to output—that is, the percentage change in total cost resulting from a 1 percent change in output. Is he correct? Why or why not?
   b. He also says that if $\alpha_1 < 1$, economies of scale are indicated, whereas if $\alpha_1 > 1$, diseconomies of scale are indicated. Is he correct? Why or why not?
   c. According to Tacke's president, the value of α^3 can be estimated by regressing log (TC/P_K) on log Q and log (P_L/P_K). Is he correct? Why or why not?

8. Engineers sometimes rely on the "0.6 rule," which states that the increase in cost is given by the increase in capacity raised to the 0.6 power; that is,

$$C_2 = C_1(X_2/X_1)^{0.6}$$

where C_1 and C_2 are the costs of two pieces of equipment, and X_1 and X_2 are their respective capacities.

   a. Does the 0.6 rule suggest economies of scale?
   b. Some experts have stated that in the chemical and metal industries, the 0.6 rule can be applied to entire plants rather than individual pieces of equipment. If so, will the long-run average cost curve in these industries tend to be negatively sloped?
   c. Can you think of a way to test whether this rule is correct?

9. The Dijon Company's total variable cost function is

$$TVC = 50Q - 10Q^2 + Q^3$$

where Q is the number of units of output produced.

   a. What is the output level where marginal cost is a minimum?
   b. What is the output level where average variable cost is a minimum?
   c. What is the value of average variable cost and marginal cost at the output specified in the answer to part (b)?

10. The Berwyn Company is considering the addition of a new product to its product line. The firm has plenty of excess manufacturing capacity to produce the new product, and its total fixed costs would be unaffected if the new product were added to its line. Nonetheless, the firm's accountants decide that a reasonable share of the firm's present fixed costs should be allocated to the new product. Specifically, they decide that a $300,000 fixed charge will be absorbed by the new product. The variable cost per unit of making and selling the new product is $14, which is composed of the following:

Direct labor	$8.20
Direct materials	1.90
Other	3.90
Total	$14.00

   a. Should the Berwyn Company add the new product to its line if it can sell about 10,000 units of this product at a price of $25?
   b. Should it add the new product if it can sell about 10,000 units at a price of $20?
   c. Should it add the new product if it can sell about 10,000 units at a price of $15?

  d. What is the minimum price for the new product that will make it worthwhile for Berwyn to add the new product to its line?

11. The Jolson Corporation produces 1,000 wood cabinets and 500 wood desks
per year, the total cost being $30,000. If the firm produced 1,000 wood
cabinets only, the cost would be $23,000. If the firm produced 500 wood desks
only, the cost would be $11,000.

  a. Calculate the degree of economies of scope.
  b. Why do economies of scope exist?

12. The Smith Company made and sold 10,000 metal tables last year. When output was between 5,000 and 10,000 tables, its average variable cost was $24. In
this output range, each table contributed 60 percent of its revenue to fixed
costs and profit.

  a. What was the price per table?
  b. If the Smith Company increases its price by 10 percent, how many tables
  will it have to sell next year to obtain the same profit as last year?
  c. If the Smith Company increases its price by 10 percent, and if its average
  variable cost increases by 8 percent as a result of wage increases, how
  many tables will it have to sell next year to obtain the same profit as last
  year?

APPENDIX A: BREAK-EVEN ANALYSIS AND OPERATING LEVERAGE

Managers must continually compare alternative systems of production.
Should one type of plant be replaced by another? How does your plant stack
up against your competitor's? Break-even analysis can be extended to help
make such comparisons more effective. In this appendix we show how managers can analyze how total cost and profit vary with output, depending on
how automated or mechanized a plant may be. This is an important topic
because top-level managers often have to make such comparisons.

At the outset it is essential to recognize that some plants, because they are
much more mechanized than others, have relatively high fixed costs but relatively
low average variable costs. Consider firms I, II, and III in Figure 5.8. Firm I's plant
has fixed costs of $100,000 per month, which are much higher than those of the
plants operated by firm II or III; however, its average variable cost of $2 is much
lower than that of firm II or III. Essentially firm I has substituted capital for labor
and materials. It has built a highly automated plant with high fixed costs but low
average variable cost.

At the opposite extreme, firm III has built a plant with low fixed costs but
high average variable cost. Because it has not invested a great deal in plant and
equipment, its total fixed costs are only $25,000 per month, which is much less
that for firm I or II. However, because of the relatively low level of mechanization

FIGURE 5.8

Break-Even Analysis and Operating Leverage

Firm I has relatively high fixed costs and low variable costs; firm III has relatively low fixed costs and high variable costs; and firm II is in the middle.

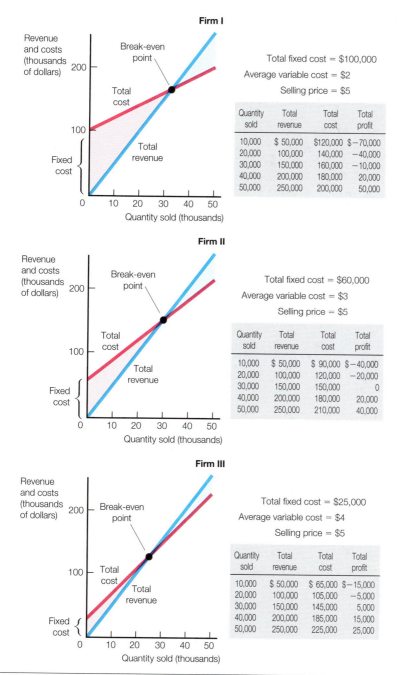

Firm I

Total fixed cost = $100,000

Average variable cost = $2

Selling price = $5

Quantity sold	Total revenue	Total cost	Total profit
10,000	$ 50,000	$120,000	$−70,000
20,000	100,000	140,000	−40,000
30,000	150,000	160,000	−10,000
40,000	200,000	180,000	20,000
50,000	250,000	200,000	50,000

Firm II

Total fixed cost = $60,000

Average variable cost = $3

Selling price = $5

Quantity sold	Total revenue	Total cost	Total profit
10,000	$ 50,000	$ 90,000	$−40,000
20,000	100,000	120,000	−20,000
30,000	150,000	150,000	0
40,000	200,000	180,000	20,000
50,000	250,000	210,000	40,000

Firm III

Total fixed cost = $25,000

Average variable cost = $4

Selling price = $5

Quantity sold	Total revenue	Total cost	Total profit
10,000	$ 50,000	$ 65,000	$−15,000
20,000	100,000	105,000	−5,000
30,000	150,000	145,000	5,000
40,000	200,000	185,000	15,000
50,000	250,000	225,000	25,000

at its plant, firm III's average variable cost is $4—considerably higher than at the other two firms. Relative to firm I, firm III uses more labor and materials and less capital.

Firm II's plant occupies a middle position (between firms I and III) in this regard. Its total fixed cost of $60,000 is less than firm I's but more than firm III's, and its average variable cost of $3 is greater than firm I's but less than firm III's. It has not automated its plant to the extent that firm I has, but it has automated more than firm III.

In comparing these plants, an important issue to consider is the degree of operating leverage, which is defined as the percentage change in profit resulting from a 1 percent change in the number of units of product sold. Specifically,

$$\text{Degree of operating leverage} = \frac{\text{Percentage change in profit}}{\text{Percentage change in quantity sold}}$$

$$= \frac{\Delta\pi/\pi}{\Delta Q/Q}$$

$$= \frac{\Delta\pi}{\Delta Q}\left(\frac{Q}{\pi}\right) \quad \text{or} \quad \frac{d\pi}{dQ}\left(\frac{Q}{\pi}\right) \tag{5.8}$$

where π is the firm's profit, and Q is the quantity sold.

The degree of operating leverage, because it measures how a given change in sales volume affects profit, is of great importance. If firm I is selling 40,000 units per month, and if we let $\Delta Q = 10,000$ units, the degree of operating leverage equals

$$\frac{\Delta\pi}{\Delta Q}\left(\frac{Q}{\pi}\right) = \frac{\$50,000 - \$20,000}{10,000}\left(\frac{40,000}{\$20,000}\right) = 6$$

because Figure 5.8 shows that if $\Delta Q = 10,000$ units, $\Delta\pi = \$50,000 - \$20,000$. (Why? Because if Q changes from 40,000 to 50,000 units, π changes from $20,000 to $50,000.) Thus a 1 percent increase in quantity sold gives a 6 percent increase in profit.

If both the total revenue curve and the total cost function are linear, as in Figure 5.8, a simple way to calculate the degree of operating leverage when output equals Q is to use the following formula:

$$\text{Degree of operating leverage} = \frac{Q(P - AVC)}{Q(P - AVC) - TFC} \tag{5.9}$$

where P equals selling price, AVC equals average variable cost, and TFC equals total fixed cost. It can be shown that if both the total revenue curve and the total cost function are linear, equation (5.9) yields the same result as equation (5.8). Thus for firm I, if $Q = 40,000$, equation (5.9) says that the degree of operating leverage equals

$$\frac{Q(P - AVC)}{Q(P - AVC) - TFC} = \frac{\$40,000(\$5 - \$2)}{40,000(\$5 - \$2) - \$100,000}$$

$$= \frac{\$120,000}{\$120,000 - \$100,000} = 6$$

because P equals \$5, AVC equals \$2, and TFC equals \$100,000. The result is the same as in the previous paragraph. (In both cases it is 6.)

It is interesting and important to compare the degree of operating leverage of the three firms; this comparison reveals a great deal about how these plants differ. If $Q = 40,000$, the degree of operating leverage for firm II equals

$$\frac{Q(P - AVC)}{Q(P - AVC) - TFC} = \frac{\$40,000(\$5 - \$3)}{40,000(\$5 - \$3) - \$60,000} = 4$$

STRATEGY SESSION: Water, Water, Not Everywhere

China is growing at close to a double-digit rate in GDP each year. Water is an essential element of that growth, and the price of water (set by local water bureaus) has not changed since the establishment of the People's Republic of China in 1949. As demand has increased rapidly, supply has not kept pace, and the country is facing acute shortages. Shortages are reportedly hindering agricultural and manufacturing production. Our knowledge of supply and demand tells us that the market will increase prices if a shortage exists. Centrally controlled economy planners also know this, so the Chinese are increasing the price of water.

The increase in prices is designed to curb quantity demanded through conservation and to encourage investment in new supply. Because water has been so cheap for so long, many Chinese habitually waste water. Chinese officials have stated that they will increase the price to their estimation of what the market will bear. Beijing plans to virtually double the price of its water. It's estimated that approximately two-thirds of China's cities are short of water. Some cities are rationing water with a quota of the old cheap water and rapidly increasing prices for water greater than the rationed amount. It is estimated that China's production functions use 5 to 10 times more water than the production functions for the same goods in developed countries.

The supply side can be improved by replacing leaky pipes and water mains. Twenty percent of China's water is lost through leaks. Foreign entrepreneurs and water experts are entering the Chinese market hoping to invest and use their expertise to make money in the water supply market.

Source: "To Conserve Water, China Lifts Its Price," *The Wall Street Journal*, June 14, 2004.

For firm III, it equals

$$\frac{Q(P - AVC)}{Q(P - AVC) - TFC} = \frac{\$40,000(\$5 - \$4)}{40,000(\$5 - \$4) - \$25,000} = 2.67$$

Thus a 1 percent increase in sales volume results in a 6 percent increase in profit at firm I, a 4 percent increase in profit at firm II, and a 2.67 percent increase in profit at firm III. Clearly firm I's profit are much more sensitive to changes in sales volume than are firm III's profit; firm II is in the middle in this regard.

APPENDIX B: MEASUREMENT OF SHORT-RUN COST FUNCTIONS: THE CHOICE OF A MATHEMATICAL FORM

Smart managers understand the need to estimate cost functions for their informational value. In business these are often called cost curves. One step in estimating a cost curve is to choose the mathematical relationship between output and cost. As a first approximation, managers often assume that short-run total cost is a linear function of output, which means marginal cost tends to be constant in the relevant output range (see Figure 5.9). In fact, this simple linear approximation often fits the data for particular firms and plants quite well in the short run. However, managers

---

FIGURE 5.9

Average Cost and Marginal Cost: Linear Total Cost Function
Marginal cost is constant.

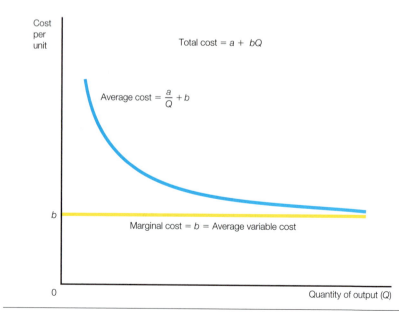

FIGURE 5.10

Average Cost and Marginal Cost: Quadratic Total Cost Function
Marginal cost increases as output rises.

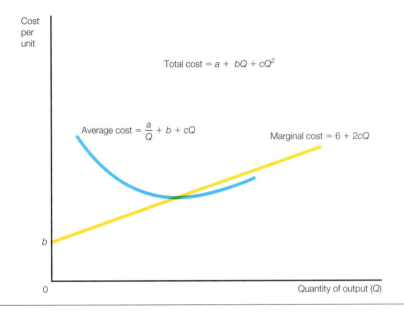

need to note that although marginal costs may vary little over a wide range of output, it is inconceivable that they do not eventually rise with increases in output. Therefore, a linear function is likely to be appropriate only for a restricted range of output.

It is also possible to assume total cost is a quadratic or cubic function of output. If the quadratic form is chosen, marginal cost increases with output, as shown in Figure 5.10. If the cubic form is chosen (and c is large enough), marginal cost first decreases then increases with output, as shown in Figure 5.11. Whether these forms are better than the linear form depends on whether they fit the data better. In many cases, they fit the data slightly better than the linear form.

Key Steps in the Estimation Process
When managers have chosen a mathematical form and decided on their data set, the following six items should be given careful thought:

1. *Definition of cost*: As we said at the beginning of this chapter, the relevant concept of cost for managers is opportunity cost, not cost based on accounting data. We must be careful to ensure that the accounting data—or engineering data, for that matter—on which an estimated cost function is based are reasonably indicative of opportunity costs. If not, adjust the data. For example, suppose his-

FIGURE 5.11

Average Cost and Marginal Cost: Cubic Total Cost Function
Marginal cost first falls then rises as output increases.

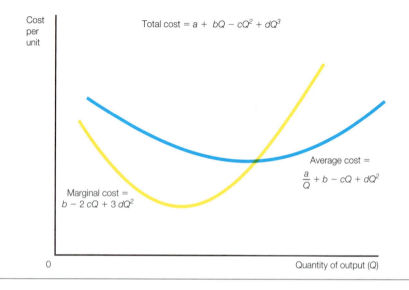

Cost per unit

Total cost = $a + bQ - cQ^2 + dQ^3$

Average cost = $\dfrac{a}{Q} + b - cQ + dQ^2$

Marginal cost = $b - 2cQ + 3dQ^2$

0

Quantity of output (Q)

torical data regarding a firm's depreciation costs are based on tax laws rather than on opportunity costs of the relevant equipment. Managers need to revise the cost data to better reflect both opportunity costs and tax conventions.

2. *Correction for price level changes*: When managers use time series data to estimate cost functions, it is important that changes over time in the input prices be recognized and measured. What managers need is a cost function based on next year's input prices if next year is the period to which the analysis pertains. Because historical data are based on input prices at various times in the past, we need a price index to allow us to adjust our historical cost data for changes in various input prices. Moreover, because various inputs may experience quite different rates of inflation, managers should construct a separate price index for each major input. Using these price indexes, managers can convert the available historical cost data into cost data reflecting next year's input prices, not those of the past.

3. *Relating cost to output*: For an estimated cost function to be reasonably accurate, it is important that cost data distinguish properly between costs that vary with output and those that do not. For many types of equipment, as well as other assets, depreciation depends on both the passage of time and the extent of use, with the result that it is difficult or impossible to determine solely from accounting data how much the depreciation cost varies with output alone. Also, some costs do not vary with output so long as output does not exceed a critical level. Above

this critical level, these costs may increase considerably. For example, up to some output level, managers need just one machine tool of a particular type; but beyond that output level they need to obtain an additional machine tool.

4. *Matching time periods*: Major errors sometimes occur because cost data do not pertain to the same time periods as output data. To see what mayhem this can cause, suppose we were to plot a firm's 2009 cost against its 2008 output. Would the resulting chart be a good estimate of the firm's cost function? Of course not. Instead managers need to relate a firm's costs in a particular period to its output in that same period. Managers need to modify this guideline in cases in which some costs of producing output in one period do not arise until subsequent periods. These delayed costs must be recognized, measured, and charged against the period in which the output occurred. For example, the costs of maintenance and repairs, when they are delayed, should be treated in this way.

5. *Controlling product, technology, and plant*: Managers need to estimate a firm's cost function on the basis of a fixed definition of the firm's product, as well as on a fixed level of technology and (for short-run cost functions) a fixed scale of plant. This means that managers should be careful to ensure that the firm's product mix does not significantly change over time. Also, the observations used in the analysis should not cover so long a period that they pertain to different levels of technology (or different scales of plant).

6. *Length of period and sample size*: Although managers should prefer a larger sample size, they cannot extend the data gathering phase too long. No simple rule

FIGURE 5.12

Relationship between Total Cost and Output, Cross Section

STRATEGY SESSION: The Value of Time and the Full Price of Transportation

Transportation economists have written for years about the full cost of using a transportation mode. It's not just the fare or the gas and parking costs but also the time spent on accessing and egressing the mode; the costs associated with unreliable transport time; safety costs; the ability to pursue other activities while being transported; and so on. Generally the most important cost component (at least for higher-income people) is travel time.

We can get a feel for this by observing what happens in markets where consumers have options. Take State Route 91 in California, for example. Toll lanes were built in the median of an existing freeway. The freeway is heavily congested and often takes two hours to drive in peak periods. In the toll lanes, however, the same trip takes a half hour. The cost? $11. So what's saving an hour and a half worth? At least $7.33/hour (that is, 11/1.5) or a rational driver wouldn't use such lanes. The lanes are continuously priced so that a "free flow" (a flow at the posted speed limit) is maintained. This is supply and demand at work. If too many cars want to use the toll lanes so that the posted speed can't be maintained, the toll is increased (and users can choose whether or not to enter the lanes if they wish). Likewise, if the toll lanes can tolerate more cars and still maintain the posted speed limit, the tolls are lowered.

If $11 seems steep, consider that such a policy encourages car pools. Cars with three or more occupants can use the toll lanes for 50 percent of the toll during evening rush hour and for free at all other times. Cars with multiple occupants can split the toll,

mitigating some of its impact. California also is pricing Interstate 15 in San Diego. The states of Washington, Virginia, and Texas are now considering toll roads. The Bush administration proposed congestion pricing in the 2007 State of the Union message. Singapore has been using congestion pricing for over 35 years, and the system was adopted two years ago in London and more recently in Stockholm. Mayor Bloomberg of New York City has recently proposed an $8 prime time weekday toll for Manhattan south of 86th Street.

But offers to save time are not limited to highways. You've perhaps experienced a long delay in an airport security line. Would you like to bypass such lines? Even if the line isn't long, you have to report to the airport early because the line might be long. In such cases you spend long times in the secure area of the airport—time you probably would rather spend elsewhere.

A firm called Verified Identity Pass will allow (for a fee of $99.95 per year) British Airways travelers to avoid the typical security wait. Certain airports (Orlando, Indianapolis, Cincinnati, and San Jose) are interested in establishing lanes where passengers have been pre-cleared and only have to verify their identity by a fingerprint or an iris scan. If you were a businessperson flying the New York–London route 10 times a year, you'd pay perhaps $10 to avoid a half-hour delay each time you flew. A weekly commuter on the same route would pay only $2 to save that half hour.

The time spent in security, the airlines' cutting service to small airports, and the fact that virtually all service between small airports is through a hub airport (with the resulting waiting time for connecting flights) is spawning another industry: an air taxi service. With the production of very light jets at the relatively low price of $1.8–$2.4 million, which can fly up to 1,200 miles nonstop and can land at over 5,000 U.S. general aviation airports (there are general aviation airports almost everywhere), several entrepreneurs are contemplating entering the air taxi service market.

Why do they believe this will be lucrative? Because of the full costs of travel via conventional carriers to and from as well as between small markets. Such a service will allow customers to fly directly from origin to destination, transforming many trips to home and back in a day rather than the current two–three day trips with their accompanying meals and hotel accommodations.

Such taxis will be easy to catch at the general aviation airports in the suburbs of big cities; but taxis may be unwilling to fly to locations where generating return fares will not be easy.

Several airlines now fly the lucrative New York–London route offering all business-class service. They are pricing this service in the $1,975 range compared with the business-class services offered by the legacy carriers, such as British Airways, Virgin Atlantic, and American Airlines, which charge around $5,925. While the legacy carriers go to London Heathrow, the new carriers go to Stansted (farther from central London). In addition, connections at Stansted are mostly with discount carriers (like Ryanair); so after transatlantic luxury, a beyond-London traveler would face minimal service.

But why wouldn't a London-destined business traveler want to save $3,950 on her fare? It's the full pricing again. British Air runs 10 round-trips per day, and Virgin offers five round-trips per day, whereas the all-business-class airlines usually offer one. Many businesspeople value the ability to go when they want to; this is called schedule delay and is measured by the difference between when the customer wants to go and when the carrier is scheduled to leave. And don't forget the legacy carriers' loyalty awards and frequent-flier miles. One can go anywhere in the world on British Air. Finally, because this service caters to business travelers, they aren't paying the bill (the company is); and a business expense is tax deductible, so the cost difference isn't as great as it initially appears.

Are there hidden full costs for nontransportation goods and services? Because most goods take time to consume and may require other expenditures (say, user assembly time and electricity and repair costs), all rational decision makers should consider the full costs of each product and service.

Sources: "Paying on the Highway to Get Out of First Gear," *The New York Times*, April 28, 2005, at www.nytimes.com/2005/04/28/natural/28tll.html; "For a Price, a Faster Way through Local Airports," *The New York Times*, December 5, 2006, at www.nytimes.com/2006/12/05/nyregion/05screen.html; "Standing on a Runway Hailing an Air Taxi," *The New York Times*, February 28, 2006, at www.nytimes.com/2006/02/28/business/28road.html; "Trans-Atlantic Luxury for Less," *The New York Times*, February 21, 2006, at www.nytimes.com/2006/02/21/business/21complete.html; and "Get Moving on Traffic Relief," *The New York Times*, May 25, 2007, at www.nytimes.com/2007/05/25opinion/25fri2.html.

can specify the best length of time. In deciding how long to wait, managers need to consider issues like the level of technology change, seasonal effects, and product changes.

Nature and Limitations of Available Data

Having chosen a mathematical form, we must select the type of data to use in estimating a cost function. One possibility is to use time series data. Another possibility is to use cross-section data and relate the total costs of a variety of firms (during the same period) to their output levels. Figure 5.12 plots the 2008 output of eight firms in a given industry against their 2008 total costs. Here, too, regression analysis can be used to estimate the relationship. A third possibility is to use engineering data to construct cost functions.

Regardless of which types of data are used, there are a number of important issues in estimating cost functions. Accounting data, which are generally the only cost data available, suffer from a number of possible deficiencies. Accountants may use arbitrary allocations of overhead and joint costs. The depreciation of an asset is determined largely by tax laws rather than economic criteria. Many inputs are valued at historical cost and do not include opportunity cost.

Engineering data also may contain possible issues. An inherent arbitrariness is involved in allocating costs jointly when producing more than one product in multiproduct firms.

PART 4

MARKET STRUCTURE AND
SIMPLE PRICING STRATEGIES

CHAPTER 6

PERFECT COMPETITION

We are at a natural point to review our path. We first looked at behavior in simple markets and the laws of supply and demand that govern them. We next focused on the supply side of the market, looking at production and cost structures. Our goal was to provide tools and understanding to help managers improve their operating efficiency. Now we want to switch to the demand side and examine managerial behavior and pricing decisions. Only after managers understand both sides of the market can they consider maximizing profit.

Our decision model, like most rational models, assumes managers want to maximize firm value. In the strictest sense this means maximizing profit, though we believe value is more than a simple financial measure. Managers can bring value to their firms by thinking about long-term reputational effects. All decisions have short- and long-term consequences; the foresight to maximize firm value is the benchmark by which managerial ability is judged.

Managers live within a constrained world. They make decisions subject to the limits imposed by technology, resources, economics, politics, and avarice. A dominant constraint in pricing decisions is the structure of the market. Market structure is important because it largely determines the potential pricing power of managers. We say potential because many managers fail to price optimally. We discuss this further when we introduce sophisticated pricing in Chapter 8.

Managers should classify markets based on their degree of pricing power. At one end is a perfectly competitive market in which managers have no market power. The other end is anchored by monopoly markets, where managers face no competition and possess plenty of market power.

We begin by examining pricing behavior in perfectly competitive markets. From a strategic view, these markets are less interesting because individual managers have no effect on price. Instead they are ruled by the "invisible hand" described by Adam Smith. Managers are price takers: They accept the decisions of the aggregate market. However, perfectly competitive markets serve as good benchmarks to evaluate any value created by managers. They also lay the groundwork for our journey through more strategically interesting markets where managers must consider and anticipate the actions of others (consumers and rivals) in setting prices.

In many markets managers operate with no market power. For example, as a small participant in a large market where the market supply and demand curves determine the price, the manager maximizes the firm's profit given the market-determined price. Other examples occur when the government sets the price (either via price controls or by virtue of being in a regulated industry) or where the firm is a follower firm in a market where a price leader sets the market price. Managers with no market power have no control over price; they are at the whim of the market.

If you find yourself in such a market, here is what you should expect. You will still face the supply-side challenges of efficient production and cost control. This is true for all managers at all times. From the demand side, managers must choose the profit-maximizing output when the price is given. In all other markets, managers can vary both output and price.

In perfectly competitive markets, managers cannot overrule the price set by the interaction of the aggregate market demand and supply curves. An individual manager cannot influence the market price. It is often suggested that the farmer is in this position. While not controlling price, the farmer does decide on quantity—that is, how much of each crop to plant. This decision must be made months before the crop comes to market. To minimize risk, a farmer may sell a crop for future delivery, but most do not. After the crop is planted, the price may change as conditions influencing demand (tastes, income) and supply (weather, crop disease) change. The farmer makes a second quantity decision at harvest time: How much of the crop to harvest. Farmers may also stop growing a crop before it matures, replow, and plant another crop because of changes in market prices. What is common in all these cases is that the farmer makes quantity decisions only, and they are based on a price over which the farmer has no control.

MARKET STRUCTURE

This situation of a price-taking producer is one of four general categories of market structure we investigate. We preview all four categories in this section, then

Perfect competition When there are many firms that are small relative to the entire market and produce similar products.

Monopolistic competition When there are many firms and consumers, just as in perfect competition; however, each firm produces a product that is slightly different from the products produced by the other firms.

Monopoly Markets with a single seller.

Oligopoly Markets with a few sellers.

spend the rest of this chapter discussing the perfect competition (price taker) category. As we pointed out in Chapter 1, a market consists of a group of firms and individuals that buy or sell some good or service. Economists have generally found it useful to classify markets into four broad types: perfect competition, monopoly, monopolistic competition, and oligopoly. In **perfect competition** and **monopolistic competition** there are many sellers, each of which produces only a small part of the industry's output. **Monopoly** markets, on the other hand, consist of only a single seller. **Oligopoly** is an intermediate case where there are a few sellers; this is the most prevalent category in present-day business. Hence American Water (which serves 16.2 million customers in 32 states and Ontario), if it is the only supplier of water in a particular market, is a monopoly. And because there are only a few automobile manufacturers, the market for automobiles is an oligopoly.

Market structures vary substantially in the extent to which managers can control price. Managers in perfectly competitive markets have no control over price. For example, a farmer producing corn has no control over the price of corn. On the other hand, a monopolist is likely to have considerable control over price. In the absence of public regulation, American Water would have considerable control over the price of water in the locations it serves. A manager operating under monopolistic competition or oligopoly is likely to have less control over price than a monopolist and more control over price than a manager in a perfectly competitive market.

These market structures also vary in the extent to which the firms in an industry produce standardized (that is, identical) products. Firms in a perfectly competitive market all produce identical products. One farmer's wheat is essentially the same as another farmer's. In a monopolistically competitive industry like shirt manufacturing, firms produce somewhat different products. One firm's shirts differ in style and quality from another firm's shirts. In an oligopoly, firms sometimes, but not always, produce identical products; for example, in steel and aluminum they do, whereas in cars, they do not. And in a monopoly there can be no difference among firms' products because the industry contains only one firm.

Barriers to entry Barriers that determine how easily firms can enter an industry, depending on the market structure.

How easily firms can enter an industry differs from one market structure to another. In perfect competition **barriers to entry** are low. For example, only a small investment is required to enter many parts of agriculture. Similarly, there are low barriers to entry in monopolistic competition. But oligopolies such as automobile manufacturing and oil refining tend to feature considerable barriers to entry: It is very expensive to build an automobile plant or an oil refinery. In a monopoly entry is blocked; if entry occurs, the monopoly no longer exists.

Market structures also differ in the extent to which managers compete on the basis of advertising, public relations, and different product characteristics, rather than price. In perfect competition there is no nonprice competition. (If every farmer produces identical corn and has to accept the market price, why devote funds to advertising?) In monopolistic competition considerable emphasis is placed on managers using nonprice competition. Much of this nonprice competition centers around the ability of managers to differentiate their products; this differentiation gives managers the power to overrule the market price. Managers of oligopolies that produce differentiated products also tend to rely heavily on nonprice competition, whereas managers of oligopolies that produce nondifferentiated products do not. For example, computer firms try to increase their sales by building better computers and by advertising, whereas steel companies do little advertising. Monopolists also engage in advertising and public relations, although these activities are directed not at capturing the sales of other firms in the industry (no other firms exist) but rather at increasing total market demand and insulating the firm from the negative connotations sometimes associated with monopoly.

Table 6.1 summarizes many key features of each market structure. Be sure to look over this table before proceeding further. This chapter discusses perfect competition. Chapter 7 covers monopoly and monopolistic competition. Chapters 8 and 9 extend the monopoly model to consider sophisticated monopoly pricing strategies. Chapter 10 considers oligopoly.

TABLE 6.1

Characteristics of Perfect Competition, Monopolistic Competition, Oligopoly, and Monopoly

Market Structure	Examples	Number of Producers	Type of Product	Power of Firm over Price	Barriers to Entry	Nonprice Competition
Perfect competition	Some sectors of agriculture	Many	Standardized	None	Low	None
Monopolistic competition	Retail trade	Many	Differentiated	Some	Low	Advertising and product differentiation
Oligopoly	Computers, oil, steel	Few	Standardized or differentiated	Some	High	Advertising and product differentiation
Monopoly	Public utilities	One	Unique product	Considerable	Very high	Advertising

---

FIGURE 6.1

Determination of Price in a Perfectly Competitive Market

Equilibrium price is $10, and equilibrium quantity is 24,000 units.

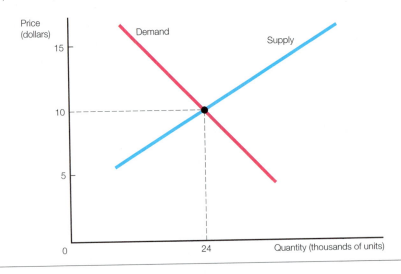

MARKET PRICE IN PERFECT COMPETITION

In a perfectly competitive industry, market price, as we saw in Chapter 1, is determined by the intersection of the market demand and supply curves. The market demand curve shows the total amount that individual buyers of the commodity will purchase at any price; the market supply curve shows the total amount that individual suppliers of the commodity will supply at any price. Figure 6.1 shows the market demand and supply curves for a good produced in a perfectly competitive market. As is ordinarily the case, the market supply curve slopes upward to the right; that is, price increases generally result in higher industry output because managers find it profitable to expand production. Also, in accord with Chapters 1 and 2, the market demand curve slopes downward to the right; that is, price increases generally result in less product being demanded.

To determine the equilibrium price, which is the price that will eventually prevail in this market, we must find the price at which market supply equals market demand.[1] The demand curve in Figure 6.1 is

$$P = 22 - 0.5Q_D \tag{6.1}$$

where P is the price (in dollars) of this good and Q_D is the quantity demanded (in thousands of units). The supply curve in Figure 6.1 is

$$P = 4 + 0.25Q_S \tag{6.2}$$

1. Recall from Chapter 1 that an equilibrium price is a price that can be maintained. If conditions do not change, the actual price tends to equal the equilibrium price.

where Q_S is the quantity supplied (in thousands of units). Because the equilibrium price is at the level where Q_D (the quantity demanded) equals Q_S (the quantity supplied),

$$P_D = 22 - 0.5Q = 4 + 0.25Q = P_S$$
$$0.75Q = 18$$
$$Q = 24$$

Substituting 24 for Q_D in equation (6.1), we find that $P = \$10$. (If we substitute 24 for Q_S in equation (6.2), we get the same result.) Therefore, as shown in Figure 6.1, price is expected to equal $10, and output is expected to equal 24,000 units.

Although Figure 6.1 shows that both total quantity demanded and total quantity supplied depend on price, this does not mean an individual manager can affect price. According to the market demand curve in equation (6.1),

$$P = 22 - 0.5Q_D$$

If 1,000 firms are in this market, each produces, on the average, only 24 units of the product. Even if an individual firm doubles its output (from 24 to 48 units), the effect on price is minuscule. Specifically, an output increase of 24 units results in a price reduction of only 1.2 cents, or about 0.1 percent.[2] This means that managers in this market essentially face a horizontal demand curve. No matter how many units one manager sells, the market price remains the same. Whereas the demand curve for the output of the entire industry slopes downward to the right (as shown in Figure 6.1), the demand curve for the output of any single firm is regarded as horizontal (at a price of $10 in this case).

SHIFTS IN SUPPLY AND DEMAND CURVES

Shifts in the market supply or demand curves result in price changes (recall Chapter 1). For example, if the supply curve in Figure 6.1 shifts to the left, the price is expected to rise. Shifts in market supply and demand curves have significant consequences for firm performance, and managers must try to anticipate them and respond as best they can.

For present purposes, managers must understand the factors affecting the supply and demand curves of the products they buy and sell. There is no need here to dwell at length on the factors causing shifts in demand curves; they have been discussed in Chapter 2. But it is worth recalling from Chapter 1 that two of the most important factors causing shifts in supply curves are technological advancements and changes in input prices. Improvements in technology tend to shift a product's supply curve to the right because they often permit managers to reduce their costs. On the other hand, increases in input prices tend to shift a product's supply curve to the left because they push up the firm's costs.

2. If output increases by 24 units, Q increases by 0.024 because Q is measured in thousands of units. If Q increases by 0.024, P falls by $0.5(0.024) = 0.012$, according to the demand curve in equation (6.1). P is measured in dollars, so this amounts to 1.2 cents.

PROBLEM SOLVED: Responding to Supply Shifts in Natural Gas

Consider the price increase in the United States for natural gas in 2003. Due to the lack of drilling activity and low inventories, natural gas prices in mid-2003 were around $6 per million British thermal units. This price was about twice the historical norm. *The Wall Street Journal*[a] reported that at one time the United States had the cheapest natural gas prices in the world. Because natural gas is the main raw material in the manufacture of many chemicals, U.S. chemical producers exported more chemicals than were imported. In 1999 the chemical industry had a foreign trade surplus of over $8 billion. Because of the increase in the price of natural gas, that trade surplus had changed to an expected deficit of $9 billion in 2003. As Greg Lebedev, a top executive of the American Chemistry Council, put it, "The competitiveness of the U.S. chemical industry is predicated on natural gas pricing. It is an absolute sea of change."

Managers took several actions to counteract the increase in the price of natural gas due to decreases in its supply. Many chemical-producing plants were shut down. Analysts estimated that over a dozen large chemical plants in the United States were closed in 2003. Managers also tried to recoup some of their additional costs by passing them on to buyers. For example, in the choline chloride market (also dependent on natural gas for production), prices increased 75 percent. Prices also increased in the methanol, caustic soda, and titanium dioxide markets. Finally, some production was moved to countries where natural gas was cheaper. For example, in 2003 the price of natural gas in Saudi Arabia was around $1 per million British thermal units.

[a]T. Herrick, "Natural Gas Cooks Chemical Sector—Rising Prices Force Firms to Cut Jobs, Shut Plants as Output Moves Abroad," *The Wall Street Journal*, June 18, 2003, p. A2.

THE OUTPUT DECISION OF A PERFECTLY COMPETITIVE FIRM

How much output should managers at a perfectly competitive firm produce? As we discussed previously, managers in a perfectly competitive firm cannot affect the market price of their product, and they must sell any output (within their capabilities) at the market price. To illustrate the manager's situation, consider the example in Table 6.2. The market price is $10 per unit, and the manager can produce as much as she chooses. Hence the firm's total revenue at various output rates is given in column 3 of Table 6.2. The firm's total fixed cost (1), total variable cost ($2Q + Q^2$), and total cost ($1 + 2Q + Q^2$) are given in columns 4, 5, and 6 of Table 6.2. Finally, the last column shows the firm's total profit.

Figure 6.2 shows the relationship between total revenue and cost and output. The vertical distance between the total revenue and total cost curves is the profit at the corresponding output. Below one unit of output and above seven units of output, this distance is negative. Because the manager can sell either large or small volumes of output at the same price per unit, the total revenue curve is a straight line through the origin with a slope equal to the fixed price. (Specifically, $TR = P^*Q$; because the price is constant, total revenue is proportional to quantity.)

TABLE 6.2

Cost and Revenues of a Perfectly Competitive Firm

Units of Output Period	Price (Dollars)	Total Revenue (Dollars)	Total Fixed Costs (Dollars)	Total Variable Costs (Dollars)	Total Cost (Dollars)	Total Profit (Dollars)
0	10	0	1	0	1	−1
1	10	10	1	3	4	6
2	10	20	1	8	9	11
3	10	30	1	15	16	14
4	10	40	1	24	25	15
5	10	50	1	35	36	14
6	10	60	1	48	49	11
7	10	70	1	63	64	6
8	10	80	1	80	81	−1
9	10	90	1	99	100	−10

FIGURE 6.2

Relationship between Total Cost and Total Revenue of a Perfectly Competitive Firm

The output rate that would maximize the firm's profit is four units per time period. The profit (total revenue minus total cost) equals $15.

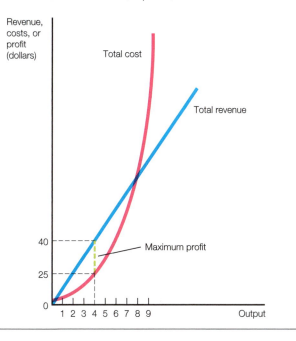

Because a manager in a perfectly competitive firm takes the price as given, the slope of the total revenue is always the market price.

The firm's profit (π) is expressed as total revenue (TR) minus total cost (TC):

$$\pi = TR - TC$$

It follows that

$$\frac{\Delta\pi}{\Delta Q} = \frac{\Delta TR}{\Delta Q} - \frac{\Delta TC}{\Delta Q}$$

If

$$\frac{\Delta\pi}{\Delta Q} = 0$$

then

$$\frac{\Delta TR}{\Delta Q} - \frac{\Delta TC}{\Delta Q} = 0$$

so

$$\frac{\Delta TR}{\Delta Q} = \frac{\Delta TC}{\Delta Q}$$

QUANT OPTION

$$\pi = TR - TC$$

$$\frac{d\pi}{dQ} = \frac{dTR}{dQ} - \frac{dTC}{dQ}$$

To maximize profit,

$$0 = \frac{dTR}{dQ} - \frac{dTC}{dQ}$$

so

$$\frac{dTR}{dQ} = \frac{dTC}{dQ}$$

or

$$MR = MC$$

Here $\Delta TR/\Delta Q$ is the firm's marginal revenue. It represents a change in total revenue when the output changes by a small amount (usually $\Delta Q = 1$). The firm's total revenue is price times quantity or PQ. Therefore, marginal revenue is $\Delta TR/\Delta Q = P$. So the firm's marginal revenue is the product's price. This is not surprising. If the firm sells five units, its total revenue is $5P$; if it sells six units, its total revenue is $6P$; if it sells seven units, its total revenue is $7P$; and so on. Every time another unit is sold, total revenue rises by P. In this case $P = \$10$, so the firm's marginal revenue (always equal to price for a price taker) is $\$10$.

Consider the firm's total cost ($TC = 1 + 2Q + Q^2$). Therefore, $\Delta TC/\Delta Q = 2 + 2Q$, and $\Delta TC/\Delta Q$ is called the firm's marginal cost. It represents a change in the total cost (or variable cost) when output changes by a small amount (usually by $\Delta Q = 1$).

The condition $\Delta TR/\Delta Q = \Delta TC/\Delta Q$ is restated as $MR = MC$; that is, to maximize profit, the manager must set marginal revenue equal to marginal cost (if marginal cost is increasing). In the case of a price taker, the profit-maximizing condition reads $P = MC$ (because $P = MR$). This is why managers want to avoid these markets: The nature of competition is to grind the price down to marginal cost. The competitive pressure is relentless. There is no above-normal economic profit, nor should managers expect any (except in the short run). Clearly managers should never produce output where the marginal cost is greater than the marginal revenue. Hence

$$P = 10 = 2 + 2Q = MC \text{ or } Q = 4 \tag{6.3}$$

Table 6.2, Figures 6.2 and 6.3, and equation (6.3) show that managers maximize the firm's profit at four units per time period. At this output level, the profit figure in the last column of Table 6.2 is the highest; the vertical distance between the total revenue and cost curves in Figure 6.2 is the largest; and the profit curve in Figure 6.3 is the highest.

It is worthwhile to present the marginal revenue and marginal cost curves as well as the total revenue and total cost curves. Table 6.3 shows the firm's marginal revenue and marginal costs at each output rate.

QUANT OPTION

Of course the marginal revenue of the firm is $dTR/dQ = P$ because Q is not a function of P. The marginal cost is

$$dTC/dQ = 2 + 2Q$$

FIGURE 6.3

Relationship of Profit and Output of a Perfectly Competitive Firm

The output rate that maximizes profit is four units per time period. To maximize profit, the slope of the profit function ($\Delta\pi/\Delta Q$) must be zero.

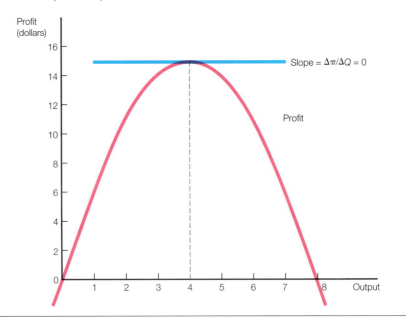

Figure 6.4 shows the resulting marginal revenue and marginal cost at each output rate. Because the manager takes the price as given, it is constant for all output levels ($P = MR$). Hence the marginal revenue curve is also the firm's demand curve, which (for the reasons discussed already) is horizontal.

The central point to note is that managers maximize profit at the output where the price (or marginal revenue) equals the marginal cost. Both the numbers in Table 6.3 and the curves in Figure 6.4 indicate that the price equals the marginal cost at an output rate of four units, which we know from Table 6.2, Figures 6.2 and 6.3, and equation (6.3) to be the profit-maximizing output.

3. Recall from Chapter 5 that in the short run, $MC = W/MP$, where W is the fixed wage of labor and MP is the marginal product of labor. Therefore, if the marginal cost is increasing, the marginal product of labor must be decreasing. A price-taking situation, therefore, implies diminishing marginal productivity of labor in the short run.

SETTING THE MARGINAL COST EQUAL TO THE PRICE

Earlier we showed that if managers want to maximize firm value, they should set price equal to marginal cost when marginal cost is increasing. As we can see in Table 6.3 and Figure 6.4, this is true.[3]

TABLE 6.3

Marginal Revenue and Marginal Cost: Perfectly Competitive Firm

Output per Period	Marginal Revenue	Marginal Cost[a]
0	10	2
1	10	4
2	10	6
3	10	8
4	10	10
5	10	12
6	10	14
7	10	16
8	10	18

[a]This column was calculated from $MC = 2 + 2Q$. This assumes that output can be sold and produced in noninteger, continuous amounts. Many goods meet this criteria—for example, gasoline, deli meats, and bulk agricultural products. Although these goods are priced on a per-unit basis (by the gallon, per pound), seldom do we purchase integer units. Other goods are produced and consumed only in integer units, such as cars, televisions, and compact disks. In this case, the marginal cost for output level n is calculated as the total cost at output level n minus the total cost for output level $n - 1$. For instance, the total cost at $Q = 3$ is 16, at $Q = 4$ is 25, at $Q = 5$ is 36 (see Table 6.2). Therefore, the marginal cost at $Q = 4$ is 9 and at $Q = 5$ is 11 (as opposed to 10 and 12 shown in this table). Under these conditions, the manager wants to produce the fourth unit because the marginal revenue from doing so ($10) exceeds the marginal cost ($9). However, the manager would not produce the fifth unit because the marginal cost of doing so ($11) exceeds the marginal revenue ($10). Therefore, the manager produces four units in the integer output case and in the continuous output case.

Managers in perfectly competitive markets often accrue negative profits, even if they satisfy the preceding rules ($P = MC$ and MC increasing). If the price is P_2 in Figure 6.5, the short-run average total cost exceeds the price at all possible outputs. Because the short run is too short (by definition) to permit the manager to alter the scale of plant, all she can do is to produce at a loss or discontinue production. The decision to close a plant should answer one question: Does the product's price cover the average variable costs? For any output where price exceeds average variable costs, managers should produce, even though the price does not cover average total costs. If there is no output rate at which price exceeds the average variable cost, the manager is better off shutting the plant. Hence if the average variable cost curve is as shown in Figure 6.5, the manager will produce if the price is P_2 but not if it is P_1.

It is essential to recognize that if managers shut a plant, they still incur fixed costs. Therefore, if the loss from producing is less than the firm's fixed costs (the

FIGURE 6.4

Marginal Revenue and Marginal Cost of a Perfectly Competitive Firm

When output is at the profit maximizing level of four units, price (= marginal revenue) equals marginal cost.

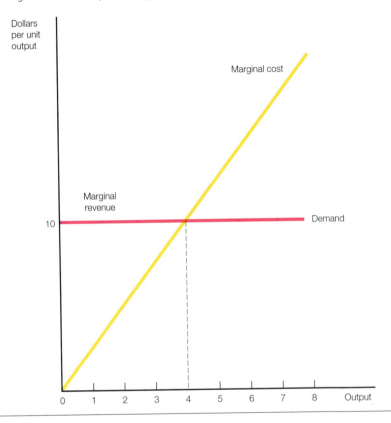

loss of shutting down), it is more profitable (a smaller deficit) to produce than to discontinue production. Another way of expressing this is if the loss per unit of output is less than the average fixed cost—that is, if $ATC - P < AFC$, where ATC is average total cost, P is price, and AFC is average fixed cost. This is true if $ATC < AFC + P$ because P is merely added to both sides of the inequality. Subtracting AFC from both sides results in $ATC - AFC < P$. $ATC - AFC$ is the average variable cost; thus it is better to produce than to shut down production if the price exceeds the average variable cost.

Managers must manage the cash flow they control, which is total revenue (because managers control the Q of $P*Q$). They must also manage variable cost because it is a function of Q. But the fixed cost is not part of controllable short-run

FIGURE 6.5

Short-Run Average and Marginal Cost Curves

If the price is P_0, the firm will produce an output of X; if price is P_2, it will produce an output of Y; and if price is less than P_3 (that is, when P_3 equals the minimum of average variable cost), the firm will produce nothing.

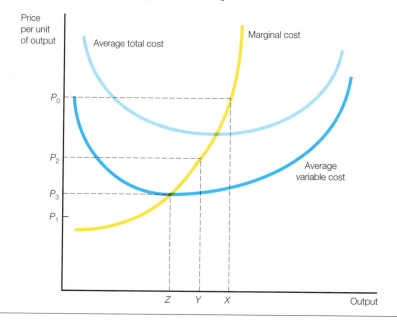

cash flow. Thus managers want TR to exceed VC by as much as possible—that is, maximizing the controllable cash flow. If VC exceeds TR, you shouldn't produce because your controllable cash flow is negative. If TR exceeds VC, you should produce because your controllable cash flow is positive. Dividing both sides in the preceding sentence by Q yields $TR/Q = P > VC/Q = AVC$. Thus in addition to $P = MC$, P must exceed AVC.

The manager will be indifferent at P_3, the price that is equal to the minimum point of average costs (output Z). The point (Z, P_3) is called the **shutdown point** because at that point, the price equals the minimum average variable cost. Price is also equal to marginal cost because it intersects with average variable cost at this point. The future is clear: At this price, the manager loses money equal to fixed cost if he produces, or he loses that money if he shuts down. At any price below P_3, the manager shuts the plant. Therefore, the marginal cost curve (above the minimum average variable cost) is the supply curve of the firm; that is, if the price is P_2, the firm produces Y, and if the price is P_0, the firm produces X. These points (Y, P_2) and (X, P_0) are also points on the firm's marginal cost curve.

Shutdown point When the price equals the minimum average variable cost.

STRATEGY SESSION: Forecasting the Price of Salmon

Managers at a large diversified food firm set out to forecast the price of fresh salmon three years ahead. Such a forecast is needed because these managers must decide whether they should enter the business of supplying salmon. The firm's analysts estimate the quantity of fresh salmon to be supplied three years ahead. Because of substantial plans to expand the production of farmed Atlantic and Pacific salmon in Canada, Chile, Japan, and Ireland, this projected supply is considerably greater than the actual current supply. In addition, the analysts estimate the quantity of fresh salmon that is demanded three years ahead. Their results show that if the price of salmon remains unchanged over the next three years, the quantity supplied will exceed the quantity demanded by about 15 percent at the end of the three-year period.

The firm's analysts also estimate the price elasticity of demand for fresh salmon to be about −1.5. This estimate, too, is based on the techniques described in previous chapters. Like the other estimates presented here, it is regarded as rough but useful.

Before they can determine whether to enter the salmon market, managers need to estimate the future price of salmon. (The firm's analysts believed that the quantity supplied three years hence will be approximately equal to their estimates, regardless of whatever changes occur in price during this three-year period.) Using the previous estimates, they envision that the quantity demanded will increase by 15 percent to reduce the gap between quantity supplied and quantity demanded. Because they estimate that the price elasticity of salmon is −1.5, a 10 percent decrease in price will increase the quantity demanded by about 15 percent.

This section is based on an actual case, although the numbers and situation have been disguised somewhat.

PROBLEM SOLVED: The Kadda Company

As an illustration, consider the Kadda Company, a perfectly competitive firm with the following total cost function:

$$TC = 800 + 6Q + 2Q^2$$

where TC is the total cost (in dollars) and Q is the firm's output per day. The firm's marginal cost is therefore

$$\Delta TC/\Delta Q = MC = 6 + 4Q$$

If the price of Kadda's product equals $30, the manager should set output so that

$$MC = \Delta TC/\Delta Q = 6 + 4Q = 30 = P \qquad (6.4)$$

In other words, the manager should set marginal cost equal to price ($30). Solving equation (6.4) for Q, we find the manager should set output equal to six units per day. To make sure the price is not less than average variable cost at that output, we note that because the firm's total variable cost equals $6Q + 2Q^2$, its average variable cost (AVC) equals

$$AVC = (6Q + 2Q^2)/Q = 6 + 2Q$$

Therefore, if $Q = 6$, average variable cost equals $6 + 2(6)$ or $18, which is less than the price of $30.

QUANT OPTION

Kadda's marginal cost is

$$dTC/dQ = MC = 6 + 4Q$$

QUANT OPTION

For a maximum to occur, the sign of the second derivative of the profit function must be negative:

$$\frac{d^2\pi}{dQ^2} = d\left(\frac{\frac{d\pi}{dQ}}{dQ}\right)$$

$$= d\left(\frac{\frac{dTR}{dQ}}{dQ}\right) - d\left(\frac{\frac{dTC}{dQ}}{dQ}\right)$$

$$= \frac{dMR}{dQ} - \frac{dMC}{dQ} < 0$$

Because $MR = P$ and doesn't change as Q changes,

$$\frac{dMR}{dQ} = 0$$

Thus dMC/dQ must be positive because it has a negative sign in front of it and the whole equation must be negative.

To summarize, if the manager maximizes profit or minimizes loss, the output is set so the short-run marginal cost equals the price and the marginal cost is rising. But this proposition has an exception: If the market price is below the firm's average variable costs at every output level, the manager minimizes loss by discontinuing production.

ANOTHER WAY OF VIEWING THE PRICE EQUALS MARGINAL COST PROFIT-MAXIMIZING RULE

If a firm has one fixed input (say capital) and one variable input (say labor), how much of its variable input should it utilize? This is an important question for managers of firms large and small. To answer it, we must define the marginal revenue product of the variable input and the marginal expenditure of the variable input.

Marginal revenue product (MRP) The amount an additional unit of the variable input adds to the firm's total revenue.

The **marginal revenue product** (MRP) is the amount an additional unit of the variable input adds to the firm's total revenue. The input adds to total revenue because it allows managers to produce more output. Letting MRP_L be the marginal revenue product of the labor input,

$$MRP_L = \Delta TR/\Delta L \tag{6.5}$$

where ΔTR is the change in total revenue resulting from a change of ΔL in the amount of labor input used by the firm. It can easily be proven that MRP_L equals labor's marginal product times the firm's marginal revenue. To see this, note that marginal revenue (MR) equals $\Delta TR/\Delta Q$, where ΔQ is the change in the firm's output, and that

$$MRP_L = \Delta TR/\Delta L = (\Delta TR/\Delta Q)(\Delta Q/\Delta L)$$

Because $\Delta Q/\Delta L$ equals labor's marginal product (MP_L), it follows that

$$MRP_L = (MR)(MP_L) \tag{6.6}$$

which is what we set out to prove. Let's view the intuition. If managers use ΔL more labor, they produce ΔQ more units of the firm's product—that is, the marginal product of labor. If managers take these additional ΔQ units to market, they will generate ΔTR in revenue (marginal revenue). The marginal revenue per unit times the number of units gives the additional revenue obtained by managers as the result of using an additional unit of labor.

The **marginal expenditure** (ME) is the amount an additional unit of labor adds to the firm's total costs. That is, letting ME_L be the marginal expenditure on labor,

$$ME_L = \Delta TC/\Delta L \tag{6.7}$$

where ΔTC is the change in total cost resulting from a change of ΔL in the amount of labor. If managers can buy all the labor they want at the price of $10 per unit, ME_L equals $10. In some cases, however, managers must pay a higher price for labor to get more of it; in such cases, ME_L exceeds the price of labor (as we will show in the monopsony section of Chapter 7). Note that $\Delta TC/\Delta L$ can be written as $(\Delta TC/\Delta Q)(\Delta Q/\Delta L)$, where $\Delta TC/\Delta Q$ is the change in the firm's total cost (ΔTC) divided by the firm's change in output (ΔQ). $\Delta TC/\Delta Q$ is the firm's marginal cost (MC), or the change in the firm's total cost as its output is changed by a small amount.

QUANT OPTION

In more technical terms,

$$MRP_L = dTR/dL$$

and

$$ME_L = dTC/dL$$

To maximize profit, managers should use labor where its marginal revenue product equals its marginal expenditure. In other words, managers should set

$$MRP_L = ME_L \qquad (6.8)$$

Again, let's view the intuition. To maximize profit, managers need to expand any activity as long as the marginal benefit exceeds the marginal cost. They should stop expanding it when the marginal benefit (in this case MRP_L) equals the marginal cost (in this case ME_L). To generalize this further, rewrite equation (6.8) as

$$\left(\frac{\Delta TR}{\Delta Q} \right)\left(\frac{\Delta Q}{\Delta L} \right) = \left(\frac{\Delta TC}{\Delta Q} \right)\left(\frac{\Delta Q}{\Delta L} \right)$$

or

$$\frac{\Delta TR}{\Delta Q} = \frac{\Delta TC}{\Delta Q}$$

or

$$MR = MC$$

We have again verified one of the most important rules of managerial economics: Managers should stop expanding output when marginal revenue equals marginal cost.

In the case of perfect competition, $MR = P$. So our rule becomes $P \times MP_L = ME_L = P_L$, where P_L is the price of a unit of labor. Consider the intuition once again. Hiring another unit of labor costs managers P_L. That laborer generates MP_L additional output, which, when managers take it to market, generates $P \times MP_L$ additional revenue for the firm. Managers should continue to hire more labor as long as $P \times MP_L > P_L$, and they won't hire labor if $P \times MP_L < P_L$. The stopping rule to maximize profit is $P \times MP_L = P_L$. Dividing both sides by MP_L gives $P = P_L/MP_L$. As was shown in Chapter 5, $P_L/MP_L = MC$. Thus to maximize profit in the perfectly competitive market, managers should expand production until $P = MC$.

PRODUCER SURPLUS IN THE SHORT RUN

Producer surplus The difference between the market price and the price the producer is willing to receive for a good or service (the producer's reservation price).

In Chapter 3 we examined consumer surplus and saw that it equals the difference between the market price and the price consumers are willing to pay (their reservation price). Now we introduce a parallel idea, called producer surplus, from the supply side of the market. **Producer surplus** is the difference between the market price and the price the producer is willing to receive for a good or service (the producer's reservation price). As we showed in our analysis of a perfectly competitive market, a producer's reservation price is the marginal cost of producing a good or service (above the break-even point of the firm). Panel A of Figure 6.6 shows this surplus in the shaded area. The firm's profit before accounting for fixed cost (its variable cost profit = $P^*BC'D' = P^*BE$) is just total revenue (P^*Q^*) minus variable cost ($D'C'Q^*O$). But the variable cost is also just the area under the marginal cost up to output Q^*; that is, EBQ^*O. This variable-cost profit is also the shaded area in Panel A of Figure 6.6; that is, P^*BE. Note the difference between profit (P^*BCD) and producer surplus. To arrive at a producer surplus, managers subtract only the variable cost from the total revenue, whereas to calculate their profit, they subtract both the fixed and variable costs from total revenue. Hence the variable-cost profit is larger than profit (by the level of fixed cost), and producer surplus and variable-cost profit are the same. Because the perfectly competitive firm's marginal cost represents its supply curve, we can view producer surplus as the difference between the supply curve and the price received for the good (area b in Panel B of Figure 6.6).

Figure 6.7 shows the market equilibrium. Just as market demand is the horizontal summation of individuals' demand curves for the product, market supply is the horizontal summation of individual firms' supply curves for the product. Using the results for consumer surplus, we can see from Figure 6.7 that the market equilibrium price of P^* yields a consumer surplus of A and a producer surplus of B.

The sum of A and B, the total surplus, is the economist's measure of social welfare at the price P^* and the quantity Q^*. To understand this idea, think about the total benefit and cost that consumers and producers assign to the goods in the market. For consumers, this is the area beneath the demand curve, left of the equilibrium quantity—that is, the total amount consumers are willing to pay for the goods (areas A, B, and C in Figure 6.7). For producers, the total variable cost of supplying quantity Q^* is the area beneath the supply curve and left of the equilibrium quantity (area C in Figure 6.7). In the market consumers pay and producers receive P^*. Yet P^* is less than the total benefit and greater than the variable cost of the goods. In this sense the market exchange generates value for participants, represented by consumer, producer, and total surplus. In this case the difference between what the demanders are willing to spend (A, B, and C) and what the suppliers are willing to receive (C) is the measure of social welfare—that is, $A + B$.

FIGURE 6.6

Producer Surplus and Variable-Cost Profit

Producer surplus for the firm is its variable-cost profit, or total revenue minus variable cost. Producer surplus for the market is the area above the supply curve but below the price received for the good because the supply curve is the horizontal summation of the competitive firms' marginal cost curves.

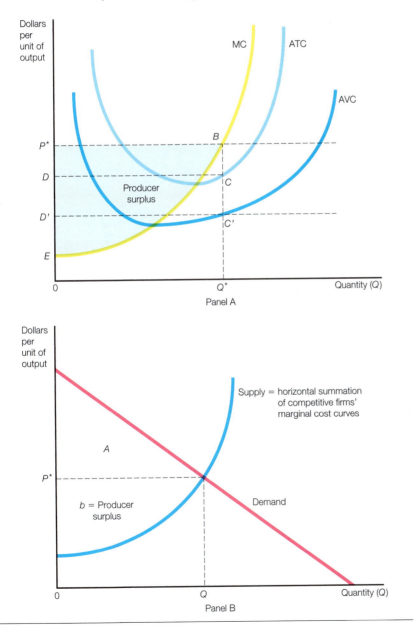

FIGURE 6.7

Market Social Welfare (A + B) of a Perfectly Competitive Price Policy, P*

Social welfare at a given price (P*) is measured by the sum of the consumer surplus (A) and the producer surplus (B).

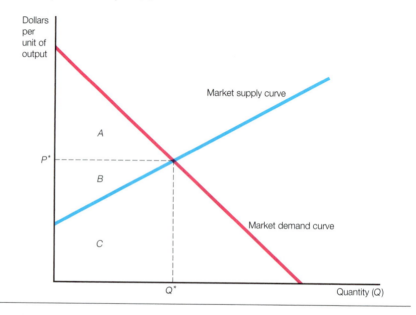

Clearly the magnitude of the total surplus and its distribution between consumers and producers depend on the shape of the demand and supply curves. For instance, keeping the equilibrium at P*, Q*, a more gently sloped supply curve reduces producer surplus, whereas a more gently sloped demand curve reduces consumer surplus. But the thing to remember is that market exchanges, generally speaking, provide opportunities for gains; and as we see later, savvy managers can devise ways to capture a greater share of those gains for their firms.

We use this measure of social welfare to show the rationale of antitrust policy and the gains from trade in Chapter 16.

LONG-RUN EQUILIBRIUM OF THE FIRM

In the long run, how much will managers of a competitive firm produce? The long-run equilibrium position of the firm is at the point where its long-run average total cost curve[4] equals the price. If the price exceeeds the average total cost, economic profit is earned and new firms enter the industry. This increases supply, thereby driving down price and hence profit. If the price is less than the average total costs for any firm, that firm will exit the industry. As firms exit, supply falls,

4. This is also called the *long-run average cost curve.* Because all costs are variable in the long run, there is no need for an adjective in front of average costs, as there is in the short run, to distinguish between average total, average variable, and average fixed costs. There are only average costs in the long run.

causing price and profit to rise. Only when economic profit is zero (which means that long-run average cost equals price) is a firm in long-run equilibrium.

Recall from Chapter 1 that economic profit is not the same as accounting profit. Economic profit is profit above and beyond what the owners could obtain elsewhere from the resources they invest in the firm. Therefore, long-run equilibrium occurs when the owners receive no more (and no less) than they could obtain elsewhere from these resources.

More specifically, the price must equal the *lowest value* of the long-run average total cost. That is, in equilibrium managers produce at the minimum point on their long-run average cost curves. To see why, note that if managers maximize their profit, they must operate where price equals long-run marginal cost. Also, we just saw that they must operate where price equals long-run average cost. If both of these conditions are satisfied, it follows that long-run marginal cost must equal long-run average cost. And we know from Chapter 5 that long-run marginal cost is equal to long-run average cost only at the point at which long-run average cost is a minimum. Consequently this point is the equilibrium position of the firm.

To illustrate this equilibrium position, consider Figure 6.8. When all the adjustments are made, price equals G. Because price is constant, the demand curve is horizontal, and therefore the marginal revenue curve is the same as the demand curve, both being GG'. The equilibrium output of the firm is V, and its optimally sized plant is described by the short-run average and marginal cost curves AA' and MM'. At this output and with this plant, we see that long-run marginal cost

FIGURE 6.8

Long-Run Equilibrium of a Perfectly Competitive Firm

In long-run equilibrium, the firm produces an output of V, and price = marginal cost (both long-run and short-run) = average cost (both long-run and short-run).

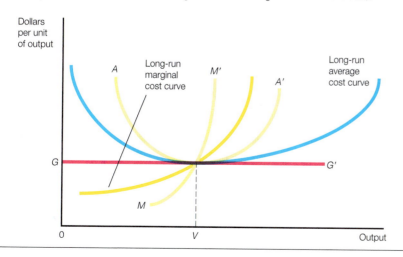

PROBLEM SOLVED: Output at the Bergey Company

For example, suppose the Bergey Company's long-run average cost curve is

$$AC = 200 - 4Q + 0.05Q^2 \qquad (6.9)$$

where AC is long-run average cost (in dollars) and Q is the firm's output per day. Because the Bergey Company operates in a perfectly competitive market, its output in the long run equals the value of Q that minimizes AC. Note from Figure 6.8 that the slope of the long-run average total cost curve when it is a minimum is $\Delta AC/\Delta Q = 0$; that is, GG' is tangent to AC at the output level V in Figure 6.8.

Forming $\Delta AC/\Delta Q$ from equation (6.9) and setting it $= 0$ gives $Q = 40$. Therefore, if managers at Bergey maximize profit, in the long run they will maintain an output of 40 units per day.

As indicated previously, the average cost equals the marginal cost at this output. To see this, note that because total cost equals Q times AC,

$$TC = Q(200 - 4Q + 0.05Q^2)$$
$$= 200Q - 4Q^2 + 0.05Q^3$$

where TC is total cost.

The firm's marginal cost is $MC = \Delta TC/\Delta Q$. Therefore, $MC = \Delta TC/\Delta Q = 200 - 8Q + 0.15Q^2$. Because $Q = 40$,

$$MC = 200 - 8(40) + 0.15(40)^2 = 120$$

Also, inserting 40 for Q in equation (6.9),

$$AC = 200 - 4(40) + 0.05(40)^2 = 120$$

Therefore, marginal cost equals average cost when $Q = 40$. (Both marginal cost and average cost equal $120. This means that the long-run equilibrium price is $120.)

equals short-run marginal cost equals price. This ensures that the manager maximizes profit. Also, long-run average cost equals the short-run average cost equals price; this ensures that economic profit is zero. Because long-run marginal cost and long-run average cost must be equal, the equilibrium point is at the bottom of the long-run average cost curve.

THE LONG-RUN ADJUSTMENT PROCESS: A CONSTANT-COST INDUSTRY

Having looked at the behavior of managers at a perfectly competitive firm in the short and long runs, we turn to the long-run adjustment process of a perfectly competitive industry. We assume that this industry is a *constant-cost industry*, which means that expansion of the industry does not increase input prices. Figure 6.9 shows long-run equilibrium under conditions of constant cost. The top panel shows the short-run and long-run cost curves of a typical firm in the industry. The bottom panel shows the demand and supply curves in the market as a whole, D being the original demand curve and S the original short-run supply curve. We assume the industry is in long-run equilibrium, with the result that the price ($6 per unit) equals the minimum value of the long-run (and short-run) average cost.

FIGURE 6.9

Long-Run Equilibrium in a Constant-Cost Industry

A constant-cost industry has a horizontal long-run supply curve, as shown in panel B. If demand shifts upward from D to D_1, the consequent increase in price (to $7 per unit) results in the entry of firms, which shifts the supply curve to the right (to S_1), thus pushing the price back to its original level ($6 per unit).

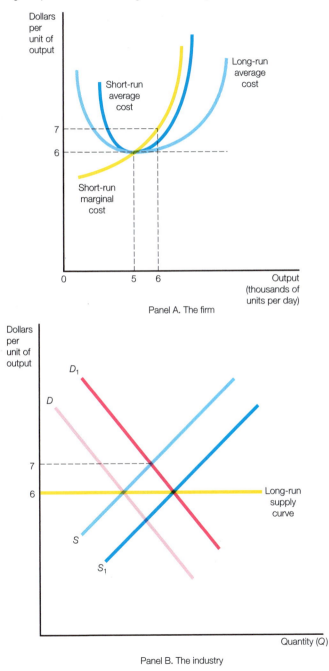

Panel A. The firm

Panel B. The industry

Suppose now that the demand curve shifts to D_1. In the short run, with the number of firms fixed, the product price rises from $6 to $7 per unit; each firm expands its output from 5,000 to 6,000 units per day; and each firm makes economic profit because the new price, $7, exceeds the short-run average costs of the firm when the output is 6,000 units per day. The result is that firms enter the industry and the supply curve shifts to the right. In a constant-cost industry, entrance of new firms does not influence the costs of existing firms. The inputs used by this industry are used by other industries as well, and new firms in this industry do not bid up the price of inputs and hence raise the costs of existing firms. Neither does the entry of new firms reduce existing firms' costs.

Hence a constant-cost industry has a horizontal long-run supply curve. Because output can be increased by increasing the number of firms producing 5,000 units of output per day at an average cost of $6 per unit, the long-run supply curve is horizontal at $6 per unit. So long as the industry remains in a state of constant costs, its output can be increased indefinitely. If price exceeds $6 per unit, firms enter the industry; if price is less than $6 per unit, firms leave the industry. Therefore long-run equilibrium can occur in this industry only when price is $6 per unit. And industry output can be raised or lowered, in accord with demand conditions, without changing this long-run equilibrium price.

THE LONG-RUN ADJUSTMENT PROCESS: AN INCREASING-COST INDUSTRY

Not all industries are constant-cost industries. Next we consider the case of an *increasing-cost industry*, which occurs when industry expansion increases input prices.[5] An increasing-cost industry is shown in Figure 6.10. The original conditions are the same as in Figure 6.9: In panel B, D is the original demand curve, S is the original supply curve, $6 per unit is the equilibrium price, and LL' and AA' in the top panel are the long-run and short-run average cost curves of each firm. As in Figure 6.9, the original position is one of long-run equilibrium because price equals the minimum value of long-run (and short-run) average cost.

Assume now that the demand curve shifts to D_1, with the result that the product price goes up and the firms earn economic profit, attracting new entrants. More and more inputs are needed by the industry, and in an increasing-cost industry, the prices of the inputs rise with the amount used by the industry. Therefore, the cost of inputs increases for established firms as well as entrants, and the average cost curves are pushed up to $L_1L'_1$ and $A_1A'_1$.

If each firm's marginal cost curve is shifted to the left by the increase in input prices, the industry supply curve tends to shift to the left. But this tendency is more than counterbalanced by the increase in the number of firms, which shifts the industry supply curve to the right. The latter effect *must* more than offset the former effect because otherwise there would be no expansion in total industry

5. In addition to constant-cost and increasing-cost industries, there are also decreasing-cost industries, which are the most unusual case, although quite young industries may fall into the category. External economies, which are cost reductions that occur when an industry expands, may be responsible for the existence of decreasing-cost industries. For example, the expansion of an industry may improve transportation and reduce the costs of each firm in the industry. A decreasing-cost industry has a negatively sloped long-run supply curve.

FIGURE 6.10

Long-Run Equilibrium in an Increasing-Cost Industry

An increasing-cost industry has a positively sloped long-run supply curve, as shown in panel *B*. After long-run equilibrium is achieved, increases in output require increases in the price of the product.

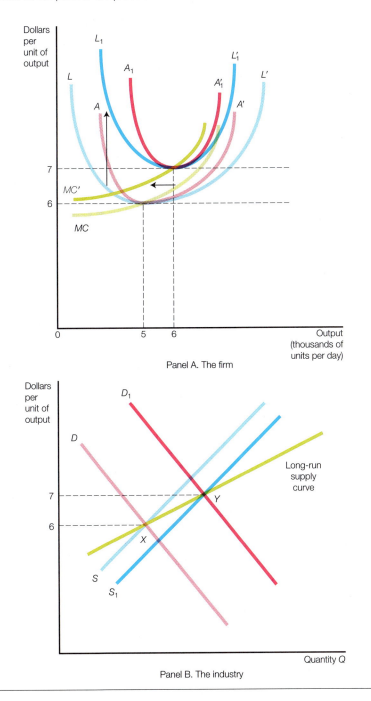

Panel A. The firm

Panel B. The industry

output. (No new resources would be attracted to the industry.) This process of adjustment must go on until a new point of long-run equilibrium is reached. In Figure 6.10 this point is where the price of the product is $7 per unit and each firm produces 6,000 units per day.[6]

An increasing-cost industry has a positively sloped long-run supply curve. That is, after long-run equilibrium is achieved, increases in output require increases in the price of the product. For example, points X and Y in Figure 6.10 are on the long-run supply curve for the industry. The difference between constant-cost and increasing-cost industries is this: In constant-cost industries, new firms enter in response to an increase in demand until the price returns to its original level; whereas in increasing-cost industries, new firms enter until the minimum point on the long-run average cost curve has increased to the point where it equals the new, higher price.[7]

Finally, some industries are neither constant-cost nor increasing-cost industries: They are decreasing-cost industries. Their long-run supply curves are negatively sloped. For further discussion of these industries, which are encountered less frequently than constant-cost or increasing-cost industries, see footnote 5.

HOW A PERFECTLY COMPETITIVE ECONOMY ALLOCATES RESOURCES

It is important for managers to understand how a competitive economy allocates resources. Without such an understanding, they cannot interpret or anticipate the fundamental changes that may occur. To illustrate this allocation process, we take a simple case: Consumers become more favorably disposed toward corn and less favorably disposed toward rice than in the past. What happens in the short run? The rising demand for corn increases its price and results in some increase in the output of corn. However, corn output cannot be increased substantially because the capacity of the industry cannot be expanded in the short run. Similarly, the falling demand for rice reduces its price and results in some reduction in the output of rice. But the output of rice cannot be curtailed greatly because firms continue to produce as long as they can cover their variable costs. Because of the increased price of corn and the decreased price of rice, corn producers earn economic profit and rice producers show economic loss. Producers reallocate resources to correct this imbalance.

When short-run equilibrium is achieved in both the corn and rice industries, the reallocation of resources is not yet complete because there has not been enough time for producers to build new capacity or liquidate old capacity. In particular, neither industry operates at minimum average cost. The corn producers may operate at greater than the output level where average cost is a minimum; and

6. We cannot be sure that the firm's new output exceeds its old output as shown in Figure 6.10. It is possible for its new output to be less than or equal to its old output.

7. This is not the only way in which equilibrium can be achieved in increasing-cost industries. It is also possible that the increase in input prices (due to the expansion of industry output) raises average cost more than the increase in demand raises average revenue. Therefore, firms may experience losses, some may leave the industry, and the remaining firms may produce more.

the rice producers may operate at less than the output level where average cost is a minimum.

What occurs in the long run? The shift in consumer demand from rice to corn results in greater adjustments in output and smaller adjustments in price than in the short run. In the long run, existing firms can leave rice production and new firms can enter corn production. As firms leave rice production, the supply curve shifts to the left, causing the price to rise above its short-run level. The transfer of resources out of rice production ceases when the price has increased and costs have decreased to the point where loss no longer occurs.

Whereas rice production loses resources, corn production gains them. The short-run profit in corn production stimulates the entry of new firms. The increased demand for inputs raises input prices and cost curves in corn production, and the price of corn is depressed by the movement to the right of the supply curve because of the entry of new firms. Entry stops when economic profit is no longer being earned. At that point, when long-run equilibrium is achieved, more firms and more resources are used in the corn industry than in the short run.

SUMMARY

1. Managers of perfectly competitive firms set output levels so that price equals marginal cost. If there is an output level where price exceeds average variable cost, it pays the firm to produce in the short run, even though price does not cover average total costs. But if there is no output level where price exceeds average variable cost, managers are better off to produce nothing at all. In the long run, managers produce at the minimum point on their long-run average total cost curve. The price tends to be at the level where the market demand curve intersects the market supply curve. The short-run supply curve of a perfectly competitive firm is its marginal cost curve above the point of the minimum average variable cost.

2. Producer surplus is equivalent to the firm's variable-cost profit—that is, total revenue less variable costs. The producer surplus is the difference between the price a seller receives for its product and the seller's reservation price (the minimum price at which it would sell its product). This is a measure of welfare from a producer's perspective. When combined with the consumer surplus introduced in Chapter 3, the sum of the producer and consumer surpluses gives a measure of social welfare. We can use this measure to compare the benefits of different pricing proposals and the benefits of trade (as shown in Chapter 16).

3. A constant-cost industry has a horizontal long-run supply curve; an increasing-cost industry has a positively sloped long-run supply curve. If a constant-cost industry expands, there is no increase (or decrease) in input prices; if an increasing-cost industry expands, there is an increase in input prices.

wwnorton.com/studyspace

PROBLEMS

1. The Hamilton Company is a member of a perfectly competitive industry. Like all members of the industry, its total cost function is

$$TC = 25,000 + 150Q + 3Q^2$$

where TC is the firm's monthly total cost (in dollars) and Q is the firm's monthly output.

   a. If the industry is in long-run equilibrium, what is the price of the Hamilton Company's product?

   b. What is the firm's monthly output?

2. In 2008, the box industry was perfectly competitive. The lowest point on the long-run average cost curve of each of the identical box producers was $4, and this minimum point occurred at an output of 1,000 boxes per month. The market demand curve for boxes was

$$Q_D = 140,000 - 10,000P$$

where P was the price of a box (in dollars per box) and Q_D was the quantity of boxes demanded per month. The market supply curve for boxes was

$$Q_S = 80,000 + 5,000P$$

where Q_S was the quantity of boxes supplied per month.

   a. What was the equilibrium price of a box? Is this the long-run equilibrium price?

   b. How many firms are in this industry when it is in long-run equilibrium?

3. The Burr Corporation's total cost function (where TC is the total cost in dollars and Q is quantity) is

$$TC = 200 + 4Q + 2Q^2$$

   a. If the firm is perfectly competitive and the price of its product is $24, what is its optimal output rate?

   b. At this output rate, what is its profit?

4. The supply and demand curves for pears are

$$Q_S = 10,000P$$

$$Q_D = 25,000 - 15,000P$$

where Q_S is the quantity (tons) supplied, Q_D is the quantity (tons) demanded, and P is the price per pear (in hundreds of dollars per ton).

   a. Plot the supply and demand curves.

   b. What is the equilibrium price?

   c. What is the equilibrium quantity?

5. The White Company is a member of the lamp industry, which is perfectly competitive. The price of a lamp is $50. The firm's total cost function is

$$TC = 1{,}000 + 20Q + 5Q^2$$

where TC is total cost (in dollars) and Q is hourly output.
   a. What output maximizes profit?
   b. What is the firm's economic profit at this output?
   c. What is the firm's average cost at this output?
   d. If other firms in the lamp industry have the same cost function as this firm, is the industry in equilibrium? Why or why not?

6. The long-run supply curve for a particular type of kitchen knife is a horizontal line at a price of $3 per knife. The demand curve for such a kitchen knife is

$$Q_D = 50 - 2P$$

where Q_D is the quantity of knives demanded (in millions per year) and P is the price per knife (in dollars).
   a. What is the equilibrium output of such knives?
   b. If a tax of $1 is imposed on each knife, what is the equilibrium output of such knives? (Assume the tax is collected by the government from the suppliers of knives.)
   c. After the tax is imposed, you buy such a knife for $3.75. Is this the long-run equilibrium price?

CHAPTER 7

MONOPOLY AND
MONOPOLISTIC COMPETITION

The question faced by most managers is how to set prices and output when they have market power. As we will see, when managers possess market power, they have the ability to overrule the invisible hand described by Adam Smith. In these markets the equilibrium price set by the intersection of the supply and demand curves is rarely seen. We will first investigate this important issue by looking at how managers act when they have monopoly power. Managers with monopoly power do not have to consider the actions of market rivals because there are none. For example, US Airways is the only carrier flying between Ithaca, New York, and Philadelphia, Pennsylvania. In the winter Kubel's Restaurant is the only restaurant open in Barnegat Light, New Jersey. Only one supermarket may be open all night long in your area. The Philadelphia Gas Works is the only supplier of natural gas in Philadelphia, Pennsylvania.

The market demand curve for air travel between Ithaca and Philadelphia *is* the demand curve for US Airways. The market demand for winter restaurant meals in Barnegat Light *is* the demand curve seen by managers at Kubel's. Likewise, the market demand for overnight supermarket shopping and natural gas in Philadelphia are the demand curves facing those firm managers. Monopolies have no intramarket competition, and firm demand is equal to market demand.

The demand faced by managers of monopolies is downward-sloping; that is, as price increases, quantity demanded decreases. Managers with market power face a pleasantly more complex decision relative to those in perfectly competitive markets. They must decide both price and quantity; they are no longer passive price takers. Relative to managers of perfectly competitive firms, they have more strategic power and are rewarded with higher economic profit. We now want to look at how managers maximize profit in such an environment.

Although being a monopolist comes with some degree of market power, it does not give managers carte blanche; they need to manage the demand characteristics of their product. If no one wants to fly between Ithaca and Philadelphia or shop at 3 A.M. or eat in a restaurant in the winter in Barnegat Light, the manager's monopoly power is virtually worthless. And even if managers create demand for their products, they still must efficiently manage costs and resources. Finally, monopolists still must worry about potential competitors. It is only 183 miles between Ithaca and Philadelphia, so driving or taking a bus is an option for many consumers. And though Barnegat Light has only one winter restaurant, a restaurant exists in a town four miles away, and home-cooked meals are a substitute. Many grocery stores are open all day and in the early evening, so customers can easily shop at times other than 3 a.m. Consumers need not heat their homes or hot water with gas; many choose to use oil or electricity. Cross elasticities (see Chapter 2) can tell us what goods, locations, and times are substitutes for a "monopoly" product.

So even when there is no intramarket competition, managers must work hard if substitute products, locations, and times exist. Managers need to understand product, spatial, and temporal competition, or they can make serious mistakes. Also, the higher the profit, the more others will test your market defenses and try to enter your market. Finally, if managers do too good a job and generate what is viewed as excess profit, authorities may try to regulate their actions in some way.

In this chapter we examine issues the monopolist manager must consider in choosing the optimal price and quantity combination. We show how market power changes the thought process of managers, though the decision rule remains to produce where marginal revenue equals marginal cost. This simple rule dictates managerial behavior in all market structures.

We also show the profit-maximizing rule for managers in monopolistic competitive markets. In these markets managers still have market power, but they must deal with intramarket rivals. Although managers still face a downward-sloping demand curve, a lack of entry barriers allows others into the market. The world is more complicated; managers must consider the actions of these rivals in choosing their optimal strategy. Industries such as shirt manufacturing approximate monopolistic competition.

STRATEGY SESSION: The Newspaper Industry in Detroit

Relatively few cities in the United States have rival newspapers that are separately owned and commercially independent. Consider Detroit: In early 1989 the *Detroit Free Press* and the *Detroit News* obtained approval from the U.S. Court of Appeals to establish a newspaper monopoly in Detroit. Arguing that the *Free Press* was a failing newspaper, they took advantage of a special exemption from antitrust law, permitted under the Newspaper Preservation Act of 1970. (This exemption was created to keep alive competing editorial voices in major cities). The two newspapers were allowed to continue to print newspapers under their own names. But all commercial operations would be merged. Such arrangements are called JOAs or joint operating agreements.

Because the merged newspapers were legally permitted to fix prices and allocate markets as they pleased, they constituted a monopoly, even though their newspapers were printed under two different names. The result was a substantial increase in profit. Before they combined, each lost more than $10 million a year; after they combined, experts estimated that they would make more than $150 million a year. This is eloquent testimony to the effect of monopoly on profit.

The reasons for this increase in profit were summarized as follows by *The New York Times*: "The formation of the monopoly enterprise would end an all-out war for control of advertising and circulation dollars, sending . . . rates skyrocketing for readers and advertisers."[a] This, of course, is entirely consistent with our discussion in this chapter. A monopolist, free from the constraints imposed by direct competition, can set a higher price—and obtain a higher profit level—than it could if it had to compete with rival firms.

However, even a monopoly is not guaranteed a profit. In July 1995 about 2,500 reporters, editors, press operators, drivers, and other workers of the *Detroit Free Press* and *Detroit News* struck over job cuts, wages, and work rules. This strike continued for over 18 months and cut heavily into the profit of the merged newspapers.[b]

Detroit isn't the only city that has received legal permission to have a JOA: In total, twenty-eight have been granted since 1970. But only nine existed in 2008. In fifteen cases one of the papers folded. In two of the cases the papers ultimately completely merged; and in two cases the JOA was terminated, resulting in two completely independent papers today. For the surviving JOAs, in four cases the agreements are between morning and evening papers that are not temporal competitors (and these are in smaller cities: Charleston, WV; Fort Wayne, IN; Tucson, AZ; and York, PA). Thus although the intention of the 1970 act was to preserve editorial competition, it has been temporally successful only in Denver, Detroit, Las Vegas, Salt Lake City, and Seattle, where morning papers have joint presses, distribution, and sales but compete on editorial policy. Students of the 1970 act have concluded that the law merely postponed the inevitable: Virtually every paper that failed was the evening paper.

The lesson here is one of market definition. Although production monopolies were formed in several local newspaper markets, consumers were moving away from newspapers to evening local and network news TV broadcasts, then to 24-hour cable news TV, and then to the Internet for their news. People still want to be informed, but they want news on demand and less in a print format. The news market is much more broadly defined than it was prior to 1970; so most of the monopolies created were short-lived.

[a]*The New York Times*, September 18, 1988.
[b]*The New York Times*, February 20, 1997.

PRICING AND OUTPUT DECISIONS IN MONOPOLY

The monopolist behaves differently than the perfect competitor of Chapter 6. An unregulated monopolist maximizes profit by choosing the price and output where the difference between total revenue and total cost is the largest. For example, consider a monopolist with a demand curve of

$$P = 10 - Q$$

where P is the price per unit of the product and Q is the number of units demanded at that price. The monopolist has a total cost curve of

$$TC = 1 + Q + 0.5Q^2$$

The monopolist's total revenue is $TR = PQ$, or

$$TR = (10 - Q)Q = 10Q - Q^2$$

The total revenue and total cost for the monopolist at various levels of output are shown in Table 7.1. The manager maximizes profit at the output where total revenue exceeds total cost by the greatest amount. Figures 7.1 and 7.2 show the situation graphically.

Under monopoly, as under perfect competition, managers maximize profit if they set output at the point where marginal cost equals marginal revenue. As can

TABLE 7.1

Cost, Revenue, and Profit of a Monopolist

Output	Price (Dollars)	Total Revenue (Dollars)	Variable Cost (Dollars)	Total Cost (Dollars)	Total Profit (Dollars)	Variable-Cost Profit (Dollars)
0	10	0	0	1	−1	0
1	9	9	1.5	2.5	6.5	7.5
2	8	16	4	5	11	12
3	7	21	7.5	8.5	12.5	13.5
4	6	24	12	13	11	12
4.5	5.5	24.75	14.625	15.625	9.125	10.125
5	5	25	17.5	18.5	6.5	7.5
6	4	24	24	25	−1	0
7	3	21	31.5	32.5	−11.5	−10.5
8	2	16	40	41	−25	−24
9	1	9	49.5	50.5	−41.5	−40.5
10	0	0	60	61	−61	−60

FIGURE 7.1

Total Revenue, Total Cost, and Total Profit of a Monopolist

To maximize profit, the monopolist chooses an output rate of three units per period of time and a price of $7.

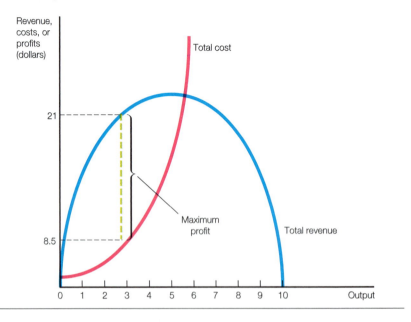

FIGURE 7.2

Profit and Output of a Monopolist

To maximize profit, the monopolist chooses an output rate of three units per time period and makes a profit of $12.5.

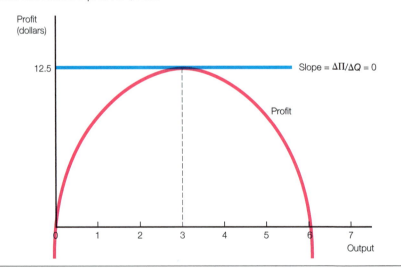

be seen in Figure 7.2, profit is maximized when $\Delta\pi/\Delta Q = 0$. Recall from Chapter 6 that $\pi = TR - TC$ (that is, profit equals total revenue minus total cost) and that

$$\frac{\Delta\pi}{\Delta Q} = \frac{\Delta TR}{\Delta Q} - \frac{\Delta TC}{\Delta Q} = 0$$

which implies that $MR - MC = 0$ or that $MR = MC$.

Let us investigate the situation in Table 7.1 and Figures 7.1 and 7.2 in greater detail. The marginal revenue $= MR = \Delta TR/\Delta Q = 10 - 2Q$.

Note that with a linear demand curve, the marginal revenue curve has the same dollar intercept as the demand curve (10) but it falls at twice the speed; that is, the marginal revenue curve has twice the slope of the demand curve. This is always true for linear demand curves (which we almost always use for illustrative purposes—of course, in the real world, demand curves could take any form that shows an inverse relationship of price and quantity). Therefore, a demand curve of $P = 250 - 12.5Q$ has a corresponding marginal revenue curve of $MR = 250 - 25Q$.[1]

The total cost function is $TC = 1 + Q + 0.5Q^2$. Therefore, marginal cost $= MC = \Delta TC/\Delta Q = 1 + Q$.

Setting marginal revenue equal to marginal cost gives

$$MR = 10 - 2Q = 1 + Q = MC, \text{ or } Q = 3 \tag{7.1}$$

and hence $P = 10 - 3 = \$7$.

Unlike firms in a perfectly competitive market, the firm's marginal revenue is no longer constant; nor is it equal to price. Recall from Chapter 3 that

$$MR = P\left[1 + \left(\frac{1}{\eta}\right)\right]$$

$$= P\left[1 - \left(\frac{1}{|\eta|}\right)\right]$$

$$= P - \left(\frac{P}{|\eta|}\right) \tag{7.2}$$

QUANT OPTION

For those in the know, the monopolist's marginal revenue is

$$dTR/dQ = MR = 10 - 2Q$$

The monopolist's marginal cost is

$$dTC/dQ = MC = 1 + Q$$

---

1. Total revenue would be $TR = (250 - 12.5Q)Q = 250Q - 12.5Q^2$ and so $MR = dTR/dQ = 250 - 25Q$.

TABLE 7.2

Marginal Cost and Marginal Revenue of a Monopolist

Price	Output	Marginal Cost[a]	Marginal Revenue[b]	Total Profit[c]	Elasticity
10	0	1	10	−1	−∞
9	1	2	8	6.5	−9
8	2	3	6	11	−4
7	3	4	4	12.5	−2.33
6	4	5	2	11	−1.5
5.5	4.5	5.5	1	9.125	−1.22
5	5	6	0	6.5	−1
4	6	7	−2	−1	−0.67
3	7	8	−4	−11.5	−0.43
2	8	9	−6	−25	−0.25
1	9	10	−8	−41.5	−0.11
0	10	11	−10	−61	0

[a]The marginal cost is calculated from the equation $MC = 1 + Q$. This assumes that the product is produced in continuous amounts, like gasoline. If the product can be produced only in discrete amounts, like cars, the marginal cost for output n is defined as the total cost of producing n units minus the total cost of producing $n - 1$ units. Using the total cost information from Table 7.1, the marginal cost of producing two units is $2.5 (that is, $5 − $2.5); the marginal cost of producing three units is $3.5 (that is, $8.5 − $5); and the marginal cost of producing four units is $4.5 (that is, $13 − $8.5). Why does this differ from the marginal cost of $5 shown for output 4 in the table? Because the costs differ if you can produce continuously as opposed to only in discrete integer units.

[b]The marginal revenue is calculated from the equation $MR = 10 − 2Q$. This assumes that the product can be sold in continuous amounts, like gasoline. If the product can be sold only in discrete amounts, like cars, the marginal revenue for output n is defined as the total revenue from selling n units minus the total revenue of selling $n - 1$ units. Using the total revenue information from Table 7.1, the marginal revenue of selling two units is $7 (that is, $16 − $9); the marginal revenue of selling three units is $5 (that is, $21 − $16); and the marginal revenue of selling four units is $3 (that is, $24 − $21).

[c]Note that using the discrete marginal revenue and the marginal cost gives the same result as the continuous analysis; that is, the profit-maximizing output is three units. In the discrete case, the firm would clearly produce the second unit because the marginal revenue exceeds the marginal cost ($7 > $2.5) and hence would increase profit. Likewise, it would produce the third unit because the marginal revenue exceeds the marginal cost ($5 > $3.5) and hence would increase profit. However, the firm would not produce the fourth unit because the marginal revenue is exceeded by the marginal cost ($3 < $4.5) and hence would decrease profit.

Where MR is marginal revenue, P is price, and η is the price elasticity of demand. Because $\eta < 0$, the marginal revenue equals price minus $P/|\eta|$. Hence marginal revenue is price minus something positive—so price must exceed marginal revenue. In addition, no rational manager produces where marginal revenue is negative. (This implies that selling another unit decreases total revenue; because producing another unit would increase total costs, the manager could not maximize profit.) If managers are to produce where marginal revenue equals marginal cost, a negative marginal revenue implies a negative marginal cost. Total costs increase (not decrease) when managers increase production. If marginal revenue is positive, then from equation (7.2), $\eta < -1$ (that is, $|\eta| > 1$), which implies an elastic demand.[2] Thus a monopolist will not produce in the inelastic range of her demand curve if she is maximizing profit.

Table 7.2 and Figure 7.3 present the marginal revenue and marginal cost numbers for these functions; they substantiate that profit is maximized when marginal revenue equals marginal cost.

Note at the optimal output of three units (price = \$7), the demand is elastic (-2.33) and the marginal revenue is positive (\$4). It is also true that in a monop-

---

FIGURE 7.3

Marginal Revenue and Marginal Cost of a Monopolist

At the monopolist's profit-maximizing output (three units), the marginal cost equals the marginal revenue (at \$4).

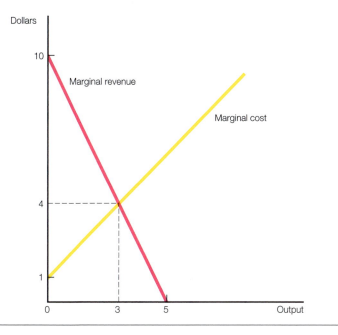

2. From equation (7.2), if $|\eta| > 1$, then $1/|\eta| < 1$ and $[1 - (1/|\eta|)] > 0$. This makes $MR > 0$, because P must be positive.

oly, price must exceed average variable cost if managers are to maximize profit (and from Table 7.1, we calculate that at a production of 3 units, AVC is equal to $2.5; that is, $AVC = VC/Q = \$7.5/3 = \$2.5$). If not, the monopolist is not covering variable cost and should shut the operation to reduce losses to only fixed cost.

It is easy to graphically show the price and output decision facing managers. Figure 7.4 shows the demand curve, the marginal revenue curve, the marginal cost curve, the average total cost curve, and the average variable cost curve faced by managers. To maximize profit, managers need to produce the output Q_M where the marginal cost curve intersects that of marginal revenue. If the monopolist produces Q_M, she will set a price of P_M. Because she is the only member of her market, her firm's demand curve is the industry demand curve. This is in contrast to perfect competition, where the demand curve for a firm's output is horizontal. The demand curve for the monopolist's output slopes downward to the right, as shown in Figure 7.4.

In Figure 7.4 managers generate profit per unit of $P_M - ATC$. This, multiplied by the number of units, Q_M, is the shaded area of the figure. Note also that $P_M > AVC$ to fulfill the second managerial rule of profit maximization.

Relative to managers in perfectly competitive markets, monopolists choose a higher price and lower output. This lets them charge a price higher than marginal

---

FIGURE 7.4

Output and Price Decisions of a Monopolist

In equilibrium, the monopolist produces Q_M units of output and sets a price of P_M. (Note that, in contrast to perfect competition, the demand curve slopes downward to the right.)

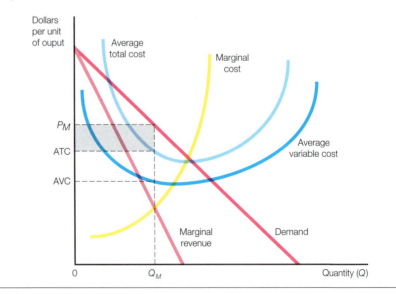

PROBLEM SOLVED: The McComb Company

To illustrate how managers choose price and output to maximize profit, consider the situation facing managers at the McComb Company, a monopolist producing and selling a product with the demand curve

$$P = 30 - 6Q \qquad (7.4)$$

where P is price (in thousands of dollars) and Q is the firm's output (in thousands of units). The firm's total cost function is

$$TC = 14 + 3Q + 3Q^2 \qquad (7.5)$$

where TC is total cost (in millions of dollars).

From the demand curve in equation (7.4), we determine the firm's total revenue (in millions of dollars), which is

$$TR = PQ = (30 - 6Q)Q = 30Q - 6Q^2$$

Therefore, marginal revenue equals $\Delta TR/\Delta Q = 30 - 12Q$.

From the total cost function in equation (7.5), we determine that marginal cost is

$$\Delta TC /\Delta Q = 3 + 6Q$$

Setting marginal revenue equal to marginal cost gives us

$$MR = 30 - 12Q = 3 + 6Q = MC$$

This means that $Q = 1.5$. Inserting 1.5 for Q in the demand equation (7.4), we find that $P = 30 - 6(1.5)$, or $21. So to maximize profit, managers should set a price of $21,000 and produce and sell 1,500 units. Doing so will result in profit equal to $[30(1.5) - 6(1.5)^2] - [14 + 3(1.5) + 3(1.5)^2] = \$6.25$ million.

---

cost and hence generate economic profit. Managers in perfectly competitive markets can only set price equal to marginal cost. In the preceding example, if managers were forced to behave as a perfect competitor, they would set price equal to marginal cost; that is, $P = 10 - Q = 1 + Q = MC$. This yields $2Q = 9$ or an output of 4.5 and a price of 5.5; that is, $P = 10 - 4.5$. Therefore, output is curtailed under monopoly (from 4.5 to 3), price is increased (from $5.5 to $7), and profit is increased (from $9.125 to $12.5)—see Table 7.1.

To see that the monopolist's price exceeds marginal cost, recall that

$$MR = P[1 - (1/|\eta|)]$$

and that the monopolist sets marginal revenue equal to marginal cost. Therefore,

$$MC = P\left[1 - \left(\frac{1}{|\eta|}\right)\right] \text{ or} \qquad (7.3)$$

$$P = \frac{MC}{\left[1 - \left(\frac{1}{|\eta|}\right)\right]}$$

Because $|\eta| > 1$, it follows that $[1 - (1/|\eta|)] < 1$, which means P must exceed MC.

What happens when a franchiser with monopoly power has a different objective than a franchisee's? Consider the case of McDonald's, where the franchiser makes its money by collecting a percentage of each store's gross sales or total revenues (formally called a *royalty*). Therefore the franchiser wants to maximize the total revenue from the sales of its hamburgers by having each store maximize its total revenues (and by adding more stores). We assume that franchisees wish to maximize their profit. To do so, the franchisee would set $MR = MC$ (in the elastic range of demand where $|\eta| > 1$). But maximizing total revenue requires that $MR = 0$ (and that $|\eta| = 1$). Because the objectives of the franchiser and the franchisee cannot be accomplished with the same pricing policy, they are in conflict. The situation is depicted in the figure.[a]

Note that this conflict exists in other situations such as book publishing. Authors generally receive a percentage of book sales as a royalty. Therefore, authors would like publishers to maximize total revenues. Publishers, on the other hand, want to maximize profit. Hence the authors' objective would entail lower book prices than the publishers', don't blame us for the high price of this book!

The royalty rates[b] (as a percentage of monthly sales) for some popular franchises are shown here:

McDonald's	4% of gross sales
DQ Grill and Chill Restaurants	4% of gross sales
DQ Treat Centers	6% of gross sales
Motel 6	4% of gross room revenues
Studio 6	5% of gross room revenues
UPS Store	5% of gross sales and gross commissions
Ben and Jerry's	3% of gross sales
Jiffy Lube	5% of gross sales

In addition, there is generally a marketing or sales promotion fee (for advertising) of 2–6 percent of sales for most franchises as well as a one-time franchise fee. Papa John's, however, has a royalty fee of 5 percent of *net* sales (and hence the incentives of the franchiser and franchisees are aligned).

[a]*Business Week*, June 2, 1997.
[b]Company Web sites, May 2008.
A monopolist produces at $P_{Franchisee}$, $Q_{Franchisee}$ as dictated by the rule that marginal revenue equals marginal cost. A revenue maximizer produces where marginal revenue is zero ($P_{Franchiser}$, $Q_{Franchiser}$)—that is, where $|\eta| = 1$.

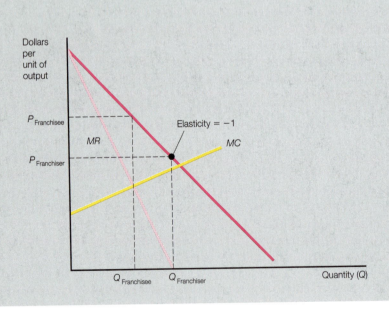

The extra profit earned by monopoly managers is generated by their ability to choose a price greater than marginal cost, whereas the perfect competitor merely charges the marginal cost. Of course managers in both markets must choose a price that is higher than average variable cost.

COST-PLUS PRICING

Unfortunately academic studies of pricing behavior consistently suggest that many managers do not price optimally. Instead they use the simple heuristic of **cost-plus pricing** (see Strategy Session: Pricing Behavior of Managers, page 210).

Many managers act as if cost is the primary driver of price. Although this simple strategy guarantees that price is higher than the estimated average cost, it does not necessarily optimize profit. The behavior has many variations but follows a guiding principle: Price is set as a function of cost. Managers first allocate unit costs conditional on a given output level (such as 70 percent capacity). Then they add a profit margin. This margin is generally a percentage of costs and is added to the estimated average costs. The markup is meant to cover costs that are difficult to allocate to specific products and as a return on firm investment.

Cost-plus pricing Simplistic strategy that guarantees that price is higher than the estimated average cost.

STRATEGY SESSION: Using Patents to Maintain Market Power

The U.S. government often tries to break up monopolies; but one government institution, the patent system, is designed to grant firms monopoly power over their inventions and product innovations. The government grants companies patents for 20 years. This gives the patent holder the exclusive rights to an invention or new product for the life of the patent. Because companies apply for a patent before a product is on the market, the effective life of a patent can be significantly less than 20 years. For drugs, the effective average patent protection is about 12 years.

Thanks to the monopoly granted by the patent system (and the anticipated monopoly profit from a popular product), drug companies are willing to invest significant funds in research and development (R&D). It is estimated that a successful new drug averages

approximately $350 million in development costs. Without patent protection, it is doubtful whether drug companies would undertake highly problematic and expensive R&D.

What do managers at drug companies do price-wise with their patent-generated monopoly power? One test is to compare the price of drugs just as drugs come off patent with the price of the generics that then appear on the market. For example, Bristol-Myers Squibb's heart drug Capoten sold for 57 cents per pill, and the generic sold for 3 cents. This suggests at least a 19 times markup.

Source: "With Patents Expiring on Big Prescription Drugs, Drug Industry Quakes," *The Wall Street Journal*, August 12, 1997.

In basic algebra, the percentage markup of this strategy is expressed as:

$$\text{Markup} = (\text{Price} - \text{Cost})/\text{Cost} \qquad (7.6)$$

Profit margin The price of a product minus its cost.

where the numerator (Price − Cost) is the **profit margin.** If the cost of a paperback book is $4 and its price is $6,

$$\text{Markup} = (6 - 4)/4 = 0.50$$

or 50 percent. If we solve equation (7.6) for price, the result is

$$\text{Price} = \text{Cost} (1 + \text{Markup}) \qquad (7.7)$$

which is the pricing formula described in the previous paragraph. In the case of the paperback book,

$$\text{Price} = 4(1 + 0.5) = \$6$$

because the markup is 50 percent.

STRATEGY SESSION: Pricing Behavior of Managers

Surveys of financial officers of large manufacturing companies suggest behavioral differences that vary across countries. When asked to rank factors that influence market price, the majority of officers in U.S. companies said product cost was the primary driver of price. These managers were also more likely to use full unit cost instead of variable cost. Managers in Japan, Ireland, and the United Kingdom showed different behavior. They listed market factors as the primary driver of price.

The use of a cost-plus heuristic explains the behavior of American managers. This heuristic requires greater knowledge of cost; hence managers focus on product cost to set price, and the nature of competition is an afterthought. In contrast, behavior in Japan, Ireland, and the United Kingdom suggests that managers focus first on market competition and then on cost.

This market focus is further refined by Japanese managers. Surveys find that Japanese managers are more likely to use value engineering in pricing decisions. In *value engineering* managers first go to the

market and look at the products of rivals. They determine a price they think must be received in the market for their product to succeed. Then they go back to the design engineers and ask whether the product can be built within the price constraint.

Although it is arguable whether a cost-plus policy is consistent with a market focus, the use of this heuristic is widespread. For example, an entire software industry provides programs to help managers optimize their cost-plus pricing decisions (for example, see www.acornsys.com). Cost-plus purchase programs are even seen as a competitive advantage (as an example, see www.monettech.com/products).

Sources: P. Blayney and I. Yokoyama, "Corporate Analysis of Japanese and Australian Cost Accounting and Management Practices," Abacus 6 (1997), pp. 33–50; M. Cornick, W. Cooper, and S. Wilson, "How Do Companies Analyze Their Overhead?" *Management Accounting*, June 1988, pp. 41–43; and C. Drury, S. Braund, P. Osborne, and M. Tayles, "A Survey of Management Accounting Practices in UK Manufacturing Companies," Association of Chartered Certified Accountants publication, London, 1993.

Managers may also choose a **target return** they hope to earn, which determines the markup. For example, General Electric at times has established a target rate of return of 20 percent. Under a target rate of return pricing, price is set equal to

$$P = L + M + K + (F/Q) + (\pi A/Q) \qquad (7.8)$$

where P is price, L is unit labor cost, M is unit material cost, K is unit marketing cost, F is total fixed or indirect costs, Q is the number of units managers plan to produce during the relevant planning period, A is total gross operating assets, and π is the desired profit rate on those assets. If managers estimate unit labor cost at $2, unit material cost at $1, unit marketing cost at $3, total fixed cost at $10,000, output at 1,000 units, with assets of $100,000 and a target rate of return of 15 percent, they should set price at

$$P = 2 + 1 + 3 + (10,000/1,000) + [0.15(100,000)/1,000] = \$31$$

One issue facing managers who produce more than one product is the charge for indirect cost, or overhead. Often managers use the heuristic of allocating this cost among the firm's products on the basis of their average variable costs. If a firm's total annual indirect costs (for all products) are estimated to be $3 million and the total annual variable costs (for all products) are estimated to be $2 million, indirect costs would be allocated to products at a rate of 150 percent of variable costs. For example, if the average variable cost of product Y is estimated to be $10, managers should add a charge of 1.50 × $10, or $15, for indirect cost. Adding this charge to the average variable cost, the manager estimates the fully allocated cost of $10 + $15, or $25. Managers then set a price that is higher than this cost to generate profit. For example, if the markup is 40 percent, the price is 1.40 × $25, or $35.

COST-PLUS PRICING AT THERMA-STENT

Cost-plus pricing is widely used in medical group purchasing organizations. Therma-Stent is a producer of graft stents. Managers set price by estimating the average production costs (including indirect ones). They then add a 40 percent markup to set the product's market price:

Factory cost/unit = $2,300 (at production of 20,000)
40 percent markup = $920
U.S. list price = $3,220

Using the heuristic eases the complexity of setting price by ignoring market considerations. For instance, price is set without considering prices of rival products. This pricing scheme works better when products are differentiated. Therma-Stent produces graft stents that are unique in form and surface structure.

COST-PLUS PRICING AT INTERNET COMPANIES AND GOVERNMENT-REGULATED INDUSTRIES

Managers at many online companies seem to have adopted a cost-plus pricing scheme. Consider Onsale, an online computer store. Managers have structured a pricing policy called "At Cost" where they sell products based at the wholesale price plus a fixed transaction fee (the markup).[3]

Online sellers in other product lines have adopted the same pricing scheme. Managers at bybb.com sell major household appliances (GE and Hotpoint washers, dryers, refrigerators, and ovens) and electronics (Toshiba, Mitsubishi, and Sony TVs and MP3 players) on a cost-plus basis, where the purchaser is shown the wholesale price of the item.[4]

Many automobile dealers also use a cost-plus pricing scheme, though they tend to make it difficult for consumers to accurately determine cost. Auto dealer invoices contain some items such as area allowances, which are hard for the novice consumer to interpret, and manufacturer givebacks are not included in the invoice. Therefore consumers do not see the true price the dealer paid for the car. In addition, many customers trade in their old vehicles. In haggling with a customer, the dealers are concerned with how much money they can make in the package—the trade-in plus the sale of the new vehicle. This makes buying from the auto dealer harder than buying from the appliance seller (where trade-ins are nonexistent).

Government regulators also use cost-plus pricing in industries they regulate or control. For instance, the Coal Ministry in India recently allowed Rajmahal coal to be priced at cost plus Rs143 per tonne after meeting production costs.[5] The danger of such a pricing scheme in a government-controlled industry is that, when the profit is guaranteed, firm managers may lose the incentive to be cost efficient. This tends to create a larger government regulatory bureaucracy to monitor costs.

CAN COST-PLUS PRICING MAXIMIZE PROFIT?

The important question we need to consider is how good a heuristic cost-plus pricing is for managers to use. So far it seems unlikely that cost-plus pricing will often maximize profit. Indeed, this pricing technique seems simple-minded in that it does not explicitly account for important factors on both the demand and supply sides. It certainly does not explicitly consider the extent of demand or the product's price elasticity, including the pricing behavior of rivals. On the supply side it looks at average, not marginal, cost. Nevertheless, if applied well, cost-plus pricing may result in managers almost maximizing profit. The possibility that cost-plus pricing is sometimes a good heuristic revolves around what factors managers consider in determining the size of the percentage markup or the target rate of return. For example, why was the markup on the paperback book cited earlier 50 percent? Why not 25 percent or 150 percent?

In choosing a markup to maximize profit, managers must estimate the book's price elasticity of demand. To understand why this is true, recall from equation (7.3) that

3. "Egghead Whips Up a $400 Million Deal with Onsale," *San Francisco Chronicle*, July 15, 1997.

4. Cost Appliances and Electronics: Lowest Prices on the Web, found at www.bybb.com.

5. B. Sanyal, "Cost-Plus Pricing Helps Rajmahal Expansion," August 26, 1996; found at www.hindubusinessline.com/1996/08/26/BLFP.08.html.

$$MC = P\left[1 - \left(\frac{1}{|\eta|}\right)\right]$$

Dividing both sides of the equation by $1 - (1/|\eta|)$, we get

$$P = MC\left\{\frac{1}{\left[1 - \left(\frac{1}{|\eta|}\right)\right]}\right\}$$

So in setting price, if managers want to maximize profit, they need to understand how marginal cost and price elasticity of demand are associated. Formally, managers need to set price so it equals the product's marginal cost multiplied by

$$\left\{\frac{1}{\left[1 - \left(\frac{1}{|\eta|}\right)\right]}\right\}$$

Intuitively, equation (7.7) says that in cost-plus pricing, managers choose a price equal to cost multiplied by (1 + Markup). If managers use marginal (not average) cost, then a markup of

$$\text{Markup} = 1/(|\eta| - 1) \tag{7.9}$$

will maximize profit.

Put differently, a manager can maximize profit using cost-plus pricing with a markup equal to the value specified in equation (7.9). As equation (7.9) clearly shows, the optimal markup depends on the product's price elasticity of demand. To help managers think about this, we have constructed Table 7.3, which shows the profit-maximizing markup corresponding to elasticity values. For example, if

---

TABLE 7.3

Relationship between Optimal Markup and Price Elasticity of Demand

Price Elasticity of Demand	Optimal Percentage Markup of Marginal Cost
−1.2	500
−1.4	250
−1.8	125
−2.5	66.67
−5.0	25
−11.0	10
−21.0	5
−51.0	2

PROBLEM SOLVED: The Humphrey Corporation

To illustrate how managers can use cost-plus pricing and maximize profit, consider the Humphrey Corporation, a seller of office furniture. One of Humphrey's major products is a metal desk for which the company pays $76 per desk, including transportation and related costs. Although managers at Humphrey face a variety of overhead and marketing costs, these costs are essentially fixed, so marginal cost is approximately $76. Given that many firms in Humphrey's geographic area sell reasonably comparable desks, Humphrey's managers estimate that the demand for desks is fairly price elastic—about −2.5. On the basis of Table 7.3, managers should choose a markup of 66.67 percent to maximize profit.

According to equation (7.7), the optimal price is

$$\text{Price} = \text{Cost}(1 + \text{Markup})$$
$$= 76(1 + 0.6667)$$
$$= \$126.67$$

So if managers want to maximize profit, they should choose the price of $127 per desk. In so doing, managers will approximate profit-maximizing behavior. Behavior is only approximated because values of factors like marginal cost and price elasticity of demand must be estimated. Recognizing that this is the case, Humphrey's managers should be prepared to slightly alter the price once they see the market reaction to it.

a product's price elasticity of demand equals −1.2, the optimal markup is 500 percent. If its price elasticity is −21, the optimal markup is only 5 percent. Table 7.3 should be studied carefully because it provides useful information to help managers choose an effective pricing policy.

Note the negative association between elasticity and markup. As the price elasticity of demand decreases (in absolute value), the optimal markup increases. Table 7.3 shows this clearly. To see that the inverse relationship in Table 7.3 between markup and price elasticity is reasonable, ask yourself the following question: If the quantity demanded of a product is not very sensitive to its price, should I set a relatively high or low price for this product? Obviously you should set a high price if you want to make as much money as possible. Since this is what Table 7.3 tells us, it accords with common sense.

THE MULTIPLE-PRODUCT FIRM: DEMAND INTERRELATIONSHIPS

Managers at monopolies that produce multiple products face a more complex decision. Managers need to recognize that a change in the price or quantity sold of one product may influence the demand for other products. For example, if the Akkina Company produces and sells two products, X and Y, its total revenue (that is, sales) is represented as

$$TR = TR_X + TR_Y \tag{7.10}$$

where TR_X is its total revenue from product X and TR_Y is the total revenue from product Y. The marginal revenue from product X is

$$MR_X = \frac{\Delta TR_X}{\Delta Q_X} - \frac{\Delta TR_Y}{\Delta Q_X} \qquad (7.11a)$$

and the marginal revenue from product Y is

$$MR_Y = \frac{\Delta TR_Y}{\Delta Q_Y} - \frac{\Delta TR_X}{\Delta Q_Y} \qquad (7.11b)$$

The last term in each of these equations represents the demand interrelationship between the two products. In equation (7.11a), the last term shows the effect of an increase in the quantity sold of product X on the total revenue from product Y. This effect can be positive or negative. If products X and Y are complements, this effect is positive because an increase in the quantity sold of one product increases the total revenue from the other product. On the other hand, if products X and Y are substitutes, this effect is negative: An increase in the quantity sold of one product reduces the total revenue of the other product.

Managers who do not understand or pay proper attention to demand interrelationships of this sort can make serious pricing mistakes. For example, if product X is a fairly close substitute for product Y and the division of the Akkina Company producing product X launches a campaign to increase its sales, the results may be good for the division but bad for the company as a whole. Why? Because the resulting increase in product X's sales may occur largely at the expense of product Y's sales.

PRICING OF JOINT PRODUCTS: FIXED PROPORTIONS

In addition to being interrelated on the demand side, some products also have interrelated production characteristics. For example, products sometimes are pro-

---

QUANT OPTION

The marginal revenue from product X is

$$MR_X = \frac{\partial TR_X}{\partial Q_X} - \frac{\partial TR_Y}{\partial Q_X}$$

and the marginal revenue from product Y is

$$MR_Y = \frac{\partial TR_Y}{\partial Q_Y} - \frac{\partial TR_X}{\partial Q_Y}$$

PROBLEM SOLVED: Pricing Steaks at the Palm Restaurant

If you want a steak in New York, a top-notch place to go is the Palm restaurant, owned by the Palm Management Corporation, which has 11 Palm restaurants in 10 cities, all with the same menu. The price of a steak at each of these 11 restaurants in 1993 was as follows:

New York	$27.00	Chicago	$22.00
(two restaurants)			
East Hampton	26.00	Houston	23.00
Philadelphia	24.00	Dallas	23.00
Washington	24.00	Las Vegas	25.00
Miami	24.50	Los Angeles	26.00

Problems

1. According to Bruce Bozzi, co-owner of the Palm Management Corporation, "People are very price-conscious in Chicago, and our manager there knows what we have to charge to be competitive." Assuming that the market for restaurant food is monopolistically competitive in each of these cities, is the demand curve for steak at the Palm restaurant in Chicago the same as at the Palm restaurant in New York? If not, how does it differ?

2. Bozzi also states, "Our labor costs are highest in New York. We figure labor at around $8 per customer. That's nearly double what we pay in some other cities. Utilities are also high. It costs us $7,000 a month for garbage removal for the two restaurants." Is the marginal cost curve for steak at the Palm restaurant in New York the same as at the Palm restaurant in Chicago? If not, how does it differ?

3. Why is the price higher in New York than in Chicago?

4. If marginal cost is 20 percent higher in New York than in Chicago and the price elasticity of demand is −3 in New York and −4 in Chicago, what would you expect to be the percentage price differential between New York and Chicago?

Solutions

1. No. On the basis of Bozzi's statement, the demand curve is more price elastic in Chicago than in New York. A 1 percent price increase is likely to reduce the quantity demanded by a larger percentage in Chicago than in New York.

2. No. The marginal cost curve is lower in Chicago than in New York.

3. As pointed out on page 207, the profit-maximizing price equals

$$P = MC \div \left(1 - \frac{1}{|\eta|}\right)$$

where MC equals marginal cost and $|\eta|$ equals the absolute value of the price elasticity of demand. (This is true under any market structure.) Because MC is higher and η is less elastic in New York than in Chicago, the profit-maximizing price is higher in New York than in Chicago.

4. If P_C is the price in Chicago and P_N is the price in New York, MC_C is the marginal cost in Chicago and MC_N is the marginal cost in New York, and η_C is the price elasticity of demand in Chicago and η_N is the price elasticity of demand in New York,

$$\frac{P_C}{P_N} = \frac{MC_C \div \left(1 - \frac{1}{|\eta_C|}\right)}{MC_N \div \left(1 - \frac{1}{|\eta_N|}\right)}$$

$$= \frac{MC_C \div \left(1 - \frac{1}{|-4|}\right)}{1.2 MC_C \div \left(1 - \frac{1}{|-3|}\right)} = 0.74.$$

Therefore, we would expect the price in Chicago to be about 26 percent below the price in New York.

For further discussion, see *The New York Times*, April 28, 1993. All prices refer to filet mignon.

duced in a fixed ratio, as in the case of cattle, where beef and hide are obtained from each animal. In such a situation there is no reason to distinguish between the products from the point of view of production or costs; managers should think of them as a bundle. One hide and two sides of beef might be such a bundle in the case of cattle because they are produced from each animal. With such jointly produced products, there is no economically correct way to allocate the cost of producing each bundle to the individual products.

To determine the optimal price and output of each such bundled product, managers need to compare the marginal revenue generated by the bundle to its marginal cost of production. If the marginal revenue—that is, the sum of the marginal revenues obtained from each product in the package—is greater than its marginal cost, managers should expand output. Assuming there are two joint products (A and B), Figure 7.5 shows the demand and marginal revenue curves for each, as well as the marginal cost of the bundled product (AB) in the fixed proportion in which it is produced.[6] The **total marginal revenue curve** is the vertical summation of the two marginal revenue curves for the individual products

Total marginal revenue curve
The vertical summation of the two marginal revenue curves for individual products.

FIGURE 7.5

Optimal Pricing for Joint Products Produced in Fixed Proportions (Case 1)

The price of product A is set at P_A, the price of product B is set at P_B, and output is set at Q.

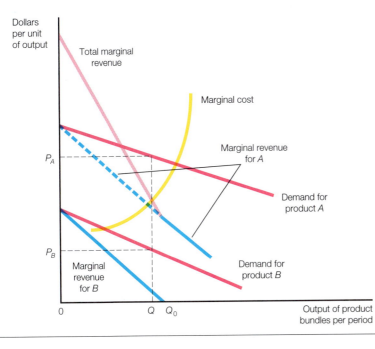

6. For simplicity, we assume that the demand curve for product A is not influenced by the price of product B and vice versa.

PROBLEM SOLVED: Profit Maximizing at Humphrey

Humphrey managers now face the following situation. They manufacture two different conference table legs that are cut from the same piece of metal. They differ in their design but are jointly produced in equal quantities. That is, for every unit of the modern design produced, Humphrey also produces a unit of classical design. Managers face the total cost function

$$TC = 100 + Q + 2Q^2 \qquad (7.12)$$

where Q is the number of units (in tens) of output. (Each unit contains one classic leg and one modern leg.) The demand curves for the firm's two products are

$$P_A = 200 - Q_A \qquad (7.13)$$
$$P_B = 150 - 2Q_B \qquad (7.14)$$

where P_A and Q_A are the price and output (in tens) of the modern leg and P_B and Q_B are the price and output (in tens) of the classic leg.

Humphrey managers need to know how many units of each leg they should produce to maximize profit. The firm's total revenue is equal to the total revenues from its two products:

$$TR = P_A Q_A + P_B Q_B \qquad (7.15)$$

Substituting the right sides of equations (7.13) and (7.14) for P_A and P_B, respectively, it follows that

$$TR = (200 - Q_A)Q_A + (150 - 2Q_B)Q_B$$
$$= 200Q_A - Q_A^2 + 150Q_B - 2Q_B^2$$

Assuming that Humphrey managers want to sell all they produce of both products, $Q_A = Q_B = Q$ because a unit of one product is produced whenever a unit of the other product is produced. Therefore,

$$TR = 200Q - Q^2 + 150Q - 2Q^2$$
$$= 350Q - 3Q^2 \qquad (7.16)$$

To obtain total profit, π, managers must subtract the total cost in equation (7.12) from the total revenue in equation (7.16):

$$\pi = (350Q - 3Q^2) - (100 + Q + 2Q^2)$$
$$= -100 + 349Q - 5Q^2$$

To maximize profit, we need to set $\Delta\pi/\Delta Q = 0$:

$$\Delta\pi/\Delta Q = 349 - 10Q = 0$$

or

$$10Q = 349$$

(A and B) because each AB bundle of output yields revenues from both products. Consequently, the profit-maximizing output in Figure 7.5 is Q, where the total marginal revenue equals marginal cost. The optimal price for product A is P_A, and the optimal price for product B is P_B.

Note that the total marginal revenue curve coincides with the marginal revenue curve for product A at all outputs beyond Q_0 in Figure 7.5. This is true because managers should never sell product B at a level where its marginal revenue is negative. A negative marginal revenue means managers can increase revenue by selling fewer units. Therefore, if the total output exceeds Q_0, managers should sell only part of the product B produced; specifically, they want to sell the amount corresponding to an output of Q_0 product bundles. Consequently, if output exceeds Q_0, the total marginal revenue equals the marginal revenue of product A alone.

or

$$Q = 34.9$$

In other words, to maximize profit, Humphrey managers should produce 34.9 (tens of) legs of each design. Equation (7.13) tells managers they need to choose a price of $165.10 to sell 34.9 (tens of) modern legs:

$$P_A = 200 - 34.9 = \$165.10$$

And equation (7.14) tells managers they need to price classic legs at

$$P_B = 150 - 2(34.9) = \$80.20$$

to sell 34.9 (tens of) of them.

Managers are not quite through with the analysis yet. As indicated, we assume that Humphrey sells all it produces of both products. To see whether this is true, we must see whether, if $Q = 34.9$, the marginal revenues of both products are nonnegative. Only then will Humphrey managers sell all that is produced of both products (recall Figure 7.6). From equations (7.13) and (7.14), we find that TR_A, the total revenue from product A, equals

$$TR_A = P_A Q_A = (200 - Q_A)Q_A = 200Q_A - Q_A^2$$

and that TR_B, the total revenue from product B, equals

$$TR_B = P_B Q_B = (150 - 2Q_B)Q_B = 150Q_B - 2Q_B^2$$

Hence the marginal revenue of product A is

$$MR_A = \Delta TR_A / \Delta Q_A = 200 - 2Q_A = 130.2$$
$$\text{(when } Q_A = 34.9\text{)}$$

And the marginal revenue of product B is

$$MR_B = \Delta TR_B / \Delta Q_B = 150 - 4Q_B = 10.4$$
$$\text{(when } Q_B = 34.9\text{)}$$

Because both marginal revenues (MR_A and MR_B) are nonnegative when Q_A and $Q_B = 34.9$, the assumption underlying the analysis is valid.[a]

---

[a]If one product's marginal revenue had been negative when Q_A and Q_B equaled 34.9, the optimal solution would have involved producing more of this product than is sold, as indicated in Figure 7.6. The firm would sell only the amount of this product where the marginal revenue is zero. The marginal revenue for the other product would be used to determine its optimal amount level, as shown in Figure 7.6.

QUANT OPTION

$$d\pi/dQ = 349 - 10Q = 0 \text{ so that } 10 = 349 \text{ or } Q = 34.9$$

The marginal revenue for product A is

$$MR_A = dTR_A/dQ_A = 200 - 2Q_A = 130.2 \text{ (when } Q_A = 34.9\text{)}$$

The marginal revenue for product B is

$$MR_B = dTR_B/dQ_B = 150 - 4Q_B = 10.4 \text{ (when } Q_B = 34.9\text{)}$$

FIGURE 7.6

Optimal Pricing for Joint Products Produced in Fixed Proportions (Case 2)

The price of product A is set at P_A, the price of product B is set at P_B, and not all of product B is sold.

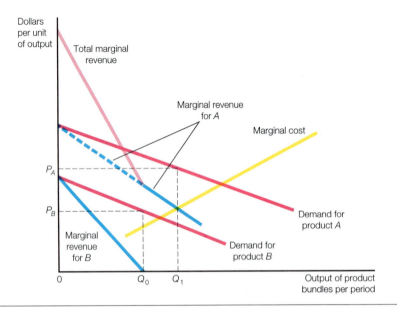

What should managers do if the marginal cost curve intersects the total marginal revenue curve to the right of Q_0 in Figure 7.5? In particular, suppose managers face the situation shown in Figure 7.6, where the marginal cost curve is lower than in Figure 7.5 (but the other curves are the same). The profit-maximizing output is Q_1, where the marginal cost and total marginal revenue curves intersect. All of product A produced is sold, the price being P_A; but not all of product B is sold. Instead the amount sold is limited to the amount of output Q_0, so that the price of product B is P_B. The "surplus" amount of product B (that is, $Q_1 - Q_0$) must be kept off the market to avoid depressing its price.

OUTPUT OF JOINT PRODUCTS: VARIABLE PROPORTIONS

Having discussed the case in which two joint products are produced in fixed proportions, we turn to the case in which they are produced in variable proportions. This generally is a more realistic case, particularly if a manager is considering a fairly long period. Even cattle's proportions of hides and beef can be altered because the animals can be bred to produce more or less beef relative to hide.

FIGURE 7.7

Optimal Outputs for Joint Products Produced in Variable Proportions

The optimal point, which must be at a point where an isorevenue line is tangent to an isocost curve, is at point M, where profit per day is $7,000.

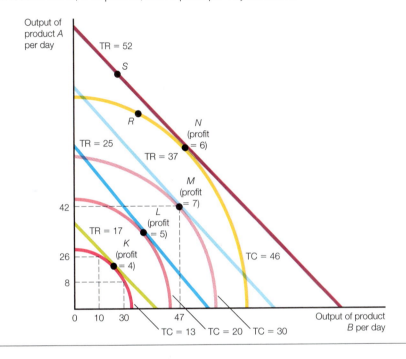

Suppose a firm produces and sells two products, A and B, and that each **iso-cost curve** (labeled TC in Figure 7.7) shows the amounts of these goods produced at the same total cost. The isocost curve labeled $TC = 13$ shows the various combinations of outputs—for example, 26 units of product A and 10 units of product B or 8 units of product A and 30 units of product B—that can be produced at a total cost of $13,000 per day.

Also included in Figure 7.7 are **isorevenue lines** (labeled TR), each of which shows the combinations of outputs of the two products that yield the same total revenue. For example, the isorevenue line labeled $TR = 52$ shows the various combinations of outputs, such as those corresponding to points S or N, that yield a total revenue of $52,000 per day. Other isorevenue lines show the output combinations that yield total revenues of $17,000, $25,000, and $37,000, respectively.

The problem facing the manager is to determine how much of products A and B to produce. The first step toward solving this problem is to observe that if

Isocost curve Curve showing the amounts of goods produced at the same total cost.

Isorevenue lines Lines showing the combinations of outputs of products that yield the same total revenue.

an output combination is at a point where an isorevenue line is *not* tangent to an isocost curve, it *cannot* be the optimal output combination. To see this, note that if an output combination is at a point where an isorevenue line is not tangent to an isocost curve (say point *R*), it is possible to increase revenue (without changing cost) by moving to a point (on the same isocost curve) where an isorevenue line *is* tangent to the isocost curve (say point *N*). Therefore, any output combination that is not at a tangency point cannot be the profit-maximizing output combination because we indicated how profit can be increased if the firm is at such a nontangency point.

Given that this is the case, we find the optimal output combination by comparing the profit level at each tangency point and choosing the point where the profit level is the highest. For example, four tangency points are shown in Figure 7.7: points *K*, *L*, *M*, and *N*. As indicated in Figure 7.7, the profit levels corresponding to these four points are $4,000, $5,000, $7,000, and $6,000, respectively. So if we must choose among the output combinations on the isocost curves in Figure 7.7, the optimal output combination for this firm is point *M*, where the managers produce and sell 42 units of product *A* and 47 units of product *B* per day and make a profit of $7,000.

MONOPSONY

Monopsony Markets that consist of a single buyer.

Whereas monopoly occurs when there is one seller, **monopsony** occurs when there is one buyer. As in monopoly, the monopsonist controls price. Consider the market for busboys for New York City restaurants. There are many restaurants and many aspiring busboys. If a restaurant wants to hire an additional busboy, it can pay the prevailing wage for busboys, and that wage won't change as a result of its hiring. However, consider The Company in a company town. When it wishes to hire another worker, because it employs such a large proportion of the labor force, it will influence the wage.

The demand for labor is labor's marginal revenue product—that is, the incremental revenue that an additional worker will generate for The Company and the additional benefit of hiring another worker. Formally, it is The Company's marginal revenue multiplied by the marginal product of labor. It is downward-sloping because marginal revenue falls as output increases and because labor's marginal

---

QUANT OPTION

The marginal cost of hiring another worker is

$$dC/dQ = c + 2eQ$$

product falls as more labor is employed (recall the law of diminishing marginal productivity from earlier in the book). Denote the labor supply curve as $P = c + eQ$, where P is the wage of labor and Q is the number of workers willing to work at that wage. Note that it is upward-sloping, reflecting the influence that the monopsonist has on the prevailing wage rate; that is, to hire another worker, The Company must increase the wage to entice a worker either into the workforce or away from another job (and by so doing will have to pay all its workers the new higher wage).

The Company's total expenditure on labor (total cost) is

$$C = PQ = (c + eQ)Q = cQ + eQ^2$$

To maximize profit, managers will equate the marginal benefit of hiring another worker with the marginal expenditure (marginal cost) of hiring another worker:

$$\Delta C/\Delta Q = c + 2eQ = MC$$

Figure 7.8 shows the optimal amount of labor and the wage paid by the monopsonist. The marginal benefit equals the marginal expenditure at point X with Q_1

FIGURE 7.8

Optimal Monopsony Pricing

The optimal number of workers hired under monopsony is less (Q_1) than the optimal number of workers hired under perfect competition (Q_2); and the optimal wage under monopsony (P_1) is less than the optimal wage under perfect competition (P_2).

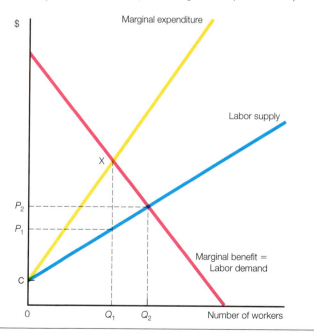

workers. Dropping down to the labor supply curve yields a wage of P_1. Note that the monopsonist restricts the amount of labor hired (Q_1) and pays a lower wage (P_1) than it would if the labor market were perfectly competitive (Q_2 and P_2).

MONOPOLISTIC COMPETITION

We now turn our attention to monopolistic competition. From a managerial point of view, a central characteristic of monopolistic competition is product differentiation. Unlike perfect competition, in which all managers sell an identical product, firms in monopolistic competition sell similar but not identical products. Hence consumers can associate specific products with a given firm. For example, in retail markets both American Apparel and Gap sell similar tank tops for women. Managers at each firm make their tank tops slightly different (color, fabric, design). Managers could also offer different services or use different distribution channels to differentiate their products. Due to the differences among their products, managers have some control over product price, though price differentials are relatively small because the products of other firms are so similar.

In perfectly competitive markets, the firms included in an industry are easy to determine because they all produce an identical product. But when managers can differentiate their products, it is not as simple to accurately define an industry. Each firm produces a somewhat different product. Nevertheless, it is often useful to group together firms that produce similar products and call them a **product group**. We can define a product group called *neckties* or *toothbrushes* or *shirts*. The process by which we combine firms into product groups is somewhat arbitrary; there is no way to decide how close a pair of substitute products must be to belong to the same product group. Clearly the broader the definition of a product group, the greater the number of firms included.

Product group Group of firms that produce similar products.

In addition to product differentiation, other conditions must be met for an industry to qualify as one of monopolistic competition:

1. *There must be many firms in the product group.* The product must be produced by perhaps fifty to a hundred or more firms, with each firm's product a fairly close substitute for the products of the other firms in the product group.

2. *The number of firms in the product group must be large enough that each firm expects its actions to go unheeded by its rivals and unimpeded by possible retaliatory moves on their part.* Hence, when formulating their own price and output policies, they do not explicitly concern themselves with their rivals' responses. If there are many firms, this condition normally is met.

3. *Entry into the product group must be relatively easy, and there must be no collusion, such as price fixing or market sharing, among managers in the product group.* It generally is difficult, if not impossible, for a great many firms to collude.

Price and Output Decisions under Monopolistic Competition

If each firm produces a somewhat different product, it follows that the demand curve facing each manager slopes downward to the right. That is, if the firm raises its price slightly, it will lose some, but by no means all, of its customers to other firms. And if it lowers its price slightly, it will gain some, but not all, of its competitors' customers.

Figure 7.9 shows the short-run equilibrium of a monopolistically competitive firm. Managers, in the short run, set price at P_0 and output at Q_0 because this combination of price and output maximizes profit. We can be sure this combination of price and output maximizes profit because marginal cost equals marginal revenue at this output level. Economic profit is earned because price, P_0, exceeds average total cost, C_0. As in the case of monopoly and perfect competition, price must exceed average variable cost for profit to be maximized (clearly this occurs in Figure 7.9—average variable cost lies below average total cost).

One condition for long-run equilibrium in these markets is that each firm make no economic profit or loss because entry or exit of firms will occur other-

---

FIGURE 7.9

Short-Run Equilibrium in Monopolistic Competition

The firm will set its price at P_0 and its output rate at Q_0 because marginal cost equals marginal revenue at this output. It will earn a profit of $P_0 - C_0$ per unit of output.

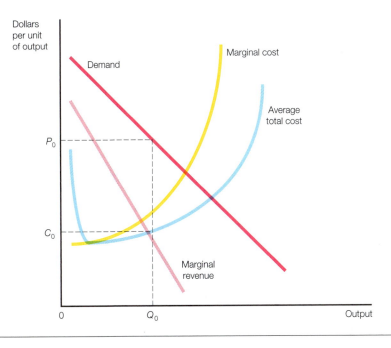

FIGURE 7.10

Long-Run Equilibrium in Monopolistic Competition

The long-run equilibrium is at price P_1 and output Q_1. There is zero profit because long-run average cost equals price. Profit is maximized because marginal cost equals marginal revenue at this output.

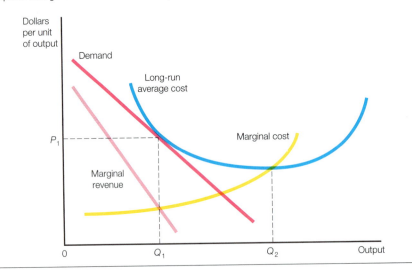

wise—and entry and exit are incompatible with long-run equilibrium. Another condition for long-run equilibrium is that each firm maximize its profit. At what price and output are both these conditions fulfilled? Figure 7.10 shows that the long-run equilibrium is at a price of P_1 and an output of Q_1. The zero economic profit condition is met at this combination of price and output because the firm's average cost at this output equals the price, P_1. And the profit maximization condition is met because the marginal revenue curve intersects the marginal cost curve.[7]

ADVERTISING EXPENDITURES: A SIMPLE RULE

Managers in monopolistic competition, as well as in other market structures, spend huge amounts on advertising. How much should a profit-maximizing manager spend on advertising? This section derives a simple rule to help managers answer this question.[8] The quantity a firm sells of its product is assumed to be a function of its price and the level of its advertising expenditures. We assume diminishing marginal returns to advertising expenditures, which means that beyond some point, successive advertising outlays yield smaller increases in sales. (Table 7.4 shows an illustrative case in which successive increments of $100,000

7. The seminal work in the theory of monopolistic competition was E. Chamberlin, *The Theory of Monopolistic Competition* (Cambridge, MA: Harvard University Press, 1933).
8. This rule, put forth by R. Dorfman and P. Steiner, applies to monopolistic or oligopolistic (see Chapter 10) firms as well as monopolistically competitive firms.

TABLE 7.4

Relationship between Advertising Expenditures and Quantity

Advertising Expenditures (Millions of Dollars)	Quantity Sold of Product (Millions of Units)
0.8	15.0
0.9	17.0
1.0	18.5
1.1	19.5
1.2	20.0

in advertising outlays result in smaller increases in quantity sold. For example, the quantity sold increases by 2 million units when advertising expenditures rise from $800,000 to $900,000, but by only 1.5 million units when they rise from $900,000 to $1 million.)

Let P be the price of a unit of the product and MC the marginal cost of production. If we assume that neither price nor marginal cost is altered by small changes in advertising expenditure, managers realize an increase in gross profit of $(P - MC)$ from each additional unit of product. Why is this the *gross* profit of selling an additional unit of output? Because it takes no account of whatever additional advertising expenditures are required to sell this extra unit of output. To obtain the net profit, managers must deduct these additional advertising outlays from the gross profit.

To maximize net profit, a manager must set advertising expenditures at the level where an extra dollar of advertising results in extra gross profit equal to the extra dollar of advertising cost. Unless this is the case, a manager can increase the firm's total net profit by changing advertising outlays. If an extra dollar of advertising results in more than a dollar of increase in gross profit, the extra dollar should be spent on advertising (because this increases the total net profit). If the extra dollar (as well as the last dollar) of advertising results in less than a dollar's increase in gross profit, advertising outlays should be cut.[9] Therefore, if ΔQ is the number of extra units of output sold as a result of an extra dollar of advertising, the manager should set advertising expenditures so that

$$\Delta Q(P - MC) = 1 \qquad (7.17)$$

because the right side of this equation equals the extra dollar of advertising cost and the left side equals the extra gross profit resulting from this advertising dollar.

If we multiply both sides of equation (7.17) by $P/(P - MC)$, we obtain

$$P\Delta Q = P/(P - MC) \qquad (7.18)$$

9. For simplicity, we assume that the gross profit resulting from an extra dollar spent on advertising is essentially equal to the gross profit resulting from the last dollar spent. This is an innocuous assumption.

Because the manager is maximizing profit, he is producing an output level at which marginal cost (MC) equals marginal revenue (MR). Therefore, we can substitute MR for MC in equation (7.18), the result being

$$P\Delta Q = P/(P - MR) \qquad (7.19)$$

Using equation (7.2), we can show that the right side of equation (7.19) equals $|\eta|$, the negative of the price elasticity of demand for the firm's product.[10] The left side of equation (7.19) is the marginal revenue from an extra dollar of advertising (it equals the price times the extra number of units sold as a result of an extra dollar of advertising). To maximize profit, the manager should set advertising expenditure so that

$$\text{Marginal revenue from an extra dollar of advertising} = |\eta| \qquad (7.20)$$

This rule can be very helpful to managers.[11] Consider managers at the Humphrey Corporation, who estimate that the price elasticity of demand for its product equals -1.6. To maximize profit, managers must set the marginal revenue from an extra dollar of advertising equal to 1.6, according to the rule in equation (7.20). Suppose managers believe an extra $100,000 of advertising will increase sales by $200,000. This association implies that the marginal revenue from an extra dollar of advertising is about $200,000/$100,000, or 2.0 rather than 1.6. Because the marginal revenue exceeds the absolute value of the price elasticity, managers can increase profit by advertising more.[12] To maximize profit, managers should increase advertising to the point where the marginal revenue from an extra dollar of advertising falls to 1.6—that is, the absolute value of the price elasticity of demand.

USING GRAPHS TO HELP DETERMINE ADVERTISING EXPENDITURE

A simple graphical technique can help managers identify optimal advertising expenditures. Take the case of the Hertzfeld Chemical Company. Curve A in Figure 7.11 shows the relationship between a product's price elasticity of demand and the amount managers spend on advertising. Managers should think of price elasticity as a proxy for the effectiveness of their differentiation strategies. Advertising is a strategic variable managers use to convey their differentiating message. The graph shows a curvilinear association between advertising and price elasticity. With little or no advertising, differentiation is slight between rival products; hence the price elasticity is high (in absolute value).

But because effective advertising can induce consumers to attach economic value to product attributes, increases in advertising spending reduce the product's price elasticity (in absolute value) considerably (by decreasing the product's perceived substitutability with other goods).[13] For any advertising level, the B curve shows the marginal revenue from an extra dollar of advertising. Because the A curve

---

10. Recall from equation (7.2) that $MR = P[1 - (1/|\eta|)]$. Therefore, $[1 - (1/|\eta|)] = MR/P$ and $1/|\eta| = 1 - (MR/P)$; this means that $|\eta| = 1/[1 - (MR/P)] = P/(P - MR)$ which is the right side of equation (7.19).

11. However, this rule is based on many simplifying assumptions and is not a complete solution to this complex problem.

12. Had Humphrey's managers believed that the marginal revenue from an extra dollar of advertising was *less* than the price elasticity of demand, a *reduction* in the firm's advertising expenditures would increase profit.

13. This is true for some products, but not for others. In some cases the absolute value of price elasticity of demand is directly, not inversely, related to the amount spent on advertising.

FIGURE 7.11

Optimal Advertising Expenditure

The firm's optimal advertising expenditure is *R* if the marginal revenue curve is *B* (or *S* if the marginal revenue curve is *B'*).

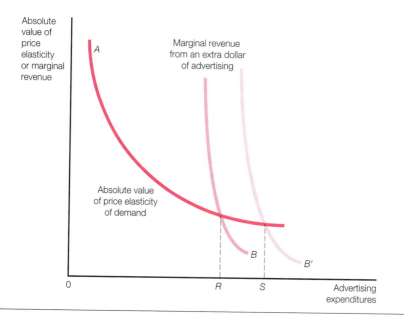

intersects the *B* curve when Hertzfeld's advertising expenditure is *R* dollars, this, on the basis of equation (7.20), is the estimated optimal advertising spending.

Clearly the optimal advertising level depends on the position and shape of the *B* and *A* curves. For example, suppose Hertzfeld's *B* curve shifts rightward to *B'*, as shown in Figure 7.11. Such a shift might occur if managers increase advertising effectiveness. Because advertising is more effective, marginal revenue increases, so managers want to increase their ad spending. Hence we see the optimal level of advertising increases (to *S* dollars in Figure 7.11).

ADVERTISING, PRICE ELASTICITY, AND BRAND EQUITY: EVIDENCE ON MANAGERIAL BEHAVIOR

Promotions and advertising tend to be two sides of the same coin. Although they both seek to improve market performance, promotions appeal to the price-sensitive, whereas ads build brand loyalty. Promotions use a price-oriented message to test the limits of brand loyalty; advertising illuminates brand worth and does not mention price. Both strategies persuade purchasers by influencing the price sensitivities of consumers. Promotions increase price elasticity and, in the long run, limit the price consumers are willing to pay for brand quality. Understanding these effects on consumer behavior certainly helps managers better understand the consequences of their actions.

So can we find real-world evidence of the effectiveness of these strategies? Yes. A large body of evidence shows that promotions increase the price elasticities of consumers.[14] These studies also show that the change in elasticities varies across consumers and time. In addition, brand loyalty does protect against promotions: Promotional strategies have less effect on the elasticities of brand loyalists relative to nonloyalists. And promotion is characterized as decaying in time. Short-term change is greater, as if consumers operate with a high discount rate; or they may have short memories.

Mela, Gupta, and Lehmann report on a mature good market in which the ratio of advertising to promotions shifted from spending $250 million on advertising and offering promotions less than 10 percent of the time to spending less than $100 million on advertising and giving discounts more than 25 percent of the time. They found that the price elasticity of the average nonloyalist was twice that of the average brand loyalist. Loyalty is measured as frequency of repeat purchases. A drop in advertising messages affects all consumers, but the effect is much greater on the nonloyal crowd. In fact, a drop in advertising leads to a larger number of nonloyalists. Without reinforcement, a brand is eroded by price. Frequent promotions encourage nonloyalists to look for them, so their price sensitivities increase. The effect of promotions on the price sensitivity of nonloyalists is four times that of loyalists.

Pauwells, Hanssens, and Siddarth report on the soup and yogurt markets. They studied buying habits over a two-year period by analyzing purchases of over 690,000 ounces of yogurt and 535,000 ounces of soup. In both markets they found the effects of a promotion on price sensitivities was the greatest within the two-week period following its announcement. After this initial period, the effect grew weaker. The frequency of promotions also varied across firms, as did the amount of the discounts. These findings indicated that promotions are used more frequently by managers whose brand is weaker.

14. K. Pauwells, D. Hanssens, and S. Siddarth, "The Long-Term Effects of Price Promotions on Category Incidence, Brand Choice, and Purchase Quantity," *Journal of Marketing Research* 39 (November 2002), pp. 421–436; C. Mela, S. Gupta, and D. Lehmann, "The Long-Term Impact of Promotion and Advertising on Consumer Brand Choice," *Journal of Marketing Research* 34 (May 1997), pp. 248–262.

SUMMARY

1. Under monopoly, a manager maximizes profit by setting output at the point where marginal revenue equals marginal cost. It does not follow that managers in monopoly markets always earn significant profit. If the monopolist cannot cover its variable costs, it, like a perfectly competitive firm, will shut down, even in the short run.

2. An industry that is monopolized generally sets a higher price and a lower output than if it were perfectly competitive. The perfectly competitive firm oper-

ates at a point where price equals marginal cost, whereas the monopolist operates at a point at which marginal revenue equals marginal cost (and price exceeds marginal cost).

3. Empirical studies indicate that cost-plus pricing is used by many managers. In this approach, a manager estimates the cost per unit of output (based on some assumed output level) and adds a markup to include costs that cannot be allocated to any specific product and to provide a return on the firm's investment. On the surface, it is questionable whether this approach can maximize profit; but if marginal cost (not average cost) is really what is being marked up and the size of the markup is determined (in the appropriate way) by the product's price elasticity of demand, cost-plus pricing can approximate profit maximization.

4. Firms generally sell more than one product. It is important for managers to recognize the demand interrelationships among the products they sell. Also, products are often interrelated in production. If two products are produced jointly in fixed proportions, the profit-maximizing output occurs where the total marginal revenue curve (the vertical summation of the marginal revenue curves for the individual products) intersects the marginal cost curve for the bundle of products, assuming the marginal revenue of each product is nonnegative.

5. If two products are produced jointly in variable proportions, we can construct isocost curves, each of which shows the combinations of outputs that can be produced at the same total cost. Also, isorevenue lines can be constructed, each of which shows the combination of outputs that yield the same total revenue. For an output combination to be optimal, it must be at a point where an isorevenue line is tangent to an isocost curve. To determine which output combination is optimal, we compare the profit levels at the tangency points. The tangency point where profit is the highest is the optimal output combination.

6. Monopsony occurs when there is only one buyer. Analogous to monopoly, the monopsonist restricts the amount purchased to less than what would occur if perfect competition existed and decreases the price paid relative to the price that would prevail under perfect competition.

7. In contrast to perfect competition, where all firms sell an identical product, firms under monopolistic competition sell somewhat different products. Producers differentiate their products from those of other producers. Therefore, the demand curve facing each firm slopes downward to the right—and is not horizontal, as it would be under perfect competition. Each firm sets marginal revenue equal to marginal cost if it maximizes profit.

8. Managers of monopolistically competitive firms spend large amounts on advertising. To maximize its profit, a manager should set an advertising level so the marginal revenue from an extra dollar of advertising equals the absolute value of the price elasticity of demand (under the conditions discussed).

9. Advertising of price changes may increase the price elasticity of demand for the product whose price has changed. This happens because the advertising

makes consumers more aware of the price changes. Measures of brand loyalty are useful in guiding decisions concerning promotional activities to increase sales of particular brands.

wwnorton.com/studyspace

PROBLEMS

1. Harry Smith owns a metal-producing firm that is an unregulated monopoly. After considerable experimentation and research, he finds that the firm's marginal cost curve can be approximated by a straight line, $MC = 60 + 2Q$, where MC is marginal cost (in dollars) and Q is output. The demand curve for the product is $P = 100 - Q$, where P is the product price (in dollars) and Q is output.
   a. If Smith wants to maximize profit, what output should he choose?
   b. What price should he charge?

2. The Wilson Company's marketing manager has determined that the price elasticity of demand for its product equals -2.2. According to studies she carried out, the relationship between the amount spent by the firm on advertising and its sales is as follows:

Advertising Expenditure	Sales
$100,000	$1.0 million
200,000	1.3 million
300,000	1.5 million
400,000	1.6 million

   a. If the Wilson Company spends $200,000 on advertising, what is the marginal revenue from an extra dollar of advertising?
   b. Is $200,000 the optimal amount for the firm to spend on advertising?
   c. If $200,000 is not the optimal amount, would you recommend that the firm spend more or less on advertising?

3. The Coolidge Corporation is the only producer of a particular type of laser. The demand curve for its product is

$$Q = 8,300 - 2.1P$$

and its total cost function is

$$TC = 2,200 + 480Q + 20Q^2$$

where P is price (in dollars), TC is total cost (in dollars), and Q is monthly output.
   a. Derive an expression for the firm's marginal revenue curve.

   b. To maximize profit, how many lasers should the firm produce and sell per month?

   c. If this number were produced and sold, what would be the firm's monthly profit?

4. The Madison Corporation, a monopolist, receives a report from a consulting firm concluding that the demand function for its product is

$$Q = 78 - 1.1P + 2.3Y + 0.9A$$

where Q is the number of units sold, P is the price of its product (in dollars), Y is per capita income (in thousands of dollars), and A is the firm's advertising expenditure (in thousands of dollars). The firm's average variable cost function is

$$AVC = 42 - 8Q + 1.5Q^2$$

where AVC is average variable cost (in dollars).

   a. Can we determine the firm's marginal cost curve?

   b. Can we determine the firm's marginal revenue curve?

   c. If per capita income is $4,000 and advertising expenditure is $200,000, can we determine the price and output where marginal revenue equals marginal cost? If so, what are they?

5. The Wilcox Company has two plants with the marginal cost functions[15]

$$MC_1 = 20 + 2Q_1$$
$$MC_2 = 10 + 5Q_2$$

where MC_1 is marginal cost in the first plant, MC_2 is marginal cost in the second plant, Q_1 is output in the first plant, and Q_2 is output in the second plant.

   a. If the Wilcox Company minimizes its costs and produces five units of output in the first plant, how many units of output does it produce in the second plant? Explain.

   b. What is the marginal cost function for the firm as a whole?

   c. Can we determine from these data the average cost function for each plant? Why or why not?

6. If the Rhine Company ignores the possibility that other firms may enter its market, it should set a price of $10,000 for its product, which is a power tool. But if it does so, other firms will begin to enter the market. During the next two years it will earn $4 million per year, but in the following two years it will earn $1 million per year. On the other hand, if it sets a price of $7,000, it will earn $2.5 million in each of the next four years because no entrants will appear.

   a. If the interest rate is 10 percent, should the Rhine Company set a price of $7,000 or $10,000? Why? (Consider only the next four years.)

15. This question pertains to the chapter appendix.

    b. If the interest rate is 8 percent, should the Rhine Company set a price of $7,000 or $10,000? Why? (Consider only the next four years.)

    c. The results in parts (a) and (b) pertain to only the next four years. How can the firm's managers extend the planning horizon?

7. During recessions and economic hard times, many people—particularly those who have difficulty getting bank loans—turn to pawnshops to raise cash. But even during boom years, pawnshops can be profitable. Because the collateral that customers put up (such as jewelry, guns, or electric guitars) is generally worth at least double what is lent, it generally can be sold at a profit. And because usury laws allow higher interest ceilings for pawnshops than for other lending institutions, pawnshops often charge spectacularly high rates of interest. For example, Florida's pawnshops charge interest rates of 20 percent or more *per month*. According to Steven Kent, an analyst at Goldman, Sachs, pawnshops make 20 percent gross profit on defaulted loans and 205 percent interest on loans repaid.

    a. In late 1991 there were about 8,000 pawnshops in the United States, according to American Business Information. This was much higher than in 1986, when the number was about 5,000. Indeed, in late 1991 alone the number jumped by about 1,000. Why did the number increase?

    b. In a particular small city, do the pawnshops constitute a perfectly competitive industry? If not, what is the market structure of the industry?

    c. Are there considerable barriers to entry in the pawnshop industry? (*Note:* A pawnshop can be opened for less than $125,000, but a number of states have tightened licensing requirements for pawnshops.)

8. In 1996 dairy farmers, hurt by a decade of low milk prices, began reducing their herds. Subsequently Kenneth Hein, a Wisconsin farmer, said he was getting $16 per 100 pounds of milk, rather than $12, which he had gotten earlier.[16]

    a. Why did the price increase?

    b. Dairy cattle are often fed corn. When Hein got $16 per 100 pounds of milk, he paid $5 a bushel for corn; but when he got $12 per 100 pounds of milk, he paid $2.50 a bushel for corn. Does this mean that Hein made less money when the price of milk was $16 than when it was $12?

9. The demand for diamonds is given by

$$P_Z = 980 - 2Q_Z$$

where Q_Z is the number of diamonds demanded if the price is P_Z per diamond. The total cost (TC_Z) of the De Beers Company (a monopolist) is given by

$$TC_Z = 100 + 50Q_Z + 0.5Q_Z^2$$

16. *Philadelphia Inquirer*, September 14, 1996.

where Q_Z is the number of diamonds produced and put on the market by the De Beers Company. Suppose the government could force De Beers to behave as if it were a perfect competitor—that is, via regulation, force the firm to price diamonds at marginal cost.

a. What is social welfare when De Beers acts as a single-price monopolist?

b. What is social welfare when De Beers acts as a perfect competitor?

c. How much does social welfare increase when De Beers moves from monopoly to competition?

10. The Hassman Company produces two joint products, X and Y. The isocost curve corresponding to a total cost of $500,000 is

$$Q_Y = 1,000 - 10Q_X - 5Q_X^2$$

where Q_Y is the quantity of product Y produced by the firm and Q_X is the quantity of product X produced. The price of product X is 50 times that of product Y.

a. If the optimal output combination lies on this isocost curve, what is the optimal output of product X?

b. What is the optimal output of product Y?

c. Can you be sure that the optimal output combination lies on this isocost curve? Why or why not?

11. The McDermott Company estimates its average total cost to be $10 per unit of output when it produces 10,000 units, which it regards as 80 percent of capacity. Its goal is to earn 20 percent on its total investment, which is $250,000.

a. If the company uses cost-plus pricing, what price should it set?

b. Can it be sure of selling 10,000 units if it sets this price?

c. What are the arguments for and against a pricing policy of this sort?

12. The Morrison Company produces tennis rackets, the marginal cost of a racket being $20. Because there are many substitutes for the firm's rackets, the price elasticity of demand for its rackets equals about -2. In the relevant range of output, average variable cost is very close to marginal cost.

a. The president of the Morrison Company feels that cost-plus pricing is appropriate for his firm. He marks up average variable cost by 100 percent to set price. Comment on this procedure.

b. Because of heightened competition, the price elasticity of demand for the firm's rackets increases to -3. The president continues to use the same cost-plus pricing formula. Comment on its adequacy.

13. The Backus Corporation makes two products, X and Y. For every unit of good X that the firm produces, it produces two units of good Y. Backus's total cost function is

$$TC = 500 + 3Q + 9Q^2$$

where Q is the number of units of output (where each unit contains one unit of good X and two units of good Y) and TC is total cost (in dollars). The demand curves for the firm's two products are

$$P_X = 400 - Q_X$$
$$P_Y = 300 - 3Q_Y$$

where P_X and Q_X are the price and output of product X and P_Y and Q_Y are the price and output of product Y.

a. How much of each product should the Backus Corporation produce and sell per period?

b. What price should it charge for each product?

APPENDIX: ALLOCATION OF OUTPUT AMONG PLANTS

Many firms own and operate more than one plant. In this appendix we show how the managers of these firms should allocate output among various plants. This is an important decision, and our results have major direct practical value. We consider the case of the Johnson Company, a monopolist; but our results are valid for any firm that exercises market power.

The Johnson Company, a monopolist that makes a particular type of fixture, operates two plants with marginal cost curves shown in columns 2 and 3 of Table 7.5, output being shown in column 1. Clearly, if the managers decide to produce only one unit of output per hour, they should use plant I because the marginal cost between zero and one unit of output is lower in plant I than in plant II. Hence for the firm as a whole, the marginal cost between zero and one unit of output is $10 (the marginal cost between zero and one unit for plant I). Similarly, if the

---

TABLE 7.5

Costs of the Johnson Company

Output per Hour	Marginal Cost[a] Plant I (Dollars)	Marginal Cost[a] Plant II (Dollars)	Marginal Cost for Firm[a] (Dollars)	Price (Dollars)	Marginal Revenue[a] (Dollars)
1	10	14	10	40	—
2	12	18	12	30	20
3	14	22	14	26	18
4	20	26	14	23	14
5	24	30	18	20.8	12

---

[a]These figures pertain to the interval between the indicated output and one unit less than the indicated output.

managers decide to produce two units of output per hour, both should be produced in plant I, and the marginal cost between the first and second units of output for the firm as a whole is $12 (the marginal cost between the first and second units in plant I). If managers decide to produce three units of output per hour, two should be produced in plant I and one in plant II, and the marginal cost between the second and third units of output for the firm as a whole is $14 (the marginal cost between zero and one unit of output for plant II). Alternatively, all three could be produced at plant I (the marginal cost between the second and third units of output in plant I is also $14).

Going on in this way, we can derive the marginal cost curve for the firm as a whole, shown in column 4 of Table 7.5. To maximize profit, the manager should find the output level at which the marginal revenue equals the marginal cost of the firm as a whole. This is the profit-maximizing output level. In this case it is three or four units per hour. Suppose managers choose to produce four units.[17] To determine what price to charge, they must estimate what price corresponds to this output on the demand curve. In this case, the answer is $23.

At this point we have solved most of the Johnson Company's problems, but not quite all. Given that managers will produce four units of output per hour, how should they divide this production between the two plants? The answer is that they need to set the marginal cost in plant I equal to the marginal cost in plant II. Table 7.5 shows this means that plant I would produce three units per hour and plant II would produce one unit per hour. The common value of the marginal costs of the two plants is the marginal cost of the firm as a whole; this common value must be set equal to the marginal revenue if the firm maximizes profit.

Many managers use this technique to allocate output among plants. For example, electric power companies have developed computer programs to facilitate the job of allocating electricity demand (or "load") among plants in accord with this theoretical rule. These programs allow a central dispatcher, who is in constant communication with the plants, to compute quickly the optimal allocation among plants. The result has been millions of dollars of savings.

As a further illustration, consider the Chou Company, which has plants at Altoona, Pennsylvania, and at High Point, North Carolina. The total cost function for the Altoona plant is

$$TC_A = 5 + 9Q_A + Q_A^2$$

where TC_A is the daily total cost (in thousands of dollars) at this plant and Q_A is its output (in units per day). The total cost curve for the High Point plant is

$$TC_H = 4 + 10Q_H + 0.5Q_H^2$$

where TC_H is the daily total cost (in thousands of dollars) at this plant, and Q_H is its output (in units per day).

17. The firm is indifferent between producing three or four units. If it produces four, its total revenue is $92,000 ($23 × 4$) and its variable cost is $50,000 ($10 + 12 + 14 + 14$), yielding a variable-cost profit of $42,000. If it produces three, the total revenue is $78,000 ($26 × 3$) and the variable cost is $36,000 ($10 + 12 + 14$), yielding a variable-cost profit of $42,000. Because both plants already exist, their fixed costs must be paid and therefore are irrelevant in the short run. In the long run (if demand were predicted to remain constant), the firm could divest itself of plant II.

The Chou Company's demand curve is

$$P = 31 - Q$$

and its total revenue is

$$TR = PQ = (31 - Q)Q = 31Q - Q^2$$

Therefore the Chou Company's marginal revenue curve is

$$MR = \Delta TR/\Delta Q = 31 - 2Q$$

Note that $Q = Q_A + Q_H$, P is price, and MR is the marginal revenue (in thousands of dollars per unit).

To maximize profit, managers must choose a price and output such that

$$MC_A = MC_H = MR \tag{7.21}$$

where MC_A is the marginal cost (in thousands of dollars) at the Altoona plant and MC_H is the marginal cost (in thousands of dollars) at the High Point plant.

The Altoona plant's marginal cost is

$$MC_A = \Delta TC_A/\Delta Q_A = 9 + 2Q_A$$

The High Point plant's marginal cost is

$$MC_H = \Delta TC_H/\Delta Q_H = 10 + Q_H$$

According to equation (7.21), MC_A must equal MC_H. Therefore,

$$9 + 2Q_A = 10 + Q_H$$

or

$$Q_H = -1 + 2Q_A$$

Also, because equation (7.21) states that MC_A must equal MR,

$$
\begin{aligned}
9 + 2Q_A &= 31 - 2(Q_A + Q_H) \\
&= 31 - 2(Q_A - 1 + 2Q_A) \\
&= 33 - 6Q_A
\end{aligned}
$$

or

$$8Q_A = 24$$

Consequently, $Q_A = 3$. And because $Q_H = -1 + 2Q_A$, it follows that $Q_H = 5$. Moreover, $P = 23$ because $P = 31 - (Q_A + Q_H)$. In a nutshell, managers should charge \$23,000 per unit and produce three units per day at the Altoona plant and five units per day at the High Point plant.

PART 5

SOPHISTICATED MARKET PRICING

CHAPTER 8

MANAGERIAL USE OF
PRICE DISCRIMINATION

Price discrimination is common across many markets and products. A car dealership aims to sell each vehicle for the highest price it can get (as long as that price is higher than its reservation price). Airline managers segment their markets and sell the same seats at significantly different prices depending on when the tickets are purchased, whether the tickets are refundable, penalities for changing flight plans, and the like. College administrators use a price discrimination policy by awarding financial aid; there is a wide variety of aid packages within the student population.

In general, managers try to identify submarkets on the basis of an individual's price elasticity of demand. A car dealership is an example of first-degree price discrimination, where the dealer attempts to extract the reservation price of each buyer. In effect each buyer is a submarket. The airlines use one general pricing model to divide the market into at least two submarkets: a relatively price-insensitive business class and a relatively price-sensitive leisure class. Airlines are an example of third-degree price discrimination, where each airline tries to extract the average reservation price of those similar in price sensitivity. The airline pricing model is compromised somewhat by Internet firms such as Expedia, which search airline databases for the lowest fares. This gives the consumer more information about the range of fares available and enables the consumer to potentially get a lower fare than that available from dealing directly with the carrier.

MOTIVATION FOR PRICE DISCRIMINATION

Consider Figure 8.1, which shows the profit-maximizing price and quantity for a single-price monopolist. By charging price P_M, the monopolist sells Q_M units. But aside from the customer whose reservation price was P_M, all other purchasing customers in area AB of the demand curve value the good at a price higher than P_M, but they are asked to pay only P_M for it. Consumers can retain a significant amount of consumer surplus—money they are willing to pay the producer but are not asked to do so. The amount of that consumer surplus is V (the area shaded in dark blue).

Consumers in area BC of the demand curve are unwilling to spend P_M for the good but have reservation prices that exceed the marginal cost of producing the

---

FIGURE 8.1

Single-Price Monopolist Profit-Maximizing Outcome

The single-price monopolist prices at P_M and produces and sells Q_M units. Consumers in region AB are willing to pay a higher price than P_M yet are not asked to do so. Consumers in region BC are unwilling to pay a price as high as P_M but will pay a price higher than it costs the producer to make the good. Both these situations are potentially profitable sales that are not made.

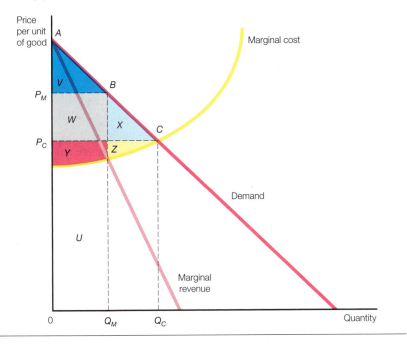

good and hence represent potential profitable sales. These sales are not made by the single-price monopolist, who curtails output at Q_M, whereas profitable sales could continue up to Q_C. The amount of profit represented by those potential sales is $X + Z$.

Instead the single-price monopolist settles for a variable-cost profit of $W + Y$: the gray plus red areas where total revenue is $P_M Q_M = W + Y + U$ and variable cost is the area U, under the marginal cost curve (as shown in Chapter 5).

If the monopolist raises the price above P_M to capture some of the consumer surplus in area V, area $X + Z$ becomes greater. If the manager lowers the price below P_M to capture some of the potential profit in area $X + Z$, area V becomes bigger. We know that managers cannot increase profit by deviating from P_M because it is the profit-maximizing price for the single-price monopolist. If the manager is going to capture some (or all) of region V and some (or all) of region $X + Z$, she cannot do it with a single-price strategy. Managers can capture surplus from area V and profit from areas $X + Z$ only with a strategy that involves two or more prices. We now explore what those strategies should be. Their motivation is capturing the additional profit in area V and areas $X + Z$. If the benefit of capturing that profit exceeds the costs of doing so (remember that sophisticated pricing is more costly to implement than simple single pricing), then our manager should do so.

PRICE DISCRIMINATION

Price discrimination occurs when the same product is sold at more than one price. For example, an airline may sell tickets on a particular flight at a higher price to business travelers than to college students. An automobile dealer may sell the exactly equipped make and model at different prices on the same day to different buyers. Even if the products are not precisely the same, price discrimination is said to occur if similar products are sold at prices that are in different ratios to their marginal costs. If managers sell boxes of candy with a label (costing 2 cents) saying "Premium Quality" in rich neighborhoods for $12 and sell the same boxes of candy without this label in poor neighborhoods for $5, this is price discrimination. Differences in price among similar products are not evidence of discrimination unless these differences do not reflect cost differences.

First-Degree Price Discrimination

Managers need to master three basic types of price discrimination: first, second, and third degree. The auto dealer is an example of the first degree, whereas the airline and candy firm are examples of the third degree. Selling electricity to certain customers is an example of the second degree. By examining price discrimination in a bit more detail, managers can better understand how to use all three types.

Consider again the diagram of a simple monopoly (single-price) profit maximizer shown in Figure 8.1. To reiterate, consumers in segment AB of the demand

In general, Americans hate to haggle. They do so at car dealers (and detest the experience), in real estate transactions, in dealings with contractors for home repairs, in contract negotiations, and at flea markets; but most of their purchases involve posted prices, and most Americans accept that. However, haggling is the norm in many places around the world, and more haggling is drifting into the United States. What gives?

According to a *Consumer Reports* National Research Center survey of over 2,000 shoppers, 61 percent bargained for products such as cell phones, furniture, medical bills, home electronics, household appliances, jewelry, antiques, and the like during the previous three years. In the home furnishings category, 94 percent reported paying less than the posted price. Of those who negotiated successfully, 61 percent reported savings of between $50 and $99; 26 percent reported savings of between $1 and $49; and 14 percent reported savings of $100 or more.

Our MBA students play a series of managerial economics games against each other and MBA students at INSEAD's campuses in Fontainebleau and Singapore. Because they are French, INSEAD Fontainebleau gave a bottle of fine French champagne to the team that scored the highest. We decided to do the same. We teach 12 sections and hence needed 12 bottles. One of our faculty members went to several New Jersey liquor stores and negotiated a price for the champagne that was significantly below the posted price.

Here are *Consumer Report's* tips for hagglers:

1. Use the power of timing. For service contracts, negotiate for discounts and perks at the time of the initial contract or at its renewal.

2. Offer cash. Credit and debit card companies charge merchants 2–8 percent for card use.

3. Look for flaws—scratches and dents that don't impair the performance of the product and can be hidden or covered by the purchaser.

4. Buy multiple units and ask for a quantity discount.

This opportunity to haggle is good news for consumers who don't buy goods at their posted prices because they are above their reservation prices. But it's got to be a good deal for the sellers too. Otherwise why would sellers negotiate?

However, it's potentially not good news for people who don't mind posted prices. If buying a bar stool becomes more like buying a car, many people are going to hate shopping. Even if you accept the posted price of the stool (which you know is high relative to the seller's reservation price given your car-buying experience), you'll worry that you paid too much; and you'll worry that your neighbor will quiz you about what you paid and then humble you when she tells you what she paid. At least when you both paid the same posted price, you felt equal to her.

Source: "Haggle Even at Stores; Survey Shows It Works," *Philadelphia Inquirer*, May 18, 2008, p. M-2.

curve are willing to pay more than the single monopoly price of P_M. Consumers in segment BC of the demand curve are willing to pay more for the good than it costs the producer to produce it—that is, the firm's marginal cost.

The simple monopolist makes a variable-cost profit of $W + Y$, as shown in Figure 8.1, and leaves the consumer surplus of V with the consumers of segment AB. If managers could perfectly price discriminate (another term for first-degree

PROBLEM SOLVED: Honest Sanjay's Use of First-Degree Price Discrimination

We now view an example of first-degree price discrimination versus simple monopoly pricing. Honest Sanjay sells used cars. The market demand for Sanjay's used cars is $P = 12 - Q$, where P is the price in thousands and Q is the quantity of cars sold per month.

Sanjay has two strategies of selling cars. He can set a price and merely pay a general manager to write the paperwork. The total cost of selling each car under such an arrangement is $2 (thousand), so Sanjay's marginal cost is $2 (thousand). This is also Sanjay's average variable cost of selling a car. Sanjay faces fixed costs of $5 (thousand) per month.

To maximize profit under simple monopoly pricing, Sanjay should set marginal revenue equal to marginal cost. Sanjay's total revenue is $TR = PQ = (12 - Q)Q = 12Q - Q^2$. Sanjay's marginal revenue, $MR = \Delta TR / \Delta Q$, is

$$MR = 12 - 2Q$$

Setting Sanjay's marginal revenue equal to his marginal cost,

$$MR = 12 - 2Q = 2 = MC$$

gives $Q = 5$, which implies that the price of cars is $P = 12 - 5 = 7$ or $7,000.

Sanjay's total revenue per month is $35 (that is, $PQ = (\$7)(5) = \$35,000$), variable costs are $10 (that is, $(AVC)Q = (\$2)(5) = \$10,000$), and fixed costs are $5 (thousand), resulting in a monthly profit of $20 (thousand) from simple monopoly pricing.

Sanjay could also sell cars the more common way—customers haggling with salespeople. Sanjay can hire a slick salesforce. By chatting with customers, a salesperson can pretty well estimate a customer's reservation price of a car; for example, salespeople often come right out and ask a customer how much the customer is looking to spend or are more subtle by asking, "What do you do for a living? Do you want to drive the car home tonight?" Salespeople who are not good at estimating customers' reservation prices tend not to be employed for long in the automobile business. A general manager is still needed to write the paperwork, and the salespeople are paid strictly on commission: $1 (thousand) for each car they sell. Under this model of sales, Sanjay's marginal cost is $3 (thousand) per car. The haggle model is first-degree price discrimination in action. As mentioned, practicing price discrimination does carry costs not incurred by managers charging a single price.

Under this model, Sanjay sells cars up to the point where the reservation price equals marginal cost:

$$P = 12 - Q = 3 = MC \text{ or } Q = 9$$

price discrimination), they would charge the consumers in segment AB their reservation prices, capturing all the consumer surplus and turning it into producer surplus (that is, variable-cost profit). Note that when managers can perfectly discriminate in segment AB, the firm's variable-cost profit increases to $V + W + Y$.

First-degree discrimination lets managers expand sales. Because managers are not constrained by a single price, they can serve consumers in segment BC. This increases variable-cost profit by $X + Z$ because the reservation price of the consumers in segment BC exceeds the additional cost of producing the units involved: $Q_C - Q_M$. By perfectly discriminating in both the AB and the BC segments, managers increase the firm's variable-cost profit (and hence its profit) by $V + X + Z$.

First-Degree Price Discrimination

The first-degree price discriminator captures all consumer surplus *J* and turns it into producer surplus (variable-cost profit).

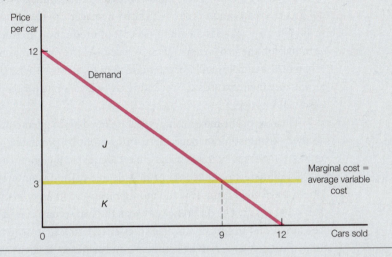

All consumer surplus (*J* in the figure shown) is captured. Sanjay's profit is total revenue (*J* + *K*) less total cost (variable cost, *K*, plus fixed cost). In this case total revenue is $67.5[a] (thousand), variable cost is $27 ((*AVC*) (*Q*) = ($3)(9) = $27,000), and fixed cost is $5 (thousand), resulting in a profit of $35.5 (thousand).

Sanjay prefers the haggle model over the simple monopoly posted-price model (because $35.5 > $20).

Presumably this explains why most auto dealers have not switched to the posted-price model and continue haggling to sell cars.

[a]The area of trapezoid *J* + *K* is one-half the height (9) times the sum of the trapezoid's two sides (12 + 3). Therefore 0.5(9)(15) = 67.5.

QUANT OPTION

Sanjay says, for those in the know, that marginal revenue is

$$dTR/dQ = 12 - 2Q$$

This is precisely all the area we saw that the simple monopolist was not exploiting in Figure 8.1. The potential for this additional profit gets creative managers thinking about pricing strategies to capture it.

If managers can capture all of $V + X + Z$, we say they are practicing discrimination of the first degree. As a manager, you always want to find ways to use first-degree price discrimination. In essence, the strategy allows managers to charge each consumer his or her reservation price. By so doing, they guarantee that consumer surplus is zero. Clearly managers are willing to do this up to Q_C units in Figure 8.1. The additional revenue managers generate by selling an additional unit of product is the reservation price of the consumer. Managers sell to a consumer as long as the reservation price (which the manager can charge and the consumer is willing to pay) exceeds the marginal cost of production. In essence, in perfect discrimination the firm's demand curve becomes the firm's marginal revenue curve. Therefore, managers will not sell more than Q_C items because the marginal cost of producing them exceeds the revenue they will generate for the firm—that is, their reservation price.

Thus the profit-maximizing rule developed in Chapters 6 and 7 holds. The perfectly discriminating manager maximizes profit by producing until marginal revenue (represented by the demand curve) is equal to the output's marginal cost.

One interesting outcome of first-degree price discrimination is that it produces the same output as if the monopolist were in a perfectly competitive market—that is, Q_C. The difference between the two scenarios is in the distribution of consumer and producer surplus. In essence, using first-degree price discrimination, the manager gets to bake the cake and eat it too. In Figure 8.1, under perfectly competitive pricing (P_C), consumer surplus is $V + W + X$ and producer surplus is $Y + Z$. Because total welfare is the sum of consumer and producer surplus, social welfare is V through Z. Under first-degree discrimination, consumer surplus is zero (it has all been captured) and producer surplus is V through Z. Therefore, the welfare is the same under both pricing mechanisms, V through Z, but consumers benefit under perfect competition and producers get *all* the benefit of first-degree price discrimination. Because the output is the same in each pricing scheme, social welfare is identical.

For first-degree price discrimination, managers usually must have a relatively small number of buyers and must be able to estimate the maximum prices they are willing to accept. In addition, other conditions must hold that are elaborated on when we discuss third-degree price discrimination. For these reasons, the two-part tariff method of pricing (discussed later) is a simpler way to operationalize first-degree price discrimination.

The general retail market in the United States is not well suited to first-degree price discrimination. The market is predominantly posted price, so there is no haggling (with the exception of car buying, home buying, dealing with housing contractors, and yard sales). In other cultures haggling is more prevalent. For example, in the bazaars of Asia, buyers are expected to haggle with sellers. In the finest pearl establishments of Hyderabad, India (a pearl capital of the world), transactions are all done by haggling (unless an unsuspecting tourist from a no-haggle country is uninformed enough to pay the price listed for the pearls). Negotiation is much more prevalent in business-to-business transactions in the United States.

Second-Degree Price Discrimination

Second-degree price discrimination is most common in utility pricing. According to some authorities, second-degree price discrimination plays an important role in the schedule of rates charged by many public utilities—gas, water, electricity, and others.[1]

Consider a gas company, *each* of whose customers has the demand curve shown in Figure 8.2. The company charges a high price, P_0, if the consumer purchases fewer than X units of gas per month. For an amount beyond X units per month, the company charges a medium price, P_1. For purchases beyond Y, the company charges an even lower price, P_2. Consequently the company's total revenues from each consumer are equal to the shaded area in Figure 8.2 because the consumer purchases X units at a price of P_0, $(Y - X)$ units at a price of P_1, and $(Z - Y)$ units at a price of P_2.[2]

The manager, by charging different prices for various amounts of the commodity, increases revenues and profit. After all, if she charged only a single price

---

FIGURE 8.2

Second-Degree Price Discrimination

The company charges a different price (P_0, P_1, or P_2) depending on how much the consumer purchases, thus increasing its total revenue and profit.

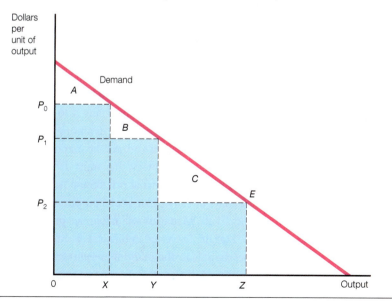

1. Of course, this assumes for simplicity that each consumer purchases Z units and that each price considered exceeds the firm's marginal cost. Also, other simplifying assumptions (which need not concern us here) are made in this and the next paragraph.
2. R. Davidson, *Price Discrimination in Selling Gas and Electricity* (Baltimore: Johns Hopkins University Press, 1955) and C. Cicchetti and J. Jurewitz, *Studies in Electric Utility Regulation* (Cambridge, MA: Ballinger, 1975).

and wanted to sell Z units, she would charge a price of P_2. Thus the firm's total revenue would equal the rectangle $0P_2EZ$, which is considerably less than the shaded area in Figure 8.2. By charging different prices, managers increase profit relative to a single-price strategy. Unlike first-degree price discrimination, managers leave a consumer surplus of $A + B + C$. Because second-degree (and third-degree) discrimination occurs at the group level and not that of the individual, consumers retain some surplus.

Third-Degree Price Discrimination

We now consider the most common form of price discrimination: third-degree price discrimination. Three conditions must hold true for this pricing strategy to succeed. Demand must be heterogeneous, managers must be able to identify and segregate the different segments, and markets must be successfully sealed. As we have previously discussed, individuals within a market have different preferences toward a product. The differences in their price elasticity of demand may be due to differences among classes in income levels, tastes, or the availability of substitutes. For example, the price elasticity of demand for the boxes of candy discussed earlier may be lower (in absolute value) for the rich than for the poor.

Think of it like this. Managers would prefer to identify the preferences of individuals (first-degree price discrimination). For various possible reasons, they can't (or don't want to because it is too expensive). So they choose the next best alternative, which is to identify individuals with similar traits and group them together. Managers then appeal to the group.

Students are a good example of third-degree discrimination. Students have relatively limited income, so they tend to have high price elasticities of demand—they are price sensitive. Thus many times they are sold a good or a service at a lower price. They get a discount, and all they must do is to show student identification.

Buyers of the product must fall into classes with considerable differences in price elasticity of demand for the product. Managers must then identify and segregate these classes at moderate cost. Also, buyers must be unable to transfer the product easily from one class to another; otherwise people could make money by buying the product from the low-price classes and selling it to the high-price classes, making it difficult to maintain the price differentials among classes. We call these latter two conditions the ability to *segment* and *seal* the market.[3]

If managers want to use a third-degree strategy, they must decide how much output to allocate to each class of buyer, and at what price. Suppose there are only two classes of buyers. Managers have already chosen total output, so they need to allocate output across the two markets. Managers will maximize profit by allocating the total output so that the marginal revenue in one class is equal to the marginal revenue in the other. For example, if the marginal revenue in the first class is $25 and that in the second class is $10, the allocation is not optimal. Managers

3. Segmenting and sealing can have another meaning. In 2000 customers of Amazon.com discovered (via an Internet chat room) that they had been charged significantly different prices by Amazon for the same DVD. When they expressed their displeasure and made the price differences public, Amazon announced that it no longer would engage in such pricing. If the customers had not discovered the price differences, they would have been satisfied (as revealed by their purchase of the DVD), and Amazon could have continued selling the same product at different prices. See David Streitfeld, "On the Web, Price Tags Blur," *Washington Post*, September 27, 2000.

STRATEGY SESSION: Why Do Women Pay More?

Two individuals walk into a hair salon. They have equal length hair and want the same amount cut and the same hairstyle. Yet one pays more for the service than the other. The same two individuals walk into a dry cleaning establishment. One tenders a white silk dress shirt, as does the other—except in the latter case the shirt is called a *blouse*. The bill for the first shirt is less than for the second. In some states, like Pennsylvania, Massachusetts, and California, laws prohibit price discrimination based on gender. A consumer advocacy group surveying Philadelphia business establishments found that women paid a premium at 4 of the 14 dry cleaners they randomly surveyed and at 18 of the 22 hair salons randomly surveyed. For a standard shirt, the maximum difference was $2.45. At hair salons the difference could be double. A California study suggested that gender pricing could cost an additional $1,351/woman/year for a total of $15 billion more than men.

The law, however, states that if the price differs, it must be for a reason other than gender. We must then ask this question: Is the good or service exactly the same and, if not, do the price differences reflect the cost of service differences? Not surprisingly, businesses found not in compliance argued that women were more expensive to serve than men—hence the price difference. Another explanation was that what currently is sold under a one-number rubric, like a haircut, is really a bundle of products. Were the law to be enforced, one hair salon owner stated that she would just unbundle the product and charge separately for the actual cutting of the hair, the gelling, the blow drying, and the styling. Because many men get nothing more than the cut and many women get more than just the cut, women would pay more than men.

Source: "Being a Woman: It Can Cost You in PA," *Philadelphia Inquirer*, March 5, 1999.

can increase profit by allocating one less unit of output to the second class and one more unit to the first class. In fact, managers want to allocate so the marginal revenue of both classes is equal. When this is true, the ratio of the price in the first class to that in the second class equals

$$\frac{P_1}{P_2} = \left[\frac{1 - \left(\frac{1}{|\eta_2|} \right)}{1 - \left(\frac{1}{|\eta_1|} \right)} \right]$$

(8.1)

where η_1 is the price elasticity of demand in the first class and η_2 is that in the second class.[4] We can now see why it does not pay to discriminate if the two price elasticities are equal: $|\eta_1| = |\eta_2|$ implies that $P_1 = P_2$. Moreover, segments with a lower (absolute values) price elasticity are charged a higher price.

Turning to the more realistic case in which managers choose total output, it is obvious they must look at costs as well as demand in the two classes. The manager will then optimize profit when the marginal cost of the entire output is

4. Recall from equation (2.15) that marginal revenue equals $P[1 + (1/\eta)]$, where P is price and η is the price elasticity of demand. Therefore, if marginal revenue is the same in the two classes, $P_1[1 - (1/|\eta_1|)] = P_2[1 - (1/|\eta_2|)]$. Hence $P_1/P_2 = [1 - (1/|\eta_2|)]/[1 - (1/|\eta_1|)]$.

STRATEGY SESSION: That Darling Little Mouse Is Really a Price Discriminator

It's been a long, cold winter in Green Bay. Let's reward the kids with a spring break vacation at Disneyland and Disney California Adventure Park. They'll love Mickey, Minnie, Donald, and Snow White, and it'll be warm. Family A of four (two adults, two kids ages 5 and 7) packs up and heads for Anaheim.

It's another day in paradise. Should we go to the ocean, take a ride to the mountains, or go to Disneyland and Disney California Adventure Park? So many choices for the Los Angeles family, and so many times those same choices are available. Family B of four (two adults, two kids ages 5 and 7) hops in the family car and heads for Anaheim.

Both families buy the One-Day Park Hopper (which lets them visit both parks). The bill for the Griswolds from Green Bay is $312. The bill for the family from Los Angeles is $292. It costs Disney the same to serve the Los Angeles family as the Green Bay family. So why the $20 price difference?

And how can Disney tell the two families apart? It's the Wisconsin driver's license that family A is carrying and the driver's license showing a Southern California address that family B is carrying. That's how the market is sealed. How is it segmented?

The Griswolds came all the way from Green Bay to see Mickey, and Dad's not going to disappoint those children for a mere $20. On the other hand, family B could have gone to the ocean or the mountains or could see Mickey tomorrow. Simply put, the Griswolds had a much less elastic demand than family B, who had plenty of substitutes.

That mouse is a clever third-degree price discriminator!

Sources: http://disneyland.disney.go.com/disneyland/en_US/reserve/ticketListing?year=2007 for Southern California prices and http://disneyland.disney.go.com/disneyland/en_US/reserve/ticketListing?name=TicketListin for other prices.

---

equal to the common value of the marginal revenue in the two classes. The firm's profit (π) is

$$\pi = TR_1 + TR_2 - TC$$

where TR_1 is the total revenue from class 1, TR_2 is the total revenue from class 2, and TC is the total cost. The total cost is a function of the total amount of the good (Q) produced and sold, and it is allocated Q_1 to class 1 and Q_2 to class 2.

The monopolist has two output choices, so profit is maximized when $\Delta\pi/\Delta Q_1 = 0$ and $\Delta\pi/\Delta Q_2 = 0$. Note that $\Delta\pi/\Delta Q_1 = (\Delta TR_1/\Delta Q_1) - (\Delta TC/\Delta Q_1)$ and $(\Delta TR_2/\Delta Q_1) = 0$ because revenues in class 2 are independent of sales in class 1. Likewise, $\Delta\pi/\Delta Q_2 = (\Delta TR_2/\Delta Q_2) - (\Delta TC/\Delta Q_2)$ and $(\Delta TR_1/\Delta Q_2) = 0$ because revenues in class 1 are independent of sales in class 2. These two relationships are rewritten as

$$\Delta\pi/\Delta Q_1 = MR_1 - MC = 0$$
$$\Delta\pi/\Delta Q_2 = MR_2 - MC = 0$$

(8.2)

Note that both $\Delta TC/\Delta Q_1$ and $\Delta TC/\Delta Q_2$ equal MC (and not MC_1 and MC_2) because the plant manager knows only that producing another unit incurs additional costs. It is the marketing or sales department's job to decide whether the good is destined for class 1 or class 2 demanders.

The equations (8.2) state that to maximize profit, managers must choose output so $MR_1 = MC$ and $MR_2 = MC$, implying that $MR_1 = MR_2 = MC$. Had there been n classes of demanders, the profit-maximizing rule would be $MR_1 = MR_2 = \ldots = MR_n = MC$. To see this in the two-class case, consider Figure 8.3, which shows D_1, the demand curve in class 1; D_2, the demand curve in class 2; R_1, the marginal revenue

FIGURE 8.3

Third-Degree Price Discrimination

To maximize profit, the firm produces a total output of Q units and sets a price of P_1 in the class 1 market and P_2 in the class 2 market.

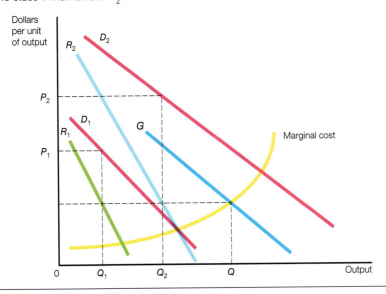

curve in class 1; R_2, the marginal revenue curve in class 2; and the firm's marginal cost curve. The curve representing the horizontal summation of the two marginal revenue curves is G. This curve shows, for each level of marginal revenue, the total output needed if marginal revenue in each class is to be maintained at this level. The optimal output is shown by the point where the G curve intersects the marginal cost curve because marginal cost must be equal to the common value of the marginal revenue in each class. If this were not true, profit could be increased by expanding output (if marginal cost were less than marginal revenue) or contracting output (if marginal cost were greater than the marginal revenue). Therefore, managers produce an output of Q units and sell Q_1 units in the class 1 market and Q_2 units in the class 2 market. The price is P_1 in the class 1 market and P_2 in the class 2 market. This results in a higher profit than if the firm quoted the same price in both markets.

STRATEGY SESSION: Mickey Mouse Pricing at Amusement Parks

Going to an amusement park used to mean paying the admission charge (and perhaps an additional fee inside the park to ride the hot new attraction); but that was it. The prices were transparent. But now you need a scorecard to know how to play and what prices are available. Attendance fell after 9/11. Despite that, most parks raised their base gate prices.

But in general, that gate price is the highest one to get into a park. There are Web-based sales with 17–27 percent discounts for those who purchase on the Web and print their tickets. Others offer further discounts for the observant buyer. For instance, the gate price at Knott's Berry Farm in California is $43, $35 online, and $28.95 on its all-you-can-eat barbecue days. King's Dominion north of Richmond, Virginia, has a $43.99 gate price, a $34.99 online price, and a $29.99 four-day advance purchase price. Five rival parks in California (Disney and Knott's included) teamed together to sell City Pass, which allowed admission to all five parks at a substantial discount. Multiday and annual passes are also generally available only online.

Some of the discounts are cost-based. Online tickets save a park money by not having more sales personnel at the gates and eliminate queues at entrances that annoy customers.

The parks are also exploring other types of tickets. For instance, some people do not want to use a park's attractions but would rather watch others use them—such as grandparents who wish to see their grandchildren enjoy the attractions but who would rather skip riding the "Rebel Yell" roller coaster. The full price may deter onlookers from coming to the park, but a reduced price can mean additional profit because they don't contribute much to costs, are likely to consume high markup concessions and souvenirs, and might preclude the whole family from attending if they didn't attend.

More diverse pricing structures can be based on both the cost and demand sides of the equation.

Source: "A New Twist in Theme Park Pricing," *The Wall Street Journal*, June 24, 2004.

Managerial Use of Third-Degree Price Discrimination

Perhaps the most frequently cited example of third-degree price discrimination is the case of airline tickets. The airlines often charge a lower fare for essentially the same ticket if it is purchased in advance, if there is a penalty if the trip is canceled or changed, or if the trip includes a Saturday night stay. For example, in early 2008 the price of a round-trip coach ticket from New York to San Francisco ranged from about $312 to $688 for flights leaving and returning on similar dates.

One reason for these price differences is that the price elasticity of demand for business travel is much less elastic than that for vacation travel. Business travelers must meet with clients, suppliers, and associates at particular times, often as soon as possible. Regardless of the price of an airline ticket (so long as it remains within reasonable bounds), many of these trips would be well worth making. On the other hand, vacation travelers often plan their trips well in advance, are relatively flexible with regard to the timing of their trips, and are sensitive to moderate differences in ticket price. From the discussion in the previous section, it seems likely that the airlines, to maximize profit, would like to set higher prices for business travelers than for vacation travelers. And this is the effect of the price differences just cited because business travelers are much less likely than vacation travelers to buy their tickets ahead of time or to include a Saturday night stay,[5] and they desire the flexibility of being able to change their flight schedules.

At the same time, it is also worth noting that because the airlines can reduce their costs if demand is predictable (as a result of better scheduling of equipment and personnel), they may enjoy savings if travelers buy their tickets in advance. Also, if a ticket is not refundable, it clearly benefits the airline more than a ticket that is refundable, even though the penalty involved in changing it may be relatively small.

In recent years entrepreneurs have stepped in with a business model that mitigates some of the airlines' ability to practice third-degree price discrimination. Internet firms such as Expedia scour airline databases continuously looking for cheap fares. Consumers use Expedia and its competitors, such as CheapTicket or Travelocity, to view such fares. These additional information sources can lead to lower fares than if the customer dealt with the air carrier alone. This is not always the case, however. In addition, customers must take the time to search the sites. Because airlines change fares continuously, if the sites are not updated frequently, the customer may not get the cheapest fare. A recent search of two such sites visited within seconds of each other revealed a $500 difference between the cheapest fares from Philadelphia to Hyderabad, India. Because the airlines release the sale of these seats to the sites, they are still falling into a managerial pricing plan (that plan, however, would be different if the sites were not present). In addition, some sites, like Priceline, follow more of a first-degree strategy. Consumers are asked to

5. Because of the events of September 11, 2001, and a business recession that started in the second quarter of 2001, business travel on the airlines fell precipitously. Many airlines relaxed certain restrictions, including the Saturday night stay, in an attempt to woo back the business traveler.

STRATEGY SESSION: Yield Management and Airline Performance

A recent survey has shown that yield management is a major factor in airline profitability. The managers of American Airlines used yield models to generate over $1 billion in savings over a three-year period. Yield management models are a nice example of how mathematical models apparently capture the complexity of our social structure, using only a few variables. They also show how the intellectual effort of managers generates profit for the firm.

Yield management models are complex pricing mechanisms. They are dynamic in the sense that prices respond to customer behavior. At any time several classes of seats are priced at different levels. Prices at each level depend on a real-time demand forecasting model that analyzes market behavior and then optimizes pricing behavior. The firm prices as if it were practicing third-degree price discrimination.

The models can handle the complexity of reality only by looking at a simplified version of it—as if life is abridged. Yield management models focus on a few key variables and ignore everything else. Most focus on overbooking, discount allocation, and traffic management. Managers build models that look at the revenue potential of a complex menu of price and itinerary pairs.

For example, consider overbooking. Airlines must overbook because some customers never claim their reservations. If they did not overbook, then some aircraft that should fly full based on demand (customer behavior) would fly with unused capacity. So managers build models that balance the trade-offs between the increased revenue of more passengers and the costs of having passengers take the next flight (ideally).

Modeling the situation is not easy. Clearly reputational costs with customers are involved if overbooking becomes too common. There are also real economic costs. Passengers not permitted to board the plane because of overbooking must be compensated. Many are given vouchers for discounts on future flights, and some must be fed or given hotel rooms.

Managers build the models to maximize expected net revenue. The optimal overbooking rule is to overbook until the expected marginal revenue from one more passenger on a flight is equal to the marginal cost of an additional overbooking. The actual point chosen reflects concerns for customer satisfaction, so it is constrained a bit.

Other variables are modeled using similar decision rules. For example, in discount allocation models, the objective is to balance the expected marginal revenue of a specific fare request against the expected marginal net revenue of all other fares. To see how sophisticated the models are, consider the inclusion of "sell-up" probabilities. These probabilities are used in discounting models to predict which customers will buy a higher-priced ticket if they are not offered a low price.

The models require sophisticated hardware and software to operate efficiently. Computerized reservation systems like SABRE play an integral part in yield management. These systems interface with the market; their ability to capture and analyze data allows the models to constantly update pricing levels. They also control seat inventory.

Given the competitive nature of the airline market, airlines have not been able to keep all the surplus generated by yield management programs. The programs generate some benefits for airline customers, mainly in the form of lower ticket prices and more efficient use of equipment.

Sources: "Yield Management—A Growth Key Driver," www.airlinesgate.free.fr; "Airline Ties Profitability Yield to Management," *The Travel Tightwad*, May 28, 2002, at www.elliot.org.

name their target price (say X). If the cost of the seat to Priceline was price Y (less than X), then managers have created a surplus of $X - Y$.

USING COUPONS AND REBATES FOR PRICE DISCRIMINATION

One way managers can implement a price discrimination strategy is with coupons and rebates. Basically these devices reduce the price of products. But why don't managers simply reduce prices? Primarily because coupons are used to price discriminate. Not all consumers use coupons. Of 291.9 billion coupons distributed in the United States in 1995, only 5.8 billion were redeemed. A certain segment of consumers (20 to 30 percent) regularly uses coupons in buying goods and services. This demand segment is more price sensitive and on the more elastic part of the demand curve. Hence managers use coupons and rebates to price discriminate because other consumers (on the less elastic part of the demand curve) are willing to pay more—that is, to buy the good without a coupon.

By estimating the elasticity of demand, managers can figure out how coupons should be priced. Suppose managers at the Barnegat Light Fish Company sell their product, a special blend of crab cake, in a market where managers think two types of consumers exist: a more affluent group (R) with an estimated price elasticity for Barnegat Light crab cakes of -2 ($|\eta_R| = 2$) and a less affluent group (S) with an estimated price elasticity for Barnegat Light crab cakes of -5 ($|\eta_S| = 5$). Managers at the fish company choose a posted price (P) but then issue a coupon for $\$X$ off in the newspaper local to the consumer types. Every buyer pays the nominal price of P per unit for Barnegat Light crab cakes on the grocers' sales receipt; but at the bottom of the sales receipt, an $\$X$ credit appears for those who tender a coupon. Thus although all buyers pay the same price P, in reality buyers without coupons pay P while coupon tenderers pay $P - X$. What should the values of P and X be? As we saw, to maximize profit, the marginal revenue in each market should be equal and they, in turn, should equal Barnegat Light's marginal cost (MC). Therefore,

$$P[1 - (1/|\eta_R|)] = (P - X)[1 - (1/|\eta_S|)] = MC$$

Suppose Barnegat Light's marginal cost is a constant $2:

$$MR_R = P[1 - (1/2)] = P/2 = 2 = MC \text{ or } P = \$4$$

and

$$MR_S = (4 - X)[1 - (1/5)] = (4 - X)(0.8) = 2 = MC$$

or

$$3.2 - 0.8X = 2 \text{ or } X = \$1.5$$

PROBLEM SOLVED: Third-Degree Price Discrimination

To illustrate how price discrimination is used, suppose a drug manufacturer sells a major drug in Europe and the United States. Because of legal restrictions, the drug cannot be bought in one country and sold in another. The demand curve for the drug in Europe is

$$P_E = 10 - Q_E \tag{8.3}$$

where P_E is the price (in dollars per pound) in Europe and Q_E is the amount (in millions of pounds) sold there. The demand curve for the drug in the United States is

$$P_U = 20 - 1.5Q_U \tag{8.4}$$

where P_U is the price (in dollars per pound) in the United States and Q_U is the amount (in millions of pounds) sold there. The total cost (in millions of dollars) of producing the drug for sale worldwide is

$$TC = 4 + 2(Q_E + Q_U) \tag{8.5}$$

The firm's total profit (π) from both Europe and the United States is

$$
\begin{aligned}
\pi &= P_E Q_E + P_U Q_U - TC \\
&= (10 - Q_E)Q_E + (20 - 1.5Q_U)Q_U - [4 + 2(Q_E + Q_U)] \\
&= 10Q_E - Q_E^2 + 20Q_U - 1.5Q_U^2 - 4 - 2Q_E - 2Q_U \\
&= -4 + 8Q_E - Q_E^2 + 18Q_U - 1.5Q_U^2 \tag{8.6}
\end{aligned}
$$

To maximize profit with respect to Q_E and Q_U, we must set $\Delta\pi/\Delta Q_E = 0$ and $\Delta\pi/\Delta Q_U = 0$. Hence $\Delta\pi/\Delta Q_E = 8 - 2Q_E = 0$ and $\Delta\pi/\Delta Q_U = 18 - 3Q_U = 0$.

Solving these equations for Q_E and Q_U, we find that managers should sell 4 million pounds of the drug in Europe and 6 million pounds in the United States.

To find the optimal prices in Europe and the United States, we substitute 4 for Q_E and 6 for Q_U in equations (8.3) and (8.4); the result is that managers set a European price of $6 per pound and a U.S. price of $11 per pound. Substituting these values of P_E and P_U, as well as the foregoing values of Q_E and Q_U, into equation (8.6), we find that the firm's profit equals

$$\pi = -4 + 8(4) - 4^2 + 18(6) - 1.5(6^2) = 66$$

or $66 million.

Note that if we use the graphical technique shown in the previous section, we will obtain identical results. Whether the graphical technique or the mathematical technique is used, the answer is the same.

How much additional profit do managers generate? If price discrimination were not possible (perhaps because the submarkets could not be segmented and sealed), P_E would equal P_U. Letting this common price be P, it follows from equation (8.3) that $Q_E = 10 - P$, and from equation (8.4) that $Q_U = (1/1.5)(20 - P) = (40/3) - (2/3)P$. Therefore, the firm's total amount sold in Europe and the United States combined is

$$
\begin{aligned}
Q = Q_E + Q_U &= (30/3) - (3/3)P + (40/3) - (2/3)P \\
&= (70/3) - (5/3)P
\end{aligned}
$$

which implies that[a]

$$P = 14 - 0.6Q \tag{8.7}$$

[a]This means that $(5/3)P = (70/3) - (3/3)Q$ or $5P = 70 - 3Q$ or $P = 14 - 0.6Q$.

QUANT OPTION

To be elegantly fashionable, setting $\partial\pi/\partial Q_E = 0$ and $\partial\pi/\partial Q_U = 0$ will maximize profit. Hence $\partial\pi/\partial Q_E = 8 - 2Q_E = 0$ and $\partial\pi/\partial Q_U = 18 - 3Q_U = 0$.

for $P \leq \$10$ or for $Q \geq 20/3$. (For $P \geq \$10$ or $Q \leq 20/3$, $P = 20 - 1.5Q$ because only the United States purchases the drug if the price exceeds $10.) Hence managers generate profit of only

$$\pi = PQ - TC$$
$$= (14 - 0.6Q)Q - (4 + 2Q)$$
$$= 14Q - 0.6Q^2 - 4 - 2Q$$
$$= -4 + 12Q - 0.6Q^2 \qquad (8.8)$$

because $Q = Q_E + Q_U$.

To maximize profit, the manager selects Q so that $\Delta\pi/\Delta Q = 0$. Therefore,

$$\Delta\pi/\Delta Q = 12 - 1.2Q$$

Solving for Q, we find if managers do not engage in price discrimination, they choose output of 10 million pounds of the drug (which is the same as the output produced when they discriminated).[b] Substituting 10 for Q in equations (8.7) and (8.8), it follows that

$$P = 14 - 0.6(10) = \$8$$
$$\pi = -4 + 12(10) - 0.6(10^2) = \$56$$

Therefore, if managers do not engage in price discrimination, profit is $56 million rather than the $66 million they earn by using price discrimination.

Because 10 million pounds are produced under both pricing schemes, the cost of production is the same in both cases: $4 + 2(10) = \$24$. So the total revenues are $80 (= 64 + 16) when there is no discrimination and $90 (= 66 + 24) when there is discrimination.

With no discrimination, the average revenue per unit is just the price (80/10 = $8); but with discrimination, the average revenue per unit is $9 (90/10). The profit-enhancing property of third-degree discrimination is that it raises the average revenue above the price on the demand curve for a given quantity.

If segmenting and sealing the market are possible but costly, the preceding example tells us that managers should be willing to pay up to the difference in the profit of the two pricing schemes (but no more) to segment and seal—that is, up to $10 million.

Finally, note that at a price of $6, 4 million pounds of the drug are sold in Europe (from $Q_E = 10 - 6$) and that at a price of $11, 6 million pounds are sold in the United States (from $Q_U = (40/3) - (2/3)11$). Also, note that $\Delta Q_E/\Delta P_E = -1$ and $\Delta Q_U/\Delta P_U = -2/3$. Recall from Chapter 2 that elasticity is $|\eta| = (P/Q)(\Delta Q/\Delta P)$. So $|\eta_E| = (6/4)(|-1|) = |-1.5|$ and $|\eta_U| = (11/6)(|-2/3|) = |-1.22|$. Therefore, the price is raised (from $8 to $11) for the less elastic demander and lowered (from $8 to $5) for the more elastic demander—just as we would expect from equation (8.1).

---

[b] If the demand curves are curvilinear, the output of the third-degree discriminator and the single-price monopolist are not necessarily the same, and it's possible that prices fall in all markets.

You might think that a car is a car. Clearly a Prius isn't a Hummer. But if you rent a Prius and I rent a Prius from the same company on the same day at the same counter at the same time, isn't a Prius a Prius? Apparently not if you're from Australia, India, Canada, or Brazil.

A *Financial Times* reporter in 2004 went on the Avis Web site and pretended to book a car rental for four days for a four-door compact car from Los Angeles International Airport. As part of the booking process, you are asked for your home country. The reporter experimented with different countries and received the following rate quotes:

Country	Rate
Australia	$198
India	$198
United Kingdom	$162
France	$159
Germany	$156
South Africa	$156
United States	$153
Canada	$132
Brazil	$120

While the United Kingdom, France, Germany, South Africa, and the United States all trade within a narrow band, the 82 percent premium for Australians over Brazilians is very large. Car companies call this "source market pricing," and it's based on the "dynamics of the market" according to an Avis spokesperson, who also described it as depending "on the number of competitors in the market and what those competitors are doing in that market at that moment. It is a pure demand and supply issue."

It sure looks like third-degree price discrimination to us. How is the market segmented and sealed? That's easy. You have to show your passport to rent the car.

Source: "Hire Companies' Quick Getaway Comes under Scrutiny," *Financial Times*, February 3, 2004.

Managers should price crab cakes at $4 per unit and offer a $1.50 off coupon. The more affluent buyers pay $4/unit for the crab cakes, and the less affluent ones clip the coupon and pay $2.50/unit for the *same* crab cakes. Those who are more price elastic (the less affluent in this case) use coupons; the less price elastic people (the affluent in this case) do not. So by issuing coupons (or rebates) managers can price discriminate (and increase their profit).

PEAK LOAD PRICING

The demand for goods or services may shift with the time of day, week, or year. For example, the demand for highway and transit services is greatest during the morning and evening rush hours, lower during midday, and lower still overnight. Roads to resorts are likely to see greater demand on the weekend than during the week. And Miami Beach hotels have greater demand in February when it is cold in the northern United States than in the summer when it's warm almost everywhere in the United States.

Because these temporal differences in demand are coupled with a plant capacity that does not change over the demand cycle, managers facing these demand conditions should charge different prices in the peak (high ones $= P_p$) and in the trough (low ones $= P_T$). The rule to follow is that marginal revenue equals marginal cost. However, the marginal revenue curves differ because the service demand curves change between the peak and trough. The marginal cost is usually high in the peak because the supplier is operating at or near capacity, and it is usually low in the trough because much excess capacity exists. Note that this is not the same as third-degree price discrimination. Both the third-degree price discrimination and peak trough situations have separate marginal revenues for each demand class; but in third-degree price discrimination, the demand classes share the *same* supplier capacity at the *same* time. Therefore, marginal cost in third-degree price discrimination is a function of $Q_1 + Q_2$; that is, the two demands are interdependent in how they influence marginal cost. But in the intertemporal demand case, the demanders use the *same* capacity at *different* times. Therefore, there are separate levels of marginal cost for Q_1 and Q_2; that is, the demands are independent in their influence on marginal cost. The optimal solution for third-degree price discrimination is $MR_1(Q_1) = MR_2(Q_2) = MC(Q_1 + Q_2)$, whereas the optimal solution for peak–trough pricing is $MR_1(Q_1) = MC_1(Q_1)$ and $MR_2(Q_2) = MC_2(Q_2)$. The parentheses indicate "a function of." These conditions are shown in Figure 8.4.

The Strategy Session box discusses peaks and troughs in electricity demand. Consider the situation on roadways. The Texas Transportation Institute reports that Americans suffered 4.2 million hours of delay on congested roadways in the 85 largest metropolitan areas of the United States in 2005.[6] This indicates severe auto congestion in some areas. The worst is in Los Angeles, where the typical driver could save 72 hours per year if he or she could drive at free flow rates on the roadway—that is, at the posted speed limit. (The next most congested places are San Francisco, Washington, DC, and Atlanta, all at 60 hours per year—but Los Angeles is 20 percent *more* congested than they are.) One reason why such levels of congestion exist is that roadways, in general, are not peak–trough priced in the United States. Singapore has used peak–trough pricing in its central city since the 1970s. In 2003 London instituted a £5 (now £8, and the pricing area has expanded geographically) price for driving in central London. Initial reports are that driving has decreased by 20 percent. (Are you surprised by the direction of this change? Having studied managerial economics, we hope you are not.) State Route 91 in Orange County, California, has priced newly constructed lanes (where

6. David Schrank and Tim Lomax, *The 2007 Urban Mobility Report* (College Station: Texas Transportation Institute, Texas A & M University, September 2007).

STRATEGY SESSION: The Future is Now: The Futures Market for Super Bowl Tickets

Your team is going to the Super Bowl. You'd like to go. You could have bought tickets way in advance of the game, but you didn't know your team was going until they won their league championship game (and you're only interested in being there if your team is playing). So you go online and see if you can buy tickets on eBay, or you call a ticket broker, or you go to the Super Bowl city on game day and seek a ticket scalper outside the stadium. You could have bought the tickets before you knew who was in the game and then sold them on eBay if your team did not make the game.

But a new market has grown up for you. Commodities have had futures markets for years. Now there's a futures market for Super Bowl tickets. In such markets both buyers and sellers can lock in a price and reduce uncertainty. If you wait until your team makes it, you don't know what the ticket price will be.

Yoonew.com, The Ticket Reserve.com, and SuperbowlOption.com sold options on the 2006 Super Bowl. A client pays X for the option of getting a ticket for the game. If his or her team makes the Super Bowl, he or she gets a ticket. If not, the option is worthless. The futures contracts are for a specific team, so the price will vary from team to team based on the likelihood of that team making the Super Bowl. Prices change as more information becomes available. For instance, if a team clinches their division crown, that guarantees them a slot in the playoffs (and increases their chances of being in the Super Bowl). This raises the price of their option. If the team wins the first round of their divisional playoffs, this puts them a step closer to the Super Bowl and hence increases the price of their option. If they win the second-round playoff game, they are in the Super Bowl. Even then the value of the option will change based on the collective demand of fans to see the game (because the supply is fixed—the stadium has a certain capacity). Data suggests that gambling odds from SportingbetUSA explained 96 percent of the variability in one options market's prices.

Alan Krueger, an economist at Princeton, gives the following example of how the market works. Suppose there's a 10 percent chance a fan's team will reach the Super Bowl, and a futures contract costs $250, whereas a ticket when the Super Bowl participants are known is $2,500. Note that the expected value of a $2,500 ticket is $250 ($0.1 \times \$2,500$). Suppose a risk-loving fan would pay $2,500 for a ticket to see his team play and a risk-averse fan would pay $250 for a futures contract. But there's more. A risk-averse fan will be willing to pay more for a futures contract. As with an insurance policy, ticket futures sell at a premium over their expected value because they help risk-averse fans hedge against uncertainty.

What premium? The fan could guarantee a ticket to the Super Bowl by buying a futures contract on every team in a conference. This is a sure thing. If fans were risk-neutral, the sure-thing price would equal the price the tickets were expected to be at game time (say $2,500). The excess of the sure-thing price over $2,500 is a measure of the market valuation of insuring against risk. For the 2006 Super Bowl, the premium for a sure-thing ticket ranged from 35 to 60 percent during the season (which is not far from the risk premium in some lines of regular insurance). However, this premium fell substantially as the playoffs advanced. Krueger hypothesizes that this occurred because fans overestimated their teams' chances of getting in the Super Bowl earlier in the season.

Source: "Wait Till Next Year, but Lock In the Ticket Price Now," *The New York Times*, February 2, 2006, at www.nytimes.com/2006/02/02/business/02scene.html.

FIGURE 8.4

Determination of Peak and Trough Prices

The optimal peak price (P_P) is determined by where the peak marginal revenue equals the firm's marginal cost; the optimal trough price (P_T) is determined by where the trough marginal revenue equals the firm's marginal cost.

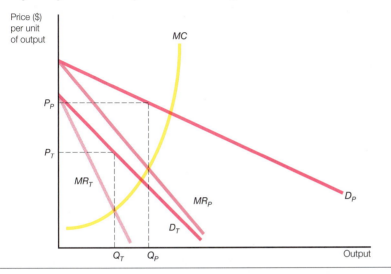

the price varies in real time to keep the lanes operating at free flow level) and kept the existing lanes free (where rush hour traffic moves at 10–25 mph). Many transit systems run 10 times as much equipment during peak rush hours compared to off-peak periods. However, many transport systems charge a flat fee to use the system, independent of the time of use. In fact, many systems actually reward peak use by selling weekly or monthly passes at a discount compared to purchasing single rides for each commute. Therefore, some peak riders actually pay less per ride compared with off-peak riders—just the opposite of what we stated was optimal.[7] Some systems, such as the Metro system in Washington, DC, practice peak–trough pricing.

Another version of intertemporal pricing exists. Some consumers have to read the best-selling book on *The New York Times* list as soon as it reaches that position (or perhaps before it reaches that position if they are truly trendsetters). Others must see the latest Harry Potter or Daniel Day-Lewis movie the first weekend it opens (or soon thereafter). Such individuals can discuss the book or movie at the next cocktail party or around the water cooler and be judged "worthy" by their peers. These people have a high demand to be "with it" and hence pay a high price for hardcover books and first-run movies.

7. Such a pricing policy may be related to the fact that transit's competition (the highway system) has a zero price during peaks and troughs.

STRATEGY SESSION: Why Do Your Laundry at 3 A.M.?

Gertrude Stein once wrote that "a rose is a rose is a rose." In most states a kilowatt-hour is a kilowatt-hour—but not in Florida, Pennsylvania, Washington, and Wisconsin. These states allow electric utilities to practice time-of-day pricing to residential customers who opt to be charged in this way. Otherwise consumers can stick with the traditional plan, where they pay the same flat rate per kilowatt-hour all the time for power. In the new pricing schemes, prices of a kilowatt-hour can change every several hours. (A Pennsylvania utility, Allegheny Power, is experimenting with rates that change every hour.) Not surprisingly, in these states it costs more to consume a kilowatt-hour in the peak periods, when demand is greatest, and less during the trough periods, when demand is the lowest. Many states have allowed time-of-day pricing for commercial and industrial customers for quite some time.

In Florida, Gulf Power of Pensacola charges 4.2 cents per kilowatt-hour at night, on weekends, and on holidays. Demand is less during those periods because the 9-to-5 workday crowd is not at work. Gulf charges 10 cents per kilowatt-hour on weekday afternoons when residential and commercial power demand peaks because of air conditioning use. A third rate is a "critical rate" of 30.9 cents when sup-

plies of kilowatt-hours go extremely short (less than 1 percent of the time). These rates compare to the alternative residential plan of a flat 6.3 cents per kilowatt-hour regardless of the time. A customer utilizing the plan estimates that he shaved $600 off his annual power bill by shifting a third of his power consumption to the off-peak periods. In Washington Puget Sound Energy estimates that running the same dishwasher in the off-peak time saves a user 25 percent off the peak rate. With about one-third of customers participating in the off-peak plan, Puget Energy Inc. (the biggest residential time-of-use provider) estimates that peak demand has been cut by 5 percent. This saves the energy company big money. If it cannot handle peak loads, it enters the power grid market to buy the required power at spot market rates (which are usually expensive) or brings its least efficient (most expensive) capacity on line. By restricting the quantity demanded in the peak via pricing, it need not resort to these expensive alternatives. In addition, by bolstering trough demand, it utilizes its capital plants better.

Source: "Cut Your Electric Bill: Do Laundry at 3 A.M.," *The Wall Street Journal*, August 22, 2002.

Others have an interest in such books or movies but not at the prices that the trendsetters will pay. After about a year, the paperback version of the best seller appears at 20–40 percent of the price of the hardcover book. And after about six months, the DVD of the movie is available for purchase for less than two admissions to the first-run movie theater (and you can see it again and again, pause while you do something else, and rewind to see a favorite scene).

So book and movie suppliers realize that there are leaders and followers in the markets for their services and have figured out how to cater to both with high prices for those who cannot wait and low prices for those who can.

STRATEGY SESSION: A Change from Markup Pricing to Sophisticated Pricing

Parker Hannifin produces over 800,000 individual parts. Many (about a third) are virtually one of a kind with limited or no competition. How should these items be priced? Until 2001 the answer was cost plus (the cost of making the part plus a 35 percent markup). Sophisticated computer models costed out an item and then added on 35 percent (approximately, with some discretion given to sales where competition and hence price comparisons were easier for clients).

This pricing mechanism created several results counter to the best profit interests of the firm. First, if Parker became more efficient and reduced its costs, it automatically reduced its price. This might make sense if competitors were lowering their prices or if lowering Parker's prices would yield more profitable business; but if there was limited competition, this was a missed profit opportunity. Second, if Parker improved its product at the same cost and thus added value to the customer, Parker maintained its price and got nothing for its value-enhanced product. It's estimated by Thomas Nagle of the Monitor Group that as many as 60 percent of U.S. manufacturers use cost-plus pricing.

When Donald Washkewicz became CEO of Parker in 2001, he decided to practice strategic pricing (defined as basing prices on determining what a customer was willing to pay as opposed to what it costs to make a product). Since Parker implemented strategic pricing, operating income increased by $200 million, net income increased by $543 million, return on invested capital increased to 21 percent (from 7 percent), and Parker's share prices rose by 88 percent (all in the 2002–2006 time frame).

Washkewicz views the change of corporate culture as being like pulling teeth. His vice president of corporate strategic pricing defines it as messing with the company's DNA. Washkewicz had to terminate some executives who couldn't get with the new program. Now each of the company's 115 divisions has at least one pricing guru to implement its strategic pricing. One guru describes the previous cost-plus pricing policy as one where no one asked, Why not a 45 percent markup?

Parker has divided its 800,000 products into five categories. A core product is highly competitive with many external reference prices. Prices in this category fell modestly (in some cases by 3 percent) but also increased (in some cases by 5 percent). Two classes (B and C) of partially differentiated (from the market) products exist. In B the differentiation adds value to the customer; prices here increased by 0–5 percent. In C the products were niche in nature with no close competitors; here prices increased by 0–9 percent. The differentiated product systems were tailored to improve customer profitability and productivity, and prices in this category increased by 0–25 percent. The last category was custom designed, and only Parker could do it. Here prices increased by over 25 percent.

Although some customers balked at the price increases, virtually all stuck with Parker, especially because Parker promoted the value-added properties of its products to customers. Adopting strategic pricing also has impacted how Parker thinks about new product development. One dimension now considered is the ability of each product to yield a pricing premium.

With the financial gains shown by Parker, one wonders what the other 60 percent of companies that practice cost-plus pricing are thinking.

Source: "Seeking Perfect Prices, CEO Tears Up the Rules," *The Wall Street Journal*, March 27, 2007, p. 1.

TWO-PART TARIFFS

Two-part tariff When managers set prices so that consumers pay an entry fee and then a use fee for each unit of the product they consume.

Often managers will implement a first-degree price discrimination strategy through a **two-part tariff**. Managers set prices so that consumers pay an *entry fee* and then a *use fee* for each unit of the product they consume. Two-part tariffs are common in the business world. Membership fees for golf clubs are the entry fee, and a greens fee for playing a round of golf is the use fee. Wireless phone users are asked to pay an initial fee and then are charged monthly fees in exchange for access to the network. Some are even charged a use fee for each message unit. Other examples include razors and blades, health clubs, and computer printers. An innovative (and lucrative) use of a two-part tariff is the personal seat license (PSL) for sports stadiums. While the stadium is being constructed, fans are asked to pay a PSL. This is a fixed fee (usually thousands of dollars) that gives the fan the right to purchase tickets to attend a game. It is also an important source of revenue for construction costs. In effect, managers use PSLs to generate revenue from an asset that hasn't yet been built.

One key decision facing managers is to set the appropriate fixed upfront fee and variable usage fee to maximize profit. The upfront fee is designed to extract consumer surplus, so managers use it for first-degree price discrimination. One example is a country club (which actually practices a three-part tariff). Before you can play a round of golf, you must be approved for membership. With that comes a one-time initiation fee, then yearly dues. Both payments are made before you can play and are independent of the number of rounds you play. (Indeed, you may never play. You may have joined merely to improve your image.) In this sense the initiation fee and the dues are like the fixed costs managers face. But should you wish to play a round of golf, having been selected as a member and being a member in good standing, you must also pay a greens fee (that is, a use fee for the service the club provides). The greens fee is analogous to the variable costs managers face. Eating clubs, tennis clubs, health clubs, and amusement parks all practice similar pricing policies. In some amusement parks, one fee (the entry fee) gets you inside the park, where the fee to go on the rides (the use fee) is zero for many rides; but some rides (the newest or the most popular) often require additional fees for rides taken.

Managers in other markets also use two-part tariffs. Walmart's Sam's Club is one example. After paying a membership fee, members are admitted to a Sam's Club store, where they pay individually for every item purchased. As another example, it is estimated that Costco earns over 50 percent of its profit from its entry fee. This bodes well for Costco customers because it means individual items are being priced close to marginal cost.

Managers at Internet service providers also use this pricing strategy. For a fixed monthly fee (the entry fee), customers get access to the Internet. Then they are charged for each time unit they are online (the use fee). In many cases the use

STRATEGY SESSION: Making Them Pay Twice: Personal Seat Licenses for Sports Teams

Charlotte, North Carolina, is a city on the move. It is the banking capital of the southeastern United States. One way that many upcoming cities "get on the map" is to obtain a professional sports franchise. Charlotte acquired a National Football League franchise for the Carolina Panthers. But it needed a stadium. How should it finance such a large capital expense?

Enter Max Muhlemann. Charlotte was excited about its new team, and fans were supportive. Muhlemann suggested that the Panthers sell personal seat licenses for the new stadium. The concept was that a fan would have to purchase a personal seat license to be able to purchase a ticket to see the Panthers play football. The personal seat license was an entry fee. The use fee was the price of a game ticket.

Demand for the licenses was strong; they sold for prices that reflected the desirability of the seats. The average price of a personal seat license was $2,400. The Panthers sold 62,500 personal seat licenses. That's $149 million received by the team *before* a game was ever played in the stadium. That's $149 million in consumer surplus that fans were willing to spend just for the *right* to purchase tickets to see the games. After obtaining the personal seat license, the holder would buy a game ticket at a price no different than other football teams charge. The big difference was that other teams were not collecting the consumer surplus as the Panthers were.

The use of personal seat licenses to finance new stadiums and stadium improvements is growing. The New York Jets and the New York Giants are building a $1.6 billion new stadium to be shared by both teams in New Jersey. Although this has not yet been announced, virtually all commentators and fans expect both teams to use personal seat licenses to help finance the stadium. If they sell them, it is expected that all 9,200 club seats (the category below luxury suites) would be sold as personal seat licenses, along with a number of other seats. Twelve

NFL teams have used seat licenses since the mid-1990s and have raised almost $900 million in the process. The Philadelphia Eagles sold 29,000 such licenses at prices ranging from $1,800 to $3,700 and raised $70 million toward the cost of their new field. Dallas has sold one for its yet-to-be-built stadium at $150,000. Other Dallas luxury seats are going for $16,000, $35,000, $50,000, and $100,000. The Cowboys' senior vice president for sales and marketing has said that "it was an internal feeling that that was what the market could bear"—which is what price discrimination is all about. Half of the Dallas licenses sold in a four-month period. It is estimated that the Cowboys could raise $300 million. The Chicago Bears sold 45 percent of their seats with the highest price being $10,000. The remaining 55 percent of the seats carried no licenses.

Although some fans complain about the licenses because of an active resale market, other fans (in cities where attendance and demand for tickets are high) view the licenses as an appreciating asset. Some Chicago fans (of the 55 percent who did not have to purchase licenses) approached the Bears *and requested that their seats be licensed.* The Bears did so. The licenses are resold in many ways. One is via seasonticketrights. com. Its founder reports that the average gain on the resale of a Bears license is about $8,300 (which shows that the Bears underpriced their licenses). To demonstrate that fans have a higher reservation price than they are currently charged, one Giants fan who currently pays $80 per game ticket says, "I'm going to buy my tickets whether there are licenses or not. Do I want to pay? No." But he says he will.

Source: F. Klein, "Growing Plague: Buying the Right to Buy a Ticket," *The Wall Street Journal.* Sept. 26, 1996, and "Jets and Giants Fans May Pay for the Right to Pay for Tickets," *The New York Times*, March 22, 2008.

STRATEGY SESSION: Costco and the Two-Part Tariff

"People laughed at the idea of charging someone to shop at your warehouse, but our membership fees are north of $1 billion per year," states Joel Benoliel, a senior vice president at Costco. There are more than 24 million members in the United States and Canada. Current yearly membership fees are $50 per person, per family, or per business and $100 for an executive membership (which entitles the customer to other services). Note that 24 million members at $50 per member is $1.2 billion, and because some are executive members, that $1.2 billion is a conservative estimate.

Steve Hoch, a professor of marketing at the Wharton School, states that most of Costco's profit is from the annual membership fee (the entry fee). But profit also occurs from the markup of items' costs. There is a scale advantage here too: The larger the Costco membership, the larger the item quantities Costco buys. That greater buying power gives Costco a lower cost of obtaining items and the ability to offer items at lower prices.

Source: "24 Rolls of Toilet Paper, a Tub of Salsa, and a Plasma TV," *The New York Times*, January 28, 2007.

---

fee is zero for the first X minutes; but after those X minutes are over, a per minute fee is assessed. In some places, such as France, Internet customers pay for each minute used. Most wireless phone plans, as well as landline phone services, use a similar pricing strategy.

We start with a simple example to demonstrate this pricing principle. Suppose all demanders for a service are perfect clones; *each* demander has the same demand curve for the service. That is, they all have the same preferences. We assume the demand curve is linear of the form $P = a - bQ$, where P is the price per unit and Q is the number of units demanded at price P. In addition, we assume managers face a constant marginal cost of production.

The profit-maximizing optimal two-part tariff requires managers to price the use fee equal to the marginal cost and to price the entry fee equal to the consumer surplus. So managers must choose their use fee before they can determine the entry fee. Consider the situation in Figure 8.5. The use fee (P^*) equals MC. At that use fee, the demander wishes to consume Q^* units. The resulting consumer surplus is A^*, and that is the optimal entry fee.[8] Note the use fee covers the manager's variable cost of serving the consumer (because $MC = AVC$ and $(AVC)Q^* = VC$), and the variable-cost profit of the firm for serving this consumer is $A^* + P^*Q^* - (AVC)Q^* = A^*$ (because $AVC = P^*$). Multiplying A^* by the number of clones and subtracting the firm's fixed cost gives managers their profit.

Intuitively, a two-part tariff lets managers act as first-degree price discriminators. Managers capture the entire consumer surplus through the entry fee and convert it into producer surplus (variable-cost profit). Note that managers produce until price equals marginal cost.

8. Technically, $A^* - \varepsilon$ will break the indifference of the consumer to joining or not joining. Hereafter we'll call it A^*, recognizing that the nonambiguous entry fee is $A^* - \varepsilon$.

FIGURE 8.5

Optimal Two-Part Tariff When All Demanders Are the Same

The optimal two-part tariff when all demanders are clones is a use fee equal to marginal cost ($P^* = MC$) and an entry fee equal to the consumer surplus resulting from such a use fee (A^*).

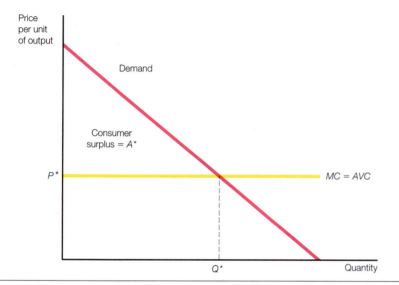

A two-part tariff is simpler for managers to implement than first-degree price discrimination because they need not charge individuals different prices for each unit of the good consumed. This pricing strategy also gives managers two other advantages. First, the entry fee is collected up front at the beginning of the demand period; first-degree price discrimination collects the price from the consumer at the time of each individual consumption of the product or service. Money now is worth more than the same amount of money later. Second, although most managers understand that there are some units for which consumers will pay a high price (like the first round of golf after a long Minnesota winter) and some units for which consumers will pay a low price (a round of golf in a downpour), at any given time managers are not certain of consumers' reservation prices. With the two-part tariff, all a manager must know is that sometime over the demand period, consumers will show variance in their reservation prices. By using a two-part tariff strategy, managers need not worry about this variance in behavior. They have already collected their surplus with the entry fee.

Managers also use two-part tariffs to get customers to reveal their preferences. Because costs are associated with getting customers to reveal their demand functions, many managers offer a pricing menu to customers. Consider the wireless phone industry. Managers offer customers different plans that vary in monthly

---

STRATEGY SESSION: Verizon Local Calling Plans

Telephone service is a classic example of a two-part tariff. A subscriber pays the phone company a monthly fee for the privilege of receiving a dial tone. This fee must be paid regardless of whether there are zero, tens, or hundreds of incoming or outgoing calls per month. It is an entry fee for having the service available (although one could avoid this fee by using pay phones, albeit at a higher use fee for outgoing calls).

Managers of phone companies are becoming more adept at using sophisticated pricing strategies. Consider Verizon's local calling plans in New Jersey. Because Verizon managers do not know, with certainty, the demand curve of individual consumers, they let the consumers reveal their preference function by offering a menu of pricing plans. Although most of the plans are primarily two-part tariff pricing, managers combine this pricing strategy with bundling and price discrimination.

In 2008 Verizon offered the following local calling plans in New Jersey:

- *Low-use message rate service*—$5.20/month: This plan has a monthly allowance of 20 message units per month with every unit over 20 costing $0.10/unit. A message unit is a local call of five minutes.
- *Moderate message rate service*—$7.40/month: This plan has a monthly allowance of 75 message units per month with every unit over 75 costing $0.065/unit.

- *Flat-rate service*—$8.95/month: This plan gives the consumer unlimited message units of local outgoing calls during the month.
- *Verizon local package*—$25.99/month: This plan gives the consumer unlimited message units of local outgoing calls during the month and a choice of up to three calling features.
- *Verizon local service package extra*—$29.99/month: This plan gives the consumer unlimited message units of local outgoing calls during the month and a choice of four or more calling features.
- *Verizon regional package unlimited*—$38.00/month: This plan gives the consumer unlimited message units of local outgoing calls, unlimited message units of regional outgoing calls, and a choice of up to three calling features.
- *Verizon regional package*—$42.95/month: This plan gives the consumer unlimited message units of local outgoing calls, unlimited message units of regional outgoing calls, and five calling features including home voice mail.

Special features include unlimited directory assistance and calling features. Features include caller ID, three-way calling, and call waiting.

Source: www.verizon.com, accessed on 3/24/2008.

charges and use fees. Customers choose the plans they believe are optimal for them; hence they reveal their preferences.

A Two-Part Tariff with a Rising Marginal Cost

What if managers face marginal costs that are upward-sloping rather than constant? The optimal rule for managers remains the same: Charge a use fee equal to marginal cost and an entry fee equal to the resulting consumer surplus. The only difference here, relative to constant marginal cost, is that managers realize

PROBLEM SOLVED: Two-Part Tariff Pricing

Let's demonstrate the use of a two-part tariff pricing strategy. Managers at C-Pal Industries face 100 identical individuals, each with a demand curve of $P = 10 - Q$. C-Pal has a constant marginal cost of $4 per unit produced and a fixed cost of $500. C-Pal's situation is depicted in the figure.

Managers at C-Pal charge a use fee of $4 $(= MC)$ for each good a consumer purchases. Consumers purchase six goods apiece; the demand can be rewritten as $Q = 10 - P = 10 - 4 = 6$. C-Pal's total revenue from the use fee from one customer is $P*Q* = ($4)(6) = 24, and C-Pal's variable cost for serving one customer is $(AVC)Q* = ($4)(6) = 24. The consumer surplus when six goods are demanded at a price of $4 for a customer is $0.5(10 - 4)6 = 18, and managers charge this as an entry fee. The total revenue from one customer is $24 + $18 = 42, and the variable cost of serving that customer is $24, yielding C-Pal a variable-cost profit of serving a customer of $42 - $24 = 18; this is the consumer surplus captured from the consumer and converted into producer surplus. Because there are 100 clones, man-agers earn a total variable-cost profit of $100($18) = $1,800$. C-Pal's profit is the variable-cost profit minus the fixed costs: $1,300 = $1,800 - 500.

One point of confusion in using a two-part tariff is what happens when a demander conceives of a two-part tariff as a one-part tariff. Consider one of C-Pal's customers. He is paying (on average) $7 for each item he consumes—that is, $4 from the use fee and $3 $(= $18/6)$ from the entry fee. But if C-Pal had merely put a flat charge on each item sold of $7, the customer would purchase only three units $(Q = 10 - P = 10 - 7 = 3)$. The individual demand curve derived in Chapter 3 shows the amount the consumer pays for *each* unit. Indeed, if C-Pal's customers face a price of $7, they will purchase only three units. But that is not the deal they have been offered. The *only* way they can buy the good is to pay an entry fee of $18 for the privilege of purchasing each unit at a price of $4. They choose to purchase six because their benefits equal their costs of doing so. That is why the two-part tariff is so clever. It extracts all the consumer surplus (which a single price does not).

A Two-Part Tariff Example: C-Pal Industries

C-Pal's optimal two-part tariff entails charging a use fee of $4 $(= MC)$ for each item consumed and an entry fee of $18.

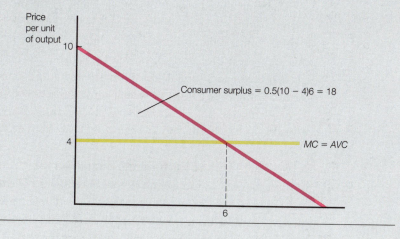

FIGURE 8.6

Optimal Two-Part Tariff When Marginal Cost Is Rising

The optimal two-part tariff is to charge a use fee P^* equal to marginal cost and an entry fee equal to the resulting consumer surplus (A^*). The firm's variable-cost profit is now $A^* + X^*$ because the firm's use revenues now exceed its variable cost (Y^*).

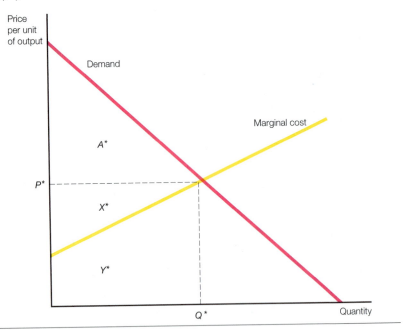

additional profit from the use fee (see area X^*) as well as their entry fee, as shown in Figure 8.6.

Charging a use fee of P^* results in selling Q^* to the consumer. This yields revenues of $P^*Q^* = X^* + Y^*$ from the use fee. The variable cost of selling Q^* units to the customer is the area under the marginal cost curve (Y^*). Therefore, the revenue from the use fee more than covers the variable-costs of serving the customer, and managers earn a variable-cost profit from serving the customer of X^* from the use fee. The entry fee is the consumer surplus that results from charging the use fee of P^* (that is, A^*). Hence the variable-cost profit of serving this customer is $A^* + X^*$.

A Two-Part Tariff with Different Demand Curves

In most markets consumers do not all have identical demand functions. What is the optimal two-part tariff when there are multiple types of demanders in the market? Consider the case with relatively strong and weak demanders. The strong demander is willing to purchase more units than the weak at any given price. Man-

STRATEGY SESSION: Scientific Pricing—Even for Great Art?

A number of firms have been practicing scientific pricing for some time. Airlines have milked their databases to learn the booking trends on routes each hour until takeoff and how those booking rates respond to price changes at various times. They also factor in forward-looking information such as conventions and major sporting events. Long's Drug Stores and D'Agostino Supermarkets have developed prices for specific products at specific stores (and prices for item X may differ from store to store even if the stores are close). But pricing salsa based on ethnic characteristics has got to be different than pricing Picassos, doesn't it?

Apparently not, according to David Galenson, an economist (and art lover and collector) from the University of Chicago. Galenson has developed a model to explain the value of great art, and it works fairly well. After collecting price data on works of great artists, Galenson found the following pattern. Young great artists (Gauguin, Picasso, Van Gogh) seemed to have epiphanies (something came to them and they put it down on canvas quickly). At the other end of the spectrum were the old great artists (like Cezanne), whose great paintings were modifications and evolutions of previous work. Galenson claims the same poles exist for novelists, too.

While economists understand how to model human behavior (or so we think) and use data to test the model, behaviorists feel that human behavior is too complex to be captured in a regression equation. This type of debate also rages in sports. Many professional sports teams have computerized every play of every game and look for patterns in coaches' play calling in certain situations to predict the behavior of a coach in a current situation. In addition, they document players' performances in every play. As an example, they know whether baseball player X tends to hit better against left-handed or right-handed pitchers (and which pitchers) and how he performs in pressure situations. Old-time scouts say you need a feel for the game that a computer can't give you. Some doctors also abhor "evidence-based medicine," in which data point to the diagnosis and remedy; they prefer a doctor's clinical judgment.

In the meantime, don't overpay for your next work of great art. That Picasso, painted by the old man, isn't worth much relative to the young Picasso's work; and that painting Cezanne did as a young man isn't worth as much as the work of the mature Cezanne.

Source: "The Art of Pricing Great Art," *The New York Times*, November 15, 2006, at www.nytimes.com/2006/11/15/business/15leonhardt.html.

agers should consider at least three two-part tariff pricing options. If the strong demander is willing to buy significantly more units at any price, then it is more profitable to charge a use fee equal to marginal cost and an entry fee equal to the resulting consumer surplus of the strong demander. This strategy excludes the weak demander from the market. The weak demander's consumer surplus is smaller than that of the strong demander, so the weak demander is not willing to pay the entry fee. From her point of view, the marginal cost (entry fee) is greater than the marginal benefit (consumer surplus). It is not unusual for managers to use pricing policies that exclude demanders from markets. In a single-price sce-

---

PROBLEM SOLVED: A Two-Part Tariff with Different Demands

The Will and Dylan Company has a strong demander (with a demand curve of $P_S = 8 - Q_S$) and a weak demander (with a demand curve of $P_W = 6 - Q_W$). Managers face a constant marginal cost of production of $2. They want to consider several two-part tariff pricing options in order to increase firm value. They first consider charging a use fee of $2 (the firm's marginal cost) and an entry fee equal to the resulting consumer surplus of the strong demander. We can rewrite the strong demand curve as $Q_S = 8 - P_S$. If the use fee is $2, the strong demander will purchase six units. The resulting consumer surplus is $0.5(8 - 2)6 = \$18$. The managers choose this as the entry fee. Under this strategy, managers earn a variable-cost profit of $18. Managers next consider charging a use fee of $2 and an entry fee equal to the consumer surplus of the weak demander. Because we can rewrite the weak demand as $Q_W = 6 - P_W$, if the use fee is $2, the weak demander will purchase four units. The resulting consumer surplus for the weak demander equals $0.5(6 - 2)4 = \$8$. If this is charged as the entry fee, both

demand types will pay it, and the firm's variable-cost profit will be $16.

Finally, managers consider charging a use fee greater than marginal cost and an entry fee equal to the resulting consumer surplus of the weak demander. How should managers choose the optimal use fee (P^*)? If managers charge a use fee of P^*, the strong demander will purchase $Q_S = 8 - P^*$ units and the weak demander will purchase $Q_W = 6 - P^*$ units. Because $P^* > MC = AVC$, managers will realize a variable-cost profit (of $P^* - 2$) from every unit they sell (and they sell $8 - P^* + 6 - P^* = 14 - 2P^*$ units). The variable-cost profit from the use fee is $(P^* - 2)(14 - 2P^*) = -2P^{*2} + 18P^* - 28$. With $6 - P^*$ units sold to weak demanders, their resulting consumer surplus is $0.5(6 - P^*)(6 - P^*) = 18 - 6P^* + 0.5P^{*2}$. This is the entry fee; and because both demanders will pay it, the variable-cost profit from the entry fee is $36 - 12P^* + P^{*2}$. The total variable cost profit then is

$$VC\pi = -2P^{*2} + 18P^* - 28 + 36 - 12P^* + P^{*2}$$
$$= -P^{*2} + 6P^* + 8 \tag{8.9}$$

---

nario, no consumer whose reservation price is below the market price participates in that market.

The other two pricing possibilities are used when the strong demand is not that much stronger than the weak demand. In these markets, managers should set the use fee at or above marginal cost and set the entry fee equal to the resulting consumer surplus of the weak demander. In so doing, managers cannot use first-degree price discrimination against the strong demander and this demander will realize some consumer surplus. The situation is depicted in Figure 8.7.

If managers want to exclude the weak demander, they should set the use fee equal to marginal cost ($= AVC$) and the entry fee equal to the resulting consumer surplus of the strong demander. The revenue from the use fee equals the variable cost incurred serving the strong demander. The variable-cost profit is the entry fee (areas A^* though F). If managers want to include the weak demander, they must choose the use fee P^*, which maximizes the area $2A^* + 2C + D + E$. Once P^* is chosen, it determines the consumer surplus A^*. Because both demanders are

The variable-cost profit is maximized when $\Delta VC\pi/\Delta P^* = 0$. Therefore,

$$\Delta VC\pi/\Delta P^* = 0 = -2P^* + 6$$

or

$$P^* = \$3$$

Substituting $P^* = \$3$ in equation (8.9) gives

$$VC\pi = -(3^2) + 6(3) + 8 = \$17$$

Managers compare the resulting variable-cost profit from each strategy, and choose to serve the strong demander only. This gives them the highest variable-cost profit of $18.[a]

The managers consider one last pricing option. Suppose they combine the concept of price discrimination and the two-part tariff. They calculated the consumer surplus of the weak demander when the use fee is a marginal cost (= $2) of $8, and that of the strong demander when the use fee is marginal cost which is $18. Therefore, they propose to set the use fee equal to marginal cost, charge the weak demander an entry fee of $8, and charge the strong demander an entry fee of $18. This yields a variable-cost profit of $26. Price discrimination takes place not on the use fees but on the entry fees.

Think about this last pricing policy in the real world. Clubs have full members, associate members, junior members, and the like. Each has a different initiation and dues structure. Usually there is some restriction on use (perhaps not all members can play golf on Wednesday afternoons, when the doctors play). But can you see the motivation behind these different classes of membership?

[a] If the strong demand had been $P_S = 7 - Q_S$, serving only the strong demander would yield a variable-cost profit of $12.5, whereas serving both demand types with a use fee equal to marginal cost would yield a variable-cost profit of $16. If a use fee greater than marginal cost is chosen (optimal fee $2.5) and the resulting consumer surplus of the weak demander is the entry fee ($6.125), the variable-cost profit is $16.25, which is the best of the three options considered.

QUANT OPTION

Setting $dVC\pi/dP^* = 0$ will maximize profit. Thus, $dVC\pi/dP^* = -2P^* + 6 = 0$.

---

willing to pay A^*, managers realize $2A^*$ in revenues. The revenues from the use fee more than cover the variable cost of serving the consumers. At a use fee of P^*, the weak demander wants Q_W units of the good and the strong demander wants Q_S units of the good. Area C represents the variable-cost profit managers realize from the use fee revenues from the weak demander, and area $C + D + E$ represents the variable-cost profit realized from the use fee revenues from the strong demander. Therefore, the total variable-cost profit is $2A^* + 2C + D + E$ from serving both demander types. If the use fee is set equal to marginal cost, the resulting consumer

FIGURE 8.7

Optimal Two-Part Tariff with Two Demand Types

The use fee should be set equal to marginal cost and the entry fee equal to the resulting consumer surplus of the strong demander (areas A^* through F) if areas A^* through F exceed $2A^* + 2C + D + E$. The use fee should be set equal to P^* ($>MC$) and the entry fee equal to the resulting consumer surplus of the weak demander (A^*) if $2A^* + 2C + D + E$ exceeds areas A^* through F.

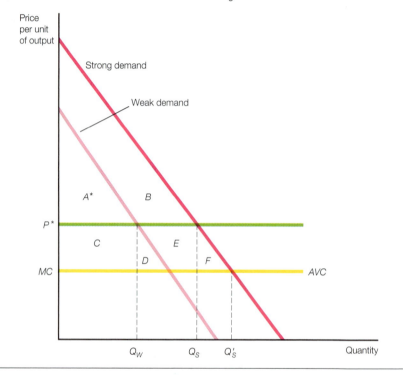

surplus of the weak demander is $A^* + C + D$. Both demanders will pay it. There is no profit from the use fee because it equals marginal cost (= average cost). The profit managers earn is thus $2A^* + 2C + 2D$. We must then compare $2A^* + 2C + 2D$ with $2A^* + 2C + D + E$ and $A^* + B + C + D + E + F$. Whichever is largest will determine the optimal two-part tariff.

Two-part tariff pricing schemes can get complicated fairly quickly. If demand curves intersect, the analysis becomes more complex than our discussion here. We treat this more difficult case in the chapter appendix. Fortunately, complex cases can be modeled so that a number of demanders with varying demand characteristics are considered. Managers need to understand the potential increase in profit due to two-part tariff pricing. Several available models examine more complex demand in markets.

SUMMARY

1. Managers practice price discrimination either when they sell physically identical products at different prices or when similar products are sold at prices with different ratios to marginal cost. The strategy works best in markets with various classes of buyers who are differentiated in price elasticities of demand; where segments can be identified and segregated with relatively low costs (lower than the added expected revenue); and where markets can be sealed so goods cannot be transferred easily from one class to another. Once managers choose a discriminating strategy, they maximize profit by allocating outputs across markets so the marginal revenues are equal to each other and to the total marginal cost. This is called third-degree price discrimination. Managers use second-degree price discrimination when they can price increments of output at different rates, usually charging higher rates for initial increments of output, then lower rates as consumption increases. First-degree price discrimination entails pricing goods at the reservation price of each consumer. This practice captures all the consumer surplus and converts it to producer surplus or variable-cost profit. It is the strategy of first choice because of this. However, it is difficult to estimate each consumer's reservation price, and this scheme is more costly to implement than the other degrees of price discrimination.

2. Two-part tariffs are a strategy to enable managers to use first-degree price discrimination. This pricing strategy has managers charge the consumer an "entry" fee for the right to pay a "use" fee to actually purchase the product. In the simplest case, where all demanders are the same, the optimal use fee is the marginal cost of the product and the entry fee is the consumer surplus available when that use fee is charged. If consumers have different demand curves, managers may exclude weaker demanders from the market and follow the preceding rule with the stronger demanders. Or managers could include all demanders by pricing the use fee at or above its marginal cost and choosing an entry fee equal to the resulting consumer surplus of the weak demander. Managers who practice price discrimination on the entry fee, while charging all consumers the marginal cost as a use fee, realize the maximum profit.

3. Consumer preferences tend to show temporal variation (by day, week, or season). To account for these variations in temporal behavioral, managers many times charge high prices during the peaks and lower prices during the troughs (as opposed to a single price across the whole temporal cycle). The rule for managers to optimize price is to set the relevant marginal revenue equal to marginal cost.

wwnorton.com/studyspace

PROBLEMS

1. Managers at the Ridgeway Corporation produce a medical device that they sell in Japan, Europe, and the United States. Transportation costs are a negligible proportion of the product's total costs. The price elasticity of demand for the

product is -4.0 in Japan, -2.0 in the United States, and -1.33 in Europe. Because of legal limitations, this medical device, once sold to a customer in one country, cannot be resold to a buyer in another country.

a. The firm's vice president for marketing circulates a memo recommending that the price of the device be $1,000 in Japan, $2,000 in the United States, and $3,000 in Europe. Comment on his recommendations.

b. His recommendations are accepted. Sales managers send reports to corporate headquarters saying that the quantity of the devices being sold in the United States is lower than expected. Comment on their reports.

c. After considerable argument, the U.S. sales manager agrees to lower the price in the United States to $1,500. Is this a wise decision? Why or why not?

d. Can you be sure that managers are maximizing profit? Why or why not?

2. Ann McCutcheon is hired as a consultant to a firm producing ball bearings. This firm sells in two distinct markets, each of which is completely sealed off from the other. The demand curve for the firm's output in the first market is $P_1 = 160 - 8Q_1$, where P_1 is the price of the product and Q_1 is the amount sold in the first market. The demand curve for the firm's output in the second market is $P_2 = 80 - 2Q_2$, where P_2 is the price of the product and Q_2 is the amount sold in the second market. The firm's marginal cost curve is $5 + Q$, where Q is the firm's entire output (destined for either market). Managers ask Ann McCutcheon to suggest a pricing policy.

a. How many units of output should she tell managers to sell in the second market?

b. How many units of output should she tell managers to sell in the first market?

c. What price should managers charge in each market?

3. The Lone Star Transportation Company hauls coal and manufactured goods. The demand curve for its services by the coal producers is

$$P_C = 495 - 5Q_C$$

where P_C is the price (in dollars) per ton-mile of coal hauled and Q_C is the number of ton-miles of coal hauled (in thousands). The demand curve for its services by the producers of manufactured goods is

$$P_M = 750 - 10Q_M$$

where P_M is the price (in dollars) per ton-mile of manufactured goods hauled, and Q_M is the number of ton-miles of manufactured goods hauled (in thousands). The firm's total cost function is

$$TC = 410 + 8(Q_C + Q_M)$$

where TC is total cost (in thousands of dollars).

a. What price should managers charge to haul coal?

b. What price should managers charge to haul manufactured goods?

c. If a regulatory agency were to require managers to charge the same price to haul both coal and manufactured goods, would this reduce the firm's profit? If so, by how much?

4. Electric companies typically have 5–10 different rate schedules for their main customer groups. The average price charged to large industrial users may differ substantially from that charged to residences. Moreover, many consumers pay a price for electricity based on the time of day they use it. For example, the prices charged by Consolidated Edison, a large New York electric utility, and Pacific Gas and Electric, a major California electric utility, are as follows:

	Price
Company and Time of Day of Electricity Use	**(Cents per Kilowatt-Hour)**
Consolidated Edison	
8 a.m.–10 p.m. (peak hours)	27
10 p.m.–8 a.m.(off-peak hours)	4[a]
Pacific Gas and Electric	
Summer	
Noon–6 p.m. (peak hours)	28.3
6 p.m.–noon (off-peak hours)	9.2
Winter	
Noon–6 p.m. (peak hours)	11.3
6 p.m.–noon (off-peak hours)	8.0

[a]Approximate figure.

Electric utilities use their cheapest generators continuously and start up their more costly ones as demand goes up. Consequently, at 3 a.m., a utility might meet its requirements from a hydroelectric dam that produces electricity for 2 cents per kilowatt-hour. However, on a hot day in August, when air conditioners are running full blast, demand would be so great that the utility would be forced to use its most costly generators—perhaps an oil-fired plant where electricity costs 7 cents per kilowatt-hour.

a. Does price discrimination occur in the market for electricity?

b. Why have some state regulatory commissions, including the Public Service Commission of New York, ordered that time-of-day rates be phased in for residential consumers?

c. In many areas, both residential and industrial consumers tend to pay a lower price per kilowatt-hour if they use more rather than less electricity. Is this price discrimination? If so, what kind of price discrimination is it?

    d. Explain why price discrimination is used by managers of electric companies.[9]

5. In the town of Oz, there are two types of tennis players: wizards and imps. Wizards and imps do not socialize, so it would be impossible to start a tennis club that both types would join. Imps have access to credit but a weak demand for tennis as follows:

$$P_I = 30 - Q_I$$

where Q_I refers to the number of games they would play if the price of a game were P_I.

    Because of their access to credit, they would be willing to pay an upfront fee to join the club.

    Wizards live from paycheck to paycheck and would be willing to pay for each tennis game as they go along. Their demand is

$$P_W = 40 - Q_W$$

where Q_W refers to the number of games they would play if the price of a game were P_W.

    There are an equal number of wizards and imps (for simplicity, assume one of each). The marginal cost of one game of tennis is a constant 2.

    You can design your tennis facility to attract either wizards or imps (but not both). Which clientele would you like to attract and what would be your profit per "person"?

6. The managers of Roosevelt's (a local yet upscale bar) are considering charging an admission fee on Thursday nights. They contemplate how to charge. Should they

    Option 1. Use just a beverage charge per beverage ordered *or*

    Option 2. Use an admission charge (a fee to enter the establishment) *and* a beverage charge per beverage ordered?

There are two types of people who frequent Roosevelt's: Over 21 Students (S) and Over 21 Student Wannabees (W). Each Student has a demand for beverages of

$$P = 8 - Q_S$$

where Q_S is the quantity of beverages demanded if the price of a beverage is P. Each Wannabee has a demand for beverages of

$$P = 8 - 2Q_W$$

where Q_W is the quantity of beverages demanded if the price of a beverage is P.

    The marginal cost of serving a beverage is a constant $2.

    For simplicity, assume there is one demander of each type. Roosevelt's must (by law) charge all customers the same admission charge and the same

9. For further discussion, see W. Shepherd and C. Wilcox, *Public Policies toward Business* (Homewood, IL: Irwin, 1979); and *The New York Times*, June 9, 1990.

per beverage charge. Beverages do not have to be sold in integer amounts and prices do not have to be in integer amounts.

a. Under option 1, what is the profit maximizing price per beverage?

b. Under option 2, what is the profit maximizing two-part tariff?

c. What is Roosevelt's profit under Roosevelt's best choice?

7. The demand for a strong demander for a round of golf is

$$P_S = 6 - Q_S$$

where Q_S is the number of rounds demanded by a strong demander when the price of a round of golf is P_S.

The demand for a weak demander for a round of golf is

$$P_W = 4 - Q_W$$

where Q_W is the number of rounds demanded by a weak demander when the price of a round of golf is P_W.

The cost of providing an additional round of golf to either type of golfer is a constant 2.

There is one golfer of each type.

The club has decided that the best pricing policy is a two-part tariff. However, it's your job to tell the club the optimal entry fee and the optimal use fee to maximize the club's profit. The club cannot price discriminate on either the use or the entry fee. The club's fixed cost is 1.

What are the club's optimal use fee and the optimal entry fee?

8. The University Museum has two types of visitors. One type is University employees; and the other type is people non-affiliated with the University. All University employees have identical annual demands for Museum visits, given by

$$P_P = 30 - Q_P \qquad \textit{(for each University employee)}$$

where Q_P is the number of visits demanded if the price is P_P per visit. Non-affiliated people all have identical annual demands for Museum visits, but differ from University employees:

$$P_N = 100 - Q_N \qquad \textit{(for each non-affiliated person)}$$

where Q_N is the number of visits demanded if the price is P_N per visit. The Museum can identify University employees by their University ID card, while a non-affiliated person does not possess a University ID.

The University's profit-maximizing Museum is contemplating two different pricing policies:

Policy 1

· For University employees: An annual membership fee and an additional price-per-visit. (Only University employees are eligible for this membership plan.)

- For non-affiliated visitors: A single price-per-visit, with no membership fee. (This price per visit is not necessarily the same as the University employee price per visit.)

Policy 2

- This policy would offer a *different* price-per-visit for each type of visitor, but no membership fees at all.

The museum has a constant marginal cost of 6 per visit, regardless of the visitor's type. For simplicity, assume that there is one University employee and one non-affiliated person in the target population.

How much more profit does the best policy yield than the other policy?

APPENDIX: TWO-PART TARIFF WITH INTERSECTING DEMANDS

Managers may find themselves executing a two-part tariff pricing strategy in markets where demand curves intersect. In such a case determining the optimal use price and entry price may entail searching back and forth among the demand curves, as we show in the following example.

There are two types of demanders in our market. Consumer 1 has a demand curve of

$$P_1 = a_1 - b_1 Q_1$$

and consumer 2 has a demand curve of

$$P_2 = a_2 - b_2 Q_2$$

Marginal cost is constant at c.

Managers can estimate the consumer surplus for any demander i when the use fee is set at marginal cost. Consumer surplus when the use fee is equal to marginal cost is

$$CS_i = (a_i - c)^2/2b_i$$

where $i = 1, 2$.

One fact managers can estimate is whether double the consumer surplus for the smaller consumer surplus demander is greater than the consumer surplus for the larger consumer surplus demander. If so, then the optimal entry fee *if marginal cost is the use fee* is the consumer surplus of the lower consumer surplus demander. If not, then the optimal entry fee *if marginal cost is the use fee* is the consumer surplus of the higher consumer surplus consumer. However, it is possible that a use fee (P^*) greater than marginal cost will lead to the highest profit.

The profit margin under such a use fee is $P^* - c$. The quantity consumed in market i at price P^* is

$$Q_i = (a_i - P^*)/b_i$$

and therefore the total amount consumed by both consumers at price P^* is

$$Q = [a_1b_2 + a_2b_1 - (b_1 + b_2)P^*]/b_1b_2$$

yielding profit from the use fee of

$$[(a_1b_2 + a_2b_1)(P^* - c) - (b_1 + b_2)P^{*2} + c(b_1 + b_2)P^*]/b_1b_2$$

that is, $(P^* - c)Q$.

The consumer surplus resulting from the choice of P^* as the use fee would be

$$CS_i = (a_i - P^*)^2/2b_i$$

If double the resulting consumer surplus for the demander with the lower consumer surplus exceeds the resulting consumer surplus of the demander with the higher consumer surplus, managers will choose the smaller consumer surplus as the entry fee. How can we determine which consumer surplus is relevant?

Suppose $a_1 > a_2$. We can portray the decision by managers when seeking the best use price greater than marginal cost as dividing the range of $a_2 > P_{Use} > MC$ into regions to determine the relevant entry fee to charge. a_2 is an upper boundary because demander 2 will not participate in the market if the use fee is higher than a_2. MC is a lower boundary because managers will never produce unless the price they can charge for output at least covers marginal cost. When a P_{Use} exists such that $CS_1 = CS_2$, either consumer surplus is the relevant entry fee. Equating the two consumer surplus values gives

$$P = [(a_1b_2 - a_2b_1) \pm [2(a_1^2b_2^2 + a_2^2b_1^2) - (a_1 - a_2)^2b_1b_2]^{0.5}]/(b_2 - b_1)$$

where $A = a_1b_2 - a_2b_1$, $B = (a_1 - a_2)(b_1b_2)^{0.5}$, and $C = b_2 - b_1$.

The relationship between CS_1 and CS_2 as a function of use fee (P^*) appears in Figure A.1 for the case where $(A + B)/C < (A - B)/C$. (This is the case examined in the first example here.)

Between MC and $(A + B)/C$, $CS_2 > CS_1$, so the consumer surplus of consumer 1 (if the optimal use price is in this range) will be charged to both demanders. The entry price will thus be

$$P_{Entry} = (a_1 - P^*)^2/2b_1$$

and the profit from the entry fee will be

$$\pi_{Entry} = (a_1 - P^*)^2/b_1$$

because both demanders will pay it.

The profit earned is

$$\pi = [(a_1b_2 + a_2b_1)(P^* - c) - (b_1 + b_2)P^{*2} + c(b_1 + b_2)P^*$$
$$+ (a_1^2b_2 - 2a_1b_2P^* + b_2P^{*2}])/b_1b_2$$
$$\Delta\pi/\Delta P^* = [(a_1b_2 + a_2b_1) - 2(b_1 + b_2)P^* + c(b_1 + b_2) - 2a_1b_2 + 2b_2P^*]/b_1b_2 = 0$$

Solving for P^* gives

$$P^* = a_2b_1 - a_1b_2 + c(b_1 + b_2)/2b_1$$

It must be checked that the resulting P^* lies in the range of

$$MC < P^* < (A + B)/C$$

Between $(A + B)/C$ and a_2, $CS_1 > CS_2$, so the consumer surplus of demander 2 (if the optimal use price is in this range) will be charged to both demanders.

QUANT OPTION

To set the record straight, profit is maximized when

$$d\pi/dP^* = [(a_1b_2 + a_2b_1) - 2(b_1 + b_2)P^* + c(b_1 + b_2) - 2a_1b_2 + 2b_2P^*]/$$
$$b_1b_2 = 0$$

The optimal use price in this range will be

$$P^* = [a_1b_2 - a_2b_1 + c(b_1 + b_2)]/2b_2$$

Of course we must check that the resulting P^* lies in the range of

$$(A + B)/C < P^* < a_2$$

Consider the following example: $P_1 = 9 - 3Q_1$, $P_2 = 8 - 2Q_2$, and $MC = 2$. Equating consumer surpluses gives

$$(A + B)/C = 3.55 \text{ and } (A - B)/C = 8.45$$

that is, $(-6 + 2.45)/-1 = 6 - 2.45 = 3.55 < (-6 - 2.45)/-1 = 8.45$. So this meets the conditions graphed in Figure A.1.

Viewing potential use fees where $MC < P^* < (A + B)/C$ gives

$$P^* = (24 - 18 + 10)/6 = 2.67$$

Because $MC = 2$ and $(A + B)/C = 3.55$, the price meets the constraints.

Viewing potential use fees where $(A + B)/C < P^* < a_2$ gives

$$P^* = (18 - 24 + 10)/4 = 1$$

Because $(A + B)/C = 3.55$ and $a_2 = 8$, this price does not satisfy the constraints.

Substituting $P^* = 2.67$ into the profit function here gives a profit of 16.5556. We must still compare this result with pricing the use fee at marginal cost and the entry fee equal to either the larger consumer surplus (if it is more than double the smaller consumer surplus) or the smaller consumer surplus (if when doubled, it is more than the larger consumer surplus). As shown in Table A.1, the best policy *if the firm sets the use fee equal to marginal cost* is to sell to both consumers at an entry fee of 8.1667 yielding a profit of 16.3333. Thus a use fee greater than marginal cost yields the highest profit.

But suppose the producer experimented with use fees (and charged the best resulting entry fee). The results appear in Table A.1.

As we can see, as price rises above marginal cost, both consumers consume the product with consumer 1's consumer surplus equal to the entry fee. At a use price of 3.55051, the consumer surpluses of each consumer are the same. At use prices higher than 3.55051, both consumers consume the product with consumer 2's consumer surplus equal to the entry fee until the use price reaches 7.93725. At that price, the profit from selling to both at an entry fee equal to consumer 2's consumer surplus equals the profit from selling to just consumer 1 with an entry fee equal to consumer 1's consumer surplus. Obviously this would be true at prices between 8 and 9, but it's best to exclude consumer 2 before the use fee reaches consumer 2's maximum reservation price.

TABLE A.1

Various Use Price and Entry Price Combinations and Their Resulting Profit

P_{Use}	CS_1	CS_2	π_{Use}	π_{Entry}	P_{Entry}	Consumer Determining Entry Fee	π
2	8.1667	9	0	16.3333	8.1667	1	16.3333
2.5	7.0417	7.5625	2.4583	14.0833	7.0417	1	16.5417
2.67	6.685	7.1111	3.185	13.37	6.685	1	16.5556
3	6	6.25	4.5	12	6	1	16.5
3.5	5.0417	5.0625	6.125	10.0833	5.0417	1	16.2083
3.55051	4.9495	4.9495	6.2667	9.899	4.9495	Either	16.165
4	4.1667	4	7.3333	8	4	2	15.3333
5	2.6667	2.25	8.5	4.5	2.25	2	13
6	1.5	1	8	2	1	2	10
7	0.6667	0.25	5.8333	0.5	0.25	2	6.3333
7.5	0.375	0.0625	4.125	0.125	0.0625	2	4.25
7.93725	0.1882	0.001	2.2896	0.002	0.001	2	2.2915
	0.1882	0.001	2.0133	0.1882	0.1882	1*	2.2915
7.95	0.1838	0.0006	2.0825	0.1838	0.1838	1*	2.2663

* In these cases only consumer 1 is served.

FIGURE A.1

The Relationship between the Demanders' Consumer Surpluses and the Use Price Chosen

The difference in the consumer surplus of demander 2 and demander 1 varies with the use price. In this example, as the use price increases above marginal cost, demander 1's consumer surplus gets closer to demander 2's consumer surplus until at use price $(A + B)/C$, the two consumer surpluses are equal. As the use price rises above $(A + B)/C$, demander 1's consumer surplus exceeds demander 2's consumer surplus. At use price a_2 until use price a_1, only demander 1 has consumer surplus.

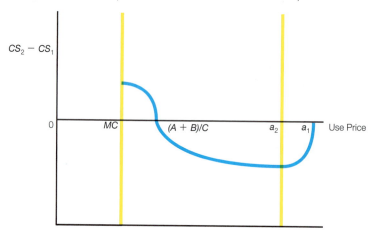

TABLE A.2

Various Use Price and Entry Price Combinations and Their Resulting Profit

P_{Use}	CS_1	CS_2	π_{Use}	π_{Entry}	P_{Entry}	Consumer Determining Entry Fee	π
2	8.1667	4	0	8.1667	8.1667	1*	8.1667
2.67	6.685	2.7778	1.407	6.685	6.685	1*	8.09
2.95	6.1004	2.2494	1.9158	6.1004	6.1004	1*	8.0163
3	6	2.25	3.5	4.5	4	Either	8
3	6	2.25	2	6	6	1*	8
3.05	5.9004	2.1756	2.0825	5.9004	5.9004	1*	7.9829
4	4.1667	1	3.333	4.1667	4.1667	1*	7.3333
5	2.6667	0.25	4	2.6667	2.6667	1*	6.6667
6	1.5	0	4	1.5	1.5	1*	5.5

* In these cases only consumer 1 is served.

A Different Relationship between the Demanders' Consumer Surpluses and the Use Price Chosen

In this case there is no user fee where the consumer surpluses are the same. Here we get a "corner solution," where the optimal use fee is at marginal cost.

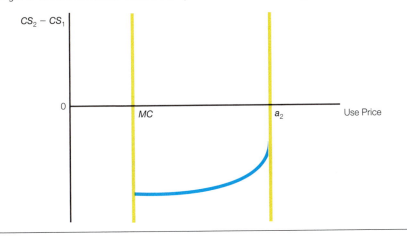

Consider a second example where the second demander's demand is $P_2 = 6 - 2Q_2$. Then $(A + B)/C = -7.348$, which makes no sense, and $(A - B)/C = 7.348$, which exceeds a_2. In this case the graph looks like Figure A.2.

The supporting figures for Figure A.2 are shown in Table A.2.

In this case the best solution is to set the use price equal to marginal cost and the entry fee equal to the resulting consumer surplus of consumer 1 and not serve consumer 2. The weaker demand of demander 2 significantly constrains the profitability of the firm.

CHAPTER 9

BUNDLING AND INTRAFIRM PRICING

Simple bundling When managers offer several products or services as one package so consumers do not have an option to purchase package components separately.

Mixed bundling Allows consumers to purchase package components either as a single unit or separately.

Negative correlation When some customers have higher reservation prices for one item in the bundle but lower reservation prices for another item in the bundle, whereas another group of customers has the reverse preferences.

Simple bundling occurs when managers offer several products or services as one package so consumers do not have an option to purchase package components separately. An example of simple bundling is the inclusion of a service contract with a product. **Mixed bundling** allows consumers to purchase package components either as a single unit or separately. The bundle price is generally less than the sum of the components. Season tickets to sporting events or the value meals of McDonald's are examples of a mixed bundling strategy.

Bundling is best used when there is wide variance in consumers' price sensitivity of demand and when market conditions make it difficult to price discriminate. Managers increase profit by leveraging the different valuations (reservation prices) consumers have for a product. Managers prefer to form bundles so as to create negative correlations across consumers. **Negative correlation** exists when some customers have higher reservation prices for one item in the bundle but lower reservation prices for another item in the bundle, whereas another group of customers has the reverse preferences. By bundling together the products, managers (under certain conditions) can make a greater profit than by selling the products separately.

Consumers often encounter bundling when managers offer distinct goods or services together at a packaged price. Economists distinguish between simple (pure) bundling, when the goods are offered only in the package, and mixed bundling, when the goods have a packaged price as well as stand-alone prices.

Examples abound. Entertainers as diverse as professional sports teams and opera companies commonly practice mixed bundling, offering tickets to individual performances as well as season tickets, subscriptions of tickets to multiple (but not all) performances, and other bundles. A record company bundles 12 songs of your favorite recording artist on a CD, and you must buy the CD (the bundle) to obtain the several songs you want (and hence obtain more songs that you do not want as much, if at all). This product is a pure bundle.

THE MECHANICS OF BUNDLING

Why do managers commonly use bundling? One reason is that it can increase the seller's profit if customers have varied tastes. In addition, it is a way to emulate perfect price discrimination when perfect price discrimination is not possible (because knowing individual reservation prices is either too difficult or expensive to pursue) or it is not legal to charge multiple prices for the same product. With a bundle, we need not know the reservation price of each consumer for each good (as in perfect price discrimination) but only the distribution of all consumers' reservation prices over the goods.

Managers need to consider other issues in choosing bundling schemes. For example, is the worth of the bundle to consumers the sum of their reservation prices for the separate goods in the bundle? That is, are the goods independent? This will be our assumption. However, we can easily envision cases of complementarity of the goods, where the goods as a bundle have a value greater than the sum of the separate reservation prices—such as software and hardware. We can also envision cases of goods, where the goods as a bundle have a value less than the sum of their separate reservation prices. And what about demand? We will assume consumers purchase no more than one unit of any good either separately or in a bundle. From the cost side, managers need to consider whether there are economies of scope or scale in the production of two goods. We will assume production costs are the same regardless of whether the goods are produced for sale separately or as a bundle; that is, the cost of a bundle is the sum of the individual costs of the two goods. A last issue is whether the goods are sold in secondary markets. We will assume that consumers do not resell the goods.

Of course managers can always sell the goods as separate items. If managers cannot price discriminate but must charge a single price for each good, we'll assume that price is the simple monopoly profit-maximizing one.

We can investigate the three possible pricing scenarios in the following three figures. Figure 9.1 shows the separate price strategy. Managers choose the optimal simple monopoly prices for good 1 and good 2 (the ones that maximize profit). Call them $p_1^\#$ and $p_2^\#$. Figure 9.1 shows the resulting consumption behavior of consumers depending on their reservation prices. For example, consumers in the upper right cell buy both goods given their high reservation prices for the goods.

STRATEGY SESSION: Bundling Carbon Credits with Gas Sales

Gazprom is a Russian energy firm that sells natural gas to Europe and has profited handsomely. But now it has figured out how to make even more profit. A London subsidiary (Gazprom Marketing and Trading) has invested in a Brazilian biomass power plant (Propower do Brasil) that earns Gazprom Marketing and Trading carbon dioxide emission credits (because biomass uses renewable resources and is "carbon neutral" because it emits as much carbon when used as fuel as was absorbed when it was a crop). Gazprom will then bundle those credits with natural gas and sell the combination as a single product to electric utilities in Europe. The utilities need these credits to burn natural gas.

The ability to make this bundle has come about because of the 1997 Kyoto Protocol on climate change, which gave Russia a massive amount of these credits, and a 2005 European Union program of "cap and trade" that allows "dirty" utilities (heavy polluters) to purchase carbon dioxide credits that permit them to pollute and "clean" utilities (low polluters) to sell pollution credits they don't need. Although

Russia is one of the largest producers of greenhouse gases because of antiquated technology, relatively small investments will enable them to significantly reduce emissions. This gives Gazprom access to a large amount of Russian pollution credits (the Brazilian pollution credits are just Gazprom's test of the bundled market). To facilitate the activity, Gazprom's banking subsidiary has established a carbon trading unit (Carbon Trade and Finance) with Dresdner Bank. Carbon Trade and Finance will then invest in modern efficient equipment at Russian polluting firms and thus earn the credits that Gazprom will use to bundle with its natural gas.

It's estimated that the value of carbon credits in Russia is in the range of $40 to $60 billion. The fly in the ointment? If the Kyoto Protocol is not extended, the carbon credits could be worth nothing.

Source: "Russian Energy Giant to Bundle Carbon Credits with Gas Sales," *The New York Times,* April 25, 2007, at www.nytimes.com/2007/04/25/business/worldbusiness/25carbon.html.

Figure 9.2 shows the strategy of pure bundling. Here managers choose the optimal pure bundle price (the one that maximizes profit). Call it $p_B^\#$. Consumers located to the right of the $p_B^\#$ line in Figure 9.2 buy the bundled product.

Figure 9.3 shows the strategy of mixed bundling. Managers choose the optimal pure bundle price ($p_B^\star$), the optimal separate price for good 1 ($p_1^\star$), and the optimal separate price for good 2 ($p_2^\star$); these prices are set to maximize profit. Figure 9.3 shows the resulting consumption behavior of consumers depending on their reservation prices. This is a good example of how managerial actions influence the behavior of consumers. By increasing the purchase options, managers can track behavior in specific sectors of the market.

The optimal solution is the *greatest profit of the profit-maximizing solutions yielded by separate pricing, pure bundling, and mixed bundling*. The manager chooses the action that maximizes profit. These figures do not show the cost of producing the goods to keep things simple. Obviously, although the figures show

FIGURE 9.1

Price Separately

Whether consumers purchase goods separately depends on their reservation price for the good relative to the prices charged by the seller.

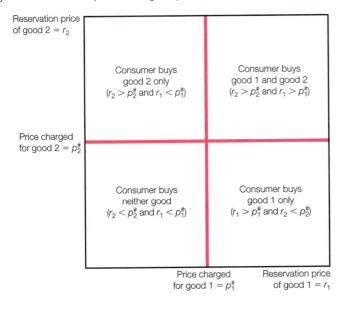

FIGURE 9.2

Pure Bundling

Whether consumers purchase the bundle depends on the sum of their reservation prices for the goods relative to the bundled price charged by the seller.

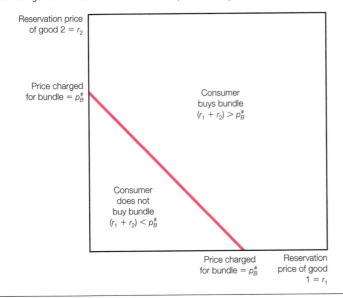

FIGURE 9.3

Mixed Bundling

Whether the consumer purchases the goods separately or as a bundle depends on the consumer surplus (the difference between consumers' reservation prices, or sum of their reservation prices, and the price charged by the seller). Consumers choose the goods or bundles that maximize their consumer surplus.

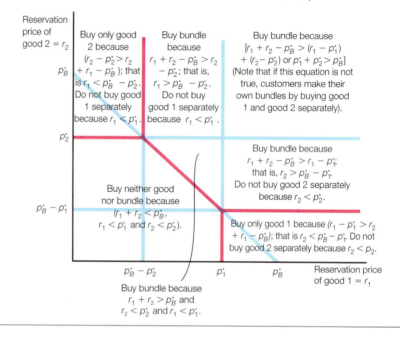

the buyers' intentions, their realized transactions are a subset of those shown because certain pricing actions are precluded by the manager's profit-maximizing behavior. Solving for the profit-maximizing solutions for Figures 9.1 and 9.2 is easy because of the more limited choices of consumers. Figure 9.1 considers only individual reservation prices for the goods; and only the sum of each consumer's reservation prices is a candidate price for the pure bundle in Figure 9.2. Any other prices would unnecessarily leave consumer surplus on the table (and a profit-maximizing seller always wants to convert such consumer surplus into producer surplus).

The more difficult calculation is determining the best mixed bundle prices. As we show next, the optimal prices do not have to be a reservation price of a good or a bundle. The solution is derived either by educated trial and error or via a computer program[1] that searches all separate prices and pure bundle prices and chooses the combination yielding the highest profit. Trial and error can be done in simple cases with few consumers and goods. Cases with many consumers and goods require a computer program. Critical to mixed bundling is creating a

1. Hanson and Martin ("Optimal Bundle Pricing," *Management Science* 36, no. 2 (1990), pp. 155–174) have developed such a program, as have the authors.

credible mixed bundle. **Credibility of the bundle** means that managers correctly anticipate which customers will purchase the bundle or the goods separately.

The following example shows the three types of bundling strategies when reservation prices of consumers are perfectly negatively correlated; that is, all the reservation prices lie on a line of slope -1 in the price space. Note that while the customers have a negative correlation in their reservation prices for the two goods, they exhibit *no* variation in their valuation of the bundle: They all value the bundle at $100. The consumer reservation prices are shown in Table 9.1, and the situation is depicted in Figure 9.4.

Suppose the constant unit cost of production of each good is 1. The separate price, pure bundling, and mixed bundling cases are shown in Tables 9.2, 9.3, and 9.4.

Managers can always come up with a mixed bundle by pricing the individual goods at prices at which no consumer purchases the good. In some cases, *but not this one*, it is possible to increase profit through mixed bundling. Mixed bundling, therefore, always *weakly dominates* pure bundling.

If we look at mixed bundles where customers actually consume the bundle and at least one of the goods is sold separately, the pricing strategy in Table 9.5 is the best mixed bundle.

Note that consumer *A* does not consume the bundle because at price $100, she receives no consumer surplus. However, consumer *A* consumes good 1 at $89.99 because she receives a positive consumer surplus (of $0.01). Likewise, consumer *D* does not consume the bundle because at price $100, he receives no consumer surplus. However, consumer *D* consumes good 2 at $89.99 because he receives a positive consumer surplus (of $0.01). We discuss this logic further in another example.

In the preceding case, where pure bundling is the best pricing strategy, perfect price discrimination is completely replicated as the manager extracts *all* the consumer surplus from each customer. This goal is called **extraction**. In addition, a manager can also practice **exclusion**: not selling a good to a customer who values

TABLE 9.1

Reservation Prices of Good 1 and Good 2 of Consumers *A, B, C,* and *D*

Consumer	Reservation Price		Bundle
	Good 1	Good 2	Price
A	90	10	100
B	60	40	100
C	50	50	100
D	10	90	100

FIGURE 9.4

Example of Perfect Negative Correlation of Consumers' Reservation Prices

Consumers A, B, C, and D value each good differently, but all value the bundle of the two goods at $100.

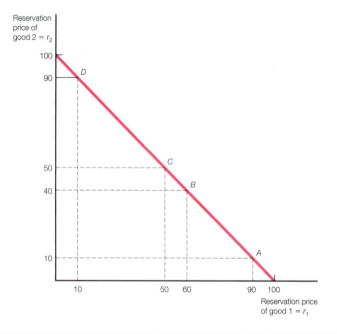

TABLE 9.2

Optimal Separate Prices for Good 1 and Good 2

Consumer	Price 1	Cost/unit	Profit/unit	Number of units	Profit
A	90	1	89	1	89
B	60	1	59	2	118
C	**50**	1	49	3	**147**
D	10	1	9	4	36

Consumer	Price 2	Cost/unit	Profit/unit	Number of units	Profit
A	10	1	9	4	36
B	**40**	1	39	3	**117**
C	50	1	49	2	98
D	90	1	89	1	89

The profit from the best separate price strategy of $P_1 = \$50$ and $P_2 = \$40$ is $264.

TABLE 9.3

Optimal Pure Bundle Price for Consumers A, B, C, and D

Consumer	Bundle Price	Cost/Bundle	Profit/Bundle	Number of Bundles	Profit
A, B, C, D	100	2	98	4	392

The profit from the best pure bundling strategy of P_{Bundle} = $100 is $392.

TABLE 9.4

Optimal Mixed Bundle Prices

Consumer	Bundle Price	Cost/Bundle	Profit/Bundle	Number of Bundles	Profit
A, B, C, D	100	2	98	4	392

Consumer	Price 1	Cost/Unit	Profit/Unit	Number of Units	Profit
None	90.01	1	89.01	0	0

Consumer	Price 2	Cost/Unit	Profit/Unit	Number of Units	Profit
None	90.01	1	89.01	0	0

The profit from the best mixed bundling strategy of P_{Bundle} = $100, $P_1 > 90, and $P_2 > 90 is $392.

the good at less than the cost of producing it. Finally, a manager may want to practice **inclusion**: selling a good to a customer who values the good at greater than the seller's cost of producing the good. Perfect price discrimination extracts all available consumer surplus, does not sell to anyone for less than cost, and sells to everyone who values the good more than cost. Thus perfect price discrimination satisfies all three of the concepts defined here. These three pricing mechanisms (price separately, pure bundling, and mixed bundling) can be compared to perfect price discrimination on the three dimensions of extraction, exclusion, and inclusion.

Pricing separately should always entail exclusion; but because of its single price per good nature, it will not fulfill complete extraction or inclusion (for nega-

Inclusion When a manager sells a good to a consumer who values the good at greater than the seller's cost of producing the good.

TABLE 9.5

Optimal Mixed Bundle Prices When Consumers Buy Bundle and at Least One of the Separately Priced Goods

Consumer	Bundle Price	Cost/Bundle	Profit/Bundle	Number of Bundles	Profit
B, C	100	2	98	2	196

Consumer	Price 1	Cost/Unit	Profit/Unit	Number of Units	Profit
A	89.99	1	88.99	1	88.99

Consumer	Price 2	Cost/Unit	Profit/Unit	Number of Units	Profit
D	89.99	1	88.99	1	88.99

The profit from the best mixed bundling strategy, where customers actually purchase the bundle and purchase at least one of the separately priced goods of P_{Bundle} = $100, P_1 = $89.99, and P_2 = $89.99, is $373.98.

tively sloped demand curves). Pure bundling can allow complete extraction (as in the preceding case); but when the sum of all demanders' reservation prices for goods does not lie on a line with a slope of -1 (that is, there is less than perfect negative correlation of reservation prices), extraction is less than complete. Mixed bundling falls someplace between pricing separately and pure bundling.

Pure bundling can also fail inclusion and exclusion. Note how the best price strategy changes when the cost of producing the goods changes. Consider the example just used but with the production cost of each good now at $11 each. Tables 9.6, 9.7, and 9.8 show the solutions for pricing separately, pure bundling, and mixed bundling.

However, if we look at mixed bundles where customers actually consume the bundle and at least one of the goods sold separately, Table 9.9 shows the best mixed bundle.

In this case the concept of exclusion dominates the concept of extraction. The pure bundle price of $100 completely extracts all consumer surplus. However, the seller sells (in the bundle) good 2 to consumer A, and A values the good at only $10, whereas it costs the seller $11 to produce good 2. Likewise, the seller sells good 1 to consumer D in the bundle, and D values the good at only $10, whereas it costs the seller $11 to produce good 1. It is better for the seller to exclude consumer A

TABLE 9.6

Optimal Separate Prices for Good 1 and Good 2

Consumer	Price 1	Cost/Unit	Profit/Unit	Number of Units	Profit
A	90	11	79	1	79
B	60	11	49	2	98
C	**50**	11	39	3	**117**
D	10	11	−1	4	−4

Consumer	Price 2	Cost/Unit	Profit/Unit	Number of Units	Profit
A	10	11	−1	4	−4
B	**40**	11	29	3	**87**
C	50	11	39	2	78
D	90	11	79	1	79

The profit from the best separate price strategy of $P_1 = \$50$ and $P_2 = \$40$ is \$204.

TABLE 9.7

Optimal Pure Bundle Prices for Consumers *A*, *B*, *C*, and *D*

Consumer	Bundle Price	Cost/Bundle	Profit/Bundle	Number of Bundles	Profit
A, B, C, D	100	22	78	4	312

The profit from the best pure bundling strategy of $P_{Bundle} = \$100$ is \$312.

from buying good 2 and consumer *D* from buying good 1. The seller can do that by practicing mixed bundling. The seller sacrifices \$10.01 in consumer revenue from each of consumers *A* and *D* by switching those consumers from a price of \$100 for the bundle to a price of \$89.99 for the separate goods (a total of \$20.02). But the seller saves \$22 in cost by not producing one unit of good 1 and one unit of good 2. This \$1.98 difference is the difference in profits between the best pure bundle profit of \$312 and the best mixed bundle profit of \$313.98. Inclusion and exclusion are practiced perfectly in this case of mixed bundling, but complete extraction is not. In general, optimal pricing solutions among these three methods entail a trade-off among the concepts of extraction, exclusion, and inclusion.

Suppose further that the cost of producing each good is now \$55. Tables 9.10, 9.11, and 9.12 show the solutions for pricing separately, pure bundling, and mixed bundling.

TABLE 9.8

Optimal Mixed Bundle Prices

Consumer	Bundle Price	Cost/Bundle	Profit/Bundle	Number of Bundles	Profit
A, B, C, D	100	22	78	4	312

Consumer	Price 1	Cost/Unit	Profit/Unit	Number of Units	Profit
None	90.01	11	79.01	0	0

Consumer	Price 2	Cost/Unit	Profit/Unit	Number of Units	Profit
None	90.01	11	79.01	0	0

The profit from the best mixed bundle strategy of P_{Bundle} = $100, P_1 > 90, and P_2 > 90 is $312.

TABLE 9.9

Optimal Mixed Bundle Prices When Consumers Buy Bundle and at Least One of the Separately Priced Goods

Consumer	Bundle Price	Cost/Bundle	Profit/Bundle	Number of Bundles	Profit
B, C	100	22	78	2	156

Consumer	Price 1	Cost/Unit	Profit/Unit	Number of Units	Profit
A	89.99	11	78.99	1	78.99

Consumer	Price 2	Cost/Unit	Profit/Unit	Number of Units	Profit
D	89.99	11	78.99	1	78.99

The profit from the best mixed bundle strategy, where customers actually purchase the bundle and at least one of the separately priced goods of P_{Bundle} = $100, P_1 = $89.99, and P_2 = $89.99, is $313.98. Therefore, mixed bundling is the best pricing strategy for the seller.

TABLE 9.10

Optimal Separate Prices for Good 1 and Good 2

Consumer	Price 1	Cost/Unit	Profit/Unit	Number of Units	Profit
A	**90**	55	35	1	**35**
B	60	55	5	2	10
C	50	55	−5	3	−15
D	10	55	−45	4	−180

Consumer	Price 2	Cost/Unit	Profit/Unit	Number of Units	Profit
A	10	55	−45	4	−180
B	40	55	−15	3	−45
C	50	55	25	2	−10
D	**90**	55	35	1	**35**

The profit from the best separate price strategy of $P_1 = \$90$ and $P_2 = \$90$ is $70.

TABLE 9.11

Optimal Pure Bundle Prices for Consumers A, B, C, and D

Consumer	Bundle Price	Cost/Bundle	Profit/Bundle	Number of Bundles	Profit
A, B, C, D	100	110	−10	4	−40

The best pure bundling strategy is any bundle price over $100. No one will buy the bundle, and the profit is $0.

TABLE 9.12

Optimal Mixed Bundle Prices at Any Pure Bundle Price over $100 (So No Bundle Is Purchased)

Consumer	Price 1	Cost/Unit	Profit/Unit	Number of Units	Profit
A	90	55	35	1	35
Consumer	Price 2	Cost/Unit	Profit/Unit	Number of Units	Profit
B	90	55	35	1	35

The profit from the best mixed bundle strategy of $P_{Bundle} > \$100$, $P_1 = \$90$, and $P_2 = \$90$ is $70.

The only reason that mixed bundling yields the same profit as separate pricing here is that a bundle price is selected so that no consumer will choose the bundle—that is, a price over $100. In cases where separate pricing is best, we can always price the bundle at a price at which no one will consume it. Therefore, mixed bundling weakly dominates pricing separately. Previously we established that mixed bundling weakly dominates pure bundling; technically mixed bundling should be a part of any bundling strategy because the profit from it is always better than or equal to that of pricing separately or pure bundling.

Although pure bundling perfectly extracts all consumer surplus in this perfectly negatively correlated reservation price example when the unit production cost is $55, it fails miserably on exclusion. Many units (five) are sold to customers who value the good at less than its cost of production. Mixed bundling, except at a price that excludes everyone from buying the pure bundle, can do no better than pricing separately. Pricing separately extracts much of the *profitable* consumer

---

FIGURE 9.5

Optimal Separate Prices in the Case of Uniformly Distributed Consumer Reservation Prices

The optimal separate prices when the uniform distribution of consumer reservation prices is between $0 and $100 for both goods are $50 for each good. Profits are $500,000.

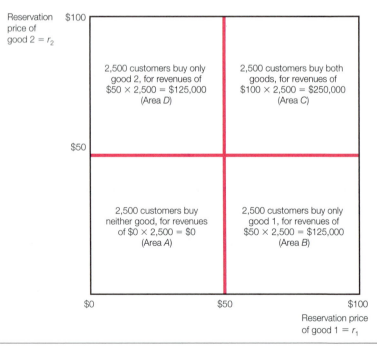

FIGURE 9.6

Optimal Pure Bundle Price in the Case of Uniformly Distributed Consumer Reservation Prices

The optimal pure bundle price when the uniform distribution of consumer reservation prices is between $0 and $100 for both goods is $81.65. Profits are $544,331.10.

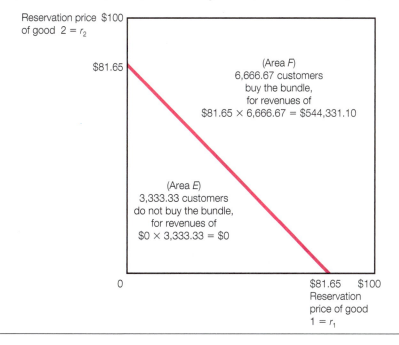

Reservation price $100 of good $2 = r_2$

$81.65

(Area F)
6,666.67 customers
buy the bundle,
for revenues of
$81.65 × 6,666.67 = $544,331.10

(Area E)
3,333.33 customers
do not buy the bundle,
for revenues of
$0 × 3,333.33 = $0

0        $81.65 $100
         Reservation
         price of good
         $1 = r_1$

surplus, excludes the right consumers, but does not include consumer B who values good 1 at $60 (the cost of production is $55).

Negative correlation of reservation prices enables a manager to fully extract all consumer surplus with a pure bundle when the cost of production is low. If we increase the production cost while keeping the reservation prices with perfectly negative correlation, initially mixed bundling is the profit-maximizing action; if production costs keep increasing, eventually separate pricing will maximize profit.

But negative correlation is not required to make bundling the best choice. Suppose customers are uniformly distributed over reservation prices for good 1 from $0 to $100 and for good 2 from $0 to $100. This would be a case of zero correlation of reservation prices. There are 10,000 such consumers. To keep things simple, suppose production costs of the goods are $0. Therefore, maximizing the total revenue is the same as maximizing profit.[2]

The best separate prices are $P_1 = \$50$ and $P_2 = \$50$, and the profit is $500,000.[3] This is shown in Figure 9.5.

2. The following examples are from "Bundling: Teaching Note," Harvard Business School, 5-795-168, rev. July 22, 1998.

3. Call the optimal price of good 1 x. Because of the uniform distribution, this also is the optimal price of good 2. When x is chosen, it determines how many customers consume each good. Consider choosing x on the horizontal axis. Everyone to the left of x does not consume good 1, and everyone at and to the right of x consumes good 1. Consider choosing x on the vertical axis. Everyone below x does not consume good 2, and everyone at and above x consumes good 2. The total area of Figure 9.5 is $100 \times 100 = 10,000$. Viewing each of the four areas created, we can calculate the percentage of the total area occupied by each of the subareas. For instance, area A occupies $x^2/10,000$ amount of the total area. Area B occupies $(100 - x)x/10,000 = (100x - x^2)/10,000$ of the total area (as does area D). Area C occupies $(100 - x)(100 - x)/10,000 = (10,000 - 200x + x^2)/10,000$ of the total area. The number of customers in each area is the percentage of the total area times 10,000. The revenue from each area is the number of customers times the price they pay. Therefore, area A generates $0x^2$ in revenue, area B generates $x(100x - x^2)$ in revenue, area C generates $2x(10,000 - 200x + x^2)$ in revenue, and area D generates $x(100x - x^2)$ in revenue, yielding a total revenue (TR) of $20,000x - 200x^2$. We maximize TR by setting $dTR/dx = 20,000 - 400x = 0$ or $x = \$50$. Total profit is $500,000.

FIGURE 9.7

Optimal Mixed Bundle Pricing in the Case of Uniformly Distributed Consumer Reservation Prices

The optimal mixed bundle pricing when the uniform distribution of consumer reservation prices is between \$0 and \$100 for both goods is P_1 = 66.67, P_2 = 66.67, and P_{Bundle} = 86.19. Profit is \$549,201.

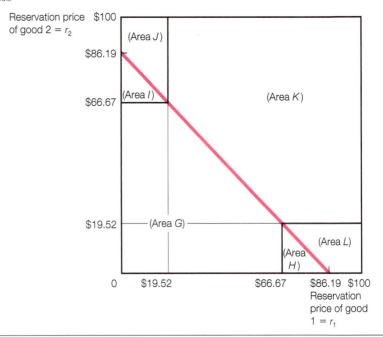

4. Call the optimal price of the bundle y. When the price of the bundle is chosen, it creates a line of slope −1 that connects the vertical axis from point y to the horizontal axis at point y. Area E has an area of $0.5(y)$ $(y) = 0.5y^2$. Its share of the whole area is $0.5y^2/10{,}000$, and hence it has $0.5y^2$ customers in it. Area F has the remainder of the customers—that is, $10{,}000 − 0.5y^2$. The total revenue generated from area E is $\$0(0.5y^2) = \$0$, and the total revenue generated from area F is $y(10{,}000 − 0.5y^2)$. The total revenue (TR) from pure bundling is therefore $10{,}000y − 0.5y^3$. Maximize TR by setting $dTR/dy = 10{,}000 − 1.5y^2 = 0$ or $y \approx$ \$81.65. Total profit is approximately \$544,331.10.

5. Call y the bundle price and x the price of good 1 (and good 2 because of the symmetry). Areas $G + H + I = 0.5y^2$. As shown in the two previous footnotes, these areas represent the number of consumers in the area.

The best pure bundle price is approximately \$81.65, and profit is approximately \$544,331.10.[4] This is shown in Figure 9.6. Even without negative correlation, bundling can increase profit over simple monopoly pricing (that is, pricing separately).

The best mixed bundle has a bundle price of approximately \$86.19, P_1 = \$66.67, and P_2 = \$66.67, yielding a profit of approximately \$549,201.[5] Therefore, mixed bundling is even better than pure bundling. This is shown in Figure 9.7. So with no negative correlation of reservation prices, the best pricing policy is mixed bundling.[6]

We may also consider quantity discounting as a form of mixed bundling. Suppose that the cost of producing the good is $1. Table 9.13 represents consumers' reservation prices for the first unit of the good and the second unit of the good. Consumers want (at most) two units of the good. Table 9.14 shows the case of separate pricing, and Table 9.15 shows the pure bundling strategy. Finally, Table 9.16 shows the best mixed bundling strategy.

TABLE 9.13

Reservation Prices for the First and Second Units of a Good by Consumers *A* and *B*

Consumer	Reservation Price of Good	
	First Unit	Second Unit
A	4	1.5
B	3.99	3

TABLE 9.14

Optimal Separate Prices for the Good

Price of Good	Cost/Unit	Profit/Unit	Number of Units	Profit
4	1	3	1	3
3.99	1	2.99	2	5.98
3	1	2	3	**6**
1.5	1	0.5	4	2

So the best separate price is $3, and the profit is $6.

TABLE 9.15

Optimal Pure Bundle Price for Two Units of the Same Good

Price of Bundle	Cost/Bundle	Profit/Bundle	Number of Bundles	Profit
5.5	2	3.5	2	**7**
6.99	2	4.99	1	4.99

So the best pure bundling strategy is a price of $5.5, and the profit is $7.

6. Bundling can also work if reservation prices are positively correlated. Consider the case where consumer *A* values good 1 at 11 and good 2 at 24, consumer *B* values good 1 at 15 and good 2 at 45, and consumer *C* values good 1 at 16 and good 2 at 15. The reservation prices are weakly positively correlated; that is, the slope of a linear regression is 0.006. The cost of good 1 is 5 and the cost of good 2 is 10. The best separate prices of $P_1 = 15$ and $P_2 = 45$ yield a profit of 55. The best pure bundle price is $P_B = 31$, yielding a profit of 48. But the best choice is a mixed bundle of $P_B = 60$, $P_1 = 16$, and not offering good 2 separately. Consumer *B* buys the bundle, consumer *C* buys good 1, and consumer *A* buys nothing. The profit is 56.

TABLE 9.16

Optimal Mixed Bundling Prices for the Case of a Single Good

Price of Bundle	Cost/Bundle	Profit/Bundle	Number of Bundles	Profit
6.99	2	4.99	1 (B)	4.99

Price of Good	Cost/Unit	Profit/Unit	Number of Units	Profit
4	1	3	1 (A)	3

So the best mixed bundle and the best overall pricing strategy are to price a unit of the good at $4 and a bundle of two goods at $6.99. This yields a profit of $7.99.

We give one final example of bundling to demonstrate how tricky calculating an optimal mixed bundle pricing package can be. The example demonstrates the point made previously about having to consider only customers' reservation prices as candidates for optimal separate prices and only the sum of customers' reservation prices as candidates for pure bundling. It also shows that in mixed bundling, the optimal prices need not be any customer's reservation price (or sum of reservation prices). And the consumer selects the good or bundle that leaves her with the greatest consumer surplus.

The complexity of solving for the optimal bundle is that managers have no $\Delta\pi/\Delta Q = 0$ formula to help derive the optimal pricing scheme. The procedure is more trial and error than derivation. The mixed bundle pricing package consists of prices for individual components and a single price for the product (or service) bundle. A manager can maximize profit even if the prices of the individual goods or the bundle are different from the reservation prices of consumers. This cannot be true when considering just separate pricing or pure bundling. Whether we deal with prices different than reservation prices or their sums depends on trade-offs from the consumers' view of consumer surplus and from the producers' view of producer surplus.

Consider the scenario in Table 9.17. There are three consumers (or consumer groups)—A, B, and C, for simplicity, with an equal number of consumers in each group, each wanting no more than one of each good at their reservation price or less—and two goods, X and Y. Both products cost a constant $4 to produce. The best separate prices are shown in boldface in Table 9.18. Therefore, the best separate pricing strategy is price X at $12 and price Y at $8, which yields a profit of $16. The best pure bundling price is shown in Table 9.19 in boldface. The best pure bundle price is $13.33, which yields a profit of $15.99.

TABLE 9.17

Consumer Reservation Prices for Good *X* and Good *Y* (in Dollars)

	Reservation Prices for Goods by Consumer		
	Good *X*	Good *Y*	Both *X* and *Y*
Consumer *A*	5.33	8	13.33
Consumer *B*	12	3	15
Consumer *C*	3	11	14

TABLE 9.18

Best Separate Price Strategy

	Cost/Unit	Profit/Unit	Number of Units	Profit
Price of *X*				
5.33	4	1.33	2	2.66
12.00	4	8.00	1	**8.00**
3.00	4	−1.00	3	−3.00
Price of *Y*				
8.00	4	4.00	2	**8.00**
3.00	4	−1.00	3	−3.00
11.00	4	7.00	1	7.00

TABLE 9.19

Best Pure Bundling Strategy

Price of Bundle	Cost/Bundle	Profit/Bundle	Number of Bundles	Profit
13.33	8	5.33	3	**15.99**
15.00	8	7.00	1	7.00
14.00	8	6.00	2	12.00

Note the negative relationship (correlation) among the customer's reservation prices. Note also that in considering separate prices, you need never consider a nonreservation price as a pricing candidate. For instance, suppose you investigated pricing good X at $5. Two customers will purchase at that price (A and B, who have reservation prices of $5.33 and $12, respectively). Your profit with such a price is ($5 − $4)2 = $2. But when you price at $5, you leave consumer surplus on the table. Consumer A is willing to pay $5.33, but you do not ask her to. As a result, you sacrifice $0.33 in profit (not only on customer A but also on customer B if you had offered good X at $5.33). By lowering your price to $5, you pick up no additional sales and sacrifice $0.66 in profit. If you do not charge the reservation prices of the customers, you cannot maximize profit using a separate price strategy. The same is true for pure bundling. Why shouldn't you consider pricing the bundle at $14.50 as one of your candidates? Because at $14.50 you get only customer B to buy the bundle, and she would have purchased the bundle at $15. You would leave consumer surplus on the table.

Consider now a mixed bundling strategy with a bundle price of $13.33, a price of good X at $10.32, and a price of good Y at $10.32. It first might appear that all customers would buy the bundle at $13.33 (because B gets consumer surplus of $15 − $13.33 = $1.67 and C gets consumer surplus of $14 − $13.33 = $0.67). But if the price of X is $10.32, consumer B gets a higher consumer surplus of $12 − $10.32 = $1.68 > $1.67 if she buys good X alone; and if the price of good Y is $10.32, consumer C gets a higher consumer surplus of $11 − $10.32 = $0.68 > $0.67 if she buys good Y alone. But consumer B does not get to consume good Y if she does not buy the bundle, and consumer C does not get to consume good X if she does not buy the bundle—doesn't that count? Yes, but they are still better off with the larger consumer surplus from consuming just one good.

Suppose consumer B has $15. If she buys the bundle for $13.33, she will have consumer surplus of $1.67 and both goods. But if she buys just good X for $10.32, she will have good X and $4.68 left over. She has $1.68 in consumer surplus from good X; and although she does not have good Y, she has $4.68 in cash ($3 of which is not part of the consumer surplus from good X). But $4.68 in cash instead of good Y is attractive to consumer B because good Y is worth only $3 to her. (She has the equivalent of good Y with the $3 in cash that is not associated with the consumer surplus for good X; recall that the definition of reservation price is that a person is exactly indifferent between a good and the amount of the reservation price.) Therefore, $4.68 in cash and good X is a better position for consumer B than $1.67 in cash and both goods (which are worth only $4.67 to her). Analogously, consumer C, starting off with $14, is better off with $3.68 in cash and good Y rather than having $0.67 in cash and both goods (because good X is worth $3 to her).

How much profit do managers earn with such a mixed bundle? Table 9.20 demonstrates the profit improvement to $17.97. The profit of $17.97 dominates

TABLE 9.20

Best Mixed Bundling Strategy

Price of Bundle	Cost/Bundle	Profit on Each	Total Number	Total Profit
13.33	8	5.33	1 (consumer A)	5.33

Price of X	Cost/Unit	Profit/Unit	Total Number	Total Profit
10.32	4	6.32	1 (consumer B)	6.32

Price of Y	Cost/Unit	Profit/Unit	Total Number	Total Profit
10.32	4	6.32	1 (consumer C)	6.32
				Sum of Profit
				17.97

the profit of $16 available from the best separate pricing strategy and the profit of $15.99 available from the best pure bundling strategy. The secret is to see if we can pull customers out of the best pure bundling strategy and increase profit with a credible bundle. The best pure bundle yields $5.33 profit per customer. We retain that net profit for customer A and pull customers B and C out at higher profit margins, thus increasing the firm's profit. In the case of separate pricing, we need to ask, Can we put some customer(s) in a bundle and do better? We sacrifice profit margin from consumer B (down from $8 in the best separate price situation), but we more than make up that loss with the tremendous gain on consumers A and C, who were yielding only $4 each under the best separate pricing strategy. (We are down $1.68 from customer B but up $1.33 from customer A and up $2.32 from customer C; so we gain $1.97, the difference between the mixed bundle profit of $17.97 and the best separate price profit of $16.)

If we price good X at $10.34, customer B does not buy it (it yields a consumer surplus of only $12 − $10.34 = $1.66, and she can get $15 − $13.33 = $1.67 by buying the bundle). So pricing good X at $10.34 and the bundle at $13.33 is not a credible mixed bundle because someone you didn't want to buy the bundle (consumer B) does.

As you can see, mixed bundling need not charge the reservation prices of a consumer for the items. But we see a lot of mixed bundling in the market—so it is important to know that experimentation plays an important role and pure bundling and separate pricing are not always the best strategies.

WHEN TO UNBUNDLE

It is important to remember that the concept of bundling entails a null case of pricing the bundled goods (services) separately. Just because bundling is the optimal pricing strategy at time t does not mean it is the optimal pricing strategy at time $t + 1$. Managers must reassess their markets periodically to see if changed conditions warrant new prices, including an unbundling of commodities.

Table 9.21 shows the reservation prices of consumers A, B, and C for goods X and Y at time t. Consumers want, at most, one of each good. The unit cost of each good is 3, and a bundle of the two goods costs the producer 6. The reservation price of a consumer for a bundle of the goods is the sum of his reservation prices for the goods. The producer cannot price discriminate.

The optimal (profit-maximizing) strategy for the producer under these conditions is to price good X at $P_X = 8.62$, price the bundle at $P_B = 10.33$, and not offer good Y separately. This policy yields a profit of 13.98. The best pure bundle would be to offer the bundle at $P_B = 10.33$, yielding a profit of 12.99. The best separate price policy would be $P_X = 9$ and $P_Y = 10$, yielding a profit of 13.

Figure 9.8 shows the best mixed bundling policy versus the best pure bundle and best separate price policies and the use of the method of "crow's feet"[7] to solve the bundling problem.

Pure bundling at $P_B = 10.33$ gives the lowest profit of the three types of pricing at 12.99. Each consumer contributes 4.33 ($= 10.33 - 6$) to the profit. If managers want to pull consumer B out of the bundle by a separate price policy, they will have to offer B a greater consumer surplus than she receives from the bundle (she currently gets 2.67 $= 13 - 10.33$) and so must offer more than 2.67 to pull consumer B from the bundle—this is shown as length b in Figure 9.8). Only good Y is a play here because consumer B is willing to pay the MC only for good X (so managers can't reduce the price and make a profit). Because B will pay 10 for good Y, if managers reduce the price of good Y to $10 - 2.67^+ = 7.33^-$, consumer B will have consumer surplus of $10 - 7.33^- = 2.67^+$; this beats the consumer sur-

7. We first saw the method of "crows feet" from our Wharton colleague Matt White.

TABLE 9.21

The Reservation Prices for Consumers A, B, and C for Good X, Good Y, and a Bundle of Good X and Good Y

| | Reservation Price | | |
	Good X	Good Y	Bundle of Good X and Good Y
Consumer A	5	5.33	10.33
Consumer B	3	10	13
Consumer C	9	2	11

plus from the bundle, so she will defect from the bundle. However, this means the profit from consumer B falls to $7.33^- - 3 = 4.33^-$, which is less than before (and without changing consumers A and C's behavior and hence their profit contribution). Thus, managers should not want to pull consumer B from the bundle.

If managers want to pull consumer C out of the bundle by a separate price policy, they will have to offer C a greater consumer surplus than he receives from the bundle (he currently gets $0.67 = 11 - 10.33$) and so must offer more than 0.67 to pull consumer C from the bundle—this is shown as length c in Figure 9.8). Only good X is in play here because consumer C is not willing to pay the MC for good Y. Because C will pay 9 for good X, if managers reduce the price of good X to $9 - 0.67^+ = 8.33^-$, consumer C will have consumer surplus of $9 - 8.33^- = 0.67^+$; this beats the consumer surplus from the bundle, so he will defect from the bundle. This means the profit from consumer C increases to $8.33^- - 3 = 5.33^-$, which is more (by 0.99^+) than before (and without changing consumers A and B's behavior and hence their profit contribution). Thus managers do want to pull consumer C from the bundle.

Pulling consumer A from the bundle lowers profits from A and also from the other consumers. To pull A from the bundle, suppose P_X is dropped to 5^- and P_Y is dropped to 5.33^-. A will buy each good separately, but profit from A drops to $5^- - 3 + 5.33^- - 3 = 4.33^{--}$ (less than before). In addition, consumer B will defect from the bundle (now getting a $10 - 5.33^- = 4.67^+$ consumer surplus from good Y), and consumer C will defect from the bundle (now getting a $9 - 5^- = 4^+$ consumer surplus from good X). Profit from B falls to $5.33^- - 3 = 2.33^-$ (much less than in the bundle), and profit from C falls to $5^- - 3 = 2^-$ (much less than in the bundle). Thus the mixed bundle is much better than the pure bundle priced at $P_B = 10.33$.

How about the separate price solution versus the mixed bundle? Consumer A purchases nothing under the optimal separate price solution of $P_X = 9$ and $P_Y = 10$ and hence contributes nothing to profit. Pulling her into a bundle at 10.33 will increase profit from her to 4.33. Consumer B buying good Y at 10 contributes 7 to profit, and consumer C buying good X at 9 contributes 6 to profit. Figure 9.8 shows that bringing consumer B into the bundle will cause B to contribute 2.67 (length b) less in profit than before ($10.33 - 6 = 4.33$ versus $10 - 3 = 7$). Pricing good X at 8.33^- will keep consumer C from joining the bundle (which he will do if the price of X remains at 9). This decreases the profit from consumer C by 0.67^+, shown as length c in Figure 9.8 ($8.33^- - 3 = 5.33^-$ versus $9 - 3 = 6$). But on net, where does it leave total profit? The mixed bundle increases profit from A by 4.33, decreases the profit from B by 2.67, and decreases the profit from C by 0.67^+ for a net increase in profit of $4.33 - 2.67 - 0.67^+ = 0.99^-$.

Thus Figure 9.8 shows the optimality of the mixed bundle pricing policy of $P_B = 10.33$, $P_X = 8.33^-$, and not offering good Y separately over the best pure bundle strategy of $P_B = 10.33$ and the best separate price strategy of $P_X = 9$ and $P_Y = 10$.

FIGURE 9.8

Depiction of Bundling Problem in Table 9.21

The bundling problem is solved by analyzing the "crow's feet" (the large blue lines) in the this figure. The "crow's feet" method is extended when the reservation price of consumer B for good Y increases from 10 to 11.

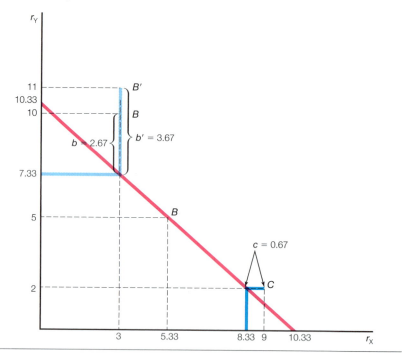

Note that the verbal explanation here is shown by the "crow's feet" (the large red lines radiating from the $P_{\text{Bundle}} = 10.33$ line in Figure 9.8).

Suppose demand conditions change. In particular, suppose consumer B's reservation price for good Y increases from 10 to 11 as shown in Figure 9.8 (with the consumer's new position shown as B'). Note that B's reservation price for the bundle has now increased to 14 (3 + 11).

If consumer B buys the bundle at 10.33, she gets a consumer surplus of 3.67 (= 14 − 10.33) and contributes a profit of 4.33 (= 10.33 − 6). However, if managers do not offer the bundle, they will make 8 (= 11 − 3) from consumer B by charging B's reservation price for good Y. At the same time, charging consumer C his reservation price of 9 for good X yields a profit of 6 (= 9 − 3) from consumer C. Consumer A will buy neither good and hence contributes nothing to profit. However, total profit is now 14 (= 8 + 6), which exceeds the profit of pure bundling at P_B = 10.33 of 12.99 and the profit of mixed bundling at P_B = 10.33, P_X = 8.33⁻, and not offering good Y separately of 13.99⁻. In fact, an increase in consumer B's reservation price for good Y to 10.98⁺ will make the unbundling policy the most profitable.

When consumer B was at point B (not B'), the separate price profit was 13.99^- $- 13 = 0.99^-$ behind the optimal (mixed bundling) pricing policy. Raising the reservation price of good Y for consumer B by 1 enables managers to profitably change their pricing policy. Again, note that the "crow's feet" tell the same story.

Here's another case where managers will want to unbundle. If consumer C's good X reservation price increases to 10 (and all other consumers' reservation prices remain the same), managers could also unbundle and sell both good X and good Y each at 10 and earn $14 (= 10 - 3 + 10 - 3)$. In fact, any combination of increases in B's reservation price for good Y and C's reservation price for good X greater than 0.98 should cause managers to unbundle the products and just sell each good separately.

Consider the new scenario where B's reservation price for good Y is 11. Suppose a bundle price of 10.33. If consumer B buys the bundle, she receives a consumer surplus of $3.67 (= 3 + 11 - 10.33)$ and yields a profit of $4.33 (= 10.33 - 6)$. To pull B out of the bundle, she'd have to be offered a consumer surplus greater than 3.67. This would entail offering good Y at a price of less than 7.33 (say 7.33^-). Such a price would yield a profit from consumer B of less than the 4.33 available from selling B the bundle at 10.33 ($7.33^- - 3 = 4.33^-$). No other consumption would be affected by dropping the price of good Y to 7.33^-, and profit is reduced by this move.

By taking away the option of the bundle from the mixed bundling scenario and just charging $P_X = 9$ and $P_Y = 11$, Figure 9.8 shows the gain in profit. For B, who bought the bundle when it was available, profit increases from $4.33 (= 10.33 - 6)$ to $8 (= 11 - 3)$ or by $3.67 (= 8 - 4.33)$ or by b' in Figure 9.8. Individual C now buys just good X for 9, yielding a profit of $6 (= 9 - 3)$, whereas under mixed bundling, he bought just good X at 8.33^-, yielding a profit of $5.33^- (= 8.33^- - 3)$. Profit from C has thus increased by $0.67^+ (= 6 - 5.33^-)$ or by c in Figure 9.8. Without the bundle available, A consumes neither good and hence the profit of $4.33 (= 10.33 - 6)$ she contributed to the firm under the mixed bundle has been lost. But the combined increase in profit from B and C of $4.34^+ (= 3.67 + 0.67^+)$ exceeds the loss in profit from A of 4.33, yielding a net gain of $0.01^+ (= 4.34^+ - 4.33)$. This is shown by the difference in the separate price profit of 14 and the mixed bundling profit of 13.99^-.

So although some form of bundling (pure or mixed) will many times increase a firm's profit, unbundling can also increase profit. It all depends on the reservation prices and the costs of production. The diagrammatic technique shows how to measure the conditions under which managers can profitably change prices.

BUNDLING AS A PREEMPTIVE ENTRY STRATEGY

In addition to being a strategy to enhance profits, bundling is also used to deter entry by potential rivals. Suppose managers at the Alpha Company have developed a bundle made up of product W and product S, which they plan to sell for $\$X$. The question for us to answer is this: What is X?

The Beta Company is developing a product (C) that is a close substitute to W. The Gamma Company is developing a product (N) that is a close substitute to S. Managers at both Beta and Gamma want to bring their products to market. Only Alpha has the financial ability to produce both products as a bundle. Alpha's entry cost to the market is 30. It would cost Beta 17 to enter the market, and it would cost Gamma 17 to enter the market. If Alpha managers were to produce each product separately, it would cost them 15 to enter each market. In all cases, these entry costs are independent of the number of units sold. Note that Alpha's entry costs are 15 for each product regardless of whether the product is sold separately or is included in a bundle.

The market for the services provided by W and C, by S and N, and for a bundle that provides both services is presented in Table 9.22. Suppose consumers regard Beta's product C as comparable to Alpha's product W and regard Gamma's product N as comparable to Alpha's product S. Consumers also regard making their own bundle (buying Beta's C and buying Gamma's N) as comparable to Alpha's bundle of W and S. The numbers in the table are the consumers' reservation prices for each product. It costs each producer 2 to distribute each product (and hence it costs Alpha 4 to distribute its bundle).

For simplicity, assume there is one of each consumer type and the table represents the long-run demand for the products. Consumers want, at most, one of each product. The companies cannot form joint ventures. The consumers' reservation prices are shown in Table 9.22.

The goods are perfectly negatively correlated. Normally this suggests a pure bundle strategy. Indeed, if Alpha is the only participant in this market, the pure bundling strategy (with a bundle price of 30) yields all consumers purchasing and

---

TABLE 9.22

The Reservation Prices for Consumers A, B, and C for Good W or C, Good S or N, and a Bundle of Good W and Good S or a Bundle of Good C and Good N

Consumer Class	Reservation Price for Product W or C	Reservation Price for Product S or N	Reservation Price or bundle W and S or C and N
A	10	20	30
B	15	15	30
C	20	10	30

a net revenue exclusive of entry costs of $(30 \times 3 - (4 \times 3) = 78$. Alpha's entry costs are 30, yielding a profit of 48. This vastly exceeds the best separate price strategy of $P_W = P_S = 15$, which yields a profit of $(15 \times 4) - (2 \times 4) - (15 \times 2) = 22$, or the mixed bundling strategy of the bundle priced at 30 and $P_W = P_N = 20$, which yields a profit of $[(30 - 4) \times 1] + [(20 - 2) \times 2] - (15 \times 2) = 32$.

But if Alpha faces the entry threat from Beta and Gamma, it cannot price the bundle at 30. If it does, Beta could enter and sell C for as little as $(23/3)$ and make money. Likewise, Gamma could enter and sell N for as little as $(23/3)$ and make money. If both Beta and Gamma priced at $(23/3)$, all three consumers would purchase C from Beta, giving Beta revenue of 23. Beta's entry cost is 17, and its cost of distributing C to the consumers would be $2 \times 3 = 6$ for a total cost of 23. The same would hold for Gamma. Both Beta and Gamma would be earning a normal profit (and zero excess profit).

If Alpha prices the bundle at slightly less than $(46/3)$, say at $(46^-/3)$, then neither Beta or Gamma can enter the market because neither can cover the $(23/3)$ cost. How will Alpha do? All three consumers will purchase Alpha's bundle at $(46^-/3)$, yielding Alpha revenue of 46^-. Alpha's cost of entry would be $15 \times 2 = 30$, and the cost of distributing the three bundles would be $4 \times 3 = 12$ for a total cost of 42. Profit would be $46^- - 42 = 4^-$. This is a far cry from 48. But it does leave Alpha as the sole producer.

The threat of entry can significantly reduce monopoly profit. But at the same time the use of bundling can preclude entry and keep a profitable market for the bundler.

STRATEGY SESSION: How *The New Yorker* Used Bundling

The New Yorker is a wonderfully written magazine with witty, informative, entertaining articles. But apparently the market for high-quality journalism has fallen on hard times as consumers have switched their cultural and media preferences.

Magazines depend on subscriptions and newsstand sales and, most of all, advertising for their revenues. And advertising revenues depend on the number of magazines sold because advertisers pay more if the circulation to their demographic group is higher.

Over the years, circulation and advertising revenues fell. It appeared that *The New Yorker* could not cover its costs with its revenues. Thus *The New Yorker's* publisher (Conde Nast) came up with a bundling strategy. Conde Nast also publishes *Architectural Digest* and *Vanity Fair* (which are doing well). The bundling strategy? If a company wanted to advertise in *Architectural Digest* or *Vanity Fair*, it also had to advertise in *The New Yorker*. This proved to be a profitable strategy, and *The New Yorker* is still publishing.

Source: "There's Less Buzz and Less Lunch at *The New Yorker*," *The New York Times*, Monday, June 28, 1999.

Despite the lack of a rigorous analytical solution, following a few simple guidelines will help managers construct more effective bundling policies:

1. If goods' reservation prices are positively correlated, pure bundling can do no better than separate pricing (but mixed bundles might).

2. If the marginal cost of producing a good exceeds its reservation price, in general you should think carefully about selling it.[8]

3. If goods' reservation prices are correlated *perfectly* negatively and the marginal cost of production of the goods is zero, pure bundling is best.

4. If goods' reservation prices are negatively correlated, as the marginal cost of production increases, mixed bundling is likely to be better than pure bundling; and as it increases further, separate pricing is likely to be better.

But everything really depends on the reservation prices and the costs of production, so remember that intelligent experimentation is the way to solve bundling pricing. The other approach, especially when the demanders or goods are many, is to use a computer program to search all three types of pricing and every price in each type for the profit-maximizing result.

TYING AT IBM, XEROX, AND MICROSOFT

One form of bundling involving complementary products is called **tying**. Tying is a pricing technique in which managers sell a product that needs a complementary product. The consumer is required, generally by contract, to buy the complementary product from the firm selling the main product. For example, during the 1950s customers who leased a Xerox copying machine had to buy Xerox paper, and customers who leased an IBM computer had to buy paper computer cards made by IBM. More recently both the United States and the European Union charged that Microsoft uses a tying strategy to force consumers to use its browser product (Internet Explorer) instead of a rival product (Netscape Navigator). Microsoft did this by tying the browser to the Windows operating system, then using its market power to force PC manufacturers to package only Internet Explorer on their machines.

Successful implementation of a tying strategy generally requires the exercise of market power. For example, IBM, Xerox, and Microsoft all had market shares above 85 percent in their respective markets. Managers engage in tying practices for several reasons. First, it is a way of practicing price discrimination. By setting the price of the complementary product well above its cost, managers can get, in effect, a much higher price from those who use it more often. For example, suppose customer A uses a Hewlett-Packard printer to print 10,000 pages per month, whereas customer B uses an HP printer to print only 1,000 pages per month. It is hard for Hewlett-Packard to price its machines to obtain more revenue from customer A, the more intensive user, than from customer B. But if HP can tie the

Tying A pricing technique in which managers sell a product that needs a complementary product.

8. Sometimes it may be more profitable to sell a good in a pure bundle even though the reservation price of a bundle buyer for a good in the bundle is less than the cost of producing the good. Consider a firm choosing between only separate pricing and pure bundling. The reservation prices for good 1 and good 2 for consumers A through F are ($70, $30), ($80, $20), ($75, $25), ($75, $15), ($84, $16) and ($90, $10), respectively. The unit cost of production of good 1 is $70 and of good 2 is $20. The optimal separate prices are $P_1 = \$80$ and P_2 either $30 or $25, yielding a profit of $40. The optimal pure bundling price of $100 yields a profit of $50. Consumers E and F, who buy the bundle, value good 2 at less than its cost and are not excluded because that would decrease the firm's profit. If mixed bundling is allowed, the exclusion problem can be solved. The bundle would be priced at $100, and good 1 would be priced at $83.99. This yields a profit of $57.98, and E and F consume only the good (good 1) they value at greater than cost.

314

STRATEGY SESSION: When Bundling Fails

AT&T customers have spoken. Would they want a cell phone, wireless service, or a free oil change bundled with their local and long distance service? The answer is a Jiffy Lube. Of the 149 bundles AT&T offers, the most popular bundle is the one with the free Jiffy Lube coupon.

This seems to be happening because many home owners do not wish to be captive to one provider for their home phone, wireless, Internet, and TV service (a monopoly fear). In addition, consumers are concerned that the prices they pay for the component services of the bundle are not transparent, making comparison shopping difficult. So one-stop shopping, at least in this field, has yet to take off.

As Adam Quinton, an analyst at Merrill Lynch, states, "Bundling works selectively. There are some bundles that are clearly very powerful, but the answer isn't necessarily to bundle everything."

Another reason for the failure of like-product bundling is that AT&T was unable to bill all services on one bill (although some phone providers are moving in this direction). The failure to do so helps consumers see their cost of services but hurts the convenience factor (two or three checks written, stamps and envelopes licked, and so on). Other consumers, by cherry-picking services from different providers, have been able to beat the bundled price. (Remember that there are transaction costs in wading through all the competing services in attempting to find the best.)

Another factor is psychological. Writing a single big check to one provider is perceived by some consumers as more expensive than writing four small checks to different providers even if the sum to the four exceeds the dollars to the one. This is something like sticker shock—with the single payment you really see how expensive it is to be "tuned into the world." In Australia, Telstra (the communications giant) purposely does not put all services into one bill for that very reason.

The AT&T experience shows that unrelated products can be bundled. But logic suggests that complementary products would seem more likely to make successful bundles.

Note, however, the proliferation of phone, cable, and Internet bundles for $99/month currently appearing.

Source: "Why 'Bundling' Its Consumer Services Hasn't Benefited AT&T," *The Wall Street Journal*, October 24, 2000.

---

sale of ink cartridges to the sale of its printer, it can get more profit from customer *A* than from customer *B* because it makes more on selling cartridges.

A 2003 notice from the Department of the Treasury warned wholesale liquor dealers that they cannot use tie-in sales when dealing with liquor retailers. Some examples of actual practices that were ruled illegal include[9]

- Requiring a retailer to purchase a regular case of distilled spirits to be able to purchase the spirits in a special holiday container.
- Requiring a retailer to purchase 10 cases of a winery's Chardonnay with 10 cases of the winery's Merlot.
- Requiring a retailer to purchase a two-bottle package of a winery's Merlot and Chardonnay to purchase cases of the winery's Merlot.

9. Department of the Treasury, Alcohol and Tobacco Tax and Trade Bureau, Industry Circular Number 2003–3, March 27, 2003.

STRATEGY SESSION: Tying Up Your Printer

Tying is a concept that links products together for the economic gain of the producer. The market for printers is competitive; therefore, printers sell for relatively low prices. This is not where a printer manufacturer's profit is made. But try running your printer without an ink cartridge.

Once they have purchased company X's printer and the included-with-the-purchase ink cartridges run out of ink, many consumers replace them with the same model cartridges from company X. That is where the printer manufacturers make their money. At Hewlett Packard in fiscal 2002, over half the printer group's revenues were from cartridges. One way that purchasers of company X's printers got around the high cost of company X's replacement cartridges was to have the original cartridges refilled. This created environmental savings (fewer cartridges in landfills), resource savings (less plastic needed to make new cartridges), and saved users lots of money when new cartridges did not have to be purchased. Printer

manufacturers got wise to this practice and started building cartridges with electronic chips in them that prevented them from being refilled.

The European Union instituted a new law in 2006 that bans companies from making products that cannot be reused because of specific design features (such as the chips in the cartridges). Nonreusable cartridges make up approximately 90 percent of the market currently.

The tying has not been perfect because "cloners" have begun to rapidly erode the printer manufacturers' share of the market in recent years with inexpensive cartridges. Still, allowing refilling of a printer manufacturer's cartridges (such refills sell at a fraction of the price of a manufacturer's cartridge) further erodes the tying profit of the printer manufacturers.

Source: "European Law May Hit Printer Makers," *Financial Times*, December 19, 2002.

Another reason managers use a tying strategy is to maintain their monopoly position. For example, Microsoft has held a market share of over 90 percent in the PC operating system market since 1991. Even a competitor the size of IBM was forced to quickly withdraw from this market after spending hundreds of millions of dollars on the OS/2 operating system. Netscape was a concern for Microsoft because its product threatened to reduce the number of application programs written for Windows. So Microsoft wanted to exclude Netscape's product. When asked the following question by a government lawyer, a Microsoft executive agreed with the lawyer's assessment:

And all I am trying to establish is that the reason for that [packaging Internet browser with Windows] was because you believed that if the customer had a choice of the two browsers side by side, the user would, in the vast majority of cases or in the majority of cases, pick Netscape for the reasons that you've identified, correct?[10]

10. From www.microsoft/presspass/trial/transcript, September 21, 1999, trial transcript.

This belief was reiterated in an internal Microsoft e-mail presented at the trial:

> It seems clear that it will be very hard to increase browser share on the merits of Internet Explorer alone. It will be more important to leverage the OS asset to make people—to make people choose Explorer instead of Navigator.[11]

In addition, managers may use a tying strategy to ensure that the firm's product works properly and its brand name is protected. To do so, the firm insists that customers use its complementary product. For example, Jerrold Electronics Corporation, which installed community antenna systems, required customers to accept five-year maintenance contracts to avoid breakdowns resulting from improper servicing of its equipment. And McDonald's franchises must buy their materials and food from McDonald's so that the hamburgers are uniform and the company's brand name is not tarnished.

TRANSFER PRICING

In some cases, transactions occur where markets do not exist; many times they involve intrafirm pricing. Say there are two divisions of a firm, where a product required as an input is produced exclusively in an upstream plant for use in a product of a downstream plant. Transfer pricing results from creating an internal market that simulates an external one and allows optimal profit-maximizing decisions by managers in both divisions of the firm. For instance, auto companies purchase inputs from their components' divisions so they can produce automobiles. When an external market exists for the product of the upstream division, the rules for the optimal transfer price determination differ because now the upstream division has the option of selling the product in the external market and the downstream division has the option of purchasing the upstream product in the external market.

Transfer pricing is prevalent. *A recent survey shows that managers in 91 percent of the *Fortune* 150 practice transfer pricing and that in one-third of the firms, managers engage in four or more instances per year of intrafirm transactions.

Consider a multidivisional firm with a downstream monopoly and an upstream provider of a component to the downstream product, such as an engine maker serving a downstream automaker. We assume initially there is no external market for engines; that is, no other engine maker can supply engines to the downstream automaker, nor can any other automaker use the engines of the upstream engine maker. Therefore, managers must decide how many engines and autos to make (these are the same because there is no external market for engines).[12] The downstream operation is subject to the discipline of the market because autos are sold in an external market. But if there is no external market for the upstream product, what price should change hands between the two divisions to pay for the upstream product? This payment, called a **transfer price**, simulates a market where no formal market exists.

Transfer price Payment that simulates a market where no formal market exists.

11. Ibid.
12. For simplicity, we assume that all the upstream product produced during the period must be sold then. In other words, no inventories of the upstream product can be carried over.

In considering transfer pricing policies, managers need to ensure that the profit-maximizing (from the point of view of the entire firm) output of the downstream and the upstream output is produced. Then they must ensure that the upstream managers have the right incentive to produce the profit-maximizing amount of the upstream product in the most efficient way.

The following notation enables us to view the transfer pricing issues facing managers. The demand curve for the downstream product is

$$P_D = P_D(Q_D)$$

where P_D is the price of the downstream product per unit, Q_D is in units of the downstream product, and the parentheses mean "function of" in this and the next equation. Recall that the impacts of complementary and substitute goods on this demand are subsumed in the intercept of the demand curve, as shown in Chapter 2.

The production function[13] of the downstream operation is defined as

$$Q_D = f(L_D, K_D | Q_U)$$

The production function is like those of Chapter 4, but it is conditional; that is, it states that Q_D can be produced with labor (L_D) and capital (K_D) *given* the critical upstream input Q_U.

This production function yields a downstream cost function of

$$TC_D = TC_D(Q_D | Q_U)$$

which is the total cost of the downstream division *exclusive* of the cost of the upstream operation.

Finally, the total cost of the upstream division is just a function of Q_U; it reads

$$TC_U = TC_U(Q_U)$$

and is typical of the cost functions we developed in Chapter 5.

The profit of the multidivisional firm is

$$\pi = TR_D - TC_D - TC_U \tag{9.1}$$

To maximize profit, we must have $\Delta\pi/\Delta Q_U = 0$. Note that Q_U is the variable that controls what the firm does. Without the critical input produced by the upstream division, nothing can be produced in the downstream division. And whatever is produced upstream equals the amount produced downstream; that is, $Q_D = Q_U$ when transfer pricing is done correctly. Although we might be tempted to put a total revenue for the upstream division in equation (9.1) ($TR_U = P_U Q_U$, where P_U would be the transfer price), it would be exactly offset by a cost item for the downstream firm (recall that TC_D is the downstream cost *exclusive* of the cost of the upstream product). Because this nets out to zero, it is not included in equation (9.1).

13. The | is not a division sign in this equation or the next one; rather, it reminds us that the functions are conditional on the amount of Q_U.

If we make the left side of equation (9.1) $\Delta\pi/\Delta Q_U = 0$, we must make the following adjustments to the right side of equation (9.1):

$$\frac{\Delta\pi}{\Delta Q_U} = \left(\frac{\Delta TR_D}{\Delta Q_D}\right)\left(\frac{\Delta Q_D}{\Delta Q_U}\right) - \left(\frac{\Delta TC_D}{\Delta Q_D}\right)\left(\frac{\Delta Q_D}{\Delta Q_U}\right) - \frac{\Delta TC_U}{\Delta Q_U} = 0$$

or

$$\left[\left(\frac{\Delta TR_D}{\Delta Q_D}\right) - \left(\frac{\Delta TC_D}{\Delta Q_D}\right)\right]\left(\frac{\Delta Q_D}{\Delta Q_U}\right) = \left(\frac{\Delta TC_U}{\Delta Q_U}\right) \tag{9.2}$$

or

$$(MR_D - MC_D)MP_U = MC_U \tag{9.3}$$

QUANT OPTION

An ode to Sir Isaac:

Setting $\partial\pi/\partial Q_U = 0$ will maximize the firm's profit. Thus,

$$\partial\pi/\partial Q_U = (\partial TR_D/\partial Q_D)(\partial Q_D/\partial Q_U) - (\partial TC_D/\partial Q_D)(\partial Q_D/\partial Q_U) - dTC_U/dQ_U = 0$$

or

$$[(\partial TR_D/\partial Q_D) - (\partial TC_D/\partial Q_D)](\partial Q_D/\partial Q_U) = (dTC_U/dQ_U)$$

or

$$(MR_D - MC_D)MP_U = MC_U$$

Note that $(\partial Q_D/\partial Q_U)$ is the marginal product of the upstream product.

Note that $(\Delta Q_D/\Delta Q_U)$ is the marginal product of the upstream product in producing the downstream product.

The intuition of equation (9.3) is straightforward. If managers produce another unit in the upstream operation, they incur an additional cost, MC_U. Producing that additional upstream product enables the conglomerate to produce MP_U more downstream units. Each additional downstream unit produced causes managers to incur additional cost in the downstream plant (MC_D) but also enables them to earn additional revenue (MR_D). If the additional net revenue earned, $(MR_D - MC_D)MP_U$, which is produced as a result of incurring the additional cost upstream, MC_U, exceeds that additional upstream cost, then managers want to produce the additional unit upstream (because profit increases). If it does not, managers do not want to produce the additional unit upstream (because profit decreases). Managers maximize profit when the additional net revenue earned downstream as a result of producing an additional unit upstream just equals the additional cost incurred in producing that unit upstream.

But MP_U equals 1 because every time one more unit is produced upstream, one more unit can be produced downstream. In situations where it would appear that the upstream firm has to produce multiple units to enable one additional unit to be produced downstream, such as four tires being required to produce one car, we treat this by requiring one bundle (of four tires) to be produced upstream in order to produce one car. Obviously the situation can also go the other way—such as one extra steer on an upstream cattle ranch enabling the downstream meat processing division to produce $X (>1)$ steaks. Here producing one more steer lets the conglomerate firm produce one more bundle of (X) steaks.

In the situation when $MP_U = 1$, equation (9.3) becomes

$$MR_D - MC_D = MC_U$$

or

$$MR_D = MC_D + MC_U \tag{9.4}$$

and the rule becomes our familiar one: The marginal revenue of the product must equal the marginal cost of producing it. That is, the marginal cost of producing the downstream product is the marginal cost of the downstream operation (remember that this excludes the cost of the upstream operation) plus the marginal cost of the upstream product.

Solving equation (9.4) for $Q_U^* = Q_D^* = Q^*$ gives the correct amount of the upstream product and downstream product produced.

Now suppose managers set the transfer price the downstream division pays and the upstream division receives for its upstream product. They tell the upstream division chief that she will receive P_U for every unit she produces. A profit-maximizing division chief (who is now a price taker) maximizes profit by setting $P_U = MC_U$, as was shown in Chapter 6. But what P_U should managers choose? Clearly it is the P_U that results in Q_U^* units being produced. This is shown in Figure 9.9.

What difference does it make what P_U managers choose? Whatever it is, would it not merely cause the upstream division to have $P_U Q_U^*$ in revenues and the downstream division to have $P_U Q_U^*$ in costs? The two terms merely cancel each other out (which is why we left them out of equation (9.1)). From the point of view of the conglomerate, profit is the same. However, *the profit of each division differs*. And because managers' bonuses are often predicated on their division's profit, these managers care about that transfer price. If the conglomerate's managers determine the optimal Q (that is, Q*) and order both divisions to produce it, then the conglomerate maximizes profit regardless of the transfer price.

FIGURE 9.9

Determination of the Transfer Price, Given No External Market for the Transferred Good

The optimal transfer price, P_U, equals the marginal cost at the optimal output, Q^*.

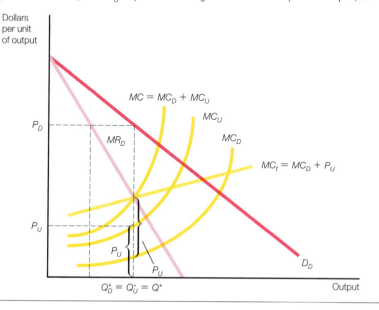

But if the managers are trying to maximize firm profit, it is critical that the correct P_U be chosen. If P_U is set too high, the upstream division will produce too much of the product (recall that in price-taking situations, the marginal cost is rising). Also, managers of the downstream division will see its marginal cost of producing another unit ($MC_D + P_U = MC_t$) as too high and therefore will produce too little downstream output. Therefore, profit will not be maximized. If P_U is set too low, managers of the downstream division will see their marginal cost of producing another unit as too low and will therefore want to produce more than the optimal output (which they cannot do because the upstream division has produced less of its output).

TRANSFER PRICING: A PERFECTLY COMPETITIVE MARKET FOR THE UPSTREAM PRODUCT

In many cases there is a market outside the firm for the product transferred from one division to the other. If this is true, the output levels of the downstream and upstream divisions no longer need be equal. If the downstream division wants more of the upstream product than is produced by the upstream division, it can buy some from external suppliers. If the upstream division produces more of its product than the downstream division wants, it can sell some to external customers. Assuming that the market for the upstream product is perfectly competitive, we can readily determine how managers should set the transfer price.

Figure 9.10 shows the optimal price and output for the firm as a whole. Because there is a perfectly competitive market for the upstream product, managers at the upstream division act as if they see a horizontal demand curve, D_U, where the price is P_U, the price of the upstream product in the external market. To maximize profit, managers at the upstream division should produce the output Q_U, where the marginal cost of the upstream division, MC_U, equals the *externally* determined market price P_U. In this sense the upstream division behaves like a perfectly competitive firm.

To maximize the firm's overall profit, the transfer price should equal P_U, the price of the upstream division in the perfectly competitive market outside the firm. Because managers at the upstream division can sell as much product as they want to external customers at a price of P_U, they have no incentive to sell it at a price below P_U to the downstream division. Similarly, because managers at the downstream division can buy as much of the upstream product as they want from external suppliers at a price of P_U, they have no incentive to buy it from the upstream division at a price above P_U.

FIGURE 9.10

Determination of the Transfer Price, Given a Perfectly Competitive External Market for the Transferred Product

The optimal transfer price, P_U, equals the market price of the transferred product.

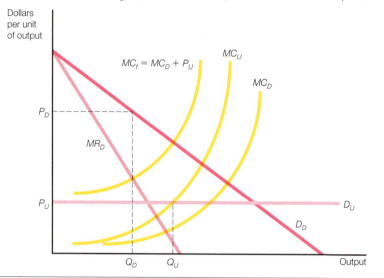

STRATEGY SESSION: Japan's Tax Man Leans on Foreign Firms

Japan's tax authority claims that foreign companies have a propensity to avoid the country's high corporate taxes by illegally shifting profit off their books in Japan.

The authority has filed claims against at least 50 multinationals totaling approximately $492.4 million in back taxes. Among the firms accused are Coca-Cola, Goodyear Tire and Rubber, Procter & Gamble, DaimlerChrysler, and Roche Holding AG. Daimler-Chrysler recently paid Japan an extra $45.87 million for taxes allegedly owed in Japan that were shifted to Germany via transfer payments.

Japanese activity in this regard has become so intense that Arthur Andersen added 10 transfer pricing specialists to its Tokyo office. Although Japan is not the only country that goes after firms that allegedly hide profit from local tax authorities, Japan's high taxes make Japan a tempting country in which to dodge taxes. In Japan about 50 percent of yearly earnings go to national and local governments. The comparable tax burden is estimated to be 41 percent in the United States and 33 percent in the United Kingdom.

Japan believes that some non-Japanese parent companies of Japanese subsidiaries overcharge the subsidiaries for use of their products or trademarks and hence transfer profit out of Japan.

But Japan is not the only country seeking back taxes. In 1993 Nissan paid approximately $144 million to the U.S. Internal Revenue Service to settle a claim that Nissan transferred part of its profit back to Japan. Nissan had a comparable problem in the United Kingdom. The auto industry has a reputation for using transfer pricing to minimize taxable profit.

The potential problem here is enormous. Approximately half the world's trade is estimated to involve goods that are subject to transfer pricing. Over two-thirds of the world's multinationals have been investigated by tax authorities regarding their transfer pricing policies.

Sources: "Japan's Tax Man Leans on Foreign Firms," *The Wall Street Journal*, November 25, 1996; "Transfer Pricing: Confusion over Tax Treatment," *Financial Tiimes*, September 2, 1997; "DaimlerChrysler Japan Forced to Pay More Tax," *Financial Times*, October 10, 2000; and "Nissan's UK Arm Hit by Tax Charges," *Financial Times*, November 8, 2000.

Managers at the downstream division, which must buy the upstream product at price P_U regardless of where it comes from, have a marginal cost of MC_t, which is the sum of the downstream division's marginal cost, MC_D, and the market-determined price of the upstream product, P_U. To maximize their own profit, managers at the downstream division must choose the output level, Q_D, where their marginal cost, $MC_t (= MC_D + P_U)$, equals their marginal revenue, MR_D. Figure 9.10 shows that the output of the downstream division, Q_D, is less than the output of the upstream division, Q_U; so the optimal solution in this case calls for the conglomerate's upstream division to sell part of its output (specifically $Q_U - Q_D$ units) to outside customers.[14]

14. Of course it is not always true that Q_D is less than Q_U. Whether this is the case depends on the shape and position of the marginal cost curves (MC_D and MC_U) and the demand curve as well as the price of the transferred product in the external perfectly competitive market. If $Q_D > Q_U$, the downstream division purchases the required $Q_D - Q_U$ units in the external market at the market-determined price of P_U.

PROBLEM SOLVED: The Orion Corporation

Consider the Orion Corporation, where an upstream chemical division (P) produces a product that it transfers to a downstream marketing division (M), which packages the basic chemical into the final product and sells it to outside customers. To illustrate how managers should calculate the optimal output rates, assume demand and cost conditions are as follows. The demand for the finished product sold by Orion's downstream marketing division is

$$P_M = 100 - Q_M \qquad (9.5)$$

where P_M is the price (in dollars per ton) of the finished product and Q_M is the quantity demanded (in millions of tons per year). Excluding the cost of the basic chemical, the marketing division's total cost function is

$$TC_M = 200 + 10Q_M \qquad (9.6)$$

where TC_M is the division's total cost (in millions of dollars).

Turning to Orion's upstream production division, its total cost function is

$$TC_P = 10 + 2Q_P + 0.5Q_P^2 \qquad (9.7)$$

where TC_P is total production cost (in millions of dollars) and Q_P is the total quantity produced of the basic chemical (in millions of tons per year). As we did earlier, we assume a perfectly competitive market for the basic chemical (the upstream output). Assume that its price in this market is $42 per ton.

Under these conditions, managers can readily determine the optimal rate for each division as well as the proper transfer price for the basic chemical. The production division can sell all the basic chemical that it wants at $42 per ton. Therefore, its marginal revenue equals $42. From equation (9.7), we see that $\Delta TC_P / \Delta Q_P = MC_P = 2 + Q_P$.

To find the output that maximizes the production division's profit, managers set its marginal revenue equal to its marginal cost:

$$MR_P = 42 = 2 + Q_P = MC_P$$

or

$$Q_P = 40$$

Hence the production division should produce 40 million tons per year of the basic chemical.

QUANT OPTION

Orion's marginal cost is $dTC_P/dQ_P = 2 + Q_P$.

THE GLOBAL USE OF TRANSFER PRICING

Transfer pricing is widespread. Many firms have policies whereby one division can buy another division's product, with the transfer price determined by various means. This observation found support in a 1992 survey of transfer pricing that targeted *Fortune* 500 firms. For domestic interdivisional transfers, the most common methods were the use of market prices, actual or standard full production

The transfer price of the basic chemical should be its price in the perfectly competitive market outside the firm. This market price is $42 per ton, and the transfer price should be the same. Also, we know from our earlier work that the marketing division's marginal cost, MC_t, is the sum of its own marginal marketing cost, MC_M, and the transfer price. That is,

$$MC_t = MC_M + P_U$$

where P_U = $42 and its own marginal marketing cost equals $MC_M = \Delta TC_M / \Delta Q_M$.

From equation (9.6), we see that $\Delta TC_M / \Delta Q_M = MC_M$ = 10. Therefore,

$$MC_t = 10 + 42 = 52$$

To maximize the marketing division's profit, managers must set its marginal cost equal to its marginal revenue. The marketing division's total revenue is

$$TR_M = P_M Q_M = (100 - Q_M)Q_M = 100Q_M - Q_M^2$$

The marketing division's marginal revenue is therefore

$$\Delta TR_M / \Delta Q_M = 100 - 2Q_M$$

Setting this expression for its marginal revenue equal to its marginal cost, we find that

$$MR_M = 100 - 2Q_M = 52 = MC_t = MC_M + P_U$$

or

$$Q_M = 24$$

Hence the marketing division should sell 24 million tons per year of the base chemical at a price of $76; that is, $P_M = 100 - 24$.

To sum up, managers at the Orion Corporation's production division should produce 40 million tons per year of the basic chemical. Of this amount, 24 million tons should be transferred to Orion's marketing division at the market price of $42 per ton, and 16 million tons (40 − 24) should be sold externally at the market price of $42 per ton. The transfer price should be the same as the market price: $42 per ton.

QUANT OPTION

Take this at face value.

Orion's marginal cost is $dTC_M / dQ_M = 10$; Orion's marginal revenue is $dTR_M / dQ_M = 100 - 2Q_M$.

---

costs, full production costs plus a markup, and negotiated prices. For international transfers, market-based transfer prices and full production costs plus a markup were the most commonly reported methods. Comparing the results to an earlier survey conducted in 1977, the shift has been to market-based prices in both the domestic and international markets.[15]

15. Roger Tang, "Transfer Pricing in the 1990s," *Management Accounting* 73, no. 8, pp. 22–26. This 1992 survey replicated one conducted in 1977.

Managers use transfer pricing to shift profits between divisions to minimize tax liability. This, done on a state-by-state and country-by-country basis, has caused government officials to investigate transfer pricing as a method of avoiding taxation. A 1999 survey by Ernst and Young showed that the number one international tax issue is transfer pricing. Firms are concerned with double taxation and onerous penalties for noncompliance. Many countries have enacted legislation enabling their tax agencies to intensify their transfer pricing inquiries and regulation enforcement. These countries feel that managers use transfer prices to decrease profit in high-tax countries, transferring this profit to low-tax countries. Items included in transfer pricing are goods, services, property, loans, and leases. Fortunately (and in line with the theory developed in this chapter), survey respondents noted that "the most important factor shaping transfer pricing policies is maximization of operating performance, not optimizing tax arrangements."[16]

Suppose the tax rate in a downstream country is α and the tax rate in an upstream country is β, where $\alpha > \beta$. Suppose the case is one of no external market for the upstream product. The after-tax profit in the downstream country is

$$(1 - \alpha)(TR_D - TC_D - P_U Q_U)$$

and the after-tax profit in the upstream country is

$$(1 - \beta)(P_U Q_U - TC_U)$$

Suppose all profits are expressed in the same currency; that is, we have adjusted for exchange rates and the P_U was set to maximize before-tax profit. The overall conglomerate's after-tax profit is

$$(1 - \alpha)(TR_D - TC_D) - (1 - \beta)(TC_U) + (1 - \beta - [1 - \alpha])(P_U Q_U)$$
$$= (1 - \alpha)(TR_D - TC_D) - (1 - \beta)(TC_U) + (\alpha - \beta)(P_U Q_U)$$

Because $\alpha > \beta$, the conglomerate's after-tax profit is higher if P_U is greater. But the optimal before-tax profit-maximizing P_U is what it is (and it could be low).

Suppose the firm, having determined the optimal $Q_D^* = Q_U^* = Q^*$, now creates a "subterfuge P_U" $= P_U^S$ for tax purposes and sets it such that

$$P_U^S = (TR_D - TC_D)/Q_U^*$$

With this P_U^S, the profit in the downstream country becomes 0 and the conglomerate's after-tax profit is

$$(1 - \beta)(TR_D - TC_D - P_U Q_U)$$

that is, all corporate profit is taxed at the lowest tax rate. Here we see the motivation of high tax rate countries to look at the transfer price policies of multinational firms.

16. "Multinationals Face Greater Transfer Pricing Scrutiny According to New Ernst & Young Survey," *Business Wire*, November 3, 1999.

Just why have transfer prices become so important on the international level? Four basic reasons exist: increased globalization, different levels of taxation in various countries, greater scrutiny by tax authorities, and inconsistent rules and laws in the various tax jurisdictions. Transfer price policies that seem to cause the fewest legal problems in the international scenario are (1) comparable uncontrolled price, in which the prices are the same or similar to "arms-length" transaction prices; (2) cost-plus prices, in which a markup used in arm's-length transactions is added to the seller's cost of the good or service; and (3) resale price, in which the resale price is used as a base for determining an arm's-length margin for the functions performed by the selling company.[17]

SUMMARY

1. Bundling is a strategy that enables managers to increase profit by selling two or more goods in a bundle. In general, bundling works better if the reservation prices of goods are negatively correlated; that is, one group has a high reservation price for one good and a low reservation price for another good relative to another group. Even so, bundling need not generate more profit relative to pricing each good separately. A pure bundle occurs when the goods are sold only as a bundle. Mixed bundling occurs when goods are sold both as a bundle and at least one good sold separately. No analytical model is available to solve the bundling pricing problem, so experimentation or a computer model is used. Managers also use bundling as an entry deterrent.

2. Many large firms are multidivisional, and one division sells its product to another division of the firm. To maximize the firm's overall profit, it is important that the price at which this transfer takes place, the so-called transfer price, be set properly. If there is no market outside the firm for the transferred product, the transfer price should equal the marginal production cost of the transferred product at the optimal output. If the outside market is perfectly competitive, the transfer price should equal the market price. Transfer prices have been used by global firms to transfer profits from high-tax countries to low-tax countries.

wwnorton.com/studyspace

PROBLEMS

1. The Locust Corporation is composed of a marketing division and a production division. The marginal cost of producing a unit of the firm's product is $10 per unit, and the marginal cost of marketing it is $4 per unit. The demand curve for the firm's product is

$$P = 100 - 0.01Q$$

17. Brenda Humphreys, "International Transfer Pricing: More Important Than Ever Before!" *Cost & Management* 68, no. 4, pp. 24–26.

where P is the price per unit (in dollars) and Q is output (in units). There is no external market for the good made by the production division.

   a. How should managers set the optimal output?

   b. What price should managers charge?

   c. How much should the production division manager charge his counterpart in marketing for each unit of the product?

2. The Xerxes Company is composed of a marketing division and a production division. The marketing division packages and distributes a plastic item made by the production division. The demand curve for the finished product sold by the marketing division is

$$P_0 = 200 - 3Q_0$$

where P_0 is the price (in dollars per pound) of the finished product and Q_0 is the quantity sold (in thousands of pounds). Excluding the production cost of the basic plastic item, the marketing division's total cost function is

$$TC_0 = 100 + 15Q_0$$

where TC_0 is the marketing division's total cost (in thousands of dollars). The production division's total cost function is

$$TC_1 = 5 + 3Q_1 + 0.4Q_1^2$$

where TC_1 is total production cost (in thousands of dollars) and Q_1 is the total quantity produced of the basic plastic item (in thousands of pounds). There is a perfectly competitive market for the basic plastic item, the price being $20 per pound.

   a. What is the optimal output for the production division?

   b. What is the optimal output for the marketing division?

   c. What is the optimal transfer price for the basic plastic item?

   d. At what price should the marketing division sell its product?

3. Knox Chemical Corporation is one of the largest producers of isopropyl alcohol, or isopropanol, as it frequently is called. Isopropanol is used to produce acetone, an important industrial chemical; it is also used to make various chemical intermediate products. Because Knox Chemical produces both acetone and these chemical intermediates, it uses much of the isopropanol it makes. One of the many tasks of Knox's product manager for isopropanol is to set transfer prices for isopropanol within the company.

   a. Knox's product manager for isopropanol generally sets the transfer price equal to the prevailing market price. Is this a sensible procedure?

   b. When the production of phenol expands rapidly, a great deal of acetone is produced because it is a by-product of the process leading to phenol. What effect do you think this has on the market price of isopropanol?

c. In producing a pound of phenol, 0.6 pound of acetone is produced. Are phenol and acetone joint products?

d. Are they produced in fixed proportions?[18]

4. The reservation prices (in dollars) of three classes of demanders (classes *A*, *B*, and *C*) for Ricky Parton's (a Latin country-western singer) compact disks are given in the table that follows:

Class	CD 1	CD 2
A	11	5
B	8	9
C	9	10

It costs $4 to produce and distribute each compact disk. The company can sell each CD separately, can put them together as a boxed set (that is, as a pure bundle), or can sell them in a mixed bundling format (offer the CDs both separately and as a boxed set). Assume that each demander wants only one of each of the CDs at the reservation price (or at any lower price) and that there are an equal number of demanders in each class. For simplicity, assume that the only costs are those mentioned here.

a. What pricing method would you advise Ricky's company to use?

b. How much better (profitwise) is the best pricing method than the second most profitable pricing method?

5. Bob and Ron's Stereo sells televisions and DVD players. They have estimated the demand for these items and have determined that there are three consumer types (A, B, and C) of equal number (assume one for simplicity) that have the following reservation prices for the two products. Bob and Ron's cost for a TV is 9 and for a DVD player is 9. It will cost Bob and Ron 18 to produce a bundle of one TV and one DVD player.

Consumer	TV	DVD Player
A	28	12
B	29	4
C	30	10

Any consumer's reservation price for a bundle of one TV and one DVD player is the sum of their reservation prices for each item. Consumers will demand (at most) one TV and one DVD player.

18. For further discussion, see E. R. Corey, *Industrial Marketing: Cases and Concepts*, 3rd ed. (Englewood Cliffs, NJ: Prentice-Hall, 1983).

  a. If Bob and Ron only consider pricing each item separately, pricing a pure bundle, or pricing a mixed bundle as their pricing policy, what price(s) would maximize their profit and what would be their profit?

  b. If Bob and Ron were able to perfectly price discriminate (that is charge different prices to different consumers, how much would their profit increase over their optimal profit in part a?

6. The University of Pennsylvania basketball team will play both the University of Kansas and Nowhere University this year on Penn's campus. Kansas is a nationally ranked team while Nowhere is just plain terrible.

  The athletic director traditionally prices each game separately. You approach him and point out that two other pricing options exist. One possibility is to offer a pure bundle, i.e., a ticket package containing one Kansas ticket and one Nowhere ticket. The second possibility is a mixed bundle. In this situation, a pure bundle is offered but admissions to the games can also be sold separately. It costs Penn a constant 5 per spectator to produce a game. It would cost Penn 10 to produce a bundle of a Kansas game and a Nowhere game.

  Three types of potential spectators exist (A, B, and C). There are an equal number of types (for simplicity, assume one of each type). Their reservation prices for each game are shown below:

Spectator	Kansas	Nowhere
A	40	13
B	49	3
C	3	30

  Penn's policy is not to price discriminate. A spectator's reservation price for a bundle of the two games is the sum of their reservation prices for each game. A spectator wants (at most) one admission to each game.

  a. What's your pricing advice to the athletic director (so that the director maximizes Penn's profit)?

  b. Given the current pricing policy of Penn, what's your advice worth to the athletic director?

7. GeeM has a sporty wheel package and a luxury interior package that it is considering offering to its auto buyers. GeeM has estimated that there are three consumer types (A, B, and C—all of equal magnitude—for simplicity, consider it one of each type). Consumers want (at most) one of each package. It costs GeeM 5 to produce a sporty wheel package and 10 to produce a luxury interior package. It will cost GeeM 15 to produce a bundle consisting of both packages.

  The following are the consumer reservation prices for each package:

Consumer	Wheels	Interior
A	11	24
B	35	12
C	18	28

A consumer's reservation price for a bundle consisting of sporty wheels and a luxury interior is the sum of the individual component reservation prices. GeeM does not price discriminate.

GeeM has solicited your help in pricing the wheel and interior package. You know that they could sell the packages separately, as a pure bundle, or as a mixed bundle.

Of those three pricing strategies, which one would maximize GeeM's profit? What are the prices (what is the price) that you suggest? How much better is the best pricing strategy than the second best pricing strategy?

8. Food For Life makes health foods for active, outdoor people. Their three basic products are whey powder, a high protein strength bar, and a meal additive that has the taste and consistency of sawdust. Research shows that consumers fall into two types (A and B) and these are described in the table below by their reservation prices for the products. Each consumer will demand no more than one unit of any product at their reservation price. The consumers will value a bundle of the products at the sum of the constituent reservation prices. Each product costs 3 to produce. A bundle of all three products costs 9 to produce. Food For Life does not price discriminate.

Consumer	Whey	Strength	Sawdust
A	10	16	2
B	3	10	13

There is an equal number of each consumer type (for simplicity, one of each type).

What pricing (profit maximizing) strategy (among pricing separately, pure bundling, and mixed bundling) would you recommend to Food For Life? Why? Only bundles of all three products need to be considered.

PART 6
THE STRATEGIC WORLD OF MANAGERS

CHAPTER 10

OLIGOPOLY

Oligopoly A market with a small number of firms.

Now we come to our last market structure, that of oligopoly. An **oligopoly** is a market with a small number of firms. As a general rule, you'd like to manage as an oligopolist; they realize relatively high profits. Think of the U.S. petroleum industry, where a few firms account for most of the industry's refining capacity. Oligopolies are strategically interesting from the managerial view. There is a tight interdependence between managers of rival firms because of the small set of players. This causes managers to explicitly consider the reactions of rivals in formulating pricing policy. When managers at Exxon Mobil raise their price of home heating oil by 1 or 2 cents per gallon, they try to anticipate the reaction of rival managers. If rivals decide against such a price increase, it is likely that Exxon Mobil managers will rescind the cut; otherwise those rivals will capture a significant number of Exxon Mobil customers. In the next chapter we offer managers game theory as a guide to this process of making strategy.

Oligopolies are global phenomena. For example, the market for commercial aircraft is dominated by Boeing and Airbus. Victoria Thieberger of *The Financial Times* writes about a duopoly in the Australian grocery market. She notes that two companies, Woolworth Ltd. and Wesfarmers Ltd., control over 80 percent of the grocery sector.[1]

There are many reasons why oligopolists are able to rule markets for scores of years. One is a high entry barrier that managers erect using their cooperative market power. Managers at smaller competitors claimed the grocery duopolists were

1. Victoria Thieberger, "Costco Plans Australia Foray to Challenge Duopoly," www.reuters.com, June 24, 2008.

using their market power to negotiate contracts that discouraged landlords from renting space to them. Thieberger also notes that managers at both companies were part of an inquiry into the setting of eerily similar prices at the rival stores.

Government fiat is another reason for duopolies. The U.S. petroleum industry was once a monopoly controlled by John D. Rockefeller. A brilliant strategist, Rockefeller transformed the industry into a design of his own making. The courts finally tore asunder what rivals could not breach.

A more common reason for oligopolies is economies of scale. Because costs decrease as output expands, only a few firms can survive in the market. Managers of these firms still achieve cost savings even when their output represents a substantial percentage of the market. Scale economies were a large part of Rockefeller's success. Even the courts could not use their power to significantly fragment the industry because of the underlying economics.

The hallmark of oligopoly strategy is its behavorial nature. In contrast to perfect competition or monopoly, for which there is a single unified model, behavior is more varied in oligopolies. This variance in choice is due to the tight interdependence between market rivals.

COOPERATIVE BEHAVIOR

Conditions in oligopolistic industries tend to encourage cooperation among rival managers. This can increase profit, decrease uncertainty, and raise barriers to discourage others from entering the market. However, maintaining cooperative behavior is difficult. There are usually incentives for cooperative parties to "cheat"; and in most countries formal collusive agreements are not enforceable.

If a collusive arrangement is made openly and formally, it is called a **cartel**. In some countries cartels are legally acceptable; but in the United States most collusive agreements, whether secret or open cartels, were outlawed by the Sherman Antitrust Act (discussed in detail in Chapter 16), which dates back to 1890. But this does not mean the government does not see the cooperative value of oligopolies. For example, airlines flying transatlantic routes are members of the International Air Transport Association, which sets uniform prices for transatlantic flights. Major League Baseball is exempted from the U.S. antitrust laws by an act of Congress.

Cartel When a collusive arrangement is made openly and formally.

If a cartel is established to set a uniform price for a particular (homogeneous) product, what price will managers charge? To answer this question, managers need to estimate the marginal cost curve for the cartel as a whole. If input prices do not increase as the cartel expands, the marginal cost curve is the horizontal summation of the marginal cost curves of the individual firms. Suppose the resulting marginal cost curve for the cartel is as shown in Figure 10.1. If the demand curve for the industry's product and the relevant marginal revenue curve are as shown there, the output that maximizes the total profit of the cartel members is Q_0. Therefore, to

FIGURE 10.1

Price and Output Determination by a Cartel

The cartel chooses a price of P_0 and an output of Q_0.

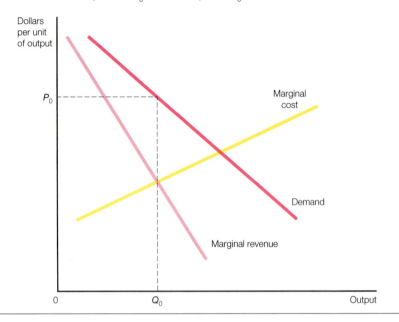

maximize profit, the cartel will choose a price of P_0, which is the monopoly price. Note that this price maximizes the profit earned by the cartel, but it says nothing about how this profit is divided among cartel members.

Cartel managers also determine the distribution of sales across members; this is the process that makes cartels rather unstable. If the purpose of the managers is to maximize the profit to the corporate entity, they should allocate sales to cartel members so that the marginal cost of all members is equal (and, in turn, equal to the cartel's marginal revenue). Otherwise cartel managers can increase corporate profit by reallocating output among members to reduce the cost of producing the cartel's total output. If the marginal cost at firm A is higher than that at firm B, cartel managers can increase profit by transferring some production from firm A to firm B.

This allocation of output is unlikely to take place, because allocation decisions are the result of negotiation between members with varying interests and capabilities. This is a political process in which managers have varying amounts of influence. Those with the most influence and the shrewdest negotiators are likely to receive the largest sales quotas, even though this raises the total cartel costs. Also, managers of high-cost firms are likely to receive bigger sales quotas than cost minimization requires because they are usually unwilling to accept the small quotas required by cost minimization. In practice, sales are often distributed in accord with a member's level of sales in the past or the extent of a member's productive capacity. Also, cartel managers might divide a market geographically, with members being given particular countries or regions.

THE BREAKDOWN OF COLLUSIVE AGREEMENTS

Let's formally see why cartels are not stable so managers understand the weakness of a cartel structure. Consider the firm in Figure 10.2. If firm managers chose to leave the cartel, they would face the demand curve of DD' as long as the other firms in the cartel maintained a price of P_0. This demand curve is very elastic; managers can significantly expand sales with a small reduction in price. Even if managers were unable to leave the cartel, they would face the same demand curve if they granted secret price concessions.

The maximum profit of managers who either leave the cartel or secretly lower their price is attained when they sell an output of Q_1 at a price of P_1: This is the output at which marginal cost equals marginal revenue. This price would result in a profit of $Q_1 \times P_1 B$, which is generally higher than the profit realized if managers conformed to the price and sales quota dictated by the cartel.[2] Managers who break away from a cartel—or secretly cheat—can increase profit as long as rival

---

FIGURE 10.2

Instability of Cartels

If the firm leaves the cartel, profit equals $Q_1 \times P_1 B$, which is generally higher than it would be if the firm adhered to the price and sales quota established by the cartel.

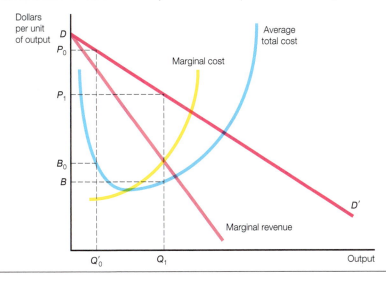

2. At price P_0, the firm will sell $Q_0' \times P_0 B_0$, which is less than $Q_1 \times P_1 B$. Because the demand curve is so elastic, total revenues increase significantly as price drops from P_0 to P_1. While the total costs increase as output increases from Q_0' to Q_1, unless they increase very rapidly, the increase in total revenue exceeds the increase in total cost.

managers do not do the same thing and the cartel does not punish this behavior. But if all managers do this, the cartel disintegrates. Hence there is a constant threat to the existence of a cartel. Its members have an incentive to cheat, and once a few do so, others may follow. Just as is true in relationships, trust is vital to a cartel's existence. As we will see, the incentive to cheat exists even in more informal cooperative endeavors.

PRICE LEADERSHIP

Price leadership In oligopolistic industries, managers at one firm have significant market power and can set their price.

In many oligopolistic industries, managers at one firm have significant market power and can set their price; rivals then follow their lead. This is called the **price leadership** strategy. Examples of industries that have seen the use of this strategy include steel, nonferrous alloys, and agricultural implements. Managers should understand what to consider when setting prices in these markets. We assume the market is composed of a large dominant firm (the price leader) and a number of small firms. Managers at the dominant firm set the price for the market but let the small firms sell all they want at that price. Whatever amount the small firms do *not* supply at that price is provided by the dominant firm.

A new version of price leadership has arisen in the retail sector with the arrival of the "big box" stores. When Wal-Mart or Home Depot come to town, the small retailers, hardware stores, lumber yards, and the like are basically victims of the prices charged by those big stores. Small stores may try to differentiate with service and high-end items; but anyone who was selling the items sold by Wal-Mart and Home Depot before their arrival must follow the prices of the big guys. Some do

---

STRATEGY SESSION: Cranberries: Where 34 Percent of the Market Producers Are Price Takers

The cranberry, that marvelous red berry that helps prevent bladder infections, has a lot of vitamin C, and contains antioxidants, is dominated by a giant growers' cooperative—Ocean Spray.

Ocean Spray is the price setter. When Ocean Spray (with a 66 percent market share) sets its price for cranberries, the other (nonmember) producers fall into line. Each year, in late September and early October, Ocean Spray sets a price for sales to supermarkets per case of 24 12-ounce bags. This price is based on anticipated and actual supply and demand conditions in the market.

Given the price that Ocean Spray sets, other producers must decide how much of the product they wish to harvest for sale, harvest to inventory, harvest for use in other products (such as juice), or leave in the bogs.

Thus Ocean Spray is the price leader, and the remaining 34 percent of the producers are followers. Whatever price is set by Ocean Spray, the followers take as given and optimize for that price.

Source: "The Case of the Vanishing Berries," *The New York Times*, November 12, 2000.

and survive, but newspapers are full of stories of the demise of small businesses that cannot compete with the prices and variety of the big box stores.

Managers of a dominant firm can readily determine what price to set. Because managers at the small firms are price takers, they act as if they are in a competitive market, taking the price as given. Hence these managers at the small firms should choose output where price equals marginal cost. Therefore a supply curve for all the small firms combined is estimated by *horizontally* summing their marginal cost curves. This supply curve is shown in Figure 10.3. The demand curve facing managers at the dominant firm is derived by subtracting the amount supplied by the small firms at each price from the total amount demanded. Thus the demand curve for the output of the dominant firm, d, is determined by finding the *horizontal* difference at each price between the industry demand curve and the supply curve for all small firms combined.

To illustrate how d is derived, suppose managers at the dominant firm set a price of P_0. The small firms supply R_0, and the total amount demanded is V_0. Therefore the output supplied by the dominant firm is $V_0 - R_0$, which is the quantity d_0 on the d curve at price P_0. In other words, d_0 is set equal to $V_0 - R_0$. The process by which the other points on the d curve are determined is exactly the same; this procedure is repeated at various levels of price.

Knowing the demand curve for the output of the dominant firm, d, and the dominant firm's marginal cost curve, M, managers can readily determine the price

---

FIGURE 10.3

Price Leadership by a Dominant Firm

Managers at the dominant firm set a price of P_1 and supply Q_1 units of the product. The total industry output is D_1.

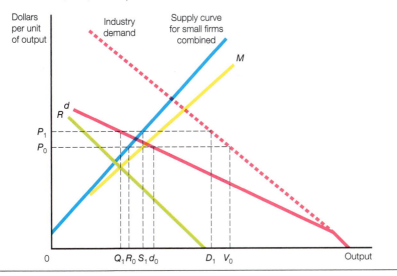

PROBLEM SOLVED: Ghoshal, Inc.: A Numerical Example

To illustrate how managers at a dominant firm can determine the price to maximize profit, consider Ghoshal, Inc., the dominant firm in an industry. The demand curve for this industry's product is

$$Q = 100 - 5P$$

where Q is the quantity demanded and P is the price. The supply curve for the small firms in this industry is

$$Q_S = 10 + P$$

where Q_S is the total amount supplied by all these small firms combined. Ghoshal's marginal cost is

$$MC = (8/3)Q_A \qquad (10.1)$$

where Q_A is Ghoshal's output.

To derive the demand curve for Ghoshal's output, we subtract Q_S from Q, the result being

$$Q_A = Q - Q_S = (100 - 5P) - (10 + P) = 90 - 6P$$
$$P = 15 - (1/6)Q_A \qquad (10.2)$$

Remembering that Ghoshal's total revenue equals PQ_A, Ghoshal's total revenue equals

$$TR = [15 - (1/6)Q_A]Q_A = 15Q_A - (1/6)Q_A^2$$

Therefore, Ghoshal's marginal revenue is

$$\Delta TR_A/\Delta Q_A = MR_A = 15 - (1/3)Q_A \qquad (10.3)$$

To maximize profit, managers at Ghoshal need to produce where marginal revenue in equation (10.3) is equal to marginal cost in equation (10.1):

$$MR_A = 15 - (1/3)Q_A = (8/3)Q_A = MC_A$$

So Q_A must equal 5. Consequently, from equation (10.2), it follows that $P = \$14.167$.

To sum up, if managers at Ghoshal want to maximize profit, they should set their price at $14.17.

QUANT OPTION

Ghoshal's marginal revenue is

$$dTR_A/dQ_A = 15 - (1/3)Q_A$$

and output that maximizes their profit. Their marginal revenue curve, R, is derived from the dominant firm's demand curve, d, in the usual way. The optimal output for the dominant firm is the output Q_1, where its marginal cost equals its marginal revenue. This output is achieved if managers set a price of P_1. The total industry output is D_1, and the small firms supply S_1 $(= D_1 - Q_1)$.

POSSIBLE BEHAVIOR IN MARKETS WITH FEW RIVALS

As we will see in the next chapter, managers need to anticipate the behavior of others. As the behavior of rivals changes, your actions often change. We now examine models of probable behavior among managers of a small number of firms. For clarity, we will explain behavior using two firms. These markets are known as *duopolies*. As we subsequently show, the results are generalizable to larger oligopolistic markets.

The two firms produce an identical product, and managers make their output decisions simultaneously. When rival managers make decisions without knowing the decisions of others, we say decision making is simultaneous. (We will formally define *simultaneous behavior* and *sequential behavior* in the next chapter.) Managers often make simultaneous decisions. When managers engage in a sealed bid auction they make decisions simultaneously. When firms enter the market at the same time and managers design plant capacity without knowing the plans of others, that too is simultaneous.

Later we consider sequential move strategies, where managers know the decisions of others before making their decisions. Managers who take action before others are called *first movers* or *market leaders*. The market leader is able to accelerate before others for several reasons. First movers often see what others don't because of business acumen, because they invent or patent a product or process, or because entrepreneurs see opportunities others do not. It may also be due to luck: Mobile phone franchises were first granted to companies via a government lottery. Also, landing slots at some airports are also allocated using a lottery.

When Rivals Are Few: Price Competition

One common strategy used by managers is that of price competition. Often price competition results in a downward spiral of price cuts, stopped only (sometimes) by the constraint of marginal cost. The great strategist Sun Tzu referred to behavior such as price wars as that of the scorched earth. Managers should try to avoid this behavior.

STRATEGY SESSION: Corporate Synergy in Conglomerates

Why do some firms organize as conglomerates whereas others produce in just one line of business? The latter argue for "core competency"—doing what they do best. The former argue for economies of scope and diversification of risk. Those who have disassembled conglomerates argue that the whole is worth less than the sum of its parts (for example, Cendent, which was built by Henry Silverman and taken apart by him). Those who favor conglomerates, such as General Electric and Siemens, argue the reverse and point to synergies of idea generation and the ability to use personnel across businesses.

On the risk diversification side, critics argue that as capital markets have become more sophisticated, global, and liquid, fund managers maintain that they can diversify risk and increase returns by purchasing securities across multiple sectors.

Source: "Less Than the Sum of Its Parts? Decline Sets In at the Conglomerate," *Financial Times*, February 5, 2007.

Consider two firms, A and B, producing identical products in a simultaneous-move scenario. Suppose both firms have identical total cost functions of

$$TC_i = 500 + 4q_i + 0.5q_i^2 \tag{10.4}$$

where $i = A, B$ and q_i is the output of firm i.

The market demand as seen by managers of both firms is

$$P = 100 - Q = 100 - q_A - q_B \tag{10.5}$$

where P is the unit price of the product, Q is the quantity demanded at price P, and $Q = q_A + q_B$.

The marginal cost of firm i is

$$MC_i = \Delta TC_i / \Delta dq_i = 4 + q_i \tag{10.6}$$

QUANT OPTION

The firm's marginal cost is

$$dTC_i / dq_i = 4 + q_i$$

If managers at both firms want to compete on price, the competition will drive price down to the level of their marginal cost. Managers should never price below marginal cost because the additional revenue made from making the last sale is exceeded by the additional cost of making that sale.

The first good demanded has a reservation price of $99—that is, $100 - 1$. This good would cost each producer $5 (that is, $4 + 1$) to produce. If managers compete on price over this customer, while they could charge as much as $99, they are willing to accept as little as $5. In fact, if there were just this one customer, and they competed on price, we expect the price to be $5. Suppose that managers at firm A offer to sell to the customer at $99 (hoping for a profit of $99 - $5 = $94). Managers at firm B would then offer to sell the product for $98 (hoping for a profit of $98 - $5 = $93). Then managers at A would counteroffer at $97. As you can see, in a series of counteroffers, the price will be bid down to $5. At that price the possibility of a profitable sale by a lower price disappears (any lower price is exceeded by the marginal cost of production).

So we can expect that price equal to marginal cost is the ultimate resolution of this pricing contest. For firm A, this means that

$$P = 100 - Q = 100 - q_A - q_B = 4 + q_A = MC_A$$
$$2q_A = 96 - q_B$$
$$q_A = 48 - 0.5q_B \tag{10.7}$$

For firm B, it means that

$$P = 100 - Q = 100 - q_A - q_B = 4 + q_B = MC_B$$
$$2q_B = 96 - q_A$$
$$q_B = 48 - 0.5q_A \qquad (10.8)$$

We determine the ultimate result of this pricing game by substituting equation (10.8) into equation (10.7) and solving for q_A (or by substituting equation (10.7) into equation (10.8) and solving for q_B):

$$q_A = 48 - 0.5(48 - 0.5q_A) = 24 + 0.25q_A$$
$$0.75q_A = 24$$
$$q_A = 32$$

Substituting $q_A = 32$ into equation (10.8) gives $q_B = 48 - 0.5(32) = 32$, which should not be surprising (because each firm has identical cost functions). Because each firm produces 32, the total output is 64 ($= Q$). Substituting $Q = 64$ into the market demand function yields a price of \$36 ($= 100 - 64$). This also equals each firm's marginal cost, \$36 (that is, $4 + 32$). Each firm has a total revenue of \$1,152 (\$36 $\times$ 32) and total costs of \$1,140 ($= 500 + 4(32) + 0.5(32^2)$), leaving managers at each firm with a profit of \$12.[3]

When Rivals Are Few: Collusion

What if our two managers both realized the dangers of a price war and instead chose to act cooperatively? How cooperative could they get? Let's take it to the limit and assume they can legally form a cartel. Under these circumstances, the market demand curve is the cartel's demand curve, and the cartel's marginal cost curve is the *horizontal* summation of each firm's marginal cost curve.[4] Rewriting each firm's marginal cost as

$$q_A = -4 + MC_A$$
$$q_B = -4 + MC_B$$

and adding q_A and q_B (that is, summing the marginal costs horizontally—adding up the quantities produced at any given marginal cost), we get

$$Q = q_A + q_B = -4 + MC_A - 4 + MC_B = -8 + 2MC$$

Rearranging yields

$$2MC = 8 + Q$$
$$MC = 4 + 0.5Q$$

which is the cartel's marginal cost.

The cartel behaves as a monopolist (see Chapter 7 and earlier in this chapter) and sets its marginal revenue equal to its marginal cost. The cartel's total revenue is

$$TR = PQ = (100 - Q)Q = 100Q = Q^2$$

3. If each was a constant-cost firm with an identical marginal cost, price competition would take the price down to that marginal cost and profit would be zero (or minus fixed costs if fixed costs exist). For example, if both firms had a marginal cost of \$4, both firms together would produce 96—that is, $4 = 100 - Q$ or $Q = 96$ (with each producing 48). Each firm's total revenue would be \$192 ($= 4 \times 48$), and both firms would have variable cost of \$192 ($= 4 \times 48$). Thus all profit would be lost to competition.

4. It is the horizontal summation because we want to measure the additional cost of producing an additional unit of output in the cartel. To produce that additional unit in the cheapest possible way, the cartel would always want to have identical marginal costs for each producer. If the marginal costs were not the same, the cartel could lower its total cost of production by shifting production from the high-marginal-cost firm to the low-marginal-cost firm until their marginal costs were equalized. See the appendix to Chapter 7 and the earlier discussion in this chapter.

The cartel's marginal revenue is therefore

$$MR = \Delta TR/\Delta Q = 100 - 2Q$$

QUANT OPTION

The cartel's marginal revenue is

$$dTR/dQ = 100 - 2Q$$

STRATEGY SESSION: Cartels Come in Many Shapes and Sizes

In 1997, every two weeks in Rutherford, New Jersey, 20 shipping line managers met and discussed what they would charge to move cargo across the North Atlantic. Although this meeting could have been composed of the managers of a single ocean shipping line discussing pricing strategy, it was not. Rather, they were executives of 20 different companies. Exempt from the U.S. antitrust laws, they collusively set rates on tens of billions of dollars of cargo. This practice has since been declared illegal.

Their monopoly power was limited because the cartel was unable to control the shipping capacity of its members, and some ocean carriers were not members of the cartel. Nevertheless, it is estimated that the cartel was able to raise rates 18 to 19 percent above competitive rates.

Of course the modern epitome of controlling supply and hence creating monopoly power is OPEC and the crude oil market. Here the ability to mark price over marginal cost is substantial. A product that costs the most efficient producer several dollars to take out of the ground is marked up as much as 25 times.

The monopoly power is so substantial because of the strong demand for the product, the inelastic-

ity of demand for the product, and the fact that the low-cost producers are members of the cartel; and although the cartel is not perfect (not all producers are members), the nonmembers are high-cost producers.

Others have tried to emulate the behavior of OPEC. Brazil and Colombia, major coffee producers, attempted a coffee cartel that failed. The major problem was that coffee has a fairly elastic demand. So when the Brazilians and Colombians withheld supply to raise prices, consumers switched to other beverages like tea and caffeinated colas. If you control the supply in a market that has many close substitutes, your monopoly power is not likely to be significant.

Cartels need not exist for goods only. They can exist for services, too. In Germany a wage-setting cartel is constitutionally sanctioned between unions and corporations. The cartel keeps wages high and labor strife low and ends up costing Germans jobs. This is exactly what we expect a monopoly to do—raise prices (wages) and restrict output (jobs).

Sources: "As U.S. Trade Grows, Shipping Cartels Get a Bit More Scrutiny," *The Wall Street Journal*, October 7, 1997; "German Wage Pact Ends Up Costing Jobs," *The Wall Street Journal*, February 19, 1997.

Setting the cartel's marginal revenue equal to the cartel's marginal cost yields

$$MR = 100 - 2Q = 4 + 0.5Q = MC$$
$$2.5Q = 96$$
$$Q = 38.4$$

Substituting $Q = 38.4$ into the cartel's demand curve gives a price of \$61.6 (i.e., $100 - 38.4$). The cartel's total revenue is \$2,365.44 (i.e., \$61.6 $\times$ 38.4). Since each firm has the same marginal cost equation, each should produce the same amount, 19.2, so that both have a marginal cost of \$23.2 (i.e., $4 + 19.2$), which, of course, equals the cartel's marginal revenue of 23.2 (i.e., $100 - 2(38.4)$). The two firms split the total revenue so that each receives \$1,182.72. Each firm has a total cost of \$761.12 ($= 500 + 4(19.2) + 0.5(19.2^2)$); hence, each firm makes a profit of \$421.6, a considerable improvement over the \$12 made when the firms competed on price. Note the cooperative behavior significantly restricts output (from 64 to 38.4) and significantly increases price (from \$36 to \$61.6); but as observed in Chapter 7, that is what monopolists do.

When Rivals Are Few: Quantity (Capacity) Competition

Unfortunately, forming a cartel is often illegal. But, strictly competing on price is a lose-lose strategy. So, what are managers to do? Well, they could compete on something other than price. Managers should try to compete on any metric that affects profit and gives them a higher profit relative to competing on price. One metric that jumps to mind is quantity (or production capacity). This type of competition is sometimes called Cournot, named after the French economist who initially derived its properties.

Cournot analysis makes the following assumptions: The rival managers move simultaneously, have the same view of the market demand, estimate each other's cost functions, and choose their profit-maximizing output conditional on their rival choosing the same.

It is thought as problematic that rival managers hold the same beliefs regarding demand. Yet, there is evidence it is more likely to occur than students think. In many situations, government- or trade-association-generated data (macroeconomic and industry-specific variables) are used by all analysts and the corporate intelligence of each firm observes the same economic landscape. Often, managers compete against one another for long periods of time. They often get to know each other through various professional associations. Nevertheless, it is possible for two (or more) managers viewing the same economic data to come up with different conclusions or assessments. With respect to knowing each other's cost functions, in some cases, good approximations of adversaries' costs are likely. For instance, in the airline industry, there are only two manufacturers of large aircraft remain (Boeing and Airbus) and only several producers of small commercial aircraft (e.g., Bombardier and Embraer). The carriers are either flying the same aircraft as their adversaries or have "speced" the aircraft (i.e., received all the operating characteristics of that aircraft from the manufacturer when the carrier considered purchasing new aircraft). Personnel are unionized (for the most part) and wage rates are well known. All carriers buy fuel, food, and other items from a limited set of suppliers. Therefore, carrier A has a fairly decent estimate of what it costs carrier B to operate its fleet (and vice versa). In addition, executive talent is mobile within the industry, and when executives leave carrier A, they carry knowledge of the company in their heads that can be useful to company B.[5]

The last assumption is that firm A optimizes their quantity (capacity) given that firm B's quantity (capacity) is fixed. This is not as restrictive as it sounds. We first formulate this situation as a series of "what-if" questions. *If* my adversary actually is going to produce quantity X, *what* quantity would I produce to maximize my profit? Which output you actually choose to produce of all the "what-if" possibilities depends on what you think your adversary will *actually* do (and your adversary is going through the same "what-if" process). By a process of deduction, managers can estimate the most logical output for rivals given profit-maximizing behavior. This is the Cournot solution, and we see that it yields a solution identical to that of game theory (see Chapter 11).

We now view the Cournot solution to the preceding case in two different ways. The first is by following a series of "what-if" scenarios. We deal with the

5. We will leave it to your ethics course to debate about what information can be revealed. To see how information is obtained about competitors, see "They Snoop to Conquer," *Business Week*, October 28, 1996. In a classic case of crossing the line, Jose Ignacio Lopez left General Motors in 1992 allegedly carrying a briefcase of GM blueprints to his new job at Volkswagen. You need no ethics course to know that this is wrong. GM sued, and in 1996 the case was settled. Lopez was forced to resign from VW, and VW was required to pay GM $100 million and purchase $1 billion worth of GM auto parts.

decisions of managers at firm A and treat this as our firm. Clearly, if firm A managers think that managers at firm B will abdicate the market to them, they should behave as a monopolist. Since the monopolist's marginal revenue is the same as the cartel's in the preceding situation (and now firm A's marginal revenue, since it is the only producer in the market), and firm A's marginal cost is $MC_A = 4 + q_A$, managers maximize profit by setting $MR = MC$ or

$$MR_A = 100 - 2q_A = 4 + q_A = MC_A$$
$$3q_A = 96$$
$$q_A = 32$$

So, if $q_B = 0$, the profit-maximizing, optimal-quantity response of firm-A managers is $q_A = 32$.

On the other hand, if managers think their rival will produce 96 units, they will only produce 4 (at most). Rewrite the market demand curve as $Q = 100 - P$. Firm A's *residual* demand curve (i.e., the market demand curve less what managers assume firm B produces), what is left for firm A after firm B managers make their production decision, is

$$q_A = 100 - P - 96 = 4 - P$$
$$P = 4 - q_A$$

Firm-A managers will produce nothing under these circumstances, since the *highest* the price could be is \$4 (when q_A is zero) and the lowest their marginal cost could be is \$4 (when q_A is zero). Therefore, the price could never be equal to or exceed firm A's marginal cost at a positive level of output. Therefore, if $q_B = 96$ is the profit-maximizing, optimal-quantity response of firm-A managers is $q_A = 0$.

Suppose firm-A managers think their rival will produce 50 units; that is, $q_B = 50$? Under these circumstances, the residual demand is

$$q_A = 100 - P - 50 = 50 - P$$
$$P = 50 - q_A$$

Firm A's total revenue is $Pq_A = (50 - q_A)q_A = 50q_A - q_A^2$. Hence, marginal revenue is

$$MR_A = \Delta TR_A / \Delta q_A = 50 - 2q_A$$

QUANT OPTION

The firm's marginal revenue is

$$dTR_A / dq_A = 50 - 2q_A$$

TABLE 10.1

Profit-Maximizing Output Responses of Managers of Firm *A* Given Their Assumptions about Firm *B* Output

If Firm *B* Produces	Then Firm *A* Produces
0	32
50	15.33
96	0

To maximize profit, you set $MR_A = MC_A$, or

$$MR_A = 50 - 2q_A = 4 + q_A = MC_A$$
$$3q_A = 46$$
$$q_A = 15.33$$

Therefore, if $q_B = 50$, the profit-maximizing, optimal-quantity response of firm-*A* managers is $q_A = 15.33$.

So, we know the optimal profit-maximizing responses for the "what-if" scenarios we investigated (see Table 10.1).

By doing more "what-if" situations, we can complete Table 10.1 for all possible firm *B* outputs between 0 and 96. But, we can get the equivalent of a full table directly with the analysis that follows.

Firm *A* maximizes profit when its total revenue (Pq_A) exceeds its total cost ($500 + 4q_A + 0.5q_A^2$) by the maximal amount. Your total revenue is

$$TR = (100 - Q)q_A = (100 - q_A - q_B)q_A = 100q_A - q_A^2 - q_Aq_B$$

Your marginal revenue is

$$MR_A = \Delta TR_A/\Delta q_A = 100 - 2q_A - q_B \tag{10.9}$$

QUANT OPTION

The firm's marginal revenue is

$$\partial TR_A/\partial q_A = 100 - 2q_A - q_B$$

To maximize profit, set $MR_A = MC_A$, or

$$MR_A = 100 - 2q_A - q_B = 4 + q_A = MC_A$$
$$3q_A = 96 - q_B$$
$$q_A = 32 - (1/3)q_B \tag{10.10}$$

Equation (10.10) is called firm A's **reaction function**; that is, it identifies for managers the profit-maximizing output to produce *given* the output of rivals at firm B. Every number in the right-hand column of Table 10.1 occurs when the corresponding number on the left–hand side of Table 10.1 is substituted into the reaction function (10.10).

Reaction function A function that identifies for managers the profit-maximizing output to produce given the output of their rivals.

Because firm B has the same cost function as firm A and both face the same market demand curve, firm B's reaction function is

$$q_B = 32 - (1/3)q_A \qquad (10.11)$$

We identify how to anticipate the profit maximizing output of a rival by substituting firm A's reaction function (10.10) into firm B's reaction function (10.11) and solving for q_A. Alternatively, we could substitute firm B's reaction function (10.11) into firm A's reaction function (10.10) and solve for q_A. The latter yields

$$\begin{aligned}
q_A &= 32 - (1/3)[32 - (1/3)q_A] \\
q_A &= (96/3) - (32/3) + (1/9)q_A \\
(8/9)q_A &= (64/3) \\
q_A &= 24
\end{aligned}$$

Substituting $q_A = 24$ into firm B's reaction function (10.11) gives

$$q_B = 32 - (1/3)24 = 24$$

Therefore, $Q = q_A + q_B = 48$ and substituting $Q = 48$ into the market demand function gives a price of \$52; that is, $100 - 48$.

Think of it like this: The only way that managers at both firms can profit maximize is if they stay on their reaction functions. Again, this function identifies for managers the profit-maximizing output conditional on the output of their rival. The only way this is possible is if we find the point of intersection between the two functions. This then represent the only quantities where what one manager wants to do is mutually consistent with what the other manager wants to do. This is known as a Nash equilibrium after Nobel laureate John Nash; subject of the book and the movie *A Beautiful Mind*.

Under the Cournot scenario, managers at each firm produce 24 units and the market price is \$52. Each firm's total revenue is \$1,248 (i.e., \$52 × 24), and each firm's total cost is \$884 (i.e., $500 + 4(24) + 0.5(24^2)$), so managers at each firm earn a profit of \$364. While this is less than each share of the monopoly (cartel) profit of \$421.6, it is considerably better than what they will earn if they compete on price (\$12). The significance of this is the powerful impact of adding just one more equal producer to a monopoly market. In this case, the price falls by 15.6 percent (from \$61.6 to \$52) and output increases by 25 percent (from 38.4 to 48). Hence, adding a competitor can have a significant impact on mitigating the power of a monopolist. Looked at from the other direction, the two firms acting as Cournot quantity competitors can retain 86.3 percent of the monopoly (cartel) profit and enhance the price-competitive profit slightly over 30–fold.

How can managers get themselves into a Cournot scenario and avoid a price-competitive scenario? Some managers cannot seem to avoid the latter; for example, the airlines constantly seem to engage in price wars, much to the detriment of their profit. On the other hand, managers who learn not to "rock the boat" or to "kill the goose that lays the golden egg" learn to compete on quantity (capacity) and not price. Examples include General Electric and Westinghouse in the marketplace for steam turbine engines and Rockwell International and others in the market for water meters.[6] As can be seen from the preceding, the stakes are high, so this quantity (capacity) competition is a strategy worth learning for managers who have only a few market rivals. Figure 10.4 is a picture of the situation just discussed.

FIGURE 10.4

Cournot Reaction Functions for Firms *A* and *B*

A Cournot equilibrium occurs where the two firms' reaction functions intersect. This is the only output combination where both firms' expectations of what the other firm will produce are consistent with their own expectations of their own optimal output. In this case, both firms produce 24 units.

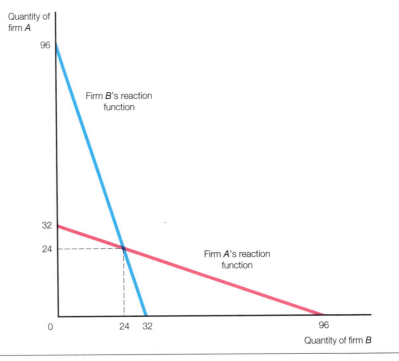

---

6. See Nancy Taubenslag, "Rockwell International," Harvard Business School Case, 9383-019, July 1983.

Such behavior tends to work well when large capital investments must be made. Once the capital investment is made, the quantity to be produced is pretty much determined. Airlines do not practice Cournot output well because it is easy to change capacity by leasing aircraft (e.g., all of Continental Airlines planes are leased). Oil refining tends to work well because it is difficult to build new refineries (expensive, environmental concerns, and no one wants one located near them— the last refinery built in the United States was Marathon-Ashland's Garyville, LA facility completed in 1976).

The Cournot Scenario with More than Two Firms

Consider a market demand curve $P = a - bQ$ with n identical firms, i.e., $Q_i = Q/n$ where a and b are parameters of the demand function and Q_i is the output of the ith firm. The marginal cost of each firm is $MC_i = c + eQ_i$, where c and e are parameters of the marginal cost function. The market demand curve can be rewritten as

$$P = a - bQ_1 - bQ_2 - ...bQ_i - ... - bQ_n$$

The total revenue for firm i is

$$TR_i = P \times Q_i = (a - bQ_1 - bQ_2 - ... - bQ_i - ... - bQ_n)Q_i$$
$$= aQ_i - bQ_iQ_1 - bQ_iQ_2 - ... - bQ_i^2 - ... - bQ_iQ_n$$

The marginal revenue of firm i is

$$MR_i = \Delta TR_i/\Delta Q_i = a - bQ_1 - bQ_2 - ... - 2bQ_i - ... - bQ_n$$
$$= a - 2bQ_i - \sum_{k \neq i}^{n} bQ_k = a - 2bQ_i - (n - 1)bQ_i$$

since all firms are the same, $Q_i = Q_k$.

QUANT OPTION

So that we do practice what we preach:

$$MR_i = \partial TR_i/\partial Q_i = a - bQ_1 - bQ_2 - ... - 2bQ_1 - ... - bQ_n$$
$$= a - 2bQ_1 - \sum_{k \neq i}^{n} bQ_k = a - 2bQ_1 - (n - 1)bQ_1$$

Further simplifying the marginal revenue gives $MR_i = a - (n + 1)bQ_i$. To maximize profit, managers will set $MR_i = MC_i$ or

$$MR_i = a - (n + 1)bQ_i = c + eQ_i = MC_i$$

STRATEGY SESSION: The Staples and Office Depot Nonmerger

In 1997 Staples proposed a merger with Office Depot. Both firms are "category killers" in the office supply business; that is, one can go to them for one-stop shopping and get almost everything to outfit and supply an office. Staples estimated that the merged firm would control 4–6 percent of the office supply market. Government antitrust officials (the U.S. Department of Justice and the Federal Trade Commission) disagreed. Staples defined the market to include Wal-Mart, K-Mart, Dell Online, Radio Shack, stores that sold office furniture, and the like—basically anyplace you could purchase a subset of the products it sold. The government defined the market as only "category killers"—that is, only stores where you could buy everything that Staples sold. The government rejected the proposed merger, partially based on studies it commissioned that showed markets with two "category killers" instead of three (the other major "category killer" was Office Max) had significantly higher prices. Likewise, markets that had one "category killer" instead of two had even higher prices. From these results, we can conclude that more competition, even when the number of competitors is quite small, can have a significant impact on prices (and hence customer well-being).

Source: W.J. Baer, director of competition, FTC, "Why the FTC Opposes the Staples Merger," *The Wall Street Journal*, April 1997.

Solving for Q_i gives

$$Q_i = (a - c)/[(n + 1)b + e]$$

Table 10.2 shows the situation when multiple firms (each of which is identical to the two Cournot firms) compete on quantity. Using the formula for Q_i above with $a = 100$, $b = 1$, $c = 4$, and $e = 1$ yields $Q_i = 96/(n + 2)$. Adding a third equal (in cost) competitor to our duopoly drops the price 31.17 percent from the cartel monopoly price and increases output by 50 percent. Having eight equal-in-cost competitors in this Cournot situation drops the price by 62.34 percent relative to the cartel monopoly price and increases output by 100 percent. Profit becomes negative after three Cournot competitors because of the high level of fixed costs ($500). If the fixed cost were lower (say $50), all situations depicted (except for high values of n) would entail positive profit.

This analysis shows just how the addition of a few entrants in a Cournot situation can bring significant price competition into the market. Even if managers of these entrants have higher costs, they still erode the market power of incumbents and generate significant downward pressure on price.

TABLE 10.2

Price, Output, and Profits with Multiple Cournot Competitors

Number of Competitors	Price	Percentage Decrease	Quantity/ Firm	Profit/ Firm	Total Quantity	Percentage Increase
Cartel	61.6		38.4	421.6	32	
2	52	15.58	24	364	48	25
3	42.4	31.17	19.2	52.96	57.6	50
4	36	41.56	16	−116	64	66.67
5	31.43	48.98	13.71	−217.92	68.57	78.57
6	28	54.55	12	−284	72	87.50
7	25.33	58.88	10.67	−329.33	74.67	94.45
8	23.2	62.34	9.6	−360.8	76.8	100
9	21.45	65.18	8.73	−385.77	78.55	104.56
10	20	67.53	8	−404	80	108.33
n	$\dfrac{4n + 200}{n + 2}$		$\dfrac{96}{n + 2}$	$(11,824 - 2,000n$ $-500n^2)/(n + 2)^2$	$\dfrac{96n}{n + 2}$	
∞	4	93.51	0	−500	96	150

STRATEGY SESSION: The Impact of More Sellers in the Market

In October 2002 Judge Barbara Jones of the Federal District Court in Manhattan upheld two AstraZeneca patents on Prilosec, a popular ulcer drug (in fact, the world's best-selling drug) that had generated $5.7 billion for AstraZeneca. However, the judge also allowed KUDco, an American unit of Schwarz Pharma, a German pharmaceutical firm, to make a lower-cost version of Prilosec long before 2007. KUDco introduced its generic version of the drug in 2002.

An important point of this ruling is its impact on pricing. "With only one generic competitor for Prilosec, there will probably be a shallower discount from AstraZeneca's price of $4 a pill, perhaps to $3 rather than $1 or $2, which would be typical under full-blown competition."

The significant conclusion is that adding just one competitor to a monopoly market can substantially reduce price (by 25 percent in this case). Although full competition (as many generics as wish to enter) would lower prices by 50 to 75 percent, a 25 percent decrease is not trivial; it shows the power of one.

Source: U. Ruling, "Prilosec May Still Face Generic Rival," *The New York Times Online,* http://www.nytimes.com/2002/10/14/business/14PLAC.html.

When Managers Move First: Stackelberg Behavior

Now consider a situation in which managers at one firm are able to implement actions prior to those of rival managers. For example, managers at firm A choose and credibly commit to a capacity decision; managers at firm B know the decision when they choose their own capacity. One behavior is described by Otto Stackelberg, and is named after him. How should managers at firm B react to the capacity decision of A managers? Well, if they want to maximize profit, they have to follow their reaction function. This function represents how B managers should act to maximize profit, given the decision of A managers. Managers cannot possibly maximize profit if they are operating off their reaction function. So, managers at firm A can anticipate the capacity choice of B managers.

Therefore, the demand curve firm A faces reads (after substituting firm B's reaction function, equation (10.11), for q_B in the market demand curve, since we can anticipate the decision of B managers)

$$P = 100 - q_A - q_B = 100 - q_A - [32 - (1/3)q_A] = 68 - (2/3)q_A$$

Firm A's total revenue is $Pq_A = [68 - (2/3)q_A]q_A = 68q_A - (2/3)q_A^2$. The firm's marginal revenue is

$$MR_A = \Delta TR_A/\Delta q_A = 68 - (4/3)q_A$$

QUANT OPTION

Firm A's marginal revenue is

$$dTR_A/dq_A = 68 - (4/3)q_A$$

Managers at firm A set marginal revenue equal to marginal cost to maximize profit:

$$MR_A = 68 - (4/3)q_A = 4 + q_A = MC_A$$
$$(7/3)q_A = 64$$
$$q_A = 27.43$$

Substituting $q_A = 27.43$ into firm B's reaction function yields

$$q_B = 32 - (1/3)27.43 = 22.86$$

Therefore, $Q = q_A + q_B = 50.29$ and substituting $Q = 50.29$ into the market demand curve gives a price of \$49.71 (i.e., $100 - 50.29$). Firm A's total revenue is \$1,363.59 (i.e., \$49.71 $\times$ 27.43), and firm A's total cost is \$985.88 (i.e., $500 + 4(27.43) + 0.5(27.43^2)$); therefore, managers earn a profit of \$377.71 (which is \$13.71 better than the simultaneous decision of Cournot). As a general managerial rule, if you have the market strength so market rivals cede you the power to move first, use it. Firm B's total revenue is $1,136.33 (i.e., $49.71 × 22.86), and its total cost is $852.65 (i.e., $500 + 4(22.86) + 0.5(22.86^2)$); therefore, the profit is $283.67 (which is $80.33 worse than under Cournot, so, managers at B do pay a penalty for moving second).

The profit situation is exactly reversed if managers at firm B moved first. In this case, where the firms have the same costs, it is worth the same amount for each firm to go first, $94.04 (i.e., the gain from going first plus the loss if you went second). In situations where the firms have different cost functions, the low-cost firm has a greater advantage than the high-cost firm in all the pricing schemes discussed here, including the first-mover situation. Managers at a low-cost firm have the most to gain by moving first. They can even afford to "purchase" the first-mover advantage, such as buy the first move from the lucky lottery winner, outbid the high-cost firm for the patent on the product, or build a bigger plant than the high-cost firm to preempt the output decision of the second mover.

Let us see how profit changes when managers face different cost functions. The two firms still face the demand curve $P = 100 - q_A - q_B$. But, now, managers at firm A face a cost function $TC_A = 500 + 4q_A + 0.5q_A^2$, while managers at firm B face one of $TC_B = 500 + 10q_B + 0.5q_B^2$ (i.e., firm B has higher costs than firm A). Firm A's reaction function is $q_A = 32 - (1/3)q_B$, and firm B's reaction function is $q_B = 30 - (1/3)q_A$. If you solve for the Stackelberg solution with managers at firm A choosing first, $P = \$51.143$, $q_A = 28.286$, $q_B = 20.571$, $\pi_A = \$433.429$, and $\pi_B = \$134.776$. If you solve for a Stackelberg solution with firm B going first, $P = \$51.429$, $q_A = 23.714$, $q_B = 24.857$, $\pi_A = \$343.551$, and $\pi_B = \$220.857$.

Now we can illustrate how lower costs leverage the advantage of moving first. If managers at firm A move first, they earn $\pi_A = \$433.429$, whereas if they wait for firm B managers to move first, they earn $\pi_A = \$343.551$. Therefore, managers at firm A gain $\$433.429 - \$343.551 = \$89.878$ by moving first. If managers at firm B move first, they get $\pi_B = \$220.857$, whereas if they go second, they earn $\pi_B = \$134.776$. Therefore, managers at firm B gain $\$220.857 - \$134.776 = \$86.081$ by moving first. Managers at firm A gain the most from going first. If this were a question of acquiring the patent rights from an inventor, managers at firm A could outbid managers at firm B for the patent (because they can afford to bid up to $89.878, whereas managers at firm B can afford to bid only $86.081). In an ascending auction where all bids are public and the auction ends with the last bid unchallenged, we would expect managers at firm A to acquire the patent and pay a little more than $86.081 for it (because they must only slightly outbid rivals to win the patent).

Oligopoly and competition among the few are so prevalent that these conditions should be studied carefully. For the first time in our analysis of firm behavior, *your optimal strategy depends on what your adversary does;* that is, in equation (10.9) your marginal revenue depends not only on what you do but also on what your adversary does. Hence the price you receive for your product depends on both your and your adversary's decisions. This is a chain of reciprocal decisions; that is, my actions depend on your actions, which in turn depend on my actions. Such interdependence of business decisions is typical of most of the economy. This mutual dependence is the basis of the management strategy formulation discussed in the game theory chapter (Chapter 11).

DUOPOLISTS AND PRICE COMPETITION WITH DIFFERENTIATED PRODUCTS

Is price competition always a lose–lose situation? We have shown that it is if there is no differentiation between market products. But what if managers can differentiate their products? Is price competition profitable? Let's view two competitors who produce *differentiated but highly substitutable products*. To keep the analysis simple, we'll assume the products have zero marginal cost. The demand for firm 1's product is expressed as

$$Q_1 = 100 - 3P_1 + 2P_2$$

where Q_1 is the quantity of firm 1's product demanded when managers price their product at P_1 per unit and managers at firm 2 price their product at P_2 per unit. Note that as managers at firm 2 price their product higher, the quantity demanded of firm 1's product increases as buyers switch. This shows that differentiation can only mitigate price competition; it is difficult to erase it as a purchase attribute. So again, the demand for firm 1's product depends not only on what managers control (their price) but also on what their rival charges (though they can influence the choices of rivals).

Analogously, the demand for firm 2's product is

$$Q_2 = 100 - 3P_2 + 2P_1$$

Managers at firm 1 want to maximize profit. In this case, this means maximizing the firm's total revenue because unit costs are 0.

As in Cournot, if managers get in a price war, they will compete prices down to marginal costs, and profit will be 0. Again, the price war is lose–lose. But is there a Cournot analog where they compete on price but don't commit economic suicide? There is, and it is called the *Bertrand model*. Firm 1's total revenue is

$$TR_1 = P_1{}^*Q_1 = P_1{}^*(100 - 3P_1 + 2P_2) = 100P_1 - 3P_1{}^2 + 2P_1P_2$$
$$= TR_{11} + TR_{12}$$

where $TR_{11} = 100P_1 - 3P_1{}^2$ and $TR_{12} = 2P_1P_2$.

To maximize total revenue, we form $\Delta TR_1 \Delta P_1 = (\Delta TR_{11}/\Delta P_1) + (\Delta TR_{12}/\Delta P_1)$ and set it equal to 0. $\Delta TR_{11}/\Delta P_1$ has the same form as when we did this earlier with respect to ΔQ—that is, $100 - 6P_1$ (same intercept of 100 and double the slope of -3). In the case of $\Delta TR_{12}/\Delta P_1$, call P_1 the initial price and P_1' the new price, so that $\Delta P_1 = P_1' - P_1$. Thus $\Delta TR_{12} = 2P_1'P_2 - 2P_1P_2 = 2P_2(P_1' - P_1) = 2P_2\Delta P_1$, and $\Delta TR_{12}/\Delta P_1 = 2P_2$. So the condition to maximize revenue (profit) for firm 1 will be

$$\Delta TR_1/\Delta P_1 = (100 - 6P_1) + (2P_2) = 0$$

or

$$6P_1 = 100 + 2P_2$$

or

$$P_1 = (50/3) + (1/3)P_2 \qquad (10.12)$$

QUANT OPTION

The revenue (profit)-maximizing condition is

$$\partial TR_1/\partial P_1 = 100 - 6P_1 + 2P_2 = 0$$

In an analogous fashion, the profit-maximizing price for managers at firm 2 is

$$P_2 = (50/3) + (1/3)P_1 \qquad (10.13)$$

Equations (10.12) and (10.13) give us two equations and two unknowns. Substituting (10.13) into (10.12) and solving yields

$$P_1 = (50/3) + (1/3) \times [(50/3) + (1/3)P_1] = (150/9) + (50/9) + (1/9)P_1$$
$$= (200/9) + (1/9)P_1$$

or

$$(8/9)P_1 = 200/9$$

Thus the optimal price for firm 1 managers to charge is $P_1 = 25$. Substituting $P_1 = 25$ in equation (10.13) gives $P_2 = (50/3) + (1/3)25 = 75/3 = 25$. Managers at both firms charge the same price because their differentiation efforts create similar impacts on the demand of others (remember their demand curves with the $+2$ in front of their rival's price). Substituting $P_1 = P_2 = 25$ into firm 1's demand curve gives $Q_1 = 100 - 3 \times 25 + 2 \times 25 = 100 - 75 + 50 = 75$ and analogously, $Q_2 = 75$. Managers at firm 1 earn total revenue (profit) of $TR_1 = P_1 \times Q_1 = 25 \times 75 = 1,875$ and analogously, $TR_2 = 1,875$. That's much nicer than the profit of 0 with the price war. The optimal solution is shown in Figure 10.5.

FIGURE 10.5

Bertrand Reaction Functions and Equilibrium for Firms 1 and 2

A Bertrand equilibrium occurs where the two firms' reaction functions intersect. This is the only price combination at which both firms' expectations of how the other firm will price are consistent with their own expectations of their own optimal price. In this case, both firms will price at 25.

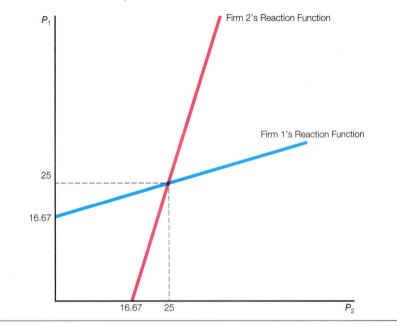

What if the managers at the two firms showed more cooperative behavior and either colluded or merged? Then the combined entity's total revenue would be

$$TR = TR_1 + TR_2 = P_1 \times (100 - 3P_1 + 2P_2) + P_2 \times (100 - 3P_2 + 2P_1)$$
$$= 100P_1 - 3P_1^2 + 2P_1P_2 + 100P_2 - 3P_2^2 + 2P_1P_2$$
$$= 100P_1 - 3P_1^2 + 100P_2 - 3P_2^2 + 4P_1P_2$$
$$= TR_{11} + TR_{22} + TR_{12}$$

where

$$TR_{11} = 100P_1 - 3P_1^2$$
$$TR_{22} = 100P_2 - 3P_2^2$$
$$TR_{12} = 4P_1P_2$$

To maximize total revenue (profit), managers will set $\Delta TR/\Delta P_1 = 0$ and $\Delta TR/\Delta P_2 = 0$.

Analogous to the procedure for deriving equations (10.12) and (10.13), we set

$$\Delta(TR_{11} + TR_{12})/\Delta P_1 = \Delta TR/\Delta P_1 = 100 - 6P_1 + 4P_2 = 0$$

or

$$6P_1 = 100 + 4P_2$$

or

$$P_1 = (50/3) + (2/3)P_2 \qquad (10.14)$$

By setting $\Delta(TR_{22} + TR_{12})/\Delta P_2 = \Delta TR/\Delta P_2 = 0$, the optimal price for P_2 is

$$P_2 = (50/3) + (2/3)P_1 \qquad (10.15)$$

QUANT OPTION

To maximize revenue (profit), the firm will set

$$\partial TR/\partial P_1 = 100 - 6P_1 + 4P_2 = 0$$

and

$$\partial TR/\partial P_2 = 100 - 6P_2 + 4P_1 = 0$$

With two equations and two unknowns, we solve by substituting (10.15) into (10.14):

$$P_1 = (50/3) + (2/3)[(50/3) + (2/3)P_1] = (150/9) + (100/9) + (4/9)P_1$$
$$= (250/9) + (4/9)P_1$$

or

$$(5/9)P_1 = 250/9$$

This results in $P_1 = 50$ and $P_2 = 50$. Substituting $P_1 = P_2 = 50$ into firm 1's demand gives $Q_1 = 100 - 3 \times 50 + 2 \times 50 = 100 - 150 + 100 = 50$ and analogously $Q_2 = 50$. Managers at firm 1 earn total revenue (profit) of $TR_1 = P_1 \times Q_1 = 50 \times 50 = 2{,}500$. Analogously, $TR_2 = 2{,}500$. Clearly collusion yields better profit, but it is also generally illegal. Managers who choose to compete on prices yield $(1{,}875/2{,}500) = 75$ percent of the collusion profit and avoid the price war (as well as jail). Note that turning this around as we did with Cournot, the entry of another competitor reduces prices (in this example by 50 percent). This is why managers need to think carefully about the effects of competition on variable profit. Consumers keep more consumer surplus and reduce producer surplus. We will further discuss strategic pricing when competition exists among a few firms in Chapter 11 ("Game Theory").

THE STICKY PRICING OF MANAGERS

The Cournot model explains why price may be "sticky"; that is, managers evolve toward the optimum and stay there. Even in markets with homogeneous products, managers show little incentive to deviate. This is especially true in markets where cost and demand have been stable or easily anticipated and managers have competed for several years. Another behavioral model explains why prices can be sticky even when products are somewhat differentiated.

Consider managers facing a limited number of competitors. They currently price at P_0 and produce Q_0. Should managers increase price, demand will be quite elastic (but not perfectly elastic because with a differentiated product, rival products are not perfect substitutes). Some customers will buy elsewhere when price increases, but other customers have a higher value for the product.

On the other hand, should managers drop their price, they could assume that demand will become less elastic because rivals will also reduce prices to protect their sales. Although lowering the price, *if* no other firm followed suit, might

---

FIGURE 10.6

The Situation of the Kinked Demand Curve

The demand curve kinks at (Q_0, P_0), with the curve being relatively elastic above the kink and relatively less elastic below the kink. The marginal revenue curve is discontinuous at Q_0 (gap BC), and the marginal cost curves intersect the marginal revenue in the gap, leading to marginal revenue equal to marginal cost and yielding an optimal price of P_0 and an optimal quantity of Q_0, despite major shifts in the marginal cost curve.

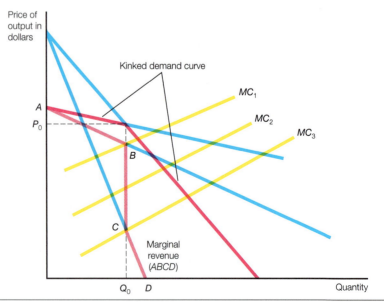

increase sales, when rivals follow a price cut, margins decrease and the increase in sales may not make up the difference.

Hence managers face a kinked demand curve at point (Q_0, P_0), with demand being gently sloped above it and steeply sloped below it. This pattern yields a discontinuous marginal revenue curve (see gap BC in Figure 10.6) at Q_0 (recall that for linear demand curves, the marginal revenue curves have the same dollar axis intercept but fall twice as fast).

Therefore, the marginal cost curves MC_1 and MC_3 (and anything in between, such as MC_2) yield the same price P_0 and quantity Q_0 for the profit-maximizing profit when they intersect the marginal revenue ($ABCD$) in the discontinuity. Thus costs can shift around quite a bit without changing the profit-maximizing price (making it sticky).

SUMMARY

1. Oligopolistic markets are characterized by a small number of firms with a great deal of interdependence, actual and perceived. A good example of an oligopoly is the U.S. oil industry, in which a few firms account for the bulk of the industry's capacity.

2. There is no single model of oligopolistic behavior; behavior depends on the circumstances and expectations. Conditions in oligopolistic industries tend to promote cooperative behavior among rivals, including collusion. Cooperation is easier to attain because the number of firms is small, and managers recognize their interdependence with rivals. The advantages to be derived by managers from collusion seem obvious: increased profit, decreased uncertainty, and a better opportunity to control the entry of new firms. However, collusive arrangements are often hard to maintain because once a collusive agreement is made, any member can increase its profit by cheating on the agreement. Also, cartels may find it difficult to identify a course of action that is agreeable to all members of the industry.

3. Another model of oligopolistic behavior is price leadership. The price leader is the dominant firm in the market. We showed how, under these circumstances, managers of the price leader will set prices to maximize profit. This model also explains pricing in an imperfect cartel (where not all producers are members).

4. When competition among a few firms exists, managers may engage in price competition. This is usually a lose–lose situation because prices are competed down to marginal costs, with severe impact on profit. Cournot competition (competition on quantity or capacity) is a strategy to capture a significant percentage of the high cartel profit and avoid the negative impact on profit of price competition. Cournot behavior exists when managers move simultaneously and engage in what-if moves; for example, what would be my profit-maximizing output response given an output by my rivals? By logically tracing all profit-maximizing responses to rivals' output choices, then putting yourself in their

position and doing the same analysis for them, behavior can become consistent across all market players. The key to competition among the few is interdependence, where your optimal output is a function not only of what you wish to do but also what your rivals wish to do.

5. If managers at one firm can act before the managers of another firm, Stackelberg behavior can explain the optimal (profit-maximizing) strategy for the first mover and all subsequent movers in this sequential game. In general, first movers see their profit improve relative to the simultaneous-move Cournot situation, and subsequent movers see their profit decrease relative to the Cournot situation. If managers of low-cost firms move first, they earn higher profits than managers of high-cost first movers. If managers can purchase the right to move first, the value they place on this purchase is their profit if they move first minus their profit if they follow.

6. Managers with differentiated products may compete on price and not compete price down to marginal cost. If a limited number of such firms compete, they can determine their and their rivals' reaction functions. Their profit-maximizing price will depend on the prices of rivals as well as their own price. Managers can deduce the optimal price they should charge because they can deduce the optimal prices of rivals. The optimal prices are considerably lower than the price the managers would charge if they formed a cartel and considerably higher than if the managers engaged in a price war.

7. Prices may be sticky (that is, tend to be stable) in oligopolies with differentiated products. This occurs because the demand curve kinks at the current price. The curve is very elastic above the current price because rivals do not follow the price increases of others; whereas it is much less elastic below the current price because rivals are likely to meet any price decreases to protect their sales. The kink in the demand curve leads to a discontinuity in the firm's marginal revenue curve. Therefore, the marginal cost can shift upward or downward considerably but still meet the marginal revenue equals marginal cost condition for profit maximization in the marginal revenue discontinuity—and thus not change the profit-maximizing price and quantity.

wwnorton.com/studyspace

PROBLEMS

1. The Bergen Company and the Gutenberg Company are the only two firms that produce and sell a particular kind of machinery. The demand curve for their product is

$$P = 580 - 3Q$$

where P is the price (in dollars) of the product, and Q is the total amount demanded. The total cost function of the Bergen Company is

$$TC_B = 410Q_B$$

where TC_B is its total cost (in dollars) and Q_B is its output. The total cost function of the Gutenberg Company is

$$TC_G = 460Q_G$$

where TC_G is its total cost (in dollars) and Q_G is its output.

a. If these two firms collude and they want to maximize their combined profit, how much will the Bergen Company produce?

b. How much will the Gutenberg Company produce?

c. Will the Gutenberg Company agree to such an arrangement? Why or why not?

2. The can industry is composed of two firms. Suppose that the demand curve for cans is

$$P = 100 - Q$$

where P is the price (in cents) of a can and Q is the quantity demanded (in millions per month) of cans. Suppose the total cost function of each firm is

$$TC = 2 + 15q$$

where TC is total cost (in tens of thousands of dollars) per month and q is the quantity produced (in millions) per month by the firm.

a. What are the price and output if managers set price equal to marginal cost?

b. What are the profit-maximizing price and output if the managers collude and act like a monopolist?

c. Do the managers make a higher combined profit if they collude than if they set price equal to marginal cost? If so, how much higher is their combined profit?

3. An oligopolistic industry selling a particular type of machine tool is composed of two firms. Managers at the two firms set the same price and share the total market equally. The demand curve confronting each firm (assuming that the other firm sets the same price) follows, as well as each firm's total cost function.

Price (Thousands of Dollars)	Quantity Demanded per Day	Daily Output	Total Cost (Thousands of Dollars)
10	5	5	45
9	6	6	47
8	7	7	50
7	8	8	55
6	9	9	65

a. Assuming that each manager is correct in believing that managers at the other firm will charge the same price as they do, what price should each charge?

b. Under the assumptions in part (a), what daily output rate should managers at each firm set?

4. James Pizzo is president of a firm that is the industry price leader; that is, it sets the price and the other firms sell all they want at that price. In other words, the other firms act as perfect competitors. The demand curve for this industry's product is $P = 300 - Q$, where P is the price of the product and Q is the total quantity demanded. The total amount supplied by the other firms is equal to Q_r, where $Q_r = 49P$. (P is measured in dollars per barrel; Q, Q_r, and Q_b are measured in millions of barrels per week.)

a. If Pizzo's firm's marginal cost curve is $2.96Q_b$, where Q_b is the output of his firm, at what output level should he operate to maximize profit?

b. What price should he charge?

c. How much does the industry as a whole produce at this price?

d. Is Pizzo's firm the dominant firm in the industry?

5. The International Air Transport Association (IATA) has been composed of 108 U.S. and European airlines that fly transatlantic routes. For many years, IATA acted as a cartel: It fixed and enforced uniform prices.

a. If IATA wanted to maximize the total profit of all member airlines, what uniform price would it charge?

b. How would the total amount of traffic be allocated among the member airlines?

c. Would IATA set price equal to marginal cost? Why or why not?

6. In late 1991 two firms, Delta Airlines and the Trump Shuttle, provided air shuttle service between New York and Boston or Washington. The one-way price charged by both firms was $142 on weekdays and $92 on weekends, with lower off-peak advance purchase fares. In September 1991 Delta increased the per-trip shuttle mileage given to members of the Delta frequent-flier program from 1,000 to 2,000 miles, even though actual mileage from New York to either Boston or Washington is about 200 miles. Moreover, Delta also offered an extra 1,000 miles to frequent fliers who made a round-trip on the same day, raising a possible day's total to 5,000 miles. Almost simultaneously, Trump changed the frequent-flier mileage it gave shuttle passengers. (It participated in the One Pass frequent-flier program with Continental Airlines and some foreign carriers.) What sorts of changes do you think Trump made? Why?

7. Two firms, the Alliance Company and the Bangor Corporation, produce vision systems. The demand curve for vision systems is

$$P = 200,000 - 6(Q_1 + Q_2)$$

where P is the price (in dollars) of a vision system, Q_1 is the number of vision systems produced and sold per month by Alliance, and Q_2 is the number of vision systems produced and sold per month by Bangor. Alliance's total cost (in dollars) is

$$TC_1 = 8,000Q_1$$

Bangor's total cost (in dollars) is

$$TC_2 = 12,000Q_2$$

a. If managers at these two firms set their own output levels to maximize profit, assuming that managers at the other firm hold constant their output, what is the equilibrium price?

b. What is the output of each firm?

c. How much profit do managers at each firm earn?

8. In Britain price competition among bookshops has been suppressed for over 100 years by the Net Book Agreement (of 1900), which was aimed at preventing price wars. However, in October 1991 Waterstone and Company began cutting book prices at its 85 British shops. According to Richard Barker, Waterstone's operations director, the decision to reduce the price of about 40 titles by about 25 percent was due to price cuts by Dillons, Waterstone's principal rival.

a. According to the president of Britain's Publishers Association, the price-cutting was "an enormous pity" that will "damage many booksellers who operate on very slim margins."[7] Does this mean that price-cutting of this sort is contrary to the public interest?

b. Why would Dillons want to cut prices? Under what circumstances would this be a good strategy? Under what circumstances would it be a mistake?

9. In the 1960s Procter & Gamble recognized that disposable diapers could be made a mass-market product and developed techniques to produce diapers at high speed and correspondingly low cost. The result was that it dominated the market. According to Harvard's Michael Porter, who made a careful study of this industry, the following were some ways in which Procter & Gamble might have signaled other firms to deter entry.[8]

Tactic	Cost to Procter & Gamble	Cost to an Entrant
1. Signal a commitment to defend position in diapers through public statements, comments to retailers, etc.	None	Raises expected cost of entry by increasing probability and extent of retaliation.
2. File a patent suit.	Legal fees	Incurs legal fees plus the probability that P & G wins the suit with subsequent cost to the competitor.

7. "British Book Shops in Price Skirmishes," *The New York Times,* October 7, 1991.

8. M. Porter, "Strategic Interaction: Some Lessons from Industry Histories for Theory and Antitrust Policy," in S. Salop, ed., *Strategy, Predation, and Antitrust Analysis* (Washington, DC: Federal Trade Commission, 1981); *The New York Times,* April 15, 1993, and March 25, 1995; and *Business Week,* April 26, 1993, and September 19, 1994.

3. Announce planned capacity expansion.	None	Raises expected risk of price-cutting and the probability of P & G's retaliation to entry.
4 Announce a new generation of diapers to be introduced in the future.	None	Raises the expected cost of entry by forcing entrant to bear possible product development and changeover costs contingent on the ultimate configuration of the new generation.

    a. In considering these possible tactics, why should managers at Procter & Gamble be concerned about their costs?

    b. Why should managers be concerned with the costs to an entrant?

    c. By the 1990s Procter & Gamble had to compete with high-quality, private-label diapers (as well as with Kimberly-Clark, which successfully entered the market in the 1970s). In March 1993 its Pampers brand had about 30 percent of the market, and its Luvs brand had about 10 percent. The price of Luvs and Pampers exceeded that of discount brands by over 30 percent. Should Procter & Gamble have cut its prices?

    d. In 1993 Procter & Gamble sued Paragon Trade Brands, a private-label producer, alleging infringement of two patents. Are lawsuits of this kind part of the process of oligopolistic rivalry and struggle?

10. Under which circumstances do managers find it profitable to increase the quality of their products? Do the benefits always exceed the costs? Why or why not?

11. The West Chester Corporation believes that the demand curve for its product is

$$P = 28 - 0.14Q$$

where P is price (in dollars) and Q is output (in thousands of units). The firm's board of directors, after a lengthy meeting, concludes that the firm should attempt, at least for a while, to increase its total revenue, even if this means lower profit.

    a. Why might managers adopt such a policy?

    b. What price should managers set if they want to maximize total revenue?

    c. If the firm's marginal cost equals $14, do managers produce a larger or smaller output than they would to maximize profit? How much larger or smaller?

12. Steve Win has purchased land from the city of Atlantic City in the Marina section. There are stories of a new casino building boom in Atlantic City (MGeeM is also talking about entering, and Gump is opening his fourth casino). Some talk is circulating that Win will subdivide his new land purchase and perhaps three casinos will be built on the site.

Suppose Win subdivides his land into two parcels. He builds on one site and sells the other to another gambling entrepreneur. Win estimates that the demand for gambling in the Marina area of Atlantic City (*after* accounting for the presence of two existing casinos in the Marina and adjusting for the rest of the casinos in Atlantic City) is

$$P = 750 - 5Q$$

where P is the price associated with gambling and Q is the quantity of gambling (think of P as the average amount that a typical patron will net the casino, an amount paid for the entertainment of gambling, and Q as the number of gamblers).

Win, of course, does not sell the other parcel until his casino is built (or is significantly far along); thus he has a first-mover advantage.

Win's total cost (TC_W) of producing gambling is

$$TC_W = 20 + 40Q_W + 15.5Q_W^2$$

where Q_W is the number of gamblers in Win's casino and the total cost (TC_R) of producing gambling for Win's rival is

$$TC_R = 10 + 50Q_R + 20Q_R^2$$

where Q_R is the number of gamblers in the rival's casino and

$$Q_W + Q_R = Q$$

Would Atlantic City have done better to sell the land as two separate parcels rather than as a single parcel to Win (given that Win was going to subdivide, Win and his rival could not collude, and Win did not have the ability to produce as a monopolist)? You may assume that Win and his rival could have been Cournot duopolists. If Atlantic City could do better, show why and by how much. Carry all calculations to the thousandths decimal point.

CHAPTER 11

GAME THEORY

Interactive When the consequence of a manager's decision
depends on both the manager's
own action and the actions of
others.

MAKING STRATEGY AND GAME THEORY

As we have seen, the managerial world is one of interactions with others. In that way it mirrors life. We now offer a tool to help managers cope with the complexities of managerial life. In fact, it is a tool to help people cope with much of life. Let us explain. We can classify all managerial decisions as either strategic or not. Nonstrategic ones do not involve other people, so their actions need not be considered. For example, managers of a shipping company can generally map the most efficient shipping route without considering what other shipping companies are doing.

Strategic decisions are fundamentally different. Characterized by interactive payoffs, they require a different cognitive frame. Payoffs are **interactive** when the consequence of a manager's decision depends on both the manager's own action and the actions of others. For example, managers decide to enter a new market. Their payoff depends on whether others follow into the market.

So when managers ponder strategic decisions, they must explicitly consider what actions others will take. And optimal choices may change depending on managerial beliefs about others. But if only life were that simple: Others are doing the same thinking about you. And this is just the first link of the expectation chain. Did you ever change a decision because you thought others expected you to take it? Making a strategic decision is like looking at yourself in a hall of mirrors; except in strategy, there are others with you.

Game theory helps managers cope with their lives, not solve all their problems. The theory is that of mathematicians who tried to bring order to the complexity of life. Game theory, their organizing framework, can help managers better understand others strategically. Through its use, managers increase their ability to anticipate the actions of others. This ability, in turn, increases the payoffs of managerial decisions—almost as if managers can look into the future.

One rule that is basic to formulating strategy is the direct result of interactive payoffs: the lack of an unconditional optimal strategy. There is no best strategy for all situations; optimality is conditional on situational parameters, many of which are controlled by managers. Though a strategic situation challenges the decision-making skills of managers, it also offers opportunities for managers to change the parameters they control to increase firm payoffs. It is the duty of managers to recognize such opportunities and act accordingly. For example, changing a relationship to the long term from the short can alter the behavior of others (as we show later in this chapter).

Like any long-standing theory, game theory furthers managers' understanding of strategy on several levels. Gravity is a theory that most of us understand, although few can cite its mathematical formula. Game theory is similar in that it illustrates principles that, if followed, will lead to better decisions.

These principles are grounded in Taoist philosophy and were recorded over 2,000 years ago in a series of classic writings, such as *The Art of War*. They are the path to strategy because they should always be followed. The mathematics of game theory clarifies why managers need to follow these principles. Those who follow will make better decisions. The most important principle managers must remember is that they control their strategic environment. Because of interactive payoffs, actions by managers will induce others to change their behavior. As we said, optimality is conditional.

So even managers who simply follow the principles and do not solve for an equilibrium will increase their decision-making ability (though not as much as those who think more rigorously). This greater clarity comes from the visual identification and organization of game parameters.

Because we want to help managers cope better with managerial life, many of the situations we discuss combine conflict with mutual dependence. Such situations are common in the business world—price wars, negotiations, intrafirm relations—and skilled managers understand the relevant considerations.

STRATEGY BASICS

Before we play a game, we need to understand the rules; consider the game of poker. There are many ways to play poker; the rules determine the specific game being played. Game parameters, such as how many cards will be dealt, the betting procedure, and which hands are better than others, define the particular game being played. The same is true for any strategic situation; the rules (parameters) define the game. Hence before managers act, they need to assess and understand the rules.

Sun Tzu said, "Strategy is the Tao of survival or extinction. One cannot but examine it." Assessment is a basic principle. Although this should seem obvious to most managers, empirical evidence shows it is not practiced. For example, the most significant difference between good and bad negotiators is how they prepare for the negotiation. Those with better outcomes prepare more thoroughly.

Game theory provides an assessment framework to help managers. All game theoretic models are defined by a common set of five parameters. Other factors may influence managerial decisions, and game theory usually recognizes these. Here are the defining, common five factors:

1. **The players:** A player is defined as the entity making a decision; entities are either individuals or groups. The decisions of all players determine the outcome. These other entities are in the hall of mirrors with you, looking at the same situation as you but from their viewpoints. Models describe both the identities of the players and their number; changes in either can alter play. Identities are important because of the diversity of the universe. You need to know exactly who is in that hall of mirrors with you. (You cannot know who is playing without a scorecard.) For example, does your behavior change when you are with your parents rather than roommates? How about a total stranger? Most of us act differently if the individual (or group of individuals) with whom we interact changes. The model explicitly recognizes this, so it requires identification. Changes in the number of players can also alter strategies.

2. **The feasible strategy set:** Managers cannot anticipate or assess an action they believe is impossible. So only actions given a nonzero probability of occurring are assessed within a model. These actions constitute the feasible strategy set. Think of it as the potential behavior of others. Behavior not in this set is outside the analytic limits of a particular game model.

It is important for managers to think carefully about the strategy set. Any strategy they don't consider, but is then played by others, puts managers at a strategic disadvantage. From a strategic view, being surprised is bad; it means that others are behaving in ways you did not anticipate. How do you know what to do if you have not assessed the situation?

3. **The outcomes or consequences:** Game models visually represent the intersection of the first two parameters as outcomes. Each player has a feasible strategy set (that is, behavior) comprising individual potential strategies. Each strategy of a player intersects all combinations of the strategies of others to form the outcome matrix. A particular outcome is defined by the strategy choice of each player. Think of the outcome matrix as a crystal ball containing all possible future states. After all players choose and play their strategies, the matrix identifies the desig-

nated state as the future. Like a fortune-teller, game theory tries to predict which state will occur before it is actually realized.

4. The payoffs: A model assigns a payoff for each player to all outcomes. So the payoff for an outcome is expressed as a vector of individual payoffs, and each possible outcome has a corresponding payoff. A player's payoff is based on his or her preferences. An inherent assumption of game theory is that players are rational: They do not wish to harm themselves. Given the choice and all other things equal, they prefer a higher payoff to a lower one. This is another reason why player identities are important. Preferences are subjective: A payoff not highly valued by one player can be highly valued by others.

5. The order of play: Timing is important in both love and war. A model specifies the order in which players reveal their chosen strategies. Models are simultaneous if all managers reveal their strategies without knowing the strategies of others. Simultaneous play is not entirely time dependent. All players need not announce their decisions at precisely the same moment. It is more a matter of information. If all players commit to a strategy before learning the strategies of others, then the game is simultaneous. Nonsimultaneous games are by definition sequential. In any sequential game, the model specifies the order of play.

One way to measure the usefulness of a model to managers is to examine how congruent it is with the real world. Here we summarize the mathematical framework to help managers decide whether it captures the nature of their world. Do managers consider the following in choosing a strategic action?

• How the outcome depends on their actions and the actions of others.
• The identities of others involved in the decisions.
• The order of play.
• How others will react to their decisions.
• The goal to achieve outcomes favorable to their preferences.

We believe most managers would answer these questions in the affirmative. That makes game theory relevant for the managerial world. Game theory formally analyzes what most managers intuitively consider when making strategy. Building a game model requires information managers already know. It asks for a finer partition of the information—a sharpening of managerial strategic focus. The theory's visual representations are tools to help managers with that focus.

VISUAL REPRESENTATION

Game models visualize interactive payoffs (outcomes) as the intersection of individual players' strategies. The representation of these payoffs takes one of two forms: matrix or extensive. The two represent the same information, although sequential games are more easily shown in the extensive form. The **matrix form**

Matrix form Form that summarizes all possible outcomes.

Extensive form Form that provides a road map of player decisions.

summarizes all possible outcomes; the **extensive form** provides a road map of player decisions.

Figure 11.1 represents a matrix form game of the following situation. Managers at two firms, Allied and Barkley, discover they both are planning to launch product development programs for competing products. They can choose to either keep spending at the currently planned level or increase it in hopes of speeding up product development and getting to market first. Expected profits are a function of the expected development costs and revenues.

Let us see how the matrix addresses the five common parameters:

1. Players: There are two players, Allied and Barkley.
2. Order of play: Simultaneous—each must reach a decision without knowing that of the other.
3. Feasible strategy set: Each player can either maintain the current spending or increase it.
4. Outcomes: Because there are two players, and each has two strategic options, there are four possible outcomes.
5. Consequences: The payoffs are listed for each player within every possible outcome. The convention in game theory is to list the row player's (Barkley) payoff first in each cell and the column player's (Allied) second. So if Allied increases spending but Barkley does not, Allied's expected profit is $3 million and Barkley's is $2 million.

Game trees Games trees are another name for extensive form games and are akin to decision trees.

Extensive form games are also called **game trees**. These are akin to the decision trees we visit in Chapter 13 and are figuratively the same. The fundamental

---

FIGURE 11.1

A Two-Person Simultaneous Game

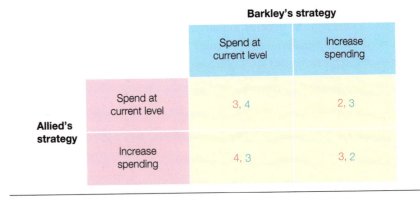

		Barkley's strategy	
		Spend at current level	Increase spending
Allied's strategy	Spend at current level	3, 4	2, 3
	Increase spending	4, 3	3, 2

difference between a game tree and a decision tree is one of strategy. A game tree is strategic; a decision tree is not. Decision trees have no interactive payoffs; payoffs are a function of the single individual and nature.

Think of any extensive form game as a decision road map. Just start at the beginning and you cannot get lost. The extensive form gives more details than the matrix form by explicitly stating the timing of choices among players. Extensive form games represent the revelation of a player strategy with decision nodes. The node specifies the player's identity and the feasible strategy set (that is, behavior). The first node (decision) of the game is represented by an open square, all other nodes are shown by a solid square. Lines from each node represent the elements of the feasible strategy set. If other players reveal strategies later in the game, the lines lead from one node to another to show the order of play. If the player is the last to reveal his or her strategy, the lines lead from the node to a payoff schedule.

Figure 11.2 shows an extensive form game representing the following situation. Managers at Allied and Barkley must choose a pricing policy for the new product. They know the other will introduce a similar competing product. Because

---

FIGURE 11.2

Allied–Barkley Pricing: Sequential

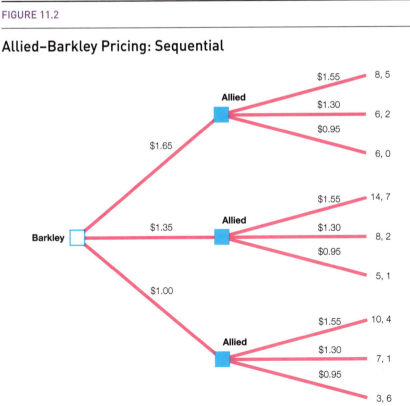

Barkley is expected to enter the market slightly sooner than Allied, Barkley managers announce their price first (note the clear square). Managers will choose one of three prices: $1.00, $1.35, or $1.65. Allied managers will reveal their price later. Because Allied is second to market, managers have possible price points of $0.95, $1.30, and $1.55. Payoffs, which represent profits, are a function of costs and revenues.

The extensive form can also show simultaneous games. It does this with information sets. All simultaneous games are played with imperfect information; that is, when revealing his strategy, a player does not know the strategies of all others. This is the nature of simultaneous situations. Figure 11.3 shows the simultaneous version of the situation depicted in Figure 11.2. The only difference between the two figures is the dotted line drawn around the Allied decision nodes. It represents Allied's information set, or knowledge at the time it reveals its strategy. The dotted line signifies that Allied managers know they are at one of the three nodes—but not which one because Barkley managers have not revealed their strategy.

These two types of models show how game theory represents strategic situations. As you see, the information required is not voluminous. But it does require

FIGURE 11.3

Allied–Barkley Pricing: Simultaneous

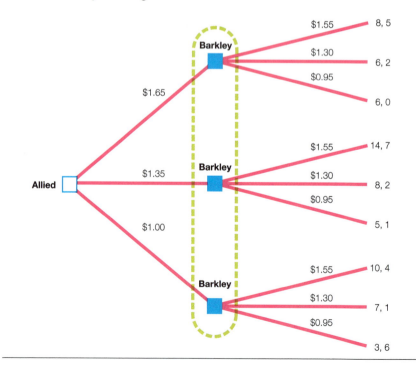

some thought and reflection. The models provide a good organizing framework. They allow managers to communicate more clearly in a common language. The models are good for examining what-if scenarios—a favorite (and helpful) pastime of managers. If this was all they offered, we think the marginal benefits of learning them would far outweigh the marginal costs. But the best is yet to come. These models let managers anticipate the future by predicting the actions of others (and those of the managers themselves). It is important to understand the models' underlying strategic principles. This knowledge gives managers greater insight into human and corporate behavior.

SOLUTION CONCEPTS

How does game theory let managers see the future? It anticipates (correctly) the behavior of others. Using principles of the Taoist tradition, the theory of games adds formal ideas and parameters. How do models anticipate behavior? Unlike crystal balls and tarot cards, the theory provides details of the underlying logic of its predictive power.

Much of the theory's predictive power comes from solution concepts, which are basically rules of behavior. The theory anticipates behavior because it believes individuals act according to prescribed rules. Before we examine some of these rules, we need to understand the concept of an equilibrium.

EQUILIBRIA

Equilibria predict behavior in the following way. In an **equilibrium**, no player has an incentive to unilaterally change his or her strategy. This rule of behavior says little about how individuals arrive at this point; but once there, no one moves unilaterally. So game models predict individual behavior for each player and identify the future (outcome). The concept of an equilibrium holds this behavior in place.

Players do not unilaterally change behavior because they cannot increase their payoff. In an equilibrium, of all possible choices (the feasible strategy set), the present choice rewards players with the highest payoff if no other player changes behavior. In other words, conditional on the choices of others, we are doing the best we can (remember—payoffs are interactive). Thus we assume that behavior is directed by our preferences. We are rational in the sense that we do not want to hurt ourselves and accept a lower payoff. Hence an equilibrium is rational, optimal, and stable. A player's behavior is directed by a preference function. Each player tries to obtain the highest payoff possible, given the actions of others. Once an equilibrium is reached, no player has an incentive to unilaterally change behavior.

Equilibrium When no player has an incentive to unilaterally change his or her strategy.

STRATEGY SESSION: The Use of Game Theory in Business

The use of game theory in the corporate world continues to increase. One example of its use is illustrated by Freight Traders Ltd., a division of Mars, Inc. Mars, Inc., is a confectionery company that holds a worldwide market share of 7.2 percent, second only to the 7.3 percent market share of Nestlé. Freight Traders is an online service (www.freight-traders.com) that uses game theory concepts to help match shippers with carriers. The service is used by over 800 carriers and 150 manufacturers.

One game theory principle used by Freight Traders is incentive compatibility. To create more efficient markets, a market organizer (like Freight Traders) wants participants to truthfully reveal their reservation prices. Of course many participants do not want to reveal this information because they want to maximize their profits. So how does one induce market participants to tell the truth? One way is to make it in their best interest to be truthful. Then they will be truthful because if they are not, they suffer adverse consequences. This is the idea underlying incentive-compatible mechanisms, which encourage honesty.

For example, Freight Traders conducts markets that use second-price auctions. This type of auction is incentive-compatible because it induces participants to truthfully reveal their reservation prices (we see why in Chapter 12). Carriers know they can bid their reservation prices and still make a profit, while manufacturers know they are obtaining the best possible prices given the current market conditions.

Managers at Freight Traders also use game theory to help clients decide the number of bidding rounds, reserve prices (minimum acceptable prices), and whether to allow negotiations between bidding rounds. Evidence of the benefits to clients is easy to find. Numico, a manufacturer of baby food and infant nutrition products, annually ships over 80,000 tons of goods. Using game theory principles, managers at Freight Traders helped the firm achieve an estimated cost savings of 12 percent. And the benefits did not end there. As John Coles, the operations director, put it, "People are immediately drawn to the financial savings, but for me, one of the biggest pluses of using Freight Traders was that it ensured a consistent approach across our

---

DOMINANT STRATEGIES

Dominant strategies A strategy whose payout in any outcome is higher relative to all other feasible strategies.

One way to tame the complexity of strategic thinking is to make it less strategic. What if managers act without regard to the actions of others? This takes managers out of the hall of mirrors and puts them in front of one mirror. Looking back at them are the only people responsible for optimizing payoffs in nonstrategy land: themselves. In these situations, if managers do not choose an optimal strategy, they have only themselves to blame.

1. A strategy is weakly dominant if it does at least as well as any other strategy for some outcomes (it is tied with another for the highest payoff) and better than any strategy for the remaining outcomes. Even if a strategy is only weakly dominant, a player would choose it.

But mathematicians cannot ignore the interactivity of life; and life suggests there are times when managers possess an option that is strategically strong relative to all others. Mathematicians represent these beliefs as **dominant strategies**. A dominant strategy is one whose payoff in any outcome is higher relative to all other feasible strategies.[1] Managers choose dominant strategies to optimize their expected return. Although the strategy choices of others still affect managerial

company, whilst retaining our flexibility and control. When this is rewarded with a 12 percent reduction to our freight bill, it makes it even more worthwhile."

Game theory is also used by insurers to estimate the risk of terrorism and the pricing of policies to cover such acts. Dr. Gordon Woo of Risk Management Solutions believes game theory can help insurers better recognize the potential targets of terrorists.

Woo argues that current models used by insurers to predict losses from natural causes are inadequate for assessing the risks of terrorist acts. Clearly insurers act as if their current models are inadequate because most exclude terrorist acts from their commercial coverage. Although some insurers offer coverage for terrorist acts, the premiums are so expensive that most businesses simply go without it.

One result of these initial game theory models showed that the probability of monetary losses at well-known landmark buildings (like the Empire State Building) is similar to the risk at ordinary office buildings. Although the landmark buildings are more likely to be attacked, they are also more likely to be better defended. This finding is counterintuitive to the insurance industry's conventional wisdom, which dictates that landmark buildings pay higher premiums for coverage against terrorist acts.

Other game theory models appear to support this finding. Game theorists have shown why it is rational for authorities to increase security at probable terrorist targets and, in turn, why rational terrorists will then target softer, less well-protected targets.

Sources: "Web-Based Freight Trading Tastes Sweet," *The Wall Street Journal*, November 29–December 1, 2002, p. R2; www. freight-traders.com; "Can the Risk of Terrorism Be Calculated by Insurers? Game Theory Might Do It," *The Wall Street Journal*, April 8, 2002, p. C1; "How to Bomb Friends and Alienate People," *Sydney Morning Herald* (online version), May 30, 2003.

payoffs, thinking about others will not change the managerial decision. A dominant strategy returns a higher payoff than any other strategy across all possible outcomes. Managers should always choose a dominant strategy if it is available.

It is easier to visually represent dominant strategies using the matrix form. Look at Figure 11.1 again. Managers at Allied have a dominant strategy to maintain the current spending level (left column). If managers at Barkley also maintain current spending, Barkley receives a payoff of $3 million; if Allied managers increase spending, the payoff is $2 million. Barkley managers also face a dominant strategy: They will increase spending. If Allied managers spend at the current level, Barkley earns $4 million; if Allied managers increase spending, Barkley earns $3 million.

We can now predict that Allied managers will maintain their current spending and those at Barkley will increase it. We have a dominant strategy equilibrium. Why will this outcome prevail? Because each manager has a dominant strategy and each is always better off playing it. Why won't they change their strategy? Any change in strategy will lead to guaranteed lower payoffs. Domination is the minimum hurdle required of rationality. If you choose dominated strategies when you know dominant ones exist, you are hurting yourself.

Dominant strategies are the stress reducers of the strategic world. They ease the mental cost of decision making and simplify the analytic process. With them, managers can ignore the actions of others. Given the hectic schedules of managers, they are a great time-saver. For example, in Chapter 12 we discuss auctions. Auction design can determine whether a dominant strategy exists for a particular auction. In auctions with no dominant strategy, managers must consider the bids of others in choosing their bids. In ones with a dominant strategy, managers need not. Good strategic managers understand the difference and do not waste time thinking about something irrelevant to a decision.

Not surprisingly, it is dominant to first look for dominant strategies in matrix games. Even if a game is not solvable through dominance, this process eliminates outcomes mapped to dominated strategies; we essentially reduce the set of playable strategies. Recall that no player should ever play a dominated strategy because he or she is always better off playing the dominant one. So we can eliminate dominated strategies from consideration. We never reach those outcomes because no dominated strategy is played. Visually, our outcome matrix is reduced by rows or columns. Mentally, the analysis is simplified because we consider fewer outcomes.

More important strategically, when managers eliminate a strategy, they reduce the set of possible outcomes. This in turn may change a formerly nondominated strategy into a dominated one. This iterative process can proceed until each player is left with only one playable strategy (that is, the situation is dominance solvable).

Figure 11.4 is the matrix form of the game shown in Figure 11.2. Managers can always model strategy as either an extensive or a matrix form game. Each game form is linked to a particular game of the other form with identical players, outcomes, and payoffs. They are like fraternal twins who act identically.

We now look at the strategies for Allied and Barkley managers. Barkley has a dominated strategy: $1.35 dominates $1.00. For any Allied strategy, Barkley managers earn more by pricing at $1.35. If Allied managers price at $0.95, $1.35 earns 5 relative to 3 for $1.00. If they price at $1.30, the ratio is 8 to 7; and if Allied manages to price at $1.55, the ratio is 14 to 10. Barkley managers should never choose $1.00, so we need not further consider its outcomes. This effectively reduces the figure's matrix to that shown in part A of Figure 11.5.

Because we eliminated Barkley's $1.00 strategy as a playable strategy, Allied managers now face a dominated strategy—two in fact: $1.55 dominates both $0.95 and $1.30. Hence the matrix is reduced to that shown in part B of Figure 11.5. Allied managers have only one playable strategy: charging $1.55. Therefore, Barkley managers now face another dominated strategy. Because 14 is greater

FIGURE 11.4

Matrix Form Representation of Figure 11.2

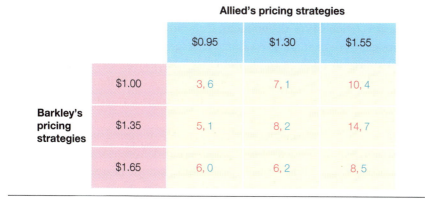

Allied's pricing strategies

		$0.95	$1.30	$1.55
	$1.00	3, 6	7, 1	10, 4
Barkley's pricing strategies	**$1.35**	5, 1	8, 2	14, 7
	$1.65	6, 0	6, 2	8, 5

FIGURE 11.5

Iterative Dominance

A. Barkley's $1.00 strategy is eliminated.

Allied's pricing strategies

		$0.95	$1.30	$1.55
Barkley's pricing strategies	**$1.35**	5, 1	8, 2	14, 7
	$1.65	6, 0	6, 2	8, 5

B. Allied's $0.95 and $1.30 strategies are eliminated.

Allied's pricing strategies

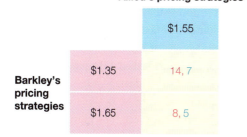

		$1.55
Barkley's pricing strategies	**$1.35**	14, 7
	$1.65	8, 5

than 8, Barkley managers will charge $1.35. So this game has a dominant strategy equilibrium: Allied managers will price at $1.55 and Barkley managers will price at $1.35.

Although both this game and the one represented in Figure 11.1 have dominant strategy equilibria, they are solved using different degrees of rationality. Most people view rationality as dichotomous: If you are not rational, you are irrational. But rationality has continuous measures. One such measure is the degree of rationality required to reach an equilibrium. Because of interactive payoffs, we have to worry about not only our own rationality but also the rationality of others. So the degree of rationality measures the number of conjectures required to reach an equilibrium.

For example, in Figure 11.1 managers can solve the game simply by knowing they are rational. If you are rational, choose your dominant strategy. No matter what others do, that is the best response. But this single degree of rationality is not sufficient to ensure that managers reach the equilibrium in Figure 11.4. When dominance is of the iterative variety, managers need to consider the rationality of others.

Let us view the game from the decision point of Barkley managers. "Well, we know we are rational. We see that $1.00 is dominated, so we will not price at $1.00. Fine; what are our beliefs about the behavior of Allied managers? Will they believe our price of $1.00 is dominated and we will not price there? If so, do Allied managers realize that pricing at $1.55 is a dominant strategy?"

In matrix form games, we measure the degree of rationality by the rounds of iterative dominance needed to reach the equilibrium. The game in Figure 11.4 requires three rounds. It is our experience that many people act rationally for games with a few degrees of rationality, but few people understand games of many degrees.

Life is complex. Domination principles help make managerial life easier. But few games have a dominant strategy equilibrium; interaction with others is generally more complicated. How can managers anticipate behavior in games without a dominant strategy equilibrium?

THE NASH EQUILIBRIUM

That is the question mathematician John Nash asked himself in the early 1950s. His answer is our most widely used solution concept: the Nash equilibrium. Similar to dominance, Nash developed guidelines for behavior that are rational, optimal, and stable. He specified behavior if players lacked a strategy that dominated all others. Here is the intuition underlying Nash's ideas.

A player's objective remains the same whether he has one or more playable strategies: to maximize the payoff. If he must choose among playable strategies, he selects the optimal one. And because payoffs are interactive, he must choose conditional on what he thinks of others. So what rule are the others following? If they are the same (rational), their goals are identical: to maximize their payoffs relative to what others will choose. Hence each will choose the strategy that maximizes his or her payoff, conditional on others doing the same. That is John Nash's prescribed behavior for players with more than one playable strategy.

Nash's concept is more transparent in its mathematical form. Let each of N players identify a strategy s^*_i, where $i = 1, 2, 3, \ldots N$. An outcome represents an array of strategies $s^* = (s^*_1, s^*_2, s^*_3, \ldots, s^*_N)$. Let $B_i(s^*)$ be the payoff to player i when s^* is chosen, with i being any player, $i = 1, 2, 3, \ldots, N$. Then a Nash equilibrium is an array of strategies such that

$$B_i(s^*_1, s^*_2, s^*_3, \ldots, s^*_N) \geq B_i(s'_1, s^*_2, s^*_3, \ldots, s^*_N) \quad \text{for all outcomes}$$

The left side of this equation states the existence of an outcome(s), defined by the array of player strategies, where all have a best response to the best responses of others. The right side states that if any player unilaterally changes strategy, she realizes a lower payoff; that is, she chooses a dominated outcome. For a complex and messy process, Nash devised an elegant solution. It treats all with equal rationality and so limits behavior. Dominance is still present, although now conditional. The solution exists for all games with a finite number of players and outcomes.

Dominance is unconditional in dominance-solvable games. We need not speculate about the behavior of others because it makes no difference. But anything less than unconditional dominance requires anticipation. And because payoffs are interactive, this anticipation requires a common vision with others. So Nash prescribes a behavioral rule. Maximize your payoff, conditional on all others doing the same. A Nash solution is dominant, conditional on this rule being followed.

Recall that an equilibrium needs to be rational, optimal, and stable. Nash's solution is rational in the sense that all players follow the prescribed behavior. It is optimal in that all try to maximize their payoffs. And it is stable because no player can unilaterally change strategy and realize a higher payoff.

Figure 11.6 illustrates the following. The numbers represent profits (in millions of dollars). Recall that Barkley entered the market first, followed by Allied. Both firms must now introduce new products. Each can choose one product of several; but because of financial constraints, only one can be supported. Managers at both firms understand this. Their choice to introduce a product is conditional on how they think the other will behave. Nash says that we all behave identically: We maximize payoffs conditional on others doing the same. We will change behavior to obtain a higher payoff but not a lower one.

Look at Figure 11.6. Remember our decision rule: Look for dominated strategies. This is quickly done. Confirm that neither firm has a dominated strategy. Now use the following algorithm. For each strategy, indicate the behavior of the other. For example, if Barkley managers know (with certainty) that Allied will introduce alpha,

---

FIGURE 11.6

New Product Introduction

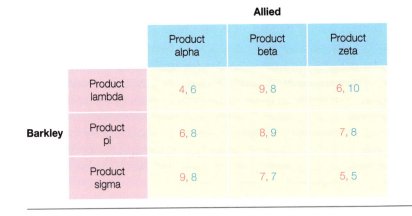

		Allied		
		Product alpha	Product beta	Product zeta
Barkley	Product lambda	4, 6	9, 8	6, 10
	Product pi	6, 8	8, 9	7, 8
	Product sigma	9, 8	7, 7	5, 5

---

what will they do? Barkley receives 4 if it introduces lambda, 6 if pi, and 9 if sigma (the first numbers in each cell of the product alpha column). Because 9 is the highest of the three payoffs, Barkley managers will introduce sigma if they know Allied will introduce alpha. Write a B in the alpha–sigma outcome. Do the same for strategies beta and zeta. Now follow the same procedure for Allied (the sequence of players makes no difference). For example, if Barkley introduces sigma, what should Allied managers choose? If Allied produces alpha it receives 8, if beta 7, and if zeta 5. So Allied managers will introduce alpha if they know Barkley will introduce sigma. Mark an A in this outcome. Do the same for strategies lambda and pi. The resulting matrix is illustrated in Figure 11.7.

Any cell with an A and a B is a Nash equilibrium. In this game the Nash solution is for Barkley to introduce sigma (and receive 9) and Allied to introduce alpha (and receive 8). Let us understand why this outcome is predicted by Nash. An A or B represents a conditional dominant strategy—a best response to a specific strategy of others. A Nash equilibrium is a meeting of the best responses—an outcome where all play conditionally dominant strategies. Beyond the reach of an individual, it is attained by the group.

Each player acts in his or her own best interest and maximizes payoffs. A player not choosing the Nash strategy is playing a dominated one (assuming others play their Nash strategies). Hence no player has an incentive to unilaterally change behavior. For example, as long as Allied produces alpha, Barkley managers want to produce sigma and receive $9 million. If they produce pi, they receive only $6 million, and if lambda, only $4 million. Allied managers face the same scenario: lower payoffs for any change in behavior. Interactive payoffs hold the two hostage to each other.

FIGURE 11.7

New Product Introduction with Other's Behavior

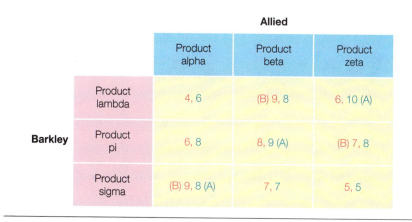

		Allied		
		Product alpha	Product beta	Product zeta
Barkley	Product lambda	4, 6	(B) 9, 8	6, 10 (A)
	Product pi	6, 8	8, 9 (A)	(B) 7, 8
	Product sigma	(B) 9, 8 (A)	7, 7	5, 5

STRATEGIC FORESIGHT: THE USE OF BACKWARD INDUCTION

A Taoist saying is, "Good strategists take care of the great while the great is small." Good managers use strategic foresight. The ancient Taoists called this the ability to see what others could not see. We define **strategic foresight** as a manager's ability to make decisions today that are rational given what is anticipated in the future. For example, a manager builds extra capacity today because she believes (correctly) that demand will increase in the near future. Strategic foresight is a principle that should always be used. Remember that the decisions of today can never affect your past—only your future. In decision making you always want to look forward. Using strategic foresight also helps managers understand that decisions have both short- and long-term consequences.

Game theory formally models strategic foresight through what is called **backward induction**. In game theory we use backward induction to solve games by looking to the future, determining what strategy players will choose (anticipation), and then choosing an action that is rational, based on these beliefs. Backward induction is most easily seen in extensive form games because of the ability to map the choices of players.

Figure 11.8 shows a game in extensive form. Recall from Figure 11.7 that Barkley managers have chosen to introduce sigma, and Allied managers have chosen to introduce alpha. They must now decide whether to expand their product lines. Either firm's managers have the choice to expand or not. Barkley is the market leader, so assume its managers will reach their decision first. After seeing the decision of Barkley managers, those at Allied decide whether to expand. Payoffs for the four possible outcomes are given in Figure 11.8.

Strategic foresight A manager's ability to make decisions today that are rational given what is anticipated in the future.

Backward induction Used in game theory, to solve games by looking to the future, determining what strategy players will choose (anticipation), and then choosing an action that is rational, based on those beliefs.

FIGURE 11.8

Allied–Barkley Expansion Decision

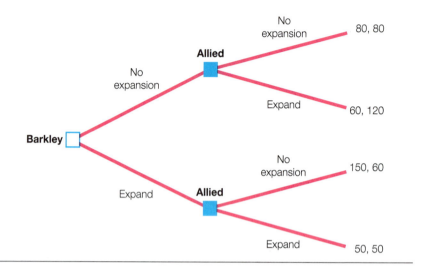

Let us see how a manager with strategic foresight can use backward induction to solve this game. The farthest left decision node represents the decision of Barkley's managers to expand or not. If they decide to expand, Allied's managers face the situation represented by Allied's bottom decision node. If Barkley does not expand, Allied faces the situation represented by the top decision node. Barkley managers use strategic foresight. They want to make a decision today that maximizes their payoff, given their vision of the future. Barkley managers realize that if they expand, Allied will receive a payoff of $50 million if it expands and $60 million if it does not.

Hence Barkley managers anticipate that if they expand, Allied will not. What if Barkley decides not to expand? Allied receives a payoff of $120 million for line expansion and $80 million if it does not expand. Thus Barkley managers anticipate that Allied will expand if they choose not to. So if they expand, they anticipate a payoff of $150 million (because Allied will not expand). If Barkley does not expand, its managers should anticipate a payoff of $60 million (because Allied will expand). Since $150 million is greater than $60 million, the managers at Barkley know they should expand their product line.

To use backward induction we must come back from the future. We anticipate the future actions of others and then choose actions that are rational, conditioned on our expected behavior of others.

Backward Induction and the Centipede Game

The usefulness of backward induction in strategic thinking is clearly shown in the simple **centipede game**. Many studies have used this game to study whether subjects use and understand backward induction. The game is shown in Figure 11.9.

Two players (*A* and *B*) participate in this sequential game. Player *A* moves first and can choose either down (*D*) or right (*R*). If player *A* chooses *D*, the game is over and both players receive a payoff of $1. If player *A* chooses *R*, then player *B* faces a similar choice. She can choose *d* or *r*. If player *B* chooses *d*, the game is over; *A* receives a payoff of $0 and *B* receives a payoff of $3. If player *B* chooses *r*, the game continues and player *A* chooses either *D* or *R* again. The game continues until one player chooses down or player *B* is asked to choose for a third time. At this point, if player *B* chooses *d*, *A* receives $3 and *B* receives $6. If player *B* chooses *r* at this point, both players receive $5. Look at Figure 11.9 and assume you are Player *A*. What strategy would you choose?

We solve the game using backward induction. The game is actually a series of six decisions. Player *A* chooses at stages 1, 3, and 5; player *B* chooses at stages 2, 4, and 6. We need to go to the end of the game and work backward from the future. Look at stage 6: Player *B* can choose down and receive $6 or choose right and receive $5. Because $6 is greater than $5, we anticipate that player *B* will choose down. Move backward to stage 5 because we now know the future. Player *A* faces the following. If *A* chooses right, he knows (anticipates correctly) that *B* will choose down, giving *A* a $3 payoff. Or *A* can choose down and receive a payoff of $3.50. Because $3.50 is greater than $3, *A* will choose down at stage 5. What should player *B* choose at stage 4 knowing this? *B* can choose down and receive a payoff of $4.50 or choose right and receive a payoff of $3.50 (because we know *A* will choose down at stage 5). Because $4.50 is greater than $3.50, player *B* will choose down at stage 4. We move backward to stage 3. Player *A* can choose down and receive a payoff of $2.50 or choose right and receive a payoff of $1.50 (since we anticipate

Centipede game A sequential game involving a series of six decisions that shows the usefulness of backward induction in strategic thinking.

FIGURE 11.9

The Centipede Game

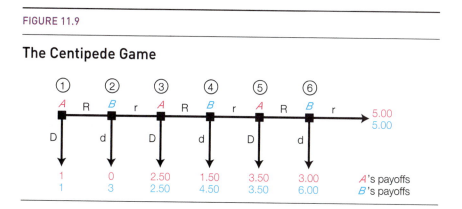

that B chooses down at stage 4). Because $2.50 is greater than $1.50, player A will choose down at stage 3. We are now at stage 2. Player B can choose down and receive a payoff of $3 or choose right and receive a payoff of $2.50 (since player A will choose down at stage 3). So player B will choose down at stage 2. Finally we find ourselves in the present; this is decision time. At Stage 1, player A can choose down and receive $1 or choose right and receive $0 (because B will choose down at stage 2). Player A will choose down at stage 1. This is the only rational choice, given our view of the future. Player A will choose down at stage 1, and both players will realize a payoff of $1. What the ancients called foresight, game theorists model as backward induction.

Now comes the real question. How do subjects behave while playing the game? Initially few subjects appear to use foresight (or they have a distorted view of the future). Subjects appear to focus on the growing size of the payoffs and try to move down this path. At some late stage, either they choose down or the person they are playing with chooses it. The next time they play, most subjects tend to choose down at an earlier stage (especially those whose partners chose down in the earlier game). By the third or fourth play sequence, most A players are resigned to the fact that they should choose down at stage 1. They do so hesitantly because they still see the path of greater payoffs. But they also know the future. Experience has shown the wisdom of backward induction.

The Credibility of Commitments

Backward induction has many uses. One is to test the credibility of commitments. From threats to promises, epithet slinging to love's rhapsody, we want to know whether we should believe others. When facing these situations, always check credibility first. That is a dominant strategy. Consider only credible commitments. A commitment is **credible** if the costs of falsely sending one are greater than the associated benefits. Managers at a company who proclaim its product is best are not credible. There is little cost to proclaiming this, and associated benefits are high. The managers can make that claim credible by offering a product warranty. A warranty increases the commitment cost (if it is falsely sent). There are many uses for such costs.

Consider the following. Recall that Barkley managers expanded their product line but Allied managers have not. Allied's managers decide to counter Barkley's product line extension by dropping the price of their product. However, they are concerned that if they drop their price, Barkley managers will follow with a price cut of their own. In fact, Barkley's managers told a common supplier of both firms that if Allied drops its price, they will drop theirs. What should Allied managers do?

Allied's managers first must consider whether Barkley's threat to drop its price is credible. They can do so by looking at Figure 11.10 and solving the game using backward induction. Barkley managers can either keep their price high or drop

Credible commitment When the costs of falsely sending one are greater than the associated benefits.

FIGURE 11.10

Does Barkley Have a Credible Threat?

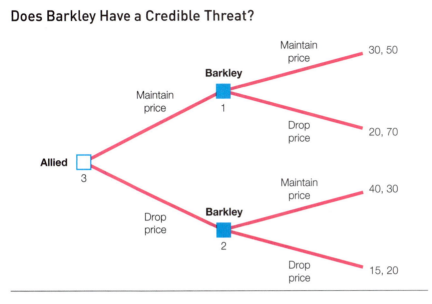

it. Allied managers have the same two strategies available to them. What happens if Allied managers drop their price? Those at Barkley can either keep their price high and earn $30 million or drop their price and earn $20 million. Because $30 million is greater than $20 million, Barkley managers should keep their price high if Allied managers reduce their price. What if Allied maintains its price? Barkley managers could keep their price high and earn $50 million or drop their price and earn $70 million. Hence Barkley managers will drop their price if Allied managers maintain their high price. Given that Allied managers can anticipate these actions from those at Barkley, how should Allied managers decide? They should drop their price. Clearly those at Barkley will not drop their price. The threat by Barkley managers to lower price is not credible, so it should be ignored. If forced to carry out the threat, Barkley managers will refuse. To do so would cost them $10 million in lost profit.

The equilibrium just described is a subgame perfect equilibrium. A **subgame** is defined as being a segment of a larger game. The subgames are marked in Figure 11.10. As you can see, within the overall game, the three constitute three separate subgames. In repeated games, all subgame perfect equilibria are also Nash equilibria, although not all Nash equilibria are subgame perfect. Nash equilibria that are based on noncredible threats are not subgame perfect. Formally, we define a subgame perfect equilibrium as a strategy profile s^* in the overall game (D) such that for any history h, the profile s^*u_h is a Nash equilibrium for the subgame $D(h)$. Intuitively this says the equilibrium for any subgame is rational, conditional on

Subgame A segment of a larger game.

387

equilibrium play in the future. For example, in the centipede game, the strategy profile of *A* choosing *D* (down) at stage 1 is rational, conditional on what we know will happen in future subgames. So that is a subgame perfect equilibrium.

REPEATED GAMES

The business world is characterized by repeated interactions. In many markets, firms and managers compete against each other for decades. Within firms, managers interact with each other over long periods. So how does a perception of future interaction affect behavior? Managers need to understand how the prospect of a future can change player actions. Again we turn to backward induction to help us understand the implications of repeated play.

We illustrate the strategic effect of repeated play using a stylized example from a class of games known as prisoner's dilemmas. Suppose Allied and Barkley produce an identical product. They also have similar cost structures. Managers at both firms must decide whether to price the product high or low. This situation is shown in Figure 11.11.

The Nash equilibrium of this game is for managers at both firms to sell their products at a low price (and earn $3 million). Although both realize they are better off if each maintains a high price, they are afraid that managers at the other firm will then drop price and steal the market. Hence managers at both firms price low. If Allied and Barkley managers compete in only one market for a single instance, we expect both of them to keep prices low. After all, that is the rational choice.

But what if they are rivals for a long time? Instead of playing this pricing game once, they play it multiple times. Should we still expect managers at both firms to price low? Each firm can see it is forfeiting $2 million per period, simply because

---

FIGURE 11.11

Pricing as a Prisoner's Dilemma

Allied's pricing strategies

		Price high	Price low
Barkley's pricing strategies	Price high	5, 5	1, 20
	Price low	20, 1	3, 3

neither can trust the other to maintain the high price. As Emerson commented, "Distrust is expensive."

Strategically, the key difference between one-shot games and those that are repeated is the presence of a future. A future introduces behavior not possible in a one-shot world. Trust, reputation, promises, threats, and reciprocity need a future to exist. A future also means that payoffs are no longer relegated to the short term because we now face longer-term implications. A betrayal of trust may create gains in the present, but these may be outweighed by future losses.

Models of repeated games reflect and account for this wider range of feasible behavior. They use the idea of a future to construct norms that let players reach mutually beneficial outcomes. For example, in the preceding situation, these norms help maintain an equilibrium where both firms price high. The risk of one firm undercutting the other is mitigated by the threat of future punishment. Of course such threats must be credible. Let us see how these models work.

The first distinction these models make is whether or not the time horizon is finite. Cooperative behavior is easier to maintain in an infinite horizon game because the future always looms. In finite horizon games, the future grows smaller as we approach the last period. So consider an infinite horizon in the game shown in Figure 11.11. If Allied and Barkley managers cooperate and price high, each receives a payoff of 5 per period. One can defect, price low, and earn 20 for a single period. The other will then price low, and each will receive 3 for the rest of the game. So the incremental earnings of 15 (20 − 5) are lost within 8 periods ((5 − 3) × 8). In fact, in an infinite horizon game, no single-period noncooperative payoff will be larger than the sum of cooperative future payoffs.

The long shadow of a future in an infinite horizon game causes the well-known result called the **folk theorem**. This theorem basically states that any type of behavior can be supported by an equilibrium (as long as the players believe there is a high probability that future interaction will occur). The support for a wide range of behaviors occurs because the future always matters in these games; hence credible threats and promises can alter the current behavior of players. Of course this makes it much harder to accurately predict behavior in games with infinite horizons.

Finite horizon games are fundamentally different because as the game progresses, the future necessarily grows shorter. Because behavior in these games is predicated on the use of credible signals of future behavior, their power diminishes as the future grows shorter. And in the last period, signals hold no power because there is no future (the last period of a repeated game is akin to a single shot); hence the Nash equilibrium is identical to that of a one-shot game. In the pricing game, this means that managers at both firms price low. Without the restraint of credible signals and a future, managers should expect others to act opportunistically.

But wait. If we know managers at both firms will price low in the last period, how should this affect their actions in the prior-to-last period? Let us again use

Folk theorem This theorem states that any type of behavior can be supported by an equilibrium (as long as the players believe there is a high probability that future interaction will occur).

backward induction. Is there any strategy managers at either firm can follow to change the low-price outcome of the last period? No: Regardless of the strategies played, managers at both firms will price low. Their strategic fate is sealed. If this is true, the rational strategy is to price low in this period, too. And just as we saw in the centipede game, similar reasoning extends backward to the first period. So the equilibrium in a repeated version of the game is identical to that of a one-shot game. Managers at both firms should price low.

But what about the looming future and the use of credible commitments? Shouldn't that change behavior? Game theorists had similar thoughts, so they developed the theory to account for these factors. This was a more difficult task relative to the infinite horizon game because they had to account for the final period.

One insight recognized by game theorists is that not everyone is opportunistic. What happens if nonopportunistic individuals are in the population and you do not know (with certainty) whether you are playing with one? How does that change predicted managerial behavior?

INCOMPLETE INFORMATION GAMES

Incomplete information games (IIG) A branch of game theory that loosens the restrictive assumption that all players have the same information.

This question established a branch of game theory called **incomplete information games (IIG)**. These games loosen the restrictive assumption that all players have the same information. The introduction of incomplete information makes it possible to derive cooperation (price high in Figure 11.11) as an equilibrium behavior. Now, when we backwardly induct, pricing low is not necessarily the predicted strategy in the last period. Nonopportunistic players may still price high in the last period because they obtain satisfaction from cooperating. They do not care that there is no future; they just want to cooperate. Instead of pricing low from the initial period, players may want to experiment in early periods by pricing high to determine whether they are playing with a nonopportunistic type.

Tit for tat Strategy that allows players to cooperate in the first period and in all succeeding periods the players mimic the preceding period's strategy of the other player.

One strategy players may use to experiment is commonly referred to as **tit for tat**. Players using tit for tat cooperate in the first period. In all succeeding periods they mimic the preceding period's strategy of the other player. For example, assume Barkley managers use a tit-for-tat strategy. In period 1 they price high. In period 2 Barkley managers mimic Allied's period 1 strategy. In period 3 they mimic Allied's period 2 strategy. So Barkley managers begin the game by pricing high. They continue to price high as long as Allied managers price high. If Allied managers price low, they price low in the following period and continue to price low until Allied managers price high again. Using this strategy, Barkley managers determine whether those at Allied are opportunistic and, if they are, suffer only one period of low payoffs.

In IIG models, players possess asymmetric information. For example, Barkley managers may know more about their cost function than managers do at Allied.

IIG models summarize this asymmetric information in the form of player types. A *type* consists of player characteristics that are unknown to others. In business, types may consist of competitive attributes, like cost functions. In personal relationships, they may consist of personality traits, like trustworthiness.

Specific types are represented by different payoff (preference) functions. So a low-cost type has a different payoff function than a high-cost type. A simple IIG model is shown in Figure 11.12. Allied managers need to decide whether to enter a product market where Barkley is an incumbent. Allied managers are uncertain of the reaction of Barkley managers if they decide to enter the market. If Barkley managers are "tough," those at Allied expect them to lower their price and defend their market. If Barkley managers are "soft," those at Allied expect them to keep their price high, thereby allowing Allied to enter the market.

FIGURE 11.12

Tough or Soft Barkley Managers

A. Barkley managers are tough.

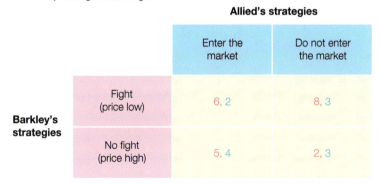

Allied's strategies

		Enter the market	Do not enter the market
Barkley's strategies	Fight (price low)	6, 2	8, 3
	No fight (price high)	5, 4	2, 3

B. Barkley managers are soft.

Allied's strategies

		Enter the market	Do not enter the market
Barkley's strategies	Fight (price low)	2, 2	3, 3
	No fight (price high)	7, 4	4, 3

PROBLEM SOLVED: Can Rating Agencies Improve a Bank's Capital Structure?

Suppose banks A and B compete with each other for a high-wealth clientele by simultaneously choosing how much capital each should hold. Because of the rich clientele, neither bank is regulated or rated by the industry rating agency Unstandard and Rich (U&R). If both banks choose HIGH capital, then consumers will perceive each to be safe and there will be little systemic risk and both banks will earn profits of 50. If both banks choose LOW capital, each will reduce its cost of capital, but each will be perceived by clients as riskier and each will earn profits of 20. If one bank chooses LOW and the other HIGH, the LOW capital bank will be able to offer more attractive terms and increase its profit to 60, while the HIGH capital bank will earn only 10.

We can use game theory to determine what capital each bank will choose. A's best choices given B's choices are bolded. B's best choices given A's choices are underlined.

		Bank A	
		HIGH capital	LOW capital
Bank B	HIGH capital	50, 50	10, <u>60</u>
	LOW capital	**60**, 10	**20**, <u>20</u>

The Nash equilibrium is both banks choosing LOW capital. It's a prisoners' dilemma game. The win-win scenario is both banks choosing HIGH capital; but this scenario will not occur given the dominant strategies of each bank to choose LOW capital.

Is it possible to change the game in a way that allows the banks to maximize profits, i.e., both choose High capital? Suppose the directors of Bank A realize that, without regulation and rating, clients do not fully realize how risky a bank will be if it carries low capital. With such a LOW rating by U&R, clients would fully realize the true risk and profits would be reduced by 15 from the numbers given above (the profit is 15 lower whatever the strategy chosen by the rival). The profits for HIGH capital are as before. The directors realize that, if they choose to be rated voluntarily, the decision is irreversible and Bank B would be forced to follow. Does the decision by the directors of Bank A to be rated by U&R advantageously change the game for the banks? Indeed, it does, as can be seen in the matrix below where A's best choices given B's choices are bolded. B's best choices given A's choices are underlined.

		Bank A	
		HIGH capital	LOW capital
Bank B	HIGH capital	**50**, <u>50</u>	**10**, 45
	LOW capital	45, <u>10</u>	5, 5

Bank A would choose to be rated. Bank B would follow. With ratings by U&R, each bank has a dominant strategy to choose high capital. Thus, both Bank A and Bank B make a profit of 50.

The lesson learned is that regulation by providing information that is valuable to both the banks and their clients can improve payoffs.

When Barkley managers are actually tough (part A of Figure 11.12), the Nash equilibrium is for Allied managers not to enter the market and for those at Barkley to price low. Of course Barkley managers will not have to price low because those at Allied will never enter the market. When Barkley managers are actually soft (part B of Figure 11.12), the Nash equilibrium is for Allied to enter the market and for Barkley to price high (allowing entry). Note that Allied payoffs are identical across parts A and B. The incomplete information is about Barkley managers, not those at Allied. Only the payoffs of Barkley managers change.

So if Allied managers know the true type of Barkley managers, their decision is easy. If Barkley managers are soft, they enter the market; if Barkley managers are tough, they stay out of the market. The problem is that they do not know the true type of Barkley managers. And knowing this, can Barkley managers influence their beliefs?

REPUTATION BUILDING

The presence of a future and incomplete information are the necessary ingredients for building reputations. In their presence, a reputation is a rent-generating asset. In the example here, if Barkley managers convince Allied managers they are tough in the early periods of the repeated game, Allied managers will stay out of the market in the later stages.

In game theory, a reputation is simply the history of behavior. Intuitively, reputation-building models parallel the human thought process. When we are unsure about the traits of others, we look to past behavior for clues. We use this information to form probabilistic beliefs regarding the traits of others. "I think I can trust him, but I wouldn't bet my life on it." In effect, we use a reputation model to infer future actions from past behavior. For example, assume a friend asks you to lend her $100. If you have previously lent money to this friend, you will recall whether she paid you back. You are more likely to lend money to a friend who repaid a previous debt. Why? Because the friend paid back the earlier debt, you perceive a higher probability that he or she will pay back this new debt. If the previous debt was not repaid, you are less likely to lend the person money again.

So in situations with futures and incomplete information, managers need to generate reputations to earn future rents. In all such situations, using backward induction, managers need to consider how current behavior will affect the future. Reneging on a debt has immediate payoffs (the debtor gains the amount lent) and long-term consequences (the lender is less likely to offer money in the future). Although these reputation models are too complex to explain here, the underlying idea is simple. In games with a future, players must consider both the present and the future. The payoff managers generate has two components: the immediate gain and its effect on future gains.

For example, suppose Barkley's managers are actually soft. They still have an incentive to act tough in early periods. Of course this will give them a lower payoff in these early periods than playing their true soft type (pricing high weakly dominates). But if they act tough early, Allied managers might not enter later because they are convinced (at least enough) that Barkley managers are truly tough. Note, though, that as the future gets shorter (as it necessarily does in finite horizon games), the value of maintaining a false reputation shrinks. So in these later periods, there is an increasing probability that Barkley managers will reveal their true type to be soft. And in the final period, Barkley managers will definitely reveal they are soft.

Examples of managerial use of reputation building are easily found. From product quality to entry deterrence, corporate culture to honest auditors, these models help explain behavior. For example, long before the recent corporate fraud scandals, game theorists modeled auditing firms as renting their reputations for being honest. The models predicted that any accounting firms involved in fraudulent activities would lose their high-quality reputations, and the value of their names would decrease toward zero. This is exactly what we saw with the implosion of Arthur Andersen after the accounting scandal at Enron.

COORDINATION GAMES

It is often profitable for managers to coordinate actions with others. Although this is certainly true for activity within a firm, it is often also true for market strategy. Managers should always consider the benefits and costs of coordination efforts. Managing a coordination effort is an important managerial task. Managers face many coordination games; it is essential that they understand how payoffs here affect behavior.

Game models represent coordination games as containing more than one Nash equilibrium. Recognizing the Nash equilibria (that is, the outcomes on which managers want to coordinate) is generally not an issue, but choosing which one to select is. We will see that as game parameters change, the impediments to coordination shift slightly. Game theory visualizes these shifts with changes in the payoff structure.

Matching Games

In matching games, players generally prefer the same outcome. However, there may be impediments to reaching this outcome. Impediments may include the inability to communicate, different ideas about how to reach an objective, or asymmetric information. The game we show in Figure 11.13 concerns coordination of product attributes.

This game has two Nash equilibria. We expect one firm to produce for the consumer market and one for the industry. Though 7, 7 is clearly inferior to 12,

FIGURE 11.13

Product Coordination Game

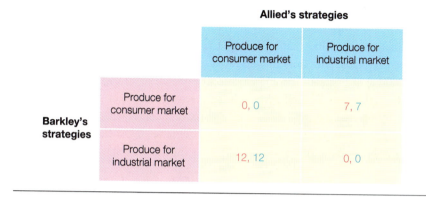

		Allied's strategies	
		Produce for consumer market	Produce for industrial market
Barkley's strategies	Produce for consumer market	0, 0	7, 7
	Produce for industrial market	12, 12	0, 0

12, it is not ruled out as a Nash equilibrium. However, note that both Allied and Barkley prefer a payoff of 12 to that of 7.

Battle of the Sexes

In this coordination game, players still want to coordinate, but they prefer different outcomes. Because of different preferences, each prefers a payoff not favored by the other. If this game is repeated, players often switch between equilibria so that both gain. However, in one-shot games like Figure 11.14, it is more difficult to predict the outcome.

FIGURE 11.14

Battle of the Sexes

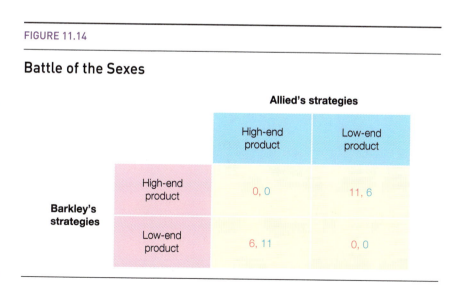

		Allied's strategies	
		High-end product	Low-end product
Barkley's strategies	High-end product	0, 0	11, 6
	Low-end product	6, 11	0, 0

Similar to the matching game, each wants to enter the submarket not entered by the other, but now the payoffs are not equal. Managers at both Allied and Barkley are better off if they produce a high-end product, so it is not clear on which outcome they will coordinate.

Assurance Games

Coordination games like that in Figure 11.15 are also known as stag hunt games. The French philosopher Rosseau tells the story of two hunters (actually poachers) who could coordinate efforts and catch a stag or renege on their agreement and each catch rabbits for himself. Although each prefers to catch the stag, that strategy carries the risk that the other will renege and the first hunter will catch nothing. So players have similar preferences for outcomes but have an associated risk.

Here we model a decision of whether to shift to new standards. Although managers at both firms prefer to shift, there is a risk if one shifts and the other does not. We say the outcome 12,12 is Pareto dominant (both players are better off) but risk dominated (if one chooses to shift and the other does not, the firm shifting receives 0).

First-Mover Games

We can also use coordination games to show the benefits of moving first. Figure 11.16 shows a sequential game in which managers at both firms want to coordinate but each has an incentive to produce a superior product (similar to the battle of the sexes). However, in this game it is possible to move first by speeding up product development. The game shows which firm managers will move first and how much they are willing to pay to speed up the process.

FIGURE 11.15

Stag Hunt or Assurance Game

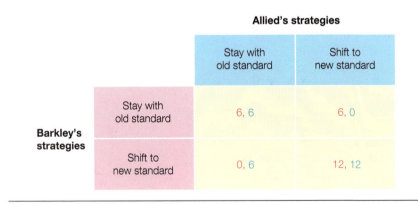

		Allied's strategies	
		Stay with old standard	Shift to new standard
Barkley's strategies	Stay with old standard	6, 6	6, 0
	Shift to new standard	0, 6	12, 12

FIGURE 11.16

First-Mover Advantage

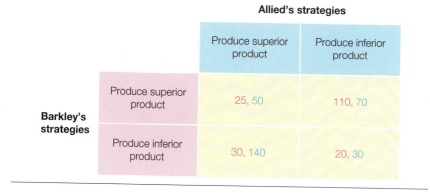

		Allied's strategies	
		Produce superior product	Produce inferior product
Barkley's strategies	Produce superior product	25, 50	110, 70
	Produce inferior product	30, 140	20, 30

In this game, managers at both firms want to introduce the superior product first. There are two Nash equilibria. Allied managers produce a superior product and those at Barkley produce an inferior one, or vice versa. Once one firm produces a superior product, the other is resigned to producing an inferior product. The question is this: Which firm's managers are willing to pay a higher price to produce the superior product? We can answer this question by looking at the incremental benefits of moving first. The incremental benefit to Allied managers of producing the superior product is the difference in payoff between producing the superior product ($140) and the inferior product ($70). This is a difference of $70. The incremental benefit to Barkley managers of moving first is $110 − $30 or $80. We would predict that Barkley will move first because it is willing to spend up to $80 to move first, whereas Allied will spend only up to $70.

Hawks and Doves

This interesting coordination game has been applied to behavior in both human and animal worlds. Assume two players are locked in a conflict. If both players act like hawks, conflict is inevitable. However, if one acts like a hawk and the other backs down (acting like a dove), conflict is avoided. If both are doves, conflict is not even threatened. The game is shown in Figure 11.17.

There are two Nash equilibria; they require one country to act like a hawk and the other to act like a dove. The issue is which country will back down and act like a dove because this country will suffer a lower payoff.

John Maynard Smith applied similar models to the animal kingdom to model when animals will fight each other. One interesting example concerns the behavior

FIGURE 11.17

Hawks and Doves

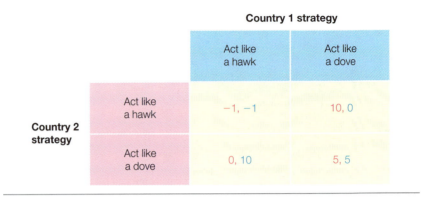

		Country 1 strategy	
		Act like a hawk	Act like a dove
Country 2 strategy	Act like a hawk	−1, −1	10, 0
	Act like a dove	0, 10	5, 5

of spiders in New Mexico. Webs are a scarce commodity within the spider community because they are difficult to build in the desert. However, a female spider needs a web to lay her eggs. Therefore, female spiders fight (or threaten to fight) over existing webs. They do so by approaching a web and violently shaking it. After each shows this force, one spider (the dove) generally leaves the web to the other spider. Rarely do the spiders actually engage in a physical fight. Smith and other biologists noted that certain physical traits account for which spider is the hawk and which is the dove. For the spiders, the two most important traits appear to be incumbency and weight. The heavier spider usually claims the web, whereas the lighter spider backs down. Smith believes that the violent shaking of the web is actually a credible signal of which spider is the heaviest.

STRICTLY COMPETITIVE GAMES

Zero-sum games A competitive game in which any gain by one player means a loss by another player.

The games we have just looked at have mixed motives in the sense that conflict interfaces with mutual dependence. However, some games are strictly competitive: Any gain by one player means a loss by another player. The net gain is always zero; what one gains, the other loses. These games are also known as **zero-sum games**. For example, slow-growth (mature) markets are characterized as zero-sum. Because the market size remains fairly constant, any increase in the share of one firm means an identical decrease in the share of another firm. Figure 11.18 shows one such example.

Zero-sum games are still solvable using Nash equilibria. In Figure 11.18 the Nash equilibrium is for Allied managers to use campaign A and Barkley managers to use campaign 2.

FIGURE 11.18

Advertising Campaigns

		Allied		
		Campaign A	Campaign B	Campaign C
Barkley	Campaign 1	−5, 5	20, −20	−22, 22
	Campaign 2	−3, 3	7, −7	4, −4
	Campaign 3	−4, 4	−6, 6	17, −17

SUMMARY

1. Strategic decisions involve interactive payoffs. Because a player's payoff depends on his or her decision and the decisions of others, that player must anticipate the actions of others in formulating an optimal strategy.

2. Game theory is a mathematical framework that can help managers anticipate the actions of others. The theory helps managers represent strategic issues by focusing on the players involved, their feasible strategies, the possible outcomes, and the payoffs associated with those outcomes.

3. In solving games, managers first need to look for dominant strategies. If they exist, managers need not consider the actions of others. Rational players always play their dominant strategy.

4. If dominant strategies do not exist, managers should try to predict the behavior of others using the solution concept of the Nash equilibrium. This concept assumes that all players do the best they can, conditional on all others doing the best they can. This is the most widely used solution concept in game theory.

5. Managers should use strategic foresight; this is the ability to make decisions today that are rational, conditional on the anticipated future behavior of others. Game theory models this foresight through backward induction. In using backward induction, we go to the end of the game to determine what strategies players will use, then choose an action for the current period that is rational given these future beliefs.

6. Managers must pay attention only to signals that are credible. Game models can determine the credibility of threats, promises, commitments, and the like.

7. Games with a future are called *repeated games.* When a future exists, players may change the strategies they select. Generally speaking, gaining cooperation from others is much easier in a repeated game.

8. Game theorists have developed incomplete information models to look at situations where there is a future and some uncertainty exists about the traits of others. Under these conditions, building a reputation is important because reputations can generate future rents.

9. The ability to coordinate is an important managerial trait. Coordination models help managers better understand the impediments to coordination and the actions necessary to decrease coordination costs.

wwnorton.com/studyspace

PROBLEMS

1. Two soap producers, the Fortnum Company and the Maison Company, can stress either newspapers or magazines in their forthcoming advertising campaigns. The payoff matrix is as follows:

		Maison Company	
		Stress newspapers	Stress magazines
Fortnum Company	Stress newspapers	$8 million, $9 million	$7 million, $8 million
	Stress magazines	$9 million, $8 million	$8 million, $7 million

a. Is there a dominant strategy for each firm? If so, what is it?
b. What will be the profit of each firm?
c. Is this game an example of the prisoner's dilemma?

2. The Ulysses Corporation and the Xenophon Company are the only producers of a sophisticated type of camera. They each can engage in either a high or a low level of advertising in trade journals. The payoff matrix is as follows:

		Xenophon Company	
		Low level	High level
Ulysses Corporation	Low level	$12 million, $13 million	$11 million, $12 million
	High level	$13 million, $12 million	$12 million, $11 million

a. Will Ulysses engage in a high or a low level of advertising in trade journals?

b. Will Xenophon engage in a high or a low level of advertising in trade journals?

c. Is there a dominant strategy for each firm?

3. *The New York Times* reports that Wal-Mart has decided to challenge Netflix and enter the online DVD-by-mail market. Because of economies of scale, Wal-Mart has a slight cost advantage relative to Netflix. Wal-Mart is considering the use of a limit pricing strategy. It can enter the market by matching Netflix on price. If it does, and Netflix maintains its price, then both firms would earn $5 million. But if Netflix drops its price in response, Wal-Mart would have to follow and would earn $2 million; Netflix would earn $3 million. Or Wal-Mart could enter the market with a price that is below Netflix's current price but above its marginal cost. If it does, Netflix would make one of two moves. It could reduce its price to below that of Wal-Mart. If it does, Wal-Mart will earn a profit of $0, and Netflix will earn a profit of $2 million. Or Netflix could keep its present price. If Netflix keeps its present price, Wal-Mart can keep its present price and earn $6 million (while Netflix earns $4 million). Or Wal-Mart can increase its price and earn $2 million while Netflix earns $6 million.

a. Draw the extensive form of this game and solve it.

b. Draw the game's matrix form and identify any Nash equilibria.

4. Two rival bookstores are trying to locate in one of two locations. The locations are near each other. Each would like to avoid a bidding war because that will drive up both of their rents. Payoffs are given in the following table:

		Borders	
		Location 1	Location 2
Barnes and Nobles	**Location 1**	10, 10	60, 40
	Location 2	25, 55	20, 20

Does either player have an incentive to bid higher for a location? If so, by how much?

5. Two soft drink producers, York Cola and Reno Cola, secretly collude to fix prices. Each firm must decide whether to abide by the agreement or to cheat on it. The payoff matrix is as follows:

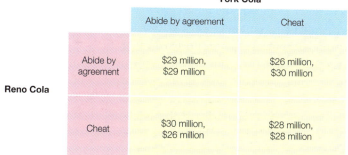

a. What strategy will each firm choose, and what will be each firm's profit?

b. Does it matter whether this agreement is for one period or for three periods?

c. Is this game an example of the prisoner's dilemma?

6. **Part 1:** Firm A currently monopolizes its market and earns profits of $10 million. Firm B is a potential entrant that is thinking about entering the market. If B does not enter the market, it earns profits of $0, while A continues to earn profits of $10 million. If B enters, then A must choose between accommodating entry and fighting it. If A accommodates, then A earns $5 million and B earns $5 million. If A fights, then both firms lose $5 million. **Draw the game in extensive form and predict the outcome.**

   Part 2: Again, consider the above game. Now, suppose the decision of B to enter is reversible in the following way. After B enters the market, and A has decided to either fight or accommodate, B can choose to remain in the market or exit. All payoffs from the above game remain the same. However, if B decides to exit the market, then B suffers a loss of $1 million, while A regains its old profits of $10 million. **Draw the game in extensive form and predict the outcome.**

7. The Rose Corporation is one of two sellers of paint. It pursues a tit-for-tat strategy. However, it has great difficulty in telling whether its rival is secretly cutting its price. What problems is this likely to cause?

8. Consider a father who is trying to discipline his child. The father insists that the child must go with the rest of the family to visit their grandmother. The child prefers to go to the movies with a friend. The father threatens to punish the child if the child doesn't visit the grandmother. If the child goes with the family to visit the grandmother, both the child and the father receive one unit of utility. If the child refuses to go to the grandmother's house, and the father punishes the child, the child receives one unit of utility, and the father receives one unit of utility. If the child refuses to go and the father relents (does not punish), the child receives two units of utility, and the father receives none.

   a. Draw this game in matrix form.

   b. Draw this game in extensive form.

   c. Solve this game via backward induction.

9. The Boca Raton Company announces that if it reduces its price subsequent to a purchase, the early customer will get a rebate so that he or she will pay no more than those buying after the price reduction.

   a. If the Boca Raton Company has only one rival, and if its rival too makes such an announcement, does this change the payoff matrix? If so, in what way?

   b. Do such announcements tend to discourage price cutting? Why or why not?

AUCTIONS

To illustrate the worth of game theory to managerial thinking, let us use it to examine behavior in auctions. All auctions, like markets, are governed by rules and procedures. Managers who understand these rules use them to create strategic advantage; for instance, they design auctions to generate higher profit or they bid more efficiently to capture greater surplus. We focus here on the auction mechanism because this parameter significantly influences behavior in auctions. We also show that managers need not abandon our sophisticated pricing strategies in auction settings. Performance-enhancing strategies like price discrimination are inherent in many auction designs. For the manager, it is a matter of understanding auction design and incentives.

It goes without saying that managers in financial services must understand auction design because this is the heart of financial markets. The growth of auctionlike mechanisms in markets outside the financial realm makes it imperative that all managers understand auction design. In 2007 the total value of goods sold at auction was over $270 billion.[1] This was a growth of 5.3 percent from 2006, which had itself grown by 7.1 percent from 2005. Auction revenues in 2008 were estimated at $278 billion. Managers will also find an understanding of auctions helpful in other areas. We will use the theory to develop behavioral implications for negotiations and monopoly markets.

1. National Auctioneers Association news release: http://www.auctioneers. org/web/2008/01/news_release_ auction_industry_1.aspx.

A SHORT HISTORY OF AUCTIONS

The first written record of an auction was the annual Babylonian marriage market described by the Greek historian Herodotus. The socially aware Babylonians structured the auction to ensure that all women who wanted husbands found them. The most beautiful women were auctioned first, their bidders being the rich who could afford to pay for beauty. Less attractive women then participated in a negative bid auction. The man with the lowest negative bid received the woman at his bid price. This price was then paid from funds generated by the beautiful women. Not only did this ensure that all willing women were married; it also gave the newlyweds financial support.

Auctions were used in ancient Greece to award mineral rights and by Roman authorities to collect debts owed by individuals. Cicero reports a court case in 80 BC involving the auctioning of goods to satisfy a debt. In 1556 the French monarch appointed an officer to appraise and auction all property left by those executed by the state. Pepys reports on a candle auction of 1660. Candle auctions gave bidders a limited time to bid (until the candle burned out); they were the forerunner of today's timed auctions on ebay.

Auctions almost caused a continuation of the War of 1812. During the war, English goods were prohibited from being imported to the United States. The end of the war saw British merchants flooding the United States with goods to satisfy pent-up demand. The goods were sold via auction because of the speed at which goods can be allocated. American manufacturers claimed the British were dumping the goods (selling them below cost) and tried to get the auctions outlawed. Newspapers and U.S. trade organizations led a spirited fight to have state legislatures abolish auctions. The fight extended to the U.S. Congress, where the Ways and Means Committee introduced a bill to ban auctions. Fortunately Congress never passed it.

Although markets grew more quickly than auctions, auctions played a major role in allocating fruits and vegetables, fish, furs, tobacco, and livestock. By the 1980s auctions were used to sell over $5 billion of goods yearly.

Auction use continued to increase and virtually exploded in the late 1990s with the increase in e-commerce. The Internet is to auctions what mass retailing is to posted prices: a highly productive marriage of technology and allocation mechanism. Internet auction use can significantly decrease organizational costs. In most auctions, if a manager is the seller, the more buyers the merrier (this idea is shown formally later in the chapter). Expected revenue does not decrease with increases in the number of bidders. So any technology that decreases the costs of bringing individuals together should increase auction use.

TYPES OF AUCTION MECHANISMS

All auctions involve a bidding process. In most auctions, a service or product is made available and buyers bid for the ownership rights. Reverse auctions occur when a buyer announces the need for a product or service and sellers bid for the right to sell the buyer the good or service (and the low bidder wins the auction). Whether using a normal or reverse auction, managers primarily use one of four auction mechanisms: the English or ascending-bid auction; the Dutch or descending-bid auction; the sealed-bid auction; and the second-price, sealed-bid auction.

English or Ascending-Bid Auction

In English auctions, the initial price is set at the seller's reservation price (called the **reserve price**). Buyers then bid against each other with a succession of higher prices until one bidder remains. This final bidder receives the good or service at his or her final stated price. There are several ways to manage this bidding procedure. An auctioneer can orally call out bids; bidders signal their acceptance of the price with a shake of their heads or a wave of their bidding cards. This method is used often by large auction houses like Christie's and Sotheby's. Another method is for bidders themselves to call out their bids. This method is used in many commodity exchanges. Individual commodities are assigned their own area, called a pit; traders of a commodity gather in the pit and call out the price at which they are willing to buy (sell) the commodity. If others wish to sell (buy) at that price, they do so. However, these pits are increasingly being replaced by more efficient electronic auctions. *The New York Times* reports that the percentage of pit trades in livestock commodities declined from roughly 90 percent of total trades in 2000 to 22 percent in 2007.[2] During this time, electronic markets hastened the closing of commodity pits in Chicago, Hong Kong, London, Sydney, and Tokyo. Exchange operators find that digital auctions have lower operating costs and generate more revenue.

Two special types of the ascending-bid auction are the Japanese auction and the ascending-bid timed auction. Much theoretical work has centered on the **Japanese auction**, in which bidders bid until the price exceeds their reservation price. They then drop out of the bidding process and do not return. Remaining bidders can thus determine who has dropped out and who remains. In the **ascending-bid timed auction**, the bidding continues for a specified time. The high bidder at the end of this period receives the good or service (assuming the bid is greater than the seller's reserve price). These timed auctions are used extensively by Internet auction sites.

A nice example of how managers influence behavior through auction design is shown in behavior at the ascending-bid auction sites of ebay and uBid. ebay managers have chosen to end auctions at preannounced times. This choice encourages the practicing of **sniping**: Bidders use programs to ensure that they submit a last-second best bid. Many times this is their only bid. uBid managers also announce a predetermined ending time. However, they use a different rule to end the auction: Auctions at uBid continue as long as there are new bids. Sniping merely extends the time the market is open; the uBid rules blunt its effectiveness as a strategy.

Reserve price The lowest price at which a seller is willing to sell a product; also called a reservation price.

Japanese auction Auction in which bidders bid until the price exceeds their reservation price.

Ascending-bid timed auction Auction in which the bidding continues for a specified time.

Sniping When bidders use programs to ensure that they submit a last-second best bid.

2. Niko Koppel, "In Chicago, a Rowdy Trading Scene Grows Quieter," *The New York Times*, October 29, 2007.

Dutch or Descending-Bid Auction

In Dutch auctions, initial prices are set very high. A price is announced and a set time passes (for example, 15 seconds). If no bidder accepts the good at that price, the price is lowered by a set interval (for example, a euro) and the procedure repeats itself. The price is lowered until one bidder accepts the announced price. A descending-bid system is often called a **Dutch auction** because it is used to sell flowers in the Netherlands, where auction halls larger than 10 football fields are used daily to auction thousands of flowers. Current offered prices are shown on a large screen, and bidders accept the prices by pushing electronic buttons. The process is very quick with over 500 transactions every hour.

Dutch auction A descending-bid system in which initial prices are set very high and are lowered by set intervals until accepted by bidders.

Sealed-Bid Auction

In these auctions, bidders submit price bids known only to themselves. So unlike an English auction, bidders do not know the valuations of others. In a first-price, sealed-bid auction, bids are opened at a preannounced time, and the highest bidder receives the item at his or her stated price. Reverse sealed-bid auctions are often used to procure goods and services. A state agency may submit a bid for highway construction, with the winning bidder being the one with the lowest bid.

Second-Price, Sealed-Bid Auction

This auction is a variant of the sealed-bid type. In a second-price auction, the highest bidder receives the good or service at the bid price of the second-highest bidder. These auctions are also called **Vickrey auctions** after William Vickrey, who wrote a seminal paper on the subject in the 1960s, which later led to his winning the 1996 Nobel Prize in economics. As we will see, second-price auctions have characteristics conducive to bidders truthfully revealing their valuations.

Vickrey auctions Second-price, sealed-bid auctions in which the highest bidder received the good or service at the bid price of the second-highest bidder.

AUCTION MECHANISM AND REVENUE GENERATION

Similar to market settings, in auctions, managers want to maximize profit. And just as differences in structural parameters like differentiation, entry barriers, and location explain variance in market power (and profitability), auction rules explain variance in generated revenues. An advantage of auctions is that relative to markets, it is easier (and less costly) for managers to influence structural parameters through auction rules. Hence it pays for managers to recognize how auction design influences revenues. We examine the effect of auction rules on revenue by first looking at a simplified model. We then relax some model assumptions to show how rules affect expected revenue.

Our baseline case assumes that bidders are symmetric and risk-neutral, and bids are based on independent signals drawn from a commonly known distribution. The behavioral implications of these assumptions follow:

- **Bidders are symmetric.** Think of a bidder as selecting a valuation (bid) from a distribution of possible bids. Symmetric bidders use similar distributions, commonly known to all. So bidders with identical reservation prices and observing the same signal submit equivalent bids. We emphasize that (as in the real world) differences in reservation prices across bidders are not constrained by this symmetry.
- **Bidders are risk-neutral.** That is, bidders bid to maximize expected values and not risk-adjusted utility. Most managers assume that individuals are risk-averse; however, evidence shows that when individuals decide as corporate agents, behavior can resemble that of risk neutrality. That said, we later show how risk-averse bidders can be strategically exploited.
- **Signals are independent.** Signals are independent in one of two ways. In **private-value auctions**, reservation prices are a function of information and utility. Because signals depend on the information space, valuation is constrained to one's own signal. Say a manager is standing next to another at an auction. Are differences in how the two value a painting a function of their own personal experience, or does what one knows (but is unknown by the other) affect the latter's valuation? The former condition sounds more plausible. This describes a private-value auction with independent signals.

In **common-value auctions**, all bidders value the good similarly. What is not known, though, is the true value of the good for which they bid. Consider the rights for minerals under a piece of land. Whatever is down there is worth about the same for all (given worldwide commodity markets), but no one knows perfectly what is there. So each bidder measures and forms beliefs about the true value. If signals are independent, then what one manager estimates does not depend on the estimates of others, although the distribution of signals is commonly known.

For any auction format, let b = bid and p = price paid by the auction winner. Expected profit is simply $(b - p)(Pr_W)$, with Pr_W = the probability of winning the auction, conditioned on bid level. Because managers want to maximize profit, optimal bids depend on valuations (reservation prices). Therefore, the expected profit for any b, Pr_W combination is given by

$$U(Pr_W, b, p) = (Pr_W)(b - p)$$

Compare these profit functions across auction formats to determine how surplus $(b - p)$ is split between buyer and seller. We show the slope of the profit function equals the conditional probability of winning for any given bid. So auction formats with identical surplus functions (conditioned on valuation) offer the same probability of winning at any given bid and hence recommend the same optimal strategies.

This relationship is the foundation for what is called the **revenue equivalence theorem**. The theorem shows that whether a manager chooses an English, Dutch,

Private-value auctions Auctions in which reservation prices are a function of information and utility.

Common-value auctions Auctions in which all bidders value the good similarly.

Revenue equivalence theorem Theorem showing that whether a manager chooses an English, Dutch, sealed-bid, or second-price, sealed-bid auction, the choice does not affect the auction's expected total surplus and hence does not affect the expected revenues.

sealed-bid, or second-price, sealed-bid auction, the choice does not affect the auction's expected total surplus and hence does not affect the expected revenues. The theorem even extends to other auction formats. As long as the format ensures an efficient allocation of goods and gives zero profit to any bidder holding zero value ($0) for the good, the surplus functions are identical, and so are the recommended bidding strategies across formats. For example, lobbying efforts can be modeled as an "all-pay" auction. All bidders pay for the good, but only the highest bidder receives it. Because this auction satisfies the stated conditions, its expected surplus is the same as any of the four standard auction formats.

BIDDING STRATEGIES

What are the optimal bidding strategies across the four auction formats? Of the four standard formats, only English auctions let bidders learn more about the reservation prices of others. In the sealed-bid format, bids of others are not revealed until after the bidding is closed. In Dutch auctions, once a bidder reveals his or her reservation price (by accepting the current price), the auction is over. But because of the ascending nature of the English auction and the public nature of bidding, bidders learn more about the reservation prices of others. Unfortunately this information is of limited value to the strategic bidder because optimal behavior is defined by a dominant strategy. And remember, good strategists do not worry about the behavior of others in using a dominant strategy because it lacks strategic value. Thus the optimal behavior in an ascending auction never changes: Managers should always be willing to bid up to their reservation prices.

If used, this guideline maximizes profit $(b - p)$. Clearly managers should never bid above their reservation prices. The maximum profit from this strategy is zero, and managers will suffer a negative profit if theirs is the winning bid. Managers do not want to bid higher than necessary because profit decreases with a bid increase. The winner in an ascending auction has to pay only the slightest bit (that is, epsilon) higher than the reservation price of the second-highest bidder. Bids significantly higher than this are inefficient (and suggest badly trained managers). The difference between the reservation prices of the top and second-highest bidders defines available surplus and therefore profit. If managers want to maximize profit, they must capture all available surplus.

The auction's dominant strategy helps managers reduce the complexity of strategic thought. Consider this strategy as a decision rule: Managers listen to any bid. If the bid is lower than their reservation price, they bid incrementally higher. If the bid is higher, they do not bid. The simplicity of the procedure highlights one component of a dominant strategy's value: process efficiencies. Managers need not consider what others might do in choosing an optimal strategy. So managers can focus (and simplify) the strategic effort, trusting the completeness of dominance.

In any ascending-price auction managers should bid to their reservation prices. If all follow this strategy, the good is sold at the reservation price of the second-highest bidder (actually at an epsilon higher). It is sold to the highest bidder, and his or her expected revenue is the total available surplus, defined as the reservation price differential between the two highest-valuation bidders.

So in an ascending auction, the highest bidder claims the item at the reservation price of the second-highest bidder. We previously noted that this is the same prediction of Vickrey auctions. Thus both English and second-price, sealed-bid auctions are ruled by the same dominant strategy. Though the two auctions differ in process, game theorists predict similar results. Of course the former format is more transparent than the latter.

We now see how the difference in bidding rules affects behavior. In English auctions, the rules allow managers to publicly bid multiple times; in a sealed-bid auction, they bid once privately. English auctions let managers respond to the bids of others; sealed-bid auctions do not. Because managers in a sealed-bid auction have only one chance to bid, they should bid their reservation prices. In both auctions, negative payoffs are nonexistent because zero becomes the manager's worst possible payoff. And the bidder who wins is guaranteed all available surplus. So while the dominant strategy is the same across formats (managers should bid to their reservation prices), the bidding rules of the second-price, sealed-bid auction require different behavior. When auctions have dominant strategies, managers should not worry about others (it achieves nothing); they should focus on their own preferences, think hard about their reservation prices, and then bid them.

Second-price, sealed-bid auctions are a good example of how auction rules influence bidding behavior. The rules in these auctions encourage all bidders to tell the truth. In fact, managers are better off if they tell the truth. In a later discussion we call such rules **incentive-compatible**. This type of rule encourages managers to reveal their true preferences.

Incentive-compatible Type of rule that encourages managers to reveal their true preferences.

Next consider the descending (Dutch) and first-price, sealed-bid auctions. Although the two operate with different bidding rules, they are strategically similar. In fact, consider them identical twins that behave differently. If we model them in their reduced normal or matrix form, they have identical strategy sets and payoffs. That is, any given bid yields the same payoff in either auction, as a function of the bids of others. And unlike the ascending or second-price formats, neither has a dominant strategy. In the Dutch or first-price, sealed-bid auctions, managers must consider what others will bid. Let us see how this design affects a manager's bid choice.

As explained earlier, bidders learn little about the valuations of others in either of these first-price auctions because bids are private until the auction is completed. But because bidders are symmetric, all know the distribution of valuations. This information lets managers estimate the bidding strategy of others. Note that it does not give them the ability to predict the bids of others—just what others would bid conditional on some privately known information.

Each bidder faces an identical decision. If a bid is not the highest, managers receive and pay nothing, so the surplus is zero. If they bid their reservation price and that bid is the highest, the surplus is still zero. A bid higher than their reservation price results in zero surplus (if the manager is lucky and loses the auction) or negative surplus if the manager wins. Managers believe there is some positive probability that their bids are the highest. So the question is this: How should managers structure their bids?

Unlike the previous auctions with dominant strategy, the set of possible strategies approaches infinity in the descending and first-price, sealed-bid auctions. Managers now must consider what others will bid. Bidding strategies become conditional on the bidding strategies of others. The world becomes more complex.

So how do managers reduce the complexity? If all bidders face the same complexity, can bidders help themselves via some constraint on bidding behavior? Economists believe they can by being rational. Rational players consider only those outcomes in which each player maximizes, given the actions of others. Remember that auction payoffs depend on the actions of all. And unless all managers are choosing their best strategies, given the actions of others, why would any one manager agree to do this? If we adopt this rule that all managers are rational, no individual has an incentive to cheat by changing strategy.

As explained in Chapter 11, in Nash equilibria, all correctly anticipate the actions of others and choose actions that maximize expected surplus. This reduces feasible strategies to a handful and allows managers to focus on fewer scenarios. We note that the Nash concept does not guarantee high payoffs for all. It simply states that given the attributes of an individual and those of others, each individual is maximizing his or her payoff.

So how should managers bid in these auctions according to Nash? Managers clearly should not bid their reservation prices. If they do, their highest possible payoff is zero. Nash assumes that managers will think about their reservation prices and discount backward. The discount should approximate their expectations of the reservation price of the second-highest bidder. Each manager will then bid an epsilon higher than this belief. Then, if her bid is the highest, she receives positive surplus; if it is not, she receives nothing. As in the ascending and second-price auctions, managers must consider their own reservation prices; but they also must consider what others will bid and base their bids on this expectation. So the decision rule for managers in these auctions is to estimate the reservation price of the second-highest bidder and bid epsilon higher.

Managerial beliefs about the reservation prices of second-highest bidders are influenced by many factors. One significant factor that should affect beliefs is the number of bidders. As the number of bidders increases, managers need to bid closer to their reservation prices. That is, increased competition reduces expected surplus in these auctions. We can be even more precise if we assume the distribution of bids is uniform. Then the optimal bidding strategy for managers is

$$b = v - \left[\left(\frac{v - L}{n}\right)\right]$$

where v is the bidder's reservation price, L is the lowest possible bid, and n is the number of bidders. For example, assume our own valuation of an item is $3, and we believe the bids will be evenly distributed between $0 and $15. Then our optimal bid if there is only one other bidder is

$$b = 3 - \left[\left(\frac{3 - 0}{2}\right)\right] = \$1.50$$

If there are two other bidders, our optimal bid is

$$b = 3 - \left[\left(\frac{3 - 0}{3}\right)\right] = \$2.00$$

And so we end where we began. In theory, the auction design should not affect expected revenue. The optimal response of bidders in each of the four designs produces the same expected revenue. Managers should bid up to their reservation prices in ascending and second-price auctions because the rules say that if they are the high bidder, they pay only the reservation price of the second-highest bidder. In descending and first-price, sealed auctions, managers consider their reservation prices and then discount back to what they believe are the reservation prices of the second-highest bidders.

STRATEGIES FOR SELLERS

Now we turn to sellers. These days many managers use auctions to sell goods, services, and assets. In these circumstances, good managerial decisions follow the standard economic rule: Maximize profit with marginal revenue equal to marginal cost. Of course some adjustments for the bidding rules must be made.

In markets, managers want to produce where $MR = MC$. This is a quantity decision that determines the pricing point. But auctions are used to sell items few in quantity (often one). The notion of quantity holds little strategic value when quantity is so limited. What determines the optimal pricing point is the distribution of reservation prices across bidders. Therefore managers want to focus on this distribution.

This is a subtle but important difference realized by the strategic manager. Consider an ascending auction. Managerial action in this format is similar to third-degree price discrimination in markets. Recall that efficient allocation is defined as the equality of marginal revenues across markets (the infamous $P_1/P_2 = [1 + (1/\eta_2)]/[1 + (1/\eta_1)]$. That is, managers maximize profit by ensuring the sale to the consumers who value the product or service the most. Total output is determined by the horizontal summation of the marginal revenue curves and its intersection with marginal cost (see Figure 12.1).

Sellers want to use a similar strategy in auctions. Consider an auction selling a unique item. The manager maximizes profit by selling to the bidder with the highest reservation price. Because the seller's marginal costs remain constant for any change in price, the higher the winning bid, the greater the surplus. The expected revenue generated by a given price is simply that price times the probability that it is the winning bid. This, of course, is determined by the distribution of reservation prices across bidders. Consider bidder i and the distribution $F(b)$. Given $F(b)$, we determine the probability that any bid b is the winning bid. This is simply $1 - F(b)$, as shown in Figure 12.1. Function b acts as a demand curve in the following way. Each point on b suggests the probability of that point being the winning bid. So if

---

FIGURE 12.1

Relationship between the Seller's Expected Revenue and the Winning Bidder's Expected Marginal Revenue

If b^* is the winning bid, the seller's expected revenue is equal to the shaded box. This is also equal to the expected marginal revenue of the bidder.

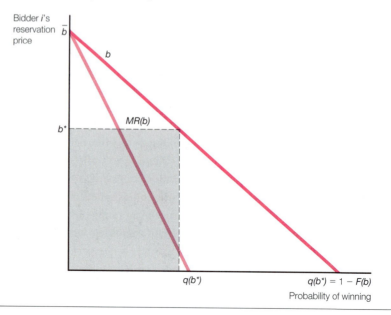

the seller were to offer the item at price b, we could predict the expected demand at b. Expected revenue then would be $b[1 - F(b)]$ or the area under the marginal revenue function for any b. Let b^* be the actual winning bid (the reservation price of the second-highest bidder). Mathematically, we can show that b^* represents the expected revenue to the seller and the expected marginal revenue to the winning bidder. That is, in ascending-bid auctions, they are equal.

What does this mean to the seller? As in third-degree price discrimination markets, managers need to sell to high-reservation-price bidders (buyers). And because they want to maximize surplus in both situations, they definitely cannot sell at any price below marginal cost. In auctions, consider marginal cost as the value at which the seller refuses to sell. This is the price at which the seller says, "If that's all others are willing to pay, I'll keep it myself." So sellers need to set a reserve price (or begin the bidding at their reserve price) for the auction. This reserve price should be the bid at which the bidder's marginal revenue is equal to the seller's marginal cost. (Recall that the bidder's marginal revenue is also equal to the auction's expected revenue.) Hence, under general conditions, managers should consider the following decision rule in setting a reserve price:

Optimal reserve price = The value of the object being auctioned off, if it does
not sell + (Managerial estimates of the highest reservation price divided by 2)

For example, if the object's value is zero if it is not sold, and a manager believes the highest reservation price is $300, he or she should set a reserve price of $150. After that, sellers should sit back and relax. Let the ascending-bid mechanism work to maximize the expected surplus. Unlike monopoly pricing, but similar to third-degree price discrimination, auctions are often more efficient than a posted-price scheme. In contrast to a posted-price scheme, auctions guarantee the highest reservation price purchase the good. Note that the managerial similarity to third-degree price discrimination is not confined to ascending auctions. All formats that are revenue equivalent to ascending auctions share this feature. The following example illustrates the efficiency of auctions.

Assume a seller has four units of output at a marginal cost of $0. The market has six consumers with reservation prices of $90, $60, $50, $40, $20, and $15. Table 12.1 shows the total available surplus broken down into consumer and seller surplus if the seller uses an auction. Table 12.2 shows the total surplus if the seller posts a $40 price.

At any posted price other than $40, the total available surplus decreases. And while the available surplus remains constant with a price of $40, relative to an auction, sellers get a lower percentage of this by using a posted price ($160 versus $174). Auction usage increases seller surplus because of its price discriminatory property. The mechanism itself gets consumers to reveal their reservation prices.

FreeMarkets.com was one of the largest business-to-business (B2B) auction services when it was purchased by Ariba in 2004. Ariba has integrated the software into its sourcing solutions program. Auctions are held for goods and services in over 190 supply verticals on a global basis. Firms, including Emerson Electric and Eaton Corp., use the Ariba/FreeMarkets auction service as part of their purchasing process and report significant savings. For example, managers at global giant GlaxoSmithKline estimate cost savings of 10 percent. How does Ariba achieve such results?

The company combines Web-based software, in-

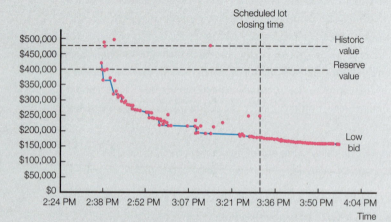

Lot summary	
Number of bidders:	16
Number of bids:	118
Historic value:	$481 thousand
Reserve value:	$397 thousand
Low bid:	$159 thousand
Potential savings:	$332 thousand (66.9%)
Savings in overtime:	$31 thousand (6.4%)

depth supply market information, market operations, and expert sourcing services to create value-added markets for its customers. Let us examine more closely how managers fashion markets to generate cost savings for customers.

Ariba's e-source technology is designed to meet the needs of large industrial customers, many with global operations. These buyers use Ariba to conduct real-time interactive auctions with selected suppliers. The auction format is that of descending price. Suppliers bid for the right to supply, generally, with the low bidder declared the winner (see the chart). The company identifies several areas of expertise: coordination, design, and services.

AUCTION COORDINATION

All online markets are controlled from a central location; this guarantees that the markets operate correctly during bidding. Ariba reduces software learning costs by using easily understood graphics and giving first-time bidders simulated trading sessions prior to the actual auction. Support is given to all bidders during auctions (in over 30 languages).

Ariba managers develop and enforce auction rules. For example, trade in many industrial markets is decided by factors other than low cost, like quality control or delivery logistics. Ariba managers work with buyers to determine the qualifications of the bidding pool. Its managers talk with those in the buying organizations about specifications, logistics, and quality. For example, all bidders could be required to be ISO-9000 certified and able to deliver within five days. Then Ariba handles bidder certification. This reduces the transaction costs to the buyer and the risk that winning (low-cost) suppliers cannot deliver promised supplies. This certification feature also helps bidders decide whether an auction is suited to their resource base.

Ariba managers have created a customer care center for all auctions. Here bidders can find such services as surrogate bidding. By agreeing to act as if they were a bidder's agent, Ariba managers reduce the transaction costs of bidders.

AUCTION DESIGN

The auction software is flexible to address the unique needs of different industrial markets. For example, some auctions are of the multicurrency type. This feature helps reduce the risks to both seller and buyer of currency fluctuations during a long-term contract. The software is also easy to integrate into a buyer's ERP/MRP system, which reduces the switching costs of buyers.

AUCTION SERVICES

Ariba managers give advice to buyers about optimal auction lotting, strategies, and design. They identify, recruit, and screen potential suppliers, ensuring that only qualified suppliers compete in the auction. Buyers are given postauction briefings by Ariba managers to analyze results and suggest changes for the future. Ariba has a global network of over 150,000 registered suppliers in 70 countries. It also supplies filters for searching its supplier database and maintains performance statistics for all suppliers.

Source: Ariba OnLine, Inc., 2008.

TABLE 12.1

Auction

Consumers	Reservation Price	Winning Bid
1	$40	$21
2	20	
3	15	
4	90	61
5	60	51
6	50	41
Total consumer surplus		66
Total seller surplus		174
Total available surplus		240

TABLE 12.2

Posted Price

Consumers	Reservation Price	Price Paid
1	$40	$40
2	20	
3	15	
4	90	40
5	60	40
6	50	40
Total consumer surplus		80
Total seller surplus		160
Total available surplus		240

VALUE OF INFORMATION

The preference-revealing nature of auctions not only guarantees buyers with the highest reservation prices purchase the good or service; it also gets buyers to identify themselves when the demand is unknown. Managers can use auctions to gather more information about demand before announcing prices.

Repurchase Tender Offers

An example of this use of auctions is **repurchase tender offers (RTOs)**. An RTO is used by managers to buy back stock shares from current shareholders. Because shareholders are not required to sell, to induce selling, RTOs generally offer a premium above the current market price. Until 1981 just about every RTO was fixed in price. Managers would announce the buyback price per share and wait to see shareholder demand at that price. Since 1981 modified Dutch auction RTOs have been the mechanism of managerial choice. And it is easy to see why: Relative to a fixed-price RTO, the modified Dutch variety generally acquires shares at a lower total cost. Several studies show that the average premium paid for fixed-price tendered shares is 15 to 20 percent, whereas those in modified Dutch auctions average 10 to 15 percent.

Unlike a fixed-price RTO, where one price is announced, in a modified Dutch one, managers announce a price range at which they are willing to repurchase tendered shares. Generally the minimum price is set at a slight premium over market, while the maximum approaches that of a fixed-price RTO. Any shareholder willing to tender reveals his or her valuations as the seller sends managers a pricing schedule (how many shares to tender at $X). Managers use the schedules of individual shareholders to construct a market supply schedule. They then determine how many shares they need and set the share price. All sellers who value the shares below that price receive the stated price. Again, note the timing differential between the fixed-price and modified Dutch auction RTOs. In the fixed-price offer, managers set a price before knowing the supply schedule; in the modified Dutch auction, they set the price after seeing the supply schedule.

Citizens First Financial Corp. (CFFC) is a savings and loan holding company with headquarters in Bloomington, Illinois. The company has roughly $325 million in assets. Its managers wanted to repurchase 391,000 shares of its stock from shareholders. On October 31, 2000, managers announced a modified Dutch auction RTO. (The share price that day was $14.) They set a price range of $15 to $17 per share—a premium above the market of 7.1 to 21.4 percent. Shareholders had until December 1 to tender their shares. On December 11, 2000, CFFC managers announced they had purchased 391,096 shares at a price of $16 (a premium of 14.3 percent above the market).

Let's look at the situation as CFFC managers may have viewed it. Many times managers repurchase shares because they believe the stock is undervalued. An RTO is used by managers to distribute company value to shareholders. RTOs annually distribute over $4 billion to shareholders. Assume CFFC managers believe their stock will be worth $20 per share in the near future. They want to buy back some shares now but do not know the valuations of shareholders. After stating their beliefs, managers construct Table 12.3 to summarize them. It shows how many shares will be tendered at different prices in three possible supply scenarios—strong, medium, and weak—and the gener-

Repurchase tender offers Offer used by managers to buy back stock shares from current shareholders.

TABLE 12.3

Shareholder Supply Schedule

Price	Strong # of Shares	Profit	Medium # of Shares	Profit	Weak # of Shares	Profit
$15	400,000	$2,000,000	310,000	$1,550,000	280,000	$1,400,000
16	415,000	1,660,000	400,000	1,600,000	315,000	1,260,000
17	600,000	1,800,000	415,000	1,245,000	400,000	1,200,000
Probability of shareholder's willingness to tender						
	0.40		0.30		0.30	

STRATEGY SESSION: The Use of Sophisticated Pricing within an Auction Format

Priceline.com is a good example of how managers can use sophisticated pricing policies within an auction format. The company was launched in April 1998 after Priceline managers helped develop software for a computer reservation system. The software allowed airline managers to make real-time adjustments to prices based on various factors, like unoccupied seats or competitor prices. Each airline sees only its own prices, but managers at Priceline can see prices across all member airlines.

Airline seats are perishable goods: Once the plane departs, empty seats are worthless because they cannot be used again. And the marginal cost of flying a plane with one more passenger is almost zero, so any price is profitable for the airline. As Brian Ek of Priceline.com states, "The airlines fly with up to 700,000 empty seats a day. Naturally they would love to sell those seats if they could without affecting their retail fare structure." Priceline.com developed an auc-tion mechanism to allow airlines to do just that. The company has sold over 5 million airline tickets since 1998.

Priceline.com uses a reverse auction mecha-nism. In reverse auctions, buyers name the price they are willing to pay for a good or service. The seller then decides whether to accept or reject this price. Price-line's auction operates as follows: A consumer speci-fies a departure date, the departing and destination airports, the price the consumer is willing to pay for a ticket, and a credit card number. All sales are final. If Priceline finds a ticket at or below that price, the consumer is obligated to purchase it. After receiving a consumer's price, Priceline examines its database to determine if any airline is offering tickets at or below that price. If there are tickets, Priceline buys them. The profit to Priceline is the difference between what the consumer is willing to pay for the ticket and the price Priceline was charged.

ated value associated with each price–supply scenario. The profit equals the difference between a tender price and the expected future value of $20.

If managers choose a fixed-price RTO, they must set the price before knowing the supply schedule. They might choose a price based on an expected value (*EV*):

$EV(\$15) = \$2{,}000{,}000(0.40) + \$1{,}550{,}000(0.30) + \$1{,}400{,}000(0.30) = \$1{,}685{,}000$

$EV(\$16) = \$1{,}660{,}000(0.40) + \$1{,}600{,}000(0.30) + \$1{,}260{,}000(0.30) = \$1{,}522{,}000$

$EV(\$17) = \$1{,}800{,}000(0.40) + \$1{,}245{,}000(0.30) + \$1{,}200{,}000(0.30) = \$1{,}453{,}500$

If CFFC managers had used such an analysis, they might have set a tender price of $15.

How might managers have increased firm value by structuring the RTO as a modified Dutch auction? If they used the auction, they would not select a tender price without knowing the supply schedule. What was the expected value

Although Priceline claims it has increased the market power of consumers (because they are free to name their own prices), many disagree with this claim. Basically Priceline's reverse auction allows airlines to practice price discrimination. Like airlines, Priceline sells tickets on the same airplane at different prices depending on the prices quoted by consumers. Say I submit a price of $300 for a ticket from New York to Chicago. If my friend submits a price of $250, she would buy an identical product at a cheaper price (assuming airlines were willing to sell tickets for $250). Priceline's reverse auction gets consumers to name their reservation prices, and Priceline then charges them these prices. So the reverse auction does not guarantee that consumers receive a product at the lowest price; it simply gives them the chance to purchase a product at their reservation prices.

Priceline's price-discriminating auction also improves on traditional price discrimination schemes by making discounts less transparent to both consumers and rivals. Airlines need not post any special rates, which reduces the probability that rivals could engage in a disastrous price war. Also, the company can practice price discrimination selectively. For example, there is some evidence that Priceline will accept lower prices from first-time customers. When those consumers subsequently bid the same price for the same product, they find their bids are rejected.

Airlines that work with Priceline also receive demand information that helps them in their pricing decisions. The company compiles all bidding information (both successful and unsuccessful) and gives this information to airlines weekly. As Ek states, "They can see all of the demand, every consumer's price offer for every route, going all the way down to $1. . . . It's a great way for the airlines to privately move more inventory that was likely to go unsold through their retail sales channels."

of the auction strategy? We use expected value because when CFFC managers announced the Dutch RTO on October 11, they did not know the supply schedule. So, if the willingness to tender was strong, they would announce a price of $15; if it was medium, they would announce a price of $16; and if it was weak, a price of $15 would be set. Hence the expected value of a modified Dutch auction RTO would be

$$EV(\text{auction}) = \$2{,}000{,}000(0.40) + \$1{,}600{,}000(0.30) + \$1{,}400{,}000(0.30)$$
$$= \$1{,}700{,}000$$

Managers are generally better off using a modified Dutch auction RTO. They get shareholders to reveal their valuations and hence can buy back shares at a lower price than if they used a fixed price. This creates value for the remaining shareholders because some shares are retired at a lower cost. And the expected number of shares tendered is

$$0.4(400{,}000) + 0.3(400{,}000) + 0.3(280{,}000) = 364{,}000$$

RISK AVERSION

As we will see in Chapter 13, most individuals are risk-averse. What are the effects of risk aversion on bidding behavior? In second-price auctions, risk preferences do not influence bidding strategy. Bidders in these auctions should always bid up to their reservation prices. However, risk preference affects bidding behavior in first-price auctions.

Consider the choices facing a risk-averse bidder in a first-price auction. The prevailing uncertainty is this: Will my bid win the auction? Because first-price auctions have no dominant strategies, managers must anticipate the bids of others and hence can only partially control this uncertainty. Their controlling mechanism is the bid price itself. A higher bid increases the probability of winning; a risk-averse bidder will pay to avoid loss, so he or she simply raises the bid by some amount of "bidding insurance." Thus risk-averse people bid higher than risk-neutral bidders. Their rush toward certainty is tempered, however, because higher bids also reduce the surplus.

If bidders are risk-averse, risk-neutral managers can increase performance through the use of auction rules. If bidders are likely to be risk-averse, then managers should use a first-price auction to capture profit generated by risk preference differences.

What if the roles were reversed—bidders are risk-neutral and sellers are risk-averse? How should this affect managerial actions? Here too the seller prefers first-price auctions. Although we know that the expected revenues from the four auction formats are equal, there is more risk in second-price auctions. That is, even though the revenue distribution means are equal, there is greater spread in possible revenues for second-price auctions. Because risk-averse managers prefer to avoid risk, they should use first-price auctions.

NUMBER OF BIDDERS

We have seen that in all auction formats, the expected bid is given by the reservation price of the second-highest bidder. Therefore managers should consider actions to increase these prices, just as they do in market settings. One possible variable that seems easily controlled is the number of bidders.

Consider how markets work. As the number of sellers increases (other factors held constant), the equilibrium price is pushed downward toward the marginal cost (or the seller's reservation price). And in perfectly competitive markets, the long-run equilibrium price is identical to the marginal cost. These markets have many sellers offering the same good or service to consumers. Auctions are the reverse of this: many buyers and one (or few) sellers. What works on the supply side also works on the demand side. The entry of more bidders (buyers) into a market must push the demand curve rightward and hence increase the price. So the more bidders a manager can induce to enter the auction, the greater is the expected surplus.

Are 1,000,001 bidders better than 1,000,000? No, that is not quite the case, although it may be true. Auctions are efficient under most conditions, so even a moderate number of bidders will make the seller's revenue approach the expected maximum valuation (conditioned on the probability function). Managers do not want to pay much to attract the 1,000,000th bidder to an auction, but the first 20 or so are important. The following example assumes the reservation prices of bidders are uniformly distributed, with the highest price being $100. A seller's expected revenue in English auctions is then given by

$$b = [(N - 1)/(N + 1)](\text{Mean reservation price of bidders})$$

where $N =$ the number of bidders. Figure 12.2 shows how a seller's expected revenue increases as the number of bidders increases.

FIGURE 12.2

Expected Revenue versus Number of Bidders

As the number of bidders increases, the expected revenue of the seller increases.

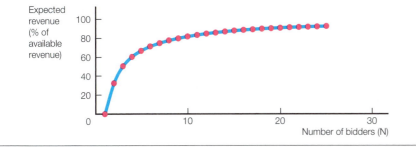

Intuitively, the expected revenue of the seller increases because of the greater competition caused by additional bidders. In placing bids, managers must consider the trade-off between the probability of winning the auction and the level of surplus (reservation price − bid price) they will realize. A lower bid results in higher surplus but a decreased probability of winning: One loses an auction if only one person bids higher. As more bidders join the auction the probability of someone bidding higher increases quickly. Hence as more bidders join the auction, bids must approach the reservation prices of bidders (and seller revenue increases). Note too that a seller's expected revenue approaches its maximal level with fewer than 30 bidders.

WINNER'S CURSE

In some auctions the value of the object or service being auctioned off is not known with certainty, although it has a common value to all bidders. For example, the U.S. government auctions the mineral rights to tracts of federally owned land. When the seller uses a sealed-bid, first-price auction in these situations, bidders are exposed to what is known as the **winner's curse**. Managers need to be aware of this possibility. The bidder with the highest estimated value bids the most and wins the auction, but the bid amount may exceed the true value of the object. Let us see why this is true.

Winner's curse When the bidder with the highest estimated value bids the most and wins the auction, but the bid amount may exceed the true value of the object.

All bidders face the same decision problem: They must estimate the value of the object without knowing the estimates of others. Suppose each bidder makes an estimate, and on average, the estimates are approximately correct. Then the distribution of bids might resemble that shown in Figure 12.3. An unbiased estimate of

---

FIGURE 12.3

The Winner's Curse

If the value of the item being auctioned is uncertain, bidders with extreme estimates of the value can bid higher than the item's true value.

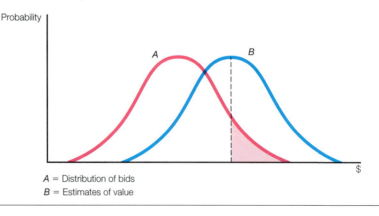

A = Distribution of bids
B = Estimates of value

STRATEGY SESSION: The Winner's Curse in Bidding for Oil Rights

During their careers, many managers find themselves in competitive bidding situations. These might entail bidding for the services of a qualified job applicant, for production inputs, to acquire another company, or to obtain a contract for corporate or personal services. When the bidding is conducted as a sealed-bid auction and it involves an object of common value, managers must be aware of the winner's curse.

An example of how costly this curse can be is shown in the accompanying table, which compiles the actual bids (in millions of dollars) of oil companies for the right to drill for oil on two tracts of government-owned land. Bids are listed in descending order of magnitude.

The table clearly shows the range of estimates of how much oil is present within these tracts of land. For tract 1, the winning bid is 87 percent higher than the second-highest bid; for tract 2, this percentage increases to 181 percent. If we examine the ratio of the high bid to the low bid in each auction, we see that for tract 1, the high bid is 10 times the low bid; for tract 2, this ratio is 109.

The natural tendency for managers is to increase their bids when more bidders enter the auction. But in these types of auctions, managers need to reduce

their bids, not increase them. Obviously the manager who submitted the winning bid for tract 2 did not follow our recommendations. In both auctions, the winning bidder suffered the winner's curse. Neither firm realized a positive return from these tracts of land.

Bids to Drill for Oil on Federal Land (in Millions of Dollars)

Tract 1	Tract 2
32.5	43.5
17.7	15.5
11.1	11.6
7.1	8.5
5.6	8.1
4.1	5.6
3.3	4.7
	2.8
	2.6
	0.7
	0.7
	0.4

the true value, if managers knew the bids of others, would be the mean shown by the dashed line. Given this distribution of values across bidders, the distribution of bids would lie to the left, say, as distribution *A*. As you can see, bidders with extreme estimates (in the right tail of *A*) bid values that exceed the best estimate of the true value. The key is that they do not know their estimates are extreme (because they do not know the estimates of others). Hence they are likely to win the auction but pay more than the object's true value.

The winner's curse is a robust phenomenon; it has been documented in many situations (see Strategy Session: The Winner's Curse in Bidding for Oil Rights). Although sophisticated algorithms for bidding behavior in these types of auctions are available, they are too complex to discuss in this text. However, managers should consider the following issues when contemplating their bids:

- What is your information relative to that of other bidders about the value of the asset? The less information managers have relative to others, the more they need to lower their bids.
- How confident are you in your estimate of the object's true value? The less confident managers are, the more they should lower their bids.
- What is the number of bidders? The more bidders in the auction, the more managers should lower their bids.

CONCERNS IN AUCTION DESIGN

In designing auctions, managers must realize that no auction design best suits all situations. Managers need to carefully consider the interface between auction design and resulting incentives. Two issues managers need to address in choosing an auction's design are the ability of bidders to collude within the auction and the attractiveness of the auction to potential bidders.[3]

The ability of bidders to collude reduces the revenue of the seller and basically overpowers the efficiency of auctions. Bidders can collude in many ways. One common way is for a group of bidders to form a *ring* in which the bidders do not bid against each other. A member of the ring is designated as the bidder, and this one person bids on the objects being auctioned. After the auction, the members of the ring meet and distribute the objects from the auction. Many times the form of the distribution is an auction among the members themselves.

Collusion is also possible in multiunit simultaneous auctions. In these auctions, multiple units of a good are auctioned off simultaneously. In the early stages of the auction, participants who collude signal each other to show what goods they desire. The colluding participants then do not bid up the prices of the identified objects. Klemperer claims this occurred in the auctioning of spectrum rights in Germany. Two large telecoms—Mannesman and T-Mobile—split the 10 available blocks. Each company acquired exactly half of the available blocks for the identical low price.

Managers also need to make their auctions attractive to potential bidders. If an auction does not attract enough bidders, the revenue raised by it can be lower than predicted. For example, if it is clear to bidders that one bidder will win the auction, others may not enter because they are sure they will not win. This happened in Glaxo's purchase of Wellcome. Though other firms were interested in Wellcome, none entered the bidding process because it was clear to them (and reinforced by Glaxo statements) that Glaxo would top any bid.

Bidders also may be deterred from entering an auction if the seller sets a reserve price that is too high or low. Setting a price that is too low can actually encourage collusion among bidders. If the price is set too low and there is a strong bidder, that bidder may find it easier (and cheaper) to collude with others to keep the price low. Basically, if the bidder does not collude, he or she faces the prospect of outbidding all other bidders, which is usually more expensive than colluding.

3. See P. Klemperer, "What Really Matters in Auction Design," *Journal of Economic Perspectives,* 16(2002), pp. 169–189.

SUMMARY

1. There are four types of auction mechanisms: English, Dutch, and first- and second-price sealed-bid auctions.

2. In common-value auctions with symmetric, risk-neutral bidders and independent signals, the auction mechanism chosen makes no difference. All mechanisms generate the same expected revenues.

3. There is no need for managers to consider the bidding strategies of others in English and second-price auctions. In English auctions, managers should bid up to their reservation prices. In second-price auctions, managers should bid their reservation prices.

4. Dutch and sealed-bid auctions have no dominant strategy. Optimal behavior in these auctions is conditioned on beliefs about the strategies of others. In each auction, managers must consider the reservation price of the second-highest bidder. Then managers need to bid just above this price.

5. When selling goods, managers should choose reserve prices that reflect this guideline:

Optimal reserve price = Value of the object being auctioned off, if it does not sell

+ (Managerial estimates of the highest reservation price divided by 2)

6. Auctions are often more efficient than posted-price schemes because they can better discriminate among consumers with differing reservation prices. Most auction designs ensure that the consumer with the highest reservation price wins the auction.

7. Auctions are useful if demand is unknown. Managers can use them to induce consumers to reveal their preferences before managers set a price. By knowing the demand before setting a price, managers increase revenues.

8. When bidding in sealed-bid, common-value auctions, managers need to recognize the tendency to bid too high. This tendency results in the winner's curse, where the high bidder wins the auction but pays more than the object's true value.

wwnorton.com/studyspace

PROBLEMS

1. Consultant.com is an Internet start-up. The company employs business professors as virtual consultants who supply answers to other companies' problems. Consultant.com wants to raise funds with a private equity issue. Unfortunately, because of fluctuations in the stock market, it is uncertain about the demand for its offering. It hopes to issue the stock at either $45 or $50. The demand is categorized into four possible scenarios. The following table shows demand for each scenario–price combination along with the beliefs regarding the probability of each possible state. Consultant.com must pay 10 percent of the generated funds to the investment bank that helped it identify potential investors. The company wants to maximize the funds raised.

Price/Share	State 1	State 2	State 3	State 4
$45	1,750	1,975	2,220	2,445
$50	1,200	1,415	2,000	2,305
Probability	0.35	0.20	0.30	0.15

What is the expected value of the stock offering if Consultant.com sets its price without knowing the future demand state? If Consultant.com can determine the future demand state by using a modified Dutch auction, what is its expected profit? If someone approached Consultant.com and told managers she could predict the future demand state, how much would that information be worth to them?

2. Your company is planning to auction off a manufacturing plant in Asia. You are asked to determine the auction design that will generate the highest revenue for the company. You believe that bidders will value the plant independently. Which design would you choose, and why?

3. There are 100 bidders in an English auction. A random sample of 40 bidders shows the following reservation prices:

Number of Bidders	Reservation Price
1	$10
3	$20
6	$30
5	$40
8	$50
6	$60
7	$70
3	$80
1	$100

Assume the bidding distribution is normal.
   a. What is the mean value of bids across the 100 bidders?
   b. What is the probability of a bid being less than $80?

4. Your company is bidding for a service contract in a first-price, sealed-bid auction. You value the contract at $12 million. You believe the distribution of bids will be uniform, with a high value of $16 million and a low value of $3 million. What is your optimal bidding strategy with
   a. 5 bidders?
   b. 10 bidders?
   c. 20 bidders?

5. The Philadelphia Eagles of the National Football League build a stadium. One revenue source during the construction of the stadium is a personal seat license (PSL), a one-time, up-front payment charged to season ticket holders before the stadium is built. It gives the buyer the right to purchase tickets for a particular seat.

   The Eagles are uncertain about demand for seats in the new stadium. They have selected three price points for PSLs ($6,000, $7,000, and $8,000). Management also has estimated that demand for PSLs could be low, medium, or high. Their beliefs are reflected in this table:

Price	Low Demand, Probability = 0.4	Medium Demand, Probability = 0.35	High Demand, Probability = 0.25
$6,000	24,500 PSLs sold	28,000 PSLs sold	40,000 PSLs sold
$7,000	21,500 PSLs sold	24,000 PSLs sold	32,000 PSLs sold
$8,000	17,500 PSLs sold	22,000 PSLs sold	25,000 PSLs sold

   Some of the stadium funding is provided by the city of Philadelphia. Because Eagles fans view PSLs as an attempt to take away consumer surplus, they resent them and have put pressure on the city government to limit their use. Therefore, the city has set a target of 25,000 seats assigned to PSLs. If the Eagles sell fewer than 25,000 PSLs, the city will grant the team a tax benefit of $10/seat for each seat under 25,000. If the Eagles sell 25,000 or more PSLs, no tax break will be given. A consulting group has told the Eagles that the team is better off using a modified Dutch auction to sell the PSLs. The group has estimated the cost of running the auction at an additional $5.1 million. Eagles management has come to you for help. The managers want to know whether they should use an auction and what the expected benefits will be. What will you tell them?

6. Your company is bidding for a broadband spectrum license. You have been asked to submit an optimal bidding strategy. You expect that bidders will have independent private values for the licenses because each bidder presently has a different structure in place. You believe the valuations for these licenses will be between $200 million and $700 million. Your own valuation is $650 million. There is some uncertainty about the auction design that will be used, so you must suggest an optimal bidding strategy for the following auction designs:
   a. Second-price, sealed-bid auction.
   b. English auction.
   c. Dutch auction.

PART 7

RISK, UNCERTAINTY, AND INCENTIVES

CHAPTER 13

RISK ANALYSIS

As you can see, the managerial world is one of interactions with others. In that sense it mirrors life. It is the way of managers to encounter risk and uncertainty, and they face decisions characterized by two conditions: a strategic nature and incomplete information. We have discussed strategy in previous chapters.

In incomplete information settings, managers do not possess all the relevant information. Hence in having made a decision, a manager cannot be sure of its outcome. Chance or the actions of others may play a role. For example, marketing a new product involves risk because managers are uncertain of the level of demand. If demand is high, profit is greater; if demand does not justify break-even volume, profit is negative. Can managers be certain the investment will reap rewards? Usually not: When they make the launch decision, the future is still uncertain.

Managers face many decisions where the tantalizing possibility of high reward is offset by higher risk. Drilling a well for oil or investing in alternative energy is risky. In making decisions, managers must form beliefs about the future. The inability to see the future can paralyze managers. Managers need to use decision tools to see through the maze of possibilities and identify sensible decisions.

In this chapter we present a variety of tools to help managers improve their decision making. We start with the concept of expected value, which summarizes a set of possible outcomes into a single representative value. We then look at decision trees. Many decisions involve myriad possible outcomes, many of which are conditional on pure chance or the actions of others. For example, a manager might wonder, "If interest rates are low and my competitor keeps prices high, then demand for my new product will be high—but what if interest rates rise, competitors' prices fall, or new entrants come into the market?" Decision trees give us a visual and intuitive guide through the web of possible consequences and allow us to structure decisions in a simple, sequential way.

We also examine techniques to reduce uncertainty. Techniques and databases can improve our ability to forecast the future. For example, the designer of a new product can conduct market research on consumer acceptance and analyze the performance of comparable products to provide more information about the likely demand. An oil company can use geological models and satellite surveys to give a clearer picture of a drilling site and its likelihood of holding oil. In short, we can invest in information about the future. We show how valuable such information is and how its quality depends on its reliability.

The other major concept we introduce is that of expected utility. People react differently to risk, much as they have differing preferences for real goods. Given a choice between a safe investment with a low rate of return and a risky investment with a high expected return, some would choose the former, others the latter; this reflects their tolerance for risk. We see how expected utility analysis can reflect risk tolerance in managerial decisions.

RISK AND PROBABILITY

In ordinary parlance, **risk** is a hazard or a chance of loss. If managers of a biotechnology firm invest $2 million in research and development knowing there is a substantial chance they will lose it if a successful product is not launched, they are making a risky investment. Moreover, the bigger the chance of loss or the greater the size of a potential loss, the more risky a particular course of action is.

To analyze risk, it is necessary to define **probability**. Suppose a situation exists in which one of a number of possible outcomes can occur. For example, if a gambler throws a single die, the number that comes up may be 1, 2, 3, 4, 5, or 6. A probability is the number attached to each possible outcome. It is the proportion of times this outcome occurs over the long run if this situation exists repeatedly. The probability that a particular die will show a 1 is the proportion of times this will occur if the die is thrown many, many times; the probability that the same die will show a 2 is the proportion of times this will occur if the die is thrown many, many times; and so on.

If a situation is repeated a large number of times, R, and if outcome A occurs r times, the probability of A is

$$P(A) = \frac{r}{R} \tag{13.1}$$

Risk Hazard or chance of loss.

Probability The likelihood or chance that something will happen.

STRATEGY SESSION: Pfizer and Its New Cholesterol Drug

Pharmaceutical company managers face decisions of great risk when developing new drugs. We illustrate how managers can use expected value by considering the following issues confronted by the managers of drug company Pfizer.

Pfizer managers had invested $1 billion developing a new, potential blockbuster drug that could add tens of billions of dollars to the company's market value. As with all drugs, managers knew there was a risk of unwanted consequences. Side effects from any drug can potentially cause injury or death, which can result in costly lawsuits. Indeed, several drug companies have lost a large part of their market value recently in such suits (consider Merck's drug Vioxx). Managers use clinical trials to help them assess the risk of new drugs. In 2006 Pfizer managers were performing trials in which some 15,003 people at high risk of cardiovascular disease were either taking the new drug or were allocated to a control group taking the existing drug Lipitor.

The trials showed that 82 people taking the new drug died compared with 51 people taking the control drug. Because of the high existing cardiovascular risk of the subjects, managers had expected some mortality. However, in evaluating the effectiveness and safety of the new drug, they needed to know whether the additional deaths were purely a statistical anomaly or whether they indicated that the new drug was indeed more risky.

The protocol managers established in advance for the trials was that if the probability that additional deaths could be attributed to the new drug exceeded 1 in 100, the trials would be stopped. A statistical analysis of the trial results showed that this threshold had been passed. In other words, managers could be 99 percent sure the results were not anomalous and did indeed reveal the new drug to be more deadly than the control drug.

The decision facing Pfizer managers involved a trade-off. If they stopped the trials, they would lose an opportunity to earn high profits. If they continued the trials and sought regulatory approval to produce and sell the new drug, the firm might face costly lawsuits from people who attributed their injury or death to an allegedly defective drug. How could Pfizer managers map out and quantify the range of outcomes arising from each decision (abandon the drug or not)? Moreover, how could Pfizer managers measure the likelihood of reaching one of these future outcomes? And after managers discussed the possible outcomes and established their beliefs, how could they organize the data to reach a sensible decision that was in the best interests of the firm and its shareholders?

In reality, Pfizer managers decided to abandon the trials, and they lost their $1 billion investment. As a result of this decision, the firm's market value fell by $21 billion.

Thus if a die is "true" (meaning that each of its sides is equally likely to come up when the die is rolled), the probability of its coming up a 1 is 1/6, or 0.167, because if it is rolled many, many times, this will occur in one-sixth of the rolls of the die.

What we have just provided is the so-called **frequency definition of probability**. However, in some situations this concept of probability may be difficult to apply because the situations cannot be repeated over and over. In 2008 Kentucky Fried

Frequency definition of probability An event's limit of frequency in a large number of trials.

Chicken was testing a new grilled chicken product to decide whether to bring it to market in early 2009.[1] This is an experiment that cannot be repeated under essentially the same circumstances. Market and other conditions vary from month to month. If KFC were to delay the introduction, the types of fast-food meals available from other firms (like McDonald's or Burger King), the prices of these competing products, the advertising campaigns of other firms, and a host of other relevant factors would probably change.

In dealing with situations of this sort, managerial economists sometimes use a **subjective definition of probability**. According to this definition, the probability of an event is the degree of confidence or belief on the part of the manager that the event will occur. If the manager believes that outcome X is more likely to occur than outcome Y, the probability of X occurring is higher than the probability of Y. If the manager believes that it is equally likely that a particular outcome will or will not occur, the probability attached to the occurrence of this outcome equals 0.50. We use this concept of probability to model managerial beliefs.

Subjective definition of probability The degree of a manager's confidence or belief that the event will occur.

1. *Yahoo! News*, March 24, 2008.

PROBABILITY DISTRIBUTIONS AND EXPECTED VALUES

Probability distribution A table that lists all possible outcomes and assigns the probability of occurrence to each outcome.

If all possible outcomes are listed and the probability of occurrence is assigned to each outcome, the resulting table is called a **probability distribution**. For example, suppose managers at Adept Technology, a San Jose, California, manufacturer of robots, think the probability is 0.6 that they can develop a new type of robot in one year and the probability is 0.4 they cannot do so in this length of time. The probability distribution is as follows:

Event	Probability of Occurrence
New robot is developed in one year	0.6
New robot is not developed in one year	0.4
	1.0

Note that the probabilities sum to 1, which must be the case if all possible outcomes or events are listed.

If Adept Technology will earn a profit of $1 million if managers develop the new robot in one year and lose $600,000 if they do not, we can readily calculate the probability distribution of profit from the new robot:

Profit	Probability
$1,000,000	0.6
−$600,000	0.4

Moreover, we can also calculate the expected value of the profit:

$$\$1,000,000(0.6) + (-\$600,000)(0.4) = \$360,000$$

The expected value is the weighted average of the profit corresponding to the various outcomes, each of these profit figures being weighted by its probability of occurrence.

In general, expected profit is expressed by the equation

$$\text{Expected profit} = E(\pi) = \sum_{i=1}^{N} \pi_i P_i \tag{13.2}$$

where π_i is the level of profit associated with the ith outcome, P_i is the probability that the ith outcome will take place, and N is the number of possible outcomes. Because $N = 2$, $\pi_1 = \$1,000,000$, $\pi_2 = -\$600,000$, $P_1 = 0.6$, and $P_2 = 0.4$ in the case of Adept Technology, equation (13.2) says precisely the same thing as the equation that precedes it.

Alan Greenspan, former chairman of the Federal Reserve System, and Robert Rubin, secretary of the treasury under the Clinton administration from 1995 to 1999, are bankers who held powerful positions. Both hold similar views of the role of risk in influencing decision making.

Greenspan describes his stewardship of the Fed as risk management. It entails "understanding the many sources of risk and uncertainty, quantifying those risks when possible, and assessing the costs associated with each." Greenspan lists his decisions to cut interest rates during the 1987 stock market crash, in the 1998 debt market crisis, and in the post 9/11/01 era as examples of such decision making. The trade-offs he assessed were the unlikely but catastrophic risks of financial meltdown or deflation versus the less serious risk that low interest rates would fuel inflation.

Rubin describes his public policy decisions as "probabilistic decision making" where he would "judge the odds of various outcomes and the possible gains and losses associated with each." Rubin says his decisions to bail out Mexico, Thailand, South Korea, Russia, and Brazil were risky, but not acting to aid those countries would have created even more dire consequences. He believes that most people (to some extent) behave as if they assigned probabilities to each outcome, even though they don't think of their decisions in those terms. Rubin, on the other hand, views such thinking as a matter of course because as a Wall Streeter, he evaluates all investments on the basis of risk and reward. He states, "You judge decisions on how sensible they were based on everything you knew at the time, not on outcomes," Putting this in the context of his Wall Street business: A trader could lose big on a single trade; but if the decision making that led the trader to that trade seemed sound, the trader's firm would allow the individual to keep trading, betting that over the long run, the trader would make money. Hindsight is 20–20. But all decisions have to be made *ex ante,* and all you have to go on when a decision is made are the facts as you know them and a logic that says that if we do *X,* then *Y* is likely to happen. Investigating all the possible *X*'s, and assessing the likely probability of the *Y*'s occurring, yield a decision model based on assessing the risks.

You can see how managers consider risk in their business and how it impacts their decision making by reading the section on risk contained in every firm's annual report and in their yearly 10-K report to the SEC.

Source: "How Two Economic Gurus Think about Risk," *The Wall Street Journal,* February 2, 2004.

COMPARISONS OF EXPECTED PROFIT

To decide which of a number of courses of action to take, managers can compare the expected profits. For example, suppose managers of the Jones Corporation, a producer of automobile tires, are thinking of raising the price of their product by $1 per tire. The managers estimate the following. If they raise the price, they will realize a profit of $800,000 if the current advertising campaign is successful, and they will incur a $600,000 loss if the campaign is not successful. Managers believe there is a 0.5 probability the current advertising campaign will be successful and a 0.5 probability it will not succeed.

Under these circumstances, the expected profit to the firm if managers increase price equals

$$\$800,000(0.5) + (-\$600,000)(0.5) = \$100,000$$

As indicated, the expected profit is the sum of the amount of money gained (or lost) if each outcome occurs times the probability of occurrence of the outcome. In this case there are two possible outcomes: (1) The firm's current advertising campaign is successful or (2) it is unsuccessful. If we multiply the amount of money gained (or lost) if the first outcome occurs by its probability of occurrence, the result is $800,000(0.5). If we multiply the amount of money gained (or lost) if the second outcome occurs by its probability of occurrence, the result is $-\$600,000(0.5)$. Summing these results, we get $100,000, which is the expected profit if the firm raises its price.

What would be the expected profit if managers at the Jones Corporation did not increase price? Suppose they believe that with no price increase, profit will reach $200,000. For simplicity, we assume that this profit level is regarded as certain if the price is not increased. If managers want to maximize the expected profit, they should not increase price because the expected profit equals $200,000 if price is not increased but only $100,000 if it is. Later in this chapter, we discuss at length the circumstances under which it is rational to maximize the expected profit—and how to proceed if it is not rational to do so.

ROAD MAP TO DECISION

When managers face risk in choosing strategy, they will often face the following scenario. They will make a choice or perhaps several among alternative strategies. The payoff of the chosen strategy will depend on the actions of others. Because it is not easy to precisely anticipate the behavior of others, managers will form beliefs about the future. To analyze any such scenario, a decision tree is useful.

Decision tree A diagram that helps managers visualize their strategic future.

A **decision tree** is a diagram that helps managers visualize their strategic future. It represents the situation as a series of choices, each of which is depicted by a fork (sometimes called a juncture or branching point). A decision fork represents a choice by which managers must commit to a strategy. A chance fork represents a point at which chance influences the outcome. To differentiate between a decision fork and a chance fork, we place a small square at the former juncture but not at the latter.

In Figure 13.1 we show the decision tree for the situation facing managers at the Jones Corporation. Managers are considering a price increase. Starting at the left side of the diagram, Jones managers must choose whether to increase price. We represent this choice as a decision node, so it is square. If managers do not institute

FIGURE 13.1

Decision Tree, Jones Corporation

If the Jones Corporation increases its price, the expected profit is $100,000. If it does not increase its price, the expected profit is $200,000.

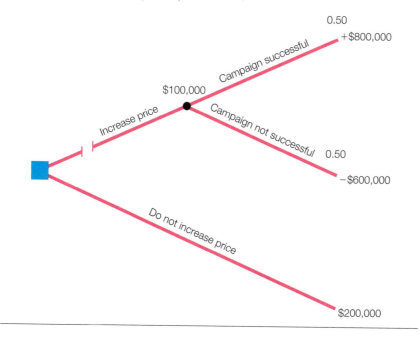

a price increase, the consequence is certain: Managers earn a profit of $200,000. Therefore, $200,000 is shown at the end of this branch. If the managers do increase price, one of two consequences will occur. The current advertising campaign is successful, customers accept the price increase, and managers earn $800,000. This is shown in the upper branch. The lower branch represents the future where the campaign is not successful, customers do not accept the price increase, and managers lose $600,000. On the basis of history, 50 percent of similar campaigns were successful, and 50 percent were not.

The tree illustrates the various options and gives managers an easy way to compare payoffs across strategies. We can then more easily determine what strategies managers should take. Begin at the right side of the decision tree, where the profit figures are located. The first step is to calculate the expected profit when managers are situated at the chance fork immediately to the left of these payoff figures. In other words, this is the expected profit to managers given that chance will influence which subsequent branch is followed. Because there is a 0.50 probability of following the branch culminating in a profit of $800,000, and a 0.50 probability

PROBLEM SOLVED: Should Tomco Oil Corporation Drill a Well?

One important business in which the concepts just presented have been applied is oil exploration. Very large amounts of money are being invested in oil exploration. Managers at oil firms use these analytical tools as an aid to decision making. To illustrate how these concepts are applied, consider the actual case faced by managers of Tomco Oil Corporation, who had to decide whether to drill a well at Blair West, a site in Kansas. The managers had information concerning the cost of drilling and the price of oil as well as geologists' reports concerning the likelihood of striking oil. The geologists' reports led the managers to believe that if a well were drilled, there was a 0.60 probability of finding no oil, a 0.15 probability of finding 10,000 barrels, a 0.15 probability of finding 20,000 barrels, and a 0.10 probability of finding 30,000 barrels.

Although these probabilities are helpful, they do not, by themselves, help managers choose whether to drill. Managers need to consider the payoff attached to each scenario. Suppose managers estimate they will realize a $90,000 loss if they find no oil, a $100,000 profit if they find 10,000 barrels of oil, a $300,000 profit if they find 20,000 barrels, and a $500,000 profit if they find 30,000 barrels. Based on these beliefs, should the managers drill the well?

Managers can answer this question by constructing the decision tree shown in the following figure. Starting at the left side of the diagram, the first choice is up to the managers who can either drill the well or not. If the branch representing not drilling is followed, the expected profit is zero, which is shown at the end of this branch. (Why? Because the firm neither gains nor loses if it does not drill.) If the branch representing drilling the well is followed, we come to a chance fork: It is uncertain whether the well will strike oil and, if it does, how much oil will it produce. The highest branch following this chance fork represents the consequence that no oil is found, in which case managers lose $90,000, shown at the end of this branch. The next branch following this chance fork represents the consequence that 10,000 barrels are found, in which case the firm gains $100,000, shown at the end of this branch. Similarly, the lowest branches following this chance fork represent the consequences that 20,000 and 30,000 barrels are found; the number at the end of each of these branches is the corresponding profit to the firm.

Having constructed this decision tree, the firm's managers can compute the expected profit to the firm if it is situated at the chance fork immediately to the left of the profit (or loss) figures. If the firm is at this fork, there is a 0.60 probability that the branch culminating in a $90,000 loss will be followed, a 0.15 probability that the branch culminating in a $100,000 profit will be followed, a 0.15 probability that the branch culminating in a $300,000 profit will be followed, and a 0.10 probability that the branch culminating in a $500,000 profit will be followed. To calculate the expected profit if the firm is situated at this fork, the firm's managers should multiply each possible value of profit (or loss) by its probability, and

of following the branch culminating in a loss of $600,000, the expected profit at this chance fork is

$$0.50(\$800,000) + 0.50(-\$600,000) = \$100,000$$

This number is written above the chance fork in question to show that this is the expected profit when the firm is located at that fork. Moving farther to the left

Decision Tree, Tomco Oil Corporation

If Tomco Oil drills the well, the expected profit is $56,000. If it does not, the expected profit is zero.

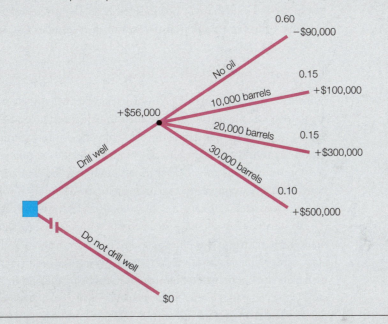

sum the results. The expected profit if the firm is situated at this chance fork equals

$$0.60(-\$90,000) + 0.15(\$100,000) + 0.15(\$300,000) + 0.10(\$500,000) = \$56,000$$

In the figure, this result is written above the chance fork in question to show that this is the expected profit if the firm is located at that fork.

Going farther along the decision tree to the left, the firm has a choice of two branches; one leads to an expected profit of $56,000, and the other leads to an expected profit of zero. So if managers want to maximize expected profit, they should choose the former branch—that is, drill the well.

along the decision tree, it is clear that managers have a choice of two branches; one leads to an expected profit of $100,000, and the other leads to a $200,000 expected profit. If managers want to maximize their expected profit, they should choose the latter branch. In other words, they should not increase price. Because the former branch (increase price) is nonoptimal, we place two vertical lines through it.

Of course this graphic procedure for analyzing the Jones Corporation's pricing problem amounts to precisely the same thing as the calculations we made in the previous section. In short, the decision tree lets you visualize complex decision problems. In the Jones case, there were only two courses of action and only two chance possibilities. However, when a decision problem gets more complicated with several choices and each choice has several possible outcomes, it is easy to get lost in the intricate maze of possibilities. A decision tree provides a simple visual map that brings order and transparency to such complex decision structures.

THE EXPECTED VALUE OF PERFECT INFORMATION

Sometimes managers can obtain information that will dispel uncertainty (to varying extents). If managers can buy such information, how much should they be willing to pay for it? We define the value of perfect information as the increase in expected profit if the manager can obtain completely accurate information concerning future outcomes. Managers generally pay for this information prior to knowing it. For example, managers at the Jones Corporation would find it worthwhile to accurately estimate how successful their advertising campaign will be.

To illustrate how managers can compute the expected value of perfect information, we return to the Jones case. We begin by evaluating the expected monetary value to managers of access to perfectly accurate information of this sort. If managers can obtain perfect information, choosing the optimal decision becomes easy. If the campaign is successful, managers will earn a profit of $800,000. If it is not successful, managers will earn $200,000. To managers with access to perfect information, the expected profit is

$$0.50(\$800,000) + 0.50(\$200,000) = \$500,000$$

Even though the managers can obtain perfect information, it is not revealed to them until after they have paid for it. We can imagine asking some forecaster to give her expert (and never wrong) opinion as to whether the advertising campaign will succeed. There is a 0.50 probability that this forecaster will tell them that the advertising campaign will be successful, in which case managers can increase price and earn a profit of $800,000. There is also a 0.50 probability the forecaster will tell managers the campaign will fail, in which case they would not increase price and would earn a profit of $200,000. So, as shown, the expected profit if managers obtain access to a perfect forecast (which is revealed after payment) is $500,000.

Recall that managers expect a profit of $200,000 if they make a decision without perfect information, not $500,000. The difference between these two amounts ($500,000 − $200,000, or $300,000) is the expected value of perfect information. It shows the amount by which the expected profit increases as a consequence of managers having access to perfect information; $300,000 is thus the managers' reservation price for this information.

PROBLEM SOLVED: Evaluating an Investment in a New Chemical Plant

To illustrate the usefulness of the expected value of perfect information, consider an actual case in which managers constructed a decision tree to determine whether a major U.S. corporation should invest in a new plant. The main product of the new plant was a brightener; but with new processing methods, a valuable by-product was produced as well. The exact amounts of both products produced were uncertain. Minute quantities of impurities in the raw materials used in the process could greatly influence the amounts of brightener and by-product produced. Also, there were uncertainties concerning the costs of raw materials and plant efficiency.

The table shows the expected value of perfect information concerning by-product quantity, impurities, raw material costs, and plant efficiency. As you can see, the critical uncertainties were those regarding by-product quantity and the level of impurities. For example, perfect information concerning by-product quantity was worth up to $6.2 million. On the other hand, information regarding raw materials and plant efficiency was much less important for this decision. Indeed, the expected value of perfect information concerning plant efficiency was close to

Expected Value of Perfect Information Concerning Factors Influencing Whether to Build New Chemical Plant

Factor	Expected Value of Perfect Information (Millions of Dollars)
By-product quantity	6.2
Level of impurities	3.9
Raw material costs	0.3
Plant efficiency	0.0

Source: Spetzler and Zamora, "Facilities Investment and Expansion Problem."

zero. Based on these results, the managers decided to research the uncertainties regarding by-product quantity and the level of impurities before committing to the construction of the new plant.[a]

[a]C. Spetzler and R. Zamora, "Decision Analysis of a Facilities Investment and Expansion Problem," in R. Howard and J. Matheson, eds., The Principles and Applications of Decision Analysis (Menlo Park, CA: Strategic Decision Group, 1984).

In many circumstances it is important that managers think about the worth of perfect information. Managers are frequently offered information by testing services, research organizations, news bureaus, credit rating agencies, and a variety of other organizations. Unless managers know how much particular types of information are worth, it is difficult to decide rationally whether they should be bought. The value of information analysis presented in this section is useful to guide such decisions because it shows the maximum amount managers should be willing to spend to obtain perfect information. The calculation of what to pay for less-than-perfect information is more complex and is not presented here. Needless to say, this amount is less than what a manager would pay if the information were perfect. And when the accuracy of the information falls below a certain level, it is worthless to managers.

As is typical of all publicly traded companies after Sarbanes-Oxley, FedEx tells investors and potential investors about its exposure to market risk. Such disclosure is caused by the failure to provide information about the true exposure to risk in the Enron, Tyco, and WorldCom cases.

FedEx states, "We have no significant exposure to changing interest rates on our long-term debt because interest rates are fixed on the majority of our long-term debt." With respect to a $500 million debt with a floating interest rate that was to mature in August 2007, FedEx stated that it did not employ interest rate hedging to mitigate the risks with respect to this borrowing. The company's reasoning was that a 10 percent increase in the interest rate on its outstanding floating-rate debt would not have a material effect on its results of operations. On May 31, 2007, it had an estimated fair value $2.4 billion in outstanding fixed-rate, long-term debt. The market risk for such debt (estimated to be $36 million as of May 31, 2006) was estimated as the potential decrease in fair value resulting from a 10 percent increase in interest rates.

FedEx also disclosed its risk due to currency fluctuations. Most of its transactions were denominated in U.S. dollars, but it had significant transactions in the euro, Chinese yuan, Canadian dollar, British pound, and Japanese yen. FedEx stated that "distribution of our foreign currency denominated transactions is that such currency declines in some areas of the world are often offset by currency gains in other areas of the world." In fact, during 2006 and 2007, FedEx believed that operating income was positively impacted due to foreign currency fluctuations. However, favorable foreign currency fluctuations also may have had an offsetting impact on the price it obtained or the demand for its services. On May 31, 2007, a 10 percent strengthening of the value of the dollar relative to the above-mentioned currencies would decrease operating income by $151 million in 2008. Note the performance of sensitivity analysis (the hypothetical 10 percent changes in interest rates and exchange rates).

Finally, FedEx disclosed its risk associated with changes in fuel prices. This was mitigated by its use of fuel surcharges passing the increased fuel costs to customers. FedEx concluded that a 10 percent increase in the price of fuel would not materially affect its earnings. However, there is a lag in the deployment of its fuel surcharges, and should a material price change occur in fuel, FedEx disclosed that its operating income might be affected.

In addition, it discussed "many risks and uncertainties":

1. Preserving the strong reputation and value of the brand.
2. Threat of technology/Internet failure on operations.
3. Assurance of adequate physical capital to handle the business volume.
4. Threat of competitors.
5. Need to effectively operate, integrate, leverage, and grow acquired businesses.
6. Ability to acquire fuel at a reasonable price.
7. Need for FedEx Ground's personnel to be classified as independent contractors.
8. Role of increased security costs.
9. Role of the international regulatory environment.

10. Role of terrorist activities on operations/economic conditions.
11. Impact of new tax, accounting, labor, and environmental rules/laws.
12. Ability to manage its cost structure.
13. Ability to maintain good relations with employees.
14. Assuring a supply of high-quality labor.
15. Managing health care and other employee benefits.
16. Managing changes in volumes, customer demand parameters, and prices charged.
17. Innovating in service and growth of product lines.
18. Controlling legal fees and avoiding liability.
19. Adapting and responding to changes in technology that impact the demand for services.
20. Responding to adverse weather conditions/natural disasters that impact system operations.
21. Responding to a pandemic.
22. Assuring accessibility to financial capital at a reasonable price.

Consider now a company in poor financial shape in Chapter 11 bankruptcy (ATA holdings—an airline that terminated operations on April 3, 2008). In its 2004 10-K report, ATA spelled out the risks that might render its forward-looking statements about the expected future of the company incorrect:

- The ability to develop and execute a revised business plan for profitable operations, including restructuring flight schedules, maintaining the support of employees, and regauging the fleet of aircraft.
- The ability to develop, prosecute, confirm, and consummate a plan of reorganization with respect to Chapter 11 cases.

- Risks associated with third parties seeking and obtaining bankruptcy court approval to terminate or shorten the exclusivity period to propose and confirm one or more plans of reorganization, for appointment of a Chapter 11 trustee, or to convert one or more assets to a Chapter 7 case.
- The ability to obtain and maintain normal terms with vendors and service providers.
- The ability to maintain contracts that were critical to its operations.
- The potential adverse effects of the Chapter 11 reorganization on liquidity or results of operations.
- The ability to attract and retain customers.
- Demand for transportation in markets in which the company operated.
- Economic conditions.
- The effects of any hostilities or act of war.
- Salary costs.
- Aviation fuel costs.
- Competitive pressures on pricing (particularly from low-cost competitors).
- Weather conditions.
- Government legislation and regulation.
- Other risks and uncertainties listed from time to time in reports the company periodically filed with the Securities and Exchange Commission.

In fact the inability to maintain a military contract and skyrocketing fuel costs ultimately did ATA in.

Sources: FedEx, Form 10-K, Annual Report, Filed July 13, 2007, and ATA Holdings Corp. 10-K for 12/31/04.

MEASURING ATTITUDES TOWARD RISK: THE UTILITY APPROACH

In discussing the behavior of managers at both Jones and Tomco Oil, we assumed that managers want to maximize expected profit. We now examine how risk affects managerial behavior. Imagine that a small business is offered the following choice:

1. A certain profit of $2,000,000.
2. A gamble with a 50–50 chance of a $4,100,000 profit or a $60,000 loss.

The expected profit for the gamble is

$$0.50(\$4,100,000) + 0.50(-\$60,000) = \$2,020,000$$

so managers should choose the gamble over the certainty of $2,000,000 if they want to maximize expected profit. However, it seems likely that many managers, especially those of small businesses, would prefer the certainty of $2,000,000 because the gamble entails a 50 percent chance that the firm will lose $60,000—a substantial sum for a very small firm. Moreover, many managers may feel they can do almost as much with $2,000,000 as with $4,100,000, and therefore the extra profit is not worth the risk of losing $60,000.

Whether the firm's managers will want to maximize the expected profit in this situation depends on their attitude toward risk. If the amount at stake in a decision is large relative to the overall value of the firm and the managers' bonuses are likely impacted, they may be overwhelmed at the thought of taking a 50 percent chance of losing $60,000, which could cost them their bonuses. On the other hand, if they manage a big corporation, the prospect of a $60,000 loss may not be unsettling; and they may prefer the gamble to the certainty of a mere $2,000,000 gain.

Fortunately we need not assume that managers want to maximize the expected profit. Instead we can construct a **utility function** for a manager that measures his or her attitude toward risk. (This concept of utility should not be confused with that discussed in Chapter 3. As we will see, it is a different concept.) From this utility function, we can identify the optimal strategy for managers conditional on their attitude toward risk.

Utility function Function used to identify the optimal strategy for managers conditional on their attitude toward risk.

Constructing a Utility Function

We define a rational manager as one who maximizes expected utility. That is, she does not want to harm herself. The manager chooses the strategy with the highest expected utility. But what (in this context) is utility? It is a value that is attached to all possible outcomes of the decision by the manager. The manager's utility function represents the level of satisfaction (or benefit or welfare) she attaches to each possible outcome. It is risk-adjusted, so it also represents risk preferences. How do managers compute **expected utility?** It is the sum of the utility of each outcome times the probability of the outcome's occurrence. For example, if a situation has two possible outcomes, *A* and *B*, if the utility of outcome *A* is 2 and the utility of outcome *B* is 8, and if the probability of each outcome is 0.50, the expected utility equals

Expected utility The sum of the utility of each outcome times the probability of the outcome's occurrence.

$$0.50(2) + 0.50(8) = 5$$

What is the expected utility if managers at Tomco Oil drill the well under the circumstances described on page 438? It equals

$$0.60U(-90) + 0.15U(100) + 0.15U(300) + 0.10U(500)$$

where $U(-90)$ is the utility that managers attach to a monetary loss of \$90,000, $U(100)$ is the utility attached to a gain of \$100,000, $U(300)$ is the utility attached to a gain of \$300,000, and so on. Because there is a 0.60 probability of a \$90,000 loss, a 0.15 probability of a \$100,000 gain, a 0.15 probability of a \$300,000 gain, and a 0.10 probability of a \$500,000 gain, the preceding formula shows the expected utility. What is the expected utility if managers do not drill the well? It equals $U(0)$ because under these circumstances, it is certain that the gain is zero.

To find the utility the manager attaches to each possible outcome, begin by ranking the utility attached to two levels of profit arbitrarily. The utility of the best consequence is set higher than that of the worst one. Managers in the oil-drilling problem might set $U(-90)$ equal to 0 and $U(500)$ equal to 50. Expected utility is an ordinal system; that is, magnitude does not matter, but rank does. Therefore, managers could set $U(-90)$ equal to 1 and $U(500)$ equal to 10. It will make no difference to the ultimate outcome of the analysis.[2]

Managers should then consider payoffs that fall between these extremes. They need to consider choices between the certainty of one of the other possible levels of profit and a gamble where the possible outcomes are the two profit levels whose utilities we set arbitrarily. In the oil-drilling case, suppose managers want to find $U(100)$. To do so, managers should consider whether they prefer the certainty of a \$100,000 gain to a gamble where there is a probability P of a gain of \$500,000 and a probability $(1 - P)$ of a loss of \$90,000. They should consider at what value of P they are indifferent between the certainty of a \$100,000 gain and this gamble. Suppose this value of P is 0.40.

If the managers are indifferent between a certain gain of \$100,000 and this gamble, the expected utility of the certain gain of \$100,000 must equal the expected utility of the gamble. (Why? Because managers maximize expected utility.) Therefore,

$$U(100) = 0.40U(500) + 0.60U(-90)$$

And because we set $U(500)$ equal to 50 and $U(-90)$ equal to 0, it follows that

$$U(100) = 0.40(50) + 0.60(0) = 20$$

2. The utility function we construct is not unique. Because we set the two utilities arbitrarily, the results vary, depending on the values of the utilities chosen. If $X_1, X_2, \ldots, X_n$ are the utilities attached to n possible monetary values, $(\alpha + \beta X_1), (\alpha + \beta X_2), \ldots, (\alpha + \beta X_n)$ can also be utilities attached to them (where α and β are constants, and $\beta > 0$).

FIGURE 13.2

Utility Function

The decision maker's utility function is useful in indicating whether particular gambles should be accepted.

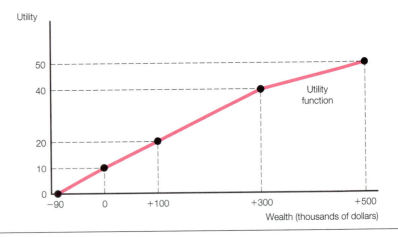

That is, the utility attached to a gain of $100,000 is 20.

Managers now have the utility measures for three wealth levels; $U(-90)$ and $U(500)$ were set arbitrarily at 0 and 50 to determine the scale of the utility function. Then we derived that on this scale, $U(100)$ must equal 20.

Using the same procedure, managers of the oil company can estimate $U(300)$ and $U(0)$, the other utilities required to calculate the expected utility if they drill the well and the expected utility if they do not drill it. For example, to obtain $U(300)$, managers should consider whether they prefer a certain $300,000 gain to a gamble where there is a probability P of a gain of $500,000 and a probability $(1 - P)$ of a loss of $90,000. Then managers should consider at what value of P they are indifferent between the certain $300,000 gain and this gamble. Suppose this value of P is 0.80. Then the expected utility of a certain $300,000 gain must equal the expected utility of this gamble:

$$U(300) = 0.80U(500) + 0.20U(-90)$$

And because $U(500)$ equals 50 and $U(-90)$ equals 0, it follows that $U(300)$ equals 40.

Utility functions of managers represent the relationship between their utility and the amount of their profit (or loss). By evaluating $U(-90)$, $U(100)$, $U(300)$, and $U(500)$ as in the previous paragraphs, managers can identify four points on their utility function, as shown in Figure 13.2. By repeated use of the procedure just described, managers can estimate many such points. (According to Figure 13.2, $U(0) = 10$.)

Once a manager estimates her utility function, it can help her decide whether to accept or reject particular gambles. Consider the actual case of Thomas Blair, president of the Tomco Oil Corporation. Using the previous procedures, an economist estimated Blair's utility function. Suppose the result is as shown in Figure 13.2 and Blair must decide whether to drill the well described on page 438. He should drill the well if his expected utility if the well is drilled exceeds his expected utility if it is not drilled. As pointed out in the previous section, his expected utility if the well is drilled is

$$0.60U(-90) + 0.15U(100) + 0.15U(300) + 0.10U(500)$$

He can use this to estimate his utility as follows. Because $U(-90)$ equals 0, $U(100)$ equals 20, $U(300)$ equals 40, and $U(500)$ equals 50, his expected utility if the well is drilled is

$$0.60(0) + 0.15(20) + 0.15(40) + 0.10(50) = 14$$

It is important to note that utility functions measure utility of "wealth" or "net worth" and not the utility of "changes in income." For example, suppose a person has wealth of $100 and is facing this choice about gambling: If the coin comes up heads, he wins $10, and he loses $10 if it is tails. Managers can pose this choice in the following form:

Expected utility of gamble =
$$0.5 \, U(\$100 + \$10) + 0.5 \, U(\$100 - \$10)$$
versus
Expected utility of no gamble = $1.0 \, U(\$100)$

With this in mind, managers at Tomco Oil should think of the values −90, 100, 300, or 500 as the wealth or net worth of the firm under the different scenarios. In other words, these figures refer to the present value of future profit, not simply the profit recorded in a single year.

If the well is not drilled, Blair's expected utility equals $U(0)$, which is 10 according to Figure 13.2. Therefore he should drill the well. Why? If he does not drill it, his expected utility is 10, whereas if he drills it, his expected utility is 14. Because he should maximize the expected utility, he should choose the action with the higher expected utility, which is to drill.

In fact, Tomco Oil Corporation did drill a well. Subsequently Blair stated, "Before we actually used decision-tree analysis to aid in our selection of drilling sites, we were skeptical as to the application of decision-tree analysis in oil exploration and field development decisions. Now we find it helpful, not only in choosing between two or more drilling sites, but also in making decisions subsequent to the choice of a drilling site."

ATTITUDES TOWARD RISK: THREE TYPES

Although managers can expect that utility increases with monetary gain, the shape of the utility function can vary greatly depending on the preferences of the individual. Figure 13.3 shows three general types of utility functions. The one in panel A is like that in Figure 13.2 in the sense that utility increases with wealth but at a decreasing rate. In other words, an increase in monetary gain of $1 is associated with smaller and smaller increases in utility as the wealth grows. Managers with utility functions of this sort are **risk averters**. That is, when confronted with

Risk averters When managers prefer a choice with a more certain outcome to one with a less certain outcome, when confronted with gambles offering equal expected wealth.

FIGURE 13.3

Three Types of Utility Functions

Utility functions assume a variety of shapes. In panel A the decision maker is a risk averter; in panel B he or she is a risk lover; and in panel C he or she is risk-neutral.

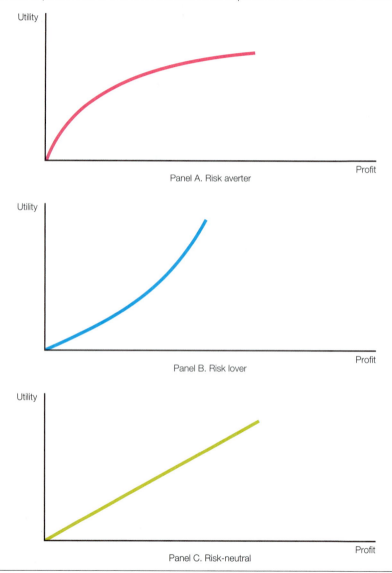

Panel A. Risk averter

Panel B. Risk lover

Panel C. Risk-neutral

3. Consider a gamble in which there is a probability of P that the gain is π_1 and a probability of $(1 - P)$ that the loss is π_2. A person is a risk averter if the utility of the gamble's expected profit, $U[P\pi_1 + (1 - P)\pi_2]$, is greater than the expected utility of the gamble, $PU(\pi_1) + (1 - P)U(\pi_2)$.

gambles offering equal expected wealth, they prefer a choice with a more certain outcome to one with a less certain outcome.[3]

Panel B of Figure 13.3 shows a case in which utility increases with wealth at an increasing rate. In other words, an increase in monetary gain of $1 is associated with larger and larger increases in utility as the wealth grows. Managers with utility functions of this sort are **risk lovers**. That is, when confronted with gambles offering equal expected wealth, they prefer a gamble with a less certain outcome to one with a more certain outcome.[4]

Finally, panel C shows a case where utility increases with wealth at a constant rate. In other words, an increase of $1 in monetary gain is associated with a constant increase in utility as the wealth grows. Stated differently, utility in this case is a linear function of wealth:

$$U = a + b\pi \tag{13.3}$$

where U is utility, π is wealth, and a and b are constants (of course $b > 0$). People with utility functions of this sort are **risk-neutral**.[5] In other words, they maximize expected wealth, regardless of risk. It is easy to prove that this is true. If equation (13.2) holds,

$$E(U) = a + bE(\pi) \tag{13.4}$$

where $E(U)$ is expected utility and $E(\pi)$ is expected wealth.[6] Consequently, because expected utility is directly related to expected wealth, it can be a maximum only when expected wealth is a maximum.

THE STANDARD DEVIATION AND COEFFICIENT OF VARIATION: MEASURES OF RISK

Risk, like many four-lettered words, carries many meanings. Some managers behave as if risk is measured in magnitude of negative outcomes. Managers need to measure risk as being related to the dispersion of the probability distribution of profit resulting from the decision. For example, suppose Jones Corporation managers must decide whether to invest in a new plant. If the probability distribution of profit resulting from the new plant is as shown in panel A of Figure 13.4, the decision to invest in the new plant is more risky relative to the probability distribution shown in panel B. Why? Because the profit resulting from the new plant is more uncertain and variable in panel A than in panel B.

As a measure of risk, managers can often rely on the **standard deviation**, σ, the most frequently used metric for dispersion in a probability distribution.[7] Managers need to consider all feasible choices and attach a payoff to each possible future. They should then input these to software that calculates the standard deviation. The software estimates the standard deviation of profit by computing the expected value of profit, $E(\pi)$ (recall equation (13.2)). It then subtracts this expected value from each possible profit level to obtain a set of deviations about this expected value. (The ith such deviation is $\pi_i - E(\pi)$.) Then we square each deviation, multiply the squared deviation by its probability of occurrence (P_i), and sum these products:

$$\sigma^2 = \sum_{i=1}^{N} P_i[\pi_i - E(\pi)]^2$$

Risk lovers When managers prefer a gamble with a less certain outcome to one with a more certain outcome, when confronted with gambles offering equal expected wealth.

Risk-neutral When a manager maximizes expected wealth, regardless of risk.

Standard deviation The most frequently used metric for dispersion in a probability distribution.

4. A person is a risk lover if the utility of the gamble's expected profit, $U[P\pi_1 + (1 - P)\pi_2]$, is less than the expected utility of the gamble, $PU(\pi_1) + (1 - P)U(\pi_2)$.
5. A person can be a risk averter under some circumstances, a risk lover under different circumstances, and risk-neutral under still other circumstances. The utility functions in Figure 13.3 are "pure" cases in which the person is always only one of these types, at least in the range covered by the graphs.
6. To illustrate that equation (13.4) is correct, suppose π can assume two possible values, π_1 and π_2, and the probability that π_1 occurs is P and the probability that π_2 occurs is $(1 - P)$. Then, if $U = a + b\pi$,

$$\begin{aligned}E(U) &= P(a + b\pi_1) \\ &\quad + (1 - P)(a + b\pi_2) \\ &= a + b[P\pi_1 + (1 - P)\pi_2] \\ &= a + E(\pi)\end{aligned}$$

because $E(\pi)$ equals $P\pi_1 + (1 - P)\pi_2$.
7. Although the standard deviation is often a useful measure of risk, it may not always be the best measure. Our discussion here and in subsequent sections of this chapter is necessarily simplified. The measures and techniques we describe are rough, but many analysts have found them useful.

449

FIGURE 13.4

Probability Distribution of the Profit from an Investment in a New Plant

The probability distribution in panel A shows more dispersion than that in panel B.

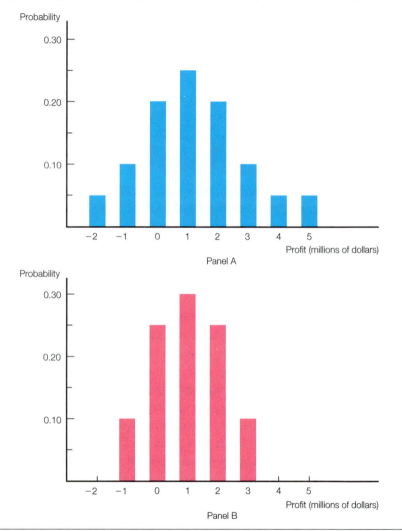

Panel A

Panel B

Taking the square root of this result, we obtain the standard deviation:

$$\sigma = \left(\sum_{i=1}^{N} P_i [\pi_i - E(\pi)]^2 \right)^{0.5} \tag{13.5}$$

As an illustration, consider managers of a company who must decide whether to invest in new process technology. According to the company's engineers, there is a

0.3 probability that such an investment will result in a $1 million profit, a 0.4 probability it will result in a $0.2 million profit, and a 0.3 probability it will result in a $0.6 million loss. Therefore the expected value of the profit from this investment is

$$E(\pi) = 0.3(1) + 0.4(0.2) + 0.3(-0.6) = 0.2$$

or $0.2 million. Based on equation (13.5), the standard deviation is

$$\sigma = [(0.3)(1 - 0.2)^2 + (0.4)(0.2 - 0.2)^2 + (0.3)(-0.6 - 0.2)^2]^{0.5}$$

$$= (0.384)^{0.5} = 0.62$$

or $0.62 million.

A larger standard deviation tends to mean greater of risk. If the standard deviation of the levels of profit resulting from the technology investment were $2 million rather than $0.62 million, there would be less certainty concerning its profitability. In other words, there would be more likelihood that its profitability would depart greatly from its expected value.

When managers use the standard deviation as a measure of risk, they implicitly assume the scale of the project is held constant. If one investment is twice as big as another, they should expect the standard deviations of the investments' profits to differ. Larger investments should have greater standard profit deviations. To take account of the scale of the project, a measure of relative risk is required. Such a measure is the **coefficient of variation**, defined as

$$V = \frac{\sigma}{E(\pi)} \qquad (13.6)$$

Coefficient of variation

$$V = \frac{\sigma}{E(\pi)}$$

For example, in the case of the new technology investment, the coefficient of variation for the profit levels is 0.62/0.2, or 3.1.

ADJUSTING THE VALUATION MODEL FOR RISK

According to the basic valuation model discussed in Chapter 1, managers must continually be concerned with the effects of their decisions on the present value of the firm's future profit, defined as

$$PV = \sum_{t=1}^{N} \frac{\pi_t}{(1 + i)^t} \qquad (13.7)$$

But the firm's managers do not know with certainty what the firm's profit in future year t (that is, π_t) will be. The best they can do is use the expected profit (that is, $E(\pi_t)$) instead. How can they adjust the formula in equation (13.7) to account for risk?

One way is to use the **certainty equivalent approach**, which is related to the utility theory developed in the previous sections. For example, consider the man-

Certainty equivalent approach
When a manager is indifferent about the certainty and gamble, the certainty equivalent (rather than the expected profit) can identify if the manager is a risk averter, risk lover, or risk-neutral.

FIGURE 13.5

Manager's Indifference Curve between Expected Profit and Risk

The manager is indifferent between gambles with the expected profit and risk shown here. Therefore, she is indifferent between the certainty of $100,000 and a gamble in which the expected profit is $200,000 and the coefficient of variation is 3.1. Similar indifference curves exist for riskless amounts other than $100,000.

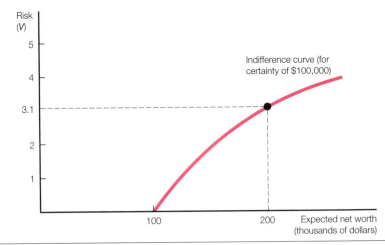

ager of the firm considering an investment in process technology. Suppose she is indifferent between the certainty of a $100,000 net worth (the net worth is the wealth of the firm) and the gamble involved in investing in the technology. If so, the certainty equivalent ($100,000), rather than the expected profit ($200,000), should be used as the right side of equation (13.7). If the certainty equivalent is less than the expected net worth, the decision maker is a risk averter; if it is more than the expected net worth, she is a risk lover; and if it equals the expected net worth, she is risk-neutral.

On the basis of the decision maker's utility function, we can construct indifference curves of the sort shown in the figure. Each such indifference curve shows the certainty equivalent corresponding to various uncertain outcomes. Figure 13.5 shows that the manager is indifferent between the certainty of $100,000 and a gamble in which the expected net worth is $200,000 and the risk, as measured by the coefficient of variation, is 3.1. Using such indifference curves, we can estimate the certainty equivalent of any uncertain situation. (In contrast to most of the indifference curves in Chapter 3, these indifference curves slope upward to the right. Why? Because the manager prefers less risk to more risk. In Chapter 3 the consumer preferred more of each commodity to less.)

In practice, of course, it is not easy to obtain such indifference curves, just as it is not easy to obtain the utility functions on which they are based. Because managers have limited time and patience, it may not be feasible to get more than a limited amount of information concerning their utility functions. Nor is it always clear which of a number of managers is the relevant one. If many managers play an important role in a particular decision and they have diverse utility curves, they may come to different conclusions. But of course this should be expected. Indeed it would be strange if managers with various attitudes toward risk did not come to divergent conclusions when facing with a choice among alternatives entailing different amounts of risk.

CERTAINTY EQUIVALENCE AND THE MARKET FOR INSURANCE

Consider managers holding mortgage debt curently worth $900 million in early 2009. They estimate there is a 25 percent chance the market will worsen and the worth of the bonds will drop to $400 million. They also estimate a 75 percent chance the market will remain relatively constant. The expected wealth of the bonds is therefore

$$0.25(400) + 0.75(900) = 100 + 675 = \$775 \text{ million}$$

If the managers are risk-averse, they may have a utility (U) function of

$$U = W^{0.5}$$

Hence the expected utility from the bonds is

$$0.25(400)^{0.5} + 0.75(900)^{0.5} = 0.25(20) + 0.75(30) = 5 + 22.5 = 27.5$$

The certainty equivalent is the monetary sum that would make the managers indifferent between selling the bonds now or holding them until the uncertainty is resolved. It is equal in expected utility to that of the gamble just calculated:

$$U = W^{0.5} = 27.5$$

Squaring both sides yields $W =$ $756.25 million. This should be the reservation price of the managers for selling the bonds at a discount.

Certainty equivalents are also used to create metrics in the insurance industry. The LBI Insurance Company provides coverage to protect individuals, such as the managers just described, against catastrophic events. LBI offers full coverage insurance—it will cover the insured's entire loss (500 in this case). LBI is risk-neutral. What premium should managers at LBI charge for this full coverage policy?

The expected payout for LBI managers is $125. They have a 25 percent chance of paying out $500 and a 75 percent chance of paying out $0. Therefore we expect a premium of at least $125, so that LBI can expect to at least break even on the policy.[8] What is the maximum that the mortgage-holding managers would pay for such a policy? This is where the certainty equivalent becomes relevant. If LBI charges

8. We are simplifying here. Although the expected payout on this policy is $125, LBI incurs other costs that it must cover if it is to stay in business, such as agents who sell policies and are paid commissions, back office staff who underwrite and process and pay claims, and executive compensation. However, insurance companies invest the premiums they receive and earn income from those investments. In this analysis we implicitly assume that the costs other than the expected payout are covered by the earnings from the invested premiums. In addition, we assume that LBI is risk-neutral. This is not an unreasonable assumption because LBI insures many individuals, and the probability of a catastrophic event occurring to its customers is close to 25 percent (if all are clones of the managers analyzed here). Thus LBI diffuses its risk by insuring many people.

STRATEGY SESSION: Pepsico Risk Management

Pepsico faces market risks due to changes in commodity prices (raw materials and energy), foreign exchange, and interest rates. But it's not just the commodity price risk that differentiates Pepsico from the risks facing FedEx. It's how it handles those risks.

Pepsico uses derivatives as cash flow or fair value hedges. It limits hedging transactions to its underlying exposure. Therefore, a change in its derivative instruments would be substantially offset by an opposite change in the value of the underlying hedged items, thus protecting the company from risk due to those hedged items. Should the value of a hedge not offset the change in the value of the hedged item, the company would not have fully protected itself against risk. This is called an *ineffective hedge*.

In addition to the use of derivatives, Pepsico protects against commodity price changes by contracts that fix prices and other pricing agreements and by diversifying geographically where it purchases commodities. In addition, it engages in productivity-enhancing endeavors with the objective of lowering its costs of doing business. The derivatives tend to be limited to no more than two years' duration and are used primarily in the natural gas, diesel fuel, and

fruit markets. Pepsico has not suffered from ineffective hedges with either these instruments or the foreign currency instruments below.

Because 44 percent of net revenue is generated outside the United States (with slightly less than half of that from Canada, Mexico, and Great Britain), the company is subject to currency fluctuation risks. Pepsico tends to enter into forward contracts of no more than two years' duration to handle this risk.

Pepsico manages its debt and investment portfolios centrally, considering investment opportunities, tax consequences, and overall financing strategies. It uses interest rate swaps and cross-currency interest rate swaps to manage interest expense and foreign exchange risk. Such instruments change the interest rate and currency of specific debt issues. When a specific debt instrument is issued, a counterpart swap instrument is entered into concurrently. The notional amounts, interest payments, and maturity dates of the swaps match the principal amounts, interest rates, and maturity dates of the original debt instruments.

Source: 2007 Pepsico Annual Report, pp. 38–39.

$143.75 for the policy, the managers would be left with $756.25 ($900 − $143.75) for sure. (If no loss occurs, they pay only the premium, so they have $900 − $143.75 = $756.25; but if the catastrophic event of 500 occurs, it is paid in full, in which case the managers would have $900 − $143.75 − $500 + $500 = $756.25.) With the policy, the managers always will have the certain wealth of $756.25 or the utility of $(\$756.25)^{0.5} = 27.5$. Notice that this is exactly the same expected utility they had with no insurance as shown earlier. Hence they are indifferent between buying the full coverage insurance policy for $143.75 and facing the gamble against nature described earlier because both give an expected utility of 27.5.

STRATEGY SESSION: The Use of Risk-Adjusted Discount Rates

Another way to introduce risk into the valuation model in equation (13.7) is to adjust the discount rate, i. This method, like that discussed in the previous section, is based on a manager's risk preferences. For example, suppose the figure shows a manager's indifference curve between expected rate of return and risk. As is evident from the fact that this curve slopes upward to the right, this manager is willing to accept greater risks only if he obtains a higher expected rate of return. Specifically, he is indifferent between a riskless investment yielding an 8 percent return and a risky investment ($\sigma = 2$) yielding an expected 12 percent return. In other words, as the risk increases, a bigger expected profit is required to compensate for the higher risk.

The difference between the expected rate of return on a particular risky investment and that on a riskless investment is called the risk premium. For example, if the manager in the figure can obtain an 8 percent return from a riskless investment, he will require a risk premium of 4 percent (12 percent minus 8 percent) to compensate for the level of risk

corresponding to $\sigma = 2$. This is the extra rate of return required to induce him to make such a risky investment. If he is offered less than this 4 percent risk premium, he will not make the risky investment.

Because the required rate of return depends on how risky an investment is, managers can adjust the basic valuation model in equation (13.7) to account for risk by modifying the discount rate, i. The adjusted version of equation (13.7) is

$$PV = \sum_{t=1}^{N} \frac{\pi_j}{(1 + r)^t} \qquad (13.8)$$

where r is the risk-adjusted discount rate. The risk-adjusted discount rate is the sum of the riskless rate of return and the risk premium required to compensate for the investment's level of risk. If the risk is such that $\sigma = 2$, the risk-adjusted discount rate would be 12 percent for the manager in the figure. This risk-adjusted rate equals 8 percent (the riskless rate) plus 4 percent (the risk premium).

Manager's Indifference Curve between Expected Rate of Return and Risk

The manager is indifferent between a riskless return of 8 percent and gambles with the expected rate of return and risk shown in the figure. Similar indifference curves exist for riskless rates of return other than 8 percent.

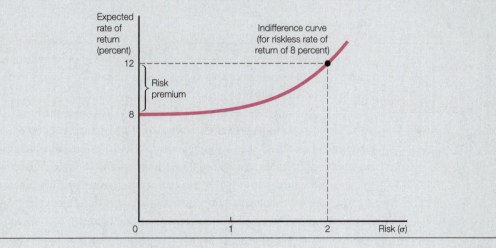

The difference between the premium that will just cover LBI's expected payout ($125) and the maximum that the managers would pay ($143.75) is called the risk premium, or the amount the managers are willing to pay the insurance company above the expected value of the loss. The risk premium is $18.75 in this case. If the premium (P) is between 125 and 143.75, the managers prefer to buy insurance (because the utility of $900 - P > 27.5$) and the insurance company will sell the policy (because the expected profit of $P - 125 > 0$). If LBI acts like a monopolist, it charges $143.75 (or epsilon below) for the policy and extracts all the managers' surplus from purchasing it.

SUMMARY

1. The probability of an event is the proportion of times this event occurs over the long run. Expected profit is the sum of the amount of money gained (or lost) if each outcome occurs times the occurrence probability of the outcome.

2. Managers can use a decision tree to graphically represent a decision problem as a series of choices, each of which is depicted by a decision fork. However, the tree also has chance forks reflecting the impact of risk on each choice. A decision tree can be used to determine the course of action with the highest expected profit. A variety of examples were discussed, including Tomco Oil Corporation's decision whether to drill an oil well at a site in Kansas.

3. The value of perfect information to managers is the increase in expected profit if they could obtain completely accurate information concerning the outcome of the relevant situation (but they do not yet know what this information will be). This is the maximum amount managers should pay to obtain such information. Methods were provided to calculate the expected value of perfect information.

4. Risk is often measured by the standard deviation or coefficient of variation of the probability distribution of profit. How managers choose to maximize expected profit depends on their attitude toward risk. We represent a manager's attitude toward risk by his or her utility function.

5. To construct such a utility function, managers initially set the utility attached to two monetary values arbitrarily. Then managers choose between the certainty of one of the other monetary values and a gamble in which the possible outcomes are the two monetary values whose utilities were set arbitrarily. Repeating this procedure over and over can estimate a manager's utility function.

6. One way managers can adjust the basic valuation model for risk is to use certainty equivalents in place of the expected profit figures in equation (13.7). To do this, construct indifference curves (based on the manager's utility function) showing the certainty equivalent corresponding to various uncertain outcomes.

7. Another way managers can introduce risk into the valuation model is to adjust the discount rate. To do this, managers should construct indifference curves between expected rate of return and risk, based on their utility functions. Using such indifference curves, managers can estimate the risk premium (if any) that is appropriate.

wwnorton.com/studyspace

PROBLEMS

1. The president of the Martin Company is considering two alternative investments, *X* and *Y*. If each investment is carried out, there are four possible outcomes. The present value of net profit and probability of each outcome follow:

Outcome	Investment X Net Present Value	Probability	Outcome	Investment Y Net Present Value	Probability
1	$20 million	0.2	A	$12 million	0.1
2	8 million	0.3	B	9 million	0.3
3	10 million	0.4	C	6 million	0.1
4	3 million	0.1	D	11 million	0.5

a. What are the expected present value, standard deviation, and coefficient of variation of investment *X*?

b. What are the expected present value, standard deviation, and coefficient of variation of investment *Y*?

c. Which investment is riskier?

d. The president of the Martin Company has the utility function

$$U = 10 + 5P - 0.01P^2$$

where *U* is utility and *P* is net present value. Which investment should she choose?

2. William J. Bryan is the general manager of an electrical equipment plant. He must decide whether to install a number of assembly robots in his plant. This investment would be risky because both management and the workforce have no real experience with the introduction or operation of such robots. His indifference curve between expected rate of return and risk is as shown in the figure.

a. If the riskiness (σ) of this investment equals 3, what risk premium does he require?

b. What is the riskless rate of return?

c. What is the risk-adjusted discount rate?

d. In calculating the present value of future profit from this investment, what interest rate should be used?

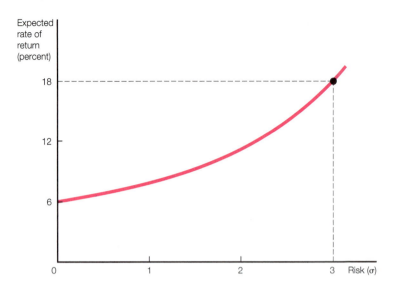

3. The Zodiac Company is considering the development of a new type of plastic. Whether the plastic will be successful depends on the outcome of a research project being carried out at a major university. Zodiac's executives have no reliable means of estimating the university research team's probability of success. Zodiac's gains (or losses), depending on the outcome of the university research project, are as follows:

Action	Outcome of University Research Project	
	Success	Failure
Zodiac develops plastic	$50 million	−$8 million
Zodiac does not develop plastic	0	0

On the basis of the information given, can you calculate the expected value of perfect information? Why or why not?

4. The Electro Corporation, which manufactures television sets, has a fixed cost of $1 million per year. The gross profit from each TV set sold—that is, the price less the average variable cost—is $20. The expected value of the number of sets the company sells per year is 100,000. The standard deviation of the number of sets sold per year is 10,000.

   a. What is the expected value of the firm's annual profit?
   b. What is the standard deviation of the firm's annual profit?
   c. What is the coefficient of variation of the firm's annual profit?

5. Richard Miller, a Wall Street trader, says he is risk-neutral. Suppose we let 0 be the utility he attaches to $100,000 and 1 be the utility he attaches to $200,000.

If what he says is true, what is the utility he attaches to (a) $400,000? (b) $40,000? (c) −$20,000?

6. The chief executive officer of a publishing company says she is indifferent between the certainty of receiving $7,500 and a gamble where there is a 0.5 chance of receiving $5,000 and a 0.5 chance of receiving $10,000. Also, she says she is indifferent between the certainty of receiving $10,000 and a gamble where there is a 0.5 chance of receiving $7,500 and a 0.5 chance of receiving $12,500.

   a. Draw (on a piece of graph paper) four points on the utility function of this publishing executive.
   b. Does she seem to be a risk averter, a risk lover, or risk-neutral? Explain.

7. The Oahu Trading Company is considering the purchase of a small firm that produces clocks. Oahu's management feels there is a 50–50 chance, if Oahu buys the firm, that it can mold the firm into an effective producer of washing machine parts. If the firm can be transformed in this way, Oahu believes that it will make $500,000 if it buys the firm; if it cannot be transformed in this way, Oahu believes that it will lose $400,000.

   a. Construct a decision tree to represent Oahu's problem.
   b. What are the decision forks? (Are there more than one?)
   c. What are the chance forks? (Are there more than one?)
   d. Use the decision tree to solve Oahu's problem. In other words, assuming that the firm wants to maximize the expected profit, should Oahu buy the firm?
   e. Before Oahu makes a decision concerning the purchase of the firm, Oahu's president learns that if the clock producer cannot be made into an effective producer of washing machine parts, there is a 0.2 probability that it can be resold to a Saudi Arabian syndicate at a profit of $100,000. (If the firm cannot be resold, Oahu will lose $400,000.)
      (1) Does this information alter the decision tree?
      (2) Can you think of three mutually exclusive outcomes if Oahu buys the firm?
      (3) What is the probability of each of these outcomes?
      (4) What is the monetary value to Oahu of each of these outcomes?
   f. Use your results in part (e) to solve Oahu's problem under this new set of conditions. In other words, on the basis of this new information, should Oahu buy the firm?
   g. Oahu's executive vice president discovers an error in the estimate of how much Oahu will gain if it buys the clock manufacturer and turns it into an effective producer of washing machine parts.
      (1) Under the circumstances in part (d), how big would this error have to be to reverse the indicated decision?
      (2) Under the circumstances in part (e), how big would the error have to be to reverse the indicated decision?

8. The National Aeronautics and Space Administration (NASA) estimated the probability of a crash of the space shuttle to be 1 in 100,000, whereas the probability was in fact closer to about 0.01–0.02. If a decision tree had been used to determine whether to attempt a launch of the shuttle, what difference, if any, would this have made?

9. The *East Chester Tribune* must decide whether to publish a Sunday edition. The publisher thinks the probability is 0.6 that a Sunday edition would be a success and 0.4 that it would be a failure. If it is a success, she will gain $100,000. If it is a failure, she will lose $80,000.

    a. Construct a decision tree corresponding to the problem, and use backward induction to solve the problem. (Assume that the publisher is risk-neutral.)

    b. List all forks in the decision tree you constructed; then indicate whether each is a decision fork or a chance fork and state why.

10. Roy Lamb has an option on a particular piece of land, and he must decide whether to drill on the land before the expiration of the option or give up his rights. If he drills, he believes that the cost will be $200,000. If he finds oil, he expects to receive $1 million; if he does not find oil, he expects to receive nothing.

    a. Construct a decision tree to represent Lamb's decision.

    b. Can you tell whether he should drill on the basis of the available information? Why or why not?
    Lamb believes that the probability of finding oil if he drills on this piece of land is 0.25, and the probability of not finding oil if he drills there is 0.75.

    c. Can you tell whether he should drill on the basis of the available information? Why or why not?

    d. Suppose Lamb can be demonstrated to be a risk lover. Should he drill? Why or why not?

    e. Suppose Lamb is risk-neutral. Should he drill?

CHAPTER 14

PRINCIPAL–AGENT ISSUES AND MANAGERIAL COMPENSATION

PRINCIPAL–AGENT ISSUES

How would you behave if we gave you millions of dollars and tickets to Las Vegas? This same question is faced by most upper-level managers. We assume managers seek to maximize value for shareholders; for the most part this is true. But managers face situations where their personal utility function conflicts with that of being an agent of the firm. This is at the heart of the **principal–agent issues** we discuss in this chapter. A conflict of interest arises when one person, the agent, makes decisions on behalf of another, the principal, in the face of uncertainty. The uncertainty is caused by imperfect monitoring of managerial behavior. In publicly held firms, managers (agents) make decisions that affect the wealth of shareholders (principals).

Principal–agent issues When managers (agents) make decisions that affect the wealth of shareholders (principals).

When the interests of the principal and agent are identical, we do not worry about this issue. For example, the captain and sailors on a ship in a storm need each other to save the ship. Because the sailors know the captain wishes to save his own life, the sailors may be confident he will make decisions that are also in the best interests of the sailors. Issues arise when interests and preferences are not identical. Hence principal–agent issues are not confined to business; we see them arise in most professions. For example, will a general, who is not on the battlefield, devise strategies that best serve the soldiers under his command? Generals may wish to win battles; soldiers prefer to stay alive. Can we be sure that elected politicians really serve their constituents and are not nudged away from that goal by interest groups? Will a plaintiff's lawyer be tempted to advise her client to go to trial (which enhances the visibility of the lawyer) rather than to accept a good settlement offer? Will a doctor prescribe treatment that is best for his patient, or might the doctor use the patient to further a research agenda or prescribe treatment that leads to the highest payment for the doctor? It is human nature to face such conflicts.

To understand the principal–agent relationship in business, we need to consider the effects of uncertainty and information. One form of uncertainty occurs because the outcomes of agents' actions are not linked in a totally deterministic way with their effort. Knowledge of results does not necessarily imply anything about effort. This lack of a direct link is caused by information asymmetry; that is, agents and principals do not share common sets of information.

The traditional corporate governance structure is straightforward. Shareholders own the firm's assets and assume the risks of doing business. Any residual from the actions of managers is split among the shareholders. Shareholders hire managers (agents) to run the business. Agents choose actions from a number of alternative possibilities (such as allocating resources within the firm). Actions affect the welfare of both the agent and the principals. However, the interests of the two parties are not necessarily identical.

Principals and agents play a noncooperative game. Principals determine rules that assign agent compensation as a function of the principal's observation of firm performance. But there is asymmetric information here: Agents (managers) have more information about the action than does the principal. This asymmetric information consists of two basic issues: The agent's action is not directly observable by the principal, and the outcome of the action is not completely determined by the agent's action.

The first asymmetric information issue is the hidden action or moral hazard. The term moral hazard arises because of insurance considerations. For example, obtaining fire insurance dulls incentives for caution and can even create incentives for arson. The most common hidden action issue in the corporate world is determining the effort of agents. Effort has a disutility to the agent but has a value to the principal because it increases the probability of a favorable outcome.

In this chapter we discuss the principal–agent issues common to most managers. Our guidelines will help managers anticipate these issues and minimize their disruptive effect. Many principal–agent issues arise under the umbrella of the firm because of the inherent conflict between the collective and individual. We show how incentive schemes like bonuses, equity, and options help converge preferences and resolve much of this conflict.

We also show why managers need to anticipate and control the incentive conflicts that arise between shareholders and creditors. For example, such conflicts might prevent managers from adopting investment projects despite the fact that they add value.

Finally, we explore the implications of principal–agent issues in looking at the evolution of product liability laws. In particular, these laws provide incentives for managers to produce safe products. However, we also show that in the information age, product liability laws may not be necessary, and the price mechanism may provide similar protections for consumers.

THE DIVERGING PATHS OF OWNERS AND MANAGERS

One of the most important principal–agent issues encountered in business is that between the owners of a firm and its managers. The owners typically are shareholders who purchase the stock as an investment, investors who simply buy shares in a mutual fund, or pensioners whose assets are invested in many companies. Most investors probably are interested in maximizing the value of their investment, which means either maximizing the income their assets yield or maximizing the value of those assets.

Clearly shareholders are concerned about the value of their shares. One question we can ask is whether managers care as much as shareholders do about maximizing share value. And if they don't, what other goals might managers have? Let us make a plausible, though not necessarily complete, list of alternative goals that may prevent managers from always taking actions to maximize firm value:

- *Minimizing effort:* Increasing profit often takes hard work. There is always disutility to work given the opportunity cost of leisure. So managers face the following question: Will I be rewarded for my hard work? Given a choice between two activities, one involving a little more effort and the other a lot more effort, which will most managers choose? The manager supplies the effort while the owner reaps the profit. Managerial behavior is largely driven by how owners structure compensation. Some examples suggest that many marginal decisions of managers tilt in favor of less effort rather than higher profit.
- *Maximizing job security:* Many decisions of managers involve risk. Often risky projects are characterized by a high potential reward or a large potential loss. Managers may be disinclined to make risky choices that could jeopardize their employment. Suppose an investment decision carries a large probability of very high returns and a small chance of failure that would cause the firm itself to fail. Shareholders, being diversified, might be inclined to accept this risk. Managers, however, might be more concerned with the downside (they do not share the upside profit and could lose their jobs given the downside risk), so they might be tempted to avoid such risky choices.
- *Avoiding failure:* Managers can be rewarded for good performance and penalized for bad results. If a risky project is undertaken, the manager is rewarded if results

(due somewhat to chance) are favorable and penalized if results are unfavorable. Often managers believe that bad results are much more likely to be noticed than good results. If so, they are disinclined to take risks.

- *Enhancing reputation and employment opportunities:* Although we argue that sometimes reputation is promoted by doing things that benefit shareholders, this is not always so. For example, a CEO with ambition to hold public office might be more concerned about showing himself to be a "good citizen" than maximizing the profit of the firm. Therefore, prices charged might be lowered below their profit-maximizing level. Alternatively, a manager might conduct contract negotiations with another firm partly with a view to establishing a personal relationship that could be a springboard to a new job.

- *Consuming perquisites:* Examples can include luxury travel, expensive artwork in the office, corporate donations to favorite charities, and employing favored people.

- *Pay:* The manager presumably works for pay; and as we shall see, both the level and structure of the compensation package become important parts of the principal–agent story.

THE PRINCIPAL–AGENT SITUATION

Figure 14.1 shows a diagram of the principal–agent situation. The principal employs an agent who performs a task that results in a benefit to the principal. The benefit is called output. The principal must pay the agent. This compensation can be a fixed sum or it can depend on the output. The level of output depends on the quantity and quality of the effort provided by the agent. If this effort were observable by the principal, the principal could simply require a certain level of effort, verify that this level of effort was provided, and compensate the agent accordingly. But effort is not always observable or measurable. The principal–agent environment is one in which effort cannot be perfectly monitored by the principal and therefore cannot be directly rewarded. The efficient solution requires some alignment of interests of the two parties. In this way, even if the principals cannot perfectly see what the agents are doing, they still can be assured that what is good for the agent is also good for the principal.

Examples of Principal–Agent Issues

Returning to a more familiar theme in this book, we believe managers generally take actions to maximize firm value. This seems reasonable because the firm's owners (shareholders) are clearly interested in the value of their shares, and this value rests on the long-term profitability of the firm. We would expect the shareholders to appoint a board of directors and management team that pursue the profit objective. However, corporate governance is more complex. A subject of considerable research is whether boards really do control managers or vice versa.

FIGURE 14.1

The Principal–Agent Problem

The principal employs an agent to undertake a task (produce output for the principal). The agent must expend effort to produce output; the more effort, the more output. Because the principal cannot observe (and therefore cannot reward) the effort, the agent tends to "shirk," or reduce effort, which in turn reduces the output for the principal.

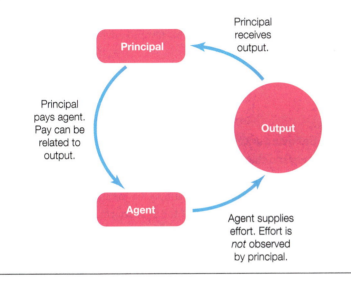

What is clear is that although managers are accountable in the long run to the owners, they still have considerable discretion in making decisions. Consider some examples.

1. Managers at a life insurance company are thinking about selling a new product through one of two distribution channels. One alternative is to use an existing distribution channel: a network of independent agents who are paid commissions. This approach is safe but has a low expected profit. The other choice is to establish an electronic distribution system. This is new and untried; but if it succeeds, profit could be very high. If the expected profit is high enough for the e-business channel, this system might be best for the shareholders. Shareholders would certainly benefit from the higher expected profit. Moreover, they probably are not too concerned about risk because most shareholders hold a number of securities and can diversify their risk. However, managers might worry more about risk because if the e-project is chosen and the firm has bad luck, the managers might lose their jobs. Therefore, managers might be tempted to play it safe with the existing distribution network even though electronic distribution could be better for shareholders.

2. Managers at many firms make charitable contributions, and it can be argued that some level of charity benefits shareholders. This visibility might stimulate demand for the firm's products and cast the firm in a favorable light with legislators and regulators. Charity also might bring some benefit in courts. For example, a car manufacturer that donates considerable sums to university safety research might find that this charitable giving is an important signal of its commitment to safety, which helps in the defense of lawsuits. Now consider a manager who has a personal agenda: He is a strong supporter of environmental causes. This manager not only increases the level of charitable giving above what is optimal for the shareholders but also redirects it to his favored environmental charity.

THE EFFECT OF RISK, INFORMATION, AND COMPENSATION ON PRINCIPAL–AGENT ISSUES

Managerial Behavior and Effort

We cannot understand the world of managers until we discuss the costs of effort. Achieving a target level of profit requires that managers incur some personal cost, which we call effort. This effort might simply be the manager's time required to attain that level of output, and the cost to the manager is the value of that time. But time is not the only dimension. Certain tasks require less pleasant work than others. Spending time with clients on the golf course may be valued differently by a manager than spending time bargaining with the union over wages. Managers may sacrifice other things to attain a profit goal. For example, to increase expected profit, a manager may cut down on perquisites and employ the best engineer rather than giving the job to her favorite niece. The cost to the manager may be a direct cost or an opportunity cost. The personal cost to the manager of making a decision reflects the quantity and quality of effort required. Given a choice among activities, most managers will exert some bias toward tasks that require less effort. Of course shareholders prefer managers to exert more effort.

We show how managers can work with owners to resolve some of these principal–agent issues. To do so, we solve profit-maximizing equations similar to those in earlier chapters. However, in earlier chapters we saw how managers often try to choose a quantity (and a price) for a given product to maximize profit, or they purchase the least costly input mix. In the principal–agent context, owners can design the manager's compensation to maximize profit; that is, owners can modify managerial behavior via compensation structures. In doing this, they recognize that how managers are compensated affects the managers' choice of effort.

We now represent the situation more precisely. The profit to the firm, π, depends on the manager's effort, e. We write this function as $\pi(e)$ to remind us of the impact of effort. For the moment we assume profit is not risky. Once the manager chooses effort, we can forecast the profit with certainty. Profit is total revenue minus total costs, and the manager's effort affects profit by changing the total revenue. Therefore we write revenue as $R(e)$ to show that it depends on effort. Finally we divide total cost between the manager's compensation, S, and all other costs, C. Profit is now written as

$$\text{Profit} = \{\text{Revenue}\} - \{\text{Costs}\}$$
$$= \{\text{Revenue}\} - \{\text{Managerial compensation} + \text{Other costs}\}$$
$$\pi(e) = \{R(e)\} - \{S + C\}$$

More effort on the part of the manager results in higher revenue. However, for the moment we assume that S is a flat salary and cannot change relative to effort. For simplification, we assume other costs are not affected by the manager's effort. We could assume that managers could reduce costs if they tried harder. But this would complicate our analysis, and the main ideas we develop will be substantially the same anyway.

   Prior to deducting the manager's salary, let $\pi(e) = R(e) - C$; and profit after deduction of salary, $\pi(e) = R(e) - S - C$, has the upward slope shown in Figure 14.2. If the owners were to choose the level of effort they wished the manager to supply, they would choose the highest feasible level. However, owners cannot sim-

---

FIGURE 14.2

The Principal–Agent Problem with a Flat Salary

Because the net benefit to the agent is the salary minus the disutility of effort, this benefit declines as effort increases. Accordingly, the agent reduces effort, which reduces revenue.

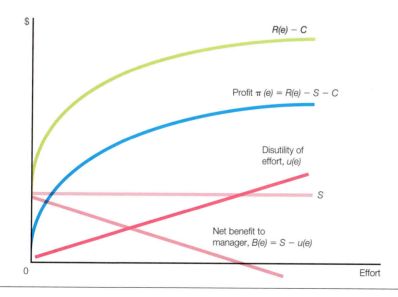

ply choose the level of effort, *e*, to maximize profit. The manager, not the owners, must choose *e*. The manager has his or her own objectives and chooses a level of effort to maximize these personal objectives. The manager is not only a member of the collective; she is also self-interested.

The objective of the manager is to maximize the net benefit of employment. The manager obtains income from employment and prefers this income to be high. To gain this income, the manager must supply effort. The cost to the manager of supplying effort is shown as the function $u(e)$; the net benefit to the manager is her compensation minus the cost in effort it took to achieve it. So there is a **disutility of effort**, which is a measure of the cost to the manager of supplying effort. At the very least, the manager must suffer an opportunity cost. More effort involves more cost, or disutility, to the manager, so $u(e)$ slopes upward. The net benefit to the manager of working at a given level of effort is now shown as

$$B(e) = S - u(e)$$

Because the salary is constant and disutility increases with effort, the net benefit, $B(e)$, must slope downward, as shown in Figure 14.2. Therefore, the manager, who bears all of the cost of effort but gets none of the reward, is better off with as little effort as possible—in this case, zero effort. In contrast, the shareholders, who get all of the benefit of the manager's effort but pay none of the cost, want maximum effort from the manager.

The incentives for managers and owners when managers are paid a straight salary are summarized in Figure 14.3. At the top of the diagram, the principal wants to maximize profit but cannot control the manager's effort. The owner pays a flat salary. At the bottom of the picture, the manager wants to maximize the net

Disutility of effort A measure of the cost to the manager of supplying effort.

FIGURE 14.3

The Principal–Agent Problem with Flat Pay

The owner pays the manager a flat salary. The manager chooses to minimize effort; therefore revenue and profit fall.

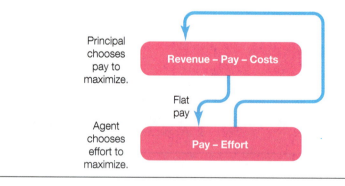

benefit of employment; but because pay is constant relative to effort, maximizing this benefit is achieved only by reducing effort. Managers tend to exert less effort when effort is not correlated to a higher net benefit.

Resolving the Incentive Conflict If Effort Is Observable

How can owners motivate managers to work harder? If owners can observe the effort provided by managers, the owners can reward managers directly in relation to the effort. Look at Figure 14.4. This is similar to Figure 14.3 except for the inclusion of incentive pay. The pay by the owners is scaled to the manager's effort. Now the manager's choice of effort is more complex. Although effort is unattractive in itself, it has the compensating advantage of increasing the manager's pay; so the manager is now persuaded to increase effort, which in turn increases revenue and profit.

To see how this works in more detail, let the owners structure the compensation in two parts. The first part, K, is a fixed amount. $U(e)$ is an additional amount that varies with managerial effort. So $U(e)$ represents the reward paid by the firm for managerial effort, while the lowercase $u(e)$ represents the monetary value of the disutility of effort to the manager. When $U(e) = u(e)$, the manager is fully compensated for effort, as we will see shortly. Because compensation now is a function of effort, we write it as $S(e)$:

$$S(e) = K + U(e)$$

FIGURE 14.4

Motivating Managers When Effort Is Observable

The owner pays incentive compensation based directly on effort. Because the agent's pay increases with effort, the agent increases his effort. This in turn increases the firm's revenue. If the increase in revenue exceeds the increase in pay, profit increases.

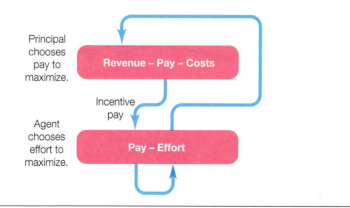

Principal chooses pay to maximize.

Revenue – Pay – Costs

Incentive pay

Agent chooses effort to maximize.

Pay – Effort

This is shown in Figure 14.5. The profit now is

$$\pi(e) = R(e) - S(e) - C$$
$$= R(e) - [K + U(e)] - C$$

which is shown in Figure 14.5. With full information regarding the actions of managers, owners can easily identify their preferred effort level as that which maximizes profit. Note that only $R(e)$ and $U(e)$ depend on effort, so the maximum is obtained by

$$\frac{\Delta\pi(e)}{\Delta e} = \frac{\Delta R(e)}{\Delta e} - \frac{\Delta U(e)}{\Delta e} = 0$$

which simply says the marginal benefit from effort (in terms of increased revenue, $R(e)$) must equal the marginal cost of compensating the managers for effort. Note that profit achieves a clear maximum in Figure 14.5 at effort level e^*. This is because profit reflects both the benefits to the shareholders and the costs to the manager for which the owners now have to pay him. The shareholders would wish to maximize profit at effort level e^*.

FIGURE 14.5

The Principal–Agent Problem with Pay as a Function of Effort

The manager is paid incentive compensation that increases with effort. Because this offsets the disutility of effort for the manager, the manager now expends more effort, which increases revenue and profit.

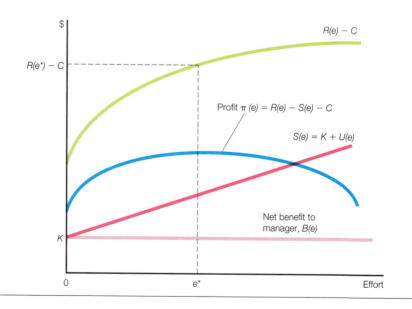

QUANT OPTION

Managers will maximize profit when

$$d\pi(e)/de = dR(e)/de - dU(e)/de = 0$$

Now what does the manager choose to do? The manager receives a net benefit, $B(e)$, equal to compensation minus the cost of effort:

$$B(e) = S(e) - u(e)$$
$$= K + U(e) - u(e)$$

If the part of compensation designed to compensate the manager for effort, $U(e)$, is exactly equal to the disutility of effort, $u(e)$, then

$$B(e) = K$$

The manager now is fully compensated for the effort supplied and is quite happy to supply any effort level. How can we get the manager to choose exactly e^*, which maximizes profit for the shareholders? The simple answer is for the shareholders to tell the manager to produce e^* in effort.

In theory, the inherently different interests of managers and owners could be accommodated if all managerial actions could simply be observed and evaluated. Managers could be given specific directions on what actions to take. For example, the owners would allow a manager to consume some perquisites because they bring benefit to the owners, but he might not be allowed to consume other perks that benefit the manager with no redeeming impact on profit.

However, this ignores the main issue. Managers, by the nature of their duty, have better information with which to make decisions than that held by shareholders. Managers are appointed precisely because they have the time and skill to make decisions. Shareholders have no time to manage every firm in which they own some shares; nor do they have the expertise to evaluate each decision. Nor can a board of directors manage every decision. Managers are generally given considerable freedom in operating discretion. In the long run, the impact of their stewardship of a firm can be inferred from how it performs. But the long run can be very long, and this permits managers considerable flexibility in balancing their own ambitions against those of the firm's owners. This discretion means that owners do not observe all the actions of the manager. In effect, it is too costly for owners to perfectly monitor managerial effort.

The weekly revenue, $R(e)$, of a retail store called Sporting Goods depends on the manager's effort, e; the more effort she provides, the higher the revenue is. The effort is the number of hours worked. However, because many of the working hours are not spent in the store, the owner does not know directly how many hours the manager actually works. Assume that even if the manager supplies no effort, revenue would equal 3,500. Effort by the manager causes revenue to increase by $100e^{0.5}$. Thus revenue can be written as

$$R(e) = 3,500 + 100e^{0.5}$$

But the manager incurs a disutility from supplying the effort of

$$u(e) = 853.55 + (7.07)e$$

In addition to paying the manager's salary, the shareholders must pay production costs of 1,000. To be persuaded to work for the store, the manager must receive a net benefit, $B(e)$, of 1,000. If she receives less, she will leave and take another job.

- How much effort, e, will the manager supply?
- How much weekly profit, $\pi(e)$, will be made?
- How much of this profit will be paid to the manager?

First, note that the owners of Sporting Goods can infer the level of effort provided by the manager from the week's revenue. This can be done by solving the revenue equation backward:

$$R(e) = 3,500 + 100e^{0.5}$$

$$\frac{R(e) - 3,500}{100} = e^{0.5}$$

$$e = \left(\frac{R(e) - 3,500}{100}\right)^2$$

The owners can pay the manager a compensation package that includes a component $U(e)$ to compensate indirectly for her effort and a bonus $\alpha\pi(e)$ related directly to profit. The profit is now

$$\pi(e) = R(e) - U(e) - C = R(e) - u(e) - C$$

Resolving the Incentive Conflict If Effort Is Not Observable: Incentive Compatibility

The nature of most principal–agent issues is that when effort is not observable by the principal, it is difficult to reward or penalize directly. The inability of owners to completely observe managerial actions gives managers some degree of freedom to pursue their own objectives, instead of always acting in the best interest of the principal.

Let us assume the firm's revenue, $R(e)$, is riskless and determined solely by the effort of the manager. The shareholders can ask, What level of effort is necessary to produce this level of revenue? In this way shareholders deduce the level of effort by observing revenue. If $R(e)$ slopes upward, as shown in Figures 14.2 and 14.5, shareholders can read backward on the graph from a given R on the vertical axis to an implied level of e on the horizontal axis. For example, if shareholders observe output level $R(e^*) - C$ in Figure 14.5, then the effort level necessary to achieve this output must have been e^*.

If the compensation component $U(e)$ is enough to compensate the manager for the disutility of her effort, $U(e) = u(e)$, she will choose to maximize her bonus, which is the same as maximizing profit:

$$\frac{\Delta\pi(e)}{\Delta e} = \frac{\Delta R(e)}{\Delta e} - \frac{\Delta u(e)}{\Delta e} = 0$$

The solution to this type of problem is now familiar. The manager simply equates the marginal benefit and marginal cost:

$$\frac{\Delta R(e)}{\Delta e} = 0.5(100)e^{-0.5} = \frac{\Delta u(e)}{\Delta e} = 7.07$$

For $R(e) = 3,500 + 100e^{0.5}$,

$$dR(e)/de = 0.5(100)e^{-0.5} = 50e^{-0.5}$$

For $u(e) = 853.55 + 7.07e$,

$$du(e)/de = 7.07$$

Setting marginal benefit equal to marginal cost yields

$$0.5(100)(e)^{-0.5} = 7.07$$

so

$$e^{0.5} = 50/7.07$$
$$e = 50^2/7.07^2$$
$$= 2,500/50$$
$$= 50$$

The manager works 50 hours per week. We can plug this effort level into the profit equation to give weekly profit:

$$\pi(e = R(e) - u(e) - C$$
$$= (3,500 + 100e^{0.5}) - (853.55 + (7.07)e) - 1,000$$
$$= (3,500 + 100(50^{0.5}) - (853.55 + (7.07)(50)) - 1,000$$
$$= (3,500 + 707) - (853.55 + 353.55) - 1,000$$
$$= 2,000$$

If the manager is to receive a net benefit, $B(e)$, of 1,000, clearly she must receive 50 percent of the profit, so $\alpha = 0.5$.

QUANT OPTION

Managers will maximize profit if

$$d\pi(e)/de = dR(e)/de - du(e)/de = 0$$

Because shareholders can infer the level of effort, observing R is as good as observing e. We can now calculate what e must have been, so we can make the same compensation payment $S(e) = K + U(e)$ as before. However, there is one snag. This ensures that the manager gets a retrospective payment that fully compensates her for effort already provided. Anticipating this reward for effort, the manager is induced to work harder. But how can the shareholders ensure the manager will choose exactly the level of effort, e^*, that they prefer?

Shareholders could make a simple but important change to the manager's compensation: Give managers a share, α, of profits, $\pi(e)$. The new compensation is $S(e) = U(e) + \alpha\pi(e)$. They replace the fixed amount K with a profit-sharing bonus.[1] Naturally, the manager does not obtain the bonus until the end of the period. Therefore, owners choose a level of bonus so the overall package is competitive and attracts and retains skilled managers. We divide the manager's compensation into two parts:

$$S(e) = (\text{Salary}) + (\text{Bonus})$$
$$= [U(e)] + [\alpha\pi(e)]$$

$\alpha\pi(e)$ is a share of profit after the salary is paid. So the profit is now

$$\pi(e) = R(e) - U(e) - C$$

This makes the bonus a real equity share in the firm.

The net benefit to the manager is now

$$B(e) = S(e) - u(e)$$
$$= U(e) + \alpha\pi(e) - u(e)$$
$$= \alpha\pi(e)$$

The last step was taken by setting the monetary compensation for effort, $U(e)$, at a level sufficient to offset the disutility of effort, $u(e)$. We have a clear alignment of the interests of the managers, who get a net benefit of $\alpha\pi(e)$, and the owners, who get the remainder $(1 - \alpha)[\pi(e)]$. Now both are interested in maximizing the net profit, $\pi(e)$.

By giving managers a share of the profits, owners converge their preferences with those of managers. Consider what level of effort owners prefer relative to what level the managers will choose. The owners get a portion of the profit, $(1 - \alpha)\pi(e)$, and the manager gets $\alpha\pi(e)$; so whatever the level of α, both shareholders and managers are happiest if $\pi(e)$ is maximized. We can think of this process in two stages:

1. The manager chooses a level of effort to maximize $\pi(e)$. This is achieved where the marginal benefit of effort equals the marginal disutility of the cost of effort.

2. The firm's owners choose a level of α such that the compensation package is competitive.

We have now introduced an important concept: **incentive compatibility**. Because the agent and the owners share in the profit of the firm, their incentives are aligned and compatible. We refer to contracts that have this alignment of interests as incentive-compatible contracts.

Incentive compatibility When the agent and the owners share in the profit of the firm; and the agent's effort maximizes the principal's profit.

1. Note that we have set part of the compensation, $U(e)$, in relation to effort. Although effort is not directly observed, the principal can infer effort from the actual level of profit.

RESOLVING THE INCENTIVE CONFLICT WHEN OUTPUT IS RISKY AND EFFORT IS NOT OBSERVABLE

The incentive issues between owners and managers change when revenue is risky and effort is not observable. With no risk, owners can infer the level of managerial effort from the firm's profit. However, when profit is risky, owners are rarely certain whether high profit is due to high effort or simply good luck (a strong economy) and whether low profit is due to low effort or bad luck. Poor management can occasionally result in short-term high profit due to random events. Similarly, determined effort can sometimes come unstuck due to the vagaries of the market.

Risk Sharing

When output is risky and effort is not observable, owners need to structure managerial compensation around two competing ideas: risk sharing and efficiency. The efficiency idea has been dealt with previously. The manager is inclined to attend to his or her own interests, so it is desirable for the firm's owners to align incentives with profit-sharing bonuses, equity participation, stock options, and similar instruments. However, the firm's profit and its equity value are uncertain. Moreover, this volatility is partly outside the control of the managers and owners. Profit and share price are affected by macroeconomic factors such as changes in interest rates, employment, inflation, foreign exchange rates, and movements in stock market indexes. Thus bonus plans impose some risk on managers.

Owners can also design managerial compensation based on who can tolerate risk at the least cost, or who is the least risk-averse. Owners tolerate risk in that managers generate some value to be divided among the stakeholders, and this value is inherently risky. The value can be expressed as the periodic profit or the value of the equity. As residual claimants, the shareholders normally get the risky profit or equity, but first they must pay the managers. Should the shareholders take out a fixed sum (a flat salary) and pay this to the managers, or should they simply give the managers a share in the risky profit or equity? For the shareholders, the riskiness of profit may not be too problematic. Most shares are owned by investors or institutions that are quite diversified. Many individual investors hold several assets in their portfolios and are concerned not about the riskiness of each stock, but about the risk in their whole portfolio. Unless the stocks are highly correlated, the risk in the portfolio can be quite modest. Therefore, investors, being able to diversify, can tolerate the risk in an individual stock. If, for example, the risk in one stock in her portfolio increased, an investor could offset this by spreading her capital over a few more stocks. Institutional investors are often much better diversified than individual investors and can easily tolerate the risk of each individual stock.

In contrast, managers are usually much less diversified. For the typical manager, the compensation received from an employer, and the equity stake in that employer, is a large proportion of his or her total wealth. Fluctuation in the value of bonuses or stock options can have a big impact on the manager's net worth. Hence we expect managers to be quite averse to risk in their compensation plan. This does not mean they will not accept a risky compensation plan. Rather, they need to be compensated for the risk; they need a **risk premium.**

Risk premium The minimum difference a manager requires to be willing to take a risk.

Comparing managers and shareholders, it seems that the riskiness of the firm's profit and equity values can be absorbed at lower cost by the shareholders than by the managers. In this view, it appears that the optimal executive compensation plan would place all risk on the shareholders—that is, pay the managers a flat salary. But what about effort?

Trading Off Risk Sharing and Efficiency

We now have two methods owners can use to align their preferences with those of managers. One method aligns the interests of the principal and the agent; that is, contracts are incentive-compatible. The other method assigns risk to the party who can bear it most easily. Can owners integrate these two methods? First they need to account for the fact that firm revenue is risky. Owners can do this by dividing revenue into two parts. The first part, $R_1(e)$, depends on the efforts of manag-

---

PROBLEM SOLVED: Two Compensation Schemes Based Solely on Risk Sharing

Consider a firm with risky equity as shown here (note that these values are before deducting for managerial compensation):

Equity = $10,000,000 (probability 0.5) or
$20,000,000 (probability 0.5)

Managers are risk-averse. We represent the manager's attitude toward risk by a utility function as shown in Chapter 13. To show risk aversion, we need to show a utility function such as that in panel A of Figure 13.4, in which utility increases at a decreasing rate as wealth increases. This type of concave utility function can be represented by a square root function as follows:

Manager's utility = $(\text{Wealth})^{0.5}$

The manager's only wealth is derived from employment. To be competitive, the firm must offer the man-

ager a compensation package that has an expected utility of 1,000; otherwise the manager will leave and find other employment. In contrast to the manager, the shareholders are risk-neutral and interested only in the expected value of the equity.

Flat Salary of $1,000,000

The manager has an expected utility sufficient to hold him or her in the job of $(1,000,000)^{0.5} = 1,000$. The shareholders have an expected equity stake, after paying the manager, of

0.5($10,000,000 − $1,000,000)
+ 0.5($20,000,000 − $1,000,000) = $14,000,000

Bonus of a Proportion, x, of the Equity

What proportion x of equity before compensation is necessary to offer the manager an expected utility of

ers: The higher the effort of managers, the higher is this component of revenue. The second part is beyond the control of the manager and depends on factors such as interest rates, economic movements, and so forth; we call this $\tilde{R}_2$. The tilde over the R shows that this component of revenue is risky. Therefore,

$$R(e) = \underset{\text{(under manager's control)}}{R_1(e)} + \underset{\text{(outside manager's control)}}{\tilde{R}_2}$$

Owners need to change the compensation structure of managers. Because they cannot observe the effort, nor can it be inferred from profit, compensation cannot depend directly on effort. Owners need to restate compensation as combining a fixed element, K, which is independent of effort, and a bonus, $\alpha\pi(e)$, which depends on profit (and effort):

$$S = K + \alpha\pi(e)$$

Correspondingly, here is the profit (note that we deduct only the direct compensation from profit—the remaining compensation, the bonus, is a share of profit):

$$\begin{aligned} \pi(e) &= R(e) - K - C \\ &= R_1(e) + \tilde{R}_2 - K - C \end{aligned}$$

1,000? We can solve this by setting the expected utility from such a bonus equal to 1,000 (the manager will receive either x times 10 million or x times 20 million):

$$\text{Expected utility} = 1,000$$
$$0.5(10,000,000x)^{0.5} + 0.5(20,000,000x)^{0.5} = 1,000$$
$$x^{0.5}[(10,000,000)^{0.5} + (20,000,000)^{0.5}] = 2,000$$
$$x^{0.5} = \frac{2,000}{7,634.4}$$
$$x = 0.06863$$

Note that the expected dollar value of the compensation paid to the manager is now 0.06863 times the expected value of equity before compensation:

Expected value of compensation
$$= 0.06863(\$15,000,000) = \$1,029,450$$

This risky compensation offers the manager the same expected utility as a flat salary of $1 million, with the manager being paid a risk premium of $29,450 to compensate for bearing the risk.

The expected value of equity remaining for the shareholders is

Expected equity to shareholders
$$= \$15,000,000 - \$1,029,450 = \$13,970,550$$

Comparing the two compensation plans, we see that both offer the manager an expected utility of 1,000, so the manager is indifferent. However, the flat salary offers shareholders an expected residual equity of $14,000,000, whereas the bonus plan leaves them with an expected equity value of only $13,970,550. Therefore, looking only at risk sharing, the flat salary is clearly preferred.

The net benefit of employment for the manager also changes because the manager is exposed to risk if she receives a bonus. The net benefit now comprises two parts. The first shows the expected utility of the manager from wealth. We show wealth as comprising only the manager's employment compensation, S.[2] The second element is the disutility of effort, $u(e)$:

2. It is easy to add in other components of wealth such as savings, financial assets, real assets, and so forth.

$$B(e) = EU(S) - u(e)$$
$$= EU[K + \alpha\pi(e)] - u(e)$$

PROBLEM SOLVED: Setting Compensation for Managers

A woman inherits the family farm when she is halfway through her MBA program. She plans to take a job in consulting and is not interested in, nor does she have the skills for, operating the farm herself. However, because the farm has been in her family for generations, she does not wish to sell it. She wants to pass it on to her children, so she decides to hire a manager. Her neighbors tell her that the going salary for a good manager is $50,000, but she is worried that such a salary will not motivate the manager to run the farm to its potential. She estimates a properly motivated manager could generate profits as shown in the table below. The profit shown in the table is profit gross of compensation costs.

In addition to the manager's effort, profit is also sensitive to the grain price. With low prices, profit is low: profit increases if grain prices move higher. With her investments and career, she is neutral toward the risk associated with farm income, hence she maximizes profit based on expected value. The manager's only source of wealth is the compensation from the farm.

Being undiversified, the manager is not risk-neutral, so he prefers to maximize expected utility. His utility function if he supplies low effort is

$$U = W^{0.5}$$

If he supplies high effort, it is

$$U = W^{0.5} - u(e)$$
$$= W^{0.5} - 46.3$$

where U is utility and W is wealth. Note that the effort he expends in working hard costs him 46.3 units of satisfaction. This represents the disutility of effort, $u(e)$.

Flat Salary

Consider first how he behaves if paid a flat salary:

Utility with low effort $= (50,000)^{0.5} = 223.6$
Utility with high effort $= (50,000)^{0.5} - 46.3 = 177.3$

Naturally, the manager's expected utility is higher if she supplies low effort. Because the manager is not rewarded for high effort, she will not work hard.

Profit and Managerial Effort

	Grain, Low-Price (Probability 0.5)	Grain, High-Price (Probability 0.5)
Low effort	$ 50,000	$150,000
High effort	$100,000	$200,000

The principal–agent incentive conflict can be presented as follows:

1. *The principal's view:* Owners must construct a compensation scheme for managers. They know they cannot perfectly observe managerial actions; so compensation cannot depend solely on effort. However, they can expect the agent to make the effort after she sees the contract terms. Therefore, they want to fashion the compensation to align their interests with that of the agent.

2. *The agent's view:* Having seen the contract terms (particularly how she will be paid), the agent selects a level of effort.

Profit-Related Compensation

When managers are paid a straight wage it is human nature not to work as hard as possible. Why would a manager expend effort if he is not paid to do so? To persuade a manager to work hard, you want to pay him a percentage of profit. If the local labor market for farm managers is efficient, you must offer compensation that generates a net 223.6 units of satisfaction. This would require a flat salary of $50,000. What percentage x of profit would achieve this? To be competitive, x should satisfy this equation:

$$\frac{\text{Expected utility with flat}}{\text{salary and low effort}} = \frac{\text{Expected utility with bonus of}}{x \text{ profit and high effort}}$$

$$223.6 = (0.5)(100{,}000x)^{0.5}$$
$$+ (0.5)(200{,}000x)^{0.5} - 46.3$$
$$2(223.6 + 46.3) = x^{0.5}[(100{,}000)^{0.5} + (200{,}000)^{0.5}]$$
$$\frac{539.8}{763.4} = x^{0.5}$$
$$x = 0.5$$

Note that the expected compensation would be $0.5[0.5(100{,}000) + 0.5(200{,}000)] = 75{,}000$. The extra $25,000 compensates the manager for both disutility of effort and risk.

So if the manager is paid 50 percent of profit and works hard, he will be just as happy as with a flat salary of $50,000 and exerting low effort. We still do not know whether the manager will choose to work hard when he gets 50 percent of profit. To see whether he will, we need to check whether the 50 percent bonus gives the manager higher expected utility with high rather than with low effort:

$$EU \text{ with high effort} = (0.5)[0.5(100{,}000)]^{0.5}$$
$$+ [0.5(200{,}000)]^{0.5} - 46.3 = 223.6$$
$$EU \text{ with low effort} = (0.5)[0.5(50{,}000)]^{0.5}$$
$$+ [0.5(150{,}000)]^{0.5} = 216$$

Therefore, the manager will choose to work hard.

The final question that needs answering is whether you, as owner, are better off paying the manager a flat $50,000 or 50 percent of profit. This is not a trivial question. This would require a flat salary of $50,000. If you pay the bonus, he will work harder, and that will increase revenues. On the other hand, you will pay him more on average if you give the 50 percent bonus (recall that average earnings with this bonus are $75,000.) To increase net profit, the extra expected revenue from high effort must exceed the additional expected compensation.

Your expected net profit will be as follows:

Flat salary: E(profit) = 0.5(50,000)
$$+ 0.5(150{,}000) - 50{,}000 = 50{,}000$$
Earnings related: E(profit) = 0.5(100,000)
$$+ 0.5(200{,}000) - 75{,}000 = 75{,}000$$

Therefore, the new 50 percent of profit plan works for both the principal and for the agent.

STRATEGY SESSION: The Value of CEO Pay

CEO pay is increasingly being questioned especially in firms where performance is poor. In many cases, shareholders receive low returns on their compensation dollars. In 2007 the CEOs of the firms in the S&P 500 earned an average of $14.2 million. This amount was over 300 times more than the average American worker earned. In 1990 CEOs earned on average over 107 times what the average worker made, and in 1980 they earned 42 times more than the average worker.

Though the use of performance-based compensation is increasing, it seems to have little effect on CEO pay even when CEOs perform poorly. For example, in 2007 KB Homes lost $929 million. Shareholders suffered huge losses as the stock price dropped from $53 at the beginning of the year to $15 toward the end of the year. Yet CEO Jeffrey Mezger still received cash bonuses totaling $6 million. Even worse was the compensation of CEOs at major financial institutions that lost billions of dollars in 2007–2008. Citigroup CEO Charles Prince was let go only after he was given a bonus of $10 million. In addition, he was granted over $1.5 million in annual perks. Stanley O'Neal of Merrill Lynch resigned in 2008 and walked away with a $161 million pay package. The Merrill board of directors then hired John Thain as the new CEO after agreeing to pay him a compensation package totaling over $83 million.

In a recent study on compensation, researchers found that 94 percent of CEOs of large firms could not be fired for poor performance without a large severance package. Another study revealed the cost to shareholders for overpaying the CEO is larger than it first appears. Because the salaries of upper-level managers are generally pegged to the CEO salary, they receive too much compensation if the CEO is overpaid. This study also revealed that while performance-based bonuses decreased in 2007, the level of discretionary bonuses (non-performance-based) increased.

Michael Jensen of Harvard Business School was an early proponent of pay for performance. He claims that boards of directors are not using the correct metrics to reward CEOs. CEO compensation does not account for the cost of capital. Jensen claims that CEO bonuses should be based on relative performance: How well did shareholders do relative to if they had invested in a company with a similar risk profile? He also advocates that CEOs pay for their stock options instead of being given them.

Sources: John Rosenthal, "Raking It In; SEC? Recession? Shareholders? Nothing Halts the Relentless Climb of CEO Salaries," *Crain's Chicago Business*, May 26, 2008, p. 18; Greg Farrell and Barbara Hansen, "Stocks May Fall, but Pay Doesn't; Many Boards Award CEOs Big Packages Despite Performance," *USA Today*, April 10, 2008, p. 1B; Louis Uchitelle, "Innovator in CEO Pay Stands by Philosophy; Flaws in Performance-Based Packages?" *The International Herald Tribune*, September 28, 2007, p. 15.

3. *Result:* At the end of the contract, the profit from the agent's activities is revealed. The agent's bonus is paid, and the remaining profit is paid to the principal.

The overall situation is illustrated in Figure 14.6. The owners pay the manager a flat salary to provide some certain income to the risk-averse manager. In addition, the manager is given a share of the profit to ensure that she will increase

FIGURE 14.6

The Principal–Agent Problem When Effort Is Not Observable

The owner pays a bonus based on profit and flat pay. Because the expected value of the bonus increases with expected effort, the agent increases that effort, which in turn increases the revenue. If the increase in revenue exceeds the increase in pay, then profit increases.

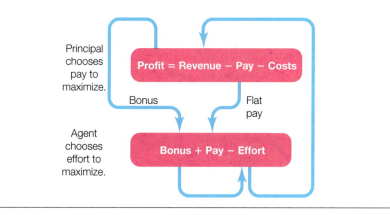

her effort, which will increase expected revenue and profit. Note that no payment relates directly to effort because this is not observable by the firm's owner. Instead the bonus motivates the manager because higher effort yields higher expected profit, and the manager gets a share of this profit.

SOME REFINEMENTS TO MANAGERIAL COMPENSATION

Figure 14.7 shows how managers behave when receiving higher utility with low effort. The higher utility function (red) shows the manager's utility of wealth when suppling low effort. The lower utility function (blue) represents the utility when managers exert high effort. It is shifted downward to show how the disutility of effort lowers overall satisfaction. Thus with a flat salary of B, the manager chooses low effort and realizes utility equals to $U(B)$.

Motivating the Manager with Profit Sharing

Figure 14.7 shows how profit-sharing schemes can affect managerial effort. These schemes give managers a straight percentage of the firm's profit. In this case the manager is paid 2 percent (1/50th) of profits. The firm's profit is

50 times A with probability 0.4
50 times C with probability 0.6

FIGURE 14.7

The Effect of Compensation Schemes on Managerial Effort

The profit sharing gives the manager a 40–60 chance of pay levels A and C, which has an expected utility of EU when the manager supplies high effort. This profit-sharing plan is designed so that working hard gives the manager the same expected utility as a flat salary of B while supplying low effort.

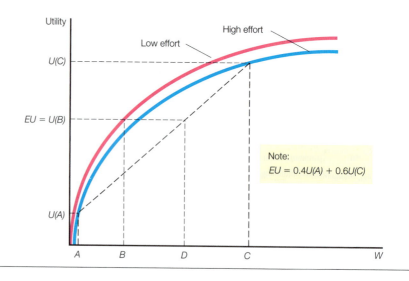

Being paid 2 percent of profit, managerial income is

A with probability 0.4 or
C with probability 0.6

The manager's expected compensation value is $(0.4)(A) + (0.6)(C) = D$ in the diagram. This scheme induces managers to work hard. The expected utility of compensation (blue line) is $(0.4)U(A) + (0.6)U(C)$, which is labeled EU in the figure. This offers exactly the same expected utility as the flat salary of B and low effort, so the manager is just as well off receiving compensation for working hard as having a flat salary and shirking. However, the expected compensation has increased from a flat value of B to an expected value of D. The difference, $D - B$, is the premium necessary to compensate the manager for the risk and disutility of effort.

Motivating the Manager with an Income Guarantee and Stock Options

Note in Figure 14.7 the manager is risking a 40 percent chance of a fall in income from B to A in accepting the profit-sharing plan. Can we achieve the same effect while protecting the manager from downside risk? Figure 14.8 shows how owners can use stock options. Suppose owners replace the incentive plan with a salary

STRATEGY SESSION: Getting the Board to Focus on the Long Term

At the urging of Warren Buffet and because of frequent criticism of corporate focus on short-term earnings, the Coca-Cola Company recently announced a new method of compensating members of their board of directors.

Typically a board member would receive a fixed fee for every board meeting or committee meeting attended. In addition, board members would receive some or all of their compensation in stock or stock options. Expenses of attending meetings would also be covered. The fee was received regardless of how the firm was performing; the stock options had value only if the stock rose during the vesting period (the time between when the option was granted and when it could be exercised) of the director. In the case of stock, payment for being on the board could go up or down depending on the stock's performance.

The Coke plan is different. If earnings per share don't increase at a rapid enough pace over a three-year period, directors will receive nothing for their service on the board. On the other hand, if the earnings per share meet or beat the standard, the board members will be rewarded handsomely. Buffet is quoted as saying, "I can't think of anything else that more directly aligns director interests with shareholder interests. As a shareholder, I love it."

Coke's previous director compensation was $125,000 per year combined in cash and stock, with added payments for those on committees. The new plan gives directors $175,000 per year in stock and no other payments. In the third year, if the earnings per share are 25.97 percent (8 percent per year compounded) or more higher than in the base year, the director will receive the value of the stock in cash at the current market price. However, if the earnings per share fail to exceed the 25.97 percent target, the director will have worked that year for nothing.

Critics of the plan note that a director in her fourth (or higher) year will have three plans working. Consider the fourth year. If the first plan looked as if it had no chance of reaching the 25.97 percent target, the director might slow down a promising project until the next year, when it could contribute to making the second plan pay off. The same reasoning holds for a first-year plan that is sure to make the target: Hold the promising project over to increase the probability that the second plan pays off.

We will see how this plan evolves. Clearly the designers feel that it is incentive-compatible between the principals (the shareholders) and the agents (the board).

Source: "Coke's Board to Get Bonus or Nothing," *The New York Times*, April 6, 2006, online at www.nytimes.com/2006/04/06/business/06place.html.

floor (a guaranteed minimum income) of E and a stock option, which has a small chance of paying a large amount of money, F.

The chances of the stock option paying off are 35 percent. Now the manager's income is either

E with probability 0.65 or
F with probability 0.35

which has an expected value of D (exactly the same as the profit-sharing plan in Figure 14.7). Note that the expected utility from this plan (if the manager works

FIGURE 14.8

Reducing Managerial Risk with Stock Options

The manager can be provided minimum compensation and strong incentives for efficiency. A flat salary of *E* is paid together with a stock option, which secures a gain of *F* minus *E* if the stock price rises sufficiently. This combination offers the manager the same expected utility as the simple profit-sharing plan in Figure 14.7.

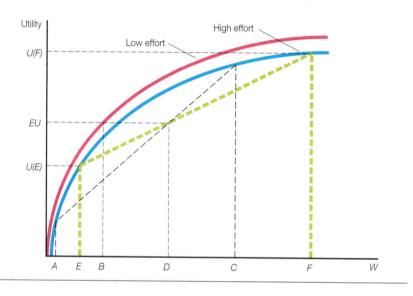

hard) is $0.65U(E) + 0.35U(F)$, which is exactly the same expected utility as from the flat salary of *B* and shirking.

Why does this scheme reduce the downside risk? First, the manager is paid a flat salary of *E*. This salary is riskless; it is paid regardless of performance. Second, the manager receives a **call option** on the firm's stock, which is at risk. This option gives managers the right to purchase the firm's shares at some future date. Moreover, the price at which the stock can be purchased (the **striking price** or exercise price) is fixed in advance (see the Strategy Session titled Call Options). These call options may have a modest value now but can be worth either nothing or a lot of money at maturity. Therefore, they offer shareholders a way of paying the managers a bonus with modest current value and high risk, with fabulous payoffs to the manager if the stock price rises significantly.

Indexed Stock Options

Both profit-sharing and stock option plans motivate managers to exert high effort; but even if they exert this greater effort, they are not guaranteed high payments. Factors beyond managerial control (such as interest rates) can affect firm performance. Hence, in introducing risk into compensation, the manager can be

Call option Option that gives managers the right to purchase the firm's shares at some future date.

Striking price The fixed price at which the stock can be purchased.

STRATEGY SESSION: Call Options

A *call option* is a contract that gives the holder the right (but not an obligation) to purchase a given number of shares of stock in a firm at a preagreed price from a counterparty (the seller of the option). The fixed price is called the *striking price* or *exercise price*.

For example, suppose you have the right to buy *x* shares in six months' time (known as *maturity*) at a striking price of $50 per share. Suppose the actual market price of the stock in six months is $42 per share. You can, if you wish, *exercise your option* to buy the stock (which is now worth $42) for the striking price of $50, but that would be silly. You can simply go to your broker and buy the stock at the going market price of $42. Why use the option to pay more than the stock is worth?

Now suppose the stock rises in price so that in six months it is worth $74. Your contract allows you to buy the stock for $50, even though it is now worth $74. You would *exercise your option* to buy the stock for $50, thus clearing a profit of $24 per share.

The value of a call option, and hence its price, depends on several features:

1. The lower the striking price, the higher the value of the option. The holder is paid the difference between the market price at maturity and the striking price (if this difference is positive); thus a lower strik-ing price increases the payoff and the current value of the call option.

2. The higher the current price of the stock, the higher its value. The higher the current stock price, the more likely the price at maturity will be above the striking price.

3. The higher the risk or volatility of the stock price, the higher the option value. Increased risk enhances the possibility that the price at maturity will be very low (downside risk) or very high (upside risk). Increased downside risk does not hurt the option holder because the option will not be exercised, but increased upside risk enhances the payoff at maturity. Thus, the risk has a one-sided positive effect.

The methodology for pricing options was developed largely by Robert Merton and Myron Scholes, who won the 1997 Nobel Prize in Economics for their work.

In summary, a call option allows managers to make a profit if the stock price rises above the strike price at the maturity date. If the stock price at maturity falls below the strike price, the option is of no value to managers. Hence the option gives managers the chance of gain without the risk of loss. Naturally such options are valuable, and managers must expect to incur a cost (effort) to buy them from the seller.

---

penalized for poor profit performance beyond her control or rewarded simply because the market as a whole takes an upturn. Indeed, much of the impressive performance of executive compensation plans in the 1990s was due as much to the bullish economy as to managerial effort and competence. Can we purge the performance yardstick of this external or exogenous risk?

One plan that has attracted attention is the indexed stock option.[3] Here the manager is given stock options, but the striking price is not fixed. Rather, it is expressed in relation to an index of stock prices, such as the Dow Jones. As the index rises, so does the striking price of the option. This ensures the manager is not

3. These are discussed in Nicholas G. Carr, "Compensation: Refining CEO Stock Options," *Harvard Business Review* 76 (1998), pp. 15–18.

STRATEGY SESSION: Imitation Is the Best Form of Flattery

European executives are asking for and getting U.S. styles and levels of compensation packages. Compensation in the last five years has risen dramatically. For instance, BP paid its top executive $18.5 million in 2005. However, investors in some countries are resisting. U.S. styles and levels of compensation have not yet reached Asia (but their executives are now voicing the same arguments given by the Europeans). Executives in Europe argue that they compete in a world economy and therefore their compensation must be comparable to world (read U.S.) executives. In 2005 Mercer Human Resources Consulting found the median CEO compensation package (salary, bonus, and stock options) was $6.8 million for the 350 largest firms in the United States. Comparable compensation for the Financial Times Stock Index 100 firms in Britain's median was $4.3 million (a difference of 58 percent). But as recently as 1998, the U.S. compensation package was four times the British compensation package. You could say that British executives were minding the gap. In France the median compensation of CEOs of the CAC-40 benchmark stock index increased from $780,000 in 1998 to $3 million in 2004. Large increases have occurred in Germany and the Netherlands as well. In some cases, such as banking and hedge funds, compensation is higher in London than in the United States.

Shareholders have more power over CEO compensation in Europe than in the United States and can actually *de facto* veto pay. Their votes are non-binding but if the Board ignores this, the Board must be aware that the shareholders vote for the Board. In addition, the press is vigilant following executives (and their family) with paparazzi type vigilance to document the excesses (from an average person's perspective) that substantial wealth makes available.

But things could be changing in the United States. Shareholders of Verizon Communications recently passed a resolution giving them an advisory role on executive compensation analogous to the situation in Europe. The board would be aware that they could be voted out if they don't go along with shareholders' wishes. But there's more. Not listening to shareholders may cause Congress to act on executive pay. The House of Representatives has passed a bill that permits nonbinding executive compensation votes by shareholders. At approximately 20 companies, shareholders have emulated Verizon's shareholders.

Because compensation includes at least three parts (salary, bonus, and stock options), it is important to see where the growth in compensation is coming from. It's mostly in incentive pay rather than base salary. Thus British executives (in addition to arguing that they compete in the global market for executives) also argue that their pay is based on adding long-term value to the firm. While base pay has risen 7–10 percent, bonus or incentive pay has risen 75–100 percent. Thus they argue that the pay raises are incentive-compatible with the objectives of the shareholders (increasing share value). The outcry in Britain is perhaps less because of this.

In France, on the other hand, there is more outrage. One investor described it as legalized greed.

Can Asia be far behind in compensation?

Sources: "U.S.-Style Pay Packages are All the Rage in Europe," *The New York Times*, June 16, 2006, at www.nytimes.com/2006/06/16/business/businessspecial/16pay.html; "A Say on Executive Pay," *The New York Times*, May 26, 2007, at www.nytimes.com/2007/05/26/opinion/26sat3.html.

rewarded simply because the market performs well. On the downside, the striking price falls as the market index falls. This ensures the manager is not penalized for poor market performance. The net effect is that the manager is handsomely rewarded if the stock price rises relative to the market. The manager's compensation is now more closely related to factors under his or her control.

PRINCIPAL–AGENT ISSUES IN OTHER CONTEXTS

Similar incentive issues exist between an insured party and the insurance company. These issues are known as issues of **moral hazard**. If you are not insured against fire, car crashes, illness, and other life contingencies, you face the possibility of sudden and possibly crippling financial losses. These uninsured risks should make you cautious. You should take care in your driving, look after your health, and protect your home by installing smoke detectors and burglar alarms. Although these safety practices can be costly or inconvenient, you are rewarded by lowering the probability, or intensity, of a financial loss. You bear the cost of safety (you pay for the smoke alarm) and reap the reward (you avoid the costs of a fire). If you are insured, there is a separation of the costs and benefits of safety. The policyholder may incur the cost and inconvenience of safety devices and preventive behavior, but the main beneficiary is the insurance firm, which now faces lower expected claim payments.

> **Moral hazard** When a party insured against risks behaves differently from the way it would behave if it were uninsured against these risks.

Insurance moral hazard can be divided into two types: ex-ante moral hazard and ex-post moral hazard. Ex-ante moral hazard refers to the tendency of insured people and firms to take less care to prevent future losses when they have insurance. The absence of smoke alarms relates to ex-ante moral hazard. Ex-post moral hazard is equally important; this refers to the reluctance of policyholders who have already suffered some misfortune to keep the cost of the event under control. Consider a firm that has bought liability insurance against defective products and has now been sued by injured customers. The policy covers both the legal cost of defending the firm against the suit and the cost of compensating the victims. Because the insurer is paying both these costs, some managerial defendants want the settlement to be generous. They see this as a way of buying back customer goodwill at the insurer's expense. Other defendants take the opposite view. Because the insurer is paying legal costs, they want the insurer to spend virtually unlimited amounts to defend the producer's reputation, even if liability seems fairly clear.[4] Had the managers been without insurance, they might well have sought to balance the incremental costs of defending a claim with the costs of making a settlement offer to the injured customers.

Asset Substitution[5]

Our discussion has centered on the stakeholders in a firm: the shareholders and the managers. But there are other stakeholders under the corporate umbrella, and principal–agent issues also exist between them. We consider now the situation

4. Although almost all insurance policies have limits on what they will pay for damages, some policies carry an unlimited obligation on the part of the insurer for legal defense costs.
5. See Hayne Leland, "Agency Costs, Risk Management, and Capital Structure," *Finance* 53, pp. 1213–1243; and Neil Doherty, *Integrated Risk Management*, chaps. 7 and 8 (New York: McGraw-Hill, 2000).

STRATEGY SESSION: The Good and Bad of Incentive Pay

A number of years ago, Sears auto repair centers offered incentive payments to auto technicians. They were compensated according to the number of repairs they did, such as brake jobs. Sears felt that the technicians weren't productive because they received the same pay whether they worked hard or not. Paying them by the jobs completed would increase their productivity, Sears reasoned. Incentive-compatible, we call it—Sears wants its workers to work hard for Sears' profit, and the technicians want to work hard to increase their compensation. It sounded like a good idea, and normally it is. But in this case, some Sears technicians decided that they could increase their compensation by doing repairs that were unnecessary. An unsuspecting and unknowledgeable consumer who is told that a car's brakes are near failure will undoubtedly authorize a repair. Many consumers were hoodwinked; when the practice was exposed, it caused great embarrassment to Sears.

Do incentive payment schemes (bonuses, stock options) create a similar incentive for potential recipients to cheat? Or do they provide the desired incentive of having them work hard for the objectives of the shareholders?

Some evidence suggests that such compensation packages (especially very large stock options packages) make it more likely that managers will misreport their numbers and make it more likely that stock option grants will lead firms to bankruptcy.

At the Academy of Management meetings in 2005, a paper compared 435 companies that were forced to restate their financial statements with comparable companies that did not have to restate their earnings. The greater the proportion of managerial pay in stock options, the greater was the probability the firm had to restate its profit. In cases where bosses received more than 92 percent of their compensation in stock options,

about 20 percent misstated their profit in a five-year period. If the firm isn't doing well, the tendency is to fake results to get compensated and to keep those who employ you happy. Likewise, if you had a good year last year, an even better year will be expected of you this year. The pressure is on.

A study by Moody's (the bond rating service) revealed that firms with the highest-paid bosses (controlling for company size and performance) experienced a greater probability of defaulting on debt or experiencing a large fall in their bond ratings. How do we know whether executives in the Moody's case were cheating? Perhaps the executives were risk takers, and the investments didn't work out. Alternative explanations are weak board oversight and that incentive pay packages "create an environment that ultimately leads to fraud." WorldCom and Enron are examples of the latter.

But do boards of directors offer enough protection against abuse? Not always. A *New York Times* editorial asked, How irresponsible does an outside director have to be before he/she faces legal responsibility for not performing duties? The editorial concluded that the answer is very, very irresponsible. It went on to imply that some boards blithely take their (not insubstantial) fees and ignore their duties. Two examples were cited: A Delaware judge harshly criticized Disney's board for the hiring and firing of Michael Eisner but concluded that no illegal acts occurred. A Krispy Kreme Doughnut's special committee of the board (composed of board members appointed after a major fall at Krispy Kreme) concluded that the prior directors did nothing illegal. Many feel that the Board had watched from the sidelines as the problems of the company occurred and rubber-stamped many decisions that should have required diligent oversight. The special committee stated that the board didn't oversee management's processes and decisions with an appropriately skeptical eye—concluding, however, that they did nothing they knew or believed was in clear conflict with the best interests of Krispy Kreme and likewise did nothing where they received improper personal benefit. These are not the only boards that did not practice due diligence and yet bore no legal consequences.

And just how strongly are the performance goals written and adhered to when it comes time to grant compensation? At the Las Vegas Sands Corporation, five top executives were overpaid (relative to the company's contracts with them) by over $2.8 million in 2005. The board said that it was okay because of the company's outstanding performance (despite the fact the capitalized value of the corporation fell by 18 percent).

It apparently is common to find instances where compensation exceeds the amounts allowed under the performance contracts approved by boards. Other examples include Halliburton, Assurant, Mothers Work, and Big Lots. Critics are concerned that standards are lowered after being initially set (so that they are easier to attain) and that they are not set high in the first place.

Some compensation packages seem to create perverse incentives. At the News Corporation, the COO was to receive a bonus of $12.5 million if earnings exceeded 15 percent in any given year but a bonus of $4.5 million if earnings *fell* by 6.25 percent and $3.52 million if earnings *fell* by 14 percent. Thus, even if the COO took off a year from managing, he would still be far from poor.

One way to circumvent transparency in bonus calculation is to have a list of vaguely defined measures that will trigger bonus payments. In addition, a board may weight these items in any way it wishes (including a zero weight). The reason for such published ambiguity, it is stated, is that rivals could calculate an executive's compensation, figure out secret company data, and put together a compensation package to woo away an executive. Critics say that carefully chosen measurement variables can trigger bonuses whether the overall firm does well or not.

An insurance company executive was well compensated despite losses to the company because of the extraordinary events caused by hurricane claims. The hurricane was called an act of God; the same act of God didn't spare the company's shareholders from a loss of capitalized value of their holdings. Owners take risks by owning a company (profits can go up or down), but executives that work in the insurance industry must take the risk that acts of God occur and may impact their compensation. When the hurricane impact was stripped out, the insurance company paid bonuses 1.72 times their target.

Other executives were paid bonuses for work that would seem to be part of their general duties, such as compliance with the Sarbanes-Oxley Act. At Mothers Work and Big Lots, bonuses were paid although both firms did not achieve the targets that would trigger the bonuses. They were paid for reasons such as other activities achieved but not listed in the performance criteria for bonus payment, to get management payroll up to the industry standard, and to keep the management team intact.

Who watches the watcher who watches the watched?

Sources: "Stock Options: Do They Make Bosses Cheat?" *The New York Times*, August 5, 2005, at www.nytimes.com/2005/08/05/business/05norris.html; "Inept Boards Need Have No Fear," *The New York Times*, August 12, 2005, www.nytimes.com/2005/08/12/business/12norris.html; "Big Bonuses Still Flow, Even If Bosses Miss Goals," *The New York Times*, June 1, 2006, at www.nytimes.com/2006/06/01/business/01bonus.html.

between equity holders and creditors. To focus our attention, we assume the board of directors has taken control of managerial compensation and aligned the interests of the shareholders and managers. Therefore, we can be reasonably assured that the managers act on behalf of the firm's owners. The new issue arises because shareholders have gained control (via their incentive-compatible schemes) of the decision-making process, but creditors have not.

Consider a drug company with an existing product line that exposes the firm to some risk. Future earnings have an expected present value (*PV*) of either 100 or 200, each with a probability of 0.5. This risk could reflect possible scenarios about consumer demand or the potential for the drug to have unforeseen side effects, resulting in a major lawsuit from injured customers. The firm has borrowed money under a bond issue, and this debt has a **face value** of 100. Even under the worst-case scenario, the firm is worth 100 and can pay back its debt. Therefore, there is no chance the firm will default. We can now see how much the equity and the bonds are worth:

Face value The principal amount of the bond.

$$\text{Overall value of the firm} = 0.5(100) + 0.5(200) = 150$$

This value can be divided between the shareholders and the bondholders, with the bondholders' obligations being met first and only what is left (the **residual claim**) going to the shareholders. Therefore, if the firm is worth 100, the debt is paid off and nothing is left for equity. If the firm is worth 200, the debt is paid off, leaving the remaining 100 for the shareholders:

Residual claim What is left of the divided value.

$$\text{Value of bonds} = 0.5(100) + 0.5(100) = 100$$
$$\text{Value of equity} = 0.5(0) + 0.5(100) = 50$$

The firm now faces a new investment decision. It can introduce a new hypertension drug. Its research has come up with two possible formulas. Formula A is moderately effective, has no adverse side effects, and is therefore unlikely to result in any consumer lawsuits. Formula B is a much more effective drug but has greater potential for unwanted side effects. If things go well, the firm could make much more money with formula B. However, if there were a lawsuit, the firm could lose money. The firm must choose which formula to produce. The capital cost of each project is 200 (as shown in Table 14.1), which will be financed by new borrowing. The third column shows the possible value that can be created. With project A, the present value, *PV*, of future earnings are a certain 220. Therefore, the net gain (net present value, or *NPV*) is 220 − 200 = 20. In contrast, project B could earn a total of only 20 (if there were a lawsuit) or 310 (if there were no lawsuit).[6] The expected *NPV* is

$$0.5(20) + 0.5(310) - 200 = -35$$

Which project should the firm choose? Clearly project A looks better because its *NPV* is a positive 20, whereas the *NPV* of B is a negative 35. However, the shareholders might look at the decision differently.

6. The earnings from the projects are independent of those from existing operations.

Project Selection Using NPV

	Capital Cost	Present Value of Earnings	Expected Net Present Value
Project A	200	220	20
Project B	200	20; probability 0.5 310; probability 0.5	−35

Value of the Firm If Project A Is Chosen

Consider the total value of the firm with each project choice. With project A, the firm has either 100 or 200 from existing operations plus an additional 220 from the project. This gives a total value of either 320 or 420. The total value is divided between the bondholders, to whom the firm owes a total of 300 (the original debt was 100, plus the firm borrowed 200 for the new project), and the shareholders. We assume that the original 100 must be paid first because it was borrowed first (it is called senior debt). The debt raised to fund the new project is junior and can be paid only after the original debt is paid.

Note in Table 14.2 that the minimum value of the firm is 320, but it owes a total of 300. Therefore, there is always enough value to pay off the debt in full.

Value of the Firm If Project B Is Chosen

If project B is chosen, the total value can be either 100 or 200 from existing operations plus either 20 or 310 from the project. This leaves possible total values of

$$100 + 20 = 120$$
$$100 + 310 = 410$$
$$200 + 20 = 220$$
$$200 + 310 = 510$$

The values of the firm and of debt and equity are as shown in Table 14.3.

TABLE 14.2

Firm Value If Project A Is Chosen

Value of the firm	0.5(320 + 420)	= 370
Old debt	0.5(100 + 100)	= 100
New debt	0.5(200 + 200)	= 200
Equity	0.5(20 + 120)	= 70

TABLE 14.3

Firm Value If Project B Is Chosen

Value of the firm	0.25(120 + 220 + 410 + 510)	= 315
Old debt	0.25(100 + 100 + 100 + 100)	= 100
New debt	0.25(20 + 120 + 200 + 200)	= 135
Equity	0.25(0 + 0 + 110 + 210)	= 80

Here is the problem. The firm borrows 200 to spend on one of these two projects. Then shareholders must choose which project to undertake. The choice should be clear. Shareholders are better off with project B, where their equity is worth 80, than with A, where their equity is worth only 70. How can what seems like the worse project actually make shareholders better off? The problem has to do with limited liability. If the firm undertakes A, it creates no risk of defaulting on the debt. Shareholders gain the full *NPV* of the new project of 20 (note that before the project is undertaken, equity is worth 50; after project A, equity is worth 70). But if B is undertaken, there is a 50 percent chance that the project will fail, resulting in a value of only 20. If that happens, the firm is bankrupt and unable to fully pay off the debt. On the other hand, if the project succeeds (is worth 310), the shareholders reap a big reward. Therefore, when things go well, the shareholders keep all the upside risk; but when things go badly, the shareholders walk away from the debt. Shareholders are playing a "heads we win, tails bondholders lose" strategy.

This illustrates an important principal–agent issue. When firms have a significant amount of debt, the shareholders tend to favor unusually risky investment decisions. It seems that the bondholders are the unwilling victims of these games. But let us look at the bondholders for a moment; they are not totally helpless. Bondholders must decide whether to lend to the firm and how much they wish to pay for the bonds. In this case the firm is trying to issue bonds with a face value of 200. If you were an investor looking at this firm, your thoughts might progress as follows:

> If I were to pay 200 to buy these bonds, what would the shareholders choose to do with the money? Well, the rational thing for the shareholders to do once they have my money is to choose project B because the shares would then be worth an expected price of 80 (compared with 70 for project A). In that case I should anticipate that B would be chosen, and my new bonds would be very risky and worth only 135 (see the value of "new debt" in Table 14.3 when B is chosen). Consequently I would be unwilling to buy these bonds for 200; rather I would pay only 135 for them, which is what they are worth.

If we follow the logic a little further, we see that managers are unable to undertake either project. Because rational bondholders anticipate that B would be chosen, they are willing to pay only 135 for the new debt issue, even though the face value is 200. Because the capital cost of project B is 200, the amount raised from the debt issue is insufficient to fund the project. Therefore the firm is unable to finance project B. Does that mean that A would be chosen? Suppose, indeed, that the managers announced their intention to choose project A. Unfortunately investors buying the new debt issue would still rationally assume that if they subscribed 200 for the issue, the shareholders would change their minds and use the 200 to fund project B. Hence investors still would subscribe only 135 for the new bond issue. The firm is unable to undertake either project. Because bondholders anticipate the shareholders' temptation to choose the risky negative *NPV* project, the firm is unable to fund either project. It is forced to sacrifice not only the expropriatory project B but also a project with a genuine positive *NPV*.

Representing the Bait and Switch in Game Theory

Figure 14.9 shows this issue in a game theory form. The shareholders must choose project A or B. Bondholders must choose either to pay the full 200 for the new debt

---

FIGURE 14.9

Will Shareholders Pull the Bait and Switch?

If bondholders pay 200, they anticipate that shareholders will choose project B. These bondholders will pay only $135 for the debt. Note that the first number at the end of each branch is the payoff for the bondholder and the second number is the payoff for the shareholder.

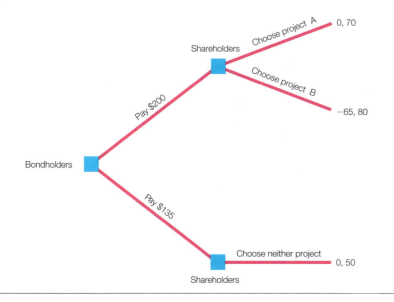

STRATEGY SESSION: **The Song of the Sirens**

A defining feature of the 2008 financial crisis was the implosion of financial institutions due to what looks like excessive risk taking. It was a quick end for some (Bear Sterns, Lehmann, Wachovia, Northern Rock Plc) and major restructuring and government aid for others (AIG, Citicorp, Fortis).

Managers of these institutions were taking on their books, increasing complex and risky securities. Indeed the level of risk of these securities can only be estimated with very sophisticated mathematical modeling and even then, the models may underestimate the true level of risk.[a] Often, managers of these institutions magnified the inherent risk in the securities they held by using a financial tactic called "leverage," whereby they borrow money to increase their holdings. Some investment banks were leveraged at a 30-to-1 ratio. For every one dollar of equity, managers held $30 of debt. In using debt, managers take on the additional risk of losing control of assets, because they are unable to repay the principle or interest on that debt.

By historical measures, the leverage risks managers at many institutions were taking were of unusually high levels.

Many observers believe compensation schemes encouraged managers to take on additional risk. This, in turn, caused them to engage in moral-hazard–like behavior. Consider the role of stock options, a common component of managerial compensation. A *stock option* is the right to purchase the firm's shares at some time in the future at an agreed price. The executive might receive a number of these options as part of his overall compensation package. We show how these are valued in the Strategy Session titled "Call Options." In theory, these options should increase managerial focus on long-term results since they expire at a future date.

From a behavioral point of view, options give managers all the upside potential from rising share prices but none of the downside loss if the share price should fall. Consequently, *these options are more valu-*

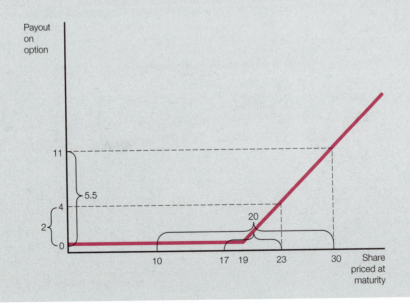

able the greater the riskiness of the underlying stock. This is illustrated in the previous diagram. Consider a firm whose share price in one year could be either 17 or 23 each with a 50-percent probability. The expected share price is therefore 0.5(17) + 0.5(23) = 20. Now an option with a strike price of 19 will have the following payoffs:

- If the share price at maturity is 17 — option pays 0 since the option is not exercised.
- If the share price at maturity is 23 — option is exercised and has net payoff of 23 − 19 = 4.

Thus, the expected payout to the manager on the option is 0.5(0) + 0.5(4) = 2.

Now suppose the manager makes a different set of decisions that result in a very different risk profile. With these alternative decisions, the share price at maturity has a 50-percent chance of being 10 and a 50-percent chance of being 30. Notice the expected share price is the same as before, i.e., 0.5(10) + 0.5(30) = 20. Now an option with the same strike price of 19 will have the following payoffs:

- If the share price at maturity is 10 — option pays 0 since the option is not exercised.
- If the share price at maturity is 30 — option is exercised and has net payoff of 30 − 19 = 11.

Thus, the expected payout to the manager on the option[b] is 0.5(0) + 0.5(11) = 5.5. By changing the riskiness of the share price without changing its expected value, the manager has substantially increased the payoffs he might receive from the option when it matures.

And herein lays the source of this moral-hazard–like behavior. Stock options provide managers with powerful incentives to make decisions that increase the stock price, which is why they are used in the first place. However, the pernicious side effect is that they also provide incentives for managers to increase the riskiness of the stock, for this too increases the value of the option.[c]

Stock options were widely used in financial institutions. In fact, most of the firms that received government support paid the highest compensation to their CEOs. Lloyd Blanfein, the CEO of Goldman Sachs received $54 million in 2007; JP Morgan CEO, James Dimon took home $30 million that year; while G. Kennedy Thompson, CEO of Wachovia received over $15 million in 2007.[d] If you believe CEOs respond to incentives, it should not be a surprise that managers sought to maximize the value of their options by trading in such risky securities and then leveraged that risk with debt financing.

[a]One of the biggest of all collapses was that of the insurance giant AIG. In addition to its regular insurance business, AIG had a special unit that "insured" mortgage debt through complex financial instruments known as credit default swaps. Despite having a very sophisticated, state-of-the-art, mathematical model to track its exposure, AIG was still unable to avoid a catastrophic failure that required a Federal Government bailout, which is currently $100 billion. See "Behind AIG's Fall, Risk Models Failed to Pass Real-World Test, " Carrick Mollenkamp, Serena Ng, Liam Pleven & Randall Smith , *The Wall Street Journal*, October 31, 2008.

[b]We need a caution on the price of the option. Pricing is quite complicated and is not simply the expected payout.

[c]See Neil Doherty, "Integrated Risk Management" McGraw Hill, 2000 for a discussion of this incentive mechanism. There are many empirical studies confirming that executives who are paid with stock options do tend to make riskier decisions. See for example Peter Tufano, "Who Manages Risk: An Empirical Examination of Risk Management Practices in the Gold Mining Industry", *Journal of Finance*, 51, pp. 1097–1137.

[d]Kang, Cecilia and Annys Shin, "Top Executives at Bruised Firms among Wall Street's Highest Paid", *The Washington Post*, 24 September 2008, p. D03.

or only 135. Because managers cannot undertake either project unless bondholders pay the full 200, shareholders have only the original equity value of 50 (from the existing product line). However, if the bondholders pay the full 200 to cover the project costs, the shareholders have equity value of 70 from choosing A and 80 from choosing B. The bondholders' payoff is the difference between what they pay for the bonds when they are issued and what they are worth. If the bondholders pay 200 and the firm chooses A, the bonds are worth 200 and the net payoff is 0. If the bondholders pay 200 and the firm chooses B, the bonds are only worth 135, leaving a net payoff of −65. If the bondholders anticipate the bait and switch, they pay only what the bonds are worth and have a net payoff of zero.

The game is sequential, with the bondholders making the first move. The bondholders anticipate that the shareholders will choose B if they pay 200. Therefore the bondholders pay only 135, and the shareholders cannot undertake either project and are left with equity of 50. Shareholders would like to make the following promise to the bondholders: If you pay 200, we promise to undertake project A. The problem is that the promise is not credible. Having received the 200, the shareholders would then have an incentive to change their minds. There is a credibility problem; shareholders have an incentive to pull a bait and switch.

Possible Solutions to the Asset Substitution Problem

There are several ways managers can avoid or minimize this problem:

- *Fund with equity:* The problem arose because managers tried to use debt to fund the project. If they can pay for the project by using internal funds or by making a new issue of shares, then the problem is mitigated or disappears.
- *Establish a reputation for protecting creditors:* If the firm follows a consistent policy of making decisions that preserve the interests of creditors, then a promise not to undertake risky projects in the future might be viewed as credible.
- *Precommit to hedge or insure risk:* Another way this problem is sometimes tackled is that the firm voluntarily commits itself to insure the risks. The problem arose because project *B* was risky, and this risk caused the possibility of default on the debt. If the risk were insured, then bondholders would be protected. Many debt instruments carry a legal obligation for the firm to insure assets.

PRODUCT LIABILITY AND THE SAFETY OF CONSUMER GOODS

Many countries have laws that protect consumers against the risks of injury from defective products. These laws serve two purposes. First, they compensate injured consumers. If a consumer is injured by a defective product, the producing firm has to pay compensation. Second, because the firm must pay compensation if products are defective, there is an incentive for the firm to make safer products. Safer products result in fewer costly lawsuits. These laws solve a principal–agent issue. The firm makes decisions on safety, but the consumer bears the costs if the product causes injury. The product liability law is incentive-compatible because it aligns the interests of the principal (the consumer) and the agent (the producer).

How Safe Would Products Be without a Product Liability Law?

How much should managers invest in making safer products. We use s to denote the expenditure undertaken to make safer products. Therefore, the cost of safety is s, and the marginal cost is simply 1:

$$\text{Total cost of safety} = s$$

$$\text{Marginal cost of safety} = \frac{\Delta s}{\Delta s} = 1$$

The benefit of safety is that it reduces the expected cost of injuries to consumers. Assume the expected cost of such injuries is

$$\text{Expected cost of accidents} = 4{,}000 - 20s^{0.5}$$

We can see that the expected cost of accidents depends on the firm's choice of s. Moreover, as s increases, the expected cost falls. This is represented as the marginal benefit of safety; because the benefit of safety is a reduction in a cost, we must remember to change the sign:

$$\text{Expected marginal benefit of safety} = \frac{\Delta[-(4{,}000 - 20s^{0.5})]}{\Delta s} = \frac{10}{s^{0.5}}$$

QUANT OPTION

Because the cost of safety is s, the marginal cost of safety is $ds/ds = 1$. The expected benefits of safety are just the negative of the expected cost of accidents—that is, $Z = -4{,}000 + 20s^{0.5}$. The expected marginal benefits of safety are then $dZ/ds = 10/s^{0.5}$.

However, in the absence of a product liability law, the firm is not required to compensate consumers for injuries suffered, and these costs fall directly on customers. The expected benefit to managers for safer products is zero. Hence the firm pays all the costs of safety and receives none of the benefits. The profit-maximizing firm chooses $s = 0$. In this case products are unusually dangerous.

Safety under a Product Liability Law

The product liability law can be rationalized as providing an incentive for managers to make safer products. To achieve this, the costs of accidents are borne by the firm, which now must compensate the victims. Therefore, the expected benefit to the firm from spending s on safety is the reduction in the expected accident cost. The level of safety now optimal for the firm is that which equates marginal cost and marginal benefit:

$$\text{Marginal cost} = \text{Marginal benefit}$$

$$1 = \frac{10}{s^{0.5}}$$

$$s = 100$$

The introduction of the law increases the firm's choice of safety from 0 to 100. Consequently the expected cost of accidents declines from $[4{,}000 - 20(0)^{0.5}] = 4{,}000$ to $[4{,}000 - 20(100)^{0.5}] = 3{,}800$. This obviously looks like a social benefit; but was the law really necessary to achieve this?

Optimal Safety under a Market Mechanism

Clearly the product liability law is incentive-compatible. But would an incentive-compatible solution evolve under private market incentives? There is a marketplace for information. Specifically, information about product safety is widely disseminated in subscription magazines, newspaper articles, and television news shows. The volume of such information is increasing, and cost and access to information are improving as it becomes available over the Internet. Moreover, if there were no product liability law, such information would be more valuable and perhaps even more widely available. Without a product liability law, consumers would bear the costs of accidents themselves, and safety would be reflected in the demand for, and therefore the price of, products.

Suppose managers sell a product in a quantity of 1,000, and customers are willing to pay a price of 30 if they knew the product was perfectly safe. The firm's revenue would then be $30 \times 1{,}000 = 30{,}000$. The total cost of the accidents is $[4{,}000 - 20(s)^{0.5}]$. With 1,000 customers, the cost to each customer is $[4{,}000 - 20(s)^{0.5}]/1{,}000 = [4 - 0.02(s)^{0.5}]$. Therefore, while the customer will pay 30 if she knows the product is safe, she will discount that price by the expected cost of accidents if information is available about product safety. Customers are willing to pay a price of only

$$\text{Price} = 30 - (4 - 0.02s^{0.5})$$

The total revenue is now

$$\text{Total revenue} = 1{,}000[30 - (4 - 0.02s^{0.5})] = 30{,}000 - (4{,}000 - 20s^{0.5})$$

The revenue is now discounted by exactly the expected cost of accidents. Assume the firm has other costs of production of 10,000. The profit of the firm is now

$$\pi = \text{Total revenue} - \text{Cost of safety} - \text{Other production costs}$$
$$\pi = 30{,}000 - (4{,}000 - 20s^{0.5}) - s - 10{,}000$$

The firm must choose the level of safety that maximizes profit, so we can set the $\Delta\pi/\Delta s$ equal to zero:

$$\frac{\Delta\pi}{\Delta s} = \frac{10}{s^{0.5}} - 1 = 0$$

When solved for s, this gives an investment in safety of $s = 100$.

Of course this is exactly the same result we got with the product liability law. This should not be a surprise. With product liability, the firm paid the full expected cost of accidents directly in lawsuits. Under the market mechanism, the firm had its revenue reduced by the full expected cost of accidents. Either way, the firm

---

STRATEGY SESSION: Moral Hazard in the Financial Market: The Rescue of the Investment Bank Bear Stearns

In 2007 Bear Stearns' stock had been trading as high as $170. But the subprime mortgage crisis severely impacted Bear Stearns, which had provided lines of credit to subprime lenders and also was the owner of EMC Mortgage. By mid-March 2008 the share price was down to $30, and fearing failure of the bank and its impact on the financial system, the Federal Reserve and rival firm JPMorgan Chase arranged a rescue plan (often called a "bailout"). Under this plan, the Fed will provide a limited guarantee of Bear Stearns' obligations, and JPMorgan purchased its rival for $10 per share. JPMorgan will bear the first part of the Bear Stearns obligations before the federal guarantee kicks in.

This is an interesting moral hazard story. Bear Stearns got into this mess by accepting high-risk activities and by not managing that risk effectively (by appropriate diversification and hedging strategies). Although the Fed perceived that a Bear Stearns failure could create a financial meltdown, bailing out the firm created an expectation that large financial institutions will not be allowed to fail (at least not when financial markets are uncertain). Will such bailouts encourage institutions in the future to take big risks? The financial system relies on prudent financial behavior. If the imprudent are allowed to avoid the dire consequences of their risky actions, they are hardly likely to exercise prudence going forward. Thus such bailouts create adverse incentives and may increase financial risk taking (and therefore the risk to the whole financial system). Bailouts thereby create a moral hazard.

The counterarguments are also couched in moral hazard terms. By receiving only $2 per share, Bear Stearns' shareholders were hardly being bailed out—they were indeed taking an enormous loss even considering the share price of just a few days earlier. In fact the offer was increased to $10 per share to make it more acceptable. This might increase the moral hazard. However, this was offset, to some extent, by reducing the value of the Fed's guarantee. Thus we can see the whole exercise as one of trade-offs. The Fed clearly did not want the bailout to be too attractive and required that the shareholders suffer considerable pain. It wanted to rescue the financial system from its mess—but without creating expectations of generous bailouts in the future.

Source: "JP Morgan Pays $2 a Share for Bear Stearns," *The New York Times*, March 17, 2008.

> ### QUANT OPTION
>
> The firm will maximize profit if
>
> $$d\pi/ds = (10/s^{0.5}) - 1 = 0$$

internalized the full cost of accidents and had an incentive to reduce these costs by investing in safety.

This shows that there are generally different methods to address principal–agent issues. One way is through the force of civil law, making firms responsible for defective products and therefore aligning the interests of firms and their customers. Another way is to appeal to market mechanisms by which self-interested customers seek out information and use this information in their purchasing decisions. Customers reward (or punish) firms by varying the price they are willing to pay according to the level of product safety. Thus price becomes a way of aligning the interests of the firm and its customers.

SUMMARY

1. A principal–agent relationship is one in which a principal employs an agent to undertake a task (such as shareholders employing managers to run a firm). The objectives of the principal and agent may be quite different. Shareholders like a high profit and high share price. Managers like such things as prestige, income, pleasant work, and perquisites. More simply, managers may wish to do as little as possible for the greatest possible reward. Therefore, we use the term effort to describe a manager forgoing his or her own objectives (the manager does not shirk) to attend the wishes of shareholders. Greater effort on the part of the manager can usually increase a firm's profit.

2. The problem for the principal is to motivate the agent to work for the benefit of the principal. Shareholders seek to get managers to supply great effort and maximize the firm's profit. If the shareholders could observe the effort of managers, this would be no problem. The managers' compensation could be scaled to the managers' effort. However, if the shareholders do not know how hard managers work, they are hard-pressed to reward them directly for effort.

3. The full principal–agent problem arises because the firm's owners lack the time or skill to observe all the actions of the manager. Owners cannot perfectly observe the manager's effort. Nor can they infer accurately the effort from the firm's revenue or profit if that profit is risky. The solution recognizes that, on average, greater effort results in higher profit. Managers are motivated by being given a share of the profit or an equity stake in the firm. However, this incentive

compensation is risky for the manager. Profit can vary for reasons outside the manager's control. Therefore, compensation usually has a fixed component and a profit-related portion.

4. A particularly powerful type of incentive compensation is the stock option. The manager is given an option to buy the firm's stock at some future date at a preagreed price. These options are risky for the manager. If the stock price falls, the options are worth nothing, but a big increase in the stock price can bring fabulous returns. The manager is penalized severely for bad firm performance and rewarded handsomely for good performance. In the bull stock market of the 1990s, stock option plans brought great wealth to many managers.

5. Another type of principal–agent problem arises between shareholders and the firm's creditors. This is known as asset substitution. Limited liability means that when a firm is bankrupt, the shareholders can walk away rather than pay the creditors. This creates an incentive for the shareholders to take on risky investments. Risk implies a chance of a large upside gain and a chance of a large downside loss. If luck is favorable, the creditors can be paid off, and all the upside gain goes to the shareholders. But if things turn out badly, the shareholders can use bankruptcy law to default on the debt. Thus high-risk projects have a "heads I win, tails you lose" quality for the shareholders. Of course risky projects hurt the creditors. This tension may lead the firm into dysfunctional investment decisions, and the firm may be forced to limit its debt financing to resolve this type of agency problem.

6. The provision of an optimal level of product safety can be viewed as a principal–agent problem. Product liability laws require firms to pay for damages caused by their products. The probability of making these payments creates an incentive for firms to make their products safer. The same level of safety can be attained by the marketplace if consumers can be cheaply informed about a product's safety level. Unsafe products would then sell at a discount relative to safe ones, and firms would be motivated to improve safety to increase their profit.

wwnorton.com/studyspace ⑤

PROBLEMS

1. Your business generates the following profits (these are stated before compensation is paid to the manager):

	Low Demand (0.3)	Medium Demand (0.4)	High Demand (0.3)
Low effort	$5 million	$10 million	$15 million
High effort	$7 million	$12 million	$17 million

You see that profit depends on both the level of effort chosen by the manager and the level of demand. The demand level is random, and the probabilities of each demand level are shown. So with low effort, expected profit is $10 million; with high effort, it is $12 million. The manager has a utility function that is either

$$\text{Utility} = (\text{Wealth})^{0.5} \text{ if effort is low or}$$
$$\text{Utility} = (\text{Wealth})^{0.5} - 100 \text{ if effort is high.}$$

Therefore -100 is the disutility of effort. You are interested in maximizing the expected profit after deduction of compensation. You consider three different compensation packages:

• A flat salary of $575,000.
• A payment of 6 percent of profit.
• A flat payment of $500,000 plus half of any profit in excess of $15 million.

Which compensation do you choose?

2. Suppose the typical Florida resident has wealth of $500,000, of which his or her home is worth $100,000. Unfortunately Florida is infamous for its hurricanes, and it is believed there is a 10 percent chance of a hurricane that could totally destroy a house (a loss of $100,000). However, it is possible to retrofit the house with various protective devices (shutters, roof bolts, and so on) for a cost of $2,000. This reduces the 10 percent chance of a loss of $100,000 to a 5 percent chance of a loss of $50,000. The homeowner must decide whether to retrofit and thereby reduce the expected loss. The problem for an insurance company is that it does not know whether the retrofit will be installed and therefore cannot quote a premium conditioned on the policyholder choosing this action. Nevertheless, the insurance company offers the following two policies from which the homeowner can choose: (1) The premium for insurance covering total loss is $12,000 or (2) the premium for insurance covering only 50 percent of loss is $1,500. The typical homeowner has a utility function equal to the square root of wealth. Will the homeowner retrofit the house, and which insurance policy will the homeowner buy? Will the insurance company make a profit (on average) given the homeowner's choice?

3. The expected profit of your firm is 1,000, plus 500 if the manager works hard. The manager receives a flat salary of 100 plus a portion x of any profit in excess of 1,300. The manager's utility function is

$$EU = [(\text{compensation})^{0.5}] \text{ if she does not work hard}$$
$$EU = [(\text{compensation})^{0.5} - 1] \text{ if she works hard}$$

What portion x must be paid to the manager to ensure that she chooses to work hard? This new compensation package must be competitive with the 100 flat salary.

4. A firm used to have productive assets that generated an income stream with a present value (*PV*) of 3,000. However, a fire occurred, and most of those assets were destroyed. The remaining undamaged assets produce an income stream that has a present value of only 1,000. Therefore the fire has reduced the value of the firm from 3,000 to 1,000. The firm could reconstruct the damaged assets for a capital cost of 1,500, which would restore the income stream to its pre-loss level (*PV* = 3,000). The firm has existing debt of 2,000, which is a senior claim. Would the shareholders choose to reinvest by issuing new equity to pay for the loss, or are they better off walking away from the firm? Would the decision made by the shareholders be in the best interests of the bondholders? In answering this question, remember that the shareholders have limited liability, and therefore the share value cannot be negative.

5. CareLess Industries has two divisions. Division 1 makes cleaning products, and the net worth of this division (*PV* of cash flows) is 500. Division 2 makes a chemical product. The net worth of division 2 is 300, absent any potential liability. However, there is a chance that division 2 could have a 700 liability for pollution damage. The potential victims have no contractual relationship with the firm. The probability of such a loss is $0.2/(1 + s)$, where s is the amount the firm spends on safety. The firm must choose the level of s. If you could sell off division 2, would you do so? What is the gain from splitting the firm in this way? Assume a separated division 2 (as a stand-alone firm) is protected by limited liability. Note also that the derivative of $a/(1 + s)$ with respect to s is $-a/(1 + s)^2$; that is, $\Delta[a/(1 + s)]/\Delta s = -a/(1 + s)^2$.

6. SubAquatics (SA) sells scuba diving equipment. Its clients typically read specialist journals and are well informed about the price, reliability, and safety of SA and competitors' products. SA has estimated that, of 100,000 units sold each year at a price of $100 each, there are $4/(1 - s)$ fatal accidents due to defective equipment. The value s is the amount spent by SA on safety in millions of dollars.

   a. Assuming that SA is fully liable for such accidents and that the average settlement of each fatal accident is $1 million, how much should SA spend on safety?

   Now assume that SA can escape this liability by selling its products at a lower price under a contract that allocates all responsibility for accidents to the purchaser (assume that courts enforce such contracts). If SA spends s (expressed in millions of dollars) on safety, the expected cost of accidents to any consumer is $[4/(1 - s)](\$1m/100,000) = \$40/(1 + s)$. Note that consumers are willing to pay $100 when all liability is assumed by SA (assuming consumers are risk-neutral),

   b. How much would consumers be willing to pay when they bear the cost of accidents?

    c. How much would SA spend on safety?

    d. Assuming that customers cannot observe the level of safety and there is no liability law, how much would SA spend on safety and how much would customers pay for the product?

7. A firm has existing operations that generate an earnings stream with a present value, *PV*, of 300 or 600, each with 0.5 probability. The firm has 250 in existing debt. The firm wishes to undertake one of the following mutually exclusive new investments:

	Capital Cost	PV of Earnings	NPV
Project *A*	400	420	+ 20
Project *B*	400	0; probability 0.5	− 50
		or	
		700; probability 0.5	

The capital cost of each project (400) is financed with new junior debt (face value 400). Is there an asset substitution problem? (Will shareholders try to choose the lower *NPV* project?) Show whether any asset substitution problem would disappear if the new project were financed with an equity issue of 400 instead of new debt.

ADVERSE SELECTION

One variable that often affects managerial performance is how quickly managers learn about relevant information. Consider the Internet. Managers can achieve almost immediate access to information about rivals' products, and sellers can reach millions of potential customers. If you wish to buy an antique clock of which only a handful may be for sale across the globe, you have a good chance of finding one of those rare sellers in the vast electronic world of ebay. If you wish to sell a used car, you want to expand the number of potential buyers to find one with a particularly high reservation price; ebay gives you such wide access. This unprecedented flow of information profoundly affects markets. Monopolies tend to break down as consumers can search and compare across many sellers. The geographical boundaries of markets are expanding, and some markets are truly global. Information fosters competition.

But information has more subtle effects on managerial behavior. We consider some of these in this chapter. Consider the differences in information between buyers and sellers. In many transactions, such as selling a car, securing a mortgage, buying health insurance, or investing in a company's stock, the buyer and seller have different information. For example, a seller of a used car usually knows more about the quality of the car than a buyer does. A borrower often knows more about his or her credit risk than does a lender. A policyholder knows more about his or her state of health than an insurer does. And "insiders" in a firm issuing shares of stock know more about the firm's prospects than the investors who may buy the stock. In these transactions, some individuals have more information than others. This chapter shows how managers can use their informational advantage to increase performance. And when managers are at an informational disadvantage, we illustrate how they can create creative defenses to mitigate their disadvantage.

THE MARKET FOR "LEMONS"

Some years ago the Nobel Prize–winning economist George Ackerlof wrote a famous paper about the market for "lemons." A "lemon" is a used car that turns out to have many faults not apparent at the time of sale–hence the sour taste. Let us call used cars that are virtually free of hidden defects "gems." The fact that some cars are lemons and some are gems may simply be random. But what Ackerlof had in mind was something a little more disturbing. A systematic process may ensure that a disproportionate number of lemons turn up in the used car market. This process arises from information differences between buyers and sellers. The basic idea is simple. Sellers know more about the hidden qualities of the cars they are selling than do buyers. If I have been driving a car, I know its defects; I know its mechanical record and whether it has been involved in accidents. Therefore, I know whether I am selling a lemon or a gem. The buyer can invest some time inspecting the car but is never going to be as well informed as the seller. The hidden qualities, good or bad, remain hidden.

Let us try to get into the mind of the buyer. How much is she willing to pay for a used car? She knows some cars are worse than average and some are better than average, but she does not know where the particular car she considers buying lies on this spectrum. So it seems safe to assume that she is willing to pay, at most, the value of a car of average quality. If the seller has a car that is a gem, he will be unwilling to sell at this average price because, known only to him, the car is really worth more than average. On the contrary, the seller of a lemon is delighted. He has a worse-than-average car and a buyer who is willing to pay a price based on average quality. If he does not blow the sale by appearing too eager, he can get a great deal. Therefore, at this average price, people tend to hold onto their gems, and the cars offered for sale are predominantly worse than average; they are lemons. And it is all because buyers are uninformed.

The picture gets worse. Buyers may not know whether a particular car is good or bad, but they can figure out what is happening. They can reason that only owners of lemons would offer their cars for sale at a price reflecting the average quality. Therefore, the selection of cars coming onto the secondhand market is not a true reflection of the overall population of cars but is mostly lemons. So buyers are not willing to offer a price that reflects the average quality. Indeed, because they can anticipate that only lemons will be sold, they are willing to buy only at a price appropriate to a lemon. Consequently no high-quality cars are offered for sale, only lemons; and the price reflects this low quality. The market for high-quality used cars has disappeared.

You might object to this analysis. Surely the seller of a high-quality car can tell the buyer, "My car is better than average, and you should pay a high price." The problem is that this statement is not credible. The buyer cannot verify this statement, so the owners of lemons have every reason to declare that their cars also are wonderful. Cheap talk is simply not convincing because it can be mimicked by the

---

PROBLEM SOLVED: Equilibrium in the Used Car Market

Of course there are many types of used cars, so let us narrow things down to the market for 2006 Toyota Camrys. Some are better than average; and *if consumers knew they were buying one of these gems*, they would be willing to pay $10,000 for it. Other are lemons; *if consumers knew they were buying a lemon*, they would be willing to offer only $5,000. The problem is that consumers do not know which car is a lemon and which a gem. So they are willing to pay a price of $7,500 reflecting the average quality.[a] Sellers, of course, know the quality of what they are selling.

At a price of $7,500,

1. Owners of gems that really are worth $10,000 would not sell for $7,500.
2. Owners of lemons that are worth $5,000 would be happy to sell for $7,500.

Therefore, only the lemons will be sold. Now consumers, even though they do not know whether any particular car is a lemon or gem, anticipate that only the owners of lemons will choose to sell. Thus buyers assume that all cars being offered are lemons and are willing to pay only $5,000. The lemon owners should still be willing to sell at $5,000 because they know this is what their cars are worth.

Is the market described here really that simple? Of course we oversimplify things somewhat. Buyers are not totally ignorant, and sellers do not know everything. For example, some sellers really do not know the quality of their cars, and it is possible that some owners of high-quality vehicles will sell at the average price. Other sellers may believe their cars to be high-quality but are willing to sell because they have an urgent need for money. Some buyers may believe they have better information or a nose for a good deal. The market is not as simple as we portrayed here, and some high-quality cars are sold in the secondhand market. But the basic ideas of adverse selection still hold in this more realistic world. If it is generally true that sellers on average are more informed than buyers, there may be some dispersion in secondhand prices, but these prices tend to converge toward the average price. Consequently, while a few people may sell gems at this price, the cars offered for sale are mostly lemons. So we still get a used car market stocked predominantly with lemons and relatively few high-quality cars.

We can now see why the term adverse selection is used. Where buyers are unable to distinguish quality, the price averages across quality groups. However, at this common price, the selection of cars being offered for sale is not representative; rather it is weighted toward the low quality—it is adverse.

---

[a]We assume there are equal numbers of lemons and gems. For example, with 100 lemons and 100 gems, the average price is [100($10,000) + 100($5,000)]/200 = $7,500. If there were different numbers, then the average price would differ. For example, with 150 gems and 50 lemons, [150($10,000) + 50($5,000)]/200 = $8,750.

owners of lemons. Later we show that there are mechanisms to separate the gems from the lemons, but these involve more sophisticated signaling.

Economists often describe a lemons market as a market failure. It is certainly desirable from everybody's viewpoint to have a vigorous market for high-quality used cars. But due to asymmetric information, this market is stunted or killed completely. As we go through this chapter, we look at how uninformed managers can compensate for their ignorance and redevelop many of these damaged markets.

ADVERSE SELECTION IN AUTOMOBILE INSURANCE

Although the term lemons was first used for cars, the term adverse selection was first used in insurance. We look now at how adverse selection arises in various insurance markets. We first look at automobile insurance; after that we look at annuities and life insurance.

If managers at the insurance firm (the insurer) can distinguish drivers according to their respective loss characteristics, each policyholder can be charged a premium that precisely matches his or her expected loss. Good drivers pay low premiums, and bad drivers pay higher premiums. Insurers take some trouble to try to tailor premiums in this way. They ask questions about observable characteristics, such as automobile type, location, or age and gender of the policyholder. And by careful statistical analysis of their databases, they determine how each of these characteristics predicts accident rates.[1] This information is then used to set premiums. But even after classifying in this way, differences in risk may remain between policyholders. For example, the insurer may set a premium based on age, gender, vehicle type, and location. But not all 22-year-old men driving sedans in Philadelphia have the same loss potential. Their skill levels and behavioral characteristics can vary substantially. So there is an effective subsidy from low-risk drivers to high-risk drivers within each class. This subsidy can have an unsettling effect.

In Figure 15.1 we consider a category of drivers in the insurance pool—say the 22-year-old men driving sedans in Philadelphia. Some are worse drivers than others. We call these respectively *high-* and *low-risk drivers*. Each policyholder has a wealth level of 125, but a loss can reduce the wealth to 25; that is, drivers can lose 100 of their wealth should the loss occur. For the high-risk group, the probability of loss is 0.75, resulting in an expected loss of 0.75 (100) = 75. For the low-risk group, the probability of loss is 0.25, resulting in an expected loss of 0.25 (100) = 25.

Perfect Information

First we show that if the insurer could distinguish between the two groups, managers could charge competitive premiums, and each group would buy insurance. The competitive premiums for each group are their respective expected losses of

1. Note that we are not saying that features such as age and gender differences *cause* differences in accident rates—only that there may be a statistical association.

FIGURE 15.1

Adverse Selection in Automobile Insurance

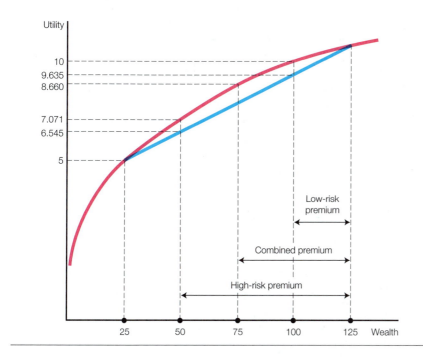

75 and 25 (in practice, the insurer would add an allowance for transaction costs and profit). Using expected utility, we can now show that each person will buy insurance. We need a utility function that reflects risk aversion. (If people were not risk-averse, why would they buy insurance?)

$$\text{Utility} = (\text{Wealth})^{0.5}$$

For the low-risk group, the utility of insuring and having wealth of 100 with certainty (derived by subtracting the premium of 25 from the initial wealth of 125)—that is, $U(100)$—is higher than the expected utility of not insuring (where wealth stays at the initial 125 without loss but falls by 100 to 25 if a loss occurs):

$$\text{Utility with insurance} = (125 - 25)^{0.5} = 10$$
$$\text{Utility with no insurance} = (0.75)(125)^{0.5} + (0.25)(25)^{0.5} = 9.635$$

Similarly, for the high-risk group,

$$\text{Utility with insurance} = (125 - 75)^{0.5} = 7.071$$
$$\text{Utility with no insurance} = (0.25)(125)^{0.5} + (0.75)(25)^{0.5} = 6.545$$

The respective positions are shown on the vertical axis of Figure 15.1.

It seems like a deal for you. Join the store's bonus club, and you'll receive instant discounts at the cash register and coupons designed just for you and not available to those who aren't members. This frees you from having to search through newspapers and clip coupons. Who could object? Many consumers have joined. But by joining, you reveal who you are and where you live. That opens up the ability to access your credit rating and estimate your income (by knowing your address, they know what census tract you live in); and of course the unit price code swipe of each purchase at the register now tracks your purchasing behavior and various prices and time periods. If you pay by credit card or check, interested parties can obtain the same information. This can occur whether you shop in a physical store or online.

What do sellers do with this information? A recent study by the Annenberg Public Policy Center at the University of Pennsylvania concluded that collection of such information leaves the consumer subject to marketplace abuse; the result can be higher prices. One midwestern grocery chain claims to have used the information to "fire" 1,500 customers. It identified these as customers who come to shop only for the loss leaders and other bargains and do not contribute to the profits of the stores. It "fixed" these customers by doing away with weekly promotions. On the other hand, Bloomingdale's was identified as having determined that 15,000 customers were very special; they were given special treatment when they were identified by their credit cards.

The study highlights two different uses of such data. One is to identify which consumers to target (such as the examples just given). The other is to use data to price discriminate among customers.

For instance, travel Web sites don't necessarily show you the best price their search engines have found (and are not by law required to do so). Stores can sell the same item at the exact same time to two individuals at different prices. Both are examples of legal price discrimination. And stores can sell information about you to other potentially interested parties.

Source: "What Stores Know about You," *Philadelphia Inquirer*, June 1, 2005, p. C1.

Asymmetric Information

Now suppose managers at the insurer are unable to distinguish between high- and low-risk drivers. However, we assume that each driver knows whether he or she is a high or low risk; in effect we each know our own driving capabilities. If there are equal numbers of low- and high-risk drivers, the insurer can break even by charging the average premium of $0.5(25 + 75) = 50$. But will each group now continue to buy insurance? It is clear that the high-risk drivers will buy insurance. If they would have bought insurance at a premium of 75, then surely they still will buy if the premium is reduced to 50:

$$\text{Utility with insurance} = (125 - 50)^{0.5} = 8.660$$
$$\text{Utility with no insurance} = (0.25)(125)^{0.5} + (0.75)(25)^{0.5} = 6.545$$

But for the low-risk group, the insurance premium has increased from 25 to 50. We can compare the expected utility with and without insurance for this group:

$$\text{Utility with insurance} = (125 - 50)^{0.5} = 8.660$$
$$\text{Utility with no insurance} = (0.75)(125)^{0.5} + (25)^{0.5} = 9.635$$

So the low-risk group will not buy the insurance. The only people who will buy insurance at the common price of 50 are the high-risk drivers. If you think a step ahead, you can see that this pricing structure is not tenable for the insurer. If only high-risk drivers buy the insurance, then each policyholder costs 75 (on

STRATEGY SESSION: Information Is Really Valuable

Would you rather pay more or less for the same item? For all economically rational people, the answer is simple: less. But it's not always easy to find out who's charging more and who is charging less. Searching the Internet rather than physically driving to various locations to see prices sounds easier—and indeed many people are using this method to search for items and prices.

But what if someone could do the search for you? IAC/InterActiveCorp has a software application at Pronto.com that allows you to click onto any of 50,000 merchants in its database. Pronto then monitors your activity on a merchant's page, shows you the prices from other merchants for the same (or similar) items, and then shows you the best deal and provides a link to that merchant. Pronto has competitors (SmartShopper, Dealio, ActiveShopper, NexTag, and WhenU among others). This process has worked in the market for airfares (via SideStep).

Why would a merchant want to be in the Pronto database—especially a high-priced merchant? Merchants can enter the database as the result of public domain information. Pronto scans catalogs and Web-based catalogs. Because it's unusual to be the low-cost provider of every item, will a merchant feel comfortable when a potential customer is wooed away by a better deal just as he or she is ready to buy? Less information is good if you are a high-priced merchant. The more consumers know, the higher their surplus should be. So far, merchants are said to prefer to be part of this trend rather than fight it.

How does Pronto make money? When a customer buys from a merchant that Pronto recommends, the merchant pays Pronto a commission ranging from 5 percent to 15 percent of the sale price. Other competitors to Pronto get paid if a customer merely clicks on a recommended merchant's page.

Should you be jumping into the market looking for where to invest in such companies? Apparently consumers are still a click away from using such Web sites. Application of Pronto requires you to download its software and lots of users are wary of doing that because the software could act like spyware—it could watch your surfing habits and store information about you. Privacy-conscious people don't value that. All the companies mentioned here claim their software does not act like spyware; but the general public is not so trusting.

Source: "Psst! You Can Get It Cheaper Over There," *The New York Times*, March 27, 2006, at www.nytimes.com/2006/03/27/technology/27ecom.html.

average) in claims but pays a premium of 50. The insurer loses 25 on average for each policy and cannot stay in business unless premiums are increased to 75. The insurer offers full insurance only at a premium of 75. Who will buy this policy? We saw that the high-risk drivers get utility of 7.071 from buying this policy but have expected utility of 6.545 if they buy no insurance. So high-risk drivers buy the insurance. Good drivers do not buy the policy as now shown:

$$\text{Utility with insurance} = (125 - 75)^{0.5} = 7.071$$
$$\text{Utility with no insurance} = (0.75)(125)^{0.5} + (0.25)(25)^{0.5} = 9.635$$

This illustration is a perfect lemons market. Because managers of the insurer cannot perfectly discriminate between high- and low-risk drivers, they offer only one type of policy, which appeals to only the high-risk drivers. An adverse selection of drivers choose to purchase insurance. The people who suffer from the information problem are the low-risk drivers, who are priced out of the market.

Managers can help restore the market in two ways so that the low-risk drivers have an appropriate choice of policies. Competition between insurers may help reduce the problem. Information about loss expectancies of individual drivers is of economic value to an insurer, so there is an incentive for managers at each insurer to invest in better information about policyholders. If an insurer acquires better information about policyholders than a rival does, that insurer can selectively attract low-risk drivers from the rival who is unable to discriminate simply by offering a lower price and admitting only low-risk drivers. Thus competition induces insurers to seek and compile information that lets them use premium structures to discriminate among risk groups. Of course insurers will never find out everything they need to know about their policyholders, and adverse selection never disappears. But in an actively competitive market, adverse selection is reduced to a level that reflects the cost of information.

The second way in which managers can help restore markets is through strategic design. We discuss this later, but we offer a teaser here. Is there any way to induce policyholders to reveal information about themselves in a credible way? Suppose managers offer a choice of A or B to each driver. Can they design these alternatives so that only a low-risk driver will choose A and only a high-risk driver will choose B? If managers can develop such a menu, they create a separating equilibrium, which we will discuss later in this chapter. Only low-risk drivers choose A, and only high-risk drivers choose B. Managers can infer what risk type each person is by the menu item he or she selects. This idea of self-selecting menus is discussed shortly.

THE MARKET FOR ANNUITIES

Another interesting adverse selection illustration is the market for annuities. Many managers have defined contribution retirement plans. Under these plans, the employer or the employee (or both) make explicit contributions to a pension plan.

STRATEGY SESSION: Information Asymmetries and Brownfields

Have you ever wondered (and worried) about those abandoned and contaminated industrial sites or gas stations that linger for years, often without being cleaned up or sold and put to use? Part of the problem turns out to be adverse selection.

The background to this problem is found in legislation enacted in 1980. The Comprehensive Environmental Response, Compensation, and Liability Act (CERCLA), commonly known as Superfund, was passed to make polluters responsible for contaminated land. Being made liable, the polluters would be responsible for the cost of cleaning up, which in many cases could be enormous. The parties who had this burden thrust upon them included not only those who put toxic materials on the land but also the owners of the land. Moreover, the liability for cleanup could pass to a new owner when the property was sold, even if the new owner did not contribute to the contamination. Does this impede the sale of such land? After all, the price that the land sells for should be discounted by the cost of cleanup, thus making it attractive for buyers to acquire and redevelop the land. However, two types of asymmetries can arise to stymie such sales.

The first of these is the so-called judgment-proof problem. If you are sued for cleanup, the amount you must pay is limited by your net worth (or if you are a firm, by the equity value of the firm). Suppose a sale were to take place in which the net worth of the seller was considerably less than the net worth of the buyer (which might be likely because the seller's business has declined to the point that the land has been abandoned). Consider that the cost of cleanup could be as much as $10 million, and there is a 50 percent chance the owner will be asked to clean up. The seller's net worth is $5 million, and the buyer

is worth $20 million. Because the seller could never have paid more than her net worth, this means the seller will have a 50 percent chance of escaping a $5 million liability and will therefore be willing to reduce the price by only 0.5 times $5 million = $2.5 million. However, the buyer will assume a 50 percent chance of paying the full $10 million and will want the price reduced by $5 million. You can easily see why they may not agree on a price: The seller is holding out for a price the buyer would be unwilling to pay, and therefore the sale may not take place, and the land will continue to lie idle.

But there is another problem. The seller knows more about the property and therefore the potential liability than the buyer. Uninformed buyers therefore are likely to be pessimistic about the likelihood and cost of cleanup and will therefore want a large price discount. At this discount, only sellers whose land is very badly contaminated are likely to sell. This creates the familiar adverse selection problem similar to the others addressed in this chapter: Only the most contaminated land will sell. In fact, even the fear that land might be contaminated may lead buyers to assume the worst, driving high-quality land from the market. But buyers can undertake an environmental audit to establish how polluted land really is. Although this may redress the information balance, the costs of such audits are high. Thus even the idea of paying for an audit because of the fear of adverse selection has a big deterrent effect on land sales.

Source: Derek B. Singer, "Brownfield Remediation as a Policy Tool in Urban Redevelopment," Working Paper EC465, Department of Economics, Middlebury College, November 2005.

The money is invested in some investment vehicle, and the value of the invested assets at retirement is available to the retiree. There is no guarantee of an income in retirement (unlike defined benefit plans). Suppose managers want to take this sum of money and convert it into an income stream that will last until they die. For example, if I knew I would live for 10 years, I could take my cash, divide it by 10 (with a little adjustment for investment income), and have a constant income stream for the rest of my life. The problem is that I cannot predict when I will die. In this savings scheme, I run out of money if I live for more than 10 years.

An annuity helps solve my problem. Even though I do not know how long I am going to live, I can buy an annuity that converts my principal into a constant income stream for the remainder of my life. Essentially, I give my cash to an annuity firm (usually a life insurance company), which in return promises to pay me a constant annual sum for as long as I live. Thus I insure against living too long and running out of money.

What are the incentives of the managers at the annuity firm? They sell many annuities. But consider 1,000 65-year-old women, all of whom buy annuities. We work through two simple examples of how annuity markets work. In the first case the health status of each individual is known both to that person and to managers at the annuity firm—perfect information. In the second case there is asymmetric information—the person knows her health status but the managers do not.

The Cost of Information Asymmetries in Annuity Markets

Annuity Markets with Full Information

Let us consider an annuity market in which managers have perfect information. Our 65-year-old women differ. All are not in the same state of health, and consequently they have different life expectancies:

- A quarter of our population is in poor health and is expected to live for only five years.
- Half are in average health and have a life expectancy of 15 years.
- A further quarter is in excellent health, with a life expectancy of 25 years.

Each person has $300,000 in capital and wishes to buy an annuity. Because the annuity firm knows each person's life expectancy, it can make the following deals (to keep things simple, we ignore interest and inflation and allow the annuity firm to break even):

- Those with a life expectancy of five years are offered an annuity of $60,000 per year. The firm receives $300,000 up front and pays five annuity payments of $60,000 = $300,000.
- Those with a life expectancy of 15 years are offered an annuity of $20,000 per year. The firm receives $300,000 up front and pays 15 annuity payments of $20,000 = $300,000.

- Those with a life expectancy of 25 years are offered an annuity of $12,000 per year. The firm receives $300,000 up front and pays 25 annuity payments of $12,000 = $300,000.

In an economic sense, this is a nondiscrimination case. Each person receives an annuity based on her own health status, and no one subsidizes anyone else. Moreover, if annuity markets were perfectly competitive, this is how managers would behave.

Annuity Markets with Asymmetric Information: Adverse Selection

Now assume the annuity firm charges everyone a premium of $300,000 and pays each person $20,000 per year until her death. This same annuity can be purchased by anyone. To see what adverse selection does to behavior in this market, we ask who knows what about each person's health. Managers of annuity firms can often find out something about health; they can ask for a medical test.[2] But what are the managers worried about when they ask for a test? They are certainly not worried about people being ill and having a five-year life expectancy. For each of these people, the firm receives $300,000 and pays five installments of $20,000, thus clearing a profit of $200,000. On the contrary, they are worried about people being "too healthy" and living too long. The annuity firm loses $200,000 on anyone who lives 25 years (it receives $300,000 and pays 25 installments of $20,000). In testing people, the managers try to spot those who are healthy and will live a long time. This is not easy. Verifying that people are ill is one thing. Identifying people who may wish to pretend they are ill but are indeed healthy is quite difficult. So the managers often lack reliable information about the health status of customers. On the other hand, each person knows a lot about his or her own health status: medical history, dietary and exercise habits, and so forth. So we have the classic information asymmetry that can lead to adverse selection. Finding health problems is easier than finding the absence of them.

Because managers do not know the health status of any particular applicant, they estimate the firm can break even if it receives $300,000 from an applicant who should be offered an annuity of $20,000. To see this, the total income for the firm is

$$1{,}000 \times \$300{,}000 = \$300{,}000{,}000$$

Here are the total annuity payments:

250 people ($\frac{1}{4}$ of 1,000) die after 5 years

$$= 250 \text{ times } \$20{,}000 \times 5 \text{ years } = \$25{,}000{,}000$$

500 people ($\frac{1}{2}$ of 1,000) die after 15 years

$$= 500 \text{ times } \$20{,}000 \times 15 \text{ years } = \$150{,}000{,}000$$

250 people ($\frac{1}{4}$ of 1,000) die after 25 years

$$= 250 \text{ times } \$20{,}000 \times 25 \text{ years } = \$125{,}000{,}000$$

$$\text{Total payments } = \$300{,}000{,}000$$

2. In practice, the annuity sum reflects some markup for the firm's profit and also accounts for investment income.

Another way to see this example is to look at the after-the-fact income statement for each group. Those dying after five years pay $300,000 for the annuity and receive (5)($20,000) = $100,000. The annuity firm makes a profit of $200,000 on each of these individuals.

Those dying after 15 years pay $300,000 for the annuity and receive (15)($20,000) = $300,000. The annuity firm breaks even on each of these individuals.

Those dying after 25 years pay $300,000 for the annuity and receive (25)($20,000) = $500,000. The annuity firm loses $200,000 on each of these individuals.

Who buys the annuity? If those in poor health believe they have a life expectancy of only five years, then five annual payments of $20,000 at an up-front cost of $300,000 are a bad deal. These people would probably be much better off simply drawing down their capital. For example, if they allow themselves $30,000 a year, they will not run out of money until after 10 years (twice their life expectancy). So those in poor health are unlikely to buy the annuity paying $20,000. Those in average health may be inclined to buy because they remove some uncertainty and get a reasonable financial deal (remember that we are ignoring interest). Those in excellent health find the annuity of $20,000 per year to be a fabulous deal—they

---

STRATEGY SESSION: Adverse Selection in the Federal Government Prescription Drug Plan

Adverse selection can bedevil both private and public programs. Consider the prescription drug plan (PDP) created by the U.S. Medicare Modernization Act of 2003. Since 2006 the PDP, as the name suggests, has provided coverage for prescription drugs. The issue arises because the plan is optional. Recent estimates have attempted to see whether enrollment will be dominated by those most likely to use the plan. Research reported at a recent meeting of health economists suggests that this is indeed the case. Excluding those enrolled in Medicare and current employer-sponsored plans, ". . . approximately 18 percent of the remaining beneficiaries will enroll in a PDP without an additional supplement. Drug expenditures for this group will be about 11 percent higher than the population average, indicating adverse selection. A similar number are predicted to enroll in a nondrug Medigap plan as well as a PDP (approximately 18 percent). These beneficiaries will have drug expenditures typically about 21 percent higher than the population average, and beneficiaries enrolling in FFS and nondrug Medigap (4 percent) will have average drug expenditures about 31 percent higher. By contrast, HMO enrollees (36 percent) and enrollees in FFS only (24 percent) will have drug expenditures about 12 percent lower than the population average."

Source: S. Pizer, A. Frakt, and R. Feldman, "Storm Clouds on the Horizon—Expected Adverse Selection in Medicare Prescription Drug Plans." Paper presented at the annual meeting of the Economics of Population Health: Inaugural Conference of the American Society of Health Economists, Madison, WI, USA, June 4, 2006.

pay $300,000 and get back $500,000. So this deal appeals to only some of our 1,000 65-year-olds. Only those in average or better-than-average health will buy the annuity.

Of course managers can anticipate that only those in average or better-than-average health will buy the policy; so if it offers an annuity of $20,000, the firm will lose money. To see this, note that managers will break even on each of the 500 people in average health and lose $200,000 on each of the people in excellent health. Therefore, they have to reduce the annuity's value until they achieve break-even costs on those choosing to buy at this reduced value.

Evidence of Adverse Selection in the Annuity and Life Insurance Markets

Managers can use a simple test to see whether annuity markets are subject to adverse selection. Recall that in the preceding illustration, the population held 1,000 people and the average life expectancy was 15 years, calculated as follows:

$$\tfrac{1}{4} \text{ (5 years)} + \tfrac{1}{2} \text{ (15 years)} + \tfrac{1}{4} \text{ (25 years)} = 15 \text{ years}$$

If the annuity was offered at $20,000, then only the 750 people in average or better-than-average health would actually buy it. Therefore, the life expectancy of the annuitants would be

$$(500/750)(15 \text{ years}) + (250/750)(25 \text{ years}) = 18.333 \text{ years}$$

If managers could observe life expectancy, they could see whether it was greater for the annuitants than for the population as a whole. The problem is that they cannot observe life expectancy. However, they can observe the actual mortality rates of populations. If the average life expectancy of annuitants is indeed higher than that for the population as a whole, managers will find that those buying annuities live, on average, longer than the population as a whole. We draw on some evidence from two colleagues at Wharton comparing the life span of annuitants with the population in the United States.[3] Figure 15.2 shows the distribution of age of death for those buying annuities and for the whole U.S. male population. The distribution for annuitants is clearly shifted to the right, indicating that they indeed live longer on average.

The Absence of Adverse Selection in Life Insurance

Whereas annuities insure people against "living too long" and running out of money, life insurance protects the survivors of people who "die too soon." If managers at life insurance firms have less information about the health status of their policyholders than the policyholders themselves, we would expect adverse selection here too. But do managers indeed have less information?

Recall that when we discussed annuities, we suggested that it might be challenging for managers to exclude those in good health; establishing the absence of

3. This is taken from David McCarthy and Olivia Mitchell, "International Adverse Selection in Life Insurance and Annuities," 2003.

FIGURE 15.2

Mortality Distributions for the U.S. Population and Annuitants

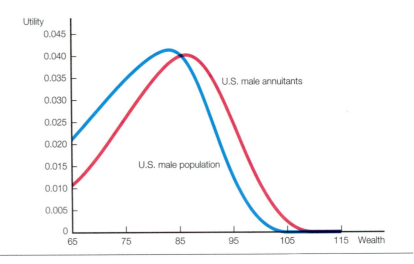

Source: O.S. Mitchell and D. McCarthy. "Annuities for an Aging World," in E. Fornero and E. Luciano, eds., *Developing an Annuities Market in Europe* (Northhampton, MA: Edward Elgar, 2003).

poor health is difficult. The evidence on annuities showed that some degree of information asymmetry exists.

Managers at a life insurance firm routinely conduct medical examinations of those seeking life insurance and turn down (or charge higher premiums to) those who do not test well. Does this action by managers significantly reduce the information asymmetries and allow them to adequately predict future health? Let us see.

In Figure 15.3 we show some evidence drawn from the United States for both men and women. These figures show the histograms of mortality—that is, how many people die in different age groups. If insurance companies did not conduct effective medical exams and there was adverse selection, we would expect that healthier people would be less inclined to buy insurance and that the mortality rates for the insured population would be higher than for the population as a whole. But this is not what we see. The distribution for the insured population is clearly shifted to the right, indicating that mortality rates are lower among those who have life insurance. This pattern can be seen for both men and women, but it is less dramatic for women. The same pattern has been observed in the United Kingdom. It appears that, far from having

FIGURE 15.3

Distribution of Age at Death Conditional on Attaining Age 25

The red line shows the distribution of age of death for the population, and the blue line shows the distribution of age of death for those purchasing life insurance.

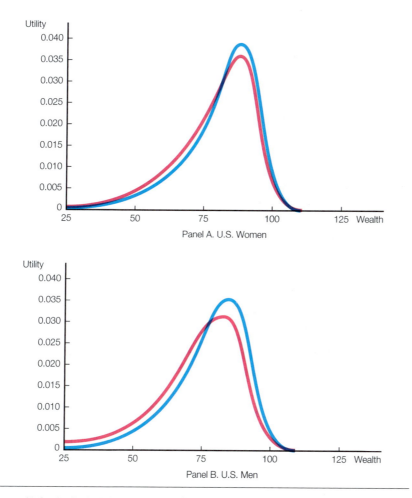

Panel A. U.S. Women

Panel B. U.S. Men

Source: McCarthy, David & Olivia S. Mitchell, "International Adverse Selection in Life Insurance and Annuities." In *Riding the Age Waves: Responses to Aging in Advanced Industrial States.* Eds Shripad Tuljapurkar, Naohiro Ogawa, & Anne Gauthier. Elsevier. *Forthcoming.*

an information disadvantage, managers at life insurance firms have been very effective in establishing the health status of their policyholders and offering insurance predominantly to those in good health.[4] There seem to be no traceable adverse selection here.

4. There is another possible explanation for these results. People who buy life insurance probably have above-average wealth. And wealth is also associated with health and longevity. Therefore, the reason that insured people live longer may have more to do with their wealth rather than insurance company screening.

RESOLVING ADVERSE SELECTION THROUGH SELF-SELECTION

While Ackerlof described the adverse selection problem, Michael Rothschild and Joseph Stiglitz laid out an elegant solution to adverse selection. (Stiglitz shared the 2001 Nobel Prize with Ackerlof and Michael Spence.) The idea behind their solution is simple. If the buyer of a secondhand car simply asks about quality, the answer is not credible. If an insurance firm simply asks how good a driver you are, you are certainly going to embellish your answer. Asking is not enough. How can an uninformed manager create credible information? Consider, for example, managers at the insurance company. They do not know whether any driver is a high or low risk. However, the insurer does know the following:

1. Some drivers are high risk and some are low risk.
2. The drivers themselves know whether they are good or bad drivers.

Managers should reason that because individuals know their own risk type, they might sometimes use this private information to reach different decisions. So managers should design policies that separate behavior between good and bad drivers. Good drivers choose one policy and bad drivers choose an alternative policy. Managers induce drivers to reveal their risk types by the policies they choose.

Let us think of a choice problem that does the trick. Managers might offer every driver who seeks insurance a choice between two policies—full insurance or a high deductible:

Full insurance When every loss is paid in full.

Deductible When the insurer does not pay the full loss but pays the loss minus some fixed amount.

- Policy A has a high premium (designed to break even if bought only by high-risk drivers) and offers **full insurance**. Full insurance means that every loss is paid in full.
- Policy B has a much lower premium but a big **deductible**. A deductible means that the insurer does not pay the full loss but pays the loss minus some fixed amount. For example, suppose the policy has a $2,000 deductible. If there is a $20,000 loss, the insurer will pay $20,000 − $2,000 = $18,000. With a $5,000 loss the insurer pays $5,000 − $2,000 = $3,000, and so forth. If the loss is less than $2,000, the insurance firm pays nothing.

Drivers who know they are bad are likely to have one or more claims, so the deductible is a big deterrent. It is much better for bad drivers to pay the higher premium and avoid the deductible. But drivers who know they are good will reason the premium saving is more important because they are unlikely to have a claim and therefore are unlikely to face the deductible. So good drivers select the cheaper deductible policy and bad drivers select the more expensive, full coverage.

Managers can also use flat and experience-related premiums to get customers to reveal their true type. Consider the following:

- Policy C has a relatively high price. Furthermore, the driver can buy the policy next year, and the year after, and so on at the same price. The premium does not go up (except for inflation) even if the driver has claims under the policy.
- Policy D starts with a high premium; in the first year the premium for policy D is higher than for policy C. However, the premium for policy D changes in future years according to the number of accidents the driver has. If there are no claims, the premium for policy D falls to a level far below that for policy C. If there are claims, the premium stays at the high level—that is, a little higher than policy C.

Now consider the reasoning of those who drive badly. They can choose either policy. But they know they are bad drivers, and there is a high chance they will crash their cars and make an insurance claim. Therefore, policy D looks unattractive. The potential premium reduction for having no claims is not really relevant given their self-knowledge. They know if they buy policy D, they always (or at least often) pay a higher premium. But good drivers see the choice differently. For them, the chance of a big premium reduction is attractive because they believe they are unlikely to have a claim. Their likelihood of getting a premium reduction more than makes up for a slightly higher premium in the first year. Accordingly, good drivers will tend to choose policy D, and bad drivers will choose policy C.

Simple Adverse Selection

In our earlier example, each driver had an initial wealth of 125 and could lose 100 with a crash. The probabilities of a crash were

Probability that bad drivers crash = 0.75
Probability that good drivers crash = 0.25

We know from this example that the market for good drivers collapses altogether. Indeed, the only policy offered is a policy offering full insurance at a premium of 0.75 (100) = 75, designed to break even for high-risk drivers. Only bad drivers buy insurance at this price. No insurance policy is offered that would appeal to good drivers. Can managers do better?

Suppose they offer the following two policies, and each driver can choose which, if any, to buy:

- Policy 1 charges a premium of 75, but it fully pays for the loss of 100 if a crash occurs. Anyone buying this policy will have a wealth of 125 minus the premium of 75 = 50. Note that because of the full insurance, the wealth of the individual is unaffected by whether the loss occurs.
- Policy 2 pays a fixed sum of 10 if a loss occurs, and the premium is 2.5. Anyone buying this policy will have the following wealth:

With no loss: 125 minus the premium of 2.5 = 122.5
With a loss: 125 minus the premium of 2.5,
minus loss of 100, plus the payment of 10 = 32.5

Clearly policy 2 is not a perfect insurance policy, but it offers some compensation for loss. Let us examine the choice facing each type of policyholder. First look at the high-risk, bad drivers. Note that high-risk drivers (and low-risk drivers later) know their probability of loss, so they use this probability when calculating expected utility:

$$\text{No insurance utility} = (0.25)(125)^{0.5} + (0.75)(125 - 100)^{0.5} = 6.545$$
$$\text{Policy 1 utility} = (125 - 75)^{0.5} = 7.071$$
$$\text{Policy 2 utility} = (0.25)(125 - 2.5)^{0.5} + (0.75)(125 - 100 - 2.5 + 10)^{0.5} = 7.043$$

For the low-risk drivers, the expected utilities are calculated using the low-risk probabilities:

$$\text{No insurance utility} = (0.75)(125)^{0.5} + (0.25)(125 - 100)^{0.5} = 9.635$$
$$\text{Policy 1 utility} = (125 - 75)^{0.5} = 7.071$$
$$\text{Policy 2 utility} = (0.75)(125 - 2.5)^{0.5} + (0.25)(125 - 100 - 2.5 + 10)^{0.5} = 9.726$$

Note that the two types of drivers choose different policies. For high-risk drivers the best choice is policy 1, which offers them a utility of 7.071 (versus 7.043 for policy 2 and 6.545 for buying no insurance). But for low-risk drivers policy 2 is the best choice, offering them a utility of 9.726 (versus 7.071 for policy 1 and 9.635 for no insurance). In making these choices, individual policyholders act in their self-interest (maximizing expected utility) and use their private information about their loss probabilities. Note also that this self-selection has taken place without managers initially being able to identify which policyholder is at low risk and which is at high risk of accidents. Hence we can call this a **self-selection menu**.

Self-selection menu When buyers act in their own self-interest and use their private information about their loss probabilities to select policies.

There are other interesting features about this solution chosen by managers. When we introduced this adverse selection problem earlier in the chapter, only one policy survived: policy 1. In that earlier analysis, the good drivers preferred self-insurance to buying policy 1. Now with the self-selection menu of policies 1 and 2, managers make the good drivers better off (they prefer the newly introduced policy 2 to self-insurance) while bad drivers are in the same position (they continue to buy policy 1). This is a clear improvement; managers improved the lot of good drivers at no cost to the bad drivers. So this menu has at least partly salvaged the marketplace by enabling low-risk drivers to get insurance.

Finally, managers need to know whether such a menu is feasible. The most immediate worry is whether managers will want to offer both policies. Because the policyholders self-select, the insurer breaks even with each policy:

- Only high-risk drivers buy policy 1. The expected claims are 0.75 (100), which matches the premium of 75.
- Only low-risk drivers buy policy 2. Hence expected claims are 0.25 (10), which matches the premium of 2.5.

Therefore, a competitive insurer can offer this choice and survive.

This solution to the adverse selection problem is called a **separating equilibrium**. It is in the interests of the uninformed insurer to offer such a choice; and the choice induces self-selection by the policyholders into their respective risk types. But note that information asymmetry still imposes a cost. The insurance coverage in policy 2 does not offer complete protection to the low-risk drivers. Although it is clearly better than no insurance, the coverage is rationed.

Separating equilibrium This solution to adverse selection induces policyholders to select their respective risk types.

USING EDUCATION AS A SIGNAL: ADVERSE SELECTION IN THE JOB MARKET

An early, and somewhat surprising, application of looking at the incentives of information was presented by the economist Michael Spence (who, as we mentioned, shared the 2001 Nobel Prize). The problem he had in mind is straightforward enough; the solution is quite clever. How can managers predict which job applicants will have good work skills? We show that applicants use education to send to potential employers a signal of labor market skills that cannot be easily measured by employers. Of course schools and universities also teach something.

Applicants have some self-awareness about their job market skills. They know their ambitions, how organized they are, and whether they are prepared to work hard and long hours. They also know something about their people skills and intellectual ability.

These traits are initially not known to a potential employer, who may learn about employee abilities only gradually and over a long period. So there is an information asymmetry. As in the insurance and annuity markets, simply asking applicants to reveal their private information does not work. Most applicants know how to prepare a résumé and hone their interview techniques. So managers need a credible method for separating those who know they have good job skills from those who lack them.

If managers believe there is a relationship between job skills and academic performance, they can craft a way to find those with good work skills. This need not be a perfect relationship; but on average, people with good job skills have an easier time overcoming academic hurdles. Consider an undergraduate degree that requires students to pass 30 courses. Many students do this in four years, but some take three years and others may take five or six because they have to repeat courses or have a smaller course load. The cost of getting a degree, therefore, varies according to the length of time it takes. These costs include the direct costs of paying for education and the opportunity costs of losing wages while not working. Direct costs mount as courses are repeated, and lost wages climb as students take longer to finish.

Consider the following example. Average direct and indirect costs per course are

High-quality job skills = \$2,000 per course
Low-quality job skills = \$3,450 per course (they take longer to finish)

Now assume that if employers knew the skill levels of applicants, they would pay the following wages:

High-quality job skills = $50,000 per year for 5 years
Low-quality job skills = $30,000 per year for 5 years

After five years, the employer can figure out an employee's job skills.

Of course employers do not know each person's job skills; but suppose employers make the following offer: All those who have taken at least x courses are paid a salary of $50,000, and those that took fewer than x courses are paid $30,000. Managers need to calculate a value of x to separate the high- and low-skilled workers.

Students know this offer stands, and they have to decide how many courses to take. So they rationally look at the costs and benefits of different degree programs. The benefit of completing x courses to any student, of high or low skill, is a wage increase from $30,000 to $50,000 for five years, giving a total benefit of $100,000 (we ignore the time value of money here). But the costs differ, being $2,000 per course and $3,450 per course for the high- and low-skilled people.

High skill:
Benefit of achieving x courses = $100,000
Cost of achieving x courses = $2,000 times x

The benefit exceeds the costs if x is less than 50.

Low skill:
Benefit of achieving x courses = $100,000
Cost of achieving x courses = $3,450 times x

The benefit exceeds the costs if x is less than 29.

So the employers choose a level of x between 29 and 50. Say they choose $x = 30$, which is the typical four-year degree program. People with low-quality skills do not choose to take the 30-course degree (the cost is $3,450 \times 30 = $103,500, and the benefit is only $100,000). But high-skilled students take the 30-course degree (the cost is $2,000 \times 30 = $60,000, and the benefit is $100,000).

By cleverly setting the 30-course standard, managers persuade people to reveal their hidden information as they choose their education. Universities now provide two functions. In addition to actual teaching, they screen people according to employment skills and endorse these skills to potential employers. Another way of thinking about this is provided by our MBA students. When asked why they go for the Wharton MBA, many reply, "Employers pay more for a Wharton MBA because they know that anyone accepted to this program and obtaining the degree must be good." Therefore, if a university wishes to signal to the market that its graduates are of high quality, it must set its standards sufficiently high to discourage low-skilled people.

PROBLEM SOLVED: Can a Government Guarantee Help Make Markets More Efficient?

Through its actions, the government can increase the efficiency of markets. This is particularly useful when markets fail because of asymmetric information. As discussed in Chapter 16, the Treasury proposed to purchase some CDOs and MBS from financial institutions. Imagine there are two kinds of mortgage-backed securities "out there": high-quality ones, and low-quality ones. A high-quality mortgage-backed security is worth 80 percent of its face value to a seller, and 90 percent of its face value to a buyer. A low-quality mortgage-backed security is worth 20 percent of its face value to a seller, and 30 percent of its face value to a buyer. Suppose that 1/3 of all mortgage-backed securities in existence are low-quality, and the other 2/3's are high-quality.

Each seller of a mortgage-backed security knows whether it is high-quality or low-quality. However, buyers cannot tell whether a mortgage-backed security is high- or low-quality before acquiring it. After acquiring it, however, they will learn its quality.

Assume that there are lots of potential buyers but only a limited supply of mortgage-backed securities; so that competition among buyers means the market price for a mortgage-backed security will equal buyers' willingness to pay for it.

Under these conditions, will high-quality and low-quality mortgage-backed securities be traded? If yes, what percentage will their price be of the securities' face value?

Readers should recognize this as a lemons problem. Initially buyers will have an expected value of the security of (2/3)*90 + (1/3)*30 = 60 + 10 = 70. When offered 70, a high-quality security holder won't sell because she values the security at 80. The low-quality holder will sell (because she values the security at 20). Ultimately, only low securities will trade and the price will be 30 percent of face value. Because this is a lemons problem, no high-quality securities will be traded.

Now imagine that the Treasury can choose to guarantee the value of a mortgage-backed security.

For a seller of a high-quality security, the expected cost of the guarantee is 15 percent of its face value. For buyers, the guarantee on high-quality securities is worth 10 percent of its face value. For low-quality securities, the guarantee is worth 70 percent of face value to buyers and costs sellers 80 percent of face value. Under such conditions, what quality of securities (if any) will sell with a government guarantee?

Only high-quality securities will trade with a guarantee, because the low-quality securities cannot afford to purchase the guarantee; therefore, the guarantee is a credible signal of quality. A guarantee bought by a high-quality holder will make the security worth 90 + 10, or 100 percent of the face value to the buyer; and a guarantee bought by a low-quality holder will make the security worth 30 + 70, or 100 percent of face value to the buyer. If the high-quality holder purchases a guarantee, it will cost her 10 percent of the face value; but if she sells the security for 100, she'll realize 100 − 10 = 90, which is greater than the 80 at which she currently values the security. If the low-quality holder purchases a guarantee, it will cost her 80 percent of the face value; but if she sells the security for 100, she'll realize 100 − 80 = 20, exactly what the security is worth to her if she holds it. Thus, the high-quality holder can purchase the guarantee and the low quality holder cannot afford to.

With the guarantee, the market price of low-quality securities will be 30 percent of face value (because it can now be identified as low-quality and buyers value it at 30 percent); and the market price of high-quality securities will be 100 percent of face value (because it can now be identified as high-quality).

So government guarantees of some securities should help markets become more efficient. As with consumer durables or services, guarantees will cause holders to reveal hidden information as to their true type and the self-selection enables the asymmetric information (lemons) problem to be solved.

Of course education has other functions in addition to sorting people according to job skills. Ideally people learn something as well. [5]

USING WARRANTIES AS SIGNALS: ADVERSE SELECTION IN THE PRODUCT MARKET

Though a consumer selects a product (and pays for it) at the time of purchase, there are many products whose quality cannot be determined until they are consumed. These products are called *experience goods.* Examples of such goods include autos, appliances, and consumer electronics. As we saw in our used car example, since consumers cannot determine quality until after their purchases, there is an incentive for low-quality producers to advertise their products as high-quality. If consumers cannot determine the true quality of the good prior to purchase, they are unwilling to pay the price of a high-quality good.

In such situations, there is an incentive for managers of firms that produce high-quality goods to signal their true quality. Hence, they want to take actions to create a separating equilibrium so consumers can accurately determine product quality. One of the most common methods managers use to create this separation is the use of a product warranty. As we see below, if constructed correctly, a warranty is a credible signal of product quality. And, there is empirical evidence showing that consumers do recognize this and are willing to pay a higher price for products that carry a credible warranty.

How Managers Can Construct Warranties to Mitigate Adverse Selection

Imagine that managers of rival firms introduce a new product that purports to perform the same function. One product is truly of high-quality, while the other is of low-quality. Consumers have a reservation price for a high-quality product and a different (and lower) one for the low-quality product, if they could determine quality prior to purchase. It costs more to produce the high-quality product and less to produce the low-quality product.

If consumers could credibly determine product quality, we'd expect a separate market for high-quality products and a separate market for low-quality products. Managers of the firm producing the high-quality product want to construct a separating mechanism so consumers can determine product quality prior to purchase. Here is how they can do so using a product warranty.

We examine two possible scenarios. In the first scenario, consumers believe that a full-coverage warranty (one that fully repairs or replaces a defective product) signals a high-quality product if the warranty is of at least X years. In the second scenario, both firms might offer a warranty, but they would be of different lengths. If both firms offer a warranty, consumers believe that whichever product has the longer warranty is the higher-quality product.

5. All the authors of this book are professors, and their jobs might depend on this caveat.

Consumers' reservation price for the high-quality good is P_H and their reservation price for the low-quality good is P_L (where $P_H > P_L$). It costs the producer of the high-quality product a constant C_H to produce a unit and it costs the producer of the low-quality product a constant C_L to produce a unit (where $C_H > C_L$). It costs the producer of the high-quality product W_H/year to honor a full-coverage warranty and it costs the producer of the low-quality product W_L/year to honor a full coverage warranty (where $W_L > W_H$, because the low-quality item needs repair/replacement more often). Y is the number of years of the warranty. Producers wish to maximize their per unit profit.

Consider the first scenario. If managers want to signal high-quality, they will issue a warranty of X years. This will cost them $W_i X$ (where $i = L$ or H). The expected warranty cost to a low-quality producer is higher since his product will suffer more defects and/or more failures. If a producer wants to signal low-quality, he will not issue a warranty. A warranty for less than X years is costly (W_L per year), but it offers no signaling value since consumers will still perceive quality as low.

If the low-quality producer issues a warranty of X years, the consumer will pay P_H (since the consumer perceives the product as high-quality) for the unit and the profit per unit will be $P_H - C_L - W_L X$, whereas if he did not issue a warranty, the consumer will pay P_L for the unit and the profit per unit would be $P_L - C_L$. The low-quality producer would not issue a warranty if $P_H - C_L - W_L X < P_L - C_L$.

If the high-quality producer issues a warranty of X years, the consumer will pay P_H for the unit and the profit per unit is $P_H - C_H - W_H X$, whereas if he did not issue a warranty, the consumer would pay P_L for the unit and the profit per unit is $P_L - C_H$. The high-quality producer will issue a warranty if $P_H - C_H - W_H X > P_L - C_H$. Thus, if $(P_H - P_L)/W_H > X > (P_H - P_L)/W_L$, then X is a credible number of years of a full-coverage warranty. The warranty is credible since the benefits to low-quality product managers of signaling high quality are less than the expected warranty cost. Bottomline: the low-quality producers can't afford to misrepresent themselves.

We now consider the second scenario where consumers view the longest warranty as a signal of high-quality. The longest warranty a high-quality producer can afford to give is one where the profit from signaling high-quality just equals the profit from not signaling at all, i.e., low-quality. This will have length Y_H where

$$P_H - C_H - W_H Y_H = P_L - C_H$$

The longest warranty a low-quality producer can afford to give is one where the profit from signaling high-quality just equals the profit from not signaling at all, i.e., low-quality. This will have length Y_L where

$$P_H - C_L - W_L Y_L = P_L - C_L.$$

PROBLEM SOLVED: Determining Warranty Length

Tole Brothers is a new entrant into the house building market. They haven't been in the market long enough to gain a reputation for the quality of the homes they build. They think of themselves as builders of high-quality homes.

In the area where they're building, a high-quality home will sell for $500,000. It will cost a builder $250,000 to build a high-quality house. A rival firm, Quality Builders can construct a house that looks like a high-quality house but soon after occupation, the owners will begin to notice the defects. If the buyers can identify such a home, they would pay $400,000 for it. It would cost Quality Builders $200,000 to construct such an inferior home.

Managers at Tole Brothers believe they can signal their homes are high-quality by issuing a warranty on the home (at no cost to the buyer) that protects the home for W years against any defects. If a defect is found, they will repair it for free. Managers estimate the expected cost of this warranty to Tole Brothers is $10,000 per year, per home. If managers at Quality Builders want to offer an analogous warranty, it will cost them $25,000 per year, per home, because the likelihood of defects is much greater in their poorly constructed homes. Should managers at Tole Brothers offer a warranty? If yes, for what duration?

If managers at Tole Brothers choose not to offer a warranty, their houses are perceived as inferior and will sell for $400,000. Since they cost $250,000 to build, Tole Brothers will make $400,000 − 250,000 or $150,000 per house.

If managers at Tole Brothers choose to offer a warranty, their houses are perceived as high-quality and sell for $500,000. It costs them $250,000 to build the house and a warranty costs $10,000 per year, per house to service. Thus, a warranty of W years would cost 10,000W. Thus, Tole Brothers' profits with a warranty is $500,000 − $250,000 − $10,000W = $250,000 − $10,000W$.

Since $W_L > W_H$, then $1/W_H > 1/W_L$, and so $Y_H > Y_L$.

Thus, the high-quality producer can afford to out-warranty the low-quality producer. But now, think strategically. If the high-quality producer issued a warranty of Y_H years, managers would dissipate all the gains of being recognized as high-quality, i.e., they would earn the same profit as if they had been perceived to be low-quality. At the same time, the low-quality producer can't afford to offer a warranty of more than Y_L years (because if managers issued a warranty of even Y_L years, they would dissipate all the gains of being perceived as high-quality). So all the high-quality producer has to do is just out-warranty the low-quality producer. A warranty of $Y_H = Y_L + \varepsilon$ will do the trick. The high-quality producer can afford to give it and the low-quality producer cannot afford to give it and so the proposed length of warranty is credible. The low-quality producer will not issue a warranty (since it doesn't provide a positive signal and mangers would incur costs of honoring the warranty). Notice the similarity to auctions. The person, who values the item most, needs just to outbid the person who values the item second most.

By setting Tole Brothers' profits with and without a warranty equal and solving for W, we get

$250,000 - $10,000W = $150,000

or $10,000W = $100,000 or W = 10.

Thus, managers at Tole Brothers could offer a warranty of up to 10 years and make more money per house than if they offered no warranty. But do they have to?

If managers at Quality Builders do not issue a warranty, their houses are perceived as inferior and will sell for $400,000. Since they cost $200,000 to build, Quality will earn $400,000 - $200,000 or $200,000 per house.

If managers at Quality decide to offer a warranty, their houses are perceived as high-quality and will sell for $500,000. It costs them $200,000 to build the house and the warranty costs $25,000 per year, per house to service. Thus, a warranty of W years will cost Quality $25,000W. Hence the managers earn a profit of $500,000 - $200,000 - $25,000W or $300,000 - $25,000W.

By setting Quality's profits with and without a warranty equal and solving for W, we get

300,000 - 25,000W = 200,000

or 25,000W = 100,000 or W = 4

Thus, managers at Quality Builders could offer a warranty of up to 4 years and make more money per house than if they offered no warranty.

Managers at Tole Brothers now must set their strategy. Suppose they offer a warranty of 4 or more years. Managers at Quality then will not offer any warranty (since they make more money with no warranty). Quality will not offer a warranty with their houses and managers will earn $200,000 per house.

Managers at Tole Brothers will earn a profit of $500,000 - $250,000 - $10,000(4$^+$) = $250,000 - $40,000$^+$ or just under $210,000 per house. This profit exceeds the $150,000 they'd make if they didn't issue a warranty and signal high quality.

Does this help explain why buyers are willing to pay an auto dealer a higher price for a pre-owned certified auto with a warranty than for the same auto they purchase from a private seller? Or, why consumers pay a higher price for electronic products from a store that offers a warranty relative to identical items on ebay that lack such a warranty?

SUMMARY

1. Adverse selection arises when one party to a contractual or economic relationship knows more than the other. For example, a seller of a used car knows more than a buyer, a policyholder knows more than an insurance company, and a borrower knows more than a lender. This puts the uninformed party at a disadvantage. For example, managers at insurance companies are unable to distinguish between safe and unsafe drivers; therefore premiums are averaged over both types. This means that good drivers subsidize bad ones, and many good drivers may

be tempted to cancel their insurance to avoid this subsidy. In the extreme case, adverse selection may bring a market crashing down as all the low-risk people are priced out of the market. Similarly, all sellers of high-quality used cars might decide to keep them rather than sell at a price reflecting average quality.

2. There are tactics managers can use to mitigate the effects of adverse selection. The obvious one is to become informed. We saw that while adverse selection exists in the annuity market, managers at life insurance companies seem to have been successful in removing the information problem by medical examinations.

3. Managers can also design a menu of contracts to let others reveal their asymmetric information; the contracts have differential appeal to different customers. For example, in insurance, a high-priced policy might offer full insurance; a low-priced policy might cover only part of the damage. Bad drivers worry about the partial coverage because they know they are likely to have an accident. On the other hand, good drivers might like the partial coverage because it is cheap, and they figure they are unlikely to be in a crash. In labor markets education is used as a signal of worker productivity; and producers might use warranties to distinguish their products from those of rivals.

wwnorton.com/studyspace ⓢ

PROBLEMS

1. Sellers of used cars know the cars' quality, but buyers do not. Imagine that used Toyota Corollas are worth $10,000 if they are of high quality and $5,000 if they are of poor quality. Although buyers may not know the quality of a specific car, they do know that 25 percent will be of poor quality. In such a market, what cars will be sold on the secondhand market and at what price?

2. The market for digital cameras is relatively new. Ajax Inc. produces what it regards as a high-quality digital camera. Knockoff Inc. produces what it regards as a low-quality digital camera. However, because the market is so new, reputations for quality have not yet developed, and consumers cannot tell the quality difference between an Ajax digital and a Knockoff digital just by looking at them.

   If consumers knew the difference, they'd be willing to pay $200 for a high-quality camera, and they'd be willing to pay $100 for a low-quality camera. It costs Ajax $85 to produce a high-quality camera, and it costs Knockoff $55 to produce a low-quality camera.

   A recent MBA hire at Ajax suggests that Ajax could differentiate its camera from Knockoff's by offering a full-coverage warranty (which would fully cover any defect in the camera at no cost to the customer). The MBA estimates that it would cost Ajax $20 per year to offer such a warranty. The MBA also estimates that it would cost Knockoff $40 per year should Knockoff attempt to copy Ajax's warranty strategy. Consumers will feel that the camera with the longest warranty is high-quality and that with the shortest warranty is low-quality. The camera companies want to maximize the profit per camera.

What is Ajax's profit per camera in the digital camera market?

3. No-State Insurance Company has made the following estimate of auto damage for several groups of potential customers who own cars worth $10,000. There are an equal number of customers in each group. No-State is risk-neutral.

Group	Initial Value of Car	Probability of Accident that Devalues Car to $5,000
A	$10,000	0.2
B	$10,000	0.3
C	$10,000	0.4

State regulation mandates that every customer must pay the same premium regardless of his or her group, and this premium must be sufficient to cover all expected claims from those who purchase insurance from No-State. There are no additional costs to the company other than paying off claims.

All consumers have the following utility function (U):

$$U = W^{0.5}$$

W is the consumer's wealth as represented by the value of the car.

What premium should No-State offer for full-coverage insurance?

4. Some people are good drivers, and others are bad drivers. The former have a 10 percent chance of crashing their cars, and the latter have a 30 percent chance. All have a total wealth of 400, but this will fall to 100 if they crash their cars. In other words, each will lose 300 of wealth if they crash. You are an insurance company manager who wishes to offer a pair of policies to all drivers. Each policy is designed to break even (zero profit) given the people who choose to buy that policy. The first policy has a premium of 90 and covers all losses (it will pay 300 in the event of a crash). The second policy has a premium of 5 and will pay 50 in the event of a crash. Who will buy which policy? Will the insurance company make a profit, break even, or lose money?

Each person has a utility function as follows:

$$\text{Utility} = (\text{Wealth})^{0.5}$$

5. Consider a market for annuities for 70-year-old men in which people differ in terms of both their expected remaining years of life and their risk preferences. Of the population of 200, half have a life expectancy of 9 years and the remaining half have a life expectancy of 11 years. We can express risk preference in the following way. The risk people are worried about is that of running out of wealth before they die. The more risk-averse you are, the higher the up-front

price you are willing to pay for the annuity. More risk-averse people are willing to pay 1.3 times x times A, where x is the expected years of life remaining and A is the dollar amount paid each year to the annuitant. Less risk-averse people are willing to pay only 1.1 times x times A. Assume that of the 100 people in each health group, half are more risk-averse and half less risk-averse.

The annuity firm sells an annuity of $50,000 per year for as long as the buyer lives, and the price of the annuity is $50,000. Because the annuity firm cannot tell whether any applicant has a short or long life expectancy, it must accept any application for its product. What is the expected profit of the annuity firm? (You may ignore discounting in this example.)

PART 8

GOVERNMENT ACTIONS AND MANAGERIAL BEHAVIOR

CHAPTER 16

GOVERNMENT AND BUSINESS

Bill Gates, chairman of Microsoft, the computer software giant, is a billionaire; yet he and other top executives of Microsoft had to be concerned with the U.S. Department of Justice's investigation of the firm's competitive practices. The government prevailed, and Microsoft was found guilty of antitrust violations. This set in motion appeals of the verdict. The government and Microsoft ultimately reached a compromise.

The government is a major player for business. Managers must be aware not only of antitrust laws but also laws about fair trade, employment, safety, environmental issues, and securities, among others. U.S. companies, which often complain about excessive government interference with their activities, are now complaining about a lack of rules in the developing countries of the world. The game of business cannot be played without rules, and the government sets the rules.

In general, economic regulation has decreased in the United States in the last 30 years. Transportation and banking are two prime examples. Previously government agencies controlled which carriers could enter and exit the transportation industries, the prices they charged, and whether they could merge. In banking, the range of services banks could provide was once heavily regulated; banks could provide banking services but not insurance or brokerage. After deregulation, transportation became like the restaurant industry—any company could enter or exit and charge what it wished.

Yet noneconomic regulation (which can have major economic costs) has grown in recent years. For instance, safety regulations and hours of service (number of hours on duty) regulations continue in the transportation industry. Laws are passed each year that affect how business is conducted.

Governments collect taxes that affect disposable income and the final prices of goods. Governments also spend money that affects the demand for goods. Tax laws affect corporate investment policy. Governments subsidize certain goods, like agricultural products, to increase their production; and governments certify whether and when certain goods can appear in the market, as in the case of drugs (both legal and illegal). Governments provide infrastructure, like roads and water and sewer lines, which are an important part of many firms' production functions.

STRATEGY SESSION: Government Actions and the Financial Crisis of 2008

While monetary and fiscal policy is the subject of a course in Macroeconomics, the nature of the financial crisis of 2008 causes us to make some comments regarding the role of government and its impact on managerial behavior.

In 2008, managers witnessed the virtual drying up of credit markets. This caused them to cut back on their investments, lay off workers, and reduce their estimates of future earnings. In 2009, managers are being squeezed on both the demand and supply side. We have emphasized that managers need to be prepared to manage during bust as well as boom times. So, what should efficient managers do?

Our answer is to follow the principles we discuss in this book. The economic environment follows a natural cycle where booms and busts must be anticipated. Managers need to be prepared for both. The optimization principles, the strategizing principles, and the information asymmetries don't change with the state of the economy; however, what ends up being a manager's best action likely does; but it still involves using the right tools to arrive at that decision.

What is the role of government as a result of the crisis? The first is monetary policy to get credit flowing so banks can lend money for working capital, so businesses have the cash to carry on their day-to-day operations (short-run) and can lend money for investment in the business (long-run). The second is fiscal policy, which is designed to invest in public infrastructure, create jobs, and generate a multiplier effect (with increases in consumption by those employed). The last will be a major push to re-regulate the segments of the economy that are blamed for precipitating the financial crisis. We can expect to see much tighter controls on financial markets, banks, investment companies, insurance companies, etc., to promote transparency (i.e., eliminate the asymmetries in information) and integrity.

The re-regulation is the result of a perceived market failure. When the financial system was significantly deregulated in the 1980s, policymakers (like Alan Greenspan) felt the financial markets would be self-regulating and that government oversight could be relaxed. The events of 2008 showed that markets can and do fail. Even Greenspan admitted he had too much trust in the ability of markets to regulate themselves. And it was basically the asymmetric information of Chapters 14 and 15 that led to the market failures.

Thus government activity is pervasive. It accounts for approximately 30 percent of our gross domestic product. If you plan to move to the top of the executive ranks, be prepared to interact not only with your colleagues and rivals but also with government agencies.

The previous chapters have shown the power of markets to allocate resources and to get things done in the economy without any intervention. In general, the authors of this book believe that the market is a good solution. However, we also believe that markets can and do fail. Negative externalities such as congestion and pollution come to mind. In those circumstances a role for outside intervention may be called for, or the market must reinvent itself and come up with a new market mechanism that corrects the failure. Sometimes the government can nudge the market in this direction. Although externality markets initially called for intervention, market-based congestion tolls and tradable emission permits are becoming more prevalent. Thus new markets can evolve to solve previous market failures. Without a governmental nudge, however, the market failure might persist.

In this chapter we discuss how actions like public regulation, antitrust policy, trade policy, price intervention, taxes, and the patent system affect managerial life. In addition, we view the role of government in providing public goods and in correcting market failures. Managers must not only understand the nature of public policy in these areas; they must understand what public policy is designed to achieve. Too frequently business executives lack the breadth of view and knowledge required to effectively promote their firms' interests in the public arena (even though over 34,750 registered lobbyists, many of them corporate, are in Washington—a number that has more than doubled since 2000).[1]

We will leave it to your course in macroeconomics to discuss federal fiscal and monetary policy, both of which have major impacts on the economy and hence on your business.

COMPETITION VERSUS MONOPOLY

The Supreme Court has stated that competition is its fundamental national policy. Many economists agree that competition is preferable to monopoly (or other serious departures from perfect competition) because it is likely to result in a better allocation of resources. As we saw in Chapter 7, a monopolist tends to restrict output, driving up the price. These economists argue that from the point of view of social welfare, it is better if a monopolist raises its output to the competitive level. (Also, in their view, monopolists are likely to be less efficient than competitive firms.) Although economists are not unanimous in this opinion, the majority seem to prefer competition over monopoly.

One way our society has dealt with these issues is to establish government commissions like the Federal Communications Commission and the Interstate

1. "The Road to Riches Is Called K Street," *The Washington Post*, June 22, 2005, p. A01.

Commerce Commission (now abolished but with some residual authority retained in the Surface Transportation Board) to regulate the behavior of monopolists. As we see in subsequent sections of this chapter, the government has tried to reduce the harmful effects of monopoly. In addition, Congress has enacted antitrust laws meant to promote competition and control monopoly. These laws too are discussed at length in this chapter. Any manager must be aware of the nature of these laws because violating them may trigger significant fines and jail sentences.

Until recently the United States went further in promoting competition than other major industrialized countries. But just because we promote competition does not mean our dedication to competition is complete. In the new millennium, the European Union seems to have taken the lead with respect to antitrust policy (in some cases pursuing cases that the United States has chosen not to prosecute). To some extent this represents a "catching up" because Europe historically has not pursued anticompetitive activities. Other countries, at our and the EU's behest, such as South Korea, Japan, and Brazil, are now taking a more active role in antitrust enforcement. But national policies are too ambiguous and rich in contradictions to be characterized so simply. The truth is that we, as a nation, have adopted many measures to promote monopoly and limit competition. For example, this is the effect of the patent system, which is designed to promote invention and innovation. In later sections of this chapter we see why the patent system is beneficial even though it creates temporary monopolies.

REGULATION OF MONOPOLY

In some areas of the economy, such as the distribution of water, it is not economical for more than one firm to exist due to important economies of scale. In such industries the single firm, a so-called natural monopolist, is in a position to charge a higher-than-competitive price for its product. Because such a price may inefficiently allocate society's resources, as well as create monopolistic profit regarded by the public as excessive and unjustifiable, government regulatory commissions often are established to limit the prices a monopolist of this sort can charge.

Consider the Acme Water Company, whose demand curve, marginal revenue curve, average cost curve, and marginal cost curve are shown in Figure 16.1. Without regulation, managers will charge a price of P_0 and produce Q_0 units of the product. By setting a maximum price of P_1, the commission can induce managers to increase output, pushing the price and output to what they would be if the industry were organized competitively. If the commission imposes a maximum price of P_1, the firm's demand curve becomes P_1AD', its marginal revenue curve becomes P_1ABR', its optimum output becomes Q_1, and it charges the maximum price of P_1. By setting the maximum price, the commission aids consumers, who pay a lower price for more of the product. By the same token, the commission takes away some of the Acme Water Company's monopoly power.

FIGURE 16.1

Regulation of Acme Water Company: Maximum Price

By setting a maximum price of P_1, a regulatory commission can make Acme increase output to Q_1.

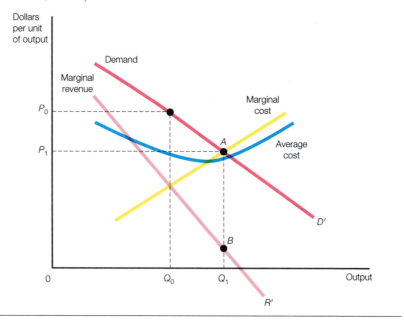

Regulatory commissions often establish the price (or the maximum price) at the level at which it equals average total cost, including a fair rate of return on the company's investment. In Figure 16.2 the price would be set by the commission at P_2, where the demand curve intersects the average total cost curve. The latter curve includes what the commission regards as a fair profit per unit of output. Considerable controversy arises over what constitutes a fair rate of return as well as what should be included in the company's investment on which the fair rate of return is to be earned.

To illustrate the workings of the regulatory process, consider the telephone industry in Michigan. The two organizational types that play a key role in regulating the telephone industry there are the firms (AT&T, Verizon, and so forth) and the Michigan Public Service Commission. AT&T is not the sole telephone company in the state, but it is a major firm that experiences direct competition from other firms in the industry. The commission, composed of three people appointed by the governor, has had authority over the telephone industry for over half a century.

General rate cases play an important role in the regulatory process. Such cases are initiated by the firms, based on company claims that earnings are too small and

STRATEGY SESSION: The Social Cost of Monopoly

Consider the following figure. A monopolist would set price at P_M and output at Q_M. Consumer surplus under a monopoly would be A; producer surplus under a monopoly would be $B + C$; hence the social welfare under a monopoly would be $A + B + C$.

If the market were perfectly competitive, price would equal marginal cost (P_C) and quantity would be Q_C. The consumer surplus under perfect competition would be $A + B + D$. The producer surplus would be $C + E$, and the social welfare $A + B + C + D + E$.

Therefore the social welfare under perfect competition is $D + E$ greater than under a monopoly. This is often called the *social welfare triangle* or *deadweight loss triangle*. The rationale for this welfare cost of monopoly is that the demanders along segment XY of the demand curve are willing to pay more than the marginal cost (ZY) of producing the goods (between the quantities $Q_C - Q_M$), yet the monopolist does not produce such socially beneficial goods (restricting output at Q_M).

Part of the rationale of antitrust policy and regulation is to ensure that society captures part or all of this $D + E$ triangle.

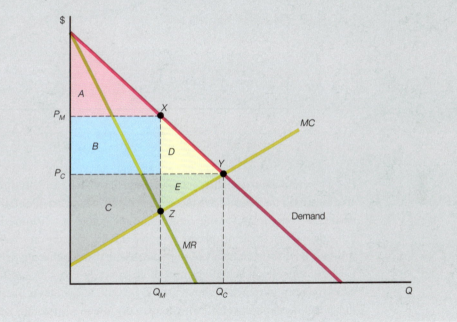

a higher price level is needed. Demand is generally assumed to be price inelastic; consequently, higher prices are assumed to result in greater revenues. The industry usually receives less than it requests (and commission decisions lag behind the industry's revenue requests). However, the fact that the commission does not approve all requests does not imply that the company is constrained much by the commission—the company may have asked for more than it thought it would receive.

FIGURE 16.2

Regulation of Acme Water Company: Fair Rate of Return

The regulated price is P_2, where the demand curve intersects the average total cost curve, which includes what the commission regards as a fair profit per unit of output.

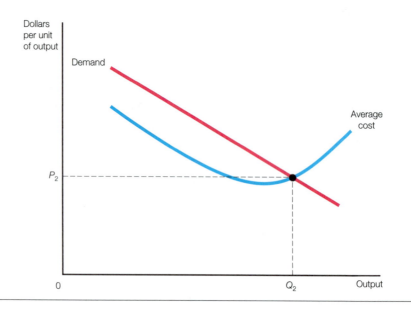

The commission tries to regulate the industry so that earnings equal a "reasonable return on the value of a firm's existing plant." Yet a host of questions concern what constitutes a "reasonable return" and the "value of a firm's existing plant." The original cost or historical cost of the plant is the measure on which most commissions base their estimates of the value of the plant; but some permit firms to use replacement cost valuations instead. In the early 1980s regulated firms often asked for a rate of return of about 10 to 15 percent. In Manitoba, in early 2004, the Public Utilities Board was allowing returns of close to 11 percent.[2] Boards look at a weighted cost of debt and risk-adjusted equity capital as a guideline to allowable returns. In many cases risk is determined by the beta from the capital asset pricing model (CAPM).

THE LONE STAR GAS COMPANY: A CASE STUDY

2. Manitoba, The Public Utilities Board Act, Order 50/05, April 8, 2005, p. 11.

As an illustration of how regulatory commissions work, we look at an actual case. In 1978 the Lone Star Gas Company (part of Enserch Corporation), which provides gas to residential and commercial customers in the Dallas–Fort Worth area,

PROBLEM SOLVED: The Trenton Gas Company

To illustrate the workings of public utility regulation, consider the Trenton Gas Company, which has assets of $300 million. The state Public Utility Commission, after considering the extent of the risks assumed by the firm and conditions in the financial markets, decides that a fair rate of return for the firm would be 10 percent. Trenton Gas is allowed to earn a profit of 0.10($300 million) = $30 million per year. This profit is not economic profit; it is an accounting profit. As stressed already, commissions try to allow firms to earn only a normal or fair rate of return, which tends to rule out economic profit.

What price and output will managers choose? To answer these questions we note that the demand curve for gas provided by the firm is

$$P = 30 - 0.1Q \tag{16.1}$$

where P is the price per unit of gas (in dollars) and Q is the number of units of gas demanded (in millions). The firm's total cost equals

$$TC = 10 + 5Q + 0.9Q^2 \tag{16.2}$$

where TC is total cost (in millions of dollars). Note that this concept of total cost does not include the opportunity cost of the capital invested in the firm by its owners. Therefore, the firm's accounting profit equals

$$\pi = (30 - 0.1Q)Q - (10 + 5Q + 0.9Q^2)$$
$$= -Q^2 + 25Q - 10 \tag{16.3}$$

where π is the firm's profit (in millions of dollars).

Because the commission has decided that the firm's accounting profit should equal $30 million, we set π equal to 30, which implies that

$$30 = -Q^2 + 25Q - 10$$
$$Q^2 - 25Q + 40 = 0 \tag{16.4}$$

which is an equation of the form $aQ^2 + bQ + c = 0$. We can use the following equation to solve for the roots of this equation:

$$Q = \frac{-b \pm (b^2 - 4ac)^{0.5}}{2a}$$
$$= \frac{25 \pm [(-25)^2 - 4(1)(40)]^{0.5}}{2(1)}$$
$$= \frac{25 \pm (465)^{0.5}}{2}$$
$$= \frac{25 \pm 21.56}{2}$$
$$= 1.72 \text{ or } 23.28$$

Because commissions generally want public utilities to serve as many customers as possible, the larger figure, $Q = 23.28$, is the relevant one. Therefore, the price is set as follows:

$$P = 30 - 0.1(23.28)$$
$$= 27.67$$

To sum up, the Trenton Gas Company's price will be $27.67, and it will deliver 23.28 million units of gas.

requested an increase in its price. The Texas Railroad Commission is the state regulatory body with authority over gas company rates. To decide whether an increase should be granted, the commission began by determining the appropriate rate base. The company's assets that were "used and useful" were identified and valued at their historical cost. After allowing for accumulated depreciation, the original cost of invested capital was calculated to be $185 million.

STRATEGY SESSION: A Dispute over a Requested Gas Rate Increase

The Boston Gas Company's request for a $17 million rate increase was examined at hearings conducted by the Massachusetts Department of Public Utilities. One consumers' group, which opposed the rate increase, argued that the gas company should be allowed a 10.5 percent rate of return, whereas the company asked for a 12.46 percent rate of return. The company also argued that because of the regulatory lag, it was receiving considerably less than the 12 percent return it was allowed by the commission. Because the previous rate increases had not become effective until almost a year after they were requested, the company earned about 9 percent, not 12 percent.

At the hearing an economist testifying for the consumers' group argued that the company's cost of equity capital was about 12 percent, whereas an economist hired by the company testified that it was about 16 percent. This was an important issue in the case. Both economists used the following equation:

$$k_t = \frac{D_1}{W} + g$$

Here k_t is the required cost of capital at time t, D_1 is the dividend paid next year, W is the firm's capitalized value, and g is the annual rate of growth in the corporate dividend, to estimate the company's cost of equity capital. The economist hired by the consumers' group assumed that the annual rate of dividend growth, g, would equal 0.01, whereas the company's economist assumed that it would equal 0.05.

If asked to advise this firm, what suggestions would you make concerning ways to reduce the adverse effects of the regulatory lag on the company's earnings? What sorts of analyses would you carry out to determine which of the two estimates of the cost of equity capital is closer to the truth?[a]

[a]For further discussion, see Barrett and Cormack, *Management Strategy in the Oil and Gas Industries*.

To establish the rate of return that Lone Star Gas should earn on this invested capital, the cost of both debt and equity capital and the percentage of each to total capitalization were estimated. The cost of capital was estimated to be 13.87 percent for common equity, 9.75 percent for preferred equity, 8.59 percent for long-term debt, and 9.98 percent for short-term debt. After weighting each of these costs of capital by the percentage of total capitalization it represented, the result was 11.1 percent. Thus the commission concluded that Lone Star Gas should earn an 11.1 percent return on its invested capital of $185 million.

To earn this return, the firm should make an annual profit of 0.111 × $185 million, or $20.535 million. Because the firm's actual profit was only about $9.8 million, the commission decided to allow the firm to raise its price to bring its profit up to $20.535 million.

EFFECTS OF REGULATION ON EFFICIENCY

Regulators try to prevent a monopoly from earning excessive profits. As we saw in previous sections, managers are permitted only a fair rate of return on their investment. A difficulty with this arrangement is that they are guaranteed this rate of return, regardless of how poorly they manage. If the regulators decide the Acme Water Company should get a 9 percent rate of return on its investment, it will get this rate of return regardless of whether it is managed well or poorly. Why is this a problem? Because unlike a competitive firm, there is no incentive for managers to increase firm efficiency.

Managers need to anticipate a regulatory process that is characterized by long delays. If they are smart, managers will use these delays to increase firm efficiency. In many regulated industries, a proposed rate change may be under review for months before a decision is made by the commission. If such a price change is hotly contested, it may take years for the required hearings and subsequent court appeals. Such a delay between a proposed price change and its ultimate disposition is called a **regulatory lag**. Long regulatory lags are often criticized by people who would like the regulatory process to adapt more quickly to changing conditions and yield more timely decisions. But an advantage of regulatory lags is that they penalize inefficiency and reward efficiency. To combat the problem of regulatory lag, some statutes require regulatory agencies to render decisions within a specific time period.

Regulatory lag A delay between a proposed price change and its ultimate disposition.

To illustrate, consider managers at a regulated company whose price is established so they can earn a 9 percent rate of return (which the commission regards as a fair rate of return). The managers develop and introduce an improved manufacturing process that cuts costs, thus increasing their actual rate of return to 11 percent. If it takes 15 months for the commission to review the prices it approved before and modify them to take account of the new (lower) cost levels, managers can earn a higher rate of return (11 percent rather than 9 percent) during those 15 months.

Although the regulatory lag restores some incentives for efficiency (and some penalties for inefficiency), it does not result in as strong a set of efficiency incentives as competitive markets. A fundamental problem with regulation is that if a regulatory commission prevents a firm from earning higher-than-average profits, there may be little incentive for managers to increase efficiency and introduce innovations.

THE CONCENTRATION OF ECONOMIC POWER

Government regulatory commissions are not the only device used by society to deal with the problem of monopoly; another device is antitrust laws. These laws reflect a feeling that excessive power lies in the hands of relatively few firms.

According to the *2008 Statistical Abstract of the United States*, manufacturing firms with more than $250,000 in assets had a total book asset value of over $6.3 trillion in 2006. According to the latest *Census of Manufacturing* (2002), the 100 largest firms employed 17.4 percent of the manufacturing workforce, paid 23 percent of the manufacturing payroll, used 16.4 percent of manufacturing production workers, created 33.7 percent of the value added in manufacturing, purchased 32.8 percent of the raw materials used in manufacturing, and made 28.5 percent of all the capital expenditures by manufacturing firms. These percentages have increased considerably since the end of World War II. Although bigness is not necessarily the same as monopoly power, there is a widespread feeling that economic power is concentrated in relatively few hands.

Antitrust laws are aimed at promoting competition and limiting monopoly. As mentioned earlier, many economists believe that competition is preferable to monopoly because competition tends to more effectively allocate resources. To measure how close a particular industry is to being perfectly competitive (or monopolized), economists have devised the *market concentration ratio*, which shows the percentage of total sales or production accounted for by the industry's four largest firms. The higher the percentage, the more concentrated the industry.

Table 16.1 shows market four-firm concentration ratios for selected nonmanufacturing industries—that is, the market share of the largest four firms. For each industry sector, the highest ratio, the lowest ratio, and the ratio of the subsector with the highest revenue of the sector are reported. These ratios vary widely from industry to industry. In the discount department store industry, the concentration ratio is very high: 95 percent. In the chiropractors industry, it is very low: 0.8 percent. The concentration ratio is only a rough measure of an industry's market structure, which must be supplemented with data on the extent and type of product differentiation in the industry, as well as on barriers to entry. Even with these supplements, it is still a crude measure because, for one thing, it takes no account of competition from foreign suppliers. Nonetheless, the concentration ratio has proven to be a valuable tool.

Herfindahl-Hirschman index An index that equals the sum of the squared market shares of all the firms in the market of manufacturing industries.

Another measure of concentration shown in Table 16.1 is the **Herfindahl-Hirschman index** (HHI), which equals the sum of the squared market shares of all the firms in the market for manufacturing industries. This index is used by the U.S. Department of Justice, Antitrust Division, and the Federal Trade Commission as a guide to determine whether they should investigate proposed mergers.[3] For example, if two firms exist in a market and each has a 50 percent share of the market, this index equals $50^2 + 50^2 = 5,000$. The HHI can range from 10,000 (a monopolist would have an HHI of 100^2) to 0 (an infinite number of atomistic competitors each with a market share approaching 0). According to the government's merger guideline, if the HHI (after the merger) will be less than 1,000, the merger is unlikely to be challenged (but this is only a guideline, so nothing is

3. See U.S. Department of Justice, Antitrust Division, *1997 Merger Guidelines* at www.usdoj.gov/atr/hmerger/11251.htm.

TABLE 16.1

Concentration Ratios and Herfindahl-Hirschman Indexes (HHI) by Economic Sectors for Largest (by Revenues) Subsector for Each Three-Digit NAICS Sector (Bold) and by Largest and Smallest Four Firm Concentration Ratio or HHI for Each Sector: 2002

	Market Share of Four Largest Firms	Herfindahl-Hirschman Index for 50 Largest (Percent) Firms
NAICS Sector		
22 Utilities		
221210 Natural Gas Distribution	18.4	
221330 Steam and Air Conditioning Supply	73.3	
311 Food Manufacturing		
3116150 Poultry Processing		773.3
3114220 Specialty Canning		2,798.5
3118110 Retail Bakeries		7.2
312 Beverage and Tobacco Product Manufacturing		
3121110 Soft Drink Manufacturing		895.7
3122210 Cigarette Manufacturing		D
313 Textile Mills		
3131130 Thread Mills		2,487.6
3132100 Broadwoven Fabric Mills		223.4
3133200 Fabric Coating Mills		218.9
314 Textile Product Mills		
3141100 Carpet and Rug Mills		1,756.4
3149120 Canvas and Related Product Mills		80.0
3149920 Tire Cord and Tire Fabric Mills		1,939.9
315 Apparel Manufacturing		
3152120 Women's, Girl's, and Infant's Cut and Sew Apparel Contractors		19.0
3152240 Men's and Boy's Cut and Sew Trouser, Slack, and Jean Manufacturing		2,514.8
316 Leather and Allied Product Manufacturing		
3161100 Leather and Hide Tanning and Finishing		782.1
3162110 Rubber and Plastics Footwear Manufacturing		2,707.2
321 Wood Product Manufacturing		
3219110 Window and Door Manufacturing		376.1
3219200 Wood Container and Pallet Manufacturing		23.8
3219910 Manufactured Home (Mobile Home) Manufacturing		685.3
322 Paper Manufacturing		
3222220 Coated and Laminated Paper Manufacturing		568.9
3222140 Fiber Can, Tube, Drum, and Similar Products		2,467.9

3222210 Coated and Laminated Packaging Paper and
    Plastics Film Manufacturing 325.9
323 Printing and Related Support Activities
3231130 Commercial Screen Printing 30.7
3231160 Manifold Business Forms Printing 372.0
3231180 Blankbook, Looseleaf Binders, and Devices
    Manufacturing 805.6
324 Petroleum and Coal Products Manufacturing
3241100 Petroleum Refineries 639.7
3241210 Asphalt Paving Mixture and Block Manufacturing 207.0
3241220 Asphalt Shingle and Coating Materials
    Manufacturing 1,061.3
325 Chemical Manufacturing
3254110 Medicinal and Botanical Manufacturing 2,703.6
3254120 Pharmaceutical Preparation Manufacturing 529.9
3259910 Custom Compounding of Purchased Resins 231.4
326 Plastics and Rubber Products Manufacturing
3261120 Plastics Packaging Film and Sheet
    (Including Laminated) Manufacturing 862.8
3261130 Unlaminated Plastics Film and Sheet
    (Except Packaging) Manufacturing 191.8
327 Nonmetallic Mineral Product Manufacturing
3272130 Glass Container Manufacturing 2,582.1
3273200 Ready-Mix Concrete Manufacturing 63.1
3279910 Cut Stone and Stone Product Manufacturing 59.4
331 Primary Metal Manufacturing
3311110 Iron and Steel Mills 656.7
3311120 Electrometallurgical Ferroalloy Product
    Manufacturing 2,195.9
3315250 Copper Foundaries (Except Die Casting) 109.4
332 Fabricated Metal Product Manufacturing
3327100 Machine Shops 3.5
3322110 Cutlery and Flatware (Except Precious)
    Manufacturing 1,946.1
333 Machinery Manufacturing
3331110 Farm Machinery and Equipment Manufacturing 1,656.8
3332950 Semiconductor Machinery Manufacturing 2,023.9
3339940 Industrial Process Furnace and Oven Manufacturing 147.3
334 Computer and Electronic Product Manufacturing
3341110 Electronic Computer Manufacturing 2,662.4
3346110 Software Reproducing 390.7
335 Electrical Equipment, Appliance, and Component
    Manufacturing

3351100 Electric Lamp Bulb and Part Manufacturing	2,757.6
3359310 Current-Carrying Wiring Device Manufacturing	292.4
336 Transportation Equipment Manufacturing	
3361120 Light Truck and Utility Vehicle Manufacturing	D
3363700 Motor Vehicle Metal Stamping	670.3
3364150 Guided Missile and Space Vehicle Propulsion Unit and Propulsion Unit Parts Manufacturing	2,761.2
337 Furniture and Related Product Manufacturing	
3371100 Wood Kitchen Cabinet and Countertop Manufacturing	317.5
3371250 Household Furniture (Except Wood and Metal) Manufacturing	2,649.2
3372120 Custom Architectural Woodwork and Millwork Manufacturing	44.6
339 Miscellaneous Manufacturing	
3399200 Sporting and Athletic Goods Manufacturing	182.2
3399410 Pen and Mechanical Pencil Manufacturing	2,159.0
3399430 Marking Device Manufacturing	199.0
42 Wholesale Trade	
4231101 Automobile and Motorcycle Merchant Wholesalers	68.2
4234901 Religious and School Supplies Merchant Wholesalers	73.0
4239401 Jewelry, Watch, Precious Stone, and Precious Metal Merchant Wholesalers	7.2
44-45 Retail Trade	
4411100 New Car Dealers	5.6
4521120 Discount Department Stores	95.0
4531100 Florists	1.7
48–49 Transportation and Warehousing	
4831120 Deep Sea Passenger Transportation	92.6
4841210 General Freight Trucking, Long-Distance, Truckload	14.7
4842204 Dump Trucking	2.4
51 Information	
5122200 Integrated Record Production/Distribution	81.0
5122400 Sound Recording Studios	9.7
5171100 Wired Telecommunications Carriers	59.7
52 Finance and Insurance	
5222940 Secondary Market Financing	98.7
5223100 Mortgage and Nonmortgage Loan Brokers	4.2
5241130 Direct Life Insurance Carriers	24.0
53 Real Estate and Rental and Leasing	
5311109 Lessors of Residential Buildings and Dwellings	6.4

5312101 Offices of Residential Real Estate Agents and Brokers	11.4
5324119 Aircraft Rental and Leasing	81.8
54 Professional, Scientific, and Technical Services	
5411101 Offices of Lawyers	2.0
5414100 Interior Design Services	1.8
5415130 Computer Facilities Management Services	71.5
56 Administrative and Support and Waste Management and Remediation Service	
5611100 Office Administrative Services	2.2
5613200 Temporary Help Services	16.4
5614501 Consumer Credit Reporting Agencies	65.7
61 Educational Services	
6115191 Technical and Trade Schools Except Computer Repair and Truck Driving Schools	16.0
6115192 Computer Repair Training	56.4
6116101 Dance Schools Including Children's and Professionals	2.9
62 Health Care and Social Assistance	
621310 Offices of Chiropractors	0.8
621491 HMO Medical Centers	78.0
6221102 General Medical and Surgical Hospitals, Except Government	11.7
71 Arts, Entertainment, Recreation	
7112111 Football Clubs	15.1
7112112 Baseball Clubs	19.5
7131102 Amusement Parks (Except Waterparks)	71.8
7139100 Golf Courses and Country Clubs	8.3
7139405 Roller Skating Rinks	3.8
72 Accommodation and Food Services	
7221100 Full-Service Restaurants	8.6
7223100 Food Service Contractors	64.4
7224100 Drinking Places (Alcoholic Beverages)	2.2
81 Other Services (Except Public Administration)	
8111110 General Automotive Repair	1.9
8123101 Coin-Operated Laundry Routes	71.0

The six-digit numbers refer to industries classified by the North American Industry Classification System, a system used by Canada, Mexico, and the United States.

D = Not disclosed because of Census Bureau disclosure rules.

Source: Concentration Ratios: 2002, U.S. Census Bureau, U.S. Department of Commerce, Economics and Statistics Administration, Various Industry Series, 2005 and 2006.

guaranteed). If the postmerger HHI will be between 1,000 and 1,800 and the index changes by less than 100 points as a result of the merger, the merger is unlikely to be challenged. Finally, if the postmerger HHI will be greater than 1,800 and the index changes by less than 50 points as a result of the merger, the government is unlikely to challenge the merger. Note that this last requirement may be hard to satisfy. For instance, if a firm with a 49 percent share wanted to merge with a firm with a 1 percent share, the HHI would increase by 99 points. A firm with a 25 percent share merging with a firm with a 1 percent share would raise the HHI by 51 points. Firms with low four-firm concentration ratios tend to have low HHIs (the HHI is not calculated for all firms here but rather for the largest 50—thus the HHI is understated). For instance, the HHI for the machine shops industry is just 3.5, whereas the HHI for the specialty canning industry is 2,798.5. Note that certain industries, such as the cigarette and light truck and utility vehicle manufacturing industries, have no published HHIs. This is because the government has rules about disclosing information about firms. If both the four-firm concentration ratio and the HHI were given, clever people could discern which firms had what share (and hence what sales levels). With so few firms in each of these industries, we can presume that their 50-firm HHIs are quite high (if not 10,000).

THE SHERMAN ACT

The first federal antitrust law, the Sherman Act, was passed by Congress in 1890. Although the common law had long outlawed monopolistic practices, it seemed to many Americans in the latter part of the 19th century that legislation was needed to discourage monopoly and to preserve and encourage competition. The formation of trusts (monopolistic combines that colluded to raise prices and restrict output) brought the matter to a head. The essence of the Sherman Act lies in the following two sections:

> Sec. 1. Every contract, combination in the form of trust or otherwise, or conspiracy, in restraint of trade or commerce among the several states or with foreign nations, is hereby declared to be illegal. Every person who shall make any such contract or engage in any such combination or conspiracy, shall be deemed guilty of a misdemeanor....

> Sec. 2. Every person who shall monopolize, or attempt to monopolize or combine or conspire with any other person or persons, to monopolize any part of the trade or commerce among the several States, or with foreign nations shall be deemed guilty of a misdemeanor.

In 1974 the Sherman Act was amended, making violations felonies rather than misdemeanors. Corporations can now be fined up to $10 million, and individuals can be fined up to $350,000 and receive prison terms of up to three years. In addition to criminal fines and jail sentences, firms and individuals can be sued for triple damages in civil suits brought by those hurt by an antitrust violation.

It is important to recognize that if executives of two or more firms in a particular industry talk about prices and agree to fix them, this is a violation of Section 1 of the Sherman Act. To illustrate this point, consider Robert Crandall, former chief executive officer of American Airlines. He called Howard Putnam, then chief executive officer of Braniff Airways, on February 21, 1982, and proposed that they raise prices. The telephone call, which (unknown to Crandall) was taped, went as follows:

> Putnam: Do you have a suggestion for me?
>
> Crandall: Yes, I have a suggestion for you. Raise your goddamn fares 20 percent. I'll raise mine the next morning.
>
> Putnam: Robert, we . . .
>
> Crandall: You'll make more money and I will, too.
>
> Putnam: We can't talk about pricing!
>
> Crandall: Oh [expletive deleted], Howard. We can talk about any goddamn thing we want to talk about.[4]

After finding out about the call, the Justice Department filed a suit accusing Robert Crandall of breaking the antitrust laws by proposing to fix prices. But because there had been no agreement to fix prices, Section 1 had not been violated. Nonetheless the court decided that a proposal of this sort could be an attempt to monopolize part of the airline industry, which is forbidden by Section 2 of the Sherman Act. American Airlines said that it would not do such a thing again.

THE CLAYTON ACT, THE ROBINSON-PATMAN ACT, AND THE FEDERAL TRADE COMMISSION ACT

During its first 20 years the Sherman Act was not regarded by its supporters as being very effective. The ineffectiveness of the Sherman Act led Congress in 1914 to pass two other laws: the Clayton Act and the Federal Trade Commission Act. The Clayton Act attempted to be more specific than the Sherman Act in identifying certain practices that were illegal because they would "substantially lessen competition or tend to create a monopoly."

The Clayton Act outlawed unjustified price discrimination, which (as you recall from Chapter 8) is a practice whereby one buyer is charged more than another buyer for the same product. However, discrimination resulting from differences in the quality or quantity of the product sold or resulting from differences

4. *The New York Times,* February 24, 1983.

in cost or competitive pressures was allowed. In 1936 the Robinson-Patman Act amended the Clayton Act. It prohibited charging different prices to different purchasers of "goods of like grade and quality" where the effect "may be substantially to lessen competition or tend to create a monopoly in any line of commerce, or to injure, destroy, or prevent competition with any person who either grants or knowingly receives the benefit of such discrimination, or with customers of either of them." The Robinson-Patman Act was aimed at preventing price discrimination in favor of chain stores that buy goods in large quantities. Small independent retailers felt threatened by the chain stores and pushed hard for this law.

The Clayton Act also outlawed the use of tying contracts that reduce competition. As Chapter 9 indicated, tying contracts make buyers purchase other items to get the product they want. For a long time IBM rented, but would not sell, its machines and insisted that customers must buy IBM ancillary equipment and use IBM maintenance services. The Supreme Court required IBM to end its tying contracts. However, not all tying contracts have been prohibited. If a firm needs to maintain control over complementary goods and services to make sure its product works properly, this can be an adequate justification for a tying contract. Also, if the tying arrangements are voluntary and informal, there is no violation of the law. Thus if a customer bought IBM ancillary equipment because that firm felt that it worked best on IBM primary equipment, this was no violation of the law so long as this customer did not have to buy IBM ancillary equipment. McDonald's requires that its franchisees buy certain products from McDonald's or from McDonald's-approved vendors. The reason is that the value of one McDonald's franchise depends on the quality of service provided by all franchises. Thus McDonald's assures the reputation of all McDonald's franchises by tying agreements.

Further, the Clayton Act outlawed mergers that substantially lessen competition; but because it did not prohibit one firm purchasing a competitor's plant and equipment, it really could not stop mergers. In 1950 this loophole was closed by the Celler-Kefauver Antimerger Act. However, this does not mean that mergers have become less prevalent. On the contrary, an epidemic of mergers in the 1980s continues to this day.

The Federal Trade Commission Act was aimed at preventing undesirable and unfair competitive practices. It established the Federal Trade Commission to investigate unfair and predatory practices and issue cease-and-desist orders. The act stated that "unfair methods of competition in commerce are hereby declared unlawful." The commission—composed of five commissioners, each appointed by the president for a term of seven years—was given the formidable task of defining exactly what was "unfair." Eventually the courts took away much of the commission's power; but in 1938 the commission acquired the function of outlawing untrue and deceptive advertising. Also, the commission has authority to investigate various aspects of the structure of the U.S. economy.

INTERPRETATION OF THE ANTITRUST LAWS

The real impact of the antitrust laws depends on how the courts interpret them, and the judicial interpretation of these laws has varied substantially from one period to another. Typically charges are brought against a firm or group of firms by the Antitrust Division of the Department of Justice; a trial is held; and a decision is reached by the judge. In major cases, appeals are made that eventually could reach the Supreme Court.

In 1911, as a consequence of the first major set of antitrust cases, the Standard Oil Company and the American Tobacco Company were forced to give up a large share of their holdings of other firms. The Supreme Court, in deciding these cases, put forth and used the famous **rule of reason**—that only unreasonable combinations in restraint of trade, not all trusts, required conviction under the Sherman Act. In 1920 the rule of reason was employed by the Supreme Court in its finding that U.S. Steel had not violated the antitrust laws even though it had tried to monopolize the industry because the court said the company had not succeeded. U.S. Steel's large size and its potential monopoly power were ruled beside the point because "the law does not make mere size an offense. It . . . requires overt acts."

Rule of reason Rule stating that only unreasonable combinations in restraint of trade, not all trusts, required conviction under the Sherman Act.

In the 1920s and 1930s the courts, including the conservative Supreme Court, interpreted the antitrust laws in such a way that they had little impact. Although Eastman Kodak and International Harvester controlled substantial shares of their markets, the Court, using the rule of reason, found them innocent on the grounds that they had not built up their near-monopoly positions through overt coercion or predatory practices.

During the late 1930s this situation changed dramatically with the prosecution of the Aluminum Company of America (Alcoa). This case, decided in 1945 (but begun in 1937), reversed the decisions in the U.S. Steel and International Harvester cases. Alcoa achieved its 90 percent of the market by means that would have been regarded as "reasonable" in earlier cases: Keeping its price low enough to discourage entry, adding capacity to take care of increases in the market, and so forth. Nonetheless the court decided that Alcoa, because it controlled practically all the industry's output, violated the antitrust laws.

Frustrating as it sometimes may be to managers, the antitrust laws are rather vague and ambiguous; consequently it is not easy to tell whether certain actions are permissible. Take the case of two breweries, Pabst and Blatz, that wanted to merge in 1958. The government objected to this merger even though the two firms together accounted for less than 5 percent of the nation's beer sales. What troubled the government was that they accounted for about 24 percent of beer sales in Wisconsin. The district court judge, agreeing with Pabst and Blatz that Wisconsin should be viewed as only part of the relevant market, dismissed the complaint; but the Supreme Court ruled against the firms. This case shows how difficult it can be to establish even the boundaries of the relevant market.

STRATEGY SESSION: Antitrust Violations: From Elevators to Breweries

The European Union's competition commissioner states that the costs of buildings and hospitals in Belgium, Germany, Luxembourg, and the Netherlands from at least 1995 to 2004 were "artificially bloated" by the actions of Otis Elevator, ThyssenKrupp, Kone, Schindler Holding, and Mitsubishi Elevator Europe in a cartel that fixed prices for the installation and maintenance of elevators and escalators. The European Union imposed fines of $1.3 billion on the five companies—the largest fines so far for price fixing in the European Union.

Heineken, Grolsch, and Bavaria (all breweries) were fined $371.56 million for price fixing in the Dutch beer market from 1996 to 1999. A fourth brewery (InBev) was a participant but "blew the whistle" on the cartel and was granted immunity from prosecution under an EU program that rewards whistleblowers. In addition to raising prices, the cartel also divided the market up among the four participants. Knowledge of and participation in the conspiracy occurred at the board of directors and managing director (CEO) level.

Although monopolization in restraint of trade is illegal, year after year in country after country, firms are found guilty of such behavior. By mid-April 2007, more than 2 billion euros in fines had been levied for antitrust violations in the European Union, surpassing the record total of 1.85 billion euros for the whole year of 2006. Because this occurs at high levels of management, it is a conscious management policy to engage in such activity.

We've seen the corporate gains from monopoly over competition in this text. The costs are the fines times the probability of being caught (the expected fine), the bad will caused by the embarrassment of being caught, and the unrecorded costs of unethical behavior and the message it sends to those who would aspire to be top management and the attitudes it engenders in peoples' everyday behavior.

Sources: "5 Elevator Makers Are Fined in Europe in Price Fixing Case," *The New York Times*, February 22, 2007, at www.nytimes.com/2007/02/22/business/worldbusiness/22lift.html; and "EU Claps Hefty Fines on Three Brewers," *Financial Times*, April 19, 2007, at www.ft.com.cms/s/1cabof72-ee13-11db-8584-000b5df10621.html.

In Chapter 1 we cited the proposed 1997 merger of Staples with Office Depot. Tom Stemberg, the CEO of Staples and instigator of the proposed merger, felt that the combined entity would have a 4 to 6 percent share of the office supply market. The government disagreed. They defined the market as "category killers" (stores that could serve all of your office supplies needs) and felt the merger would lead to two or only one category killer in many markets and that such a result would be anticompetitive. Stemberg, on the other hand, defined the market as Wal-Mart, Dell on-line, Radio Shack, Seven Elevens, local stationery stores, and the like. Again, it is difficult to define market boundaries.

Antitrust policy will change between political administrations (based on how vigorously the executive branch pursues cases) and based on the constituency of the Supreme and other courts (the judicial branch of government). Although the legislative branch can produce new laws, it has not been active in this area; the enforcement and interpretation of existing laws determine antitrust policy today.

THE PATENT SYSTEM

While the antitrust laws are designed to limit monopoly, not all public policies have this effect. The patent system is a good example. U.S. patent laws have granted the inventor exclusive control over the use of an invention for 20 years (from initial filing), in exchange for his or her making the invention public knowledge.

Three principal arguments are used to justify the existence of the patent laws. First, these laws are regarded as an important incentive to induce inventors to put in the effort required to produce inventions. Particularly in the case of the individual inventor, it is claimed that patent protection is a strong incentive. Second, patents are regarded as a necessary incentive to induce managers to carry out further work and make the necessary investments in pilot plants and other items required to bring inventions to commercial use. If an invention became public property when made, why should managers incur the costs and risks involved in experimenting with a new process or product? Managers at another firm could watch, take no risks, and duplicate the process or product if it is successful. Third, it is argued that because of the patent laws, inventions are disclosed earlier than otherwise, the consequence being that other inventions are facilitated by earlier dissemination of information.

Unlike most other goods, new technological knowledge cannot be used up. A person or firm can use an idea repeatedly without wearing it out, and the same idea can serve many users at the same time. No one need be getting less of an idea because others are using it, too. This fact creates an important difficulty for any firm that would like to make a business of producing knowledge. For an investment in research and development to be profitable, managers must be able to sell the results, directly or indirectly, for a price. But potential customers are unwilling to pay for a commodity that, once produced, becomes available to all in unlimited quantity. There is a tendency to let someone else pay for it if it then becomes available for nothing.

The patent laws, which are a way of addressing this issue, make it possible for managers to produce new knowledge and sell or use it profitably. But the patent system has the disadvantage that new knowledge is not used as widely as it should be because the patent holder, who attempts to make a profit, sets a price sufficiently high that some people who could make productive use of the patented item are discouraged from doing so. From society's point of view, all who can use an idea should be allowed to do so at a very low cost because the marginal cost of their doing so is often practically zero. However, this shortsighted policy would provide little incentive for invention.

STRATEGY SESSION: Antitrust on Both Sides of the Atlantic

The antitrust laws are on the books. Firms have internal lawyers. Why then do antitrust authorities around the world have no problem in finding candidates for violation of the laws every year? Is it because the laws are ambiguously written? Is it because managers are corrupt? Or is it a combination of both? Although some actions seem blatant after they're exposed, were they so obviously wrong when they were planned? Perhaps corrupt managers saw the expected gains of behaving unethically (increased revenues) as greater than the expected costs of so behaving (the probability of being caught and the penalty—a fine plus potential jail time). Although we don't know the reasons for the behavior listed here, such behavior attracted the attention of antitrust authorities. Note the diversity of the industries involved.

Hynix Semiconductor of South Korea has joined Samsung (also of South Korea), Infineon Technologies (Germany), and Elpida Memory (Japan) in pleading guilty to a price fixing conspiracy for dynamic random access memory chips (DRAM chips) from April 1999 to June 2000. DRAM chips are used in personal computers, printers, and other electronic devices. Thus far fines have totaled $731 million from the four companies. In addition, nine executives will serve prison terms.

In July 2004 De Beers, the world's largest diamond miner and marketer, paid a $10 million fine and pleaded guilty to engaging in monopolistic practices in a U.S. Department of Justice investigation involving industrial diamonds. This was a criminal case; parties that have been aggrieved can pursue further damages in civil suits. De Beers has agreed to settle four such cases (where they were accused of overcharging for diamonds) for $250 million. De Beers did not admit to any liability in these cases.

Fifteen makers of plastic bags were fined $324.4 million by the European Commission for colluding on prices in Belgium, Germany, Luxembourg, the Netherlands, and Spain for the last 20 years. In addition to announcing the fine, the commission released the content of documents discovered in early-morning raids on the accused firms in 2002. The commission claims that top management was aware of the pricing activity and knew it was illegal.

In a joint European Commission–U.S. Department of Justice action, air cargo carriers were raided in Europe and the United States in search of evidence of a price fixing cartel. The carriers involved are some of the largest international carriers on each continent and are names known to most as passenger airlines. Neelie Kroes (Europe's Competition Commissioner) has made cartels (which she describes as "the most damaging type of anticompetitive practice") her top priority and stated she will have zero tolerance for companies that collude. Following these actions, Sisimiza (a Tanzanian company) filed a civil suit in Illinois against 11 carriers accusing them of conspiring to fix fuel price surcharges for cargo flights.

Sources: "4 to Plead Guilty on Chip Pricing," *The New York Times*, March 2, 2006, at www.nytimes.com/2006/03/02/technology/02hynix.html; "De Beers Will Pay $250 Million to Settle Diamond Pricing Suits," *The New York Times*, December 1, 2005, at www.nytimes.com/2005/12/01/business/01diamonds.html; "15 Makers of Plastic Bags Fined over Price-Fixing Scheme," *The New York Times*, December 1, 2005, at www.nytimes.com/2005/12/01/business/worldbusiness/01plastics.html; "Big Airlines Raided in Cargo Price-Fixing Inquiry," *The New York Times*, February 15, 2006, at www.nytimes.com/2006/02/15/business/worldbusiness/15cargo.html; and "Airlines Sued over Prices," *The New York Times*, March 10, 2006, at www.nytimes.com/2006/03/10/business/10air.html.

PROBLEM SOLVED: Government Purchase of Toxic Assets

Through its actions, the government can also increase the efficiency of markets. This is particularly useful when markets fail because as discussed later in Strategy Session, "All That Glitters Is Not Gold," the Treasury proposed to purchase some CDO's and MBS from financial institutions. We show the possible outcomes of such a plan using a simplified situation.

Suppose there are only two types of risky bonds: Merely illiquid (I) types and truly toxic (T) types. Each type of bond is worth $0, if it defaults, and $1,000, if it does not default. Type I bonds have a 10-percent chance of default, and type T bonds have a 30-percent chance of default.

Assume there are only two current bondholders, each holding a different type of bond. Each current bondholder knows the type of bond they hold and is risk-averse with utility function $U = (W)^{0.5}$ where W is the bondholder's wealth. Imagine each bondholder's only wealth is its bond.

The sole buyer of these risky bonds is the U.S. Treasury. However, the Treasury does not know whether a bond is the illiquid type (I) or the toxic type (T) before buying it. Suppose the Treasury offers to buy any bond at a price of 700. Can we determine who will sell to the Treasury and what will be the Treasury's expected profit? We can do so by using our expected utility analysis.

Suppose the government offers 700 for the bond. Then a seller will have expected utility of

$$EU_{SellBond} = 700^{0.5} = 26.458$$

If the type T holder retains the bond, her expected utility is

$$EU_{RetainBondT} = 0.7*1,000^{0.5} + 0.3*0^{0.5} = 22.136$$

since 26.458 > 22.136, the type T seller will sell the bond to the government.

If the type I holder retains the bond, her expected utility is

$$EU_{RetainBondI} = 0.9*1,000^{0.5} + 0.1*0^{0.5} = 28.461$$

since 28.461 > 26.458, the type I seller will retain her bond.

So under this scheme, the Treasury will only purchase toxic bonds. Holders of type I bonds choose not to sell. If the government pays 700 and gets the type T bond

Without question, the patent system enables innovators to appropriate a larger portion of the social benefits from their innovations; but this does not mean that patents are effective in this regard. Contrary to popular opinion, patent protection does not make market entry impossible or even unlikely. Within four years of their introduction, 60 percent of the patented successful innovations included in one study were imitated.[5] Nonetheless, patent protection generally increases imitation costs. In that study, the median estimated increase in imitation cost (the cost of developing and commercially introducing an imitative product) was 11 percent. In the drug industry, patents had a bigger impact on imitation costs than in the other industries, which helps to account for the fact that patents are regarded as more important in drugs than elsewhere. The median increase in imitation cost was about 30 percent in drugs, in contrast to about 10 percent in chemicals and about 7 percent in electronics and machinery.

5. E. Mansfield, M. Schwartz, and S. Wagner, "Imitation Costs and Patents: An Empirical Study," *Economic Journal*, December 1981.

(whose expected value is 700, i.e., 0.7*1,000 + 0.3*0), the government breaks even, i.e., 700 − 700 = 0.

Now, suppose that the Treasury changes its offer to

1. Purchase any bond for the price of 700.

or

2. Purchase 25 percent of a bond for a price of 220. (In this case, the current bondholder keeps the remaining 75 percent stake in the bond.)

Each current bondholder can choose whether to accept offer 1 or 2. In this case, can we determine who will sell to the Treasury and what will be the government's profit? Again we can use our expected utility analysis. If either seller takes offer 1, her utility is

$$700^{0.5} = 26.458.$$

Suppose seller T takes offer 2. Her utility is

$$EU_{Option2T} = 0.7*(220 + 0.75*1,000)^{0.5} + 0.3*(220)^{0.5}$$
$$= 0.7*(970)^{0.5} + 0.3*(220)^{0.5} = 26.251$$

If she holds the bond, her expected utility is 22.136, as it was under the previous plan. Since 26.458 > 26.251 >

22.136, she will sell the bond to the government under offer 1.

Suppose seller I takes offer 2. Her utility is

$$EU_{Option2I} = 0.9*(220 + 0.75*1,000)^{0.5} + 0.1*(220)^{0.5}$$
$$= 0.9*(970)^{0.5} + 0.1*(220)^{0.5} = 29.514$$

If she holds the bond, her expected utility is 28.461 as it was under the previous plan. Since 29.514 > 28.461 > 26.458, she will sell the bond to the government under offer 2.

Thus, the government's expected revenue is

$$0.7*1,000 + 0.3*0 + 0.25[0.9*1,000 + 0.1*0]$$
$$= 700 + 0.25*900 = 700 + 225 = 925$$

and the government's expense is

$$700 + 220 = 920 \text{ yielding a profit of } 925 − 920 = 5$$

So, it is possible to construct a scheme where the Treasury can buy back bad bonds, increase the well-being of their holders (i.e., increase the holders' utility), and make a profit in the process. Notice that this is done by shouldering some of the risk of merely illiquid types and all of the risk of the toxic types.

TRADE AND TRADE POLICY

To ask why we have a trade policy implies that we need to ask why we trade. Once we answer that question, we can use the same tools developed in earlier chapters to explain trade policy.

Foreign Trade

First, it is important to recognize that foreign trade is of great importance to the United States (and to all but the most isolated countries of the world). There are products our citizens desire but can't produce (such as kiwis or bananas); products we can produce that can be produced less expensively or with higher quality elsewhere (most consumer electronic equipment); products we produce that others can't (jetliners for South Africa); and products we can produce less expensively or

STRATEGY SESSION: Making Whistle-Blowing Pay Off

Want to pick up a quick $195,000? The British Office of Fair Trading (the equivalent of the U.S. Department of Justice's Antitrust Division) is offering a £100,000 payment on its Web site for whistle blowers whose information leads to the apprehension and conviction of price fixing conspirators. A hotline telephone number is given. The chief executive of the office, John Fingleton, calls the practices he has been going after "shoddy, complacent, and cozy."

He has prosecuted supermarkets for their pricing practices on such items as toothpaste and tea. He is in the midst of his biggest investigation to date: 112 construction companies are accused of colluding to rig bids for construction projects involving hospitals, schools, and universities. Seventy-seven companies have already admitted wrongdoing. The conspiracy involved sharing bid information, predetermining which company would win the bid, and then having the other companies submit higher bids than the "winner." Fingleton is also investigating the pricing of cigarettes and marine hoses used in the oil industry. In 2007 he registered record fines, including a £121.5 million judgment against British Air for fuel surcharge fixing and £116 million from supermarkets and dairies for fixing the price of milk.

Why this new interest in price fixing? The trend is global (see the other Strategy Sessions describing U.S. and EU enforcement). Part of it is attributable to pressure from the United States, and increasingly the European Union, for an international crackdown on price fixing. The European Union has imposed fines of over $9.1 billion since 2005 (through the first third of 2008), which is more than it levied in the previous 15 years. South Korea, Japan, and Brazil are starting to pay attention, as is Hong Kong. This is attributed by a U.S. deputy assistant attorney general to a "growing worldwide consensus that international cartel activity is pervasive and is victimizing businesses and consumers everywhere."

Fingleton describes the situation as "a big change in Europe. And it's quite sudden." Here is a table showing the largest recent U.S. and EU antitrust fines.

United States

Company	Country	Year	Fine (Million $)
Hoffman-LaRoche	Switzerland	1999	500
Korean Air Lines	S. Korea	2007	300
British Airways	United Kingdom	2007	300
Samsung	S. Korea	2006	300
BASF	Germany	1999	225
Hynix Semiconductor	S. Korea	2005	185
Infineon Technologies	Germany	2004	160
SGL Carbon	Germany	1999	135
Mitsubishi Corp	Japan	2001	134
Ucar International	United States	1998	110

European Union

Company	Country	Year	Fine (Million £)
ThyssenKrupp	Germany	2007	480
Hoffman-LaRoche	Switzerland	2001	462
Siemens	Germany	2007	397
Eni	Italy	2006	272
Lafarge	France	2002	250
BASF	Germany	2001	237
Otis	United States	2007	225
Heineken	Netherlands	2007	219
Arkema	France	2006	219
Solvay	Belgium	2006	167

Two interesting observations emerge from the table. The average U.S. case occurred midway through 2002, whereas the average EU case occurred in 2005 (reflecting more recent activity in the European Union than in the United States); and the average value of the fines in the United States for 2007 was $300 million, whereas the average fine in the European Union in 2007 was $434 million.

Source: "Tough Protection: Competition Authorities Are Clamping Down," *Financial Times*, May 8, 2008, p. 9.

TABLE 16.2

U.S. Goods and Services by General Type: Exports and Imports 2006 and 2007 (through November) in Billions of Dollars

Product	Exports		Imports		Trade Surplus or (Deficit)	
	2006	2007	2006	2007	2006	2007
Food, feeds, and beverages	66.0	76.6	74.9	74.9	(8.9)	1.7
Industrial supplies and materials	276.0	287.8	602.0	570.9	(326.0)	(283.1)
Capital goods except automotive	413.9	406.9	418.3	407.2	(4.4)	(0.3)
Automotive vehicles, parts, and engines	107.2	111.0	256.7	238.5	(149.5)	(127.5)
Consumer goods (not food or auto)	130.0	133.7	442.9	434.4	(312.9)	(300.7)
Total goods	1,036.5	1,062.2	1,853.9	1,783.0	(817.4)	(720.8)
Services	422.6	431.2	342.8	337.1	79.8	94.1
Total goods and services	1,459.1	1,493.4	2,296.7	2,120.1	(837.6)	(626.7)

Source: Calculated from the Economic Report of the President, February 2008, Table B-106.

with higher quality (precision machine tools for Panama). As Table 16.2 shows, we exported over $1.4 trillion in goods and services in 2006 and had already exceeded the 2006 total in the first 11 months of 2007. Goods accounted for a little over a trillion dollars, with 40 percent of this in capital goods (except automotive) and 28 percent in industrial supplies and materials. We imported almost $2.2 trillion in goods and services in 2006 and were on a pace to exceed that in 2007. About $1.85 trillion paid for imports of goods, much of them capital goods (except automotive), consumer goods (nonfood, except automotive), industrial supplies and materials, and automotive vehicles, engines, and parts. As Table 16.3 shows, about 42 percent of exported goods went to our nearest neighbors (Canada and Mexico) in 2007, and slightly over 50 percent of our imports of goods were from Canada, China, Mexico, and Japan, with China's share only slightly larger than Canada's. Fifteen nations accounted for about 73 percent of all U.S. trade in goods and almost 79 percent of our trade deficit. Of our 15 largest trading partners, we ran a trade surplus in goods only with the Netherlands and Singapore. The largest trade deficits (import value minus export value) were with China ($256.3 billion), Japan ($82.8 billion), and Canada ($64.2 billion). Also of interest are the $124.5 billion

TABLE 16.3

U.S. Total Trade in Goods (Billions of Dollars) and Top Trading Partners, 2007

	Exports	Imports	Total	Percentage of Total Trade	Trade Deficit	Percentage of Deficit
Total	1,163.3	1,953.6	3,117.0	100.0	790.3	100.0
Top 15 countries	820.4	1,442.6	2,263.0	72.6	644.7	78.73
Canada	248.9	313.1	562.0	18.0	64.2	8.12
China	65.2	321.5	386.7	12.4	256.3	32.43
Mexico	136.5	210.8	347.3	11.1	74.3	9.40
Japan	62.7	145.5	208.1	6.7	82.8	10.48
Germany	49.7	94.4	144.0	4.6	44.7	5.66
United Kingdom	50.3	56.9	107.2	3.4	6.6	0.08
South Korea	34.7	47.6	82.3	2.6	12.9	1.63
France	27.4	41.6	69.0	2.2	14.2	1.80
Taiwan	26.4	38.3	64.7	2.1	11.9	1.51
Netherlands	33.0	18.4	51.4	1.6	−14.6	—
Brazil	24.6	25.6	50.3	1.6	1.0	0.01
Venezuela	10.2	39.9	50.1	1.6	29.7	3.76
Italy	14.1	35.0	49.2	1.6	20.9	2.64
Saudi Arabia	10.4	35.6	46.0	1.5	25.2	3.19
Singapore	26.3	18.4	44.7	1.4	−7.9	—

Source: Calculated from http://www.census.gov/foreign-trade/statistics/highlights/top/top0712.html.

trade deficit with OPEC countries and the $107 billion trade deficit with the European Union. Overall, we had a goods trade deficit of $790.3 billion in 2007. We traditionally run a trade surplus in services (and it was $80 billion in 2006).

Why does trade occur among countries? As economists have pointed out for over two centuries, trade permits specialization, and specialization increases output. Because the United States can trade with other countries, it can specialize in the goods and services it produces well and cheaply. Then it can trade them for goods and services that other countries are particularly good at producing. The result is that we and our trading partners benefit (as we will demonstrate next).

International differences in resource endowments and the relative quantity of various types of human and nonhuman resources are important bases for specialization. Consider countries with lots of fertile soil, little capital, and much unskilled labor. They are likely to find it advantageous to produce agricultural products, whereas countries with poor soil, much capital, and highly skilled labor probably do better to produce capital-intensive, high-technology goods. However, the basis for specialization does not remain fixed over time. Instead, as technology and resource endowments of various nations change, the pattern of international specialization changes as well. For example, the United States specialized more in raw materials and foodstuffs a century ago than it does now. India and China have the same story, but only 20 years ago they were more agrarian. (For example, the U.S. trade deficit with China in 1985 was only $6 million.)

Using Demand and Supply to Determine the Country of Import and the Country of Export

How can a manager predict whether his or her country has a comparative advantage in the production of a particular product? One important indicator is whether the country's firms can make money by producing and exporting the product. Consider the Wilton Company, the maker of a new product produced in the Netherlands and the United States—the only two countries where this product has a significant market. In the United States, the demand curve for the product is such that

$$Q_D^U = 8 - P_U \qquad (16.5)$$

and the supply curve is such that

$$Q_S^U = -2 + P_U \qquad (16.6)$$

where P_U is the price of a unit of the product (in dollars) in the United States (and $P_U \geq 2$), Q_D^U is the quantity demanded (in millions of units) per month in the United States, and Q_S^U is the quantity supplied (in millions of units) per month in the United States.

In the Netherlands, the demand curve for this product is such that

$$Q_D^N = 6 - 2P_N \qquad (16.7)$$

and the supply curve is such that

$$Q_S^N = -2 + 2P_N \qquad (16.8)$$

where P_N is the price of a unit of the product (in euros) in the Netherlands (and $P_N \geq 1$), Q_D^N is the quantity demanded (in millions of units) per month in the Netherlands, and Q_S^N is the quantity supplied (in millions of units) per month in the Netherlands.

Because the new product is being introduced for the first time in the Netherlands and the United States, managers and analysts in both countries would like to predict whether, after markets in both countries settle down, this product will be exported and, if so, by which of these two countries. To answer this question, we must begin by noting that if the cost of transporting this product from the United States to the Netherlands (or vice versa) is zero (which we will assume for simplicity), the price of this product after trade must be the same in both countries.

Why? Because if it were different, a firm could make money by purchasing it in the country where its price is lower and selling it in the country where its price is higher. As this continues, the price would rise in the former country and fall in the latter country, until eventually the price in both countries would be equal.

What do we mean by the prices in both countries being equal? Prices in the United States are quoted in dollars; prices in the Netherlands are quoted in euros. What we mean is that based on prevailing exchange rates, the prices in both countries are the same. If the U.S. dollar exchanges (at banks and elsewhere) for $2 per euro, a price of $10 in the United States is equivalent to a price of 5 euros in the Netherlands. Consequently, if this is the exchange rate, the prices in the two countries being the same means that

$$0.5P_U = P_N \tag{16.9}$$

If there is no government intervention in the market for this product and the market is competitive, the price of this product will tend to be at the level where the world total demand for the product equals the total world supply. In other words, in equilibrium

$$Q_D{}^U + Q_D{}^N = Q_S{}^U + Q_S{}^N \tag{16.10}$$

Using equations (16.5) to (16.8), we can express each of the values of Q in equation (16.10) as a function of P_U or P_N. Substituting each of these functions for each of the Q values in equation (16.10), we obtain

$$(8 - P_U) + (6 - 2P_N) = (-2 + P_U) + (-2 + 2P_N)$$

Substituting $0.5P_U$ for P_N, we find that

$$(8 - P_U) + [6 - 2(0.5P_U)] = (-2 + P_U) + [-2 + 2(0.5P_U)]$$
$$14 - 2P_U = -4 + 2P_U$$
$$18 = 4P_U$$
$$P_U = \$4.5$$

Because $0.5P_U = P_N$, $P_N = 0.5(4.5) = 2.25$ euros. In other words, the price of the product is $4.50 in the United States and 2.25 euros in the Netherlands.

Given these prices, we can determine whether the United States or the Netherlands will export the product. Based on equation (16.5), the monthly quantity demanded in the United States will be $8 - P_U = 8 - 4.5 = 3.5$ million units. Using equation (16.6), the quantity supplied per month in the United States will be $-2 + P_U = -2 + 4.5 = 2.5$ million units. Therefore, the United States will import $3.5 - 2.5 = 1$ million units per month. Based on equation (16.7), the monthly quantity demanded in the Netherlands will be $6 - 2P_N = 6 - 2(2.25) = 1.5$ million units. Based on equation (16.8), the quantity supplied per month in the Netherlands will be $-2 + 2P_N = -2 + 2(2.25) = 2.5$ million units. Therefore, the Netherlands will export $2.5 - 1.5 = 1$ million units per month.

In sum, the Netherlands will be the exporter of this new product, and its exports will equal 1 million units per month.

Analyzing the Argument for the Government's Advocacy of Free Trade Using Producer and Consumer Surplus

We now view the gains from free trade for both the United States and the Netherlands in the preceding example. To do so, we use the concepts of consumer surplus and producer surplus. Figure 16.3 shows the situation in the United States.

Before trade with the Netherlands, the price of the product in the United States was $5, and 3 million units were transacted (calculated by setting equation (16.5) equal to equation (16.6) and solving for P_U). This left U.S. consumers with a consumer surplus of $A (= 0.5 \times 3 \times 3 = 4.5)$ and U.S. producers with a producer surplus of $B + D (= 0.5 \times 3 \times 3 = 4.5)$. Because of the lower price ($4.50) after

---

FIGURE 16.3

Consumer and Producer Surplus in the United States Before and After Trade

The U.S. gain in consumer surplus is $B + C_1 + C_2$; the U.S. loss in producer surplus is B, for a net societal gain of $C_1 + C_2$ as the result of free trade. P_{AT} = price after trade; P_{BT} = price before trade; Q_{SAT} = quantity supplied after trade; Q_{DAT} = quantity demanded after trade; and Q_{BT} = quantity demanded and supplied before trade.

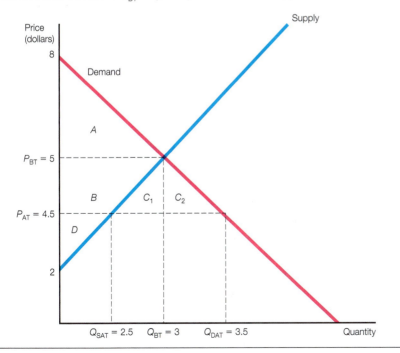

trade, consumers experience an increase in consumer surplus (now $A + B + C_1 + C_2 = 0.5 \times 3.5 \times 3.5 = 6.125$). Thus consumers gain $B + C_1 + C_2 (= 6.125 - 4.5 = 1.625)$. Prior to trade, U.S. producers received a producer surplus of $B + D$, which has now been lowered to $D (= 0.5 \times 2.5 \times 2.5 = 3.125)$ as a result of the lower price. Therefore U.S. producers lose $B (= 4.5 - 3.125 = 1.375)$ in producer surplus because of trade. The sum of the consumers' gain $(B + C_1 + C_2)$ and the producers' loss (B)—that is, $C_1 + C_2$—is the gains from trade for the United States. Its magnitude is $0.5 \times 0.5 \times 1 = 0.25 = 1.625 - 1.375$. Society is better off because social welfare has increased from $A + B + D$ to $A + B + D + C_1 + C_2$, or by $C_1 + C_2$. Although the producers have lost, in theory there are enough gains to consumers that producers could be more than compensated for their loss.

For example, suppose the U.S. government wrote the producers a check for $B + C_1$. Producers now have gained C_1 (i.e., $B + D - B + B + C_1 = B + D + C_1$ versus $B + D$ before the trade). Where did the government get the money to pay the producers? By taxing the recently better-off consumers. However, even after being taxed $B + C_1$, consumers are still better off because they have $A + B + C_1 + C_2 - (B + C_1) = A + C_2$, as compared to the A they had before trade. Thus trade makes the United States better off and, depending on how the gains are distributed, *can* make both consumers and producers better off. One role of government is to make decisions about redistribution.

Figure 16.4 shows the situation in the Netherlands. Before trade the good sold for 2 euros, and 2 million units were transacted (calculated by setting equation (16.7) equal to equation (16.8) and solving for P_N). Consumers in the Netherlands enjoyed a consumer surplus of $W + X_1 + X_2 (= 0.5 \times 1 \times 2 = 1)$, while the Dutch producers had a producer surplus of $Z_1 + Z_2 (= 0.5 \times 1 \times 2 = 1)$ for a total Dutch social welfare of $W + X_1 + X_2 + Z_1 + Z_2 (= 2)$.

After trade, the price increases to 2.25 euros. The price increase hurts Dutch consumers, and their consumer surplus falls to $W (= 0.5 \times 0.75 \times 1.5 = 0.5625)$—a loss of $X_1 + X_2 (= 1 - 0.5625 = 0.4375)$. However, the price increase benefits Dutch producers, and the producer surplus increases to $X_1 + X_2 + Y + Z_1 + Z_2 (= 0.5 \times 1.25 \times 2.5 = 1.5625)$, a gain of $X_1 + X_2 + Y (= 1.5625 - 1 = 0.5625)$. The producer gain more than offsets the consumer loss (by $Y = 0.5 \times 0.25 \times 1 = 0.5625 - 0.4375 = 0.125$). The social welfare is now $W + X_1 + X_2 + Y + Z_1 + Z_2$ (up by Y). Although the gains in each country are equal (that is, 0.125 euros in the Netherlands equals $0.25 dollars in the United States), this does not have to be the case. The point is that both countries have gained from the trade (by $C_1 + C_2$ in the United States and by Y in the Netherlands), giving each country the incentive to engage in trade.

One thing, however, must be true in this two-country, one-good trading world: The United States imports must equal the Dutch exports. The 1 million units imported are the U.S. physical trade deficit. The fiscal trade deficit is the 1 million units multiplied by the world price of $4.50, or $4,500,000. The Nether-

FIGURE 16.4

Consumer and Producer Surplus in the Netherlands Before and After Trade

The Dutch gain in producer surplus is $X_1 + X_2 + Y$, and the Dutch loss in consumer surplus is $X_1 + X_2$, for a net societal gain Y as the result of free trade. P_{AT} = price after trade; P_{BT} = price before trade; Q_{SAT} = quantity supplied after trade; Q_{DAT} = quantity demanded after trade; and Q_{BT} = quantity demanded and supplied before trade.

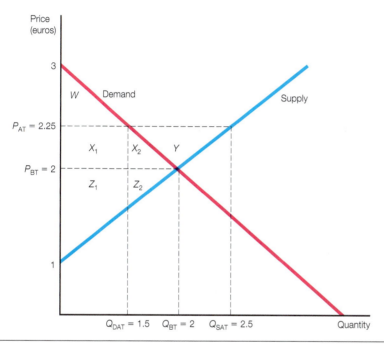

lands, on the other hand, is running a physical trade surplus of 1 million units and a fiscal trade surplus of 2.25 million euros (or $4.5 million).

How does the United States obtain the euros to import these goods from the Netherlands? We can receive euros from the Netherlands from Dutch imports of other American products; from Dutch tourists who visit the United States; and from Dutch citizens or businesses or governments that buy U.S. securities, services, real estate, and so on. In addition, we may have reserves of euros that were accrued in the past.

Use of Tariffs and Quotas to Mitigate the Gains from Trade

Although our example showed that the United States gained from trade with the Netherlands, without any redistribution of gains, the consumers gain and the producers lose. Suppose increased taxes on consumers are unpopular, so business will not receive any share of the consumer gains. There's a large loss for producers (B) and not many producers. If there are only a few producers (n) of equal size, their share of the loss is B/n—so each has a lot to lose from trade. They may have a trade association that can persuade Congress to pass legislation to curb imports of the product from the Netherlands either by placing a tariff (T) on the product (hence raising the price of the product in the United States from P_{AT} to $P_{AT} + T$ and preserving some of the before-trade producer surplus of $B + D$) or by placing a quota on imports (so that the imports allowed into the United States would be only a fraction of the $Q_{DAT} - Q_{SAT}$ imported under free trade). They may be willing to spend significant money (up to B/n per firm) to eliminate free trade.

Let's see what the impact of a quota of $\alpha(Q_{DAT} - Q_{SAT}) = Q_{DAQ} - Q_{SAQ}$ where $1 \geq \alpha > 0$ would be. This is shown in Figure 16.5.

FIGURE 16.5

Consumer and Producer Surplus in the United States Before and After Trade with an Import Quota of $Q_{DAQ} - Q_{SAQ}$ Units

The U.S. gain in consumer surplus is $B_1 + c_5 + c_6$, and the U.S. loss in producer surplus is B_1, for a net societal gain of $c_5 + c_6$, with an import quota of $Q_{DAQ} - Q_{SAQ}$ units. P_{AT} = price after trade; P_{BT} = price before trade; Q_{SAT} = quantity supplied after trade; Q_{DAT} = quantity demanded after trade; Q_{BT} = quantity demanded and supplied before trade; Q_{SAQ} = quantity supplied after quota; Q_{DAQ} = quantity demanded after quota; and P_{AQ} = price in the United States after the import quota of $Q_{DAQ} - Q_{SAQ}$ is imposed.

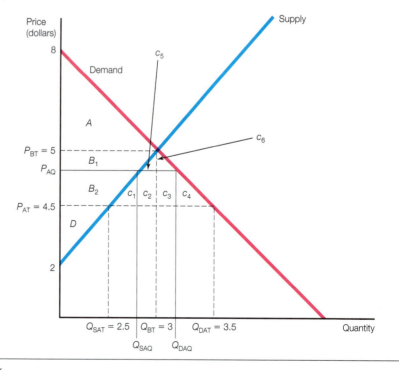

The quota raises the price in the United States to P_{AQ}. This decreases consumer surplus by $B_2 + c_1 + c_2 + c_3 + c_4$ and increases producer surplus by B_2. Instead of the social welfare under free trade of $A + B_1 + B_2 + c_1 + c_2 + c_3 + c_4 + c_5 + c_6 + D$, we now have social welfare of $A + B_1 + B_2 + c_1 + c_2 + D$ in the United States. Thus we have a loss in social welfare in the United States of $c_1 + c_2 + c_3 + c_4$, and the gains from trade have shrunk to $c_5 + c_6$. The Dutch haven't lost all their gains from free trade because of the quota. They still export $Q_{DAQ} - Q_{SAQ}$ to the United States and receive a price premium of $P_{AQ} - P_{AT}$ for each unit. Thus they capture additional producer surplus of $c_2 + c_3$ for these decreased exports. The Dutch will suffer a loss in welfare, but it isn't as drastic as it could be because of the premium of $P_{AQ} - P_{AT}$ received for the quota items. With a quota, part of our loss in welfare is transferred to the exporting country as a gain to them.

Can the U.S. government accomplish the same objective of limiting the number of imports to $Q_{DAQ} - Q_{SAQ}$ with a smaller negative effect on social welfare? Suppose the government puts a tariff of $P_{AQ} - P_{AT} = T$ on each unit of the imported product. Then the price U.S. consumers pay for the product will be P_{AQ}, U.S. demanders will demand Q_{DAQ} units, U.S. suppliers will supply Q_{SAQ} units, and $Q_{DAQ} - Q_{SAQ}$ will be imported from the Netherlands. U.S. social welfare will increase by $c_2 + c_3$ because now the U.S. Treasury will collect $T(Q_{DAQ} - Q_{SAQ})$ in revenues from the imported goods instead of letting that amount accrue to producers from the Netherlands (as with the quota). The domestic social welfare loss due to trade restrictions shrinks to $c_1 + c_4$. However, free trade would allow us to capture all of the previous $C_1 + C_2$ instead of just part of it ($c_5 + c_6$ under a quota or $c_2 + c_3 + c_5 + c_6$ under a tariff). Our conclusion is that if government wants to restrict trade, a tariff is a more efficient way (for domestic social welfare) to do so.

Trade Policy When the Market Is Not Perfectly Competitive

The previous analysis assumes that markets are perfectly competitive; they are not, as the bulk of this book has pointed out. We have suggested strategies for managers to optimize these noncompetitive situations. Likewise, there are strategies for governments to use in situations where trade involves imperfectly competitive situations.

Traditionally, economists have tended to argue that free trade is the best policy to promote the interests of society as a whole. They generally applauded the lowering of tariffs in the 1960s and 1970s and looked with disfavor on the growth of protectionism in the early 1980s. They again applauded the formation of NAFTA in the late 1980s and other free trade areas around the world. But some economists have begun to dispute these traditional beliefs. In their view, the U.S. government should control the access of foreign firms to our domestic markets, as well as promote the activities of our firms in foreign markets. For example, if particular high-technology industries generate large technological benefits for other domestic industries, the government may be justified in using subsidies or tariffs to protect and promote these industries. And if economies of scale mean that only two highly profitable producers can exist in the world market, the government may be justified in using subsidies or tariffs to increase the chances that a U.S. firm is one of the lucky pair.

According to these economists, there are strategic industries that, from the point of view of a particular country, are worth protecting in this way. However, it is difficult to identify which industries fall into this category and estimate how much the country would gain from such policies. Consequently critics of such strategic trade policies worry that special interest groups can use such policies to advance their own interests, not those of the nation as a whole. Given the vague criteria for identifying which industries should be protected, many industries can use these ideas to justify protection for themselves and their allies, regardless of whether it is merited.

That being said, let's view the use of strategic trade policy in action. There is an ongoing dispute between the U.S. government and the European Union regarding charges and countercharges of unfair government subsidization of Boeing (by the United States) and Airbus (by the European Union) in the development of commercial jet airliners. A comparable battle is being waged by Canada (Bombardier) and Brazil (Embraer) over government subsidization of regional jet aircraft.

To illustrate strategic trade policy, we can use game theoretic models. Suppose only two firms, Boeing and Airbus, are capable of producing a new 250-seat aircraft. Managers at each firm must decide whether to produce and market such a plane. Because Boeing has a head start, it can make this decision first. Figure 16.6 shows the payoff matrix for both firms. If either firm is the sole producer of the

---

FIGURE 16.6

Payoff Matrix: Airbus and Boeing

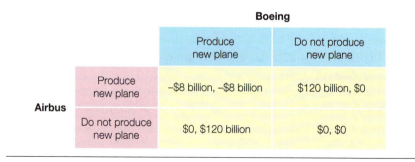

		Boeing	
		Produce new plane	Do not produce new plane
Airbus	Produce new plane	–$8 billion, –$8 billion	$120 billion, $0
	Do not produce new plane	$0, $120 billion	$0, $0

plane, it will make $120 billion; but if both firms decide to produce and market such a plane, both will lose $8 billion. Clearly Boeing managers, who have the first move in this game, will decide to produce the plane; and Airbus managers, once they realize that Boeing is committed to this course of action, will decide not to produce it.

But Boeing is a U.S. firm, whereas Airbus is a joint venture of French, British, German, and Spanish aerospace firms (with their governments' blessings and participation). If these European governments decide to pay Airbus a subsidy of $10 billion *if and only if* it produces the plane, the game has quite a different outcome. The new payoff matrix is shown in Figure 16.7, and it is clear that Airbus managers will produce the plane regardless of whether Boeing commits itself to producing it. In other words, Airbus managers now have a dominant strategy as a result of the subsidy to produce the plane. And Boeing managers, recognizing that this will be the Airbus decision, will not find it profitable to produce it. Instead they will decide against production of the plane.

In effect, the European governments have taken the profit of $120 billion away from Boeing and bestowed it on Airbus. Admittedly, they have to pay a subsidy of $10 billion, but this is relatively small for assuring a profit of $120 billion for the "home team." Because the $120 billion is profit, one could envision a subsequent $10 billion tax to compensate for the government subsidy. Without question, this example seems to indicate that government intervention of this sort can pay off. But things are not so simple: Such government actions are likely to provoke retaliation. The U.S. government may retaliate by granting a $10 billion subsidy to Boeing to produce the plane, with the result that both firms may decide to produce

---

FIGURE 16.7

Payoff Matrix: Airbus and Boeing

		Boeing	
		Produce new plane	Do not produce new plane
Airbus	Produce new plane	$2 billion, –$8 billion	$130 billion, $0
	Do not produce new plane	$0, $120 billion	$0, $0

it, although this is not economically desirable. In fact, the European Union has charged that the United States subsidizes Boeing with defense contracts because much of the U.S. flight research and applications are transferable from military to commercial aircraft.

GOVERNMENT PRICE CEILINGS AND PRICE FLOORS

Price floors Where the government will not allow a price to fall to its market level because of a belief or political pressure that the market-determined price is too low.

Price ceilings Where the government will not allow a price to rise to its market level because of a belief or political pressure that the market-determined price is too high.

Deadweight loss Social welfare under perfect competition minus social welfare under alternative pricing.

Government officials may intervene in markets domestically by enforcing prices that would not result had market forces been allowed to determine prices. We see this in the form of **price floors**, where the government will not allow a price to *fall* to its market level because of a belief or political pressure that the market-determined price is too low (minimum wage laws, agricultural price supports). We also see this in the form of **price ceilings**, where the government will not allow a price to *rise* to its market level because of a belief or political pressure that the market-determined price is too high (rent control).

We will again use our tools of producer and consumer surplus to evaluate the social welfare impacts of such government intervention in the market. Consider the impact of agricultural price supports. Figure 16.8 shows the market-clearing price (P_C) and quantity (Q_C) and the price floor (P_F) set by the government.

Suppose the government imposes the floor and suppliers, realizing that only Q_{DF} will be demanded, constrain themselves to produce only Q_{DF}. Consumer surplus is A and producer surplus (= variable profit) is total revenue ($B + G + I + J$) minus variable cost (J) or $B + G + I$. Social welfare under the price floor is $A + B + G + I$.

If the market price prevails, consumer surplus is $A + B + C$ and producer surplus is $G + H + I$, so social welfare is $A + B + C + G + H + I$. Social welfare is defined as consumer surplus + producer surplus + any government tax revenue − any government subsidy. The price floor decreases social welfare by $C + H$; this is called the deadweight loss triangle or social welfare triangle. **Deadweight loss** is defined as social welfare under perfect competition minus social welfare under alternative pricing.

In this case, consumers gain $A + B + C - A = B + C$ in consumer surplus by moving from a price floor to a market price. Producers gain $G + H + I - (B + G + I) = H - B$ by moving from a price floor to a market price. It's not clear whether producers gain or lose with a price floor in this case because $H - B$ can be positive or negative. Although it appears from Figure 16.8 that the producer will lose surplus if the price changes from the price floor to the market price, this is not necessarily true. A less elastic supply curve than the one drawn will increase H while leaving B unchanged and could make $H - B$ positive. Note the sum of the consumer gain and the producer gain $B + C + H - B = C + H$ gives the social welfare gain in moving from a price floor to the market price. Thus the deadweight loss of a price floor in this case is $C + H$.

FIGURE 16.8

Impact of a Government Price Floor

A price floor decreases social welfare by the minimum of the deadweight loss triangle ($C + H$) or the maximum of the deadweight loss triangle plus the resource cost of producing the unused output ($F + K + L$).

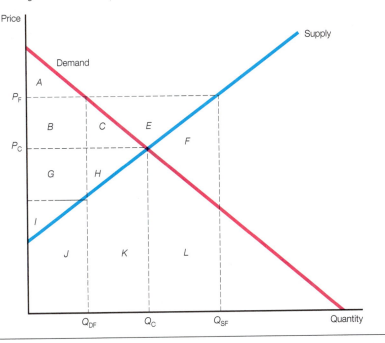

What if the suppliers produce what the supply curve tells them to do when the price is P_F: produce Q_{SF}? Because consumers will demand only Q_{DF} at that price, there will be a surplus of $Q_{SF} - Q_{DF}$ units in the market. Here's where the government comes in. The market buys Q_{DF} of the output at the price of P_F, and the government purchases the rest at the market price for a government expenditure of $C + E + F + H + K + L$.

Consumer surplus with the price floor remains at A. Producer surplus is now all the producer revenue (including revenue from the government): $B + C + E + F + G + H + I + J + K + L$, minus the variable cost of producing Q_{SF} units ($F + J + K + L$), or $B + C + E + G + H + I$. Social welfare with the price floor is consumer surplus (A) plus producer surplus ($B + C + E + G + H + I$) minus government expenditure ($C + E + F + H + K + L$) or $A + B - F + G + I - K - L$. Social welfare with market pricing is $A + B + C + G + H + I$. Deadweight loss is $A + B + C + G + H + I - (A + B - F + G + I - K - L) = C + H + F + K + L$. Thus the deadweight loss with the government subsidy of buying the unsold production at the floor price increases by the cost of producing the unsold items. This is a wasteful use of scarce resources to produce unused output.

What if the government paid the producers not to produce the output that wouldn't be sold in the market? The government saves further expense by not having to transport, store, or destroy the output. How much should it pay? How about the producer surplus the producers will earn if they had been able to sell their $Q_{SF} - Q_{DF}$ at the price of P_F: $C + E + H$? Consumer surplus with the price floor remains at A. Producer surplus is $B + G + I$ from sales to the market and $C + E + H$ from the government. Government expenditure is $C + E + H$. So social welfare with this version of the price floor is $A + B + G + I + C + E + H - (C + E + H) = A + B + G + I$. Social welfare with market pricing is $A + B + C + G + H + I$, so the deadweight loss from this pricing floor scheme is $C + H$—that is, the social welfare triangle. Thus if the government wants an agricultural support price floor, paying the farmers not to produce is the way to go.

What about a price ceiling? Consider Figure 16.9. With a price ceiling of P_{Ce}, demanders will want Q_{DCe} of the good, and suppliers will want to supply Q_{SCe}; so

---

FIGURE 16.9

Impact of a Government Price Ceiling

A price ceiling decreases social welfare by the deadweight loss triangle ($C + F$) or by the deadweight loss triangle I.

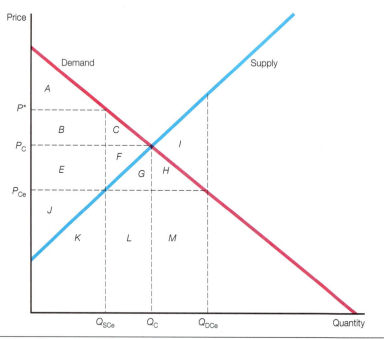

---

a shortage of $Q_{DCe} - Q_{SCe}$ exists. But because only Q_{SCe} will appear on the market, that is the relevant figure. Those lucky enough to consume the good will receive consumer surplus of $A + B + E$. The producer will receive producer surplus of J. Social welfare will be $A + B + E + J$. If the market were allowed to function, the price would be P_C. Consumer surplus is $A + B + C$, producer surplus is $E + F + J$, and social welfare is $A + B + C + E + F + J$. The deadweight loss is $C + F$.

With a market price, consumers gain $A + B + C - (A + B + E) = C - E$ in consumer surplus. This can be either positive or negative and would appear to be negative in Figure 16.9. However, a much steeper demand curve through the market equilibrium coordinates will increase C while not changing E and potentially making $C - E > 0$. With a market price, producers gain $E + F + J - J = E + F$. Social welfare thus increases by $C - E + E + F = C + F$ with market pricing.

What is the significance of P^* in Figure 16.9? With Q_{DCe} demanders trying to get Q_{SCe} units, a rationing mechanism has to be used. It could be a lottery where the lucky Q_{SCe} winners get the units. It could also be a sneaky price mechanism. For example, it's been reported that people pay "key money" (equal to $P^* - P_{Ce}$—so that quantity demanded equals the quantity of units supplied at P_{Ce}) to obtain rent-controlled apartments.

Suppose the government wants to satisfy all the demand at price P_{Ce}. Producers will satisfy all the quantity demanded and receive the ceiling price for each unit. The government will then compensate the producers for any loss they incur. Consumer surplus is $A + B + C + E + F + G + H$. Producer surplus is $J + K + L + M + I + G + H - (I + G + H + K + L + M) = J$. The government expenditure is $I + G + H$ for the producer costs not covered by the revenues from consumer purchases. Social welfare is $A + B + C + E + F + G + H + J - I - G - H = A + B + C + E + F + J - I$. The deadweight loss triangle in this case is I, where the additional $Q_{DCe} - Q_C$ items consumed over the optimal number bring benefit to consumers of $H + M$ but cost $I + H + M$ to produce.

An old TV ad stated, "It's not nice to fool with Mother Nature." Likewise, it's not nice to fool with market outcomes (except when markets fail, such as with externalities, as we will point out soon).

THE WELFARE IMPACTS OF TAXES

Suppose the government imposes a per-unit tax of t on a good. This tax drives a wedge of magnitude t between the price a seller receives and what a demander pays. Consider Figure 16.10. If there is no tax, the market price prevails, and consumer surplus is $A + B + C$, producer surplus is $E + F + G$, and social welfare is $A + B + C + E + F + G$. With the tax, the demander pays a price of P_D and consumes Q_t. On net, the supplier receives $P_S = P_D - t$. Consumer surplus is A, producer surplus is G, government tax revenues are $t \times Q_t = B + E$, and social welfare is $A + B + E + G$. The deadweight loss caused by the tax is $C + F$.

FIGURE 16.10

The Incidence and Welfare Costs of a Per-Unit Tax

A per-unit tax of t causes a deadweight loss of $C + F$. The tax is borne more by the buyer or the seller depending on their relative own-price elasticities, with the least elastic bearing more of the tax.

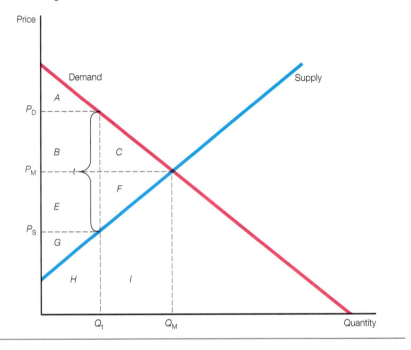

Who bears the brunt of the tax: the producer or the consumer? It depends on the relative elasticities of demand and supply. The elasticity of demand and supply through the market price equilibrium coordinates depends on the slope of the curves (recall from Chapter 2 that one definition of elasticity is $\eta = (P_M/Q_M)(1/\text{slope})$) because P_M and Q_M would be the same for all curves. A more gently sloped (more elastic) demand curve than the one depicted would decrease output and yield a lower P_D than the one depicted for a given t. Thus the demander would bear less of the tax with a more elastic demand curve. A steeper (less elastic) supply curve than the one depicted would increase output and yield a lower P_S than the one depicted for a given t. Thus the supplier would bear more of the tax with a less elastic supply curve. *The burden of the tax goes in the direction of the less elastic market participant.*

REGULATION OF ENVIRONMENTAL POLLUTION

Having looked briefly at antitrust, trade, and tax policy and the patent system, we return to the topic of government regulation. Government agencies regulate many aspects of economic life, not just the prices charged by public utility companies. Managers of firms in a wide variety of industries, ranging from steel or chemicals to paper or petroleum, must understand and cope with a huge number of government regulations to protect the environment. To illustrate the situation, consider the Reserve Mining Company (now Northshore Mining), which produces iron pellets from taconite rock. For every ton of iron pellets it manufactures, Reserve also produces two tons of waste taconite tailings, which for over a decade were dumped into Lake Superior. In 1969 Reserve found itself in a court battle, one of the most hotly debated matters being the discovery of asbestoslike fibers in the water supply of Duluth, Minnesota. When the legal battle was resolved in 1977, Reserve was granted the necessary permits to begin construction of a new dumping facility, which cost about $400 million. The price was high, but asbestos levels in Lake Superior have dropped substantially.

In the following sections we explain why our economy, in the absence of government action, is likely to generate too much pollution. Then we discuss the optimal level of pollution control and describe various forms of government regulation.

External Economies and Diseconomies

To understand why our economy is likely to generate too much pollution, we must define an external economy and an external diseconomy. An **external economy** occurs when an action by a firm or individual gives uncompensated benefits to others. For example, a firm may train workers who eventually go to work for other firms, which need not pay the training costs. Or managers may carry out research that benefits other firms, which need not pay for the research. In general, there is a tendency for activities resulting in external economies to be underperformed from society's point of view. A firm or individual that performs an action that contributes to society's welfare but receives no payment for it is likely to perform this action less frequently than would be socially desirable.

An **external diseconomy** occurs when an action by a firm or individual results in uncompensated costs or harm to others. For example, a firm may generate smoke that harms neighboring families and businesses, or a person may fail to maintain his or her property, reducing the value of neighboring houses. In general, there is a tendency for activities resulting in external diseconomies to be overperformed from society's point of view. A firm or individual that performs an action that results in costs borne by others is likely to perform this action more frequently than is socially desirable.

External economy When an action by a firm or individual gives uncompensated benefits to others.

External diseconomy When an action by a firm or individual results in uncompensated costs or harm to others.

The Genesis of the Pollution Problem

The key to understanding why our economy generates too much pollution (from society's point of view) is the concept of an external diseconomy. Firms and individuals that pollute our waterways and atmosphere are engaged in activities resulting in external diseconomies. They may pollute a river by pumping out waste materials, or pollute the air with smoke or other materials. These activities generate external diseconomies. Those that pollute (without penalty) transfer the costs of pollution to others; and as pointed out, they are likely to overpollute from a social viewpoint.

In a competitive economy, resources tend to be used in their socially most valuable way because they are allocated to the people and firms that find it worthwhile to bid most for them, assuming that prices reflect true social costs. Suppose, however, that because of the presence of external diseconomies, people and firms do not pay the true social costs for certain resources. In particular, suppose some firms or people can use water or air for nothing, but other firms or people incur costs as a consequence of this prior use. In this case, the price paid by the user of water or air is less than the true cost to society. In a case like this, users of water and air are guided in their decisions by the prices they pay. Because they pay less than the true social costs, water and air are artificially cheap for them, so that they use too much of these resources from society's point of view.

The Optimal Level of Pollution Control

Managers, like other members of society, should be able to look at matters from a social, as well as private, standpoint. They should be sensitive to the effects of their actions on society as a whole, as well as on their firm's interests. An industry generally can vary, at each level of output, the amount of pollution it generates. For instance, it may install pollution control devices like scrubbers to cut the amount of pollution it generates. In this section we determine the socially optimal level of pollution control.

The total social cost of each level of discharge of an industry's wastes, holding constant the industry's output, is shown in Figure 16.11. The more untreated waste the industry discharges into the environment, the greater are the total costs. Figure 16.12 shows the costs of pollution control at each level of discharge of the industry's wastes. The more the industry reduces the amount of wastes it discharges, the higher are its costs of pollution control. Figure 16.13 shows the sum of these two costs (the cost of pollution and the cost of pollution control) at each level of discharge of the industry's wastes.

From society's point of view, the industry should lower its discharge of pollution to the point where the sum of these two costs (the cost of pollution and the cost of pollution control) is at a minimum. Specifically, the optimal level of pollution in the industry is B in Figure 16.13. To see why this is the optimal level, note that if the industry discharges less than this amount of pollution, a one-unit increase in pollution lowers the cost of pollution control by more than it increases the cost of pollution; whereas if the industry discharges more than this amount of pollution, a one-unit reduction in pollution lowers the cost of pollution by more than it increases the cost of pollution control.

FIGURE 16.11

Pollution Cost

The cost of pollution increases as larger quantities of pollutants are emitted.

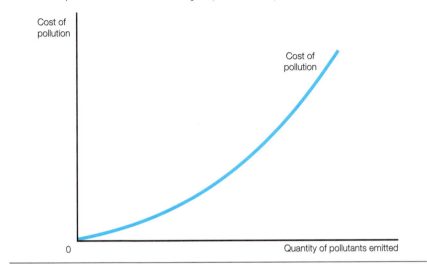

FIGURE 16.12

Pollution Control Cost

The cost of pollution control decreases as larger quantities of pollutants are emitted.

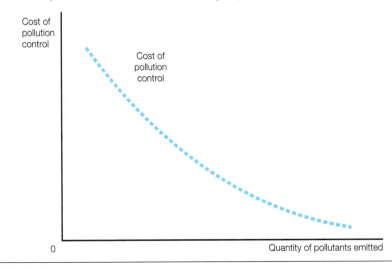

FIGURE 16.13

Sum of the Pollution Cost and the Pollution Control Cost

From the point of view of society as a whole, the optimal level of pollution in this industry is *B*.

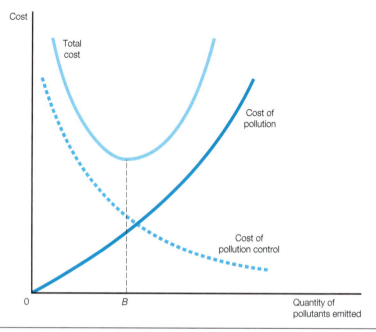

Figure 16.14 shows the marginal cost of an extra unit of discharge of waste at each level of discharge of the industry's wastes; this is designated UU'. Figure 16.14 also shows the marginal cost of reducing the industry's discharge of waste by one unit; this is designated by VV'. The socially optimal level of pollution for the industry is at the point where the two curves intersect. At this point, the cost of an extra unit of pollution is just equal to the cost of reducing pollution by an extra unit. Regardless of whether we look at Figure 16.13 or 16.14, the answer is the same: *B* is the socially optimal level of pollution.

Forms of Government Regulation

Because it does not pay all the social costs of its pollution, the industry in Figure 16.14 does not find it profitable to reduce its pollution level to *B*. One way the government can establish incentives for managers to reduce their pollution is by direct regulation. For example, the government may decree that this industry is to limit its pollution to *B* units. Direct regulation of this sort is relied on in many sectors of the U.S. economy.

Another way to induce managers to reduce pollution is to establish effluent fees. An **effluent fee** is the fee a polluter must pay to the government for discharg-

Effluent fee The fee a polluter must pay to the government for discharging waste.

FIGURE 16.14

Marginal Cost of Pollution and Marginal Cost of Pollution Control

At the socially optimal level of pollution, *B*, the cost of an extra unit of pollution is equal to the cost of reducing pollution by an extra unit.

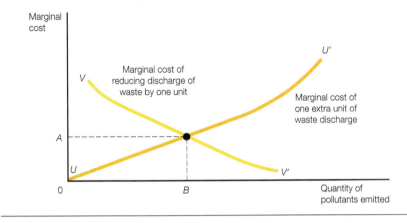

ing waste. For instance, in Figure 16.14 an effluent fee of *A* per unit of pollution discharge might be charged. If so, the marginal cost of an additional unit of pollution discharge to the industry is *A*, with the result that it cuts back its pollution to the socially optimal level, *B* units. To maximize their profits, the managers in the industry reduce pollution to *B* units because it is profitable to cut back pollution so long as the marginal cost of reducing pollution by a unit is less than *A*—and, as we see from Figure 16.14, this is the case when the pollution discharge exceeds *B*.

To illustrate the usefulness of effluent fees, consider Germany's Ruhr Valley, a highly industrialized area with limited water supplies. Effluent fees have been used in the Ruhr to help maintain the quality of the local rivers, and the results have been highly successful. But direct regulation is useful, too. Some ways of disposing of certain types of waste are so dangerous that the only sensible thing to do is to ban them. Also, it sometimes is not feasible to impose effluent fees—for example, when it is difficult to meter the amount of pollutants emitted by various firms and households.

Yet another way that the government can reduce the amount of pollution is to issue **transferable emissions permits**, which are permits to generate a particular amount of pollution. These permits, which are limited in total number so that the aggregate amount of pollution equals the level the government decides on, are allocated among firms. They can be bought and sold. Managers who find it expensive to curb pollution are likely to buy these permits; managers who find it cheap to do so are likely to sell them. The Clean Air Act of 1990 called for the use of such permits to reduce the emission of sulfur dioxide, and the Chicago Board of Trade voted to create a market for these permits (see problem 2 at the end of

Transferable emissions permits
Permits to generate a particular amount of pollution.

this chapter). An exchange for international carbon dioxide permits was formed in Amsterdam in 2005.

Consider another way of solving the problem, attributable to Ronald Coase, who won the 1991 Nobel Prize for his contributions (including this one) to economics. The Haddonfield Brewery (a microbrewery) is located downstream from the Cherry Hill Chemical Company. Cherry Hill dumps its effluent into the river. Haddonfield requires clean water to brew its beer and must therefore filter the river water before using it. This filtering costs Haddonfield $50,000, and its current profits are $200,000. Cherry Hill's current profits are $500,000. It is possible for Cherry Hill to refine the effluent before discharging it into the river so that the river water meets all standards for beer brewing. Installing and operating such a refining system would cost Cherry Hill $40,000. Coase viewed the process of controlling pollution and its costs as one that could be solved without government intervention.

Suppose there are no government laws regarding pollution. Cherry Hill can pollute at will. The value of society's output as we initially view this situation is $700,000, or $200,000 + $500,000.

Note that if Haddonfield managers paid $40,000 to Cherry Hill to refine its effluent, Haddonfield could save $10,000, increase its profits to $210,000, and hence increase the societal welfare to $710,000. The pollution is eliminated and the societal welfare is increased, and only private entities are involved.

However, such a solution could be thwarted by negotiation costs. Suppose negotiation costs for an agreement between Haddonfield and Cherry Hill are $11,000. Cherry Hill managers have no reason to negotiate or pay negotiation costs. Haddonfield managers would gain $10,000 with an agreement, but they must bear $11,000 in negotiation costs, so they will choose not to do so. It would be cheaper for them to filter the incoming water.

Suppose we impose the basic common law on this situation—not a law against pollution per se, but a law that says one is liable for the damage one causes to another. Cherry Hill's effluent causes $50,000 in damages to Haddonfield (if Haddonfield had clean water, it would not have to spend $50,000 on filtering and its profit would increase to $250,000). Given liability for the damages it causes, Cherry Hill could shut down and stop polluting. But it is very profitable, and shutting down would be foolish because it would deprive society of its output. A better solution would be for Cherry Hill to pay Haddonfield $50,000 for the damages caused; it would still have $450,000. Still a better solution would be to install the refining system and incur a cost of $40,000; Cherry Hill would still have $460,000. This eliminates any liability on Cherry Hill's part because the water is no longer polluted.

Note that in the first case, where there was no law (and no negotiation costs) and Cherry Hill could do as it wished, the ultimate solution was for Haddonfield to pay Cherry Hill to put in water refining equipment. In the latter situation, where there was a liability law, the ultimate solution was for Cherry Hill to install the refining equipment with no payment from Haddonfield. With or without the law, the private sector chooses the cheapest method to eliminate the pollution problem. In either case the societal welfare is $710,000.

The difference between the two situations is the distribution of welfare between Haddonfield and Cherry Hill. With liability, Cherry Hill gets $500,000 − $40,000 = $460,000 and Haddonfield gets $250,000. With no liability, Cherry Hill gets $500,000 + $P − $40,000 = $460,000 + $P and Haddonfield gets $250,000 − $P, where $50,000 > $P > $40,000. Previously we assumed that Haddonfield paid Cherry Hill's cost of installing the refining equipment; but with no liability laws, Cherry Hill need not abate its pollution. Clearly Cherry Hill managers must receive at least $40,000 (the cost of the refining equipment) from Haddonfield; because getting rid of the pollution is worth $50,000 to Haddonfield, Cherry Hill managers could hold out for a payment P greater than $40,000 (but Haddonfield would never pay more than $50,000 because it can do its own filtering for $50,000).

Therefore, under the no-liability scenario, Cherry Hill would get between $500,000 and $510,000, and Haddonfield would get between $210,000 and $200,000. Cherry Hill prefers the nonliable scenario and Haddonfield prefers liability; but either way, society gets social welfare of $710,000, and pollution is abated in the cheapest way.

Effects of the Regulation-Induced Cost Increase on Price and Output

Regardless of how the government induces firms to reduce pollution, the result is an increase in the firms' costs, as in the case of the Reserve Mining Company discussed earlier. Firms spend substantial amounts annually on environmental costs (both in prevention and in penalties for exceeding legal limits); for example, Du Pont is reported to have spent about $521 million (pretax) on environmental expenses in 2006.[6] It is important to recognize this and see how to determine the extent to which this cost increase is passed on to consumers in the form of a price increase—and the extent to which it will be borne by the firms. In this section we learn how this can be done. It is analogous to the incidence of a tax shown earlier.

Suppose a new regulation says that paper mills must use new methods to reduce water pollution. Assuming the paper industry is perfectly competitive, we can compare the situation in the industry after the regulation's enactment with that prior to its enactment. Before the regulation, the marginal cost function of each paper producer is assumed to be

$$MC = 20 + 40Q \tag{16.11}$$

where Q equals the number (in thousands) of tons of paper produced per week. If the price is P, managers, to maximize profit, set price equal to marginal cost, which means that

$$P = 20 + 40Q$$

6. DuPont economic, environmental, and social performance data in the *Global Reporting Initiative Format*, June 2007 Update.

or

$$Q = -0.5 + 0.025P$$

If there are 1,000 paper producers, all with the same cost function, the industry's supply curve is

$$Q_S = 1,000(-0.5 + 0.025P) = -500 + 25P \qquad (16.12)$$

Assuming that the market demand curve for paper is

$$Q_D = 3,500 - 15P \qquad (16.13)$$

we can find the equilibrium price and output of paper by setting the quantity demanded in equation (16.13) equal to the quantity supplied in equation (16.12):

$$3,500 - 15P = -500 + 25P$$
$$40P = 4,000$$
$$P = 100$$

The quantity demanded equals

$$Q_D = 3,500 - 15P = 3,500 - 15(100) = 2,000$$

And the quantity supplied equals the same amount:

$$Q_S = -500 + 25P = -500 + 25(100) = 2,000$$

In other words, before the new regulation, the price of paper is $100 per ton, and 2,000 tons are produced per week.

What is the effect of the new regulation on the price and output of paper? Suppose the regulation raises the marginal cost of producing paper by 25 percent. After the regulation, the marginal cost function of each paper producer is

$$MC = 1.25 (20 + 40Q)$$
$$= 25 + 50Q$$

To maximize profit, each firm sets marginal cost equal to price, which means that

$$25 + 50Q = P$$
$$Q = -0.5 + 0.02P$$

Hence the industry's postregulation supply curve is

$$Q'_S = 1,000(-0.5 + 0.02P)$$
$$= -500 + 20P \qquad (16.14)$$

if all 1,000 paper producers stay in the industry. (Some may drop out if they cannot avoid losses (recall Chapter 6.) To find the equilibrium price after the enact-

STRATEGY SESSION: Buying and Selling the Right to Emit Nitrogen Oxides

Nitrogen oxides help produce smog and aggravate asthma and other respiratory problems. On March 16, 1994, Public Service Electric and Gas, headquartered in Newark, New Jersey, announced that it would reduce its emissions of nitrogen oxides by 1999 by 2,400 more tons than the law requires, probably by altering a coal-fired plant in Jersey City. Northeast Utilities, which operates in Connecticut, Massachusetts, and New Hampshire, said it would purchase the rights to emit 500 of those tons. This was the first use of transferable emissions permits for an air pollutant that affects human health directly. Previous deals of this sort centered on sulfur dioxide, which helps cause acid rain.

The Clean Air Act of 1990 authorized a market in emissions permits. Firms finding it relatively expensive to cut their nitrogen oxide emissions are likely to buy pollution permits because such permits cost less than cutting their emissions. On the other hand, firms finding it relatively cheap to cut their nitrogen

oxide emissions are likely to sell pollution permits because their costs of reducing the emissions are less than what they can sell the permits for. Therefore, the reduction in the total emission of nitrogen oxides occurs at relatively low cost.

For such a scheme to work, firms must be able to buy and sell permits. In this case, Public Service Electric and Gas sold the permits to a broker, the Clean Air Action Corporation of Tulsa, Oklahoma, at cost. The Clean Air Action Corporation sold them to Northeast Utilities and others at the market price. This price is set by the supply and demand curves for permits.[a]

See the Strategy Session in Chapter 9 regarding the international trading of carbon permits, which commenced in Amsterdam in 2005.

[a]For further discussion, see *The New York Times*, March 16, 1994; and *Philadelphia Inquirer*, March 16, 1994.

---

ment of the new regulation, we set the quantity demanded in equation (16.13) equal to the quantity supplied in equation (16.14):

$$3,500 - 15P = -500 + 20P$$
$$35P = 4,000$$
$$P = 114.29$$

Hence the postregulation quantity demanded equals

$$Q_D = 3,500 - 15P = 3,500 - 15(114.29) = 1,785.71$$

And the quantity supplied equals the same amount:

$$Q'_S = -500 + 20P = -500 + 20(114.29) = 1,785.71$$

In other words, after the new regulation, the price of paper is $114.29 per ton, and 1,785.71 thousands of tons of paper are produced per week.

PROBLEM SOLVED: Auctioning Off Spectrum Rights: Australia and the United States

In 1995 the Federal Communications Commission (FCC) completed the first auction for broadband personal communications services (PCS) licenses. In designing its auction, both the FCC and its economic advisers were aware that auctions could backfire, as illustrated by a famous case in Australia. In April 1993 two licenses for satellite television service were auctioned off in Australia. When the sealed bids were received, the winners were Hi Vision Ltd. and Ucom Pty. Ltd.; their winning bids were about $140 million and $120 million, respectively. Because these bids were larger than expected and because these firms were not among the major players in the Australian television industry, the Australian government announced that the auction ushered in a "whole new era."

To the government's dismay, both Hi Vision and Ucom defaulted on their highest bids. Hence the licenses had to be reawarded at the next highest levels, which were also theirs. It soon became clear that each firm had submitted many bids, each about $5 million higher than the next. After defaulting on a number of its bids, Ucom eventually paid about $80 million for one license and $50 million for the other. An Australian politician called it "one of the world's great media license fiascos," and Bob Collins, Australia's communications minister, was almost fired.

Auctions can also be tremendously successful. In March 2008 the U.S. government announced that companies bid more than $19 billion for the portion of the wireless spectrum that will be freed as the result of the conversion to digital television by broadcasters. This was the most lucrative auction in history.

Problems

1. What are the advantages of auctions over other schemes to choose who gets licenses?

2. What was the fundamental flaw in Australia's auction of licenses?

3. To help avoid such flaws, the FCC stipulated that firms had to make down payments to the FCC; and if a high bidder were to withdraw its bid during the auction, it would be liable for the difference between its bid and the price ultimately obtained for the license. (For bids withdrawn after the auction, there would be a supplementary penalty of 3 percent.) Why would these stipulations help avoid such flaws?

Solutions

1. Auctions tend to reduce the costs and delays in choosing licenses. Hearings and lotteries, which are the principal alternative ways to allocate licenses, use a great deal of resources, particularly the time of economic, engineering, and legal consultants.

2. The fundamental flaw in Australia's auction was the lack of a penalty for default, which implied that bids were not meaningful.

3. These stipulations were aimed at preventing bidders from defaulting without penalty on their bids.[a]

[a]For further discussion, see John McMillan, "Selling Spectrum Rights," *Journal of Economic Perspectives*, Summer 1994; and "Wireless Spectrum Auction Raises $19 Billion," *The New York Times*, March 19, 2008.

Clearly the new regulation increases price (from $100 to $114.29 per ton—but note by less than the 25 percent cost increase) and reduces output (from 2,000 to 1,785.71 thousands of tons per week). This typically is the effect of such regulations, but the extent of the price increase (and the output reduction) depends on the price elasticity of demand for the product. If the price elasticity is low in absolute value, the price increase is greater (and the output reduction smaller) than if the price elasticity is high in absolute value.

PUBLIC GOODS

In addition to regulating the environment and the behavior of monopolists, the government performs various economic functions, including providing goods and services. For example, the government is responsible for national defense, a critically important product in any society. Why does the government provide some goods and not others? One important reason is that some goods—so-called public goods—are unlikely to be produced in sufficient amounts by the private (nongovernmental) sector of the economy. Therefore the government is given the task of providing these goods. Before concluding this chapter, we must describe briefly what a public good is and why the private sector is unlikely to provide a public good in sufficient amounts.

A major hallmark of a public good is that it can be consumed by one person without diminishing the amount that other people consume of it. Public goods tend to be relatively indivisible; they often come in such large units that they cannot be broken into pieces that can be bought or sold in ordinary markets. Also, once such goods are produced, there is no way to bar citizens from consuming them. Whether or not citizens contribute toward their cost, they benefit from them. Obviously this means that it would be difficult for any firm to market them effectively.

National defense is a public good. The benefits of expenditure on national defense apply to the entire nation. Extending the benefits of national defense to an additional citizen does not mean that any other citizen gets fewer of these benefits. Also, there is no way of preventing citizens from benefiting from them, whether they contribute to the cost or not. Therefore ordinary markets (such as those for wheat, steel, or computers) cannot provide national defense. Because it is a public good, national defense, if it is to reach an adequate level, must be provided by the government; the same is true for flood control, environmental protection, and other such services.

Although these services are provided by the government, this does not mean they must be produced entirely by the government. The U.S. Air Force does not produce the B-2 Stealth Bomber; Northrop Corporation (now part of Northrop Grumman) does. The U.S. Navy does not produce the F-14 fighter; Grumman (now also part of Northrop Grumman) does. Firms play a central role in developing and producing the weapons systems on which our military establishment relies, even though national defense is a public good.

STRATEGY SESSION: Entrance Fees to National Parks

The United States has many national parks, such as Yellowstone, and people frequently complain that they are overcrowded. Some economists, such as Allen Sanderson of the University of Chicago, have suggested that the solution is to raise entrance fees. They point out that when the National Park Service was set up in 1916, a family of five arriving by car could gain admission to Yellowstone for $7.50; in 1995 the price was only $10. If the 1916 price had risen in accord with the general rate of inflation, the 1995 fee would have been about $120.

According to Sanderson, "We are treating our national and historical treasures as free goods when they are not. We are ignoring the costs of maintaining these places and rationing by congestion—when it gets too crowded no more visitors are allowed—perhaps the most inefficient way to allocate scarce resources."[a]

The U.S. National Parks service has responded by charging admission to its parks. Here we show a schedule of fees taken from each park's Web site in spring 2008. Although the prices don't approach Sanderson's inflation-adjusted Yellowstone fee, they now serve as a rationing device for limited park capacity.

The U.S. National Parks Service offers a pass (America the Beautiful—National Parks and Federal Recreational Lands Pass), in cooperation with the U.S. Department of Agriculture—Forest Service, Fish and Wildlife Service, Bureau of Land Management, and Bureau of Reclamation, that allows a vehicle, the pass holder and three other adults, and an unlimited number of children under the age of 16 access to facilities run by the agencies for a year for $80. A senior citizens' version costs $10, and admission is free for citizens with permanent disabilities and park volunteers.

Here are some general entrance fees for national parks:

Acadia	Seven-day permit for auto and occupants: $20
Arches	Seven-day permit for auto and occupants: $10
	Seven-day permit for walk-ins, bike-ins, motorcycles: $5
Death Valley	Seven-day permit for auto and occupants: $20
	Seven-day permit for walk-ins, bike-ins, motorcycles: $10
Grand Canyon	Seven-day permit for auto and occupants: $25
	Seven-day permit for walk-ins, bike-ins, motorcycles: $12
Grand Teton	Seven-day permit for auto and occupants: $20
	Seven-day permit for walk-ins, bike-ins: $10
	Seven-day permit for motorcycles: $15
	Year permit: $50
	(All allow entry to Yellowstone too.)
Great Smoky Mountains	Free
Yellowstone	Seven-day permit for auto and occupants: $25
	Seven-day permit for walk-ins, bike-ins: $12
	Seven-day permit for motorcycles: $20
	Year permit: $50
Yosemite	Seven-day permit for auto and occupants: $20
	Seven-day permit for walk-ins, bike-ins, motorcycles, horseback: $10
	Year permit: $40

[a]*The New York Times*, September 30, 1995, p. 19.

FIGURE 16.15

Classification of Goods

	Nonrival	Rival
Non-Excludable	Public goods	Common property
Excludable	Marketable public goods	Private goods

Because the distinction between public and private goods is not always clear, Figure 16.15 gives a way of classifying goods.

Pure public goods have the characteristics of being nonrival (my consumption doesn't impact your ability to consume) and nonexcludable (there is no mechanism to exclude people from access). A typical entry in the northwest cell of public good would be the previously mentioned national defense. Historically lighthouses have also been put in such a category. However, technology changes things; today all the information conveyed by a lighthouse can be transmitted electronically and with a scrambled signal, so excludability is now possible—the information has moved lighthouses from the northwest corner of Figure 16.15 to the southwest corner. Some goods, such as education, bridge the two cells because they have some, but not all, of the characteristics of pure public goods. As a result, public education is in the northwest cell and private education is in the southwest cell, and consumers choose whether they want to use "free" public education or pay market prices for private education.

Certain goods are nonexcludable but rival (the northeast cell). A public sidewalk is available to anyone, but it is subject to capacity constraints, and my occupying a spot may preclude you from being on the sidewalk. We used to think of public roads as being analogous to sidewalks. Now tolls are being proposed for some existing free roads: High occupancy vehicle (HOV) lanes are being converted to HOT lanes (tolls charged for cars not meeting the vehicle occupancy criterion). Thus we have created ways to exclude consumers from some public rival goods. Finally, in the southeast corner of the matrix are private sector goods and services. Whether government provides goods in any or all of these cells is a decision made by the government or the people that elect the government. A trend toward privatization has led a number of governments to exit functions performed in the southeast corner, such as trash collection, airline operation, and prison operation.

Government agencies have a vital influence over a wide variety of industries, not just defense contractors like Northrop Grumman. This chapter has described in detail many activities of government agencies that are important to managers.

STRATEGY SESSION: All That Glitters Is Not Gold

Four months have passed since we wrote of the high commodity prices of 2008 (Chapter 1). Now, 2009 is upon us. We are in a deep global recession and commodity prices have plunged. From an all-time high of $147/bbl in July of this year, oil recently hit a 4 and a half year low at $34/bbl. Consumers are not spending; layoffs are increasing on a global scale. The credit markets are frozen. The cold state is not from lacking liquidity as governments across the globe have stimulated their economies. What is lacking is trust. That fragile gift managers sometimes bestow upon each other in the name of business. It seems the only institution trusted in the current environment is the U.S. government. People are actually paying the government to hold their money for them. Managers should never forget this lesson regarding the benefits of trust. It is necessary for those who value efficiency.

The day of free market reckoning has come and past. For the first time in our lives, we better understand what it really means to say the U.S. Government is the lender of last resort. It seems it is the only lender in some business sectors. In great market movements, there are always unintended consequences. We offer this. Prior to the crisis, if we went to cocktail parties and talked about adverse selection and moral hazard, people would change the subject or get up and leave. Now, this is what many want to discuss. We could not be more delighted to better explain these concepts to them.

The crisis provides ample examples to illustrate the usefulness of this book to the managerial world. We measure usefulness by its ability to predict behavior. Let's look at moral hazard and adverse selection, the subjects of Chapter 14 and 15. One early response from the government to the financial crisis was called the Troubled Assets Relief Program (TARP). In its initial form the money from TARP was to be used to purchase illiquid assets (toxic) held on the books by financial institutions. Many of these assets were mortgaged backed securities (MBS). These instruments,

which were designed by investment bankers, pooled mortgages of different structure (rating, length). The pool would then be segregated into what are called tranches; tranches could have different ratings in terms of risk based on its position in the repayment schedule. In turn, these securities were included in pools with those of other credit markets, like credit cards or commercial loans, as collateral for another managerially designed instrument called collateralized debt obligations (CDOs).

On October 3, 2008, Congress, by an overwhelming vote, gave $700 billion to the Treasury Department to purchase illiquid (toxic) assets like MBS and CDOs from financial institutions. One plan called for using reverse auctions to purchase the toxic assets and create a market price for them. Less than five weeks later on November 18, 2008, the Secretary of Treasury, Hank Paulson, announced the abandonment of the plan. Instead of purchasing toxic assets, the Treasury would now use fund monies to purchase equity stakes in financial institutions. What caused the Treasury to reverse its course of action? And, why were the assets toxic? These questions and many more are explained by looking at the impact of moral hazard and adverse selection on managerial behavior.

The synthetic products created by Wall Street bankers, and now illiquid, were poorly designed to protect investors from moral hazard induced behavior. This, in turn, created markets characterized by adverse selection. The securitization of mortgages (and other debt) brought unbalance to the market. Before securitization, most financial institutions held the mortgages they wrote. There was an incentive to correctly identify the appropriate level of risk because your institution would bear it. Now that chain of reasoning was broken. Mortgages written by the institution were packaged into bundles and sold to others. Managers of the firm that originated the loan could relax their lending standards because they would quickly sell the loan to others. The bankers had created a situation conducive to moral hazard-like behavior.

The Impact of Moral Hazard-like Behavior

Situations predicted by moral hazard models became reality. Some managers compounded the impact of these principles through their actions. Managerial choices at Washington Mutual Savings (WaMu) typified such behavior.

Like most mortgage originators, those originated by managers at WaMu were quickly packaged and sold to others. But, managerial behavior created additional incentives for moral hazard-like behavior. For example, upper level managers were compensated on growth numbers. And, their bonus scheme did not consider bad debt due to non-performing mortgages. Also, mortgage brokers were given greater commissions for writing more risky loans because such loans paid higher upfront fees. WaMu managers also pressured real estate appraisers to inflate property values in their reports. A founder of one such company said, "It was the Wild West. If you were alive, they would give you a loan. Actually, I think if you were dead, they would still give you a loan".[a] WaMu became one of the biggest writers of sub-prime mortgages. Managers decided to focus on a variable rate product called option ARMs. These allowed the lender to choose how much to pay each month, and were offered with low initial interest rates. By 2006 these riskier mortgages compromised 70 percent of all mortgages written. Managers focused on these mortgages because they paid higher upfront fees, and allowed WaMu to book profits on the interest due, even if the borrower chose to defer paying it. In 2005 and 2006, Kerry Killinger, the CEO, received compensation totaling $43 million due to these policies. Two years later WaMu suffered losses of billions of dollars due to bad loans and the company was sold at a great discount to JP MorganChase.

And, what about the bankers who were selling these bundled securities to investors? They also paid little consideration to reducing moral-hazard like behavior. And, their collective decisions helped to intensify the effect. They structured CDOs as private placement vehicles. The bonds were not subject to most regulatory bodies. Pricing was not transparent. There was never any public market for these products, and only those who traded them were privy to sale information. Investment banks got paid after the bonds were sold. Underwriting fees were estimated to be roughly 1.1 percent. Hence, for every $1 billion in bonds sold, bankers would receive $11 million in fees.[b] Many bankers who sold the product did not even know what assets served as the underlying collateral. One said their stated goal was to "sell as many as possible and get paid the most for every bond sold."[c]

Because the make-up of a CDO is opaque, investors depended on bond rating agencies to look more closely at the bond and rate it for risk. But, the bond raters were compensated for their services by the investment banks, and often gave AAA ratings to bonds containing sub-prime mortgages. Here, again, we see how managerial actions encourage moral hazard-like behavior.

Some bankers even described the moral hazards they were facing in documents to investors. Jill Drew describes one, "The Dillion Read fund also purchased $45 million of preferred stock in the Mantoloking trust. The hedge fund's dual role as servicer and investor gave it the incentive to load the CDO with risky investments to enhance its potential return, according to the offering document."[d]

The Impact of Adverse Selection

By late 2008, the market for MBS and CDOs did not exist. The market had failed. Pricing the instruments was difficult because few managers understood the value of the underlying collateral. The government felt it had to intervene so it created TARP. The original idea for TARP was to help create price transparency. So, the Treasury initially thought about holding an auction to establish a price for these assets. The proposed design was based on reverse auctions. In these auctions there are many sellers (financial institutions), and one buyer (the Treasury). The sellers bid the price down. For these auctions the price reflects how many cents on the dollar managers were willing to sell their debt to the government. Managers who are willing to sell at the lowest cents on the dollar would get to sell debt to the government. The auctions would not only get bad debt off the books of some firms, it would also establish some basis for pricing these bonds.

The plan had some flaws, none more important than those caused by adverse selection. The managers who held the debt clearly knew more about its composition than the government, especially because benchmarks for relative comparisons of bonds were difficult. Few trusted the ratings bestowed by rating agencies given the subsequent loss in bond value and potential for moral hazard-like behavior. And, most bonds had a unique value given the variety of mortgages in a pool.

Treasury officials anticipated creating a "market for lemons." Managers who owned the debt were like used car sellers, and the government played the used car buyer. The incentives were for the auction winners to saddle the government with their expected worst

SUMMARY

1. Commissions regulating public utilities often set price equal to average total cost, including a fair rate of return on the firm's investment. One difficulty with this arrangement is that because the firm is guaranteed this rate of return (regardless of how well or poorly it performs), there is no incentive for managers to increase efficiency. Although regulatory lag creates some incentives of this sort, they often are relatively weak.

2. The Sherman Act outlaws any contract, combination, or conspiracy in restraint of trade and makes it illegal to monopolize or attempt to monopolize. The Clayton Act outlaws unjustified price discrimination and tying contracts that reduce competition, among other things. The Robinson-Patman Act was aimed at preventing price discrimination in favor of chain stores that buy goods in large quantities. The Federal Trade Commission Act was designed to prevent undesirable and unfair competitive practices.

3. The real impact of antitrust laws depends on the interpretation of these laws by the courts. In its early cases, the Supreme Court put forth and used the famous rule of reason—that only unreasonable combinations in restraint of trade, not all trusts, required conviction under the Sherman Act. The situation changed greatly in the 1940s, when the court decided that Alcoa, because it controlled practically all the nation's aluminum output, was in violation of the antitrust laws. In the early 1980s two major antitrust cases were decided against American Tele-

performing bonds. Because of adverse selection, the Treasury was destined to purchase "lemons". The auctions might establish a price, but it would be a price for low-quality bonds.

This is one reason why Treasury officials changed their minds about how they would use TARP. The return on the monies was expected to be too low. Treasury officials recognized the dangers of adverse selection and chose to buy equity stakes in institutions themselves in return for some managerial control. The markets needed to stabilize and this was probably quicker and more transparent in showing government commitment.

In late 2008, Treasury officials did announce a program to purchase $500 billion of MBS by June 2009.

In designing the program, officials did recognize the adverse selection issues and tried to mitigate them. Only securities guaranteed by Fannie Mae, Freddie Mac, or Ginnie Mae were considered for purchase. And, securities had to be fixed rate and could not include any interest-only bonds.

[a]Goodman, Peter and Gretchen Morgenson; "Saying Yes, WaMu Built Empire on Shaky Loans", *The New York Times*, 28 December 2008, NYTimes.com
[b]Drew, Jill, "Frenzy", *The Washington Post*, 16 December 2008, p. A01.
[c]Ibid, p. 3.
[d]Ibid, p. 6.

phone and Telegraph and the IBM Corporation. The European Union has become very active in antitrust enforcement in the 2000s.

4. Patent laws grant an inventor exclusive control over the use of an invention in exchange for his or her making the invention public knowledge. The patent system enables innovators to obtain a larger portion of the social benefits from their innovations, but it frequently has only a limited effect on the rate at which imitators appear. Nonetheless, firms continue to make extensive use of the patent system.

5. Trade is a significant and growing portion of our economy. Government policy influences how free our trade is. This chapter discussed the perfect competition argument for free trade and showed the welfare impacts of tariff and quotas relative to free trade. In general, a tariff is a less harmful way to restrict trade than a quota.

6. Governments intervene with market-determined prices by imposing price floors (not allowing the price to fall to its equilibrium level) or price ceilings (not allowing the price to rise to its equilibrium level). In both situations the deadweight loss to society of such interference can be shown. A government tax on individual goods drives a wedge between the price demanders pay and the price sellers retain. The welfare impacts of price interventions and taxes can be demonstrated using the same tools (producer and consumer surplus) developd in earlier chapters.

7. An external economy occurs when an action of a firm or individual gives uncompensated benefits to others. An external diseconomy occurs when an action of a firm or individual causes uncompensated costs or harm to others. Firms and individuals that pollute our waterways and atmosphere are engaged in activities resulting in external diseconomies.

8. The socially optimal level of pollution (holding output constant) is at the point where the marginal cost of pollution equals the marginal cost of pollution control. In general, this is at a point where a nonzero amount of pollution occurs. To formulate incentives that lead to a more nearly optimal level of pollution, the government can establish effluent fees, issue transferable emissions permits, or enact direct regulations, among other things. These policies internalize the externality and make production of the externality an implicit cost to the producer.

9. Regulations (and other measures) designed to reduce pollution tend to increase the costs of the regulated firms. The price of their products generally rises, and industry output tends to drop. If the price elasticity of demand is relatively low in absolute value, more of the cost increase can be passed along to consumers in the form of a price increase than would be the case if the price elasticity of demand were relatively high in absolute value.

10. A public good can be consumed by one person without diminishing the amount of it that other people consume. Also, once a public good is produced, there is no way to bar citizens from consuming it. Public goods, such as national defense, are unlikely to be produced in sufficient quantities by the private (nongovernmental) sector of the economy. Therefore the government often is given the task of providing these goods.

wwnorton.com/studyspace

PROBLEMS

1. In 1985 United Airlines purchased Pan Am's Pacific Division for $750 million. The Department of Justice opposed the purchase, but it was approved by the U.S. Department of Transportation. The percentages of total passengers carried across the Pacific by each airline in 1984 were as follows:

Firm	Percentage	Firm	Percentage
Northeast	27.5	United	7.3
JAL	21.9	China Airlines	6.8
Pan Am	18.5	Singapore Airlines	2.9
Korean Air	9.3	Other	5.8

    a. What was the concentration ratio before the purchase? Was it relatively high?

    b. What was the concentration ratio after the purchase?

2. The Chicago Board of Trade voted to create a private market for rights to emit sulfur dioxide. The Clean Air Act of 1990 established a limit, beginning in 1995, on total emissions of sulfur dioxide from 110 power plants. Firms finding it relatively expensive to cut their sulfur dioxide emissions are likely to buy

pollution permits because such permits cost less than cutting their emissions. Given that firms can exceed their legal limits and pay fines of $2,000 per ton, do you think that the price of a right to emit a ton of sulfur dioxide exceeds $2,000? Why or why not?

3. The Miller-Lyons Electric Company is engaged in a rate case with the local regulatory commission. The demand curve for the firm's product is

$$P = 1,000 - 2Q$$

where P is price per unit of output (in dollars) and Q is the output (in thousands of units per year). The total cost (excluding the opportunity cost of the capital invested in the firm by its owners) is

$$TC = 50 + 0.25Q$$

where TC is expressed in millions of dollars.

a. The Miller-Lyons Electric Company has requested an annual rate (that is, price) of $480. If the firm has assets of $100 million, what would be its rate of return on its assets if this request is granted?

b. How much greater would the firm's accounting profit be if it were deregulated?

4. The cost of pollution (in billions of dollars) originating in the paper industry is

$$C_p = 2P + P^2$$

where P is the quantity of pollutants emitted (in thousands of tons). The cost of pollution control (in billions of dollars) for this industry is

$$C_C = 5 - 3P$$

a. What is the optimal level of pollution?

b. At this level of pollution, what is the marginal cost of pollution?

c. At this level of pollution, what is the marginal cost of pollution control?

5. Seven firms produce kitchen tables. Suppose their sales in the year 2008 are as follows:

Firm	Sales (Millions of Dollars)
A	100
B	50
C	40
D	30
E	20
F	5
G	5

    a. What is the concentration ratio in this industry?

    b. Would you regard this industry as oligopolistic? Why or why not?

    c. Suppose that firm *A* merges with firm *G*. What is the new concentration ratio in this industry?

    d. Suppose that after they merge, firms *A* and *G* go out of business. What is the subsequent concentration ratio in this industry?

6. The cost of pollution emanating from the chemical industry (in billions of dollars) is

$$C_P = 3P + 3P^2$$

where *P* is the quantity of pollutants emitted (in thousands of tons). The cost of pollution control (in billions of dollars) is

$$C_C = 7 - 5P$$

    a. What is the optimal effluent fee?

    b. If the cost of pollution control falls by $1 billion at each level of pollution, does this alter your answer to part (a)?

7. In the cardboard box industry, the minimum average cost is reached when a firm produces 1,000 units of output per month. At this output rate, the average cost is $1 per unit of output. The demand curve for this product is as follows:

Price (Dollars per Unit of Output)	Quantity (Units Demanded per Month)
3.00	1,000
2.00	8,000
1.00	12,000
0.50	20,000

    a. Is this industry a natural monopoly? Why or why not?

    b. If the price is $2, how many firms, each of which is producing output such that average cost is at a minimum, can the market support?

8. Bethlehem and Youngstown, two major steel producers, accounted for about 21 percent of the national steel market in the late 1950s, when they proposed to merge.

    a. Should the two steel companies have been allowed to merge? Why or why not?

    b. According to the companies, Bethlehem sold most of its output in the East, whereas Youngstown sold most of its output in the Midwest. Was this fact relevant? Why or why not?

    c. The district court did not allow Bethlehem and Youngstown to merge. Yet in 1985 (as we saw in problem 1), the Department of Transportation allowed United Airlines (with about 7 percent of the service between Japan and the U.S. mainland) to acquire Pan Am's Pacific Division (with about 19 percent). How can you explain this?

9. On August 28, 1991, the New York State Electric and Gas Corporation filed a request for a 10.7 percent increase in electric revenues. The reasons given to justify the increase were that the value of the firm's plant and equipment had increased by $140 million, operating costs had increased, and investors required a higher rate of return.

   a. Why should an increase in the value of the firm's plant and equipment result in an increase in the amount of revenue allowed by the Public Service Commission?

   b. Why should an increase in operating costs have the same effect?

   c. Why should the attitude of investors regarding what they require as a rate of return be relevant here?

10. During the 2000s an enormous amount of attention was devoted to global warming. According to many scientists, increases in carbon dioxide and other greenhouse gases may produce significant climatic changes over the next century. To cope with this potential problem, it has been suggested that firms reduce energy consumption and switch to nonfossil fuels. William Nordhaus, a leading expert on this topic, estimated that the worldwide costs (in 1989 U.S. dollars) of various percentage reductions in the quantity of greenhouse gases emitted into the atmosphere would be as shown in the following figure.

Cost of Greenhouse Gases in the Atmosphere

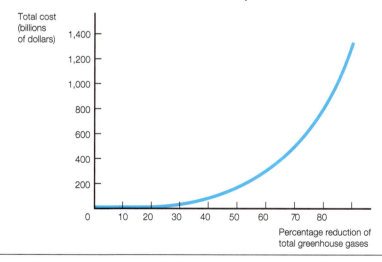

Source: R. Dornbusch and J. Poterba, eds., *Global Warming: Economic Policy Responses* (Cambridge, MA: MIT Press, 1991), p. 50.

a. Does this graph show the cost of pollution or the cost of pollution control?

b. Can this graph alone indicate the socially optimal amount of greenhouse gases that should be emitted into the atmosphere? Why or why not?

c. If world output is about $20 trillion, by what percentage would that world output be reduced if the countries of the world agreed to cut greenhouse gas emission by 50 percent?

d. The single most common policy proposed to decrease greenhouse gas emissions is a carbon tax—a tax on fossil fuels in proportion to the amount of carbon they emit when burned. Why would such a tax have the desired effect?

OPTIMIZATION TECHNIQUES

To begin this appendix, we describe marginal analysis—a powerful tool that illuminates many central aspects of decision making. Economists think at the margins. Virtually all the rules we study about optimal behavior of firms and individuals are driven by this concept.

Next, we examine the basic elements of differential calculus, including the rules of differentiation and the use of a derivative to maximize a function such as profit or minimize one such as cost. Differentiation tells us what changes will occur in one variable (the dependent variable) when a small (marginal) change is made in another variable (the independent variable). Therefore, marginal analysis can be implemented by the use of differentiation.

Finally, we examine constrained optimization, including Lagrangian multipliers. When managers want to maximize profit, such maximization or minimization is often subject to constraints (such as producing a certain amount to adhere to a contract or utilizing a certain amount of labor in a union agreement).

FUNCTIONAL RELATIONSHIPS

Frequently a relationship between economic variables is represented by a table or graph. Although tables and graphs are helpful, another way of expressing economic relationships is with equations. For example, how can the relationship between the number of units sold and the price be expressed in an equation? One way is to use the following functional notation:

$$Q = f(P) \tag{A.1}$$

where Q is the number of units sold and P is price. This equation should be read as "The number of units sold is a function of price," which means that the number of units sold *depends* on price. In other words, the number of units sold is the *dependent* variable, and price is the *independent* variable.

Equation (A.1) is useful, but it does not tell us *how* the number of units sold depends on price. A more specific representation of this relationship is

$$Q = 200 - 5P \tag{A.2}$$

This equation says that if the price equals $10, the number of units sold should be $200 - 5(10) = 150$.

MARGINAL ANALYSIS

Marginal value The change in the dependent variable associated with a one-unit change in a particular independent variable.

Marginal profit The change in total profit associated with a one-unit change in output.

The **marginal value** of a dependent variable is defined as the change in this dependent variable associated with a one-unit change in a particular independent variable. As an illustration, consider Table A.1, which shows in columns 1 and 2 the total profit of the Roland Corporation if the number of units produced equals various amounts. In this case, total profit is the dependent variable and output is the independent variable. Therefore, the marginal value of profit, called the **marginal profit**, is the change in total profit associated with a one-unit change in output.

Column 3 of Table A.1 shows the value of marginal profit. If output increases from zero to one unit, column 2 shows that the total profit increases by $100 (from $0 to $100). Therefore, the marginal profit in column 3 equals $100 if the output is one unit. If the output increases from one to two units, the total profit increases by $150 (from $100 to $250). Therefore, the marginal profit in column 3 equals $150 if the output is increased from one to two units.

The central point about a marginal relationship of this sort is that the dependent variable—in this case, total profit—is maximized when its marginal value shifts from positive to negative. To see this, consider Table A.1. So long as marginal profit is positive, the Roland Corporation can raise its total profit by increasing output. For example, if output increases from five to six units, the marginal profit is positive ($150); therefore, the firm's total profit goes up (by $150). But when marginal profit shifts from positive to negative, total profit *falls* with any further increase in output. In Table A.1, this point is reached when the firm produces seven units of output. If output increases beyond seven units, marginal profit shifts from positive to negative—and total profit goes down (by $50). So we can see that the dependent variable—in this case, total profit—is maximized when its marginal value shifts from positive to negative.

TABLE A.1

Relationship between Output and Profit: Roland Corporation

(1) Number of Units of Output per Day	(2) Total Profit	(3) Marginal Profit	(4) Average Profit
0	0	—	—
1	100	100	100
2	250	150	125
3	600	350	200
4	1,000	400	250
5	1,350	350	270
6	1,500	150	250
7	1,550	50	221.4
8	1,500	−50	187.5
9	1,400	−100	155.5
10	1,200	−200	120

Because managers are interested in determining how to maximize profit (or other performance measures), this is a useful result. It emphasizes the importance of looking at marginal values—and the hazards that may arise if average values are used instead. In Table A.1, **average profit**—that is, total profit divided by output—is shown in column 4. It may seem reasonable to choose the output level that gives the highest average profit; countless managers have done so. But this is not the correct decision if managers want to maximize profit. Instead, as stressed in the previous paragraph, managers should choose the output level at which marginal profit shifts from positive to negative.

To prove this, we need only find the output level in Table A.1 at which average profit is highest. Based on a comparison of the figures in column 4, this output level is five units; and according to column 2, the total profit at this output level equals $1,350. But we found that the output level at which marginal profit shifts from positive to negative is seven units; and according to column 2, the total profit at this point equals $1,550. In other words, the total profit is $200 higher if the output level is seven rather than five units. Thus if managers of this firm were to choose the output level at which average profit is highest, they would sacrifice $200 per day in profits.

It is important to understand the relationship between average and marginal values. Because the marginal value represents the change in the total, the average

Average profit The total profit divided by output.

value must increase if the marginal value is greater than the average value. Similarly, the average value must decrease if the marginal value is less than the average value. Table A.1 illustrates these propositions. For the first to fifth units of output, the marginal profit is greater than the average profit. Because the extra profit from each additional unit is greater than the average, the average is pulled up as more units are produced. For the sixth to tenth units of output, the marginal profit is less than the average profit. Because the extra profit from each additional unit is less than the average, the average is pulled down as more units are produced.

RELATIONSHIPS AMONG TOTAL, MARGINAL, AND AVERAGE VALUES

To further explore the relationships among total, marginal, and average values, consider Figure A.1, which shows the relationships among total, average, and marginal profit, on the one hand, and output, on the other hand, for the Roland Corporation. The relationship between output and profit is exactly the same as in Table A.1; but rather than using particular numbers to designate output or profit, we use symbols such as Q_0 and Q_1 for output levels and π_0 for a profit level. This makes the results valid in general, not just for a particular set of numerical values.

First note that Figure A.1 contains two panels. The upper panel (panel A) shows the relationship between total profit and output levels, whereas the lower panel (panel B) shows the relationship between average profit and marginal profit, on the one hand, and output levels, on the other. The horizontal scale of panel A is the same as that of panel B, so a given output level, like Q_0, is the same distance from the origin (along the horizontal axis) in panel A as in panel B.

In practice we seldom are presented with data concerning both (1) the relationship between total profit and output and (2) the relationship between average profit and output because it is relatively simple to derive the latter relationship from the former. How can this be done? Take any output level, say Q_0. *At this output level, the average profit equals the slope of the straight line from the origin to point E, the point on the total profit curve corresponding to output level Q_0.* To see that this is the case, note that the average profit at this output level equals π_0/Q_0, where π_0 is the level of total profit if the output level is Q_0. Because the slope of any straight line equals the vertical distance between two points on the line divided by the horizontal distance between them, the slope of the line from the origin to point E equals π_0/Q_0.[1] Thus the slope of line $0E$ equals the average profit at this output level. (In other words, K_0 in panel B of Figure A.1 is equal to the slope of line $0E$.) To determine the relationship between average profit and output from the relationship between total profit and output, we repeat this procedure for each level of output, not just Q_0. The resulting average profit curve is shown in panel B.

Turning to the relationship between marginal profit and output (in panel B), it is relatively simple to derive this relationship also from the relationship between

1. The vertical distance between the origin and the point E equals π_0, and the horizontal distance between these two points equals Q_0. Therefore, the vertical distance divided by the horizontal distance equals π_0/Q_0.

Total Profit, Average Profit, and Marginal Profit: Roland Corporation

The average and marginal profit curves in panel B can be derived geometrically from the total profit curve in panel A.

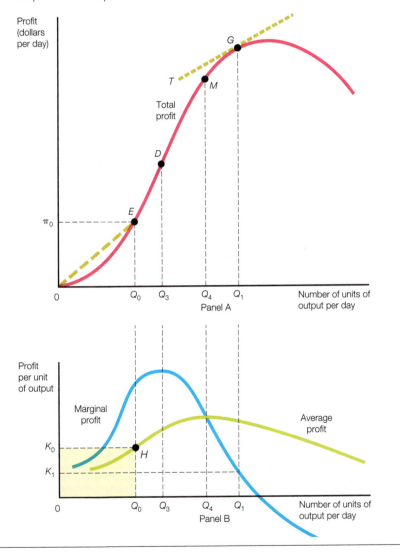

total profit and output (in panel A). Take any output level, say Q_1. *At this output level, the marginal profit equals the slope of the tangent to the total profit curve (in panel A) at the point where the output level is Q_1.* In other words, the marginal profit equals the slope of line T in Figure A.1, which is tangent to the total profit curve at point G. As a first step toward seeing why this is true, consider Figure A.2, which provides a magnified picture of the total profit curve in the neighborhood of point G.

Recall that marginal profit is defined as the extra profit resulting from a very small increase (specifically, a one-unit increase) in output. If the output level increases from Q_1 to Q_2, the total profit increases from π_1 to π_2, as shown in Figure A.2. Therefore, the extra profit per unit of output is $(\pi_2 - \pi_1)/(Q_2 - Q_1)$, which is the slope of the GK line. But this increase in output is rather large. Suppose we decrease Q_2 so it is closer to Q_1. In particular, let the new value of Q_2 be Q_2'. If output increases from Q_1 to Q_2', the extra profit per unit of output equals $(\pi_2' - \pi_1)/(Q_2' - Q_1)$, which is the slope of the GL line. If we further decrease Q_2 until the distance between Q_1 and Q_2 is extremely small, the slope of the tangent (line T) at

---

FIGURE A.2

Marginal Profit Equals the Slope of the Tangent to the Total Profit Curve

As the distance between Q_1 and Q_2 becomes extremely small, the slope of line T becomes a good estimate of $(\pi_2 - \pi_1)/(Q_2 - Q_1)$.

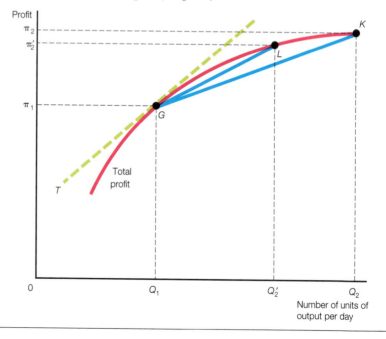

---

point G becomes a good estimate of $(\pi_2 - \pi_1)/(Q_2 - Q_1)$. In the limit, for changes in output in a very small neighborhood around Q_1, the slope of the tangent is marginal profit. (This slope equals K_1 in panel B of Figure A.1.) To determine the relationship between marginal profit and output from the relationship between total profit and output, we repeat this procedure for each level of output, not just Q_1. The resulting marginal profit curve is shown in panel B of Figure A.1.

Sometimes we are given an average profit curve like that in panel B of Figure A.1 but not the total profit curve. To derive the latter curve from the former, note that total profit equals average profit times output. Hence, if output equals Q_0, total profit equals K_0 times Q_0. In other words, π_0 in panel A equals the area of rectangle $0K_0HQ_0$ in panel B. To derive the relationship between total profit and output from the relationship between average profit and output, we repeat this procedure for each level of output. That is, we find the area of the appropriate rectangle of this sort corresponding to each output level, not just Q_0. The resulting total profit curve is shown in panel A.

Finally, two further points should be made concerning the total, average, and marginal profit curves in Figure A.1. First, you should be able to tell by a glance at panel A that the marginal profit increases as the output level rises from zero to Q_3 and that it decreases as output rises further. Why is this so obvious from panel A? Because the slope of the total profit curve increases as we move from the origin to point D. In other words, lines drawn tangent to the total profit curve become steeper as we move from the origin to point D. Because marginal profit equals the slope of this tangent, it must increase as the output level rises from zero to Q_3. To the right of point D, the slope of the total profit curve decreases as the output level increases. That is, lines drawn tangent to the total profit curve become less steep as we move to the right of point D. Consequently, because marginal profit equals the slope of this tangent, it too must decrease when the output level rises beyond Q_3.

Second, panel B of Figure A.1 confirms the following proposition: *The average profit curve must be rising if it is below the marginal profit curve, and it must be falling if it is above the marginal profit curve.* At output levels below Q_4, the average profit curve is below the marginal profit curve; therefore, the average profit curve is rising because the higher marginal profits are pulling up the average profits. At output levels above Q_4, the average profit curve is above the marginal profit curve; therefore, the average profit curve is falling because the lower marginal profits are pulling down the average profits. At Q_4, the straight line drawn from the origin to point M is just tangent to the total cost curve. Therefore, the average profit and marginal profit are equal at output level Q_4.

THE CONCEPT OF A DERIVATIVE

In the case of the Roland Corporation, we used Table A.1 (which shows the relationship between the firm's output and profit) to find the profit-maximizing output level. Frequently a table of this sort is too cumbersome or inaccurate to be useful for this purpose. Instead we use an equation to represent the relationship between the variable we are trying to maximize (in this case, profit) and the variable or variables under the control of the decision maker (in this case, output). Given an equation of this sort, we can employ the powerful concepts and techniques of differential calculus to find optimal decision solutions.

In previous sections, we defined the *marginal value* as the change in a dependent variable resulting from a one-unit change in an independent variable. If Y is the dependent variable and X is the independent variable,

$$Y = f(X) \tag{A.3}$$

according to the notation in equation (A.1). Using Δ (called *delta*) to denote change, we can express a change in the independent variable as ΔX, and we can express a change in the dependent variable as ΔY. Thus the marginal value of Y can be estimated by

$$\frac{\text{Change in } Y}{\text{Change in } X} = \frac{\Delta Y}{\Delta X} \tag{A.4}$$

For example, if a two-unit increase in X results in a one-unit increase in Y, $\Delta X = 2$ and $\Delta Y = 1$; this means the marginal value of Y is about one-half. That is, the dependent variable Y increases by about one-half if the independent variable X increases by 1.[2]

Unless the relationship between Y and X can be represented as a straight line (as in Figure A.3), the value of $\Delta Y/\Delta X$ is not constant. For example, consider the relationship between Y and X in Figure A.4. If a movement occurs from point G to point H, a relatively small change in X (from X_1 to X_2) is associated with a big change in Y (from Y_1 to Y_2). Therefore, between points G and H, the value of $\Delta Y/\Delta X$, which equals $(Y_2 - Y_1)/(X_2 - X_1)$, is relatively large. On the other hand, if a movement occurs from point K to point L, a relatively large change in X (from X_3 to X_4) is associated with a small change in Y (from Y_3 to Y_4). Consequently, between points K and L, the value of $\Delta Y/\Delta X$, which equals $(Y_4 - Y_3)/(X_4 - X_3)$, is relatively small.

The value of $\Delta Y/\Delta X$ is related to the steepness or flatness of the curve in Figure A.4. Between points G and H the curve is relatively *steep*; this means that a *small* change in X results in a *large* change in Y. Consequently $\Delta Y/\Delta X$ is relatively large. Between points K and L the curve is relatively *flat*; this means that a *large* change in X results in a *small* change in Y. Consequently $\Delta Y/\Delta X$ is relatively small.

The derivative of Y with respect to X is defined as the limit of $\Delta Y/\Delta X$ as ΔX approaches zero. Because the derivative of Y with respect to X is denoted by dY/dX, this definition can be restated as

$$\frac{dY}{dX} = \lim_{\Delta X \to 0} \frac{\Delta Y}{\Delta X} \tag{A.5}$$

2. Why do we say that Y increases by about ½ rather than by exactly ½? Because Y may not be linearly related to X.

FIGURE A.3

Linear Relationships between Y and X

The relationship between Y and X can be represented as a straight line.

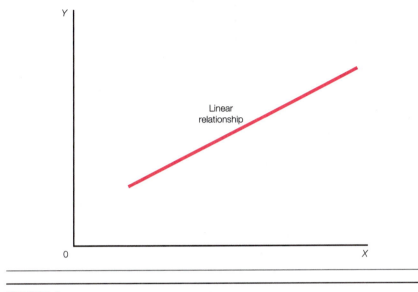

FIGURE A.4

How the Value of $\Delta Y/\Delta X$ Varies Depending on the Steepness or Flatness of the Relationship between Y and X

Between points G and H, the curve is steep, so $\Delta Y/\Delta X$ is large. Between points K and L, the curve is flat, so $\Delta Y/\Delta X$ is small.

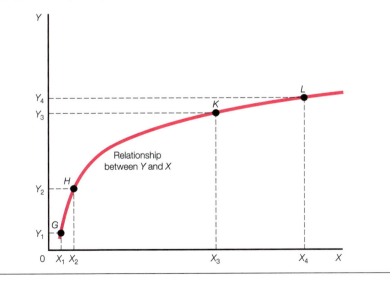

which is read "The derivative of Y with respect to X equals the limit of the ratio $\Delta Y/\Delta X$ as ΔX approaches zero." To understand what is meant by a limit, consider the function $(X - 2)$. What is the limit of this function as X approaches 2? Clearly, as X gets closer and closer to 2, $(X - 2)$ gets closer and closer to zero. What is the limit of this function as X approaches zero? Clearly, as X gets closer and closer to zero, $(X - 2)$ gets closer and closer to -2.

Graphically, the derivative of Y with respect to X equals the *slope* of the curve showing Y (on the vertical axis) as a function of X (on the horizontal axis). To see this, suppose we want to find the value of the derivative of Y with respect to X when X equals X_5 in Figure A.5. A rough measure is the value of $\Delta Y/\Delta X$ when a movement is made from point A to point C; this measure equals

$$(Y_7 - Y_5)/(X_7 - X_5)$$

which is the slope of the AC line. A better measure is the value of $\Delta Y/\Delta X$ when a movement is made from point A to point B; this measure equals

$$(Y_6 - Y_5)/(X_6 - X_5)$$

which is the slope of the AB line. Why is the latter measure better than the former? Because the distance between points A and B is less than the distance between points A and C, and what we want is the value of $\Delta Y/\Delta X$ when ΔX is as small as possible.

FIGURE A.5

Derivative as the Slope of the Curve

When X equals X_5, the derivative of Y with respect to X equals the slope of line M, the tangent to the curve at point A.

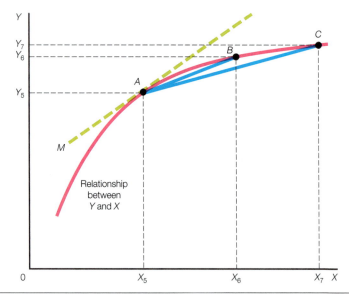

Clearly, in the limit, as ΔX approaches zero, the ratio ΔY/ΔX is equal to the slope of the line M, which is drawn tangent to the curve at point A.

HOW TO FIND A DERIVATIVE

Managers want to know how to optimize the performance of their organizations. If Y is some measure of organizational performance and X is a variable under a particular manager's control, he or she would like to know the value of X that maximizes Y. To find out, it is useful, as we will see in the next section, to know the derivative of Y with respect to X. In this section, we learn how to find this derivative.

Derivatives of Constants

If the dependent variable Y is a constant, its derivative with respect to X is always zero. That is, if $Y = a$ (where a is a constant),

$$\frac{dY}{dX} = 0 \qquad\qquad (A.6)$$

EXAMPLE Suppose $Y = 6$, as shown in Figure A.6. Because the value of Y does not change as X varies, dY/dX must be equal to zero. To see how this can also be shown geometrically, recall from the previous section that dY/dX equals the slope of the curve showing Y as a function of X. As is evident from Figure A.6, this slope equals zero, which means dY/dX must equal zero.

FIGURE A.6

Case in Which $Y = 6$

In this case, dY/dX equals zero because the slope of this horizontal line equals zero.

Derivatives of Power Functions

A power function can be expressed as

$$Y = aX^b$$

where a and b are constants. If the relationship between X and Y is of this kind, the derivative of Y with respect to X equals b times a multiplied by X raised to the $(b - 1)$ power:

$$\frac{dY}{dX} = baX^{b-1} \tag{A.7}$$

EXAMPLE Suppose $Y = 3X$, which is graphed in panel A of Figure A.7. Applying equation (A.7), we find that

$$\frac{dY}{dX} = 1 \times 3 \times X^0 = 3$$

because $a = 3$ and $b = 1$. Therefore, the value of dY/dX graphed in panel B of Figure A.7 is 3, regardless of the value of X. This makes sense: The slope of the line in panel A is 3, regardless of the value of X. Recall once again from the previous section that dY/dX equals the slope of the curve showing Y as a function of X. In this case (as in Figure A.6), the "curve" is a straight line.

EXAMPLE Suppose $Y = 2X^2$, which is graphed in panel A of Figure A.8. Applying equation (A.7), we find that

$$\frac{dY}{dX} = 2 \times 2 \times X^1 = 4X$$

because $a = 2$ and $b = 2$. Therefore, the value of dY/dX, which is graphed in panel B of Figure A.8, is proportional to X. As we would expect, dY/dX is negative when the slope of the curve in panel A is negative and positive when this slope is positive. Why? Because, as we have stressed repeatedly, dY/dX equals this slope.

We make a plea here for the actual ease of using calculus. All the calculus necessary to teach the concepts of managerial economics in this book can be summed up in one easy-to-remember formula.

If $y = kx^n$, where y is the dependent variable, i.e., its value depends on the value of x; and x is the independent variable, i.e., its value determines y's value; and n and k are parameters (just think of them as numbers), then if you want to find the impact that a change in the independent variable x has on the dependent variable y, you differentiate y with respect to x, i.e., dy/dx. Now here's the easy-to-remember formula:

$$dy/dx = nkx^{n-1}$$

In other words, when you differentiate y with respect to x, the result is nkx^{n-1}. So if $y = 4x^3$, i.e., $n = 3$ and $k = 4$, then $dy/dx = 12x^2$ with $nk = 3 \times 4 = 12$ and $n -$

FIGURE A.7

Case in Which $Y = 3X$

In this case, dY/dX equals 3 because the slope of the line in panel A equals 3.

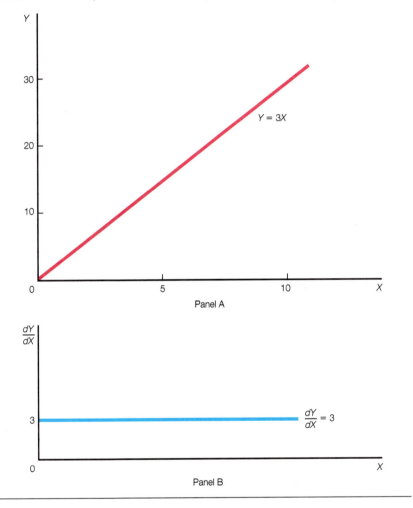

Panel A

Panel B

$1 = 2$. Memorize the formula above, and you will have all the calculus you need to understand every numerical example in the book.

Derivatives of Sums and Differences

Suppose U and W are two variables, each of which depends on X. That is,

$$U = g(X) \text{ and } W = h(X)$$

609

Case in Which $Y = 2X^2$

In this case, $dY/dX = 4X$ because the slope of the curve in panel A equals $4X$.

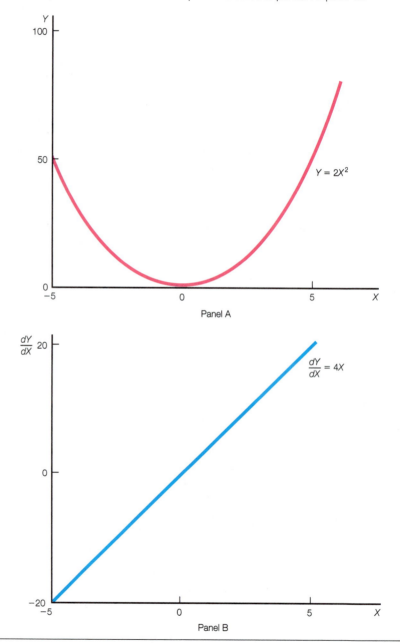

Panel A

Panel B

The functional relationship between U and X is denoted by g, and that between W and X is denoted by h. Suppose further that

$$Y = U + W$$

In other words, Y is the sum of U and W. If so, the derivative of Y with respect to X equals the sum of the derivatives of the individual terms:

$$\frac{dY}{dX} = \frac{dU}{dX} + \frac{dW}{dX} \tag{A.8}$$

On the other hand, if

$$Y = U - W$$

the derivative of Y with respect to X equals the difference between the derivatives of the individual terms:

$$\frac{dY}{dX} = \frac{dU}{dX} - \frac{dW}{dX} \tag{A.9}$$

EXAMPLE Consider the case in which $U = g(X) = 3X^3$ and $W = h(X) = 4X^2$. If $Y = U + W = 3X^3 + 4X^2$,

$$\frac{dY}{dX} = 9X^2 + 8X \tag{A.10}$$

To see why, recall from equation (A.8) that

$$\frac{dY}{dX} = \frac{dU}{dX} + \frac{dW}{dX} \tag{A.11}$$

Applying equation (A.7), we have

$$\frac{dU}{dX} = 9X^2 \text{ and } \frac{dW}{dX} = 8X$$

Substituting these values of the derivatives into equation (A.11), we obtain equation (A.10).

EXAMPLE Suppose $Y = U - W$, where $U = 8X^2$ and $W = 9X$. Then

$$\frac{dY}{dX} = 16X - 9$$

because, according to equation (A.9),

$$\frac{dY}{dX} = \frac{dU}{dX} - \frac{dW}{dX}$$

and, applying equation (A.7), we have

$$\frac{dU}{dX} = 16X \text{ and } \frac{dW}{dX} = 9$$

Derivatives of Products

The derivative of the product of two terms is equal to the sum of the first term multiplied by the derivative of the second plus the second term times the derivative of the first. Consequently, if $Y = UW$, we have

$$\frac{dY}{dX} = U\frac{dW}{dX} + W\frac{dU}{dX} \tag{A.12}$$

EXAMPLE If $Y = 6X(3 - X^2)$, we can let $U = 6X$ and $W = 3 - X^2$; then

$$\begin{aligned}
\frac{dY}{dX} &= 6X\frac{dW}{dX} + (3 - X^2)\frac{dU}{dX} \\
&= 6X(-2X) + (3 - X^2)(6) \\
&= -12X^2 + 18 - 6X^2 \\
&= 18 - 18X^2
\end{aligned}$$

The first term, $6X$, is multiplied by the derivative of the second term, $-2X$, and the result is added to the second term, $3 - X^2$, times the derivative of the first, 6. As indicated, the result is $18 - 18X^2$.

Derivatives of Quotients

If $Y = U/W$, the derivative of Y with respect to X equals

$$\frac{dY}{dX} = \frac{W(dU/dX) - U(dW/dX)}{W^2} \tag{A.13}$$

In other words, the derivative of the quotient of two terms equals the denominator times the derivative of the numerator minus the numerator times the derivative of the denominator—all divided by the square of the denominator.

EXAMPLE Consider the problem of finding the derivative of the expression

$$Y = \frac{5X^3}{3 - 4X}$$

If we let $U = 5X^3$ and $W = 3 - 4X$,

$$\frac{dU}{dX} = 15X^2 \text{ and } \frac{dW}{dX} = -4$$

Consequently, applying equation (A.13), we have

$$\frac{dY}{dX} = \frac{(3 - 4X)(15X^2) - 5X^3(-4)}{(3 - 4X)^2}$$

$$= \frac{45X^2 - 60X^3 + 20X^3}{(3 - 4X)^2}$$

$$= \frac{45X^2 - 40X^3}{(3 - 4X)^2}$$

Derivatives of a Function of a Function (the Chain Rule)

Sometimes a variable depends on another variable, which in turn depends on a third variable. For example, suppose $Y = f(W)$ and $W = g(X)$. Under these circumstances, the derivative of Y with respect to X equals

$$\frac{dY}{dX} = \left(\frac{dY}{dW}\right)\left(\frac{dW}{dX}\right) \tag{A.14}$$

In other words, to find this derivative, we find the derivative of Y with respect to W and multiply it by the derivative of W with respect to X.

EXAMPLE Suppose $Y = 4W + W^3$ and $W = 3X^2$. To find dY/dX, we begin by finding dY/dW and dW/dX:

$$\frac{dY}{dW} = 4 + 3W^2$$

$$= 4 + 3(3X^2)^2$$
$$= 4 + 27X^4$$

$$\frac{dW}{dX} = 6X$$

Then, to find dY/dX, we multiply dY/dW and dW/dX:

$$\frac{dY}{dX} = (4 + 27X^4)(6X)$$

$$= 24X + 162X^5$$

USING DERIVATIVES TO SOLVE MAXIMIZATION AND MINIMIZATION PROBLEMS

Having determined how to find the derivative of Y with respect to X, we now see how to determine the value of X that maximizes or minimizes Y. *The central point is that a maximum or minimum point can occur only if the slope of the curve showing Y on the vertical axis and X on the horizontal axis equals zero.* To see this, suppose Y equals the profit of the Monroe Company and X is its output level. If the relationship between Y and X is as shown by the curve in panel A of Figure A.9, the

Value of the Derivative When Y Is a Maximum

When Y is a maximum (at $X = 10$), dY/dX equals zero.

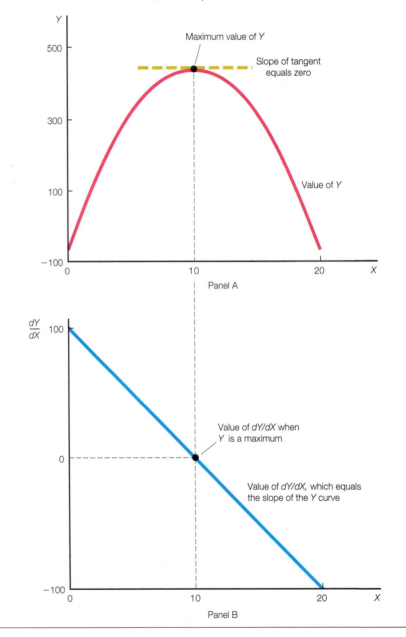

Panel A

Panel B

maximum value of Y occurs when $X = 10$, and at this value of X the slope of the curve equals zero.

Because the derivative of Y with respect to X equals the slope of this curve, it follows that Y can be a maximum or minimum only if this derivative equals zero. To see that Y really is maximized when this derivative equals zero, note that the relationship between Y and X in Figure A.9 is

$$Y = -50 + 100X - 5X^2 \qquad\qquad \text{(A.15)}$$

which means that

$$\frac{dY}{dX} = 100 - 10X$$

Therefore, if this derivative equals zero,

$$100 - 10X = 0 \qquad\qquad \text{(A.16)}$$
$$X = 10$$

This is the value of X where Y is maximized, as we saw in the previous paragraph. The key point here is that *to find the value of X that maximizes or minimizes Y, we must find the value of X where this derivative equals zero.* Panel B of Figure A.9 shows graphically that this derivative equals zero when Y is maximized.

However, on the basis of only the fact that this derivative is zero, we cannot distinguish between a point on the curve where Y is maximized and a point where Y is minimized. For example, in Figure A.10, this derivative is zero both when $X = 5$ and when $X = 15$. When $X = 15$, Y is a maximum; when $X = 5$, Y is a minimum. To distinguish between a maximum and a minimum, we must find the *second derivative of Y with respect to X, which is denoted d^2Y/dX^2 and is the derivative of dY/dX.* For example, in Figure A.9, the second derivative of Y with respect to X is the derivative of the function in equation (A.16); therefore, it equals -10.

The second derivative measures the slope of the curve showing the relationship between dY/dX (the first derivative) and X. Just as the first derivative (that is, dY/dX) measures the slope of the Y curve in panel A of Figure A.10, the second derivative (that is, d^2Y/dX^2) measures the slope of the dY/dX curve in panel B of Figure A.10. In other words, just as the first derivative measures the slope of the total profit curve, the second derivative measures the slope of the marginal profit curve. The second derivative is important because it is always *negative* at a point of *maximization* and always *positive* at a point of *minimization.* Therefore, *to distinguish between maximization and minimization points, all we have to do is determine whether the second derivative at each point is positive or negative.*

To understand why the second derivative is always negative at a maximization point and always positive at a minimization point, consider Figure A.10. When the second derivative is negative, this means the slope of the dY/dX curve in panel B is negative. Because dY/dX equals the slope of the Y curve in panel A, this in turn means the slope of the Y curve decreases as X increases. At a maximum point,

FIGURE A.10

Using the Second Derivative to Distinguish Maxima from Minima

At maxima (such as $X = 15$), d^2Y/dX^2 is negative; at minima (such as $X = 5$), d^2Y/dX^2 is positive.

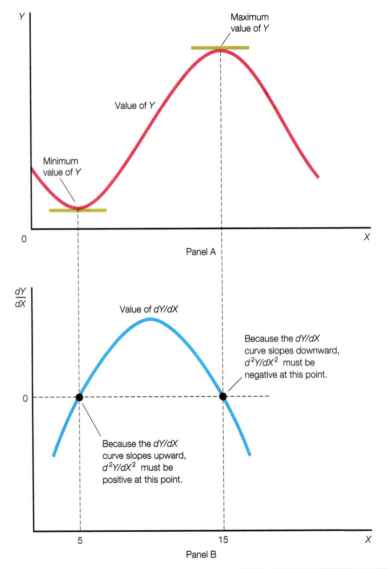

such as when $X = 15$, this must be the case. On the other hand, when the second derivative is positive, this means the slope of the dY/dX curve in panel B is positive, which is another way of saying that the slope of the Y curve in panel A increases as X increases. At a minimum point, such as when $X = 5$, this must be the case.

EXAMPLE To illustrate how we can use derivatives to solve maximization and minimization problems, suppose the relationship between profit and output at the Kantor Corporation is

$$Y = -1 + 9X - 6X^2 + X^3$$

where Y equals annual profit (in millions of dollars) and X equals annual output (in millions of units). This equation is valid only for values of X that equal 3 or less; capacity limitations prevent the firm from producing more than 3 million units per year. To find the values of output that maximize or minimize profit, we find the derivative of Y with respect to X and set it equal to zero:

$$\frac{dY}{dX} = 9 - 12X + 3X^2 = 0 \tag{A.17}$$

Solving this equation for X, we find that two values of X—1 and 3—result in this derivative being zero.[3]

To determine whether each of these two output levels maximizes or minimizes profit, we find the value of the second derivative at these two values of X. Taking the derivative of dY/dX, which is shown in equation (A.17) to equal $9 - 12X + 3X^2$, we find that

$$\frac{d^2Y}{dX^2} = -12 + 6X$$

If $X = 1$,

$$\frac{d^2Y}{dX^2} = -12 + 6(1) = -6$$

Because the second derivative is negative, profit is a maximum (at 3) when output equals 1 million units. If $X = 3$,

$$\frac{d^2Y}{dX^2} = -12 + 6(3) = 6$$

Because the second derivative is positive, profit is a minimum (at -1) when output equals 3 million units.

MARGINAL COST EQUALS MARGINAL REVENUE AND THE CALCULUS OF OPTIMIZATION

Once you know how elementary calculus can be used to solve optimization problems, it is easy to see that the fundamental rule for profit maximization—set marginal cost equal to marginal revenue—is based on the calculus of optimization. Figure A.11 shows a firm's total cost and total revenue functions. Because total profit equals total revenue minus total cost, it equals the vertical distance between

3. If an equation is of the general quadratic form, $Y = aX^2 + bX + c$, the values of X at which Y is 0 are

$$X = \frac{-b \pm (b^2 - 4ac)^{0.5}}{2a}$$

In the equation in the text, $a = 3$, $b = -12$, and $c = 9$. Hence

$$X = \frac{12 \pm (144 - 108)^{0.5}}{6} = 2 \pm 1$$

Therefore, $dY/dX = 0$ when X equals 1 or 3.

Marginal Revenue Equals Marginal Cost Rule for Profit

At the profit-maximizing output of Q_1, marginal revenue (equal to the slope of line R) equals marginal cost (the slope of line S).

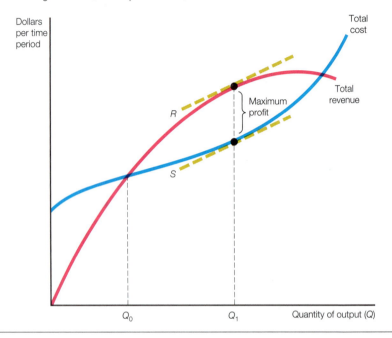

the total revenue and total cost curves at any level of output. This distance is maximized at output Q_1, where the slopes of the total revenue and total cost curves are equal. Because the slope of the total revenue curve is marginal revenue and the slope of the total cost curve is marginal cost, profit is maximized when marginal cost equals marginal revenue.

Inspection of Figure A.11 shows that Q_1 must be the profit-maximizing output. Output levels below Q_0 result in losses (because total cost exceeds total revenue) and obviously do not maximize profit. As output increases beyond Q_0, total revenue rises more rapidly than total cost, so profit must be going up. So long as the slope of the total revenue curve (which equals marginal revenue) exceeds the slope of the total cost curve (which equals marginal cost), profit will continue to rise as output increases. But when these slopes become equal (that is, when marginal revenue equals marginal cost), profit no longer will rise but will be at a maximum. These slopes become equal at an output level of Q_1, so this must be the profit-maximizing output level. After output Q_1, profit decreases because marginal cost exceeds marginal revenue.

Using calculus, we can readily understand why managers maximize profit by setting marginal cost equal to marginal revenue. The first thing to note is that

$$\pi = TR - TC$$

where π equals total profit, TR equals total revenue, and TC equals total cost. Taking the derivative of π with respect to Q (output), we find that

$$\frac{d\pi}{dQ} = \frac{dTR}{dQ} - \frac{dTC}{dQ}$$

For π to be a maximum, this derivative must be zero, so it must be true that

$$\frac{dTR}{dQ} = \frac{dTR}{dQ} \tag{A.18}$$

And because marginal revenue is defined as dTR/dQ and marginal cost is defined as dTC/dQ, marginal revenue must equal marginal cost.[4]

PARTIAL DIFFERENTIATION AND THE MAXIMIZATION OF MULTIVARIABLE FUNCTIONS

Up to this point, we have examined situations in which a variable depends on only one other variable. Although such situations exist, in many cases a variable depends on a number (often a large number) of other variables, not just one. For example, the Merrimack Company produces two goods, and its profit depends on the amount that it produces of each good. That is,

$$\pi = f(Q_1, Q_2) \tag{A.19}$$

where π is the firm's profit, Q_1 is its output level of the first good, and Q_2 is its output level of the second good.

To find the value of each of the independent variables (Q_1 and Q_2 in this case) that maximizes the dependent variable (π in this case), we need to know the marginal effect of each independent variable on the dependent variable, *holding constant the effect of all other independent variables*. For example, in this case we need to know the marginal effect of Q_1 on π when Q_2 is held constant, and we need to know the marginal effect of Q_2 on π when Q_1 is held constant. To get this information, we obtain the partial derivative of π with respect to Q_1 and the partial derivative of π with respect to Q_2.

To obtain the partial derivative of π with respect to Q_1, denoted $\partial\pi/\partial Q_1$, we apply the rules for finding a derivative (on pages 607–613) to equation (A.19), but we treat Q_2 as a constant. Similarly, to obtain the partial derivative of π with respect to Q_2, denoted $\partial\pi/\partial Q_2$, we apply these rules to equation (A.19), but we treat Q_1 as a constant.

4. Two points should be noted. (1) For profit to be maximized, $d^2\pi/dQ^2$ must be negative. (2) The analysis in this section (as well as in earlier sections) results in the determination of a *local* maximum. Sometimes a local maximum is not a global maximum. For example, under some circumstances, the profit-maximizing (or loss-minimizing) output is zero.

EXAMPLE Suppose the relationship between the Merrimack Company's profit (in thousands of dollars) and its output level of each good is

$$\pi = -20 + 113.75Q_1 + 80Q_2 - 10Q_1^2 - 10Q_2^2 - 5Q_1Q_2 \qquad \text{(A.20)}$$

To find the partial derivative of π with respect to Q_1, we treat Q_2 as a constant and find that

$$\frac{\partial \pi}{\partial Q_1} = 113.75 - 20Q_1 - 5Q_2$$

To find the partial derivative of π with respect to Q_2, we treat Q_1 as a constant and find that

$$\frac{\partial \pi}{\partial Q_2} = 80 - 20Q_2 - 5Q_1$$

Once we have obtained the partial derivatives, it is relatively simple to determine the values of the independent variables that maximize the dependent variable. All we have to do is *set all the partial derivatives equal to zero*. In the case of the Merrimack Company,

$$\frac{\partial \pi}{\partial Q_1} = 113.75 - 20Q_1 - 5Q_2 = 0 \qquad \text{(A.21)}$$

$$\frac{\partial \pi}{\partial Q_2} = 80 - 20Q_2 - 5Q_1 = 0 \qquad \text{(A.22)}$$

Equations (A.21) and (A.22) are two equations in two unknowns. Solving them simultaneously, we find that profit is maximized when $Q_1 = 5.0$ and $Q_2 = 2.75$. In other words, to maximize profit, the firm should produce 5.0 units of the first good and 2.75 units of the second good per period of time. If it does this, its profit will equal $374.375 thousand per period of time.[5]

To see why all the partial derivatives should be set equal to zero, consider Figure A.12, which shows the relationship in equation (A.20) among π, Q_1, and Q_2 in the range where π is close to its maximum value. As you can see, this relationship is represented by a three-dimensional surface. The maximum value of π is at point M, where this surface is level. A plane tangent to this surface at point M is parallel to the Q_1Q_2 plane; in other words, its slope with respect to either Q_1 or Q_2 must be zero. Because the partial derivatives in equations (A.21) and (A.22) equal these slopes, they too must equal zero at the maximum point M.[6]

CONSTRAINED OPTIMIZATION

Managers of firms and other organizations generally face constraints that limit their options. A production manager may want to minimize his or her firm's costs but may not be permitted to produce less than is required to meet the firm's con-

5. Inserting 5.0 for Q_1 and 2.75 for Q_2 in equation (20), we find that $\pi = -20 + 113.75(5) + 80(2.75) - 10(5)^2 - 10(2.75)^2 - 5(5)(2.75) = 374.375$.

6. The second-order conditions for distinguishing maxima from minima can be found in any calculus book. For present purposes, a discussion of these conditions is not essential.

Relationship among π, Q_1, and Q_2

At M, the point where π is a maximum, the surface representing this relationship is flat; its slope with regard to either Q_1 or Q_2 is zero.

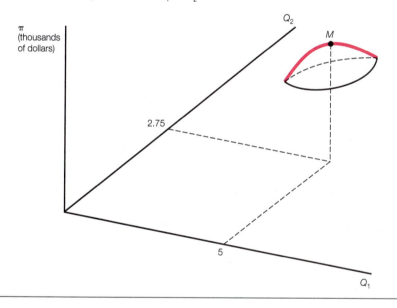

tracts with its customers. The top managers of a firm may want to maximize profits; but in the short run, they may be unable to change its product or augment its plant and equipment.

Constrained optimization problems of this sort can be solved in a number of ways. In relatively simple cases in which there is only one constraint, we can use this constraint to express a decision variable—that is, one of the variables the decision maker can choose—as a function of the other decision variables. Then we can apply the techniques for unconstrained optimization described in the previous sections. In effect, we convert the problem to one of unconstrained maximization or minimization.

To illustrate, suppose the Kloster Company produces two products, and its total cost equals

$$TC = 4Q_1^2 + 5Q_2^2 - Q_1Q_2 \qquad \text{(A.23)}$$

where Q_1 equals its output per hour of the first product and Q_2 equals its output per hour of the second product. Because of commitments to customers, the number produced of both products combined cannot be less than 30 per hour. Kloster's president wants to know what output levels of the two products minimize the firm's costs, given that the output of the first product plus the output of the second product equals 30 per hour.

This constrained optimization problem can be expressed as follows:

Minimize $\qquad\qquad\qquad TC = 4Q_1^2 + 5Q_2^2 - Q_1Q_2$

subject to $\qquad\qquad\qquad Q_1 + Q_2 = 30$

Of course the constraint is that $(Q_1 + Q_2)$ must equal 30. Solving this constraint for Q_1, we have

$$Q_1 = 30 - Q_2$$

Substituting $(30 - Q_2)$ for Q_1 in equation (A.23), it follows that

$$
\begin{aligned}
TC &= 4(30 - Q_2)^2 + 5Q_2^2 - (30 - Q_2)Q_2 \\
&= 4(900 - 60Q_2 + Q_2^2) + 5Q_2^2 - 30Q_2 + Q_2^2 \qquad\qquad \text{(A.24)} \\
TC &= 3{,}600 - 270Q_2 + 10Q_2^2
\end{aligned}
$$

The methods of unconstrained optimization just described can be used to find the value of Q_2 that minimizes TC. As indicated in earlier sections, we must obtain the derivative of TC with respect to Q_2 and set it equal to zero:

$$\frac{dTC}{dQ_2} = -270 + 20Q_2 = 0$$

$$20Q_2 = 270$$

$$Q_2 = 13.5$$

To be sure this is a minimum, not a maximum, we obtain the second derivative, which is

$$\frac{d^2 TC}{dQ_2^2} = 20$$

Because this is positive, we have found a minimum.

To find the value of Q_1 that minimizes total cost, recall that the constraint requires that

$$Q_1 + Q_2 = 30$$

which means that

$$Q_1 = 30 - Q_2$$

We know that the optimal value of Q_2 is 13.5, so the optimal value of Q_1 must be

$$Q_1 = 30 - 13.5 = 16.5$$

Summing up, if the Kloster Company wants to minimize total cost subject to the constraint that the sum of the output levels of its two products remains 30, it should produce 16.5 units of the first product and 13.5 units of the second product per hour.[7] In other words, it should produce 33 units of the first product and 27 units of the second product every two hours.

LAGRANGIAN MULTIPLIERS

If the technique described in the previous section is not feasible because the constraints are too numerous or complex, the method of Lagrangian multipliers can be used. This method of solving constrained optimization problems involves the construction of an equation—the so-called Lagrangian function—that combines the function to be minimized or maximized and the constraints. This equation is constructed so that two things are true:

1. When this equation is maximized (or minimized), the original function we want to maximize (or minimize) is in fact maximized (or minimized).

2. All the constraints are satisfied.

To illustrate how we create a Lagrangian function, reconsider the problem faced by the Kloster Company. As indicated in the previous section, this firm wants to minimize $TC = 4Q_1^2 + 5Q_2^2 - Q_1Q_2$, subject to the constraint that $Q_1 + Q_2 = 30$. The first step in constructing the Lagrangian function for this firm's problem is to restate the constraint so that an expression is formed that is equal to zero:

$$30 - Q_1 - Q_2 = 0 \qquad (A.25)$$

If we multiply this form of the constraint by an unknown factor, designated λ (*lambda*), and add the result to the function we want to minimize (in equation (A.23)), we get the Lagrangian function, which is

$$L_{TC} = 4Q_1^2 + 5Q_2^2 - Q_1Q_2 + \lambda(30 - Q_1 - Q_2) \qquad (A.26)$$

For reasons specified in the next paragraph, we can be sure that if we find the unconstrained maximum (or minimum) of the Lagrangian function, the solution will be exactly the same as the solution of the original constrained maximization (or minimization) problem. In other words, to solve the constrained optimization problem, all we have to do is optimize the Lagrangian function. For example, in the case of the Kloster Company, we must find the values of Q_1, Q_2, and λ that minimize L_{TC} in equation (A.26). To do this, we must find the partial derivative of L_{TC} with respect to each of the three variables Q_1, Q_2, and λ:

$$\frac{\partial L_{TC}}{\partial Q_1} = 8Q_1 - Q_2 - \lambda$$

$$\frac{\partial L_{TC}}{\partial Q_2} = -Q_1 + 10Q_2 - \lambda$$

$$\frac{\partial L_{TC}}{\partial \lambda} = -Q_1 - Q_2 + 30$$

7. Substituting 16.5 for Q_1 and 13.5 for Q_2 in equation (A.23), we see that the firm's total cost will equal

$TC = 4(16.5)^2 + 5(13.5)^2 - (16.5)(13.5)$
$= 4(272.25) + 5(182.25) - 222.75$
$= 1089 + 911.25 - 222.75$
$= 1,777.5$ or \$1,777.50

As indicated earlier, we must set all three of these partial derivatives equal to zero to minimize L_{TC}:

$$8Q_1 - Q_2 - \lambda = 0 \qquad (A.27)$$
$$-Q_1 + 10Q_2 - \lambda = 0 \qquad (A.28)$$
$$-Q_1 - Q_2 + 30 = 0 \qquad (A.29)$$

It is important to note that the partial derivative of the Lagrangian function with regard to λ (that is, $\partial L_{TC}/\partial \lambda$), when it is set equal to zero (in equation (A.29)), is the constraint in our original optimization problem (recall equation (A.25)). This, of course, is always true because of the way the Lagrangian function is constructed. So if this derivative is zero, we can be sure this original constraint is satisfied. And if this constraint is satisfied, the last term on the right of the Lagrangian function is zero; so the Lagrangian function boils down to the original function that we wanted to maximize (or minimize). Consequently, by maximizing (or minimizing) the Lagrangian function, we solve the original constrained optimization problem.

Returning to the Kloster Company, equations (A.27), (A.28), and (A.29) are three simultaneous equations with three unknowns—Q_1, Q_2, and λ. If we solve this system of equations for Q_1 and Q_2, we get the optimal values of Q_1 and Q_2. Subtracting equation (A.28) from equation (A.27), we find that

$$9Q_1 - 11Q_2 = 0 \qquad (A.30)$$

Multiplying equation (A.29) by 9 and adding the result to equation (A.30), we can solve for Q_2:

$$
\begin{aligned}
-9Q_1 - 9Q_2 + 270 &= 0 \\
\underline{9Q_1 - 11Q_2 = 0} & \\
-20Q_2 + 270 &= 0 \\
Q_2 = 270/20 &= 13.5
\end{aligned}
$$

Therefore, the optimal value of Q_2 is 13.5. Substituting 13.5 for Q_2 in equation (A.29), we find that the optimal value of Q_1 is 16.5.

The answer we get is precisely the same as in the previous section: The optimal value of Q_1 is 16.5, and the optimal value of Q_2 is 13.5. In other words, the Kloster Company should produce 16.5 units of the first product and 13.5 units of the second product per hour. But the method of Lagrangian multipliers described in this section is more powerful than that described in the previous section for at least two reasons: (1) It can handle more than a single constraint, and (2) the value of λ provides interesting and useful information to the decision maker.

Specifically λ, called the *Lagrangian multiplier*, measures the change in the variable to be maximized or minimized (*TC* in this case) if the constraint is relaxed by one unit. For example, if the Kloster Company wants to minimize total cost subject to the constraint that the total output of both products is 31 rather than

30, the value of λ indicates by how much the minimum value of TC will increase. What is the value of λ? According to equation (A.27),

$$8Q_1 - Q_2 - \lambda = 0$$

Because $Q_1 = 16.5$ and $Q_2 = 13.5$,

$$\lambda = 8(16.5) - 13.5 = 118.5$$

Consequently, if the constraint is relaxed so that total output is 31 rather than 30, the total cost will go up by $118.50.

For many managerial decisions, information of this sort is of great value. Suppose a customer offers the Kloster Company $115 for one of its products, but to make this product, Kloster would have to stretch its total output to 31 per hour. On the basis of the findings of the previous paragraph, Kloster would be foolish to accept this offer because this extra product would raise its costs by $118.50, which is $3.50 more than the amount the customer offers to pay for it.

COMPARING INCREMENTAL COSTS WITH INCREMENTAL REVENUES

Before concluding this appendix, we must point out that many business decisions require comparing incremental costs with incremental revenues. Typically a manager must choose among courses of action, and the relevant decision factors are the differences in costs and revenues. For example, if the managers of a machinery company are considering whether to add a new product line, they should compare the incremental cost of adding the new product line (the extra cost resulting from its addition) with the incremental revenue (the extra revenue resulting from its addition). If the incremental revenue exceeds the incremental cost, the new product line will add to the firm's profits.

Note that *incremental* cost is not the same as *marginal* cost. Whereas marginal cost is the extra cost from a very small (one-unit) increase in output, **incremental cost** is the extra cost from an output increase that may be substantial. Similarly, **incremental revenue**, unlike marginal revenue, is the extra revenue from an output increase that may be substantial. For example, suppose you want to see whether a firm's profits will increase if it doubles its output. If the incremental cost of such an output increase is $5 million and the incremental revenue is $6 million, the firm will increase its profits by $1 million if it doubles its output. Marginal cost and marginal revenue cannot tell you this because they refer to only a very small increase in output, not to a doubling of it.

Although it may seem easy to compare incremental costs with incremental revenues, in fact there are many pitfalls. One of the most common errors is the failure to recognize the irrelevance of sunk costs. Costs incurred in the past are often irrelevant in making today's decisions. Suppose you are going to make a

Incremental cost The extra cost from an output increase that may be substantial.

Incremental revenue The extra revenue from an output increase that may be substantial.

trip and you want to determine whether it will be cheaper to drive your car or to travel by plane. What costs should be included if you drive your car? Because the only incremental costs incurred will be the gas and oil (and a certain amount of wear and tear on tires, engine, and so on), these are the only costs that should be included. Costs incurred in the past, such as the original price of the car, and costs that will be the same regardless of whether you make the trip by car or plane, such as your auto insurance, should not be included. On the other hand, if you are thinking about buying a car to make this and many other trips, these costs should be included.

To illustrate the proper reasoning, consider an airline that has deliberately run extra flights that return only a little more than their out-of-pocket costs. Assume this airline faces the decision of whether to run an extra flight between city A and city B. The fully allocated costs—the out-of-pocket costs plus a certain percentage of overhead, depreciation, insurance, and other such costs—are $5,500 for the flight. The out-of-pocket costs—the actual sum this airline has to disburse to run the flight—are $3,000, and the expected revenue from the flight is $4,100. In such a case, this airline will run the flight, which is the correct decision because the flight will add $1,100 to profit. The incremental revenue from the flight is $4,100, and the incremental cost is $3,000. Overhead, depreciation, and insurance would be the same whether the flight is run or not. Therefore, fully allocated costs are misleading here; the relevant costs are out-of-pocket, not fully allocated, ones.

Errors of other kinds can also mar firms' estimates of incremental costs. For example, a firm may refuse to produce and sell some items because it is already working near capacity, and the incremental cost of producing them is judged to be high. In fact, however, the incremental cost may not be so high because the firm may be able to produce these items during the slack season (when there is plenty of excess capacity), and the potential customers may be willing to accept delivery then.

Also, incremental revenue is frequently misjudged. Consider a firm that is pondering the introduction of a new product. The firm's managers may estimate the incremental revenue from the new product without taking proper account of the effects of the new product's sales on the sales of the firm's existing products. They may think the new product will not cut into the sales of existing products; however, it may in fact do so, with the result that their estimate of incremental revenue may be too high.

DISCOUNTING AND PRESENT VALUES

When a manager chooses between two courses of action, *A* and *B*, he or she is choosing between the cash flows resulting if *A* is chosen and the cash flows if *B* is chosen. These cash flows generally occur over a number of periods. For example, if *A* is chosen, the firm may experience an outflow of $1 million this year and an inflow of $300,000 during each of the next five years. On the other hand, if *B* is chosen, the firm may experience an outflow of $1 million this year and an inflow of $250,000 for each of the next six years. How can a manager compare these two alternatives?

To answer this question, it is convenient to begin by pointing out one of the basic propositions in managerial economics: *A dollar received today is worth more than a dollar received a year from today.* Why? Because one can always invest money that is available now and obtain interest on it. If the interest rate is 6 percent, a dollar received now is equivalent to $1.06 received a year hence. Why? Because if you invest the dollar now, you'll get $1.06 in a year. Similarly, *a dollar received now is equivalent to (1.06)² dollars two years hence.* Why? Because if you invest the dollar now, you'll get 1.06 dollars in a year, and if you reinvest this amount for another year at 6 percent, you'll get $(1.06)^2$ dollars.

More generally, suppose that you can invest at a compound rate of *i* percent per year. What is the *present value*—that is, the value *today*—of a dollar received *n* years hence? Based on the foregoing argument, its present value is

$$\frac{1}{(1 + i)^n} . \tag{B.1}$$

Thus, if the interest rate is 0.10 and if $n = 4$ (which means that the dollar is received in four years), the present value of a dollar equals

$$\frac{1}{(1 + 0.10)^4} = \frac{1}{1.4641} = \$0.683.$$

In other words, the present value of the dollar is 68.3 cents.

To see that this answer is correct, let's see what would happen if you invested 68.3 cents today. As shown in Table B.1, this investment would be worth 75.1 cents after one year, 82.6 cents after two years, 90.9 cents after three years, and 1 dollar after four years. Thus, 68.3 cents is the present value of a dollar received four years hence, because if you invest 68.3 cents today, you will have exactly 1 dollar in four years.

Table B.1 shows the value of $1/(1 + i)^n$, for various values of i and n. For example, according to this table, the present value of a dollar received ten years hence is 46.3 cents if the interest rate is 0.08. To see this, note that the figure in Table B.1 corresponding to $n = 10$ and $i = 0.08$ is 0.46319.

Using this table, you can readily determine the present value of any amount received n years hence, not just 1 dollar. If you receive R_n dollars n years hence, the present value of this amount is

$$\frac{R_n}{(1 + i)^n}. \tag{B.2}$$

Thus, to determine the present value of R_n, all that you have to do is multiply R_n by $1/(1 + i)^n$. Since Table B.1 provides us with the value of $1/(1 + i)^n$, this is a simple calculation.

To illustrate, suppose you will receive \$10,000 ten years hence and the interest rate is 0.12. According to equation (B.2), the present value of this amount equals \$10,000$[1/(1 + i)^n]$. Since Table B.1 shows that $1/(1 + i)^n = 0.32197$ when

---

TABLE B.1

Value of 68.3 Cents Invested at 10 Percent Interest

Number of years hence	Return received	Value of investment
1	68.301(0.10) = 6.830¢	68.301 + 6.830 = 75.13¢
2	75.131(0.10) = 7.513¢	75.131 + 7.513 = 82.64¢
3	82.643(0.10) = 8.264¢	82.645 + 8.265 = 90.91¢
4	90.907(0.10) = 9.091¢	90.909 + 9.091 = 100.00¢

$n = 10$ and $i = 0.12$, the present value of this amount is $10,000(0.32197) = \$3,219.70$.

PRESENT VALUE OF A SERIES OF PAYMENTS

As pointed out at the beginning of this appendix, managers generally must consider situations in which cash flows occur at more than a single time. For example, investment in a new machine tool is likely to result in a cash outflow now and a series of cash inflows in the future. To determine the present value of such an investment, it is convenient to begin by considering the simple case in which you receive \$1 per year for n years, the interest rate being i. More specifically, the n receipts of \$1 occur one year from now, two years from now, ..., and n years from now. The present value of this stream of \$1 receipts is

$$\frac{1}{1+i} + \frac{1}{(1+i)^2} + \cdots + \frac{1}{(1+i)^n} = \sum_{t=1}^{n} \frac{1}{(1+i)^t}. \tag{B.3}$$

For example, the present value of \$1 to be received at the end of each of the next five years, if the interest rate is 0.10, is

$$\sum_{t=1}^{5} \frac{1}{(1+0.10)^t} = \frac{1}{(1+0.10)} + \frac{1}{(1+0.10)^2} + \frac{1}{(1+0.10)^3}$$

$$+ \frac{1}{(1+0.10)^4} + \frac{1}{(1+0.10)^5} = 0.90909 + 0.82645$$

$$+ 0.75131 + 0.68301 + 0.62092 = \$3.79. \tag{B.4}$$

To obtain each of the terms on the right in equation (B.4), we use Table B.1. For example, the final term on the right is 0.62092, which is the present value of a dollar received five years hence (if the interest rate is 0.10), according to Table B.1.

Table B.2 shows that \$3.79 is indeed the present value of \$1 to be received at the end of each of the next five years, if the interest rate is 0.10. As you can see, if you invest \$3.79 at 10 percent interest, you will be able to withdraw \$1 at the end of each year, with nothing left over or lacking. Since analysts frequently must calculate the present value of a dollar received at the end of each of the next n years, the expression in equation (B.3),

$$\sum_{t=1}^{n} 1/(1+i)^t,$$

has been tabled; the results are shown in Table B.2. For example, if you receive \$1 at the end of each of the next ten years, and if the interest rate is 0.06, the present value is \$7.36. To see this, note that the figure in Table B.2 corresponding to $n = 10$ and $i = 0.06$ is 7.3601.

TABLE B.2

Demonstration that \$3.79 (Invested at 10 Percent Interest) Provides Exactly \$1 at the End of Each of the Next Five Years

Number of years hence	Return received	Amount withdrawn	Net Value of investment
1	\$3.790(0.10) = \$.3790	\$1.00	\$3.790 + 0.3790 − 1.00 = \$3.169
2	3.169(0.10) = .3169	\$1.00	3.169 + 0.3169 − 1.00 = 2.486
3	2.486(0.10) = .2486	\$1.00	2.486 + 0.2486 − 1.00 = 1.735
4	1.735(0.10) = .1735	\$1.00	1.735 + 0.1735 − 1.00 = .909
5	0.909(0.10) = .0909	\$1.00	0.909 + 0.0909 − 1.00 = 0

More generally, if you receive R dollars at the end of each of the next n years, and if the interest rate is i, the present value is

$$\sum_{t=1}^{n} \frac{R}{(1 + i)^t} = R \sum_{t=1}^{n} \frac{1}{(1 + i)^t}. \tag{B.5}$$

Thus, the present value of \$5,000 to be received at the end of each of the next five years, if the interest rate is 0.08, is \$5,000(3.9927) = \$19,963.5, since Table B.2 shows that the value of $\sum_{t=1}^{n} 1/(1 + i)^t = 3.9927$, when $n = 5$ and $i = 0.08$.

Finally, we must consider the case in which there is a series of unequal, not equal, payments. Suppose that a payment is received at the end of each of the next n years, that the amount received at the end of the tth year is R_t, and that the interest rate is i. The present value of this series of unequal payments is

$$\sum_{t=1}^{n} \frac{R_t}{(1 + i)^t}. \tag{B.6}$$

Table B.1 can be used to help carry out this computation. For example, suppose that $i = 0.10$, that $n = 3$, and that the amount received at the end of the first year is \$3,000, the amount received at the end of the second year is \$2,000, and the amount received at the end of the third year is \$1,000. Table B.3 shows how to calculate the present value of this series of unequal payments, which in this case equals \$5,131.48.

THE USE OF PERIODS OTHER THAN A YEAR

Thus far, we have assumed that the interest or return from an invested amount is paid annually. In other words, we have assumed that a dollar invested at the begin-

---

TABLE B.3

Present Value of Stream of Unequal Payments, Where $i = 0.10$ and $n = 3$

Number of years hence	(1) Amount received R_t	(2) $\dfrac{1}{(1 + 0.10)^t}$	(1) × (2) Present value of amount received
1	$3,000	0.90909	$2,727.27
2	2,000	0.82645	1,652.89
3	1,000	0.75131	751.31
			Total $5,131.48

---

ning of a year earns interest of i percent at the end of that year. In many situations, this is not correct. Instead, interest, dividends, or other returns from an investment may be received semiannually, quarterly, monthly, or even daily. Because you earn a return in the next period on the return received in this period, the results differ from those given in previous sections of this appendix.

If interest is received *semiannually*, the present value of a dollar received n years hence is

$$\frac{1}{(1 + i/2)^{2n}},\tag{B.7}$$

where i is the annual interest rate. To understand this expression, note that the interest rate for each semiannual period is $i/2$, and that there are $2n$ semiannual periods in n years. Bearing this in mind, this expression can be derived in the same way as expression (B.1).

If interest is received *quarterly*, the present value of a dollar received n years hence is

$$\frac{1}{(1 + i/4)^{4n}},\tag{B.8}$$

where i once again is the annual interest rate. To see why this is true, note that the interest rate for each quarterly period is $i/4$, and that there are $4n$ quarterly periods in n years. Bearing this in mind, this expression can be derived in the same way as expression (B.1).

More generally, suppose that interest is received c times per year. Under these circumstances, the present value of a dollar received n years hence is

$$\frac{1}{(1 + i/c)^{cn}},\tag{B.9}$$

Table B.1 can be used to determine present values under these circumstances. To evaluate expression (B.9), let the interest rate be i/c, and let the number of years be cn; using these values, Table B.1 gives the correct answer. Thus, the present value of 1 dollar to be received 3 years hence, where the interest rate is 8 percent paid quarterly, can be obtained by finding in the table the present value of 1 dollar to be received 12 years hence where the interest rate is 2 percent. Specifically, the answer is 78.849 cents.

DETERMINING THE INTERNAL RATE OF RETURN

Previous sections of this appendix have been concerned entirely with determining the present value of a stream of cash flows. While this is of great importance in managerial economics, it also is important to calculate the internal rate of return—the interest rate that equates the present value of the cash inflows with the present value of the cash outflows. Put differently, the internal rate of return is the interest rate that makes the present value of a stream of cash flows equal zero. In other words, we want to find i where

$$R_0 + \frac{R_1}{1+i} + \frac{R_2}{(1+i)^2} + \cdots + \frac{R_n}{(1+i)^n} = 0,$$

or

$$\sum_{t=0}^{n} \frac{R_t}{(1+i)^t} = 0. \tag{B.10}$$

To solve equation (B.10) for i, it often is necessary to use trial and error (if you do not have access to a computer or calculator). The first step is to make a rough estimate of the value of i that will satisfy equation (B.10). The second step is to adjust this estimate. If the present value based on the original estimated rate of interest is *positive, increase* the value of i. If the present value based on the original estimated rate of return is *negative, reduce* the value of i. The third step is to continue to adjust this estimate until you find the value of i that will satisfy equation (B.10).

As an illustration, consider the following stream of cash flows: $R_0 = -\$5,980$, $R_1 = \$3,000$, $R_2 = \$2,000$, and $R_3 = \$2,000$. As a first step, we estimate (roughly) that the internal rate of return is in the neighborhood of 8 percent. As Table B.4 shows, the present value of this stream of cash flows, given that the interest rate is 8 percent, is \$100.12, which is positive. Thus, a higher value of i must be tried. We choose 9 percent. As Table B.4 shows, the present value of this stream of cash flows, given that the interest rate is 9 percent, is virtually zero. Thus, the internal rate of return is 9 percent.

TABLE B.4

Determination of the Internal Rate of Return

| Year | Cash flow | i = 8 percent | | i = 9 percent | |
t	R_t	$\frac{1}{(1+i)^t}$	Present value	$\frac{1}{(1+i)^t}$	Present value
0	−$5,980	1.00000	−$5,980	1.00000	−$5,980
1	$3,000	0.92593	$2,777.78	0.91743	$2,752.29
2	2,000	0.85734	1,714.68	0.84168	1,683.36
3	2,000	0.79383	1,587.66	0.77228	1,544.37
Total			100.12		0.02

If the cash flows (in years other than year 0) are all equal, there is a simpler way to determine the internal rate of return. Under these circumstances, equation (B.10) can be written:

$$R_0 + \sum_{t=1}^{n} \frac{R}{(1+i)^t} = 0,$$

where R is the cash flow in years 1 to n. Thus,

$$\sum_{t=1}^{n} \frac{1}{(1+i)^t} = \frac{-R_0}{R}. \tag{B.11}$$

Since we are given the value of $-R_0/R$, we can find the value of i in Table B.2 where the entry in the nth row equals $-R_0/R$. This value of i is the internal rate of return.

To illustrate, suppose that a machine tool costs $10,000, and that it will result in a cash inflow of $2,500 for each of the next six years. Since $R_0 = -\$10,000$ and $R = \$2,500$, the value of $-R_0/R$ is 4. Looking in the row of Table B.2 where $n = 6$, we look for the interest rate where the entry in the table is 4. Since the entry is 3.9976 when $i = 13$ percent, the internal rate of return is about 13 percent.

Finally, it is worth pointing out that if an investment yields an infinite series of equal cash flows, the present value of this series is

$$\sum_{t=1}^{\infty} \frac{R}{(1+i)^t} = R \sum_{t=1}^{\infty} \frac{1}{(1+i)^t} = \frac{R}{i}. \tag{B.12}$$

For example, if an investment yields a perpetual annual return of $4,000 per year, and if the interest rate is 8 percent, the present value of this perpetual stream of returns equals $4,000/0.08 = \$50,000$.

ANSWERS TO SELECT END-OF-CHAPTER PROBLEMS

1. Yes.

3.

Number of years in the future	Profit (millions of dollars)	$\dfrac{1}{(1+i)^t}$	Present value
1	8	0.90909	7.27272
2	10	0.82645	8.26450
3	12	0.75131	9.01572
4	14	0.68301	9.56214
5	15	0.62092	9.31380
6	16	0.56447	9.03152
7	17	0.51316	8.72372
8	15	0.46651	6.99765
9	13	0.42410	5.51330
10	10	0.38554	3.85540
			Total 77.55056

Thus, the answer is $77.55056 million.

5. a. He will receive $80(50)(\$5) = \$20,000$, from which he must pay $3,000 for the umbrellas and $3(\$3,000) = \$9,000$ for rent. Thus, his accounting profit equals $\$20,000 - \$3,000 - \$9,000$, or $8,000.

b. Since he could earn $4,000 doing construction work, his economic profit is $8,000 − $4,000 = $4,000. (For simplicity, we ignore the fact that he could have earned interest on the money he invested in this business during the summer.)

CHAPTER 2

1. a. If $Q = 20$, $P = 2,000 − 50(20) = 1,000$. Thus, price would have to equal $1,000.

b. Since $500 = 2,000 − 50Q$, $Q = 1,500/50 = 30$. Thus, it will sell 30 per month.

c. Because $Q = (2,000 − P)/50 = 40 − 0.02P$, $dQ/dP = 20.02$. Thus,

$$\left(\frac{P}{Q}\right)\left(\frac{\partial Q}{\partial P}\right) = -0.02\frac{500}{30} = -0.33.$$

d. If $-0.02\dfrac{P}{(2,000 − P)/50} = -1$,

$$-0.02\frac{50P}{2,000 − P} = -1,$$

$$P = 2,000 − P$$

$$= 2,000/2 = 1,000.$$

Thus, if price equals $1,000, the demand is of unitary elasticity.

3. a. $\dfrac{\partial Q}{\partial P}\left(\dfrac{P}{Q}\right) = \dfrac{-3(10)}{500 − 3(10) + 2(20) + 0.1(6,000)}$

$$= \frac{-30}{500 − 30 + 40 + 600} = \frac{-30}{1,110}.$$

b. $\dfrac{\partial Q}{\partial I}\left(\dfrac{I}{Q}\right) = \dfrac{0.1(6,000)}{1,110} = \dfrac{600}{1,110}.$

c. $\partial\dfrac{Q}{\partial P_r}\left(\dfrac{P_r}{Q}\right) = \dfrac{2(20)}{1,110} = \dfrac{40}{1,110}.$

d. Population is assumed to be essentially constant (or to have no significant effect on Q, other than via whatever effect it has on per capita disposable income).

6. a. Because there are lots of very close substitutes for a particular brand, but not for cigarettes as a whole. It appears that the elasticity was less than −2.

b. No. More will be said about estimating demand functions in Chapter 5.

8. No. The fact that the elasticity of demand with respect to advertising is relatively low (0.003) does not necessarily mean that an additional dollar spent on advertising would not be profitable, or that the last dollar spent was not profitable.

9. a. −3.1.

b. Decreases.

c. 2.3.

d. 0.1.

e. The quantity demanded will increase by 10 percent. (Note that Q in this problem is defined as quantity demanded *per capita*.)

CHAPTER 3

3.

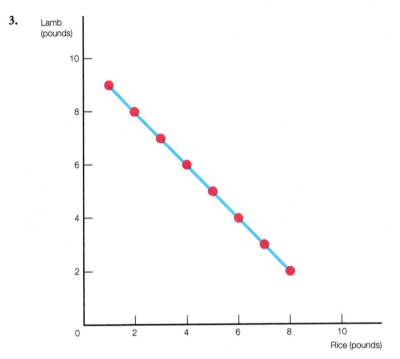

5. His budget line is as follows:

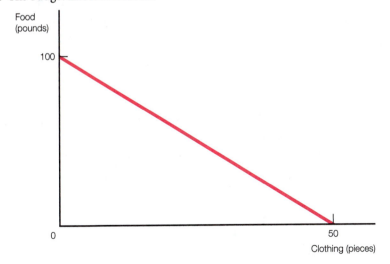

7. Maria will maximize utility at point A, where she purchases 15 units of both chips and salsa. Note that her indifference curves are 90-degree angles.

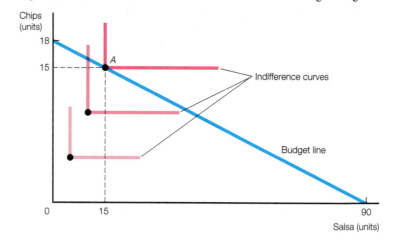

9. Since her marginal rate of substitution of opera tickets for movie tickets equals 5, and since the ratio of the price of an opera ticket to the price of a movie ticket is 10, it is impossible for her to set the marginal rate of substitution equal to the price ratio. She can increase satisfaction by substituting movie tickets for opera tickets because she is willing to give up only 5 movie tickets to get an extra opera ticket, but she has to give up 10 movie tickets to get an extra opera ticket. Thus, she will spend the entire $300 on movie tickets; she will buy 50 of them.

11. **a.** 150 miles **b.** 300 miles **c.** Yes. -0.5. **d.** $3 billion.

CHAPTER 4

1. **a.** To see whether 400 hours of skilled labor and 100 hours of unskilled labor are the optimal input combination, recall from equation (7.11) that to minimize cost, the Elwyn Company should pick an input combination where

$$\frac{MP_S}{P_S} = \frac{MP_U}{P_U},$$

where MP_S is the marginal product of skilled labor, MP_U is the marginal product of unskilled labor, P_S is the price of skilled labor, and P_U is the price of unskilled labor. Since $P_S = 10$, $P_U = 5$, and

$$MP_S = \frac{\partial Q}{\partial S} = 300 - 0.4S$$

$$MP_U = \frac{\partial Q}{\partial U} = 200 - 0.6U,$$

it follows that the Elwyn Company should pick an input combination where

$$\frac{300 - 0.4S}{10} = \frac{200 - 0.6U}{5},$$

or

$$1,500 - 2S = 2,000 - 6U$$

$$S = -250 + 3U.$$

Thus, 400 hours of skilled labor and 100 hours of unskilled labor are not the optimal input combination, because, if $S = 400$ and $U = 100$, this equation does not hold.

b. If a total of $5,000 is spent on skilled and unskilled labor,

$$10S + 5U = 5,000,$$

since $P_S = 10$ and $P_U = 5$. From the answer to part a, we know that $S = -250 + 3U$.

Solving these two equations simultaneously, $S = 392.9$ and $U = 214.3$. Thus, to maximize output, Elwyn should hire about 393 hours of skilled labor and about 214 hours of unskilled labor.

c. From equation 7.4, we know that $MP_U \cdot P$ must equal P_U, where P is the price of the product. (Under present circumstances, the marginal revenue product of unskilled labor equals $MP_U \cdot P$, and the marginal expenditure on unskilled labor equals P_U.) Thus, since

$$P = 10, P_U = 5, \text{ and } MP_U = 200 - 0.6U,$$

$$10(200 - 0.6U) = 5$$

$$U = 332.5.$$

To maximize profit, Elwyn should hire 332.5 hours of unskilled labor. (Note that we no longer assume that a total of $5,000 is spent on labor. Thus, the answer is different from that in part b.)

2. a. No.

b. 50 pounds, since half of these amounts (that is, 50 pounds of hay and 125.1 pounds of grain) results in a 25-pound gain.

c. $-(125.1 - 130.9)/(50 - 40) = 0.58$.

d. No, because it is impossible to tell (from the information given in the question) how much hay and grain can be used to produce a 25-pound gain after the advance in technology.

4. a. No.

b. General farms.

c. No.

6. a. **and b.** The average and marginal products of grain when each amount is used are calculated as follows:

Amount of grain	Average product	Marginal product
1,200	5,917/1,200 = 4.93	
		$\dfrac{7{,}250 - 5.917}{1{,}800 - 1{,}200} = 2.22$
1,800	7,250/1,800 = 4.03	
		$\dfrac{8{,}379 - 7{,}250}{2{,}400 - 1{,}800} = 1.88$
2,400	8,379/2,400 = 3.49	
		$\dfrac{9{,}371 - 8{,}379}{3{,}000 - 2{,}400} = 1.65$
3,000	9,371/3,000 = 3.12	

c. Yes. The marginal product of grain decreases as more of it is used.

7. a. To minimize cost, the firm should choose an input combination where $MP_L/P_L = MP_K/P_K$, where MP_L is the marginal product of labor, MP_K is the marginal product of capital, P_L is the price of labor, and P_K is the price of capital. Since

$$MP_L = \frac{\partial Q}{\partial L} = 5K \quad \text{and} \quad MP_K = \frac{\partial Q}{\partial K} = 5L,$$

it follows that,

$$\frac{5K}{1} = \frac{5L}{2},$$

or $K = L/2$. Since $Q = 20$, $K = 4/L$. Thus,

$$\frac{L}{2} = \frac{4}{L} \quad \text{or} \quad L^2 = 8,$$

which means that the firm should use $2(2)^{0.5}$ units of labor and $(2)^{0.5}$ units of capital.

b. If the price of labor is $2 per unit, the optimal value of K is 2, and the optimal value of L is 2. Thus, output per unit of labor is 20/2, or 10, whereas it formerly was $20/2 \times 2^{0.5}$ or $10/2^{0.5}$. Thus, output per unit of labor will rise.

c. No, because a 1 percent increase in both K and L results in more than a 1 percent increase in Q.

CHAPTER 5

1. a. It is the cheapest of these three ways of making steel. Using this method, cost per ton is $310.34, as compared with $368.86 and $401.73 with the other methods.

b. If the price of scrap rises, the cost of producing steel based on the electric-furnace continuous-casting route will increase, because this route uses scrap. Thus, the cost advantage of this route will be reduced if the price of scrap goes up.

c. It suggests that U.S. steel producers may have a hard time competing with steel producers in low-wage countries.

d. If each figure is the minimum value of long-run average cost for a particular technique, it also equals the long-run marginal cost for the technique, since marginal cost equals average cost when the latter is a minimum.

3. a. If Q is the sales volume,

$Q(\$200) - \$5,000 = \$10,000$,

so Q must equal 75.

b. Since $Q(\$250)$ 2 $5,000 5 $10,000, Q must equal 60.

c. Since $Q(\$265)$ 2 $5,000 5 $10,000, Q must equal 56.6.

5. The table is as follows:

Total fixed cost	Total variable cost	Average fixed cost	Average variable cost
50	0	—	—
50	25	50	25
50	50	25	25
50	70	$16^2/_3$	$23^1/_3$
50	85	$12^1/_2$	$21^1/_4$
50	100	10	20
50	140	$8^1/_3$	$23^1/_3$
50	210	$7^1/_7$	30

7. a. Yes. Since $(\partial TC/\partial Q)(Q/TC) = \alpha_1$, this is true.

b. Yes. If $\alpha_1 < 1$, a 1 percent increase in output results in a less than 1 percent increase in total cost, so average cost falls with increases in output; in other words, there are economies of scale. If $\alpha_1 > 1$, a 1 percent increase in output results in a more than 1 percent increase in total cost, so average cost increases with increases in output; in other words, there are diseconomies of scale.

c. If we assume that a 1 percent increase in both P_L and P_K will result in a 1 percent increase in TC, $\alpha_2 + \alpha_3 = 1$. Thus,

$$\frac{TC}{P_K} = \alpha_0 Q^{\alpha_1} \left(\frac{PL}{PK} \right)^{\alpha_2},$$

and

$$\log \left(\frac{TC}{P_K} \right) = \log \alpha_0 + \alpha_1 \log Q + \alpha_2 \log \left(\frac{P_L}{P_K} \right).$$

If this is treated as a regression equation, one can estimate the as, using the regression technique discussed in Chapter 5, subject to the caveats concerning various kinds of possible errors cited there.

9. a. Since marginal cost equals $dTVC/dQ$, it equals

$$MC = 50 - 20Q + 3Q^2.$$

It is a minimum when

$$\frac{dMC}{dQ} = -20 + 6Q = 0, \quad \text{or} \quad Q = 20/6$$

b. Average variable cost equals

$$AVC = \frac{TVC}{Q} = 50 - 10Q + Q^2.$$

It is a minimum when

$$\frac{dAVC}{dQ} = -10 + 2Q = 0, \quad \text{or} \quad Q = 5.$$

c. If $Q = 5$, average variable cost equals $50 - 10(5) + 5^2 = 25$. Marginal cost equals $50 - 20(5) + 3(5^2) = 25$. Thus, marginal cost equals average variable cost at this output level.

11. a. Using equation (9.7), $S = (23,000 + 11,000 - 30,000)/30,000 = 0.13$.

b. Production facilities used to make one product sometimes can be used to make another product, and by-products resulting from the production of one product may be useful in making other products.

CHAPTER 6

1. a. Since average cost (AC) must be a minimum, and since

$$AC = \frac{25,000}{Q} + 150 + 3Q,$$

$$\frac{dAC}{dQ} = \frac{-25,000}{Q^2} + 3 = 0.$$

Thus, $Q = \left(\frac{25,000}{3}\right)^{0.5} = 91.3$, and

$AC = 25,000/91.3 + 150 + 3(91.3) = 697.7$

so the price must be $697.7, since in long-run equilibrium, price equals the minimum value of average cost.

b. 91.3 units.

3. a. Marginal cost equals

$$MC = \frac{dTC}{dQ} = 4 + 4Q$$

Setting marginal cost equal to price, we have

$$4 + 4Q = 24$$
$$4Q = 20$$
$$Q = 5.$$

Thus, the optimal output rate is 5.

b. Profit equals total revenue minus total cost. Since total revenue equals 24Q, profit equals

$$\pi = 24Q - 200 - 4Q - 2Q^2 = -200 + 20Q - 2Q^2.$$

Because $Q = 5$,

$$\pi = -200 + 20(5) - 2(5)^2 = -200 + 100 - 50 = -150.$$

Thus, the firm loses $150 (which is less than if it shuts down).

5. a. The White Company's marginal cost is dTC/dQ = MC = 20 + 10Q. Equating this to the market price = P = 50 and solving yields the optimal output Q, i.e., P = 50 = 20 + 10Q = MC or 10Q = 30 or Q = 3.

b. The White Company's total revenue (TR) is TR = P*Q = 50*3 = 150. The White Company's total cost (TC) is TC + 1,000 + 20*3 + 5*3*3 = 1,000 + 60 + 45 = 1,105. The White Company's economic profit is TR − TC = 150 − 1,105 = −955.

c. The White Company's average total cost (ATC) is ATC = TC/Q = (1,000/Q) + 20 + 5Q = (1,000/3) + 20 + 5*3 = 333.33 + 20 + 15 = 368.33.

d. The industry is not in equilirium because the firms in the industry are losing money. In the long run, we would expect some firms to leave the industry such that in the long run, the typical firm would have long run average cost equal to long run marginal cost and no economic profits being made by any firm.

CHAPTER 7

1. a. Marginal revenue = 100 − 2Q; marginal cost = 60 + 2Q. Thus, if marginal revenue equals marginal cost, 100 − 2Q = 60 + 2Q, so Q = 10.

b. Since P = 100 − Q, P must equal 90 if Q = 10. Thus, he should charge a price of $90.

3. a. Since P = (8,300 − Q)/2.1 = 3,952 − 0.476Q,

$$MR = 3,952 - 0.952Q.$$

b. MC = 480 + 40Q. If MC = MR,

$$480 + 40Q = 3,952 - 0.952Q$$
$$40.952Q = 3,472$$
$$Q = 84.8.$$

Thus, the firm would produce 84.8 lasers per month. If Q = 84.8, P = 3,952 + 0.476(84.8) = 3,912. Thus, the price should be $3,912.

    c. The firm's monthly profit equals

$$84.8(3,912) - [2,200 + 480(84.8) + 20(84.8)^2] = \$145,012.80.$$

5. a. If the firm is producing 5 units in the first plant, the marginal cost in the first plant equals $20 + 2(5)$, or 30. Thus, if the firm is minimizing costs, marginal cost in the second plant must also equal 30; this means that

$$10 + 5Q_2 = 30$$
$$Q_2 = 4.$$

Thus, the second plant must be producing 4 units of output.

    b. Since $MC_1 = MC_2 = MC$ and the firm's output, Q, equals $Q_1 + Q_2$,

$$Q_1 = (MC_1/2) - 10$$
$$Q_2 = (MC_2/5) - 2$$
$$Q = Q_1 + Q_2 = 0.7MC - 12$$
$$MC = (1/0.7)(Q + 12).$$

    c. No, because we do not have information concerning the fixed costs of each plant. But you can determine average variable cost.

7. a. It probably tended to increase because high profits induced entry. Also, the 1990–91 recession may have resulted in more demand for the services of pawnshops.

    b. No. It is likely to be an oligopoly, since there generally is not a very large number of pawnshops in a small city.

    c. Apparently not, but licensing requirements may exist.

9. a. The total revenue (TR) for diamonds is $TR_Z = P_Z{}^*Q_Z = (980 - 2Q_Z){}^*Q_Z = 980Q_Z - 2Q_Z{}^2$. The marginal revenue for diamonds is $dTR_Z/dQ_Z = MR_Z = 980 - 4Q_Z$. The marginal cost for diamonds is $MC_Z = dTC/dQ_Z = 50 + Q_Z$. To maximize profit, the monopolist sets $MR_Z = MC_Z$ or $MR_Z = 980 - 4Q_Z = 50 + Q_Z = MC_Z$ or $5Q_Z = 930$ or $Q_Z = 186$. Substituting $Q_Z = 186$ into the demand function yields $P_Z = 980 - 2{}^*186 = 980 - 372 = 608$. Consumer surplus (CS) is then $CS_Z = 0.5{}^*(980 - 608){}^*372 = 0.5{}^*372{}^*186 = 34,596$. Total revenue is $TR_Z = 608{}^*186 = 113,088$. Variable cost is $VC_Z = 50{}^*186 + 0.5{}^*1686{}^*186 = 9,300 + 17,298 = 26,598$. So variable cost profit = producer surplus $= PS_Z = TR_Z - VC_Z = 113,088 - 26,598 = 86,490$. Social welfare is $CS_Z + PS_Z = 34,596 + 86,490 = 121,086$.

    b. If De Beers acts as a perfect competitor, they would set price $= P_Z = MC_Z$ or $P_Z = 980 - 2Q_Z = 50 + Q_Z = MC_Z$ or $3Q_Z = 930$ or $Q_Z = 310$. Substituting $Q_Z = 310$ into the demand fuction gives $P_Z = 980 - 2{}^*310 = 980 - 620 = 360$. Consumer surplus (CS) is then $CS_Z = 0.5{}^*(980 - 360){}^*310 = 0.5{}^*620{}^*310 = 96,100$. Total revenue is $TR_Z = 360{}^*310 = 111,600$. Variable cost is $VC_Z = 50{}^*310 + 0.5{}^*310{}^*310 = 15,500 + 48,050 = 63,550$. So variable cost profit = producer surplus $= PS_Z = TR_Z - VC_Z = 11,600 - 63,550 = 48,050$. Social welfare is $CS_Z + PS_Z = 96,100 + 48,050 = 144,150$.

c. Social welfare increases by $144{,}150 - 121{,}086 = 23{,}064$.

11. a. To earn 20 percent on its total investment of $250,000, its profit must equal $50,000 per year. Thus, if it operates at 80 percent of capacity (and sells 10,000 units), it must set a price of $15 per unit. (Since average cost equals $10, profit per unit will be $5, so total profit per year will be $50,000.)

b. From the information given, there is no assurance that it can sell 10,000 units per year if it charges a price of $15 per unit.

c. Unless the markup bears the proper relationship to the price elasticity of demand, the firm probably is sacrificing profit.

13. a. Backus' total revenues equal

$$TR = P_X Q_X + P_Y Q_Y = (400 - Q_X)Q_X + (300 - 3Q_Y)Q_Y,$$

and since $Q_Y = 2Q_X$,

$$TR = (400 - Q_X)Q_X + (300 - 6Q_X)(2Q_X)$$
$$= 400Q_X - Q_X^2 + 600Q_X - 12Q_X^2 = 1{,}000Q_X - 13Q_X^2.$$

Thus, the firm's profit equals

$$\pi = 1{,}000Q_X - 13Q_X^2 - 500 - 3Q_X - 9Q_X^2$$
$$= -500 + 997Q_X - 22Q_X^2$$

Setting $d\pi/dQ_X = 997 - 44Q_X = 0$, we find that the profit-maximizing value of $Q_X = 997/44 = 22.66$. Thus, Backus should produce and sell 22.66 units of product X and 45.32 units of product Y per period of time.

b. The price of product X must be $400 - 22.66 = \$377.34$, and the price of product Y must be $300 - 3(45.32) = \$164.05$.

We have assumed that Backus sells all that it produces of both products. The marginal revenue of product X equals $400 - 2(22.66) = 354.68$, and the marginal revenue of product Y equals $300 - 6(45.32) = 28.09$. Since both are nonnegative, this assumption is true if Backus maximizes profit.

CHAPTER 8

1. a. The recommendation is not correct. Profit maximization requires the marginal revenue (MR) in each market be the same and equal to margial cost. Using the relationship that $MR = P(1 + [1/\eta])$, $MR_J = P_J(1 + [1/\eta_J])$, $P_J(1 + [1/-4]) = P_J(1 + [1/4]) = 0.75P_J$, $MR_{US} = P_{US}(1 + [1/\eta_{US}]) = P_{US}(1 + [1/-2]) = P_{US}(1 - [1/2]) = 0.5P_{US}$, and $MR_E = P_E(1 + [1/\eta_E]) = P_E(1 + [1/(2-4/3)]) = P_E(1 - [3/4]) = 0.25P_E$, where $J = $ Japan, $US = $ United States, and $E = $ Europe. Thus, profit maximization requires $MR_J = MR_{US} = MR_E$ or $0.75P_J = 0.5P_{US} = 0.25P_E$. $0.75P_J = 0.75*\$1{,}000 = \$750$, $0.5P_{US} = 0.5*\$2{,}000 = \$1{,}000$, and

$0.25P_E = 0.25*\$3{,}000 = \$750$. Since $MR_J = MR_{US} = MR_E$ does not hold, this is not a profit maximizing pricing policy.

b. Since the US price is too high (see a. above), we should not be suprised that the sales (Q) in the US are below expectations.

c. The decision to lower the price in the US to $1,500 results in $MR_J = MR_{US} = MR_E$ since $MR_{US} = 0.5P_{US} = 0.5*1{,}500 = 750$. We cannot tell if this is a wise decision because we don't know if the marginal cost of the Ridgeway Corporation is 750.

d. We do not know if the Ridgeway Corporation is maximizing profit because we don't know their marginal cost. Profit maximization requires $MR_J = MR_{US} = MR_E = MC$.

3. a. The firm's profit equals $P_C Q_C + P_M Q_M - TC$, or
$$\pi = (495 - 5Q_C)Q_C + (750 - 10Q_M)Q_M - 410 - 8(Q_C + Q_M).$$
Thus,
$$\frac{\partial \pi}{\partial Q_C} = 495 - 10Q_C - 8 = 0$$
$$\frac{\partial \pi}{\partial Q_M} = 750 - 20Q_M - 8 = 0.$$
Consequently, $Q_C = 48.7$ and $Q_M = 37.1$, so
$P_C = 495 - 5(48.7) = 251.5$.

b. $P_M = 750 - 10(37.1) = 379$.

c. Yes. Under these circumstances,
$$Q_C = \frac{495 - P}{5} \text{ and } Q_M = \frac{750 - P}{10},$$
so
$$Q = Q_C + Q_M = 174 - 0.3P$$
and
$$P = (174 - Q)/0.3 = 580 - {}^{10}/_3 Q.$$
Thus,
$$\pi = (580 - {}^{10}/_3 Q)Q - 410 - 8Q$$
$$= -410 + 572Q - {}^{10}/_3 Q^2.$$
If π is a maximum,
$$\frac{\partial \pi}{dQ} = 572 - {}^{20}/_3 Q = 0,$$
so $Q = 572(3/20) = 85.8$. Consequently,
$$\pi = -410 + 572(85.8) - {}^{10}/_3(85.8^2) = 24{,}129,$$
which compares with
$$\pi = [495 - 5(48.7)]48.7 + [750 - 10(37.1)]37.1 - 410$$
$$- 8(48.7 + 37.1)$$
$$= 251.5(48.7) + 379(37.1) - 1{,}096.4$$
$$= 12{,}248.05 + 14{,}060.9 - 1{,}096.4 = 25{,}213,$$

the value of profits when price discrimination is allowed.
So profits decrease by $1,084.

CHAPTER 9

3. **a.** Yes. As stressed earlier, to maximize the firm's overall profit, the transfer price should equal the price of the product in the external (competitive market).

   b. When the production of phenol increased, the supply of acetone increased, since acetonessp was a by-product. Thus, since less isopropanol was demanded to make acetone, the demand curve for isopropanol shifted to the left (as shown below), and the price of isopropanol declined (from P_0 to P_1).

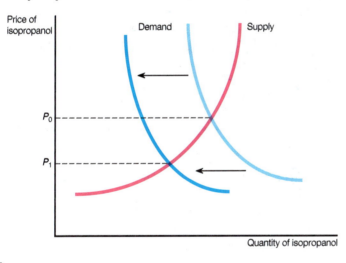

   c. Yes.
   d. Yes.

CHAPTER 10

1. **a.** They would want to set marginal revenue equal to the marginal cost of each firm, but this is impossible since Bergen's marginal cost is $410 and Gutenberg's marginal cost is $460. Because Bergen's marginal cost is always less than Gutenberg's, it will produce all the output. Equating its marginal cost to marginal revenue (MR),
   $$MR = 580 - 6Q = 410,$$
   so $Q = 170/6$. This is the output Bergen would produce.
   b. Nothing.
   c. Not unless Gutenberg receives an attractive share of the profit from Bergen's output even though it produces nothing.

3. a. $9,000. **b.** 6.

5. a. To find the profit-maximizing price, the IATA should construct the marginal cost curve for the cartel as a whole. Then, as shown in Figure 11.2, it should determine the amount of traffic (which is the output of this industry) where marginal revenue equals marginal cost. The price that will elicit this amount of traffic is the profit-maximizing price.

 b. If IATA wants to maximize profit, it will allocate this traffic among the airlines in such a way that the marginal cost of all airlines is equal. (However, for reasons discussed on page 432, it may not want to maximize profit.)

 c. No. This would not maximize profit.

7. a. Letting Alliance's profit be π_1,
$$\pi_1 = Q_1[200,000 - 6(Q_1 + Q_2)] - 8,000\,Q_1.$$
Letting Bangor's profit be π_2,
$$\pi_2 = Q_2[200,000 - 6(Q_1 + Q_2)] - 12,000\,Q_2.$$
If Alliance maximizes its profit, assuming that Bangor will hold its output constant,

$$\frac{\partial \pi_1}{\partial Q_1} = 192,000 - 6Q_2 - 12Q_1 = 0.$$

If Bangor maximizes its profit, assuming that Alliance will hold its output constant,

$$\frac{\partial \pi_2}{\partial Q_2} = 188,000 - 6Q_1 - 12Q_2 = 0.$$

Solving these equations simultaneously, $Q_1 = 196,000/18, = 10,888.89$, and
$$Q_2 = (188,000 - 196,000/3)/12 = 122,667/12 = 10,222.22,$$
so
$$P - 200,000 - 6(10,888.89 + 10,222.22) = 73,333.33 \text{ dollars.}$$

 b. Alliance's output is 10,888.89, and Bangor's output is 10,222.22.

 c. Alliance's profit is $10,888.89(73,333.33 - 8,000)$, or approximately $711.41 million.
Bangor's profit is
$10,222(73,333.33 - 12,000)$, or approximately $626.96 million.

9. a. Obviously, Procter and Gamble must be concerned with its own costs. If it adopts a tactic that is far more costly to itself than to a potential entrant, it may cost more than it is worth. If the costs of the strategy outweigh the benefits, Proctor and Gamble, on net, will lose.

 b. The point of these tactics is to raise the cost to a potential entrant, thus discouraging entry.

 c. Whether Procter and Gamble should have cut its price depends on whether the discount brands (and Kimberly-Clark, which had become a major rival) would cut their prices in response, and by how much. In fact, Procter and Gamble did reduce its price substantially (by 16 percent in the case of Luvs). According to the chairperson of Procter and Gamble, "We believe our profits are going to grow because we're going to get volume back."

d. Yes. Procter and Gamble wanted to reduce what it regarded as improper imitation of its technology. On the other hand, firms that are sued often regard such suits as attempts to intimidate them.

11. a. The size of a firm is often measured by its total revenue. Perhaps a firm might feel that a higher total revenue would make the firm more visible to investors and customers. Also, its managers may be more interested in the growth of the firm than in profits. (However, they are likely to feel that profits should not fall below some minimum level.)

b. To maximize its total revenue, it should set

$$\frac{d(PQ)}{dQ} = \frac{d(28Q - 0.14Q^2)}{dQ} = 28 - 0.28Q = 0.$$

Thus, Q should equal 100, and P should equal $14.

c. If it maximizes profit, it sets

$MR = 28 - 0.28Q = 14 = MC$

so $Q = 50$. Consequently, the firm produces 50,000 units more than it would if it maximized profit.

CHAPTER 11

1. a. Yes. Fortnum should focus on magazines, and Maison should focus on newspapers.

b. Fortnum's profit is $9 million, and Maison's profit is $8 million.

c. No.

3.

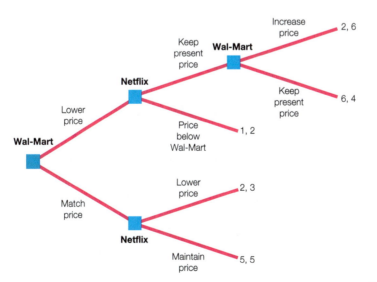

Using backward induction, the equilibrium is for Wal-Mart to lower price, Netflix to keep its present price, and Wal-Mart to respond by keeping its present price. The final payoff to Wal-Mart is 6, and Netflix receives 4.

5. **a.** Each firm will choose to cheat on the agreement. They will each earn $28 million.

 b. No, as long as the horizon is finite, behavior will not change.

 c. Yes, this is an example of prisoner's dilemma.

7. If Rose cannot ascertain the strategy of its rival then it cannot implement a tit-for-tat strategy because it will not know which strategy to play. A tit-for-tat strategy requires a player to mimic the strategy played by a rival in the previous period. For example, if Rose's rival played cheat in period n, then Rose would choose cheat in period $n + 1$.

CHAPTER 12

1. Expected Value or EV($45) $=$ 1,750($4.05)(.35) $+$ 1,975($4.05)(.20) $+$ 2,220($4.05)(.30) $+$ 2,445($4.05)(.15).

 EV($45) $=$ $2,480.63 $+$ $1,599.75 $+$ $2,697.30 $+$ $1,485.34 or $8,263.02.

 EV($50) $=$ 1,200($4.50)(.35) $+$ 1,415($4.50)(.20) $+$ 2,001($4.50)(.30) $+$ 2,305($4.50)(.15).

 EV($50) $=$ $1,890 $+$ $1,273.50 $+$ $2,701.35 $+$ $1,555.88 or $7,420.73

 EV(auction) $=$ $2,480.63 $+$ 1,599.75 $+$ 2,701.35 $+$ 1,555.88 $=$ $8,337.61.

 The value of information would be worth,

 EV($45) $=$ 1,750($4.05)(.35) $+$ 1,975($4.05)(.20) $+$ 2,220($4.05)(.30) $+$ 2,445($4.05)(.15).

 EV($45) $=$ **$2,480.63 $+$ $1,599.75** $+$ $2,697.30 $+$ $1,485.34 or $8,263.02.

 EV($50) $=$ 1,200($4.50)(.35) $+$ 1,415($4.50)(.20) $+$ 2,001($4.50)(.30) $+$ 2,305($4.50)(.15).

 EV($50) $=$ $1,890 $+$ $1,273.50 **$+$ $2,701.35** $+$ **$1,555.88** or $7,420.73

 EV(auction) $=$ $2,480.63 $+$ 1,599.75 $+$ 2,701.35 $+$ 1,555.88 $=$ $8,337.61.

 So, the value of information $=$ $8,337.61 $-$ $8,263.02 or $74.59.

3. **a.** The mean value is 67.91.

 b. (80 $-$ 67.91)/(63.64 $=$ .04573; z score of .04573 $=$ .4820. Hence the probability of a reservation price being less than 80 is approximately 19 percent.

5. If they choose to price their PSLs at $6,000, their expected revenue is: $58,802,000 $+$ $58,800,000 $+$ **$60,000** $=$ $177,602,000. If they choose to price their PSLs at $7,000, their expected revenue is: **$60,214,000** $+$ 58,803,500 $+$ 56,000,000 $=$ 175,017,500. If they choose to prices their PSLs at $8,000, their expected revenue is: $56,030,000 $+$ **$61,610,500** $+$ $50,000,000 $=$ $167,640,500. So, if they set the price and don't use an auction, they should charge $6,000/PSL. If the Eagles use a modified Dutch auction, then their

expected revenue is: $60,214,000 + $61,610,500 + $60,000 = $181,824,500. So relative to setting a price of $6,000/PSL, the auction would increase expected revenue by $4,222,500. But since auction costs are $5,100,000, the Eagles are better off pricing the PSLs at $6,000.

CHAPTER 13

1. a. The expected present value is $10.7 million, the standard deviation is $5.06 million, and the coefficient of variation is 47 percent.
    b. The expected present value is $11.0 million, the standard deviation is $1.95 million, and the coefficient of variation is 18 percent.
    c. Investment X.
    d. Investment Y, since she is a risk averter (as indicated by the fact that U increases at a decreasing rate as P rises). Investment Y has both a higher expected present value and a lower standard deviation than investment X and because $E(U_X) = 62.099 < 63.752 = E(U_Y)$, i.e., X's expected utility is less than Y's.
3. a. No.
    b. It is very conservative, as discussed on pages 558 to 559.
    c. No, because no probability distribution of the outcome can be given.
5. a. 3.   b. −0.6.   c. −1.2.
7. a.

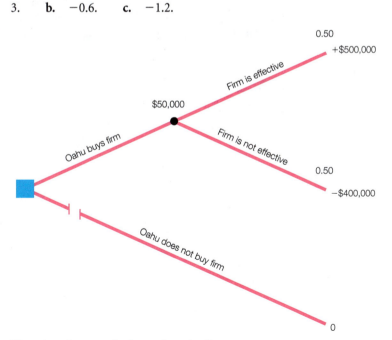

    b. There is only one: whether to buy the firm.
    c. There is only one: whether the firm becomes an effective producer of washing machine parts or not.

> **d.** Yes, it should buy the firm.
>
> **e.** (1) Yes.
>
> > (2) Three mutually exclusive outcomes are: (a) The firm becomes an effective producer of washing machine parts. (b) The firm does not become an effective producer of washing parts and is sold to the Saudis. (c) The firm does not become an effective producer of washing machine parts and cannot be sold to the Saudis.
> >
> > (3) The probability of the first outcome (in part 2) is 0.5, the probability of the second outcome is 0.5(0.2), or 0.1, and the probability of the third outcome is (0.5)(0.8), or 0.4.
> >
> > (4) The extra profit to Oahu from the first outcome is $500,000; the extra profit from the second outcome is $100,000; the extra profit from the third outcome is −$400,000.
>
> **f.** Oahu should buy the firm. The expected extra profit if it does so is 0.5($500,000) + 0.1($100,000) + 0.4(−$400,000) = $100,000.
>
> **g.** (1) If the extra profit if the firm is made into an effective producer of washing machine parts is $400,000 or less, the decision will be reversed. Put differently, if the *error* was an *overstatement* of this extra profit by $100,000 or more, the decision will be reversed.
>
> > (2) If the extra profit if the firm is made into an effective producer of washing machine parts is $300,000 or less, the decision will be reversed. Put differently, if the *error* was an *overstatement* of this extra profit by $200,000 or more, the decision will be reversed.

9. a.

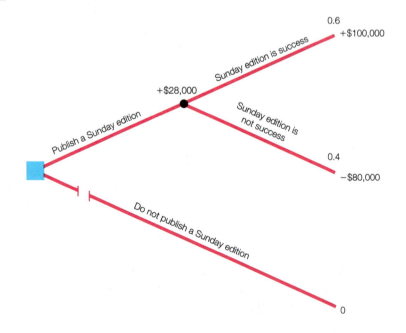

If the publisher is risk neutral, she wants to maximize expected profit. Thus, she should publish the Sunday edition.

b. Whether to publish the Sunday edition is a decision fork. Whether it is a success, if published, is a chance fork.

CHAPTER 14

1. a. Flat salary:

If effort is low, utility = 758.29. If effort is high, utility = 658.29. The manager chooses low effort since it gives higher expected utility. Your expected profit will be 0.3($5 million) + 0.4($10 million) + 0.3($15 million) − $0.575 million = $9.425 million.

b. Six percent of profit:

Expected utility of manager with

Low effort is $0.3\sqrt{0.06(\$5 \text{ million})} + 0.4\sqrt{0.06(\$10 \text{ million})} + 0.3\sqrt{0.06(15 \text{ million})} = 758.76$.

High effort is $-100 + 0.3\sqrt{0.06(\$7 \text{ million})} + + 0.4\sqrt{0.06(\$12 \text{ million})} +$

The manager chooses low effort since it gives higher expected utility. Given the manager's choice of low effort, your expected profit will be the expected profit of $10 million minus 6 percent which is

{0.3($5 million) + 0.4($10 million) + 0.3($15 million)}

(1 − 0.06) = $9.4m.

c. Five hundred thousand dollars plus half of profits in excess of $15 million:

Expected utility of manager with

Low effort is $\sqrt{(\$0.5 \text{ million})} = 707.11$.

High effort is $-100 + 0.7\sqrt{(\$0.5 \text{ million})} +$
$0.3\sqrt{^1/_2(\$17 \text{ million} - \$15 \text{ million}) + \$0.5 \text{ million}} = 762.40$.

The manager chooses high effort since it gives higher expected utility. Your expected profit will be the expected profit of $12 million minus expected compensation which is {$0.5m + 0.3(0.5($2m))} = $800,000.

{0.3($7m) + 0.4($12m) + 0.3($17m)} − $0.8m = $11.2m.

You will choose the third plan (c) since it gives highest profit after deducting the manager's compensation.

3. If the manager does not work hard, she will receive,

$[100]^{0.5} = 10$.

If the manager works hard, she will receive

$[100 + x(15,000 - 13,000)]^{0.5} - 1$.

To calculate the minimum level of x necessary to ensure that expected compensation will be higher with hard work, set the expected utility with hard work equal to that without hard work:

$[100 + x(15,000 - 13,000)]^{0.5} - 1 = 10$

$[100 + x(15,000 - 13,000)]^{0.5} \qquad = 11 \qquad$ (square both sides to get)

$[100 + x(15,000 - 13,000)] \qquad = 11^2 = 121$

$$x = \frac{121 - 100}{15,000 - 13,000} = 0.0105$$

Thus, if the manager gets a little over 0.105 times equity in excess of 13,000 she will work hard.

5. **Total value of firm:**

$$V = 500 + 300 - 700\,\frac{0.2}{1 + s} - s = 800 - \frac{140}{1 + s} - s.$$

To calculate the value of s that maximizes total value, set the derivative of value with respect to s equal to zero:

$$\frac{dV}{ds} = \frac{140}{(1 + s)^2} - 1 = 0.$$

So, $S = 10.83$.

Therefore, the value of firm is

$$800 - \frac{140}{11.83} - 10.83 = 777.3.$$

Division 1 is riskless and has a stand-alone value of 500. Since all the risk comes from division 2, we must consider the chosen level of safety of this unit as a stand-alone entity. In calculating this value recollect that its value is 300 if no liability arises. However, if a loss of 700 occurs, it simply cannot pay more than the original 300 stand-alone value (because of limited liability). So, the stand-alone value of division 2 is:

$$300 - 300\,\frac{0.2}{1 + s} - s = 300 - \frac{60}{1 + s} - s$$

Set the derivative equal to zero to maximize the division 2 stand-alone value:

$$\frac{dV}{ds} = \frac{60}{(1 + s)^2} - 1 = 0.\ \text{So, } s = 6.746.$$

So, the stand-alone value of division 2 is:

$$300 - \frac{60}{7.746} - 6.746 = 285.5.$$

Total value with split up

$500 + 285.5 = 785.5$.

So the gain from split up is $785.55 - 777.34 = 8.21$.

7. There is an asset-substitution problem. To show this, we should value the firm as a whole, and each of the stakeholders' claims, first assuming A is chosen then assuming B is chosen. We can then see which project selection leads to the higher value of equity. This is the one share-holders would naturally favor.

Value of the firm if project A is chosen:

First, note that the value of the firm will be either 720 (300 from existing operations and 420 from the new project) or 1020 (600 from existing operations and 420 from the new project) depending on the success of existing operations. This value must be divided up by first paying off old debt, next new debt, and finally equity.

Value of the firm	$0.5(720 + 1020) = 870$
Old debt	$0.5(250 + 250) = 250$
New debt	$0.5(400 + 400) = 400$
Equity	$0.5(70 + 370) = 220$

Value of the firm if project B is chosen

The value of the firm will be either 300, 600, 1000, or 1300. These figures come from the different combinations of the two possible values for the existing operations (300 and 600) and the two values for the new project (0 and 700).

Value of the firm	$0.25(300 + 600 + 1000 + 1300) = 800$
Old debt	$0.25(250 + 250 + 250 + 250) = 250$
New debt	$0.25(50 + 350 + 400 + 400) = 300$
Equity	$0.25(0 + 0 + 350 + 650) = 250$

Shareholders would like to choose B after they had creditors' money. But since investors would pay only 300 for new debt, this cannot be funded. So neither project can be undertaken if debt financing is used. The analysis can be repeated using equity financing for the new project. The values of the firm will be the same as above, but these will be allocated first to the existing debt (for which 250 is owing) and any residual will accrue to equity.

Value of the firm if project A is chosen

Value of the firm	$0.5(720 + 1020) = 870$
Old debt	$0.5(250 + 250) = 250$
Equity	$0.5(470 + 770) = 620$

Value of the firm if project B is chosen

Value of the firm	$0.25(300 + 600 + 1000 + 1300) = 800$
Old debt	$0.25(250 + 250 + 250 + 250) = 250$
Equity	$0.25(50 + 350 + 750 + 1050) = 550$

Now, shareholders will naturally choose the higher Net Present Value project A since it has the higher equity value. The asset-substitution problem is solved.

CHAPTER 15

1. First, note that buyers will not be willing to pay $10,000 for any used car since there is a chance that it is lemon. So the obvious price to contemplate is a price reflecting the average quality; i.e., there is a 75% chance the car will be "good" and worth $10,000 and a 25% chance the car will be "bad" and worth $5,000.

   Average value $(0.75)($10,000) + (0.25)($5,000) = $8,750$

   But, sellers of high quality cars, knowing there vehicles are really worth $10,000, will not be willing to sell at this price. So, only sellers of low quality vehicles will offer their cars for sale. But buyers can anticipate that only low quality cars will be offered, therefore they will only be willing to pay $5,000 for any second hand Corolla on the second hand market. Thus, only low quality cars are sold and the price is $5,000.

3. Form the following table if all are considering buying insurance:

Group	Initial Car Value	Ending Car Value If Accident	Probability of Accident	Expected Claim
A	10,000	5,000	0.2	1,000
B	10,000	5,000	0.3	1,500
C	10,000	5,000	0.4	2,000

   Thus, if all purchased insurance, the expected claims would be $1,000 + 1,500 + 2,000 = 4,500$ and hence the premium would have to be $4,500/3 = 1,500$. But this requires that ALL types buy the policy. Let's see if they will.

   Would A buy insurance if the premium was 1,500? If A self insures (does not buy insurance), his/her expected utility would be:

   $EUa = 0.8(10,000)0.5 + 0.2(5,000)0.5 = 0.8(100) + 0.2(70.711) = 80 + 14.142 = 94.142$

   If A buys a full coverage policy for 1,500, A's expected utility will be

   $EUa = (10,000 - 1,500)0.5 = (8,500)0.5 = 92.195$

   Thus, A will self insure since $94.142 > 92.195$

   Thus, the premium can not be 1,500 since A is not buying insurance.

   So, if the type A's drop out of the insurance pool, we are left with the B's and C's. If only B and C are interested in buying, the expected claims are $1,500 + 2,000 = 3,500$ and the premium must be $3,500/2 = 1,750$.

   But would B buy insurance at the premium of 1,750? If B self insures, their expected utility would be:

   $EUb = 0.7(10,000)0.5 + 0.3(5,000)0.5 = 0.7(100) + 0.3(70.711) = 70 + 21.213 = 91.213$

   If B buys a full coverage policy for 1,750, B's expected utility will be

   $EUb = (10,000 - 1,750)0.5 = (8,250)0.5 = 90.830$

Thus, B will self insure since 91.213 > 90.830.

Thus, the premium cannot be 1,750 since B is not buying insurance.

If only C is interested in buying insurance, then the premium must be 2,000

If C self insures, their expected utility would be:

EUc = 0.6(10,000)0.5 + 0.4(5,000)0.5 = 0.6(100) + 0.4(70.711)

   = 60 + 28.284 = 88.284

If C buys a full coverage policy for 2,000, C's expected utility will be:

EUc = (10,000 − 2,000)0.5 = (8,000)0.5 = 89.443

Since 89.443 > 88.284, C will buy the insurance for a premium of 2,000.

However, No-State can sell the policy for a higher price. Type C's certainty equivalent will be (88.284)2 = 7,794.11. Thus, Type C's would be willing to pay up to 10,000 − 7,794.11 = 2,205.89 for such a policy. Since the question required that the premium must be sufficient to cover expected claims and the expected claims for type C's are

0.4(5,000) = 2,000, a premium of 2,205.90 would certainly fill the bill.

5. The following table charts the maximum price people are willing to pay. Formula =

1.1(x)($50,000) for less risk averse

1.3(x)($50,000) for more risk averse

	Poor health Life expectancy = 9 years	Good health Life expectancy = 11 years
Less risk averse Pay up to 1.1 times expected value	495	605
More risk averse Pay up to 1.3 times expected value	585	715

At a price of $550,000, the product will be purchased by all those in good health and the more risk averse in poor health.

The expected profit can now be calculated

More risk averse in poor health   (50 times $550,000) − (50 times 9 times $50,000) = $5,000,000

Less risk averse in good health   (50 times $550,000) − (50 times 11 times $50,000) = $0

More risk averse in poor health   (50 times $550,000) − (50 times 11 times $50,000) = $0

TOTAL PROFIT = $5,000,000

CHAPTER 16

1. **a.** It equaled $27.5 + 21.9 + 18.5 + 9.3 = 77.2$ percent. Yes.

   b. It was $27.5 + 21.9 + (18.5 + 7.3) + 9.3 = 84.5$ percent if we simply combine United's and Pan Am's shares to approximate United's postpurchase share.

3. **a.** If $P = 480$, $Q = 260$, according to the demand curve. Thus, the firm's total revenue equals 260(480) thousand dollars, or $124,800,000. The firm's total cost equals $50 + 0.25(260) = 115$ million dollars. Thus, the firm's accounting profit is $9,800,000; this means that its rate of return is 9.8 percent.

   b. If it were deregulated, it would maximize
   $$\pi = (1/1,000)[Q(1,000 - 2Q)] - 50 - 0.25Q$$
   $$= -50 + 0.75Q - 0.002Q^2.$$
   Setting $d\pi/dQ = 0.75 - 0.004Q = 0$, $Q = 187.5$. Thus, under deregulation,
   $$\pi = -50 + 0.75(187.5) - 0.002(187.5^2) = \$20.3125 \text{ million}.$$
   So, the difference is $20.3125 2 $9.8 = $10.5125 million.

5. **a.** $220/250 = 88$ percent.

   b. Yes, because it is dominated by a few firms.

   c. $225/250 = 90$ percent.

   d. $140/145 = 97$ percent.

7. **a.** No. If price is $1, 12 firms of optimal size can exist in the market.

   b. Eight.

9. **a.** Because the commission tries to provide the firm with a "fair" rate of return on its investment.

   b. Because this increase reduced the firm's profit.

   c. See pages 645 to 646.

APPENDIX D

TABLES

TABLE D.1

Value of $\dfrac{1}{(1 + i)^n}$

					Value of i					
n	1%	2%	3%	4%	5%	6%	7%	8%	9%	10%
1	.99010	.98039	.97007	.96154	.95233	.94340	.93458	.92593	.91743	.90909
2	.98030	.96117	.94260	.92456	.90703	.89000	.87344	.85734	.84168	.82645
3	.97059	.94232	.91514	.88900	.86384	.83962	.81639	.79383	.77228	.75131
4	.96098	.92385	.88849	.85480	.82270	.79209	.76290	.73503	.70883	.68301
5	.95147	.90573	.86261	.82193	.78353	.74726	.71299	.68058	.64993	.62092
6	.94204	.88797	.83748	.79031	.74622	.70496	.66634	.63017	.59627	.56447
7	.93272	.87056	.81309	.75992	.71063	.66506	.62275	.58349	.54705	.51316
8	.92348	.85349	.78941	.73069	.67684	.62741	.58201	.54027	.50189	.46651
9	.91434	.83675	.76642	.70259	.64461	.59190	.54393	.50025	.46043	.42410
10	.90529	.82035	.74409	.67556	.61391	.55839	.50835	.46319	.42241	.38554
11	.89632	.80426	.72242	.64958	.58468	.52679	.47509	.42888	.38753	.35049
12	.88745	.78849	.70138	.62460	.55684	.49697	.44401	.39711	.35553	.31683
13	.87866	.77303	.68095	.60057	.53032	.46884	.41496	.36770	.32618	.28966
14	.86996	.75787	.66112	.57747	.50507	.44230	.38782	.34046	.29925	.26333
15	.86135	.74301	.64186	.55526	.48102	.41726	.36245	.31524	.27454	.23939
16	.85282	.72845	.62317	.53391	.45811	.39365	.33873	.29189	.25187	.21763
17	.84436	.71416	.60502	.51337	.43630	.37136	.31657	.27027	.23107	.19784
18	.83602	.70016	.58739	.49363	.41552	.35034	.29586	.25025	.21199	.17986
19	.82774	.68643	.57029	.47464	.39573	.33051	.27651	.23171	.19449	.16354
20	.81954	.67297	.55367	.45639	.37689	.31180	.25842	.21455	.17843	.14864
21	.81143	.65978	.53755	.44883	.35894	.29415	.24151	.19866	.16370	.13513
22	.80340	.64684	.52189	.42195	.34185	.27750	.22571	.18394	.15018	.12285
23	.79544	.63414	.50669	.40573	.32557	.26180	.21095	.17031	.13778	.11168
24	.78757	.62172	.49193	.39012	.31007	.24698	.19715	.15770	.12640	.10153
25	.77977	.60953	.47760	.37512	.29530	.23300	.18425	.14602	.11597	.09230

TABLE D.1

Value of $\dfrac{1}{(1 + i)^n}$ (Continued)

						Value of i					
n	11%	12%	13%	14%	15%	16%	17%	18%	19%	20%	24%
1	.90090	.89286	.88496	.87719	.86957	.86207	.85470	.84746	.84043	.83333	.8065
2	.81162	.79719	.78315	.76947	.75614	.74316	.73051	.71818	.70616	.69444	.6504
3	.73119	.71178	.69305	.67497	.65752	.64066	.62437	.60863	.59342	.57870	.5245
4	.65873	.63552	.61332	.59208	.57175	.55229	.53365	.51579	.49867	.48225	.4230
5	.59345	.56743	.54276	.51937	.49718	.47611	.45611	.43711	.41905	.40188	.3411
6	.53464	.50663	.48032	.45559	.43233	.41044	.38984	.37043	.35214	.33490	.2751
7	.48166	.45235	.42506	.39964	.37594	.35383	.33320	.31392	.29592	.27908	.2218
8	.43393	.40388	.37616	.35056	.32690	.30503	.28478	.26604	.24867	.23257	.1789
9	.39092	.36061	.33288	.30751	.28426	.26295	.24340	.22546	.20897	.19381	.1443
10	.35218	.32197	.29459	.26974	.24718	.22668	.20804	.19106	.17560	.16151	.1164
11	.31728	.28748	.26070	.23662	.21494	.19542	.17781	.16192	.14756	.13459	.0938
12	.28584	.25667	.23071	.20756	.18691	.16846	.15197	.13722	.12400	.11216	.0757
13	.25751	.22917	.20416	.18207	.16253	.14523	.12989	.11629	.10420	.09346	.0610
14	.23199	.20462	.18068	.15971	.14133	.12520	.11102	.09855	.08757	.07789	.0492
15	.20900	.18270	.15989	.14010	.12289	.10793	.09489	.08352	.07359	.06491	.0397
16	.18829	.16312	.14150	.12289	.10686	.09304	.08110	.07073	.06184	.05409	.0320
17	.16963	.14564	.12522	.10780	.09293	.08021	.06932	.05998	.05196	.04507	.0258
18	.15282	.13004	.11081	.09456	.08080	.06914	.05925	.05083	.04367	.03756	.0208
19	.13768	.11611	.09806	.08295	.07026	.05961	.05064	.04308	.03669	.03130	.0168
20	.12403	.10367	.08678	.07276	.06110	.05139	.04328	.03651	.03084	.02608	.0135
21	.11174	.09256	.07680	.06383	.05313	.04430	.03699	.03094	.02591	.02174	.0109
22	.10067	.08264	.06796	.05599	.04620	.03819	.03162	.02622	.02178	.01811	.0088
23	.09069	.07379	.06014	.04911	.04017	.03292	.02702	.02222	.01830	.01509	.0071
24	.08170	.06588	.05322	.04308	.03493	.02838	.02310	.01883	.01538	.01258	.0057
25	.07361	.05882	.04710	.03779	.03038	.02447	.01974	.01596	.01292	.01048	.0046

TABLE D.2

Value of $\displaystyle\sum_{t=1}^{n} \frac{1}{(1+i)^t}$

					Value of i					
n	1%	2%	3%	4%	5%	6%	7%	8%	9%	10%
1	.9901	.9804	.9709	.9615	.9524	.9434	.9346	.9259	.9174	.9091
2	1.9704	1.9416	1.9135	1.8861	1.8594	1.8334	1.8080	1.7833	1.7591	1.7355
3	2.9410	2.8839	2.8286	2.7751	2.7233	2.6730	2.6243	2.5771	2.5313	2.4868
4	3.9020	3.8077	3.7171	3.6299	3.5459	3.4651	3.3872	3.3121	3.2397	3.1699
5	4.8535	4.7134	4.5797	4.4518	4.3295	4.2123	4.1002	3.9927	3.8896	3.7908
6	5.7955	5.6014	5.4172	5.2421	5.0757	4.9173	4.7665	4.6229	4.4859	4.3553
7	6.7282	6.4720	6.2302	6.0020	5.7863	5.5824	5.3893	5.2064	5.0329	4.8684
8	7.6517	7.3254	7.0196	6.7327	6.4632	6.2093	5.9713	5.7466	5.5348	5.3349
9	8.5661	8.1622	7.7861	7.4353	7.1078	6.8017	6.5152	6.2469	5.9852	5.7590
10	9.4714	8.9825	8.7302	8.1109	7.7217	7.3601	7.0236	6.7101	6.4176	6.1446
11	10.3677	9.7868	9.2526	8.7604	8.3064	7.8868	7.4987	7.1389	6.8052	6.4951
12	11.2552	10.5753	9.9589	9.3850	8.8632	8.3838	7.9427	7.5361	7.1601	6.8137
13	12.1338	11.3483	10.6349	9.9856	9.3935	9.8527	8.3576	7.9038	7.4869	7.1034
14	13.0088	12.1062	11.2960	10.5631	9.8986	9.2950	8.7454	8.2442	7.7860	7.3667
15	13.8651	12.8492	11.9379	11.1183	10.3796	9.7122	9.1079	8.5595	8.0607	7.6061
16	14.7180	13.5777	12.5610	11.6522	10.8377	10.1059	9.4466	8.8514	8.3126	7.8237
17	15.5624	14.2918	13.1660	12.1656	11.2740	10.4772	9.7632	9.1216	8.5435	8.0215
18	16.3984	14.9920	13.7534	12.6592	11.6895	10.8276	10.0591	9.3719	8.7556	8.2014
19	17.2201	15.2684	14.3237	13.1339	12.0853	11.1581	10.3356	9.6036	8.9501	8.3649
20	18.0457	16.3514	14.8774	13.5903	12.4622	11.4699	10.5940	9.8181	9.1285	8.5136
21	18.8571	17.0111	15.4149	14.0291	12.8211	11.7640	10.8355	10.0168	9.2922	8.6487
22	19.6605	17.6581	15.9368	14.4511	13.1630	12.0416	11.0612	10.2007	9.4424	8.7715
23	20.4559	18.2921	16.4435	14.8568	13.4885	12.3033	11.2722	10.3710	9.5802	8.8832
24	21.2435	18.9139	16.9355	15.2469	13.7986	12.5503	11.4693	10.5287	9.7066	8.9847
25	22.0233	19.5234	17.4181	15.6220	14.9039	12.7833	11.6536	10.6748	9.8226	9.0770

TABLE D.2

Value of $\displaystyle\sum_{t=1}^{n} \frac{1}{(1 + i)^t}$ (Continued)

	Value of i										
n	11%	12%	13%	14%	15%	16%	17%	18%	19%	20%	24%
1	.9009	.8929	.8850	.8772	.8696	.8621	.8547	.8475	.8403	.8333	.8065
2	1.7125	1.6901	1.6681	1.6467	1.6257	1.6052	1.5852	1.5656	1.5465	1.5278	1.4568
3	2.4437	2.4018	2.3612	2.3126	2.2832	2.2459	2.2096	2.1743	2.1399	2.1065	1.9813
4	3.1024	3.0373	2.9745	2.9137	2.8550	2.7982	2.7432	2.6901	2.6386	2.5887	2.4043
5	3.6959	3.6048	3.5172	3.4331	3.3522	3.2743	3.1993	3.1272	3.0576	2.9906	2.7454
6	4.2305	4.1114	3.9976	3.8887	3.7845	3.6847	3.5892	3.4976	3.4098	3.3255	3.0205
7	4.7122	4.5638	4.4226	4.2883	4.1604	4.0386	3.9224	3.8115	3.7057	3.6046	3.2423
8	5.1461	4.9676	4.7988	4.6389	4.4873	4.3436	4.2072	4.0776	3.9544	3.8372	3.4212
9	5.5370	5.3282	5.1317	4.9464	4.7716	4.6065	4.4506	4.3030	4.1633	4.0310	3.5655
10	5.8892	5.6502	5.4262	5.2161	5.0188	4.8332	4.6586	4.4941	4.3389	4.1925	3.6819
11	6.2065	5.9377	5.6869	5.4527	5.2337	5.0286	4.8364	4.6560	4.4865	4.3271	3.7757
12	6.4924	6.1944	5.9176	5.6603	5.4206	5.1971	4.9884	4.7932	4.6105	4.4392	3.8514
13	6.7499	6.4235	6.1218	5.8424	5.5831	5.3423	5.1183	4.9095	4.7147	4.5327	3.9124
14	6.9819	6.6282	6.3025	6.0021	5.7245	5.4675	5.2293	5.0081	4.8023	4.6106	3.9616
15	7.1909	6.8109	6.4624	6.1422	5.8474	5.5755	5.3242	5.0916	4.8759	4.6755	4.0013
16	7.3792	6.9740	6.6039	6.2651	5.9542	5.6685	5.4053	5.1624	4.9377	4.7296	4.0333
17	7.5488	7.1196	6.7291	6.3729	6.0472	5.7487	5.4746	5.2223	4.9897	4.7746	4.0591
18	7.7016	7.2497	6.8389	6.4674	6.1280	5.8178	5.5339	5.2732	5.0333	4.8122	4.0799
19	7.8393	7.3650	6.9380	6.5504	6.1982	5.8775	5.5845	5.3176	5.0700	4.8435	4.0967
20	7.9633	7.4694	7.0248	6.6231	6.2593	5.9288	5.6278	5.3527	5.1009	4.8696	4.1103
21	8.0751	7.5620	7.1016	6.6870	6.3125	5.9731	5.6648	5.3837	5.1268	4.8913	4.1212
22	8.1757	7.6446	7.1695	6.7429	6.3587	6.0113	5.6964	5.4099	5.1486	4.9094	4.1300
23	8.2664	7.7184	7.2297	6.7921	6.3988	6.0442	5.7234	5.4321	5.1668	4.9245	4.1371
24	8.3481	7.7843	7.2829	6.8351	6.4338	6.0726	5.7465	5.4509	5.1822	4.9371	4.1428
25	8.4217	7.8431	7.3300	6.8729	6.4641	6.0971	5.7662	5.4669	5.1951	4.9476	4.1474

TABLE D.3

Areas under the Standard Normal Curve

This table shows the area between zero (the mean of a standard normal variable) and z. For example, if $z = 1.50$, this is the shaded area shown below, which equals .4332.

z	.00	.01	.02	.03	.04	.05	.06	.07	.08	.09
0.0	.0000	.0040	.0080	.0120	.0160	.0199	.0239	.0279	.0319	.0359
0.1	.0398	.0438	.0478	.0517	.0557	.0596	.0636	.0675	.0714	.0753
0.2	.0793	.0832	.0871	.0910	.0948	.0987	.1026	.1064	.1103	.1141
0.3	.1179	.1217	.1255	.1293	.1331	.1368	.1406	.1443	.1480	.1517
0.4	.1554	.1591	.1628	.1664	.1700	.1736	.1772	.1808	.1844	.1879
0.5	.1915	.1950	.1985	.2019	.2054	.2088	.2123	.2157	.2190	.2224
0.6	.2257	.2291	.2324	.2357	.2389	.2422	.2454	.2486	.2517	.2549
0.7	.2580	.2611	.2642	.2673	.2704	.2734	.2764	.2794	.2823	.2852
0.8	.2881	.2910	.2939	.2967	.2995	.3023	.3051	.3078	.3106	.3133
0.9	.3159	.3186	.3212	.3238	.3264	.3289	.3315	.3340	.3365	.3389
1.0	.3413	.3438	.3461	.3485	.3508	.3531	.3554	.3577	.3599	.3621

TABLE D.3

Areas under the Standard Normal Curve (Continued)

z	.00	.01	.02	.03	.04	.05	.06	.07	.08	.09
1.1	.3643	.3665	.3686	.3708	.3729	.3749	.3770	.3790	.3810	.3830
1.2	.3849	.3869	.3888	.3907	.3925	.3944	.3962	.3980	.3997	.4015
1.3	.4032	.4049	.4066	.4082	.4099	.4115	.4131	.4147	.4162	.4177
1.4	.4192	.4207	.4222	.4236	.4251	.4265	.4279	.4292	.4306	.4319
1.5	.4332	.4345	.4357	.4370	.4382	.4394	.4406	.4418	.4429	.4441
1.6	.4452	.4463	.4474	.4484	.4495	.4505	.4515	.4525	.4535	.4545
1.7	.4554	.4564	.4573	.4582	.4591	.4599	.4608	.4616	.4625	.4633
1.8	.4641	.4649	.4656	.4664	.4671	.4678	.4686	.4693	.4699	.4706
1.9	.4713	.4719	.4726	.4732	.4738	.4744	.4750	.4756	.4761	.4767
2.0	.4772	.4778	.4783	.4788	.4793	.4798	.4803	.4808	.4812	.4817
2.1	.4821	.4826	.4830	.4834	.4838	.4842	.4846	.4850	.4854	.4857
2.2	.4861	.4864	.4868	.4871	.4875	.4878	.4881	.4884	.4887	.4890
2.3	.4893	.4896	.4898	.4901	.4904	.4906	.4909	.4911	.4913	.4916
2.4	.4918	.4920	.4922	.4925	.4927	.4929	.4931	.4932	.4934	.4936
2.5	.4938	.4940	.4941	.4943	.4945	.4946	.4948	.4949	.4951	.4952
2.6	.4953	.4955	.4956	.4957	.4959	.4960	.4961	.4962	.4963	.4964
2.7	.4965	.4966	.4967	.4968	.4969	.4970	.4971	.4972	.4973	.4974
2.8	.4974	.4975	.4976	.4977	.4977	.4978	.4979	.4979	.4980	.4981
2.9	.4981	.4982	.4982	.4983	.4984	.4984	.4985	.4985	.4986	.4986
3.0	.4987	.4987	.4987	.4988	.4988	.4989	.4989	.4989	.4990	.4990

Source: This table is adapted from National Bureau of Standards, *Tables of Normal Probability Functions*, Applied Mathematics Series 23, U.S. Department of Commerce, 1953.

TABLE D.4

Values of *t* That Will Be Exceeded with Specified Probabilities

This table shows the value of *t* where the area under the *t* distribution exceeding this value of *t* equals the specified amount. For example, the probability that a *t* variable with 14 degrees of freedom will exceed 1.345 equals .10.

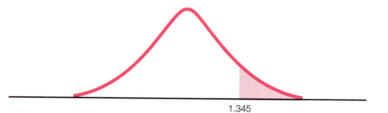

1.345

Degrees of freedom	Probability						
	.40	.25	.10	.05	.025	.01	.005
1	0.325	1.000	3.078	6.314	12.706	31.821	63.657
2	.289	0.816	1.886	2.920	4.303	6.965	9.925
3	.277	.765	1.638	2.353	3.182	4.541	5.841
4	.271	.741	1.533	2.132	2.776	3.747	4.604
5	0.267	0.727	1.476	2.015	2.571	3.365	4.032
6	.265	.718	1.440	1.943	2.447	3.143	3.707
7	.263	.711	1.415	1.895	2.365	2.998	3.499
8	.262	.706	1.397	1.860	2.306	2.896	3.355
9	.261	.703	1.383	1.833	2.262	2.821	3.250
10	0.260	0.700	1.372	1.812	2.228	2.764	3.169
11	.260	.697	1.363	1.796	2.201	2.718	3.106
12	.259	.695	1.356	1.782	2.179	2.681	3.055
13	.259	.694	1.350	1.771	2.160	2.650	3.012
14	.258	.692	1.345	1.761	2.145	2.624	2.977
15	0.258	0.691	1.341	1.753	2.131	2.602	2.947
16	.258	.690	1.337	1.746	2.120	2.583	2.921
17	.257	.689	1.333	1.740	2.110	2.567	2.898
18	.257	.688	1.330	1.734	2.101	2.552	2.878
19	.257	.688	1.328	1.729	2.093	2.539	2.861
20	0.257	0.687	1.325	1.725	2.086	2.528	2.845
21	.257	.686	1.323	1.721	2.080	2.518	2.831
22	.256	.686	1.321	1.717	2.074	2.508	2.819
23	.256	.685	1.319	1.714	2.069	2.500	2.807
24	.256	.685	1.318	1.711	2.064	2.492	2.797

TABLE D.4

Values of *t* That Will Be Exceeded with Specified Probabilities (Continued)

This table shows the value of *t* where the area under the *t* distribution exceeding this value of *t* equals the specified amount. For example, the probability that a *t* variable with 14 degrees of freedom will exceed 1.345 equals .10.

Degrees of freedom	Probability						
	.40	.25	.10	.05	.025	.01	.005
25	0.256	0.684	1.316	1.708	2.060	2.485	2.787
26	.256	.684	1.315	1.706	2.056	2.479	2.779
27	.256	.684	1.314	1.703	2.052	2.473	2.771
28	.256	.683	1.313	1.701	2.048	2.467	2.763
29	.256	.683	1.311	1.699	2.045	2.462	2.756
30	0.256	0.683	1.310	1.697	2.042	2.457	2.750
40	.255	.681	1.303	1.684	2.021	2.423	2.704
60	.254	.679	1.296	1.671	2.000	2.390	2.660
120	.254	.677	1.289	1.658	1.980	2.358	2.617
∞	.253	.674	1.282	1.645	1.960	2.326	2.576

Source: *Biometrika Tables for Statisticians* (Cambridge, U.K.: Cambridge University, 1954).

TABLE D.5

Value of an F Variable That Is Exceeded with Probability Equal to .05

	Degrees of freedom for numerator								
	1	2	3	4	5	6	7	8	9
1	161.4	199.5	215.7	224.6	230.2	234.0	236.8	238.9	240.5
2	18.51	19.00	19.16	19.25	19.30	19.33	19.35	19.37	19.38
3	10.13	9.55	9.28	9.12	9.01	8.94	8.89	8.85	8.81
4	7.71	6.94	6.59	6.39	6.26	6.16	6.09	6.04	6.00
5	6.61	5.79	5.41	5.19	5.05	4.95	4.88	4.82	4.77
6	5.99	5.14	4.76	4.53	4.39	4.28	4.21	4.15	4.10
7	5.59	4.74	4.35	4.12	3.97	3.87	3.79	3.73	3.68
8	5.32	4.46	4.07	3.84	3.69	3.58	3.50	3.44	3.39
9	5.12	4.26	3.86	3.63	3.48	3.37	3.29	3.23	3.18
10	4.96	4.10	3.71	3.48	3.33	3.22	3.14	3.07	3.02
11	4.84	3.98	3.59	3.36	3.20	3.09	3.01	2.95	2.90
12	4.75	3.89	3.49	3.26	3.11	3.00	2.91	2.85	2.80
13	4.67	3.81	3.41	3.18	3.03	2.92	2.83	2.77	2.71
14	4.60	3.74	3.34	3.11	2.96	2.85	2.76	2.70	2.65
15	4.54	3.68	3.29	3.06	2.90	2.79	2.71	2.64	2.59
16	4.49	3.63	3.24	3.01	2.85	2.74	2.66	2.59	2.54
17	4.45	3 59	3.20	2.96	2.81	2.70	2.61	2.55	2.49
18	4.41	3.55	3.16	2.93	2.77	2.66	2.58	2.51	2.46
19	4.38	3.52	3.13	2.90	2.74	2.63	2.54	2.48	2.42
20	4.35	3.49	3.10	2.87	2.71	2.60	2.51	2.45	2.39
21	4.32	3.47	3.07	2.84	2.68	2.57	2.49	2.42	2.37
22	4.30	3.44	3.05	2.82	2.66	2.55	2.46	2.40	2.34
23	4.28	3.42	3.03	2.80	2.64	2.53	2.44	2.37	2.32
24	4.26	3.40	3.01	2.78	2.62	2.51	2.42	2.36	2.30
25	4.24	3.39	2.99	2.76	2.60	2.49	2.40	2.34	2.28
26	4.23	3.37	2.98	2.74	2.59	2.47	2.39	2.32	2.27
27	4.21	3.35	2.96	2.73	2.57	2.46	2.37	2.31	2.25
28	4.20	3.34	2.95	2.71	2.56	2.45	2.36	2.29	2.24
29	4.18	3.33	2.93	2.70	2.55	2.43	2.35	2.28	2.22
30	4.17	3.32	2.92	2.69	2.53	2.42	2.33	2.27	2.21
40	4.08	3.23	2.84	2.61	2.45	2.34	2.25	2.18	2.12
60	4.00	3.15	2.76	2.53	2.37	2.25	2.17	2.10	2.04
120	3.92	3.07	2.68	2.45	2.29	2.17	2.09	2.02	1.96
∞	3.84	3.00	2.60	2.37	2.21	2.10	2.01	1.94	1.88

Degrees of freedom for denominator

TABLE D.5

Value of an *F* Variable That Is Exceeded with Probability Equal to .05 (Continued)

		Degrees of freedom for numerator									
		10	12	15	20	24	30	40	60	120	∞
	1	241.9	243.9	245.9	248.0	249.1	250.1	251.1	252.2	253.3	254.3
	2	19.40	19.41	19.43	19.45	19.45	19.46	19.47	19.48	19.49	19.50
	3	8.79	8.74	8.70	8.66	8.64	8.62	8.59	8.57	8.55	8.53
	4	5.96	5.91	5.86	5.80	5.77	5.75	5.72	5.69	5.66	5.63
	5	4.74	4.68	4.62	4.56	4.53	4.50	4.46	4.43	4.40	4.36
	6	4.06	4.00	3.94	3.87	3.84	3.81	3.77	3.74	3.70	3.67
	7	3.64	3.57	3.51	3.44	3.41	3.38	3.34	3.30	3.27	3.23
	8	3.35	3.28	3.22	3.15	3.12	3.08	3.04	3.01	2.97	2.93
	9	3.14	3.07	3.01	2.94	2.90	2.86	2.83	2.79	2.75	2.71
	10	2.98	2.91	2.85	2.77	2.74	2.70	2.66	2.62	2.58	2.54
	11	2.85	2.79	2.72	2.65	2.61	2.57	2.53	2.49	2.45	2.40
	12	2.75	2.69	2.62	2.54	2.51	2.47	2.43	2.38	2.34	2.30
	13	2.67	2.60	2.53	2.46	2.42	2.38	2.34	2.30	2.25	2.21
	14	2.60	2.53	2.46	2.39	2.35	2.31	2.27	2.22	2.18	2.13
Degrees of freedom for denominator	15	2.54	2.48	2.40	2.33	2.29	2.25	2.20	2.16	2.11	2.07
	16	2.49	2.42	2.35	2.28	2.24	2.19	2.15	2.11	2.06	2.01
	17	2.45	2.38	2.31	2.23	2.19	2.15	2.10	2.06	2.01	1.96
	18	2.41	2.34	2.27	2.19	2.15	2.11	2.06	2.02	1.97	1.92
	19	2.38	2.31	2.23	2.16	2.11	2.07	2.03	1.98	1.93	1.88
	20	2.35	2.28	2.20	2.12	2.08	2.04	1.99	1.95	1.90	1.84
	21	2.32	2.25	2.18	2.10	2.05	2.01	1.96	1.92	1.87	1.81
	22	2.30	2.23	2.15	2.07	2.03	1.98	1.94	1.89	1.84	1.78
	23	2.27	2.20	2.13	2.05	2.01	1.96	1.91	1.86	1.81	1.76
	24	2.25	2.18	2.11	2.03	1.98	1.94	1.89	1.84	1.79	1.73
	25	2.24	2.16	2.09	2.01	1.96	1.92	1.87	1.82	1.77	1.71
	26	2.22	2.15	2.07	1.99	1.95	1.90	1.85	1.80	1.75	1.69
	27	2.20	2.13	2.06	1.97	1.93	1.88	1.84	1.79	1.73	1.67
	28	2.19	2.12	2.04	1.96	1.91	1.87	1.82	1.77	1.71	1.65
	29	2.18	2.10	2.03	1.94	1.90	1.85	1.81	1.75	1.70	1.64
	30	2.16	2.09	2.01	1.93	1.89	1.84	1.79	1.74	1.68	1.62
	40	2.08	2.00	1.92	1.84	1.79	1.74	1.69	1.64	1.58	1.51
	60	1.99	1.92	1.84	1.75	1.70	1.65	1.59	1.53	1.47	1.39
	120	1.91	1.83	1.75	1.66	1.61	1.55	1.50	1.43	1.35	1.25
	∞	1.83	1.75	1.67	1.57	1.52	1.46	1.39	1.32	1.22	1.00

Source: *Biometrika Tables for Statisticians.*

TABLE D.6

Value of an *F* Variable That Is Exceeded with Probability Equal to .01

		Degrees of freedom for numerator							
	1	**2**	**3**	**4**	**5**	**6**	**7**	**8**	**9**
1	4052	4999.5	5403	5625	5764	5859	5928	5982	6022
2	98.50	99.00	99.17	99.25	99.30	99.33	99.36	99.37	99.39
3	34.12	30.82	29.46	28.71	28.24	27.91	27.67	27.49	27.35
4	21.20	18.00	16.69	15.98	15.52	15.21	14.98	14.80	14.66
5	16.26	13.27	12.06	11.39	10.97	10.67	10.46	10.29	10.16
6	13.75	10.92	9.78	9.15	8.75	8.47	8.26	8.10	7.98
7	12.25	9.55	8.45	7.85	7.46	7.19	6.99	6.84	6.72
8	11.26	8.65	7.59	7.01	6.63	6.37	6.18	6.03	5.91
9	10.56	8.02	6.99	6.42	6.06	5.80	5.61	5.47	5.35
10	10.04	7.56	6.55	5.99	5.64	5.39	5.20	5.06	4.94
11	9.65	7.21	6.22	5.67	5.32	5.07	4.89	4.74	4.63
12	9.33	6.93	5.95	5.41	5.06	4.82	4.64	4.50	4.39
13	9.07	6.70	5.74	5.21	4.86	4.62	4.44	4.30	4.19
14	8.86	6.51	5.56	5.04	4.69	4.46	4.28	4.14	4.03
15	8.68	6.36	5.42	4.89	4.56	4.32	4.14	4.00	3.89
16	8.53	6.23	5.29	4.77	4.44	4.20	4.03	3.89	3.78
17	8.40	6.11	5.18	4.67	4.34	4.10	3.93	3.79	3.68
18	8.29	6.01	5.09	4.58	4.25	4.01	3.84	3.71	3.60
19	8.18	5.93	5.01	4.50	4.17	3.94	3.77	3.63	3.52
20	8.10	5.85	4.94	4.43	4.10	3.87	3.70	3.56	3.46
21	8.02	5.78	4.87	4.37	4.04	3.81	3.64	3.51	3.40
22	7.95	5.72	4.82	4.31	3.99	3.76	3.59	3.45	3.35
23	7.88	5.66	4.76	4.26	3.94	3.71	3.54	3.41	3.30
24	7.82	5.61	4.72	4.22	3.90	3.67	3.50	3.36	3.26
25	7.77	5.57	4.68	4.18	3.85	3.63	3.46	3.32	3.22
26	7.72	5.53	4.64	4.14	3.82	3.59	3.42	3.29	3.18
27	7.68	5.49	4.60	4.11	3.78	3.56	3.39	3.26	3.15
28	7.64	5.45	4.57	4.07	3.75	3.53	3.36	3.23	3.12
29	7.60	5.42	4.54	4.04	3.73	3.50	3.33	3.20	3.09
30	7.56	5.39	4.51	4.02	3.70	3.47	3.30	3.17	3.07
40	7.31	5.18	4.31	3.83	3.51	3.29	3.12	2.99	2.89
60	7.08	4.98	4.13	3.65	3.34	3.12	2.95	2.82	2.72
120	6.85	4.79	3.95	3.48	3.17	2.96	2.79	2.66	2.56
∞	6.63	4.61	3.78	3.32	3.02	2.80	2.64	2.51	2.41

Degrees of freedom for denominator

TABLE D.6

Value of an _F_ Variable That is Exceeded with Probability Equal to .01 (Continued)

				Degrees of freedom for numerator						
	10	12	15	20	24	30	40	60	120	∞
1	6056	6106	6157	6209	6235	6261	6287	6313	6339	6366
2	99.40	99.42	99.43	99.45	99.46	99.47	99.47	99.48	99.49	99.50
3	27.23	27.05	26.87	26.69	26.60	26.50	26.41	26.32	26.22	26.13
4	14.55	14.37	14.20	14.02	13.93	13.84	13.75	13.65	13.56	13.46
5	10.05	9.89	9.72	9.55	9.47	9.38	9.29	9.20	9.11	9.02
6	7.87	7.72	7.56	7.40	7.31	7.23	7.14	7.06	6.97	6.88
7	6.62	6.47	6.31	6.16	6.07	5.99	5.91	5.82	5.74	5.65
8	5.81	5.67	5.52	5.36	5.28	5.20	5.12	5.03	4.95	4.86
9	5.26	5.11	4.96	4.81	4.73	4.65	4.57	4.48	4.40	4.31
10	4.85	4.71	4.56	4.41	4.33	4.25	4.17	4.08	4.00	3.91
11	4.54	4.40	4.25	4.10	4.02	3.94	3.86	3.78	3.69	3.60
12	4.30	4.16	4.01	3.86	3.78	3.70	3.62	3.54	3.45	3.36
13	4.10	3.96	3.82	3.66	3.59	3.51	3.43	3.34	3.25	3.17
14	3.94	3.80	3.66	3.51	3.43	3.35	3.27	3.18	3.09	3.00
15	3.80	3.67	3.52	3.37	3.29	3.21	3.13	3.05	2.96	2.87
16	3.69	3.55	3.41	3.26	3.18	3.10	3.02	2.93	2.84	2.75
17	3.59	3.46	3.31	3.16	3.08	3.00	2.92	2.83	2.75	2.65
18	3.51	3.37	3.23	3.08	3.00	2.92	2.84	2.75	2.66	2.57
19	3.43	3.30	3.15	3.00	2.92	2.84	2.76	2.67	2.58	2.49
20	3.37	3.23	3.09	2.94	2.86	2.78	2.69	2.61	2.52	2.42
21	3.31	3.17	3.03	2.88	2.80	2.72	2.64	2.55	2.46	2.36
22	3.26	3.12	2.98	2.83	2.75	2.67	2.58	2.50	2.40	2.31
23	3.21	3.07	2.93	2.78	2.70	2.62	2.54	2.45	2.35	2.26
24	3.17	3.03	2.89	2.74	2.66	2.58	2.49	2.40	2.31	2.21
25	3.13	2.99	2.85	2.70	2.62	2.54	2.45	2.36	2.27	2.17
26	3.09	2.96	2.81	2.66	2.58	2.50	2.42	2.33	2.23	2.13
27	3.06	2.93	2.78	2.63	2.55	2.47	2.38	2.29	2.20	2.10
28	3.03	2.90	2.75	2.60	2.52	2.44	2.35	2.26	2.17	2.06
29	3.00	2.87	2.73	2.57	2.49	2.41	2.33	2.23	2.14	2.03
30	2.98	2.84	2.70	2.55	2.47	2.39	2.30	2.21	2.11	2.01
40	2.80	2.66	2.52	2.37	2.29	2.20	2.11	2.02	1.92	1.80
60	2.63	2.50	2.35	2.20	2.12	2.03	1.94	1.84	1.73	1.60
120	2.47	2.34	2.19	2.03	1.95	1.86	1.76	1.66	1.53	1.38
∞	2.32	2.18	2.04	1.88	1.79	1.70	1.59	1.47	1.32	1.00

Degrees of freedom for denominator

Source: _Biometrika Tables for Statisticians._

TABLE D.7

Values of d_L and d_U for the Durbin–Watson Test

A. Significance level = .05

n	k = 1		k = 2		k = 3		k = 4		k = 5	
	d_L	d_U	d_L	d_U	d_L	d_U	d_L	d_U	d_L	d_U
15	1.08	1.36	0.95	1.54	0.82	1.75	0.69	1.97	0.56	2.21
16	1.10	1.37	0.98	1.54	0.86	1.73	0.74	1.93	0.62	2.15
17	1.13	1.38	1.02	1.54	0.90	1.71	0.78	1.90	0.67	2.10
18	1.16	1.39	1.05	1.53	0.93	1.69	0.82	1.87	0.71	2.06
19	1.18	1.40	1.08	1.53	0.97	1.68	0.86	1.85	0.75	2.02
20	1.20	1.41	1.10	1.54	1.00	1.68	0.90	1.83	0.79	1.99
21	1.22	1.42	1.13	1.54	1.03	1.67	0.93	1.81	0.83	1.96
22	1.24	1.43	1.15	1.54	1.05	1.66	0.96	1.80	0.86	1.94
23	1.26	1.44	1.17	1.54	1.08	1.66	0.99	1.79	0.90	1.92
24	1.27	1.45	1.19	1.55	1.10	1.66	1.01	1.78	0.93	1.90
25	1.29	1.45	1.21	1.55	1.12	1.66	1.04	1.77	0.95	1.89
26	1.30	1.46	1.22	1.55	1.14	1.65	1.06	1.76	0.98	1.88
27	1.32	1.47	1.24	1.56	1.16	1.65	1.08	1.76	1.01	1.86
28	1.33	1.48	1.26	1.56	1.18	1.65	1.10	1.75	1.03	1.85
29	1.34	1.48	1.27	1.56	1.20	1.65	1.12	1.74	1.05	1.84
30	1.35	1.49	1.28	1.57	1.21	1.65	1.14	1.74	1.07	1.83
31	1.36	1.50	1.30	1.57	1.23	1.65	1.16	1.74	1.09	1.83
32	1.37	1.50	1.31	1.57	1.24	1.65	1.18	1.73	1.11	1.82
33	1.38	1.51	1.32	1.58	1.26	1.65	1.19	1.73	1.13	1.81
34	1.39	1.51	1.33	1.58	1.27	1.65	1.21	1.73	1.15	1.81
35	1.40	1.52	1.34	1.58	1.28	1.65	1.22	1.73	1.16	1.80
36	1.41	1.52	1.35	1.59	1.29	1.65	1.24	1.73	1.18	1.80
37	1.42	1.53	1.36	1.59	1.31	1.66	1.25	1.72	1.19	1.80
38	1.43	1.54	1.37	1.59	1.32	1.66	1.26	1.72	1.21	1.79
39	1.43	1.54	1.38	1.60	1.33	1.66	1.27	1.72	1.22	1.79
40	1.44	1.54	1.39	1.60	1.34	1.66	1.29	1.72	1.23	1.79
45	1.48	1.57	1.43	1.62	1.38	1.67	1.34	1.72	1.29	1.78
50	1.50	1.59	1.46	1.63	1.42	1.67	1.38	1.72	1.34	1.77
55	1.53	1.60	1.49	1.64	1.45	1.68	1.41	1.72	1.38	1.77
60	1.55	1.62	1.51	1.65	1.48	1.69	1.44	1.73	1.41	1.77
65	1.57	1.63	1.54	1.66	1.50	1.70	1.47	1.73	1.44	1.77
70	1.58	1.64	1.55	1.67	1.52	1.70	1.49	1.74	1.46	1.77
75	1.60	1.65	1.57	1.68	1.54	1.71	1.51	1.74	1.49	1.77
80	1.61	1.66	1.59	1.69	1.56	1.72	1.53	1.74	1.51	1.77
85	1.62	1.67	1.60	1.70	1.57	1.72	1.55	1.75	1.52	1.77
90	1.63	1.68	1.61	1.70	1.59	1.73	1.57	1.75	1.54	1.78
95	1.64	1.69	1.62	1.71	1.60	1.73	1.58	1.75	1.56	1.78
100	1.65	1.69	1.63	1.72	1.61	1.74	1.59	1.76	1.57	1.78

TABLE D.7

Values of d_L and d_U for the Durbin–Watson Test (Continued)

B. Significance level = .025

n	$k = 1$		$k = 2$		$k = 3$		$k = 4$		$k = 5$	
	d_L	d_U	d_L	d_U	d_L	d_U	d_L	d_U	d_L	d_U
15	0.95	1.23	0.83	1.40	0.71	1.61	0.59	1.84	0.48	2.09
16	0.98	1.24	0.86	1.40	0.75	1.59	0.64	1.80	0.53	2.03
17	1.01	1.25	0.90	1.40	0.79	1.58	0.68	1.77	0.57	1.98
18	1.03	1.26	0.93	1.40	0.82	1.56	0.72	1.74	0.62	1.93
19	1.06	1.28	0.96	1.41	0.86	1.55	0.76	1.72	0.66	1.90
20	1.08	1.28	0.99	1.41	0.89	1.55	0.79	1.70	0.70	1.87
21	1.10	1.30	1.01	1.41	0.92	1.54	0.83	1.69	0.73	1.84
22	1.12	1.31	1.04	1.42	0.95	1.54	0.86	1.68	0.77	1.82
23	1.14	1.32	1.06	1.42	0.97	1.54	0.89	1.67	0.80	1.80
24	1.16	1.33	1.08	1.43	1.00	1.54	0.91	1.66	0.83	1.79
25	1.18	1.34	1.10	1.43	1.02	1.54	0.94	1.65	0.86	1.77
26	1.19	1.35	1.12	1.44	1.04	1.54	0.96	1.65	0.88	1.76
27	1.21	1.36	1.13	1.44	1.06	1.54	0.99	1.64	0.91	1.75
28	1.22	1.37	1.15	1.45	1.08	1.54	1.01	1.64	0.93	1.74
29	1.24	1.38	1.17	1.45	1.10	1.54	1.03	1.63	0.96	1.73
30	1.25	1.38	1.18	1.46	1.12	1.54	1.05	1.63	0.98	1.73
31	1.26	1.39	1.20	1.47	1.13	1.55	1.07	1.63	1.00	1.72
32	1.27	1.40	1.21	1.47	1.15	1.55	1.08	1.63	1.02	1.71
33	1.28	1.41	1.22	1.48	1.16	1.55	1.10	1.63	1.04	1.71
34	1.29	1.41	1.24	1.48	1.17	1.55	1.12	1.63	1.06	1.70
35	1.30	1.42	1.25	1.48	1.19	1.55	1.13	1.63	1.07	1.70
36	1.31	1.43	1.26	1.49	1.20	1.56	1.15	1.63	1.09	1.70
37	1.32	1.43	1.27	1.49	1.21	1.56	1.16	1.62	1.10	1.70
38	1.33	1.44	1.28	1.50	1.23	1.56	1.17	1.62	1.12	1.70
39	1.34	1.44	1.29	1.50	1.24	1.56	1.19	1.63	1.13	1.69
40	1.35	1.45	1.30	1.51	1.25	1.57	1.20	1.63	1.15	1.69
45	1.39	1.48	1.34	1.53	1.30	1.58	1.25	1.63	1.21	1.69
50	1.42	1.50	1.38	1.54	1.34	1.59	1.30	1.64	1.26	1.69
55	1.45	1.52	1.41	1.56	1.37	1.60	1.33	1.64	1.30	1.69
60	1.47	1.54	1.44	1.57	1.40	1.61	1.37	1.65	1.33	1.69
65	1.49	1.55	1.46	1.59	1.43	1.62	1.40	1.66	1.36	1.69
70	1.51	1.57	1.48	1.60	1.45	1.63	1.42	1.66	1.39	1.70
75	1.53	1.58	1.50	1.61	1.47	1.64	1.45	1.67	1.42	1.70
80	1.54	1.59	1.52	1.62	1.49	1.65	1.47	1.67	1.44	1.70
85	1.56	1.60	1.53	1.63	1.51	1.65	1.49	1.68	1.46	1.71
90	1.57	1.61	1.55	1.64	1.53	1.66	1.50	1.69	1.48	1.71
95	1.58	1.62	1.56	1.65	1.54	1.67	1.52	1.69	1.50	1.71
100	1.59	1.63	1.57	1.65	1.55	1.67	1.53	1.70	1.51	1.72

TABLE D.7

Values of d_L and d_U for the Durbin–Watson Test (Continued)

C. Significance level = 0.01

	k = 1		k = 2		k = 3		k = 4		k = 5	
n	d_L	d_U	d_L	d_U	d_L	d_U	d_L	d_U	d_L	d_U
15	0.81	1.07	0.70	1.25	0.59	1.46	0.49	1.70	0.39	1.96
16	0.84	1.09	0.74	1.25	0.63	1.44	0.53	1.66	0.44	1.90
17	0.87	1.10	0.77	1.25	0.67	1.43	0.57	1.63	0.48	1.85
18	0.90	1.12	0.80	1.26	0.71	1.42	0.61	1.60	0.52	1.80
19	0.93	1.13	0.83	1.26	0.74	1.41	0.65	1.58	0.56	1.77
20	0.95	1.15	0.86	1.27	077	1.41	0.68	1.57	0.60	1.74
21	0.97	1.16	0.89	1.27	0.80	1.41	0.72	1.55	0.63	1.71
22	1.00	1.17	0.91	1.28	0.83	1.40	0.75	1.54	0.66	1.69
23	1.02	1.19	0.94	1.29	0.86	1.40	0.77	1.53	0.70	1.67
24	1.04	1.20	0.96	1.30	0.88	1.41	0.80	1.53	0.72	1.66
25	1.05	1.21	0.98	1.30	0.90	1.41	0.83	1.52	0.75	1.65
26	1.07	1.22	1.00	1.31	0.93	1.41	0.85	1.52	0.78	1.64
27	1.09	1.23	1.02	1.32	0.95	1.41	0.88	1.51	0.81	1.63
28	1.10	1.24	1.04	1.32	0.97	1.41	0.90	1.51	0.83	1.62
29	1.12	1.25	1.05	1.33	0.99	1.42	0.92	1.51	0.85	1.61
30	1.13	1.26	1.07	1.34	1.01	1.42	0.94	1.51	0.88	1.61
31	1.15	1.27	1.08	1.34	1.02	1.42	0.96	1.51	0.90	1.60
32	1.16	1.28	1.10	1.35	1.04	1.43	0.98	1.51	0.92	1.60
33	1.17	1.29	1.11	1.36	1.05	1.43	1.00	1.51	0.94	1.59
34	1.18	1.30	1.13	1.36	1.07	1.43	1.01	1.51	0.95	1.59
35	1.19	1.31	1.14	1.37	1.08	1.44	1.03	1.51	0.97	1.59
36	1.21	1.32	1.15	1.38	1.10	1.44	1.04	1.51	0.99	1.59
37	1.22	1.32	1.16	1.38	1.11	1.45	1.06	1.51	1.00	1.59
38	1.23	1.33	1.18	1.39	1.12	1.45	1.07	1.52	1.02	1.58
39	1.24	1.34	1.19	1.39	1.14	1.45	1.09	1.52	1.03	1.58
40	1.25	1.34	1.20	1.40	1.15	1.46	1.10	1.52	1.05	1.58
45	1.29	1.38	1.24	1.42	1.20	1.48	1.16	1.53	1.11	1.58
50	1.32	1.40	1.28	1.45	1.24	1.49	1.20	1.54	1.16	1.59
55	1.36	1.43	1.32	1.47	1.28	1.51	1.25	1.55	1.21	1.59
60	1.38	1.45	1.35	1.48	1.32	1.52	1.28	1.56	1.25	1.60
65	1.41	1.47	1.38	1.50	1.35	1.53	1.31	1.57	1.28	1.61
70	1.43	1.49	1.40	1.52	1.37	1.55	1.34	1.58	1.31	1.61
75	1.45	1.50	1.42	1.53	1.39	1.56	1.37	1.59	1.34	1.62
80	1.47	1.52	1.44	1.54	1.42	1.57	1.39	1.60	1.36	1.62
85	1.48	1.53	1.46	1.55	1.43	1.58	1.41	1.60	1.39	1.63
90	1.50	1.54	1.47	1.56	1.45	1.59	1.43	1.61	1.41	1.64
95	1.51	1.55	1.49	1.57	1.47	1.60	1.45	1.62	1.42	1.64
100	1.52	1.56	1.50	1.58	1.48	1.60	1.46	1.63	1.44	1.65

Source: J. Durbin and G. S. Watson, "Testing for Serial Correlation in Least Squares Regression," *Biometrika 38* (June 1951).

INDEX